# PLANNING FOR TEACHING

# planning
# for teaching
## AN INTRODUCTION TO EDUCATION

## ROBERT W. RICHEY

Dean of Continuing Education
Director of Summer Sessions, and
Professor of Education, Indiana University

## FIFTH EDITION

## McGRAW-HILL BOOK COMPANY

New York   St. Louis   San Francisco   Düsseldorf
Johannesburg   Kuala Lumpur   London   Mexico
Montreal   New Delhi   Panama   Rio de Janeiro
Singapore   Sydney   Toronto

# PLANNING FOR TEACHING:
## An Introduction to Education

1234567890KPKP798765432

This book was set in Caledonia and Helvetica by Black Dot, Inc.
The editors were Samuel B. Bossard, Robert C. Morgan, and Helen Greenberg;
the designer was Rafael Hernandez;
and the production supervisor was Sally Ellyson.
The drawings were done by John Cordes, J & R Technical Services, Inc.
The printer and binder was Kingsport Press, Inc.

**Library of Congress Cataloging in Publication Data**

*Richey, Robert William, 1912–*
   **Planning for teaching.**

   Includes bibliographies.
   1.  Teaching as a profession.   I.   Title.
LB1775.R52 1973        371.1'0023        72-3976
ISBN 0-07-052342-8

# CONTENTS

# PREFACE

The content of this book, from the beginning, has been a response to the questions and concerns expressed by students in their introductory course in education. For example, the first edition was the result of four years of intensive experimentation with content materials based upon the questions expressed by over 4,000 students. In planning for this edition, students in the first class-meeting of their introductory course were asked to indicate the questions and concerns which they wished to have considered. A very careful analysis was made of the more than 10,000 questions which they submitted. I wish to thank the students, as well as their instructors, for their generous contributions and thoughtful suggestions for making this edition even more meaningful and relevant to those planning to become educators. I also wish to thank especially the following people for excellent depth reviews of the fourth edition and/or their penetrating reviews of the manuscript for the fifth edition: Dr. Robert L. Burton, Associate Dean, College of Education, University of Missouri; Dr. Norman R. Dixon, Professor of Higher Education and of the Foundations of Education, University of Pittsburgh; Dr. Howard G. Getz, Assistant Professor of Education, Eric/Crier Resources Center, Illinois State University; Dr. James E. Hertling, Director of Programs, Division of Continuing Education, Indiana University; Dr. Walter A. Nelson, Professor and Chairman of the Department of Elementary Education, San Fernando Valley State College, Northridge, California; and Dr. George Ryden, Southwestern State College, Weatherford, Oklahoma.

Although this edition represents a major revision of the book, every effort has been exerted to maintain the same clearly defined purposes as were used in the preceding four editions—to help a student in (1) gaining a valid and comprehensive understanding of what is involved in a teaching career, (2) acquiring a breadth of knowledge that usually is not formally included in general and educational psychology courses, in general and special methods courses, or in student teaching, (3) engaging in a variety of activities that will provide greater meaning or a rationale for subsequent professional course work to be taken, (4) seeing clearly the tasks which lie ahead in developing into an effective teacher, (5) gaining a reasoned dedication to the profession, and (6) planning with care and insight for teaching and for professional growth after entering the profession. Emphasis is placed upon self-analysis, self-direction, inquiry, and personal involvement in planning an effective and successful career in education.

These purposes are in keeping with Standard 3 of the *Standards for Accreditation of Teacher Education* adopted in January, 1970, by the National Council for Accreditation of Teacher Education which states: "The institution owes it to the student to determine as objectively and systematically as possible specific strengths and weaknesses as they affect his continuing in a teacher education program." Students need assistance "in assessing their strengths and weaknesses and in planning their programs of study. Prospective teachers need to be informed about professional organizations and agencies as well as current school problems. They also need to know about the wide variety of options available to them in teaching."

In this revision, the first chapter has been modified greatly and is addressed primarily to the problems of change and the challenges that educators will face in the future. Chapter 2 has been condensed considerably in order to allow for new content on teacher competencies. In Chapter 3, greater stress is placed upon the changes being made in teacher education, certification, and accreditation. The variety of new opportunities that are emerging for educators is emphasized in Chapter 4. Chapter 5 has been recast and retitled in order to focus upon the changing role of the teacher. Chapter 6, "Educational Technology, Change, and Transition," constitutes an addition to the book. The last half of Chapter 7 is a new section concerned with the development of competency skills essential in creating positive conditions for learning. Recent court cases have been added to Chapter 8, "Legal Liabilities and Responsibilities of Teachers." In Chapter 9 additional attention is given to the changing role of professional organizations, especially in their efforts to improve the profession. The material on the economic, organizational, and financial concerns of teachers (Chapters 10 to 13) has been condensed and updated, with more attention being given to the role of the teacher. In discussing historical development of schools in America (Chapter 14), sections have been added concerning the education of minority groups. Modifications have been made in Chapter 15, and the contributions of Piaget, Gagné, and Bloom have been added. In addition to other changes,

Chapter 16 includes new sections on who determines the objectives of education, the taxonomy of objectives, and performance objectives. The section on controversial issues and problems in education, which has been recast and expanded into two chapters (17 and 18), includes such additional concerns as vocational education, student unrest, relevance of school experiences, student governance, sex education, drug education, accountability, performance contracting, equalization of educational opportunities, national assessment, educational deprivation, and racism. Although changes have been made in the content of the last chapter, its primary purpose is to encourage the prospective teacher to assess his gains from having read the book, and to formulate plans for moving effectively into the teaching profession.

The present arrangement of the chapters by parts provides much flexibility and offers an instructor a variety of approaches to an introductory course. For example, an instructor might wish to give early consideration to Part 5, "Historical and Philosophical Concerns," or to Part 4, "Organizational, Administrative, and Financial Concerns." Another instructor might wish to start with some of the controversial issues and problems discussed in Part 6. There might be good reasons to consider Part 3, "Professional and Economic Concerns," before Part 2, "Instructional and Legal Concerns." With the possible exceptions of Chapter 1, Part 1, and Chapter 19, the order in which the various parts of the book are considered is a matter for the instructor to decide. Resource Sections containing checklists, selected readings, 16 mm film lists, and other relevant materials are located at the end of each part.

All the content has been brought as nearly up-to-date as possible in order to reflect recent changes, developments, and trends. Projections on such matters as school and college enrollments, demands for teachers, the gross national product, salaries, and school finance are presented. Data from the 1970 census has been incorporated where possible and appropriate. Special efforts have been made to include research findings on teachers and teaching, and to indicate probable changes in the role of schools and of teachers. Greater attention has been given to such topics as curricular innovations, ecology, differentiated staffing, middle schools, flexible scheduling, nongradedness, educational technology, performance objectives, accountability, national assessment, performance contracting, vouchering, and the education of blacks and other minority groups. The need for humanizing the educational process has been emphasized. Topics have been approached from the point of view of encouraging students to explore them further and to expand their understandings of the teaching profession. Efforts have been made to help students become skilled observers of our changing society, the teaching profession, student behavior, and teaching-learning situations. The needs of both elementary and secondary school teachers are taken into consideration, with some attention being given to teaching on the college level.

The annotated lists of suggested readings at the end of Chapters 1 and 19 and in the Resource Section for each part have been radically updated with the hope that the student will be encouraged to read beyond the confines of this book, to pursue special interests, and to acquaint himself with many other books and periodicals in the field of education. The highly selective annotated lists of 16 mm films, also located at the end of Chapters 1 and 19 and in the Resource Section for each part, have been confined to fairly recent films, even though some of the older films listed in the fourth edition also would be helpful to students in grasping the concepts and principles involved.

A number of changes have been made in the end-of-chapter materials. The Questions for Consideration are designed to stimulate thoughtful concern and discussion on basic ideas, concepts, problems, issues, and plans for teaching. The Activities to Pursue, which emphasize the *doing,* are designed to encourage students to work independently or in groups along lines of special interest in their exploration of teaching as a profession.

As another new feature of this edition, a Problem Situation for Inquiry has been included at the end of each chapter. The primary purpose in using problem situations is to enable students, through group participation, discussion, and debate, to gain skill in identifying relevant factors stated (as well as those not stated) in a problem situation, sensing the variety of possible solutions to a problem, weighing the various issues involved, and deciding upon what would appear to be the most appropriate course of action for coping with a given set of circumstances. An instructor may wish to use other problem situations, appropriate for each chapter, with which he or his students are familiar.

The breadth of topics covered in this book is so great and the changes taking place in the field of education are so rapid that it is virtually impossible for an author to revise such a book without the assistance of authorities in various fields of education. Drs. Edward G. Buffie and John W. Vaughn of Indiana University revised Chapter 5 of the fourth edition, which has been divided into Chapters 5 and 6 of this edition. Drs. James E. Weigand, Roger T. Cunningham, DeWayne Kurpius, James D. Russell, Doris A. Trojcak, Ronald D. Anderson, Donald L. Troyer, Odvard E. Dyrli, and Alfred DeVito prepared material on developing teacher competencies which is contained in the last part of Chapter 7. Dr. Lowell C. Rose, Executive Secretary of Phi Delta Kappa, updated and revised Chapters 8, 17, and 18. Dr. Maurice A. McGlasson of Indiana University revised Chapter 9. Dr. Philip G. Smith of Indiana University made valuable additions to Chapter 15. Dr. James E. Hertling of Indiana University revised Chapters 12 and 13, contributed the sections on minority group education in Chapter 14, made valuable contributions to Chapters 16 and 19, revised the Glossary, prepared the problem situations, and served as a sounding board and critic in the preparation of the manuscript. Dr. Norman Dixon, of the University of Pittsburgh, carefully checked the entire manuscript for relevance on the education of minority groups and made many excellent suggestions. The author is deeply grateful to these people for their excellent contributions and fine cooperation in revising the book.

Mr. William J. Cuttill and others of the Audio-Visual Center of Indiana University were most helpful in updating the lists of 16 mm films. Mrs. Don David assisted in proofreading the manuscript.

Appreciation is extended to the many publishers, and especially to the National Education Association and the American Association of Colleges for Teacher Education, for their willingness to grant permission to use various materials. Miss Virginia Stephenson of the Research Division, National Education Association, was most helpful in locating and in forwarding current relevant publications.

As has been true in the preceding four editions of this book, the greatest contribution of all has come from my wife Eloise, who typed most of the manuscript, checked on many details, proofread, criticized copy, made many helpful suggestions, and endured another revision. To her I am forever grateful.

**Robert W. Richey**

# TO THE STUDENT

Anyone interested in teaching usually wishes to become the most competent teacher possible. The supply of teachers today adds incentive for a prospective teacher to excel in his preparation for entering the profession. An introductory course in education, therefore, should be designed to help a student in (1) gaining a valid and comprehensive understanding of what is involved in a teaching career, (2) acquiring a breadth of knowledge that usually is not formally included in general and educational psychology courses, in general and special methods courses, or in student teaching, (3) engaging in a variety of activities that will provide greater meaning or a rationale for subsequent professional course work to be taken, (4) seeing clearly the tasks which lie ahead in developing into an effective teacher, (5) gaining a reasoned dedication to the profession, and (6) planning with care and insight one's preparation for teaching, as well as his professional growth after entering the profession.

*Planning for Teaching* is designed to assist you in accomplishing the above stated purposes of an introductory course in education. The book is divided into six integral parts. Each part is preceded by an overview designed to assist you in sensing clearly the relations of the chapters involved to the central purpose of the book. Part 1 should help you understand and gain skill in planning a career in teaching. The arrangement of the four chapters in Part 1 should assist you in grasping the logical sequences of some fundamental steps involved in career planning. Professional competencies and certification requirements are examined, and the wide range of opportunities that a career in education provides are explored with the hope that your interests and abilities may best be utilized and your success and happiness in the profession proportionately increased. The needs for both prospective elementary and secondary school teachers are taken into consideration.

Part 2 is concerned with such vital questions as: What are the normal duties and responsibilities of teachers and how might they change in the future? What are some of the newer instructional patterns and procedures? How will educational technology affect the work of teachers? How can a prospective teacher gain skill in guiding the learning process? What are some of the legal liabilities and responsibilities of teachers?

Part 3 is concerned with the status of teaching as a profession, the role of professional organizations in the improvement of the profession, and the obligations and responsibilities of teachers in the profession. Such realistic matters as salary, sick leave, tenure, tax deductions, retirement, and other fringe benefits are considered. Part 4 explores the complex structure of school organization and the ways in which schools are administered and financed. The point is made that success and happiness in teaching are enhanced through an understanding of the different patterns of school organization, administration, and finance, thoroughly enabling a teacher to work more effectively toward the full realization of the school's function in society.

Part 5 explores some of the historical forces that have shaped our educational system, the development of modern concepts of education, and the purposes of education in American democracy. In Part 6 some of the persistent and current problems and issues in education are examined. You are encouraged to plan ways in which you may aid in the solution of these problems and contribute effectively to the fuller realization of the school's function in a democratic society.

In Chapter 19 you are encouraged to assess some of the gains you have made from reading this book and to formulate further plans for moving effectively and happily into the teaching profession.

**Robert W. Richey**

# PLANNING FOR TEACHING

# 1 | THE CHALLENGE OF TEACHING

Congratulations upon your interest in becoming a member of the teaching profession. In addition to being the largest of the professions, teaching may be considered to be basic to all the other professions. In other words, other professions are made possible through the work of teachers in elementary and secondary schools, colleges, and universities.

Becoming a successful teacher presents a greater challenge today than at any previous time in history. Students expect more from schools and their teachers than they did in earlier days. Pressures applied by them, as well as by parents and by the profession itself, to find improved ways of teaching have led to the development of new programs and instructional strategies such as inquiry approaches, simulation games, contract approaches, computer-assisted instruction, and programmed learning materials. Teachers are being challenged to utilize new approaches in an effort to improve learning results. Furthermore, schools and teachers today are dealing with a clientele which is considerably more knowledgeable than previous students due to such factors as mass media, population mobility, population shifts from rural to metropolitan areas, and the economic ability to travel widely.

But a genuine challenge serves to attract people equipped to accept and meet the challenge. As a result, better-qualified persons today are being attracted to teaching. They also have the benefit of improved teacher preparation programs. For those who are personally and professionally qualified, teaching offers a genuine challenge and an opportunity to make a major contribution to the improvement of society.

In addition to the increased challenge, your interest in the possibilities of becoming a teacher also is commendable in view of the frequent criticisms that are being voiced about schools and teachers. It is not uncommon to hear that schools are irrelevant and have failed in their mission of educating the youth of America. You may have read about the abundance of requests for increased school taxes which have been defeated by voters. You may have heard about some school districts which, frustrated in their efforts to provide an effective educational program, have contracted with private business firms to operate all or part of their instructional programs. You may have sensed some anger upon the part of the general public toward teachers who engage in collective bargaining over salaries and working conditions. You may have been told that it will be very difficult, if not impossible, to get a position as a teacher. In the face of what might appear to be discouraging conditions, your interest in pursuing a career in the teaching profession therefore is commendable.

In some respects this negative climate may seem to be a function of the times. In contrast to the optimistic growth pattern of the past, Stinnett makes the following assessment of the current scene [256:5–6][1]:

Something has gone sadly awry. On every hand the quality of life is diminished by blight, pollution, noise, and over-crowding. Our streams are fouled, our soils eroded, our forests cut down, our traffic snarled. As one quipster put it, "not only is there no God, but try getting a plumber on weekends."

Man may walk on the moon in safety and security, but not on the streets and in the parks of our big cities. There is hunger in the midst of plenty; poverty abrades the nation's conscience. Riots, violence, pickets, marches, and dissent mar our days and nights. We seem suddenly to have come upon visions of our limitations; earlier visions of better tomorrows seem now obscured or jaded. The infinity of our powers and possibilities seems, at least momentarily, to be giving way to frustration. We despair that there are no more mountains to climb, no more rivers to cross, no more virgin forests to devastate. Above all, we have lost our identity in the anonymity of the mob. The individual is only a number in the soulless conscience of an error-prone computer.

The much-ballyhooed American goal of uninterrupted, eternal growth—in GNP, in ever bigger cars, in income, in large cities, in population—is proving to be a delusion. The price of bigness is too big to pay. Our cities are becoming unlivable and ungovernable. Population growth, already outrunning our natural resources, is still climbing danger-ously. We can no longer believe in the gospel of growth. Faith in the miracles of technol-ogy has sustained our giddiness. But technology cannot defy the limitations of nature. For every technological advance there have been corresponding adverse effects—fouled air, polluted waters, impossible transportation problems.

Within this negative context it might be easy for any teacher aspirant to become discouraged. But so frequently the abundance of criticism tends to blur the massive educational accomplishments of the past and the vision of the future. It is true that there are many weaknesses and problems existing in our educational system and in the profession which warrant critical analyses. And constructive criticism should always be encouraged, since it serves many useful purposes. "But criticism that is based on erroneous assumptions, that uses slogans rather than facts, or that takes the form of wild accusations does not further the public interest" [196:13]. It may be helpful, therefore, to note briefly some

[1]References indicated by number are listed in an alphabetical reference section beginning on page 619.

The advent of the space age highlights the importance of quality education in a demanding and rapidly changing world. *(Photograph from National Aeronautics and Space Admininstration.)*

contributions of the American school system, as well as some future challenges facing teachers, as a means of gaining perspective for planning a career in education.

## SOME POSITIVE CONTRIBUTIONS OF AMERICAN EDUCATION

Teachers, and the school systems in which they work, do not pretend to make exclusive claims for the tremendous gains that have been made in our society. But few people would ever deny that they have played a significant role in making possible the rapid and monumental growth of our nation.

From the founding of the first common school in America, largely of the public subscription type, a hardy breed of poorly educated, poorly equipped teachers kept the feeble flame of learning alive, under the most adverse circumstances, until the founding of our state school systems. . . .

With the advent of special schools for the preparation of teachers, there went out from these substandard institutions an ever enlarging stream of dedicated people, to plant and nurture the seeds of the American dream. By present standards, their preparation was meager, their learning sketchy. But they made up in zeal and devotion to the goals of this country for their deficiencies in scholarship . . . under great handicaps, they were able to impart a significant measure of learning, enough to enable the people to become self-governing people, thus developing and nurturing one of the world's few constitutional democracies [258:2].

## Unification of the Nation

It is difficult to comprehend the prodigious task with which the public schools have been confronted in their attempts to fulfill one of the greatest dreams a society has ever dreamt—universal educational opportunities. Inscribed on the base of the Statue of Liberty is the following:

> Give me your tired, your poor,
> Your huddled masses yearning to breathe free,
> The wretched refuse of your teeming shore,
> Send these, the homeless, tempest-tossed, to me:
> I lift my lamp beside the golden door.

In response to this open-door approach, more than 30 million immigrants have come to our shores—vastly different in backgrounds and culture. Through the process of bringing these people into our schools, teachers over the years have been able to impart a measure of literacy to them and assist them in becoming a part of the developing American culture—its ideals, behavorial patterns, customs, hopes, and aspirations.

Just as the purposes of the American school are unprecedented, so are its achievements. To it the American people owe the unity which has enabled them to master a continent and to forge from immigrant diversity a single people. It has helped to prevent the formation of rigid class barriers. It has fostered the diversification of talents, the ingenuity, and productivity which has brought this society to the highest level of economic prosperity ever known. On it are based many of the great American scientific and technological advances. And, perhaps most important of all, the spiritual stamina and fervor for freedom which have preserved individual liberty and guarded equality of opportunity through war and hardships have been derived from American education. This majestic record has set the standard against which the rest of the world judges the value of universal education [53:6–7].

Although much remains to be done in American society in recognizing and unifying people whose races, religions, creeds, national origins, as well as ethnic, cultural, and economic backgrounds, are so diversified, undoubtedly public schools will continue to be perhaps the most effective integrating and unifying force within our total society.

## Opportunities for Education

Throughout the years educators have fought vigorously for the establishment, preservation, and improvement of the free public school system. This fight has been based upon a fundamental tenet of a democratic society—respect for the dignity and worth of the individual. In a democratic society each individual should have the opportunity to achieve the promise that is within him—to be worthy of a great society and capable of strengthening it. Education is the medium through which this belief can best be realized. In other words, a democratic society is committed to the proposition that educational opportunities must be provided for all youth in our society [Figure 1–1].[2]

The greatness of a nation may be manifested in many ways—in its purposes, its courage, its moral responsibility, its cultural and scientific eminence, the tenor of its daily life. But ultimately the source of its greatness is in the individuals who constitute the living substance of the nation.

A concern for the realization of individual potentialities is deeply rooted in our moral heritage, our political philosophy, and the texture of our daily customs. It is at the root of our efforts to eliminate poverty and slums at home and to combat disease and disaster throughout the world. The enthusiasm with which Americans plunge into projects for human betterment has been considered by some critics to be foolishly optimistic. But

[2]Figure credits may be found on page 39 and at the end of each Resource Section following each part of the book.

FIGURE 1–1   Per cent of youth 15 to 19 years of age enrolled in school in various countries. The United States excels by far other countries in the percentage of secondary school youth engaged in formal education.

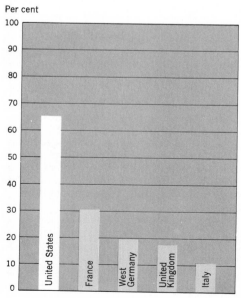

though we may have gone to extremes in a naive belief that we could cure all of mankind's ills, we need not be ashamed of the impulse. It springs from our deepest values. We do not believe that men were meant to live in degradation and we are foes of the poverty and ignorance which produces that result. We deplore the destruction of human potentialities through disease, and we are prepared to fight such destruction wherever we meet it. We believe that man—by virtue of his humanity—should live in the light of reason, exercise moral responsibility, and be free to develop to the full the talents that are in him.

Our devotion to a free society can only be understood in terms of these values. It is the only form of society that puts at the very top of its agenda the opportunity of the individual to develop his potentialities. It is the declared enemy of every condition that stunts the intellect, moral and spiritual growth of the individual. No society has ever fully succeeded in living up to the stern ideals that a free people set themselves. But only a free society can even address itself to that demanding task [208:1].

In commenting upon some accomplishments in American education, a prominent state superintendent of public instruction has presented the following comparisons [196:13]:

Public education in America is essentially free and is, in many respects, almost universal. Our concept of what these basic features are has been expanding for the past hundred years, and we strive to make the reality match the concept. In 1870, high school graduates composed only two per cent of the population of 17-year-olds. This percentage has increased by leaps and bounds; by 1968 it was almost 77 per cent. The numbers of graduates make interesting reading too: In the year 1869–1870, it was 16,000; in 1967–1968 it was 2,672,000. In this period U.S. population increased approximately fivefold, whereas the number of high school graduates increased 167 times.

It is instructive to note how we compare with other nations in retaining students through the final year of high school. The United States retains 70 per cent of its age cohorts. Japan holds second place, retaining 57 per cent. England and Germany retain 12 and 11 per cent respectively.

These data hold considerably more meaning than the mere percentages suggest. Scholars have developed a retentivity index to show the relative chances that students from families with different occupational backgrounds will reach the last grade of the secondary school. This index shows that the U.S. is less selective or discriminatory than other nations. For example, more than two-and-a-half times as many pupils from working class families reach the final year of secondary school in the United States as in England. As a more extreme example, the same ratio for the U.S. and Germany is more than seven to one.

Thus the United States provides education for a greater percentage of its young people than do most industrial nations. And it does so with the least social bias.

When we look at data for higher education, we find again that the U.S. provides substantially more opportunities for its citizens to enroll in institutions of higher education and to earn degrees than do other advanced nations. The UNESCO Statistical Yearbook for 1967 shows that the U.S. has 2,840 students enrolled in higher education per 100,000 population. In a list of seven industrial nations, the Soviet Union is second, with 1,674. The other five are Canada, 1,651; Japan, 1,140; France, 1,042; Germany, 632; and England, 480.

Reports on the number of graduates per 100,000 population for the year 1960 again show the U.S. with a commanding lead; the figure is 268. In the same year Japan was second with 165. The other five industrial nations were reported as follows: Soviet Union, 163; United Kingdom, 133; Canada, 128; Germany, 78; and France, 55.

These data for the secondary schools and for higher education emphasize that the

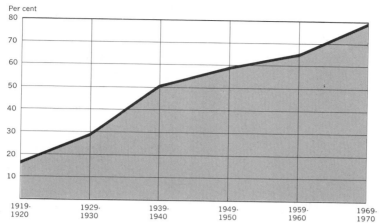

FIGURE 1–2   Percentage of 17-year-olds who graduate from public and nonpublic schools in the United States. What factors have fostered this phenomenal increase?

U.S. makes educational opportunities substantially more available to its citizens than do other major nations. The figures confirm that public education is almost universal at the elementary and secondary levels. But this result has been achieved only after many decades.

Other evidence of educational opportunities is to be found in the fact that American schools have become almost universally coeducational at all levels. "The U.S. has been in the forefront in recognizing the educational rights of the female and in providing opportunities for women to develop their full potential. Unfortunately, it is true that we have not been as successful in utilizing the talents of women as in developing them" [196:14].

Polley calls attention to another contribution of the American educational system [196:14–15]:

American education has not been stratified in the European sense, and largely because of that fact it has produced another outstanding achievement: social mobility. Social mobility contributes not only to a healthy and growing economy but to the maintenance of a free political system. Sons of immigrant fruit peddlers become owners of restaurants or doctors; sons of poor farmers become university presidents or bankers; and the sons of police officers and plumbers are elected mayors or members of Congress. Without a system of comprehensive and high quality education, social mobility would be a far less significant factor in our economic and political life.

While the goal of equal educational opportunities for all has not been reached, much progress, especially in recent years, has been made. As will be indicated in other sections of this book, many complex factors are involved in achieving this goal. Indeed, it must be a concern of the total society.

## Economic Returns of Education

The economic returns of education are reflected in the unparalleled economic growth of this nation. Although the people of the United States constitute only about 6 per cent of the world's population and occupy less than 7 per cent of the world's land area, they create over one-half of the world's wealth, produce over 40 per cent and consume nearly one-third of the total energy produced in the world, and own one-half of the world's telephones, radios, and television sets [66:iv]. "We provide more material things, such as food, clothing, and houses, more health services, more cultural and recreational outlets for more people than any other nation, past or present" [285:1].

The striking relationship between education and economic growth in various nations throughout the world is revealed through a comparison of educational development, natural resources, and per capita income. As may be noted in Table 1–1, Denmark and Colombia present an interesting contrast. Colombia has abundant natural resources. Until recently, it had neglected education. Its per capita income in 1965 was the equivalent of $284. A century ago Denmark had a very low per capita income, and its soil was not rich. It had few minerals, and the growing season was short. But the people decided to place much emphasis upon developing good schools for their children. The per capita income in 1965, in contrast with Colombia's, was $2,066. Likewise, Brazil, very rich in natural resources but low in education, produced only $270 per capita. On the other hand, Switzerland, with limited resources but a well-

FIGURE 1–3    Relationship between lifetime income of men and the level of education.

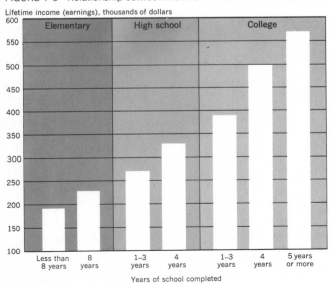

TABLE 1–1 **RELATIONSHIP OF NATURAL RESOURCES, EDUCATION, AND INCOME IN SELECTED COUNTRIES**

| Nation | Natural Resources | Educational Development | Per capita Income, 1965 |
|---|---|---|---|
| Brazil | High | Low | $ 270 |
| Colombia | High | Low | 284 |
| Denmark | Low | High | 2,066 |
| Mexico | High | Low | 455 |
| New Zealand | High | High | 1,986 |
| Switzerland | Low | High | 2,343 |
| United States | High | High | 3,501 |

*Source: What Everyone Should Know about Financing Our Schools,* National Education Association, Washington, 1968, p. 8.

developed educational program, ranked first in Europe in per capita income in 1965. Similar examples can be illustrated by many other countries. They show clearly that regardless of natural resources, the development of educational potential increases per capita income.

The manifold ways in which good schools strengthen society are summarized in the booklet *Education Is Good Business* [66:46–47]:

1. Well-documented evidence indicates that schools have made a magnificent contribution to our economic growth. More education means a more highly skilled work force; gains in worker efficiency achieved through education have accounted for 20 to 23 per cent of our growth in national product. Education is the base upon which the quality of research and development activities of American industry rests; the "advance of knowledge" achieved through research accounts for an additional 20 per cent of our prosperity.
2. Investments in education, accordingly, mean bigger markets for American businessmen. Rising markets give us strength in our economy.
3. Just as we want our economy to be generally strong, we want the many special benefits that education-based research helps to provide: freedom from disease, better communications, faster travel, clean water, and clear air in our growing cities.
4. We want a national government and an economic structure that can cope with chronic unemployment, a problem which appears to be characteristic of periods of rapid technological change. We believe that education, properly directed, is the chief means whereby people can find new kinds of jobs when the old kinds disappear. Labor, industry, and government must be sensitive to this fact.
5. For our whole system of government to function properly, we need strength and fiscal stability in our local governments. Good education is an important safeguard against economic stagnation and decay of local areas.
6. Of great importance are the benefits that education yields to the student as an individual. For the student, the zealous pursuit of education leads to higher income; the opportunity to choose among a variety of interesting and challenging kinds of work; a greater chance to participate in on-the-job training (in order to keep one's skills fresh and up-to-date); and, finally, job security.

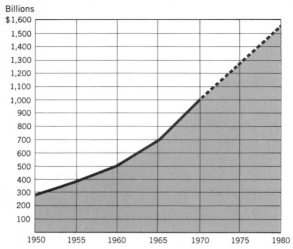

Billions

FIGURE 1–4   Past and projected gross national product. In comparison with other countries, the United States has a high standard of living, and is capable of raising this standard. Approximately 4 per cent of the GNP is expended for public elementary and secondary education. In what way has public education contributed to the enormous growth of the GNP?

7.  By no means, however, are all the individual benefits of education in material form. Education promotes stability of family life, the improvement of educational opportunities for one's children through the early learning experiences that educated parents offer their boys and girls, and a vastly greater capacity to enjoy leisure. Furthermore, the attainment of full cultural maturity may be a central purpose of education.
8.  Education is one of the chief ways by which we come to value human life in all its complexity. Through education, our children are led to develop a feeling of compassionate regard for their fellowmen—to be willing, on the one hand, to walk the extra mile to alleviate our neighbor's distress; and to be able, on the other, to share gracefully our friend's happiness in times of joy.

Frequent criticisms are made of our educational system. Much of this criticism is sincere and justified. Some of it is mixed with half-truths, misinformation, and ill-founded generalizations. There are those who would have us believe that European educational systems are far superior to our public school system. But it should be remembered that [122:4]:

The educational system which is criticized today is the same one from which came the people who built the first atomic bomb, who flew the first airplane, who launched the first atomic submarine, who led the world in thermonuclear experiments, who developed mass industrial production of automobiles, bathtubs, and telephones. And, by the way, gave the world sulfa drugs, terramycin, and Salk vaccine.

Yet, in the face of this phenomenal growth, problems remain. Many are still hungry, poorly housed and clothed, in need of medical attention and more education. To these and other problems, teachers must address themselves as they guide the educational growth of future generations.

## Promotion of the Democratic Way of Life

The founding fathers clearly recognized that education is fundamental to the preservation of freedom and self-government. For example, George Washington, in his "Farewell Address" in 1796, strongly encouraged the spread of knowledge: "Promote then, as an object of primary importance, institutions for the general diffusion of knowledge. In proportion as the structure of a government gives force to public opinion, it is essential that public opinion is enlightened." Thomas Jefferson warned that "if a nation expects to be ignorant and free in a state of civilization it expects what never was and never will be." He felt that "if the condition of man is to be progressively ameliorated . . . education is the chief instrument for effecting it." Indeed, almost every president of the United States has made strong statements regarding the importance of education. In recent years especially, they have worked vigorously to provide various types of federal support in order that the public schools, colleges, and universities might be better able to fulfill their mission.

In order to perpetuate and to strengthen our democratic way of life, youth must gain a clear understanding of the values and traditions that have emerged from mankind's search for desirable ways of living. They must have an operational understanding of the democratic ideals and values that guide free people in acting responsibly, so that, ultimately, the welfare of society is seen as the combined welfare of all individuals. Factual knowledge alone does not ensure wise decision making since

FIGURE 1-5   Trends in the level of educational attainment of persons 25 years old and over in the United States. Between 1940 and 1969, the proportion of high school and college graduates more than doubled, raising the median number of school years completed by persons 25 years of age and over from 8.6 to 12.1. What effect will this trend have upon schools and the role of the teacher?

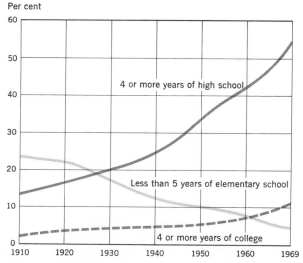

decisions are made largely in terms of the ideals and goals an individual cherishes. How can our schools do an even better job in meeting this basic need in a free world?

John W. Gardner, in his book titled *Excellence* [95:159–160], sounds a warning which has significance for all teachers as they work with boys and girls:

The importance of competence as a condition of freedom has been widely ignored (as some newly independent nations are finding to their sorrow). An amiable fondness for the graces of a free society is not enough. Keeping a free society free—and vital and strong—is no job for the half-educated and the slovenly. Free men must be competent men. In a society of free men, competence is an elementary duty. Men and women doing competently whatever job is theirs to do tone up the whole society. And a man who does a slovenly job—whether he is a janitor or a judge, a surgeon or a technician—lowers the tone of the society. So do the chiselers of high and low degree, the sleight-of-hand artists who always know how to gain an advantage without honest work. They are the regrettable burdens of a free society.

Individual competence, however, is not enough to ensure a strong, vibrant, creative, and productive society. Teachers should help boys and girls value the dignity of work and the establishment of high standards of performance in all phases of life. Youth must learn to accept the responsibility for setting their own high standards of performance, for serving as their own hard disciplinarians, and for demanding quality performance upon the part of their fellowmen. They must feel that satisfaction at the level of mediocrity will result in the decay of the ideals that have made this country great. They must feel a sense of pride in and dedication to their work and to the basic ideals of our society.

In the history of our country we have never faced a period in which the demand for education has been greater. It seems obvious that, barring world catastrophe, the demands for educated intelligence will increase.

In order to add strength to our nation and survive the strong threats to our way of life, increasing numbers of our most able young people must become teachers. Our future welfare rests so heavily upon the quality and quantity of education received by the young that only the best should teach. We, as a nation, can afford no less since our most important resources are the capacities, the energy, and the character of our people.

Alvin C. Eurich very effectively summarized the challenge with which we are faced [72].

America still means promise; it is still a land of opportunity. At this juncture of our history perhaps our greatest opportunity is in the education of our children. If we fail in this, we fail all succeeding generations. But there can be no bright future—as there never has been in any field—if we maintain the status quo. We cannot stand still. Every nation in the history of mankind has been defeated totally and miserably when it strove merely to protect what it had. New nations, including our own, have risen to the top through hardship and struggle, through ingenuity and the courage to create new patterns.

Innovation has been basic to our economic well-being and growth. It is also basic to education, for creative imagination in education will determine our future and the future of our children.

## AMERICAN LIFE IN TRANSITION

In view of these major contributions, one may ask "Why do some people feel that major changes should be made in the American school system?" A great portion of the answer to this question lies in the fact that we are in a major period of transition which appears to have begun in the 1940s and has continued to accelerate. This transition essentially is "a move from an industrial to a post-industrial society, from a pluralistic to a more centrally (or technocratically) directed nation in which traditional concepts, institutions, and practices are being challenged, negotiated, traded, or held on to" [56:5].

In making its forecast for the 1970s and 1980s, the National Industrial Conference Board indicated that this transition which we are encountering is compounded by the following complex considerations [56:5]:

(1) the rate of change which is shrinking research and planning time; (2) outdated criteria used to examine new problems and opportunities; (3) micro and piecemeal ways of dealing with problems at macro scale; (4) public insistence on "instant" solutions and leader impatience with problems that demand attention over longer periods of time; (5) inexperience in bringing about large-scale collaboration on the part of leaders in and between the private and public sectors; (6) the pushing and pulling on the part of those who, through fear or selfish interests, resist change, and those who want to lead and accelerate it; (7) competing demands for scarce talents and resources, and the increasingly frequent absence of needed skills; (8) uncertainty on the part of decision makers and institutions as to the nature of their new roles and responsibilities in a changing society; (9) the temporary inability of our systems of checks and balances, of regulations and controls, to function effectively during the transition; and (10) the question of how to regularize the irregular.

The American school system, an agency of society, is being affected by the profound changes which have been taking place during this period of transition and which will continue to occur in the future. Educators are becoming more aware of these changes as phenomenal events draw attention to the new conditions under which we live. The increasing use of automation and computerization, the expanding use of atomic energy, the phenomenal growth of population, the explosion of knowledge, the launching of communication satellites, the landing of men on the moon, and a host of other sensational developments have been experienced within the space of a third of a century. These have focused attention upon the rapid, pervasive, and fundamental changes in our cultural scene.

Educators can appreciate and aid in planning the proper role of the schools in today's affairs only when they understand the consequences of these basic changes in living conditions. This understanding will help avoid the tendency of educators to impose upon youth the same values, beliefs, and modes of behavior that have characterized the past—thereby transmitting increasing incompetence for dealing with the future. In the swift flow of change there are those among us who would have us feel that whatever exists is irrelevant—that only tomorrow is relevant [258:1].

How does our contemporary culture differ specifically from that of the past? An examination of some of these differences may provide clues to the new competencies that will be required of youth in order to make creative approaches to, and to deal more adequately with, the changing character of the future. The statements that follow should be considered as only the beginning of many with which all thoughtful prospective teachers should be concerned.

1. *Community life has been affected increasingly by industrial and technological processes.* Inventions and new ways of making the basic commodities of life have moved from hand manufacture to a machine process which is largely automatic and highly technical in nature. Through mass production, enormous factories now turn out great quantities of products. The simple agrarian life and modes of production of our forefathers (and in many other parts of the world today) are in sharp contrast with this industrial and technological proficiency. We note the creation of "new relationships between people, education, and work, with technical skills and knowledge, mental alertness, and creative capacities taking priority over capacities to endure hard physical labor" [127:2]. To what extent has the school's curriculum been modified in order to reflect these changes?

2. *Extreme ease of production has led to a high standard of living for many.* In spite of the range of differences existing within our society, we now enjoy the highest standard of living in the world. The results of

FIGURE 1–6  Number of farms in the United States. Between 1952 and 1970 the number of farms declined from 5.2 million to 2.9 million—resulting in a corresponding decrease in rural population.

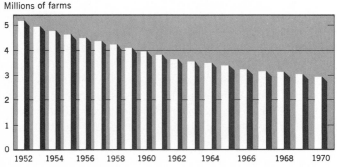

Millions of farms

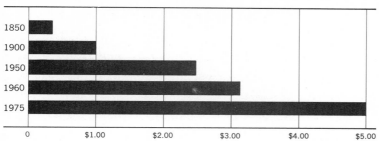

FIGURE 1–7    Changes in productivity of workers, 1850–1975. In 1975 each worker will produce almost twelve times as much as the worker of 1850.

our scientific and industrial knowledge have provided us with more of the material things than ever before. As compared to the past, we live in better houses, take more and longer vacation trips, engage in more outdoor activities, dine out more often, attend more sports activities, read more books, periodicals, and newspapers, listen to more records, engage in more hobbies, and attend more concerts, art galleries, and museums. In brief, the pattern of our lives has changed very significantly as a result of this increase of abundance.

3.   *Modern living has become increasingly urban.* In 1950, 59 per cent of our population lived in urban areas. This percentage had increased to over 70 in 1970. The major portion of the remaining 30 per cent live in nonfarm rural locations and commute to urban areas for employment. During this period of time, decided increases have occurred in such occupational groups as professional and technical workers, proprietors and managers, clerical and sales workers, skilled and semiskilled workers, and service workers. For the most part, these occupations are located in urban areas. What changes in the character of living and the education needs of youth have resulted from this increase in urbanization?

4.   *Vast differences exist in the educational opportunities afforded children.* Large numbers of boys and girls, especially those living in the slum sections of cities, may be considered to be educationally disadvantaged. Often finding little relevance in the school experiences, many of them either drop out or graduate from school without any hope of continuing their education, regardless of their abilities. They may experience major difficulty in finding employment and a role to play in an increasingly complex, technological society. To what extent are teachers attempting to understand the backgrounds and values held by disadvantaged children and their families? To what extent are teachers respecting the racial and ethnic differences which these boys and girls hold and, at the same time, helping them to become effective citizens?

5.   *Increased standardization of policies, procedures, and products has resulted in increased pressures toward conformity.* The frontiersman

and the farmer lived close to the land. Their welfare depended heavily upon the use of individual initiative, hard work, and ingenuity in solving problems and in improving their status in life. Mechanization, unionization, standardization, and pressures toward conformance tend to inhibit individuality and creativity at a time when these qualities are especially needed. To what extent is the school assisting the young in making creative approaches to the solution of the increasingly complex problems in our society?

6. *Productivity, new markets, new economic and distributive occupations, communication, and urbanization have been influenced by new patterns of ownership.* Yesterday's society was characterized mainly by individual ownership and direct proprietary control over the means of production. Today the ownership of industry is diffused. The stockholder or bondholder rarely understands or manages to any appreciable degree the enterprises in which his money is invested. Labor groups have become highly organized and are corporate in character. The forces which direct our economic and productive affairs are corporate groups that are increasingly directed by professional managerial experts. Today the individual functions more and more in terms of the group with which he comes in contact. Youth has difficulty in being able to identify, to find purpose, to develop feelings of responsibility, to become effective citizens.

7. *Our population has become highly mobile.* Modern transportation facilities and a generally high standard of living in an economy which is extremely productive make it possible for people to move about with great ease. This means that people no longer may be educated to fit the requirement of only one restricted community. They are much more in touch with each other and consequently know more about how others live. Personal aspirations are altered as the possibilities of a better life are experienced firsthand.

Millions of workers change jobs every year. Today, approximately 20 per cent of all the families in the United States move yearly to gain better jobs, health, or climate, or for other reasons. Much of the mobility of people is "from the open country and small towns and villages to large centers of population and from the centers of cities to the suburbs, with the inevitable consequences of culture clashes that shake institutions, disturb long-established customs, set values in new perspective, color political action, disrupt systems of school support, and leave indelible marks on the behavior patterns and characters of children" [127:3].

8. *We are now living in a highly interdependent world community.* A dislocation in one major industry today may affect the industrial actions, health, and economic well-being of large numbers of people in distant areas. War today is a concern of all the people; depression is global in proportions. We now face the need for the skills and knowledge necessary to enable us to live together in this complex, interdependent

society—accepting without prejudice people of other races, creeds, and religions.

9.   *The older controls in our social life no longer operate as they did in our earlier agrarian period.* The family, for instance, was at one time an institution around which centered the production and marketing of goods, personal services, recreation of all members, and a large part of the group's education and worship. Today practically all these activities are performed through some other community institution or organization. The parent used to supervise the chores of the young, but today if work is available, children are generally without the supervision of a parent or teacher. What is the responsibility of the school in providing for these learnings?

10.   *Today's community life for many has become highly imper-sonal compared with small-town agrarian life in the past.* In the con-temporary metropolitan area the individual is often unknown to his neighbor; personal identity frequently is lost in the confusion of urban life. Here one is less accountable for his actions, less subject to the pressures of a society in which every individual is well known by his neighbors. The problems of finding an adequate sense of belonging and adequacy seem to become more difficult under such conditions. Why are there 20 million mentally ill persons in our society, 6 million alcoholics, 44,000 suicides a year, increasing incidence of juvenile delinquency and drug addiction? To what extent are schools responsible for promoting desirable physical and mental health in this world?

11.   *Technological advancements have made possible greater amounts of leisure time.* Since 1859, the amount of leisure time for the average worker in our society has increased from 12 to 52 hours per week. Today Americans spend more income for leisure-time pursuits than for all public elementary and secondary schools. In spite of the constructive benefits that have been derived from the increased amount of leisure time available to the average individual, some questions having educational significance may be raised. How can we account for the low state of physical fitness of children, youth, and adults throughout America? Why, according to the late J. Edgar Hoover, has serious crime reached the highest point in history, and, why is it increasing four times as fast as the population? How constructively do those over 65 years of age spend their time? Why have so many homes, the basic unit in our society, dis-integrated because of the high divorce rate?

12.   *American society has become one in which an understanding of totalitarianism and an ability to meet its challenge are imperative.* With the current trend toward dictatorship, an enlightened citizen should study the significance of the suppression of the individual's thoughts and actions, not only in the international scene but also in our domestic affairs, and be prepared to oppose tyrannies over free men's self-government. This ability to lay bare the basis of totalitarianism is of

crucial importance today; in our technological society the bigotry of the demagogue may immediately reach a whole people rather than be merely disseminated by word of mouth from one speaker to a handful of others. The forces which make for tyranny over the minds of men may use the devices of modern science for their own purposes. To find ways of disclosing the purposes and evaluating the efforts of totalitarianism of all kinds is an imperative need in modern society.

13.   *The citizen today needs to make finer and more subtle discriminations in what he says and hears than did his ancestors.* Through radio, movies, television, and the press, modern citizens receive opinions and attitudes which tend to be uncritical expressions of emotion and exhortation rather than critically examined statements of conviction. "Different ethnic, racial, and cultural groups of people are vigorously struggling for recognition, full rights, fair employment practices, nondiscrimination in housing, and higher levels of living. Pressure tactics, emotional displays, and florid propaganda displace reason and the exercise of sober judgment in approaches to the solution of common problems" [127:3].

We are asked to distinguish between groups, interests, and pressures whose purposes are not always explicit and whose avowals may be different from the intentions which underlie them. To avoid a feeling of hopelessness, anxiety, and frustration, it is necessary to have the techniques and skills by which a thoughtful evaluation may penetrate to the real significance of what goes on in contemporary society. What is the difference between liberal and subversive activities, indoctrination and education, freedom and license, control and dictatorship?

These characteristics of modern living are of course not exhaustive of the changes that have occurred in our culture, but they are representative. They reveal some of the modern conditions with which prospective teachers are faced. They set the stage on which teachers are to act. They define the requirements of the context in which teachers must develop professional proficiencies. If schools are to keep pace with the conditions of modern life, they should consider how well they will be able to meet the demands of the contemporary social scene. To what extent have educators been aware of the pervasive changes of modern living, and to what extent have they defined the content and methods of formal education in terms of these conditions?

## THE CHALLENGE OF THE FUTURE

The changing nature of our culture, as indicated in the preceding section, represents only a prelude to the rate and the scale of change that may take place in the future. We will be encountering the future so rapidly that the ordered and familiar patterns of living may seem to be inadequate to provide direction for us [240:67]. Toffler maintains that this rate of change may become so great that we may experience a state of future shock—"the dizzying disorganization brought on by the premature arrival of the future" [282:13]. In his opinion, "it may well be the most important disease of tomorrow"—a breakdown in communication, a misreading of reality, an inability to cope [282:13]. This possibility raises some fundamental problems for mankind: How much change can he accept and assimilate? How can he retain some familiar clues that, in the past, have guided him into the future? How can he gain and maintain any sense of competence for determining the direction in which this change will take place?

Increasing attention is being given to forecasting the future—sometimes called *futuristics.* As the National Industrial Conference Board points out, many current acute problems—air and water pollution, transportation, inner-city deterioration—might have been lessened if better forecasting had been done twenty or thirty years ago [56:1]. Unless we do more long-range forecasting and planning in all areas—business, industry, government, education, etc.—we will be "backing into the future" [56:1].

The purpose of forecasting is to enable people to make better choices. In brief, it is the process of (1) anticipating what occurrences are possible and assessing their probabilities; (2) identifying the occurrences that can be controlled and the extent of such control; and (3) evaluating alternative future possibilities, considering varying degrees of control that are within our power [56:2]. It is a deliberate process of planning the future rather than planning for the future.

Educators are faced with the challenge of being in the forefront of forecasting the future and planning educational programs that will enable their products—the students—to live constructively in a world that will become increasingly different from the world of today. Unfortunately much of the curriculum in schools today is geared to the past, with little attention being given to the futuristic type of thinking and skill development that future generations must have if, perhaps, they are to survive. Furthermore, with the "premature arrival of tomorrow," it seems certain that education in the future will not be a straight-line extrapolation of the past (Lecture of Alvin Toffler, Indiana University, April 26, 1971).

A number of educators are devoting much thought to education in the future. For example, Donald N. Michael, in his challenging book *The Next Generation* [158], indicates some changes that most likely will take place within the next few years and which will affect greatly the role of the school in society and the work of teachers. Much of the discussion that follows is adapted from three lectures he gave to prospective teachers in an introductory education course.[3]

A generation is a convenient span of time in terms of which teachers

[3]Permission granted by Donald N. Michael.

can project on probable changes since (1) the pace of change in politics, technology, society, and the world is so great that it is difficult to make useful predictions much beyond this period of time; (2) this is the period in which you as a teacher will assume major responsibilities as a citizen and as a mediator, moderator, and transmitter of the culture to the pupils you will teach; and (3) the next generation of young people will share, to a greater or lesser degree, the various value systems that exist in today's society. If we go much beyond this time period, it is highly probable that the people who will be growing up and becoming adults will be emphasizing values that are importantly different from those we share.

The speculations that follow apply basically to the United States. What may happen in regard to the rest of the world is vague, extremely complex, and uncertain. It should be held in mind, however, that what happens to us in the future may be affected enormously by what happens in the rest of the world. Michael feels that "whether we live or die over these years may depend more upon what happens in the emerging nations, for example, than on what we do at home."

What, then, may happen during the next few years that has significance for a teacher? Many of these probable happenings are well known and represent only the continuation of current visible trends. *But frequently it is as important to be encouraged to think further upon matters with which we may be familiar as it is to be exposed to new ideas and information.*

1. *Our population will increase considerably, and its composition will change significantly.* The population of the United States reached the historic point of 200 million November 20, 1967. By 1985 it is expected to

FIGURE 1–8   Past and projected population of the world. Note that the population approximately doubled between 1760 and 1880 (120 years) and again between 1880 and 1960 (80 years). What new educational problems will arise if the population doubles between 1960 and the year 2000 (40 years)?

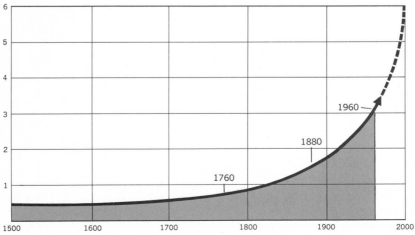

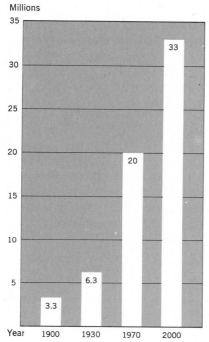

FIGURE 1–9  Growth in the number of people over 65 years of age in the United States. What educational needs does this increasing population age group present, and how should schools and teachers attempt to meet these needs?

be between 235 and 250 million, with the strong probability of increasing to over 300 million by the turn of the century. In 1975 almost 50 per cent of the population will be less than 25 years of age, and this percentage is expected to increase. In 1970 there were approximately 20 million people 65 years of age and older. It is predicted that this 65 and older age group will grow to 25 million in 1985 and from 28 to 33 million by the year 2000. This condition increases the polarization of our population. We face the increasing problem of meeting the pre-work force needs of the young and the needs of those who are retired. Definite trends toward lowering the age of retirement will increase the percentage of the population who are in the post-work force. From an educational standpoint these two large populations represent decidedly contrasting needs and conflicting value systems. Both between and within these groups there are the well-educated and the ill-educated, the haves and the have-nots, the laggards and the leaders, the concerned and the indifferent. These vast contrasts pose enormous educational problems with which educators will need to grapple. What changes will need to be made in our educational structure to meet the challenge which this situation will present?

    2.  *A much greater percentage of our population will be living in*

*urban areas.* By 1980, approximately 80 per cent of the population in the United States will be living in urban areas, with about 70 per cent living on approximately 5 per cent of the land area. Most of them will be living in four major urban areas, called megalopoli, which will consist of smaller cities that have become fused together. One such area will stretch from Maine to Virginia; another, from Minneapolis and Chicago to Buffalo; a third, from San Francisco to San Diego; and a fourth, from Miami, Florida to Houston, Texas. As a result, there will be unprecedentedly large urban complexes—a situation historically unfamilar, especially to the older generations.

As towns and cities fuse together across state lines, the conventional forms of city and state government will be inadequate to meet the problems and potentials of the regional cities. During this time period, interesting and hopefully successful experiments in new forms of government, school districting, and the like will emerge. At the same time, some urban areas will be growing while others will be decaying—each presenting different needs and value patterns. Density populations in metropolitan areas may reach 700 per square mile as compared to 400 in 1970. If present trends continue, further problems most likely will be generated with respect to crime, pollution, transportation, polarization of black-white communities, housing, simple privacy, social interaction, natural beauty, outdoor recreation, individual freedom, and equal economic and educational opportunities.

How will these changes affect the perspectives and values of youth as well as parents and other adults? In what ways may the organization and financing of school systems be changed? What changes may need to be made in teacher certification procedures, in programs of instruction, and in the preservice and in-service preparation of teachers?

3. *It will become increasingly difficult for the individual to establish and maintain identity, dignity, and purpose in life.* With the trend toward urbanization and the formation of very large cities, parents and children may be less inclined to identify themselves with other people, as well as institutions and communities. Interpersonal relationships may become highly transient. Physical uprooting of families most likely will increase because of the need for parents to change jobs more often. Values may change and life-styles may become more complex. Increased feelings of isolation may exist in the midst of great numbers of people, rapid communication, and transportation. It may become increasingly difficult for the individual to relate to others, to feel a cause or purpose in life, to sense a feeling of adequacy and worth. All these probable conditions may result in the teacher having to play an increasingly significant role in helping youth to establish identity as well as values in terms of which they will direct their lives. How will teachers be able to provide more humanizing experiences for their students without sacrificing opportunities for the students to gain the fundamental knowledge and skills needed

for effective living? How will teachers aid in the development of the twenty-first-century man described by Goodlad [102:4]:

We would have him be a man with a strong sense of himself and his own humanness, with awareness of his thoughts and feelings, with the capacity to feel and express love and joy and to recognize tragedy and feel grief. We would have him be a man who, with a strong and realistic sense of his own worth, is able to relate openly with others, to cooperate effectively with them toward common ends, and to view mankind as one while respecting diversity and difference. We would want him to be a being who, even while very young, somehow senses that he has it within himself to become more than he now is, that he has the capacity for lifelong spiritual and intellectual growth. We would want him to cherish that vision of the man he is capable of becoming and to cherish the development of the same potentiality in others.

4. *The influence of parents upon the educational growth of their children may decrease.* A number of factors will affect the relationship between parents and children. For example, there may be more physical separation of parents and children. More mothers may find it necessary to work, either to satisfy career aspirations or to supplement the family budget. Greater emphasis undoubtedly will be given to preschool experiences which may lessen the contacts of parents with children under six years of age. Ease of transportation may cause children and youth to spend more time away from home in camping, using recreational facilities, traveling, and studying abroad.

There is the possibility, however, that advanced technology may tend to return the family to the center of the stage as a basic learning unit. As Goodlad points out [102:4]:

Each home could become a school, in effect, via an electronic console connected to a central computer system in a learning hub, a videotape and microfilm library regulated by a computer, and a national educational television network. Whether at home or elsewhere, each student, of whatever age, will have at the touch of a button access to a comprehen-

FIGURE 1–10  Past and projected number of women in the work force. The trend toward more women being in the work force will continue. How should the public schools seek to meet their vocational needs? What are the implications for the education of children of working women?

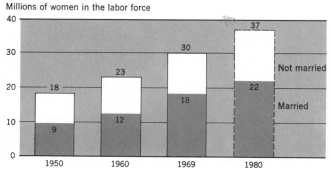

Millions of women in the labor force

sive "learning package," including printed lessons, experiments to be performed, recorded information, videotaped lectures, and films.

5. *There may be a definite increase in the number of women in the labor force.* Between 1969 and 1980 the number of women in the labor force is expected to increase from a total of 30 million to a total of 37 million—employed either full-time or on a part-time basis [121:5]. It is estimated that 22 million of these 37 million women in 1980 will be married. A relatively high percentage of them will be between the ages of 20 and 44 years, having children under 18 years of age at home. In what ways may the educational needs and objectives of girls change? How may the work of a teacher be affected by this tendency for an increasing number of mothers to work at least part-time in the labor force? What are the implications for the establishment of day-care centers?

6. *The percentage of culturally deprived children may increase, especially in the central part of large metropolitan cities.* By 1980, 50 per cent of the children living in the central part of our large metropolitan cities may be considered to be culturally deprived. Unless rather drastic measures are taken to curtail the development of this condition, a very significant percentage of young people will never be able to develop fully their potential for effective democratic living. Benjamin Bloom, in his book *Stability and Change in Human Characteristics,* finds that the intellectual and emotional deprivation of many children begins early. From his studies [28:104–105], he finds that half of a person's "intellectuality," as well as general intelligence, is formed by the age of four. By the age of six, when a child enters school, he has developed as much as two-thirds of the intelligence he will have at maturity. Even with regard to purely academic achievement, at least one-third of the development at age 18 has taken place prior to a child's entrance into the first grade at school. If children are deprived of early intellectual stimulation, they may never reach the heights of which they might be capable.

Bloom maintains that the environment has a maximum impact on the development of a specific trait during the period of time in which that trait experiences the most rapid growth. For example, a starvation diet would not affect the height of an eighteen-year-old, but could severely retard the growth of a one-year-old baby—a loss that might never be recovered. Other studies indicate that poor diet in very young children also can permanently damage intellectual growth.

What measures are being taken and what new steps should be taken in order to overcome the problems of cultural deprivation of people in our society? How can educators help in solving this problem?

7. *In terms of the way we shall be living (life-styles), there will be opportunities for greater diversity in the midst of conformity.* A study of life in various communities will reveal that the level of anonymity for the individual tends to increase as the population of a city increases. As the population of urban areas increases, therefore, people will have greater

freedom to experiment with the styles of living they desire. They will be developing and experimenting with different sets of values which will affect how they live, what they aspire to, how they want their children educated, what kinds of education they want for themselves, and where they want to live.

Within this context of anonymity, the individual may become increasingly self-centered and demanding. He may tend to use people with careless indifference of the consequences to them; take from the material world whatever he wishes, but seldom if ever give anything in return; insist upon being permitted nearly everything and being held accountable for nothing; become increasingly disrespectful of law and order— frequently resorting to violence, lawlessness, and crime; and become insensitive to the need for any environmental controls.

Concurrent with this probable change in life-styles, there may be a tendency for values to become negotiable items. As the National Industrial Conference Board points out [56:51]:

Goals, values, and ethics in U.S. society are being questioned, modified, and traded. This state of flux grows out of and accompanies transitions from a "yesterday" controlled by adults to a "today" dominated by young people; from a production to a service economy; from a concern for quantity and status to a quest for quality and equality. Schizoid situations proliferate. "The establishment" sees traditional values as eroding; the young believe that many of these values have lost their relevance, and that "the establishment" obstructs change. The sweep of power from individuals and single units to groups and conglomerates, from a pluralistic power base to a powerful apex, throws up in its wake serious questions concerning cherished American ideals. The question is: Which values will be traded and which held?

Teachers will have the opportunity to work with students who represent a greater variety of life-styles. They will be confronted with the more difficult task of helping youth as well as adults clarify their values in terms of which their behavior will be governed and to build more meaningful concepts of freedom and responsibility in a democratic society.

8. *More and more demands will be made for high-level social competence.* In the past our lives have been related basically to our local environments. In the future our lives will be affected more by our continental and world environments. So many things will be happening in so many places that the environment in which teachers and students live will become quite complex. The number of significant social interactions will become almost overwhelming.

Only recently have we begun to take seriously first-class citizenship for blacks, as well as the recognition of the need to do something about poverty in our society. There are many other social requirements which we must set for ourselves. We are only beginning to recognize that we must be more humane and prepare sensible and meaningful lives for older people. There are questions regarding air and water pollution, traffic control, population control, conservation of resources, etc. All these interact with one another, and all these have assets and liabilities with regard to carrying out each of them. A teacher will not be able to concentrate totally on the discipline he is teaching or on the community in which he is located. To be a good teacher, he will have to transcend subject-matter disciplines as well as local attachments. These conditions will put a much greater burden upon teachers than in the past, when life was less complex, less closely coupled, and less loaded with events of enormous implication.

9.  *Leisure will become an increasingly important part of the lives of many.* Automation, shorter work weeks, earlier retirement, and longer life-spans will provide even greater amounts of free time for the individual to spend as he wishes. Increasing affluence will extend the scope of ways in which he may choose to spend this free time. Free time, therefore, will become a very important part of life. It will take on a legitimacy and a significance that our Protestant ethic-oriented society has not had in the past. Even though work will still be considered a moral obligation of the individual, leisure will be considered a more virtuous part of life. For some people, increased free time will present a wonderful opportunity in which they may grow—a time for personal fulfillment. For others it may be a period of boredom, frustration, and anxiety—or a time for dangerous and sometimes criminal activities as a way of getting a "kick" out of life. If children are to avoid the undesirable results of increased leisure time, they need to learn before they grow up how to find

FIGURE 1–11   Projected changes in the spending of family income. Between 1968 and 1980, it is estimated that the amount of money spent on nondurables (clothing, food, paper goods, etc.) will increase 50 per cent; expenditures for services (laundry, restaurants, recreation, health, repairs, etc.) will increase 75 per cent; but expenditures for durables (cars, appliances, furniture, etc.) will increase 100 per cent. At the turn of the century, about half of the average wage earner's weekly pay was spent on food. In 1980 less than one-fifth of his wages will be needed for food. What are the social, economic, and educational implications of these changes?

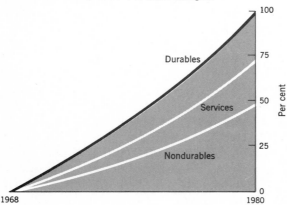

personal enrichment in their free time. Toynbee, the great historian, warns that never in the history of man has any nation been able to accumulate a vast amount of leisure time for its people and survive.

How to help both young and old learn to use leisure time for personal enrichment and fulfillment presents exciting and important opportunities for the teacher. How will the work of a teacher be affected? How might the role of the school in the community change? What changes may be made in the school's curriculum? Will cocurricular activities in the school take on added significance? What changes might take place in the use of the school's library, auditorium, playground, or fine arts and music departments? Will the use of the school's facilities tend to follow the 24 hours per day pattern of operation that more industries and businesses may adopt as a result of automation? What new requests for the services of teachers may be made by industries, businesses, recreation centers, and government agencies?

10. *We will become increasingly aware of the need for environmental controls.* Although environmental scientists have been concerned for some time about the serious, perhaps irreversible, deterioration of the ecological conditions that support life on this earth, mankind received its first shocking realization of the problems on Christmas Eve 1968 when the astronauts sent back pictures of the earth. For the first time, in the words of Von Braun, "We saw the beautiful little blue silver sphere on which we live shining forth against the blackness of infinity. The peoples of the earth saw for the first time how finite our habitat really is; they sensed its essential frailty" [262:5].

The threat to human survival comes from several interrelated problems: (1) the explosive increase in human population; (2) an awesome increase in man's ability to alter the environment (largely through the release of vast quantities of gaseous, liquid, and solid effluent), and (3) rapid depletion of resources that are in finite supply. If man is to survive, it is imperative that all three of the problems be dealt with simultaneously [295:10].

Although the population of the United States is only a fraction of the world's population, we proportionately are by far the most serious "pollutants" since we are the largest per capita consumers of goods and materials. What should be the role of educators in assisting mankind to establish bases for survival?

11. *The educational attainment of our population will continue to rise.* Between 1965 and 1985 the percentage of men 25 years of age and over who have completed four years or more of college is expected to increase from 11.4 to 19.4 per cent, and the increase for women is expected to be from 6.4 to 9.7 per cent [204:1]. During this period of time the total number of high school graduates is expected to rise from about 47 million to 87 or 88 million among persons 25 years old and over. At the same time it is anticipated that there will be a sharp reduction in the percentage of persons 25 years old and over who have had less than five

When viewed from the surface of the moon, the earth appears as a giant space ship carrying its own life support system. Learning how to preserve this finite system has become a major educational responsibility. *(Photograph from National Aeronautics and Space Administration.)*

years of formal schooling. The expected increase in the median years of school completed by those 25 years old and over may also serve as an indicator of improvement in educational attainment. Between 1960 and 1985 the median is expected to increase from 10.5 to 12.4 years of formal schooling [204:2]. What effect may this expected increase in educational attainment have on the pupils as well as on the parents and other adults with whom teachers will work? How will our economy and social structure be affected?

12.  *Both basic and applied knowledge will expand at a very rapid rate.* "If we start with the birth of Christ as the base point, it is estimated that man's knowledge doubled for the first time around 1750. The second doubling of man's knowledge occurred by 1900. . . . With the acceleration of an industrial and business economy, man's knowledge doubled a third time by 1950 and a fourth time by 1960" [155:11]. We may expect this trend in the expansion of knowledge to continue, especially when we consider that, for example, 90 per cent of all the scientists who have lived since the dawn of history are living and working today [56:21]. Bentley Glass, a distinguished scientist and past national president of Phi Beta Kappa, states [96:44]:

The obsolescence of education in rapidly developing fields of knowledge has become about equal in rate to the obsolescence of an automobile. In five to seven years it is due for a complete replacement. It follows that our times, to a degree generally quite unrecognized, demand a major reconstitution of the educational process, which must become one of life-long renewal. Perhaps a month out of every year, or three months every third year, might be an acceptable new pattern. Indeed, instead of cramming the educational years of life into adolescence and early maturity, a more efficient plan might be to interrupt education with work periods after elementary school, high school, and college. In any case, programs of continuing education for all professional people must become mandatory, and the educational effort and expenditures must be expanded by at least a third to permit adequate retraining and reeducation.

How will the school system be affected by the continuing education needs of all ages of people? What kinds of skills and attitudes should teachers attempt to develop in students so that they may be effective citizens, competent to deal with the problems they will face in life? What implications does this rapid increase in knowledge have for the in-service education of teachers—how can they be relevant in content, process, and procedures?

13. *Significant technological changes will take place as a result of more automation and the use of computers.* The term "cybernation" refers to the use of computers in automation. Through the use of a procedure known as numerical control, computers will replace many skilled workers who, in the past, have designed and fabricated complex components for such things as shipbuilding and automobile manufacturing. Much of what is called design work, in such areas as architecture and engineering, is a fairly routine task of working through a series of alternatives. This type of design can now be done by computers. As a result, a person may try out different models of how an airplane might be designed, how a certain kind of economic system might operate, how a particular national strategy might be construed, or how some type of educational program might function. In other words, a computer may be used to try out various ideas and refine them before they are actually put into operation.

It is easy to see that job opportunities, as well as the lives of many people, will be affected greatly by cybernation.

Many unskilled workers will lose out to machines, and some extension of the antipoverty program may be needed to provide them with the services they cannot afford. However, some unskilled jobs will remain and some new ones will be created. Automation will turn some jobs that now require skill into jobs that merely require watching a meter or a dial; other jobs which now require a high level of skill will be split into simpler ones that will be done in part by semiskilled workers and in part by machines.

Many skilled workers will be forced to retrain. Already, skilled machinists' jobs have begun to be abolished as computer-controlled machine tools take over their tasks. Gradually, many bank clerks, office workers, auditors, draftsmen, and middle-level managers and engineers will find their work being done by computers [159:8–9].

The work of highly creative persons will not be threatened by cybernation. Rather, they will have more latitude for being creative. For example, creative people in such areas as economics, political science,

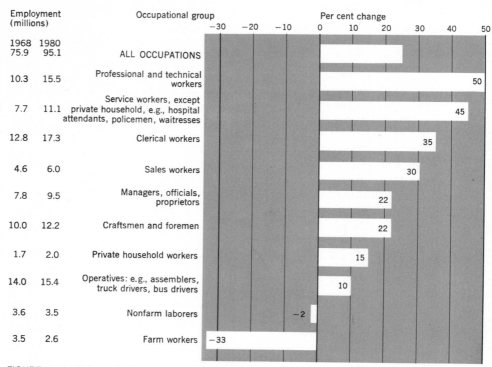

| Employment (millions) 1968 | 1980 | Occupational group | Per cent change |
|---|---|---|---|
| 75.9 | 95.1 | ALL OCCUPATIONS | |
| 10.3 | 15.5 | Professional and technical workers | 50 |
| 7.7 | 11.1 | Service workers, except private household, e.g., hospital attendants, policemen, waitresses | 45 |
| 12.8 | 17.3 | Clerical workers | 35 |
| 4.6 | 6.0 | Sales workers | 30 |
| 7.8 | 9.5 | Managers, officials, proprietors | 22 |
| 10.0 | 12.2 | Craftsmen and foremen | 22 |
| 1.7 | 2.0 | Private household workers | 15 |
| 14.0 | 15.4 | Operatives: e.g., assemblers, truck drivers, bus drivers | 10 |
| 3.6 | 3.5 | Nonfarm laborers | −2 |
| 3.5 | 2.6 | Farm workers | −33 |

FIGURE 1–12 Estimated changes between 1968 and 1980 in occupational groups. What are the educational implications of these changes?

and the behavioral sciences will be able to conceptualize about man and his environment in a much higher and different manner from that which is available without the assistance of the computer. Likewise, the demand for people in most of the professions will increase greatly, and the hours of work per week will tend to be longer than at present.

The person who does a routine kind of physical or mental work, on the other hand, will be potentially subject to displacement. This means that, in the years ahead, we shall find many people being continually displaced from their jobs, having to learn new jobs, and having to live in a number of different locations and to learn new ways of life. It means that children will grow up recognizing the fact that many of them will have two or three careers which will involve seven or eight different jobs during their work years. It means that they may spend a significant amount of their lives in school being retrained and reeducated. Obviously, the vocational education programs in our schools will need to undergo considerable reorientation. It also means that the demands upon teachers and vocational counselors will increase greatly. How should teachers attempt to counsel and educate youth for a work world that is becoming so complex—when many of the jobs that will exist in the year 2000 are not now known? How can we absorb effectively another 15 million into the labor force during the 1970s and early 1980s in spite of the decreasing number of man-hours required for the production of goods?

14. *There will be a decided increase in management technology.* Management technology refers to a set of procedures, techniques, and approaches to organizing, on a national scale and over long periods of time, the manpower brawn and brains to accomplish major tasks. In other words, brain power may be organized administratively and procedurally in much the same way as men have been organized to use their muscles in the past. Management technology makes it possible to plan ahead and to undertake activities that may literally change the nation in terms of how various resources and agencies are used.

Management technology started after World War II as a new approach to the development of our weapons system, and has been applied more recently to the space program, to city building and rebuilding, to oceanography, to the construction of school buildings, and in a number of other areas. Undoubtedly this trend will continue. This means that more and more people will be meshed in larger and larger administration

FIGURE 1–13 Estimated percentage changes between 1968 and 1980 in various industries. State and local government and service industries will experience the most rapid gains. What effect will these changes have upon the occupational needs of youth?

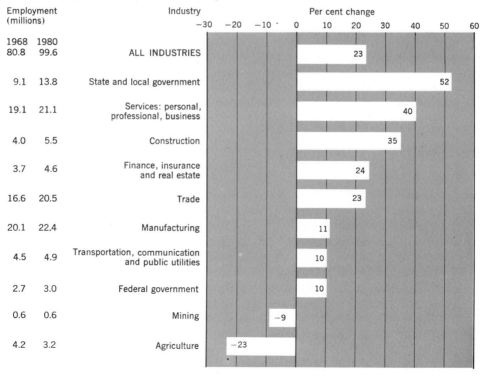

complexes. How will an individual in this type of complex maintain a sense of loyalty, dignity, and worth? What new skills, understandings, and attitudes will be needed?

15. *We probably will experience a greater degree of social engineering.* The term "social engineering," refers to the systematic application of social science to the organization, control, direction, and motivation of man and his institutions. The computer enables the social scientist to do two things he has never been able to do before. First, he can build enormously complex models about man and his institutions. In the past, his work was done using only simple models because he was unable to keep the many variables in mind and manipulate them. But the computer has the capacity to manipulate very large numbers of variables. This means that very complex and subtle models of how men behave in groups and organizations can be conceived of and simulated on computers. Second, by virtue of the computer, he can collect data about society as it is now, check the computer models against them, and determine whether the models represent reality. In the past the social scientist was not able to do this type of verification, since it took a long time to collect the data and to process them. Because of the rapid processing of data, there exists the potential for developing far more sophisticated social sciences.

We inevitably will have available, for good or for bad, many more opportunities to control or be controlled than we have had in the past. More funds will be available for research to evaluate and understand what is happening as growth takes place in federal programs dealing with such areas as education, poverty, unemployment, pollution, population, counterinsurgency, and guerrilla warfare. It will be necessary to conduct this research in order that we will not flounder in our own complexity. This raises a basic problem of determining who is going to do the job of deciding what is to be controlled as well as that of controlling it. What are going to be the ethical bases for deciding what is to be controlled? Who is to be controlled and under what circumstances? This kind of power carries with it a potential for corruption, even for destroying our whole democratic system. Since education is bound to be affected to some extent, this profound ethical question will confront teachers in the future.

16. *There may be an increasing professionalization of the government and all activities having to do with the planning and administration of society.* Almost everyone will admit that, as our population increases, the task of governing ourselves will become more complex. We note the increasing role being played by the government in solving the complex and technical problems faced by our society. The solution of many of these problems calls for the services of people who are highly competent in governmental affairs. Perhaps the greatest challenge for our society over the years ahead is going to be meeting the increasing professionalization of the government and of all other activities having to do with the

planning and administration of our society. This condition raises the very important question of the role played by the citizen who is not part of the professional governmental processes by which our society will be conducted. Is there a danger of following the same plan that has been formally approved in Russia for the establishment of a national computer network for the collection and processing of information essential for the control, the planning, and the management of the country's economy—in fact, all aspects of that nation's life? How will teachers be able to face the critical challenge of helping pupils and adults identify themselves with and play significant citizenship roles in the direction of the nation and in other democratic processes?

17. *Major and dramatic advancement most likely will be made in biological engineering.* It is generally agreed that the developments in biological science and their application over the next two decades will be at least as spectacular as the development of atom smashers and the like in the field of physics. One development will be that of the increased ability to alter brain processes, modify personality, and control behavior through the use of chemical agents, drugs, and electronic devices. Krech [139:48] feels that in the not too distant future teachers will be "talking about enzyme-assisted instruction, protein memory consolidators, antibiotic memory repellers, and the chemistry of the brain." There is much evidence that memories can be enhanced or wiped out. Biologists probably will be able to change characteristics that might be inherited. They may be able to predetermine the sex of a baby. They will be able to help the aged to revitalize their memories, skills, and abilities. They undoubtedly will find ways to manipulate the emotional and cognitive characteristics of human beings.

This raises several questions: Who has the right to make these changes? What are the implications of these advancements for dealing with behavior problems, psychological disorders, juvenile delinquency, potential school dropouts, crime, and the like? Will there be possibilities of motivating more young people to develop their capacities for democratic living to the fullest extent possible? What new educational needs and economic and social complexities may arise if it becomes possible to revitalize the memories and abilities of older people?

## Some Major Professional Challenges Facing Teachers

In addition to those already mentioned, what are some other major professional challenges which the future holds for teachers?

1. How should a teacher balance his role between being the agent for conserving the styles of the past and acting as the cutting edge for disrupting traditions and inventing new ones? It has always been a

question whether the task of education is to prepare people to fit the society or to prepare them to change the society. In the past, teachers have been able to be rather casual about the problem because the nature of society did not change very fast. But the future is going to change society fast and radically, and a teacher is going to be confronted perpetually with the problem of determining his role as a conserver of the past and as an innovator so far as the future is concerned.

2.  What will be an appropriate role model for a teacher? In the future the status of the teacher in society will increase because the welfare of society will be more and more dependent on education of all sorts and at all ages.

Education will be available almost on a cradle-to-grave basis. More children of all economic groups will attend nursery school and kindergarten. Post-high school education will be more widely available and, with increased recognition that a well-educated population is a national necessity, government subsidies for higher education will be more general.

Many different kinds of institutions will provide opportunities for lifelong education. Community colleges, vocational schools, centers for instruction in recreation activities, and institutions attached to industry, business, and government will cater to all individuals, regardless of age: Indeed, we will see more and more intermingling of age groups as education becomes a general condition of living rather than just early preparation for it [159:11–12].

As a result of these highly probable conditions, a teacher will play an exceedingly important role in the lives of his pupils as well as in those of many adults. To his pupils a teacher will be an expression of adulthood and the opportunities which being an adult presents. Expressing the adult world through what one teaches and relating it to society become a very interesting, difficult, and challenging task for the teacher.

3.  How should a teacher attempt to promote the growth and development of wisdom in his pupils? We shall need people who are more than skilled engineers, scientists, and technicians. We shall need people who are humanists, who have the intuition that is necessary to understand the human predicament, and who have the insight to do the things that the large society with its high aspirations sets for itself. It is going to take wise men and women, indeed, to act in such ways that save the individual from being lost sight of in the mass. In the past we have been able to bumble through and manage to get along with only a few wise people. No man could do very much good or evil to mankind. But this will not be the case in the future. To do good in the future will require more than technological skill. It will require wisdom. "Without wisdom, technical brilliance alone could lead to social or physical disaster and the destruction of the democratic way of life. Somehow, our schools and homes must educate for and practice wisdom, compassion, courage,

tolerance of uncertainty, and appreciation of the unique and different" [159:14].

## SUMMARY

In the first part of this chapter an attempt was made to indicate briefly some contributions that education has made in the growth and development of our nation. More than ever before in the history of mankind, our future progress will depend upon how well schools fulfill their role. Stated differently, the need for quality education has never been greater, and, in the years to come, the need will increase still more. This, therefore, constitutes one of the important reasons for becoming a teacher.

The second part of the chapter was concerned with a number of changes that have taken place in our culture during the past quarter of a century. These changes have called for major modifications to be made in school organization, procedures, and practices.

In the third part of the chapter, an attempt was made to indicate some of the technological and social changes that may take place in the future and the need for teachers to help those of the next generation acquire the knowledge, skills, and attitudes that will enable them to deal successfully with the increasing complexity of life. Teachers face the challenge of discovering new ways of helping youth as well as adults gain the competencies they will need to cope adequately and effectively with the complexity of problems they will face and to preserve and refine the basic freedoms that characterize our way of life. Never in the history of mankind has the need for education been greater. Never have teachers faced so great a challenge.

## QUESTIONS TO CONSIDER

1. What features of the American school system have especially contributed to the phenomenal growth and success of America?
2. Have you ever experienced any school practices and procedures that showed a lack of respect for the dignity and worth of the individual? How will you attempt to avoid the use of such practices and procedures?
3. Does the concept of equal educational opportunity mean that all pupils should receive the same kind and amount of education?
4. John W. Gardner has stated: "At this moment in history, free institutions are on trial." What evidences would support (or not support) such a statement?
5. In the second part of this chapter you noted some major changes that have taken place in our society. What educational implications do you see in each of these changes?
6. In an age of advancing technology, upon what bases can you defend a program of general education as a part of your college education?

7.  How will technological changes that may take place during the next few years affect the function of the school and the role of the classroom teacher?
8.  If greater emphasis is placed upon helping youth "learn how to learn," how will the nature of the teacher's work change?
9.  How will you attempt to educate youth for the effective use of leisure time?
10. In what ways should public schools attempt to meet the educational needs of adults?

## PROBLEM SITUATION FOR INQUIRY

The school system in Bayview is faced with a crisis. The school district treasury has been depleted, and the regular distribution of tax funds from the state will not be available for three months. The district has gone to the voters of Bayview four times during the last two years asking for additional taxes to operate the schools. Each time the voters have rejected the proposal. A fifth vote is to be taken within the next four weeks. If the issue is not approved by two-thirds of the voters, it will be necessary to close the schools in Bayview for a period of two months until the distribution of taxes is received from the state.

Bayview is a retirement community in which a large number of the residents do not have children attending the Bayview schools. An analysis of the previous four defeats indicates that the request for new taxes has been defeated by the segment of the community which does not have children enrolled in the schools.

If you were the superintendent of the Bayview school district, what would you do in an effort to convince *all* the voters that education is a worthwhile community investment?

## ACTIVITIES TO PURSUE

1.  List what you consider to be the major challenges that teaching holds for you. Discuss these challenges with some of your college teachers, or with other students who plan to teach, to see whether they agree with your challenges.
2.  Read *Future Shock,* by Alvin Toffler, and *The Next Generation,* by Donald N. Michael. Discuss the contents of each with your colleagues. Make a list of implications for education which emerge from their projections.
3.  Make a list of new opportunities that will open to teachers during the next few years as a result of technological and social changes that most likely will occur. Check your list with some of your colleagues and professors.
4.  Confer with some leading executives in business and industry regarding their views on the importance of education to our economy. Ask them to indicate what educational responsibilities their businesses and industries may need to assume in the future.
5.  Confer with employment agencies in your community regarding the changes in employment patterns they have noticed during the past few years. What changes do they anticipate so far as the future is concerned?
6.  Visit one or more preschool projects especially designed for culturally deprived children. Observe the kinds of activities being provided for children, and discuss with the teachers what they hope to accomplish.
7.  Talk with one or more social workers and with those working in various welfare agencies regarding the importance of education. What solutions do they see for welfare problems? In their opinions, how will the lives of children whose parents are on welfare be affected?
8.  Discuss with your colleagues the educational role, if any, that our federal government should take in alleviating the problems of people who are culturally deprived, who are unemployed, who have unequal educational opportunities.
9.  Ask some Appalachian whites, blacks, Puerto Ricans, Chicanos, or American Indians

how education can improve their lives and their people. Discuss your findings with your colleagues.

10. Discuss with your colleagues the changes that most likely will take place in the United States within the next 10 to 20 years. What modifications in the elementary and secondary school curriculum do these changes suggest?

## OTHER SOURCES OF IDEAS AND INFORMATION FOR CHAPTER 1

### Suggested Readings

Boyer, William H.: "Education for Survival," *Phi Delta Kappan,* vol. 52, no. 5, pp. 258–262, Phi Delta Kappa, Bloomington, Ind., January, 1971. Stresses the importance of planning in terms of the future.

Darling, Charles M., III: *Prospectives for the 70's and 80's,* National Industrial Conference Board, Inc., New York, New York, 1970. An experimental forecast conducted by the National Industrial Conference Board and the Opinion Research Corporation.

Fantini, Mario D.: "Schools For the 70's: Institutional Reform," *Today's Education,* vol. 59, no. 4, pp. 43–44 and 60–62, National Education Association, Washington, April, 1970. Discusses various changes that schools may make in order to meet the changing needs of society.

Gardner, John W.: "Uncritical Lovers, Unloving Critics," *The Journal of Educational Research,* vol. 62, no. 9, pp. 396–399, Dembar Educational Research Services, Inc., Madison, Wis., May–June, 1969. Reflects upon education from 300 years ago to 300 years in the future.

Goodlad, John I.: "The Future of Learning: Into the 21st Century," *Bulletin,* vol. 24, no. 1, pp. 1, 4–5, American Association of Colleges for Teacher Education, Washington, March, 1971. Discusses the changes that will need to take place as we move toward the twenty-first century.

Krech, David: "Psychoneurobiochemeducation," *Phi Delta Kappan,* vol. 50, no. 7, pp. 370–375, Phi Delta Kappa, Bloomington, Ind., March, 1969. Indicates how biochemists, neurologists, psychologists, and educators can combine forces to add to the intellectual stature of man.

"The New Shape of America," *Life,* vol. 70, no. 1, pp. 2–104, Special Double Issue, Time Inc., Jan. 8, 1971. An excellent analysis of the changing nature and current status of our society.

Polley, Ira: "What's Right with American Education?" *Phi Delta Kappan,* vol. 51, no. 1, pp. 13–15, Phi Delta Kappa, Bloomington, Ind., September, 1969. A prominent state superintendent of public instruction indicates some of the massive achievements of education in the United States.

Rich, John Martin: *Education and Human Values,* Addison-Wesley Publishing Company, Inc., Reading, Mass., 1968. Indicates the important role that education should play in helping students develop democratic values.

Shane, Harold G., and Owen N. Nelson: "What Will the Schools Become?" *Phi Delta Kappan,* vol. 52, no. 10, pp. 596–598, Phi Delta Kappa, Bloomington, Ind., June, 1971. Presents the results of what 333 school persons feel will happen in a quarter of a century hence.

Stinnett, T. M.: "Reordering Goals and Roles: An Introduction," in *Unfinished Business of the Teaching Profession in the 1970's,* pp. 1–7, Phi Delta Kappa, Bloomington, Ind., 1971. A challenging treatment of a number of problems facing the teaching profession.

Toffler, Alvin: *Future Shock,* Random House, New York, 1970. An excellent presentation of problems we may encounter as a result of "the premature arrival of tomorrow," which has enormous implications for education.

Wagar, J. Alan: "Growth Versus the Quality of Life," *Science,* vol. 168, pp. 1179–1184, American Association for the Advancement of Science, Washington, June 5, 1970. Indicates that our widespread acceptance of unlimited growth is not suited to survival on a finite planet.

"What Schools Can Do about Pollution," *Today's Education,* vol. 59, no. 9, pp. 14–29, National Education Association, Washington, December, 1970. A special feature in which various educators discuss what schools can do about pollution.

## Suggested 16 MM Films

*America: The Edge of Abundance* (National Educational Television, 59 min). Explores the far-reaching economic and social consequences of the increasingly automated and computer-oriented society in the United States as viewed by British television. Traces America's growth from an agricultural base to a manufacturing society and focuses on automation. Shows the immense problems of retraining and suggests that leisure will become the new business. Concludes that American values must be reexamined.

*America's Crises: The Community* (National Educational Television, 59 min). Evaluates the cultural, educational, religious, and physical aspects of America's cities and towns. Focuses on the small New England fishing community of Provincetown and compares it with San Jose, California, a booming Western community in the midst of accelerated growth. Discusses their similarities and differences, shows the effects of change, and suggests the problems that must be solved.

*America's Crises: The Individual* (National Educational Television, 59 min). Examines the problem of the individual in a complex society by looking at various areas of American life in relation to man's needs for self-identification. Probes the effects of government planning in agriculture on individual initiative and community identification.

*America's Crises: The Parents* (National Educational Television, 59 min). Presents a documentary report on the changing problems of America's parents today and their attempts to find identity, meaning, and purpose in their lives. Features frank interviews with parents and children. Shows the effects of rural-urban-suburban social change and presents interviews with Benjamin Spock, Betty Friedan, and Paul Popenoe.

*Education for a Free Society* (National Educational Television, 29 min). Indicates that we need education that deliberately tries to cultivate the following three freedoms: "freedom from"—the condition of being free from constraint; "freedom of"—freedom of thought, of religion, of speech, and of press; and "freedom to"—the opportunity to make choices and to act on those choices.

*Education for National Survival* (National Educational Television, 29 min). Emphasizes the fact that our national strength depends more on a high level of educational achievement than on any other factor.

*Information Explosion* (Ohio State University, 34 min, color). Presents a series of examples of the significance, scope, and importance of free communications in such areas as government, industry, and the professions. Suggests that educators must concentrate on an accurate perception of how local and mass media really affect children, and that both teachers and students must be taught early to discriminate.

*Man's Impact on the Environment* (Modern Learning Aids, 23 min, color). Reveals how man has caused dangerous changes in his environment. Shows that man is the single most important factor affecting the "balance of nature." Explains the tragic consequences of man's almost complete encroachment upon his environment.

*National Goals, No. 2* (New York University, 29 min). Presents a discussion of economic growth as a national goal. Reviews the causes and effects of inflation, unemployment, and rate of growth. Points out the effect of education in producing new employment patterns. Compares American and Soviet rates of expansion. Discusses problems of automation, standards of living, and individual initiative in our economic position.

*Philosophies of Education: Education for National Survival* (National Educational Television, 29 min). Emphasizes the fact that our national strength depends more on a high level of educational achievement than any other factor. We must come to realize this, and we must be willing to spend a larger proportion of our national income on education. We must provide an educational challenge for our young people, and we must discover the best talent and see to it that this talent is developed to the highest possible degree.

*The Population Problem: A Time for Decision* (National Educational Television, 60 min). Analyzes United States population trends from colonial days to the present. Focuses particularly on the baby-boom era, the increasing number of senior citizens, and the present and future problems to be faced in housing, rising crime, overcrowded schools, unemployment, and poverty.

*View of America from the 23rd Century* (National Educational Television, 21 min, color). Dramatizes how present-day American institutions might look when viewed from the perspective of the twenty-third century. Shows that man increasingly rages against his institutions because they have been designed to resist rather than to facilitate change.

*Why We Learn* (Aims Instructional Media Services, 7 min, color). Describes modern knowledge as the accumulation of all man's knowledge. Cites learning as the key to the future.

## FIGURE CREDITS

FIGURE 1–1 (*Source: 200 Million Americans,* U.S. Department of Commerce, Bureau of the Census, Washington, November, 1967, p. 57.)

FIGURE 1–2 (*Source:* Data from "Ranking of the States 1971," *Research Report 1971–R6,* National Education Association, Research Division, Washington, 1971, p. 28.)

FIGURE 1–3 (*Source:* Adapted from "Does Increased Education Produce Increased Income?" *NEA Research Bulletin,* vol. 46, no. 4, National Education Association, Research Division, Washington, December, 1968, p. 103.)

FIGURE 1–4 (*Source:* Data from *Statistical Abstract of the United States,* U.S. Department of Commerce, Bureau of the Census, Washington, 1970, p. 312, and *The Realities of School Finance,* American Association of School Administrators, Washington, 1970, p. 10.)

FIGURE 1–5 (*Source:* Kenneth A. Simon, and W. Vance Grant, *Digest of Educational Statistics,* U.S. Office of Education, National Center for Educational Statistics, Washington, 1970, p. 10.)

FIGURE 1–6 (*Source:* "Farms in U.S.," *The Wall Street Journal,* Dow Jones and Company, Inc., New York, Mar. 30, 1971, p. 1.)

FIGURE 1–7 (*Source:* Arnold B. Barach, *USA and Its Economic Future,* Twentieth Century Fund, Inc., New York, 1964, p. 3.)

FIGURE 1–8 (*Source:* Harrison, Brown, and E. K. Fedorov, "Too Many People in the World?" *Saturday Review,* Feb. 17, 1962, p. 18.)

FIGURE 1–9 (*Source:* Data from "Our No. 1 Priority," *NRTA Journal,* vol. 20, no. 96, National Retired Teachers Association, Ojai, California, July–August, 1970, p. 4.)

FIGURE 1–10 (*Source:* J. D. Hodgson, "Manpower Patterns of the 70's," *Manpower,* vol. 3, no. 2., U.S. Department of Labor, Washington, February, 1971, p. 5.)

FIGURE 1–11 (*Source:* Reprinted by permission from *Changing Times,* the Kiplinger Magazine,

FIGURE 1–12   (*Source:* "Economic Status of the Teaching Profession, 1970–71," *Research Report 1971–R4,* National Education Association, Research Division, Washington, 1971, p. 10.)

FIGURE 1–13   (*Source:* "Economic Status of the Teaching Profession, 1970–71," *Research Report 1971–R4,* National Education Association, Research Division, Washington, 1971, p. 11.)

# 1 perceiving, planning, and preparing

Part 1 of this book is concerned with the nature and process of career planning in an increasingly complex and interdependent society, not only as this planning relates to you personally but also as it pertains to the lives of those whom you may teach. Even though emphasis is placed upon planning a career in teaching, it is to be recognized that this aspect of planning is only a phase of the total process of life planning.

As a background for planning a career in education, the preceding chapter was concerned with some major contributions that the school system has made in the preservation and progressive improvement of American society. Since the 1940s significant changes have been taking place in the American culture which have called for changes to be made in the process of educating American youth. These changes in addition to the sweeping changes projected for the future provide exciting challenges for those preparing to teach.

Recognizing that we shape our tomorrows by the way we handle the problems and decisions of today, Chapter 2 provides a rationale and framework for planning a career in the teaching profession. Chapter 3 is concerned with the preservice programs of teacher education and with certification requirements for entering the profession. Factors affecting the supply and demand for teachers as well as the wide range of opportunities within the profession are emphasized in Chapter 4.

The remaining parts and their respective chapters are designed to build added meaning into the content of Part

1. As you proceed through the book, you may wish to refer to Part 1—especially Chapter 2—from time to time in order to maximize your effectiveness in planning your professional career.

# 2 | PLANNING A CAREER IN THE TEACHING PROFESSION

As may be concluded from reading Chapter 1, the task of preparing for a successful career in the teaching profession is far more demanding today than it was in the past. Furthermore, due to the inevitable changes that will take place in the role of teachers in tomorrow's schools, the task of maintaining a high level of success will be increasingly demanding and difficult.

Some students, unfortunately, have not given careful consideration to their decisions to become teachers, or to the basic attributes required for successful teaching, or to the means by which they can develop into the most competent teachers possible, or to the specific types of positions for which they might prepare. Some prospective teachers have decided to teach in secondary schools because, having been recently graduated, they are more familiar with this level. But if they had investigated other levels, such as early childhood education, they might have found themselves more interested in and more qualified to work with young children. Other students have decided to teach in high school largely because they feel that secondary teachers have more prestige than elementary teachers. Still others find themselves majoring in English or social studies because they are not familiar with opportunities in other areas, such as speech or hearing therapy, special education, or library science, in which they might have been interested and well qualified.

Planning for teaching involves much more than being admitted to a program of teacher education, passing the required number of courses for certification, and securing a teaching position upon graduation. A career in education is a phase of life planning which involves fundamental values of life and which is integrally related to home life and citizenship. The completion of collegiate professional training is only an initial phase in the professional life of an educator and does not ensure professional success regardless of the quality of the courses completed. The full realization of values inherent in a teaching career depends largely upon the extent to which the individual attempts to realize those values.

## The Nature of Career Planning

Planning is essentially a continuous life process in which action is directed by an individual's critically reasoned values and goals. It involves the constant weighing of these values and goals.

All career planning obviously must be tentative in nature in order to adjust to changing conditions and demands. In fact, the very essence of planning is one of continuous change, modification, and adaptation. Therefore, many of the initial details of any master plan or blueprint which you may formulate for your career will change as the years pass. But a master plan will give direction to your professional growth. The details will enable you to expend energy efficiently and to gain greater realization of your goals in life.

## SUGGESTED STEPS IN PLANNING
## A CAREER IN EDUCATION

The broad outline of steps to be followed in planning a career in education is no different from that to be followed in planning for any career. Consequently, not all your efforts will be lost if, after thoroughly exploring teaching as a profession, you come to the thoughtful conclusion that this is not the lifework for which you are best suited. Your efforts will make it easier for you to plan in terms of another occupational objective.

## Importance of Values and Goals in Career Planning

An individual normally seeks to do the things that seem important to him. In other words, the things he values provide the foundation for his goals. It is important, therefore, that an individual's vocational goals be consistent with what he desires, strives for, and approves in life.

Values are the intangible bases for behavior. They constitute the foundation for the things we cherish in life. They may be expressed in such terms as freedom, equality, individualism, dignity of man, self-respect, democracy, cooperativeness, service to mankind, the golden rule, prestige, trustworthiness, dependability, thrift, and open-mindedness.

Values are acquired. They are cultural—learned through experience [242:71].

Man's behavior is governed by the values he has come to accept during the years of cumulative experiences that make up his lifetime. What he thinks, what he looks upon as "good," and what he does are controlled and restricted by the chains forged by his values: uplifting or debasing, humane or bestial—whatever his experience has made them.

Since the life experiences of no two individuals are the same, the values they hold will not be identical. On the other hand, every society has certain values which characterize it, and the individuals who have grown up in that society tend to hold those values in common. In America, respect for the uniqueness and worth of the individual, freedom, equality, and shared responsibility for the common good are examples of common basic values. Since the school is concerned with developing, strengthening, and transmitting values considered to be desirable in this society, it is important for a teacher to have a clear and functional understanding of them.

Many people have never consciously examined their basic values or tested the internal consistency of them. As a result, their behavior may seem to be inconsistent in various kinds of situations, and they may have difficulty in working effectively with others. A recent study of teacher attitudes as a function of values indicates that teachers with consistent educational values, whether they be extremely emergent or extremely traditional, were more sure of their classroom practices and displayed more approval of school practices than other teachers [69:461–462]. Since the teacher as a person is the most important single factor in the classroom, it is extremely important for him to have a clearly reasoned and consistent set of values which is in harmony with the tenets of a democratic society.

Since your values will range from mild preference to intense convictions, it will be relatively easy for you to identify your major values, such as service to mankind, and to use them as criteria for testing your career choice. It is more difficult to analyze all your values in great detail and to derive a whole pattern of criteria for testing teaching as a career. If you construct this pattern as completely as you can, you will be much more certain of your decision.

Each occupation has its unique pattern of inherent values that may be pursued by an individual who engages in that occupation. If you discover that teaching fails to meet a significant number of the tests you establish, you have an obligation to yourself and to the teaching profession to explore the possibility of preparing for some other occupation. Hence, the first and perhaps the most difficult step in planning a career in education is to answer as accurately and as completely as possible the following questions:

1. What do I value in life?
2. Why are these my values?

3. Are these values desirable?
4. Are these values internally consistent?
5. What life goals emerge from my values?
6. Can I best realize my life goals through a career in education?

## Importance of Self-appraisal in Planning for Teaching

Cervantes advised, "Make it thy business to know thyself, which is the most difficult lesson in the world." His advice is certainly appropriate for anyone engaged in the process of planning a career. Furthermore, understanding oneself is essential for understanding others. Two psychologists report the following about the relationship of self-understanding to the understanding of others [134:6]:

What the teacher sees in the student, the way he feels about him, and what he derives from his dealings with him will be influenced not only by the kind of person the student is but also the kind of person the teacher is and by the kind of situation that is created when the two are together. To the extent that the student's behavior, as seen by the instructor, reflects the instructor's own perceptions and attitudes, he will be unable to understand the student unless he understands himself. Similarly, the way in which the instructor interprets or evaluates a student's attitudes or conduct will be influenced by his own values, likes, and dislikes. The greater this influence is, the more the instructor's perception of his student will be a reflection of himself rather than an objective, or unbiased, reaction. Therefore, it is essential for the instructor to take stock of his own involvement and, as far as possible, make allowance for it.

Jersild and Associates feel that understanding oneself and others involves more than an intellectual process [134:9]:

One can master the facts, principles, and laws contained in a hundred books on psychology and still understand neither oneself nor others. Self-understanding requires integrity rather than mere cleverness. It involves emotion. To know oneself, one must be

FIGURE 2–1   Major steps involved in planning a career.

1   CLARIFICATION OF
Values   Goals   Wants

2   ANALYSIS OF
Career requirements

3   SELF-ANALYSIS
Strengths   Weaknesses

4   PLANS FOR CAREER
College   Intermediate   Later life

able to feel as well as think. One must be able to recognize feelings, face them, and deal with them in constructive ways; and this is something quite different from reading or talking about them with detachment.

## Influence of Requirements upon Planning for Teaching

Perhaps no career imposes more varied requirements on the successful worker than does teaching. Although general competency as a citizen seems to include most of the requirements for success in many careers, it is only the first requisite in teaching. Above and beyond this requirement lie the many aspects of special expertness demanded of the teacher. The basic concern at this point is to emphasize the need for an analysis to be made of the requirements which a career as a teacher imposes. This analysis should include a stocktaking of your present qualifications. If the analysis of all your qualifications reveals certain deficiencies which you cannot or do not wish to remove, you again have warning of trouble ahead. Likewise, revelation of unusual strengths in this analysis should bear a strong implication for your future, and your plans in the field of education should involve use of these special strengths.

A subsequent section of this chapter should provide you with an understanding of the competencies you normally should have in order to be a successful teacher. Certification requirements prescribed for teachers by the respective states are discussed in Chapter 3. Chapters 5 and 6 contain a rather clear indication of what will be required in order to perform adequately in schools in the future. Chapters 7, 15, 16, 17, and 18 will also provide a rather comprehensive understanding of what a teacher needs in order to fulfill the broad functions of education in a democratic society.

## Influence of Other Factors upon Planning for Teaching

Many other factors should be taken into consideration in order to plan a career in education wisely. Various sections of this book are designed to help you in this regard. For example, Chapters 10 and 11 are concerned with the various economic aspects that may be involved, such as salary, sick leave, retirement, and tenure. Chapter 4 should assist you in exploring the vast range of opportunities in the field of education. Should you be a nursery school or kindergarten teacher? Would you like teaching in the elementary school? Would you enjoy teaching in the emerging middle school, or the junior high school? Would you be interested in high school teaching? Could you teach on the college level? Should you do specialized teaching, i.e., teaching the gifted, the physically handicapped, the culturally different, the mentally retarded, or the emotionally disturbed? What opportunities are there for supervisory or administrative positions, for teaching disadvantaged children, for teaching in differentiated staffing situations, for teaching overseas? Explore this wide range of opportunities so that your abilities and interests may best be utilized and your success and happiness in the profession may be proportionately increased.

To plan a career competently, you should learn about the school system—how the schools developed, how they are organized (Chapter 12) and financed (Chapter 13), what changes may be expected during the time you will be associated actively with them (Chapters 5, 6, and 7), what crucial problems schools are faced with today (Chapters 17 and 18), and how and to what extent you may contribute to the solution of these problems. As you continue your reading and planning, you will discover other factors which should be investigated and evaluated.

## Further Suggested Procedures for Planning a Career in Education

In order to do a really effective job in planning for teaching, you may wish to engage in the following major activities:

*Put your plans on paper.* Many people have found that the act of writing out their plans is in itself of great help to them. The necessary labor involved in selecting and weaving in the various ideas causes planners to be more critical and objective. This procedure—often called "writing the planning paper"—has been used in colleges and universities for a number of years with considerable evidence of worthwhile results.

Many students experience difficulty in getting started in the writing of their plans. This is understandable in view of the fact that planning is, or at least should be, the most highly individual task that any student can undertake. By virtue of differences in backgrounds, values absorbed, and goals desired, each student differs from every other student. Unfortunately, our school system and our social setting are such that the average student has had little encouragement to come to grips with himself. Furthermore, most students seem to experience difficulty in writing the things which they have always thought about.

There is no specific method of approach to prescribe for *all* students faced with the planning of a life career. An individual should begin his planning in any manner which will bring the greatest benefit. Some students, for example, start by listing their strong points; others list their weaknesses, e.g., the things over which they worry. Some choose to list the major decisions with which they are or will be faced and to indicate the many aspects of their present and future life that may be affected by these decisions. Other students choose to study critically those previous experiences that have caused them to be the way they are today. In the latter approach, the student does not attempt to write an autobiography but rather attempts to isolate those aspects of his background that he believes have a bearing upon his problem of planning a life's work.

It would seem logical for an individual to first indicate all the things that he values in life, i.e., those things which are central to his beliefs and behavior. Directly or indirectly, values are involved in every decision you make, now and in the future. You may find it helpful to group them under major headings such as the following, which are merely suggestive.

*Intellectual values*—such as scholarship, truth, knowledge, opportunities for self-expression, high standards of morals and ethics, clear and logical thinking

*Physical and personal values*—such as health and vitality, attractiveness, pleasing personality, and successful marriage and family life

*Occupational values*—such as service to mankind, intellectual stimulation, prestige, contacts with others, favorable working conditions, a reasonable degree of financial security, industriousness, self-sufficiency, opportunities for advancement, opportunities for creativeness, and opportunities for combining your occupation harmoniously with family life

*Adjustment values*—such as sense of personal worth, respect for human personality, tolerance, self-respect, independence, friendship, sense of humor, happiness, cooperativeness, and opportunities for choice and self-direction

*Social values*—such as social approval, stability, honesty, generosity, loyalty, kindness, fairness, justice, and impartiality

*Aesthetic values*—such as beauty, attractiveness of surroundings, and appreciation of cultural influences

*Recreational values*—such as ample time to devote to recreational activities, freedom to participate in a wide variety of activities, and stimulation to develop interests

You may also use an objective instrument such as the Allport-Vernon Scale of Values to help clarify your beliefs.

In addition to listing your values, you may wish to check to see whether they are consistent with each other and analyze each critically to determine why you hold it, as well as whether it is desirable to continue to hold it. In order to gain an adequate understanding of the origin of these values, it may be helpful to dip critically into your background. Early childhood experiences are much more important than one is inclined to suspect, so far as the formation of his values is concerned.

Any analysis of values will automatically necessitate a consideration of goals. The balance sheet that you construct of your values and goals should assist you greatly in being objective and facile in the other aspects of your planning.

**Talk to others about your background, values, and goals**   You doubtless have discussed your life plans at length with your parents, your public school teachers, your school friends, and various older adults in your home community; and you will probably want to consult these people again, especially your parents, as you continue with your planning.

In view of the fact that college provides a superb opportunity for anyone to extend greatly his contacts, avail yourself of this resource for planning. In your beginning course in education you will contact many other students interested in the same career possibilities that you are.

Both in and out of class you will have the opportunity to share your values, goals, and plans and to think them through critically. Participating in activities such as the Student National Education Association provides additional opportunities for engaging in intelligent, meaningful, and fruitful discussions. Seek out college instructors as well as specialists in other fields, from whom you may receive valuable aid. In short, avail yourself of every possible opportunity to analyze and appraise your background, values, and goals. It is primarily through this process that your thinking is deepened and clarified, your horizons are extended, and your planning is directed. Furthermore, the act of engaging in these experiences should enable you to gain facility in helping the pupils whom you may teach to do likewise.

Perhaps one of the most effective ways for anyone to analyze his competencies for teaching is to use various checklists or self-rating scales that have been prepared. One of these scales is located in the Resource Section for Part 1 of this book. In using this checklist, please keep in mind that the ratings should not be considered final and that they represent only your present competencies. You should be able to do much to improve your ratings for teaching fitness through carefully planned future experiences.

After you have rated yourself, you might wish to ask your adviser or some other competent person who knows you well to rate you on this same scale. Compare these ratings and discuss especially those that differ greatly. Your adviser or friend might be able to help you formulate plans whereby you may remove any weaknesses and increase the strengths that you have for teaching.

**Obtain objective data on your specific abilities**   In using the preceding checklist, you perhaps felt the need for objective data to support some of the relatively subjective judgments you made, especially if the appraisal of someone else differed appreciably from your own rating. You should be able to locate considerable objective data to help you appraise yourself. Data on physical health may be obtained from your college health clinic or your family physician. A speech department or clinic can give you objective data concerning your speech and hearing. A good personality test administered and interpreted by a clinician can supply emotional stability and personal adjustment data.

Practically every college and university today requires entering students to take a battery of tests. Ordinarily the registrar's office, the guidance department, or some other agency administering the entrance tests will be glad to help you obtain these results. You are almost certain to find results on your English test. English tests usually cover at least three aspects of reading: vocabulary, speed of reading, and level of comprehension. If your English scores are low, you may wish to visit a reading clinic for consultation and advice.

Many colleges encourage students to take some type of occupational-preference or interest test. Such tests attempt to indicate fields in which a particular person would likely experience happiness and success. Although the results of these tests are not conclusive, they do indicate vocational preferences or interests worthy of consideration.

Many students pursuing a specialized course in college tend to neglect their personal development along broad cultural lines. Educators generally agree that a teacher should have a well-rounded background in addition to the other requirements for teaching. Therefore, you may wish to take a test that will indicate your achievement in each of the broad fields of knowledge and plan to strengthen, either through course work or through independent study, areas in which you appear especially weak.

You may think of other kinds of test data that you will need in developing your plans. If your college does not provide the various tests for which you find a need, you can apply at the nearest testing agency. The cost is comparatively low, and the service usually includes a profile as well as an interpretation of the scores.

Please remember that objective test data have limitations. In order to ensure profitable use of the information, a careful evaluation by a qualified person of the purpose and the results of each test is an essential part of any testing program.

You may wish to develop a graphic picture of the information obtained by constructing a profile chart or psychograph of all your test results. A psychograph also would help your adviser gain a better picture of you.

**Formulate your plans for the future**  Planning for the future involves preparing for three rather clearly defined periods: the years in which you are still in college; the first five or ten years after graduation, during which time you are becoming adjusted to your life's work; and your later life, which extends into old age.

If you are a senior or graduate student, it is obvious that the amount of planning which you can do while still in college is fairly limited. You are faced more immediately with the need for detailed plans for the second period, the first five or ten years after graduation.

The material that follows is roughly divided into these three periods, and a few suggestions are given for your consideration.

**Years in college**  As indicated previously, college is an unusual environment in which you are able to take advantage of many learning opportunities that may not be present in future surroundings. For this reason your plans during the college years may differ significantly from other plans you may make.

If you feel, for example, that you need to improve your ability to work cooperatively and harmoniously with others, you can become an active member in some of the many campus activities at your disposal. You may wish to assume positions of leadership and responsibility and participate in various discussion groups to develop the characteristics of a mature thinker. There are also many opportunities on campus and in the community, such as convocations, concerts, special lectures, and forums, that will help you acquire a broad cultural education.

Other plans may include attempts to develop skills and insights for working with children. These include observing and participating in as many classroom situations as possible, working as a volunteer or paid teacher aide, taking part in camp and club activities with children, and acting as playground director or camp counselor during the summer.

**Years immediately after college**   The years following graduation present a variety of major decisions and problems for which tentative plans should be made. There is the matter of locating a position. What type of setting would be most desirable for you—rural or urban? Near your home or a considerable distance from home? An inner city or suburban setting? In-state or out-of-state? As will be noted in Chapter 3, certification requirements are increasing so rapidly that some thought should be given to plans for completing a master's degree.

For this period of time, consideration should be given to plans for living an interesting social, civic, cultural, and recreational life. Prospective periods of summer employment provide many opportunities for gaining valuable experience and intellectual growth. Plans also need to be made for gaining future financial security through insurance, investments, and retirement plans. Continued professional growth is essential for anyone remaining in the profession for a number of years.

**Years in later life**   There is much merit in doing some "intelligent dreaming." Many people find added enjoyment, happiness, and security during their later years of life as a result of long-range planning.

A wide variety of cultural and recreational interests, a concern with civic and professional activities, a wise use of the increased time at your disposal, and an enlarged circle of friends can do much to promote wholesome adjustment at this time. Leisure time can become extremely boring and devasting to an individual. It takes a considerable amount of long-range planning and the development of skills, attitudes, and interests to make these years become a period of constructive fulfillment to an individual and to society.

## COMPETENCIES FOR TEACHING

A prospective teacher is normally very much concerned with the competencies essential to success in teaching. Having identified these competencies, he also is concerned with the ways in which he can become the most competent teacher possible.

In recalling the many teachers you have had, you might select those who stand out as having been especially effective and analyze their characteristics carefully. As you study each of these teachers, write down the reason or reasons why you consider them outstanding. Have your friends engage in the same kind of activity. Compare and contrast your list with theirs.

In making this analysis you will probably note considerable difference in the personalities of the teachers. Some may have been quiet, gentle, and warm. Others may have been outgoing and aggressive. Whatever their differences, it is safe to conclude that there is no *one* personality which teachers must have in order to ensure success. Further study also may reveal that because of variations in situations, there is no *one* method of teaching that will ensure success. Each of your outstanding teachers probably had a distinct personality, as well as a distinct style of teaching.

The differences to be found in the characteristics of effective teachers should not be alarming to you. Nor should you be discouraged if educators tell you that they are not absolutely certain of the competencies that will ensure anyone's success in teaching. It is true that they know

What teacher competencies will be needed in order to fully develop this child's abilities for living effectively and constructively in our society? *(Photograph by Joe Di Dio, National Education Association.)*

something about the abilities required, but they hesitate to say with complete conviction that a particular individual will be a very successful teacher and that another will be unsuccessful.

One reason why it is difficult to predict teaching success is that a teacher deals with the most complex thing in the world—the human being. A successful teacher must be able to affect people in such ways that desirable changes occur in behavior. He must be able to encourage the individual to think and to make intelligent decisions; he must guide his behavior with increasing effectiveness toward constructive, democratic ends. The complexity of the interaction of the teacher with his pupils is so great that superior teaching assumes the characteristics of an art which cannot be fully analyzed. Horace Mann recognized this fact when he wrote in his *First Annual Report* in 1853, the following: "Teaching is the most difficult of all arts and the profoundest of all sciences. In its absolute perfection it would involve a complete knowledge of the whole being to be taught, and of the precise manner in which every possible application would affect it."

In planning a career in education, you should examine searchingly the competencies which generally are conducive to success in teaching. This analysis should serve as a background from which you will be able to formulate specific and long-range plans for meeting these requirements to the highest degree possible.

## Identifying the Competencies for Teaching

Hundreds of studies have been made of the personal and professional characteristics of teachers in an attempt to establish which traits are the most desirable for teachers to possess and those which are definite handicaps. Several techniques have been used to identify these traits. You may wish to study these traits carefully, to analyze yourself in terms of them, and then establish specific and detailed plans for meeting as many of these requirements as possible while you are in college. It will not be possible to meet all of them at this time, since some require a lifetime of experience, study, and effort.

**Studying the critical behaviors of teachers**   Ryans has published the results of an extensive and rigorous scientific analysis of teacher characteristics. This study was sponsored by the American Council on Education [225:1–416]. As an initial step in the study, teacher supervisors, college teachers, school principals, teachers, student teachers, and students in education methods courses were asked to make analytical reports on teacher behavior in specific situations which make a difference between success and failure in teaching. These reports served as a basis for the construction of a "critical incidence" blank upon which significant behavior relative to teaching might be recorded. The more than 500 critical incidents submitted by the participants in the study were reduced to the following list of generalized behaviors [225:82]:

## Generalized Descriptions of Critical Behaviors of Teachers

| Effective Behaviors | Ineffective Behaviors |
|---|---|
| 1. Alert, appears enthusiastic. | 1. Is apathetic, dull, appears bored. |
| 2. Appears interested in pupils and classroom activities. | 2. Appears uninterested in pupils and classroom activities. |
| 3. Cheerful, optimistic. | 3. Is depressed, pessimistic; appears unhappy. |
| 4. Self-controlled, not easily upset. | 4. Loses temper, is easily upset. |
| 5. Likes fun, has a sense of humor. | 5. Is overly serious, too occupied for humor. |
| 6. Recognizes and admits own mistakes. | 6. Is unaware of, or fails to admit, own mistakes. |
| 7. Is fair, impartial, and objective in treatment of pupils. | 7. Is unfair or partial in dealing with pupils. |
| 8. Is patient. | 8. Is impatient. |
| 9. Shows understanding and sympathy in working with pupils. | 9. Is short with pupils, uses sarcastic remarks, or in other ways shows lack of sympathy with pupils. |
| 10. Is friendly and courteous in relations with pupils. | 10. Is aloof and removed in relations with pupils. |
| 11. Helps pupils with personal as well as educational problems. | 11. Seems unaware of pupils' personal needs and problems. |
| 12. Commends effort and gives praise for work well done. | 12. Does not commend pupils, is disapproving, hypercritical. |
| 13. Accepts pupils' efforts as sincere. | 13. Is suspicious of pupil motives. |
| 14. Anticipates reactions of others in social situations. | 14. Does not anticipate reactions of others in social situations. |
| 15. Encourages pupils to try to do their best. | 15. Makes no effort to encourage pupils to try to do their best. |
| 16. Classroom procedure is planned and well organized. | 16. Procedure is without plan, disorganized. |
| 17. Classroom procedure is flexible within overall plan. | 17. Shows extreme rigidity of procedure, inability to depart from plan. |
| 18. Anticipates individual needs. | 18. Fails to provide for individual differences and needs of pupils. |
| 19. Stimulates pupils through interesting and original materials and techniques. | 19. Uninteresting materials and teaching techniques used. |
| 20. Conducts clear, practical demonstrations and explanations. | 20. Demonstrations and explanations are not clear and are poorly conducted. |
| 21. Is clear and thorough in giving directions. | 21. Directions are incomplete, vague. |
| 22. Encourages pupils to work through their own problems and evaluate their accomplishments. | 22. Fails to give pupils opportunity to work out own problems or evaluate their own work. |
| 23. Disciplines in quiet, dignified, and positive manner. | 23. Reprimands at length, ridicules, resorts to cruel or meaningless forms of correction. |
| 24. Gives help willingly. | 24. Fails to give help or gives it grudgingly. |
| 25. Foresees and attempts to resolve potential difficulties. | 25. Is unable to foresee and resolve potential difficulties. |

Admittedly some value or subjective judgments were involved in the formulation of these descriptive statements; however, the list does tend to objectify the types of behavior that make a difference in the success or failure of teachers.

Ryans points out that there is an increasing amount of evidence that certain characteristics may contribute to the model of the teacher. Data growing out of various research in which quite different approaches and criteria have been used suggest the following list of generalizations regarding the characteristics of outstanding teachers [225:366]:

Superior intellectual abilities, above-average school achievement, good emotional adjustment, attitudes favorable to pupils, enjoyment of pupil relationships, generosity in the appraisal of the behavior and motives of other persons, strong interests in reading and literary matters, interest in music and painting, participation in social and community affairs, early experiences in caring for children and teaching (such as reading to children and taking a class for the teacher), history of teaching in family, family support of teaching as a vocation, and strong social service interests.

**Questioning pupils** Another technique that has been used extensively is that of questioning pupils regarding the qualities of teachers they admire. It has been found that boys and girls who have spent considerable time with a teacher are able to pass rather valid judgments regarding his competence [297:3]. A talk with some students after the first week of a school term will reveal that they have the teacher "sized up" with amazing accuracy.

Witty [299:386] analyzed approximately 12,000 letters on "The Teacher Who Has Helped Me Most" that were submitted by pupils from grades 2 to 12 all over the nation. The teacher traits mentioned most frequently by the pupils, in the order of their frequency, were the following: (1) cooperativeness, democratic attitude; (2) and (3) kindliness and consideration for the individual, patience; (4) wide variety of interests; (5) an attractive general appearance and pleasing manner; (6) fairness and impartiality; (7) sense of humor; (8) good disposition and consistent behavior; (9) interest in pupil's problems; (10) flexibility; (11) use of recognition and praise; (12) unusual proficiency in teaching a particular subject.

Witty summarized his findings by stating that "these boys and girls appear to be grateful to the school in proportion to the degree that it offers security, individual success, shared experience, and opportunities for personal and social adjustments. And these are precisely the factors which promote good learning."

Witty conducted three additional nationwide contests in an attempt to verify and expand the findings gained from the first contest. He found that the twelve traits mentioned previously were cited consistently, although their order varied from year to year [298:312].

In a somewhat similar study, Williamson asked 2,000 Colorado high school seniors to identify the most effective and the least effective teacher they had experienced during their school career and to indicate specifically why the teacher was most or least effective. Comments concerning their most effective teacher were categorized into the following six areas according to frequency of occurrence: (1) interest in the student, (2) interesting class management, (3) enthusiasm for teaching, (4) students required to work, (5) impartiality by teacher, and (6) respect for student opinion [297:4]. Their comments on their least effective teacher fell into the following categories: (1) practiced poor class management, (2) showed favoritism, (3) was uninterested in students, (4) was a poor disciplinarian, (5) knew material but could not communicate it to the students, (6) did not enjoy teaching, and (7) did not respect the student or his opinions [297:5]. Sample comments of the students, which are contained in the report of this study [297:4–7], are worth reading.

**Analyzing biographies of outstanding teachers**   Another method of gaining understanding of competencies for teaching is to read carefully some of the many biographies as well as fiction books that have been written on outstanding teachers. You may remember, for instance, the heartwarming story of Hilton's *Goodbye, Mr. Chips.* Biographies can be helpful in gaining an understanding of the artistic qualities that characterize outstanding teaching as well as the human factors that have rich meaning in the lives of boys and girls. Discussion of these and other books may prove profitable. What seemed to be the life values of the teachers mentioned? What did they consider the job of the teacher to be? How were they able to stimulate the interest of boys and girls and to guide their growth toward desirable ends?

**Analyzing statements of competencies and research studies**   Educators singly and in groups have developed lists of competencies for teaching, based upon their experiences as teachers and their observations of, and work with, other teachers. These lists often take the form of rating scales used in evaluating the work of teachers on the job and of students engaged in their student teaching. You may wish to see the scale on which your success in student teaching will be appraised and to study carefully the competencies involved. By having a clear understanding of these competencies you will be able to plan specific experiences that you should gain prior to your student teaching.

Hamachek [113:341–345] recently completed a study of the voluminous research that has been done on teacher effectiveness and considerations which enhance or restrict this effectiveness. He found that most of the research was aimed at investigating teacher effectiveness from one or more of the following dimensions of teacher personality and behavior: (1) personal characteristics, (2) instructional procedures and interaction styles, (3) perceptions of self, and (4) perceptions of others.

In summarizing the research on the personal characteristics of good or effective teachers, Hamachek states:

Effective teachers appear to be those who are, shall we say, "human" in the fullest sense of the word. They have a sense of humor, are fair, empathetic, more democratic than autocratic, and apparently are more able to relate easily and naturally to students on either a one-to-one or group basis. Their classrooms seem to reflect miniature enterprise operations in the sense that they are more open, spontaneous, and adaptable to change [113:341–342].

In discussing the instructional procedures and interaction styles of good versus poor teachers, Hamachek points out that Flanders (85) found that "classrooms in which achievement and attitudes were superior were likely to be conducted by teachers who did not blindly pursue a single behavioral-instructional path to the exclusion of other possibilities. In other words, the more successful teachers were better able to range along a continuum of interaction styles which varied from fairly active, dominative support on the one hand to a more reflective, discriminating support on the other" [113:342]. In summarizing the research on classroom behavior interaction patterns, and teaching styles, Hamachek indicates that good or effective teachers seem to reflect more of the following behaviors [113:342]:

1. Willingness to be flexible, to be direct or indirect as the situation demands.
2. Ability to perceive the world from the student's point of view.
3. Ability to "personalize" their teaching.
4. Willingness to experiment, to try out new things.

Effective communication and interaction involves more than words. *(Photograph by Joe Di Dio, National Education Association.)*

5.  Skill in asking questions (as opposed to seeing self as a kind of answering service).
6.  Knowledge of subject matter and related areas.
7.  Provision of well-established examination procedures.
8.  Provision of definite study help.
9.  Reflection of an appreciative attitude (evidenced by nods, comments, smiles, etc.).
10. Use of conversational manner in teaching—informal, easy style.

The way teachers see, regard, and feel about themselves (self-perception) has an enormous impact on both their professional and personal lives. Ryans [226:1,486–1,490] found that the more emotionally stable teachers (1) more frequently named self-confidence and cheerfulness as dominant traits in themselves, (2) said they liked active contact with other people, (3) expressed interest in hobbies and handicrafts, (4) reported their childhoods to be happy experiences. After reviewing several research studies, Combs [45:70–71] concludes that good teachers typically see themselves as follows [113:342–343]:

1.  Good teachers see themselves as identified with people rather than withdrawn, removed, apart from, or alienated from others.
2.  Good teachers feel basically adequate rather than inadequate. They do not see themselves as generally unable to cope with problems.
3.  Good teachers feel trustworthy rather than untrustworthy. They see themselves reliable, dependable individuals with the potential for coping with events as they happen.
4.  Good teachers see themselves as wanted rather than unwanted. They see themselves as likable and attractive (in a personal, not physical sense) as opposed to feeling ignored and rejected.
5.  Good teachers see themselves as worthy rather than unworthy. They see themselves as people of consequence, dignity, and integrity as opposed to feeling they matter little, can be overlooked and discounted.

Hamachek sketches the following interrelated generalizations about how good teachers differ from poor teachers in the way they perceive others [113:343]:

1.  They seem to have generally more positive views of others—students, colleagues, and administrators.
2.  They do not seem to be as prone to view others as critical, attacking people with ulterior motives; rather they are seen as potentially friendly and worthy in their own right.
3.  They have a more favorable view of democratic classroom procedures.
4.  They seem to have the ability and capacity to see things as they seem to others—i.e., the ability to see things from the other person's point of view.
5.  They do not seem to see students as persons "you do things to" but rather as individuals capable of doing for themselves once they feel trusted, respected, and valued.

The importance of the teacher's attitude toward pupils is reflected in the research published by Rosenthal and Jacobson, titled *Pygmalion in the Classroom.* The research suggests strongly that children who are expected by their teachers to gain intellectually in fact do show greater intellectual gains after one year than do children of whom such gains are not expected [224:121]. What the teacher "said, by how and when she said it, by her facial expressions, postures, and perhaps her touch, the teacher may have communicated to the children of the experimental group that she expected improved intellectual performance. Such communications together with possible changes in teaching techniques may have helped the child learn by changing his self concept, his expectations of his own behavior, and his motivation, as well as his cognitive style and skills" [224:108]. Teachers who have low expectations of pupils tend to inhibit their progress by: (1) limiting the amount of material a pupil can learn—partly because the teacher does not try to teach him as much and partly because the teacher gives up more easily and quickly, and (2) stifling a pupil's motivation and giving him a feeling of alienation [100:52].

## Teacher-competency Self-appraisal Forms

Self-appraisal forms can prove to be helpful in appraising one's competency for teaching. Two of these forms have been included in the Resource Section for Part 1. Other forms may be obtained from your teacher-placement office to use in self-appraisal.

One of the forms in the Resource Section is concerned with the teacher's personality. Each prospective teacher should give careful attention to a study of the probable effects of his personality upon his success as a teacher. Please keep in mind that what you are as a person will be the most potent subject matter that will be in your classroom. To paraphrase Emerson, "I cannot hear what you *say*, when what you *are* thunders so loud!"

There has been some significant research completed on types of teacher personalities and their effects upon various groups of children [118:1–82]. Heil and his associates developed and applied what is called a "Manifold Interest Schedule" to over fifty public school teachers of grades 4, 5, and 6 and measured the progress of their children against the personality types of teachers identified by the schedule. It was found that children with a teacher having one type of personality made 50 per cent more academic progress than did children with a teacher having a decidedly different personality.

Another instrument called the "Children's Feeling Test," developed by Professor Heil and his associates, made it possible to identify four categories of children's personalities. One type of teacher appeared to have a deleterious effect upon children of the least well-adjusted category, whereas another type had a definitely beneficial effect upon such children.

As a result of this study, Heil and his associates concluded that the teacher's type of personality appears to have much effect on the progress of his pupils. Furthermore, it appears that the clear overriding factor in determining children's academic achievement is a positive and definite personality [118:66–68].

## Some Implications for Your Planning

The school of today requires far more of teachers than did the school of yesterday. This fact is understandable when one considers the expanding function of the school in American life. In earlier days the school in this country was limited primarily to teaching boys and girls the fundamental skills of reading, writing, and arithmetic. The home, the church, and the community provided most of the other learnings essential for effective citizenship. Life was relatively simple. Today, however, life is much more complex. This is due especially to the tremendous technological advancements that have been made. Great changes have also taken place in our social, economic, and political lives. The function of the school must change and expand in order to meet the needs of youth today and tomorrow. These changes give rise to new and broader requirements for teachers.

The teacher today understands the cultural context in which all education takes place. He sees clearly the significance of industrialization, urbanization, corporativeness, economic planning, cultural lags, cultural fragmentation, the growth of a scientific attitude toward problems, and other outstanding characteristics of the contemporary American scene as they affect the lives of the people. He has the ability to understand modern problems in terms of historical conditions, to recognize the recurrent nature of many educational concerns, to use the resources of the past when faced with the problems of the present, and thus to discriminate between worthy traditional solutions and those solutions which are no longer pertinent. He understands the process whereby values are inculcated for the guidance of our conduct and judgments. He demonstrates, through his attitudes, skills, and habits, a basic understanding of democracy as a way of perpetuating the values of our culture, as a process by which each may develop his best self, as a method for solving problems, and as a process of disciplining himself for the betterment of our common lives. He possesses a critical understanding of the function of communities as agencies directing human growth and of the school as one agency by which society seeks to provide for its continued expansion as well as for the development of the individual. He sees the school as an institution which is charged with a major responsibility in determining the direction and character of this growth. He recognizes that the manner in which he goes about the teaching of boys and girls is determined by what he conceives to be the real function of education.

Educational research, during the past several years, has revealed new insights regarding human behavior and the learning process. The teacher of today needs an extensive understanding of the nature of individual development in all its various aspects so that he may recognize and anticipate the increasing needs of the student and provide the conditions which will promote his maximum growth. He is aware of the ways in which people are alike and of the ways in which they differ. He understands how the individual may become more like others and yet remain unique as he attains maturity. He comprehends thoroughly the nature of human learning, both in terms of the learner's habits, attitudes, skills, and abilities and in terms of his own role as an effective guide in the learning process. It is essential, furthermore, for him to possess expert skill in guiding the education of others toward desirable ends.

## PERSONAL GROWTH TOWARD TEACHING

Much of your personal growth toward effective teaching is concerned with intangibles that are not learned in formal ways. In fact, you may get little direct help in this regard from the formal courses you take in your preparation for teaching. You do have available in your college environment, however, many resources that you may use. The amount of growth you make will depend largely upon you. Only a few areas for personal growth are discussed in this chapter, primarily for illustrative purposes.

### Skill in Oral Communication

Teachers whose voice and speech are pleasing to others tend to be more effective in the classroom. Although most people have acceptable speech, almost everyone can improve his speech if he knows his own special needs. There is the true story of a young first-grade teacher who complained to her principal, "I can't underthand why tho many of my children lithp." Children are great and often unconscious imitators. It is doubly important, then for teachers to perfect their speech—not only to improve their effectiveness in communication but also to serve as an adequate model for pupils.

Each prospective teacher should make arrangements with a speech therapist for a voice and speech test. A therapist will be able to help you with suggestions about pronunciation, tone quality, pitch, speed, and enunciation.

If professional help is not available, you can record your voice on tape. Certain problems may be obvious at once. How do you like your voice? Is your voice too high or too low to be pleasant? Are your words monotonous? Are there nervous pauses and repetitions? Do you speak too fast or too slow to be distinctly understood? Do you hesitate on the pronunciation of words? Do you speak with expression appropriate to the speech? Are you sure of the correctness of your grammar? The checklist on voice and speech that appears in the Resource Section for Part 1 may help you appraise yourself systematically.

A recording on video tape would help you check your speech as well as physical mannerisms. One of the advantages of engaging in micro-teaching activities that are also video taped is to study how you look and sound to others and how you can improve the total act of communicating and interacting with others.

## Skill in Decision Making

A teacher is forced to make many decisions each day. These decisions have an effect upon the lives of his pupils and their parents, his colleagues, and other community members, as well as upon his personal and professional life.

During your college career you have many opportunities to improve your skill in decision making. It is a skill to which conscious effort should be directed. While many decisions are simply a matter of picking the things which are of greatest interest and importance at the moment, other decisions involve the making of value judgments, the careful selection of activities in the light of their real worth.

Teaching requires a high degree of skill in working with others—colleagues, pupils, parents, and other community members. Many opportunities exist within a college environment for the further development of this skill. *(Photograph by Joe Di Dio, National Education Association.)*

## Skill in Group Participation

Much of a teacher's life involves group work with colleagues, parents, and other community members. Likewise, the teacher is concerned with helping his pupils gain skill in effective group work. In order to be truly successful in his work, therefore, a teacher must have a high degree of skill in group work. Membership in clubs, fraternities or sororities, church and welfare organizations, civic groups, sports groups, and professional societies provides opportunities for you to gain skills of good group membership.

In order to increase your effectiveness as a group participant you may find it helpful to check yourself in regard to some questions titled "Am I a Good Group Participant?" which appear in the Resource Section for Part 1.

One application of the principles of group participation can be a class discussion of some of the topics or problems found at the end of each chapter in this book. In order to get started, your instructor may temporarily assume leadership in helping your group select its subjects. After this initial step, he may wish to turn over his role to members of the group as quickly as possible so that they may gain leadership experience.

All members of the group should help decide how the group will attack the topic. Such projects as reading in the library, interviewing, bringing resource people to the classroom, writing reports, viewing films, having panel discussions, and the like may be involved. It may seem desirable for small groups to work on certain aspects of the problem and to report their findings to the entire group.

## Skill in Group Leadership

There is a significant difference between being a group participant and serving as discussion group leader. Since the latter more nearly approximates the role you will play as a teacher, gain as much leadership skill as possible while in college in your course work and cocurricular activities. As a group leader keep in mind the following:

1. Help the group define the problem clearly—its nature and scope or delimitations.
2. Encourage all participants to share their thinking, information, and experience.
3. Provide opportunity for all points of view to be expressed.
4. Keep the discussion directed to the problem.
5. Help group members to clarify their thinking and to summarize their progress.
6. Utilize all resources represented in the experience of group members.
7. Strive to develop a cohesive and productive group.
8. Avoid trying to save time by telling the group the right answer.

Keep in mind that the leader is not a group instructor; he is a guide trying to arrange conditions so that each member will do creative thinking. Group discussion is not a debating society. While disagreements are to be expected, the task of the group is to find more truth than each member brings to any group meeting—a cooperative quest in which thinking is creative rather than combative.

## Skill in the Effective Use of Time

You may recall Shakespeare's advice, "Let every man be master of his time. . . ." You undoubtedly recognize the wisdom of planning your personal time, and understand desirable procedures that may be used. For this reason the only points to be made are that the problem of using time effectively is ever present, that you need to check periodically to see whether or not you are using your time most profitably, that skill in the wise use of time may be gained as you work intelligently upon the problem and plan accordingly, that provision should be made for a well-balanced program of activities which takes into consideration all aspects of your personal growth, and that skill gained in the effective use of your time while in college will pay high dividends in your work as a teacher and as a citizen.

## SUMMARY

As you think about yourself as a part of society, you recognize the role which planning plays in this increasingly complex and interdependent culture. You sense that an intelligent application of the process necessitates your becoming skilled not only in planning your own life, but also in helping those whom you teach to do likewise.

Several steps have been suggested for use in outlining the details of your plans for teaching. Your first responsibility is to be certain of the things in life that really seem important to you—your values. These values largely determine the things you seek to accomplish. You then examine the possibilities of a career in education to see if it holds promise of your being able to fulfill these needs and if you can meet the requirements for such a career. You then develop detailed schemes for moving from where you are to where you want to go, keeping in mind that plans are always tentative, and that modifications are made as unforeseen factors develop.

This chapter also has been concerned with competencies for teaching and with personal growth toward teaching. The results of several studies on teacher competencies have been presented so that you could compare them, note similarities, and evaluate yourself in terms of them.

No one can expect to meet all the competencies for teaching to the highest degree, either at the time of graduation or at the end of a lifetime teaching career. But with each year of experience, it is a teacher's professional obligation to move to a fuller realization of his potential. Weaknesses can be eliminated, and strengths can be made stronger; hence there is always the horizon of greater fulfillment. You may wish to study yourself in the light of those qualities that seem characteristic of effective teachers and then plan to acquire the ones you now appear to lack. The suggestions given here should point the way to many other possibilities.

Careful planning and conscientious execution of those plans will assist you in becoming a worthwhile citizen, a well-adjusted person who knows how to work with others. Such a person can become important in his own right and can justify the investment of time and energy needed to help him take his place in his chosen profession.

## QUESTIONS TO CONSIDER

1. In your opinion, what values should a person have in life if he plans to teach?
2. "Values are acquired parts of an individual's life." What are some of the implications of this statement for the experiences you will plan for your pupils, and the personal influence you will attempt to exert upon your pupils?
3. In what ways do the values held in common by people in America differ from those that characterize people in an autocratic society?
4. In what ways might long-range planning have improved the lives of some of your friends?
5. Some people feel that group planning and work reduces everyone to the level of mediocrity. Is this necessarily true? If not, how can group work contribute to the development of the unique talents of an individual?
6. In addition to a thorough grounding in subject matter, what specific understandings, skills, and techniques are, in your opinion, essential to success in the teaching profession?
7. From your observations what are the most common weaknesses of beginning teachers? How can you avoid such weaknesses when you begin teaching?
8. Do you feel that your image of yourself often is reflected in how others see you? Can you present any evidence to support this point, and what are its implications for your success as a future teacher?
9. In what ways does a teacher's personality affect the progress of his pupils? Can you recall incidents that support your point of view?
10. Does a school administrator or supervisor have the right to criticize a teacher for being untidy or inappropriately dressed? If so, why?
11. What qualities of voice and speech in teachers are conducive to good discipline in the classroom?

## PROBLEM SITUATION FOR INQUIRY

Louise, a 23-year-old recent college graduate, has been certified to teach in her home state. Her undergraduate studies took her five years to complete because she worked part-time to supplement the support which her widowed mother provided her.

Louise has received several job offers to teach at the secondary school level. Her long-range goal, however, is to teach at the college level. To achieve such a position would require additional work at the graduate level and would postpone much-needed income.

The problem, then, for Louise is to decide whether to accept a position at the secondary school level where she will receive a substantially lower salary over a long period of time, or to undertake graduate studies for a postponed, but more financially rewarding and more stimulating career. If you found yourself in a position similar to that of Louise, what would you do? Why?

## ACTIVITIES TO PURSUE

1. Make a list of the things you really value in life. After careful study, try to arrange them in descending order according to their importance to you. Reflect upon your past experiences and try to determine why you attach importance to each of your values. Examine them carefully to see whether they are compatible with each other. Opposite this list indicate all the values you see in education as a career. Compare and contrast these two listings to determine the extent to which they seem compatible.

2. Question seriously some of your close friends regarding what they value most in life. In what ways do the values they hold differ from yours? How do you account for these differences? In what ways are their career plans being affected by their values?

3. Talk to some people who have been very successful in their careers. Question them regarding long-range plans they have followed in order to gain success. Study also the careers of some people who have not been very successful. What differences do you find in the career planning done by successful and unsuccessful people?

4. Talk with people who have retired. You will find some who are happy and well adjusted in their retirement and others who are not. Attempt to determine whether long-range planning, or the lack of it, accounts to some extent for the differences.

5. Assume that you as a teacher should be skilled in helping your pupils plan together in the effective solution of common problems. Consider some college activities in which you might engage for purposes of increasing your skill in this regard.

6. As suggested previously, collect as many objective data as possible on your special abilities for teaching. Study these data carefully, seeking help from your college instructors if needed; formulate plans for overcoming your weaknesses and building up your strengths.

7. Prepare a paper on "What I Value in Life," "What Life Means to Me," "My Philosophy of Life," or on a similar topic suggested in this chapter.

8. Interview informally a number of boys and girls about the qualities that they think teachers should have. Have them also indicate the qualities which they dislike the most in teachers. Check your findings against those listed in this chapter.

9. Draw a line vertically through the center of a piece of paper. On the left-hand side, list the factors that characterize the teacher whom you most disliked while in school. On the right-hand side, list the factors that characterize the teacher you liked best. At the bottom of the page, list the characteristics of the teacher who was of most value to you. Compare and contrast the characteristics listed for all three in an effort to determine common elements. Check your results against the findings listed in this chapter.

10. Check yourself on the "Checklist of Important Factors in the Teacher's Personality" which appears in the Resource Section of Part I, and underline the qualities or traits in which you need to improve. Try to formulate some first steps to take in overcoming your weaknesses.

11. Consult your director of student teaching regarding competencies against which you will be evaluated in your student teaching. Secure copies of any forms that may be used, and study them carefully. Formulate specific plans for overcoming any weaknesses that may be revealed from a study of these forms.

12. Discuss with an experienced school superintendent the qualities he looks for when he is employing teachers. Also ask him to list the main weaknesses of beginning teachers.

13. Consult with the counseling services on your college campus to locate the various agencies which may be of service to you in your program of self-improvement.
14. Explore your college catalog in an effort to find those courses that may be taken to broaden your interests or help overcome a personality problem. Consider taking courses in mental hygiene, philosophy and ethics, science fields that are new to you, arts and crafts, camp counseling, folk dancing, sports, speech improvement, writing, or dramatics.
15. If possible, do some microteaching and have it recorded on video tape. Study the recording carefully to discover any improvements you might make in your speech, mannerisms, appearance, and probable affect upon others.
16. In your future group activities carefully appraise the extent to which you fulfill the characteristics of a good group member. Formulate ways to strengthen any characteristics in which you find yourself to be weak.
17. Keep an accurate record of how you spend your time during a fairly normal week of school. At the end of the week analyze the distribution of your time to see whether you are making the best use of it. You may wish to discuss the results with your friends and instructors and to plan ways of gaining more value from the free time you have available.

# 3 | TEACHER EDUCATION, CERTIFICATION, AND ACCREDITATION

One of the distinguishing characteristics of a profession is the requirement that its future members undergo a relatively long period of professional preparation to acquire the knowledge, skills, and techniques unique to that profession. This normally means successfully completing a prescribed program in higher education. As Stinnett [225:404–405] points out:

The most effective way to assure that persons admitted to practice are competent is through a formal, rigorous, scholarly, prescribed program of preparation. This is why any profession must be constantly concerned with the collegiate and university programs that prepare its members. It is the only way that reasonable standards can be enforced for admission to practice, and it is the only way the members of a recognized profession can be protected from the competition of unqualified persons.

The same conditions pertain to teaching, and the reasons given above indicate why the professional education of teachers is of prime concern to every member of the profession.

## Programs for Teacher Education

Since more people are engaged in teaching than in any other profession in the world, it is to be expected that institutions of higher education are engaged in the preparation of more students for teaching than for any other profession. Even in the large state universities, normally over one-third of the undergraduates are in teacher education programs. Of more than 2,000 institutions of higher education in the United States, approximately 1,250 are approved for the preparation of teachers. Of these institutions, 1,137 are accredited by regional associations, and 470 of them were accredited by the National Council for Accreditation of Teacher Education in 1970. The list of approved teacher education institutions in 1970 included 180 public and 172 private universities, 206

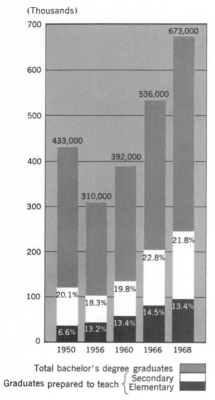

(Thousands)

FIGURE 3–1   Percentage of all college graduates who have prepared to teach. Over one third of all bachelor's degree graduates in American colleges and universities are prepared to teach.

public and 636 private general or liberal arts colleges, 5 public and 11 private teachers colleges, and 36 junior colleges [254:38].

It is significant to note the steady change taking place in the institutions preparing teachers.

After a bitter struggle extending over a period of 130 years, teacher education has fought its way into the mainstream of higher education. The separate, single-purpose teacher education institution (normal schools, teachers colleges, state colleges of education) have virtually disappeared. Only 5 such public institutions and 11 private ones remain out of a total of more than 300 normal schools existing at the turn of the century, and perhaps as many as 150 teachers colleges and state colleges of education in 1930 [254:6].

## Importance of Teacher Education

One of the reasons why some colleges and universities have been slow in accepting teacher education as a central function has been due to the feeling that "anyone who knew his subject would be able to teach it." Strange as it may seem, there are some professors on college campuses, especially those in subject-matter areas, who voice this same feeling and express grave doubts about the value of professional education courses. In fact, they may vociferously condemn such courses, and the student preparing to teach often is either confused or inclined to develop negative attitudes toward the importance of professional education courses. Often the violence of the controversy over the relative importance of subject-matter courses to professional courses is directly proportional to the lack of understanding of the field being condemned.

Some critics point to the fact that, on the college level and in private schools, one finds good teachers who have not taken any courses in education. The fallacy of this argument lies in the fact that these teachers are excellent in spite of their deficiencies. One may ask the question, "How much better might they have been?"

The fallacy of the belief that an effective teacher needs only a thorough knowledge of subject matter may be illustrated in various ways. As Chandler [41:5] points out, a passenger who has traveled extensively by air may feel that his experience qualifies him to pilot a plane. He may know much about aerodynamics, theory of flight, engines, flight patterns, regulations, schedules, etc. But if he should attempt to take charge of a flight, without having gone through the necessary long and intensive program of training, he immediately would discover the difference between being a pilot and flying as a passenger. Chandler feels that "the difference between lay teaching and professional teaching is comparable to the contrast between the recommendations of home remedies given by a layman for the sick and injured and the professional medical prescription and advice given by a doctor" [41:5].

There are other reasons why some prospective teachers may feel that a thorough knowledge of subject matter is about the only requirement for successful teaching. Unfortunately most of these students have attended schools in which attention has been given to little more than the sheer mastery of assigned subject matter. Furthermore, there is an element of security to be found by some students in assuming that the function of the teacher is to teach subject matter per se. These students, more than any others, have need for professional education courses.

Educational researchers, such as Smith at the University of Illinois and Turner and Fattu at Indiana University, have conducted some sophisticated research that sheds light upon the controversy. Turner and Fattu, for example, have worked upon the assumption that any profession, to be worthy of the name, possesses an extensive and growing body of systematic, organized, and abstract knowledge which can be mastered only over an extended period of time by individuals who are selected for their aptitude and perform an essential public service better than any other group can perform such service. As a case in point, medical men ultimately justify their claim to professional status by being best able to solve problems within their domain because they are more competent than any other group in medical diagnosis and treatment. Similarly, teachers should be more competent than any other group in solving problems within their domain. Their research [284:1–29] clearly indicates that (1) teachers who have had a methods course perform better than those who have had none; (2) bachelor's degree graduates from teacher education programs perform significantly better than graduates in other areas including liberal arts; (3) teachers who have had teaching experience perform significantly better than those without such experiences; (4) teachers with one year of experience perform significantly better than those with no experience; (5) teachers with three to five years experience perform significantly better than those with one year of experience; and (6) teachers in large school districts where in-service teacher education is supported perform significantly better than those in small districts.

## General Pattern of Teacher Education

It is perfectly understandable, in the light of American education's brief and rapid development, that considerable variation exists in the specific nature of programs to be found in teacher education institutions today. There are, however, some characteristics that are common to most teacher education programs for the elementary and secondary levels. These programs may be studied in terms of three major areas: general education, subject-matter specialization, and professional education.

There has been considerable controversy, especially during recent years, over the proportionate distribution of general and specialized course work and of professional education course work. Some of the critics seem to feel that a four-year teacher education program consists almost entirely of methodology or professional education. They bitterly condemn the "educationist" for most of the weaknesses in the American school system upon the grounds that almost all of a prospective teacher's education involves "learning how to teach." The facts of the case are these: approximately three-fourths of a prospective elementary teacher's preparation for teaching and approximately five-sixths of a prospective secondary school teacher's preparation involve study in the various subject areas. It would not seem excessive to devote from one-sixth to one-fourth of a student's time in college to a consideration of what education is for, of what young children and adolescents are like, and of how effective learning can best be promoted, as well as to gain some experience under expert guidance. Educators, in their feverish efforts to keep the amount of professional education to a minimum, realize that anything short of this proportionate amount does violence to any program designed to produce effective teachers. Those in other professions (medicine, dentistry, law, engineering, business administration) insist

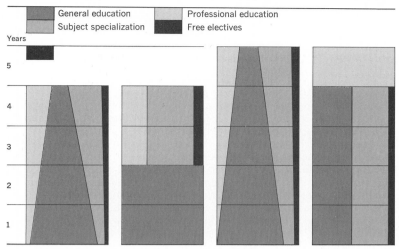

FIGURE 3–2   Four prevailing program patterns of teacher education in the United States. What are the advantages and disadvantages of each pattern?

upon devoting a significantly higher percentage of their respective preparatory programs to professional education.

The committee of the National Commission on Teacher Education and Professional Standards which prepared the report *New Horizons for the Teaching Profession* feels that general education, specialization in one or more teaching fields, and professional education should be viewed as interrelated parts of a total program [172:59].

General education, specialization in a teaching field, and professional education can and should make an important contribution to helping the student to develop intellectual curiosity, a positive attitude toward learning, and a disposition to examine, inquire, and analyze; to build skills of logical analysis and of reasoned and orderly consideration of ideas; to gain understanding of and competence in using the different forms of reasoning employed in various fields; and to deepen respect for all areas of knowledge.

Further, a student should have opportunity in all parts of his program to become acquainted with resources for continuing inquiry and to build facility in their use. No part of a teacher education program is complete if it fails to give direct attention to helping the student derive principles and generalizations and to examine his actions on the basis of them. Important skills basic to effective interpersonal relationships must be a deliberate focus, not in one aspect of a program but throughout the total of planned experiences of every student.

Any discussion of the parts should be viewed in terms of the above desired outcomes of the total program.

**General education**   General education refers to the broad fields of knowledge, such as the humanities, the life and physical sciences, and the social and behavioral sciences, that are designed to help you solve personal problems and those of the society in which you live. General education is focused upon the needs and responsibilities which men have in common. It is designed to help a prospective teacher become a more alert, cultivated, and responsible individual and citizen [146:39].

Members of the teaching profession as persons need the same general education important for all thoughtful people. For the educator as a professional, however, general education has unusual urgency. *The teacher stands before his pupils in a special way, as a symbol and example of the educated person in the best sense of that term.* If he is a rounded and informed person, with a lively curiosity in many fields, he will stimulate students to join him in these interests. Further, his broad educational background will make him sensitive to pupil interests. Then, too, the teacher's central and critical role in the twentieth century, that of helping learners to intellectualize their experiences, gain new insights and develop the motivation to continue to learn and the ability to cope with the unknown, requires a new dimension in his own general education [146:40].

The college campus may offer many opportunities for anyone to expand his cultural background, such as concerts, lectures, plays, and art exhibits. There also is the library with a wealth of books, periodicals, magazines, and newspapers from which one can gain breadth of understanding of the past as well as the present. There is much that can be done before graduation to develop the rich general background which one owes to himself and to the pupils he will teach.

**Subject-matter specialization**  An elementary teacher usually is responsible for teaching virtually all subject fields. Although some schools do have special teachers in such areas as art, music, and physical education, it is common practice for the elementary teacher to assume responsibility for these special subjects. As a result, he needs a thorough grounding in more areas of learning than does the secondary teacher. The elementary teacher needs to develop enough depth of understanding in each of these areas to guide children into increasingly rich and challenging learning experiences. There is the feeling that a prospective elementary teacher also would profit from an intensive study of a special field and would become a more valuable teacher. The changing patterns of school organization and instructional procedures, such as team teaching and programmed learning, are emphasizing the need for elementary teachers who have subject area specialties.

A secondary teacher is certified in one or more subject areas. He is responsible for bringing to his pupils a large store of knowledge in the courses he teaches. For this reason he takes a greater amount of advanced work in one or more subject areas than does the elementary teacher.

Although larger schools have sufficient classes in English, for example, to occupy a teacher's full time, secondary teachers frequently begin teaching in small schools where it usually is necessary to teach in at least two subject fields. It is highly desirable, therefore, to be certified in more than one subject, unless you wish to become a special teacher in such fields as fine arts, music, vocational home economics, or agriculture. By very careful planning, it may be possible to complete the certification requirements for a third or a fourth subject area. For example, some course work may be used to meet general education requirements, and some of the work needed for a major or minor may be applicable toward the requirements of a third or fourth certification area. Often only a small amount of additional work may be needed to increase the number of subject areas for certification.

The information contained in Chapter 4 should help you to make an intelligent and firm decision with regard to a field or fields of specialization. In view of the current oversupply of teachers, you also may wish to consult the education placement office to determine the probable demand for teachers having the specializations in which you are interested.

Institutions vary considerably in regard to the number of course credits required for majors and minors. If you anticipate teaching in another state, you should consult the specific state requirements for certification in the subject areas you elect in order that you may meet these requirements, if possible, upon graduation.

**Professional education**   During the past three or four decades rapid strides have been made in the professional education of teachers. This progress has been fostered especially by far-reaching research in the field of psychology. Techniques similar to those of the social psychologist, sociologist, and anthropologist have assisted educators in expanding the areas of investigation to include the more intangible aspects of education. Hundreds of studies have been made on such problems as the learning process, individual differences in pupils, methods of evaluating pupil progress, curriculum organization, child growth and development, utilization of community resources and instructional media. Educational philosophers have provided clarification of the function of the school in society. The cooperative efforts of public school and teacher education personnel have helped to clarify the professional needs of the teacher. All these factors, and many others, have aided in establishing the professional education of teachers as a unique and scientific function.

The various statements of competencies listed in Chapter 2 indicate many qualities required of a successful teacher. It is this body of specialized knowledge, skills, and techniques that distinguishes teaching as a profession. Professional education courses are designed to assist students in developing the essential requirements for membership in the profession.

Teacher education institutions differ considerably in the specific ways in which they attempt to develop the professional competencies of teachers. This variation results from such factors as differences in state certification requirements, continued experimentation in the preparation of teachers, and rapid developments in teacher education. Any student who anticipates transferring to another institution during the time of his preparation for teaching should exercise great care in selecting his courses. Differences in requirements are so great among institutions that credits awarded at one college may not meet the specific demands of another. Whenever a transfer is anticipated, a student should check on the acceptability of the course work to be taken prior to the transfer. Careful planning along these lines often saves disappointment and delays in accepting desired teaching positions.

In spite of variations in the details of professional programs for teachers, there is a fairly common pattern in evidence. The programs generally can be divided into the following major areas, although the emphasis on each varies among institutions as well as within institutions according to the area or level of specialization:

1. Introduction to education
2. General and educational psychology
3. Human development
4. General methods
5. Special methods
6. Student teaching

Much of the remaining portion of this book should help a prospective student sense more clearly the rationale of these areas. The values, insights, understandings, and skills gained in the sequence of professional courses required for certification will be affected greatly by the extent to which a student recognizes the crucial need for each.

Students in elementary education generally are required to take more professional course work, mostly in special methods, than are students in secondary education. Elementary teachers tend to be more concerned with a child's total development, whereas secondary teachers are more concerned with the teaching of their areas of specialization. The professional preparation of elementary and secondary teachers is usually similar in the initial stages. Differentiation designed for specialization normally occurs when prospective teachers take special methods courses and student teaching.

Institutions differ considerably with respect to the length of time during which a student will take his professional education. Some institutions concentrate the program in the last year of college work. It is more common, however, to reserve professional education courses for the last two years of a four-year program. Currently there is a trend to spread a prospective teacher's professional learning throughout his entire college career so as to provide more opportunity to relate professional course work to firsthand experiences in working with pupils. Creative teaching does not consist of a "bag of tricks" and "cookbook recipes." Only time can provide the experiences from which prospective teachers may gain deep insights into human beings, the nature of the learning process, and creative ways of guiding children into expanding areas of effective living.

The authors of *New Horizons for the Teaching Profession* feel that not all professional education should be postponed to the fourth year of teacher preparation for the following reasons [146:65]: "(1) there is need for ideas about teaching to mature and to be tested before the student undertakes responsibility for the trusteeship of the teacher, and (2) when the student has selected teaching as his profession, the motivation that comes from exploring what is involved in teaching enhances rather than detracts from the values gained from work in general education."

A number of institutions are requiring students to observe many teaching-learning situations, beginning with their first year of college. Case studies of children and participation in classroom situations are part of other professional education courses and are studied prior to a period of supervised student teaching.

There is much that can be done to gain a greater understanding of the behavior, interests, abilities, individual differences, and general characteristics of children. Many students participate in such valuable activities as teaching Sunday school classes, serving as camp counselors, working in youth centers or settlement houses, serving as life guards or playground supervisors, or baby sitting. College courses have much greater meaning when a student is able to relate the concepts and principles discussed to the rich and varied experiences which he has had with children.

## Five-year Programs in Teacher Education

A growing number of educators, professional organizations, and state certification offices are reflecting the feeling that it is more difficult for a person to learn enough in four years to gain the competence needed to teach today's youth. This point of view is expressed by Stinnett in the following manner [263:16]:

The teaching profession is now driving vigorously for universal acceptance and enforcement of the five-year preservice program of preparation. Actually, what will evolve is a six-year program. The five-year preservice regimen will equip the beginning teacher for initial service in the form of a full-time, full paid internship in the sixth year. Having had professional preparation including student teaching, in the five-year sequence the beginning teacher will pursue the internship year on an apprentice certificate and as an integral part of the teacher education program.

Although a few teacher education institutions already have experimented with programs of five consecutive years of preparation for teaching, there does not seem to be any mass shift away from the

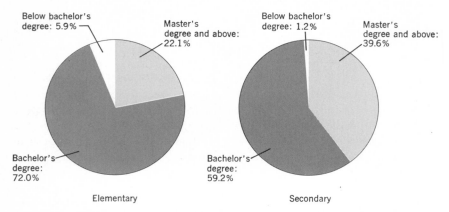

FIGURE 3–3   Estimated national distribution of public school teachers in 1970 according to their highest level of academic preparation. What changes in the distribution may be expected in the future?

four-year bachelor's degree program followed by a master's degree program. Harap, for example, is not optimistic about its adoption for the following reasons [114:21]:

It is clear that the four-year sequence will remain as the dominant pattern of training for teaching for many years to come. Arguments for the four-year liberal arts-professional education sequence are powerful; it is unhurried and proceeds as a planned, step-by-step sequence; it permits the college graduate to begin contributing to society sooner; a four-year program, followed by several years of experience in teaching, is an assurance of more profitable graduate study both in the individual's teaching field and in education; the financial investment of the fifth year is an unreasonable expectation for great numbers of prospective teachers, particularly women whose teaching careers may be short; not all prospective teachers are able to profit from graduate study.

## Performance-based Approaches to Teacher Education

Perhaps as a result of such factors as (1) the desire to change the pattern of teacher education programs with the hope of preparing better teachers, (2) the current stress being placed upon the use of performance objectives, (3) the emphasis upon accountability, and (4) the application of technology in the field of education, a number of institutions are contemplating or are experimenting with what has been termed performance-based teacher education programs. The concept seems to connote [154:3]:

A program designed *specifically* and *explicitly* to provide the prospective teacher with learning experiences and instruction that will prepare him to assume a specified teaching role. Successful completion of the program is accomplished when, and only when, the teacher candidate demonstrates that he is competent to assume the role for which he has prepared: that is, he must provide satisfactory evidence, not only that he possesses specified requisite knowledge, but also that he can carry out in practice specified teacher tasks and functions. It is the degree of specificity and explicitness in program design and in competence to be demonstrated that tends to distinguish performance-based programs from traditional programs.

The programs designed thus far have been confined to the professional studies component, with no attempt having been made to include the general studies and specialized studies components of teacher education. The professional studies component usually consists of:

A collection of performance-based instructional units requiring much independent study by the prospective teacher. Specific behavorial objectives are defined prior to instruction, in terms indicating the kinds of evidence regarding performance that would be acceptable to show that the objectives had been attained. Both the objectives and the kinds of evidence are made explicit to the learners at the outset of the program. For each performance objective, the learning of the prospective teacher is guided by periodic assessment and feedback [154:3].

In his study of performance-based teacher education programs, Massanari [154:3] noted some promising practices. Objectives are being given sharper focus. Responsibility for learning is being shifted from the teacher to the learner. Instruction is being individualized. Alternative routes to achieve the stated objectives can be chosen by the learner. The prospective teacher is provided feedback as he works toward attaining each objective. Practical experiences, in either simulated or real-life situations, tend to be related closely to the theory being studied. The instructor is viewed more as an enabler of learning than a dispenser of knowledge. The program is less *time*-oriented than standard programs—time becomes a variable rather than a constant, which enables each prospective teacher to take as long as he needs to attain the stated objectives.

Massanari [154:6 and 8] also identified some problems and concerns that are central to performance-based teacher education programs. Problems can arise from focusing on specific teaching behaviors at the expense of concern for the teacher's total performance. Some basic questions arise, such as: Can performance criteria be established that deal with generic elements of teaching? Who should establish these objectives? Can such objectives be established in the affective domain, and can they be assessed? What constitutes broad involvement in designing and evaluating programs? How can we obtain evidence to show whether or not better teachers can be prepared through this procedure? What is the relationship between teaching behavior and pupil learning? What is the relationship between performance-based certification and performance-based preparation programs?

## Teacher Education in Transition

Teacher education programs, like public school programs, have always been criticized. Much of this criticism stems from differences in the conceptions that individuals have with respect to the function of education—what it is supposed to do, and how the task should be accomplished. Chapter 15, "Development of Modern Concepts of Education," reveals some of the fundamental differences that exist today in the conceptions held by educators.

During the past several years, teacher education programs have been criticized increasingly. For example, as a result of the effort of a special task force that initially was concerned with the education of disadvantaged youth, the American Association of Colleges for Teacher Education published *Teachers for the Real World*, in which it was maintained that [249:9]:

Education is beyond repair! What is needed is a radical *reform*. This reform is to include the nature of the schooling process, the systems which control educational policy, and the institutions which prepare persons to be teachers. In teacher training, reform must be undertaken in the selection of teachers. There must be more adequate representation of the poor, the black, the Mexican, and the Indian in teaching ranks.

The current situation of remoteness of the prospective teacher from the realities of classroom practice must be reformed. Prospective teachers must be brought into contact with reality through various training experiences and actual encounters with children in the classroom.

The report contains a comprehensive plan in which current teacher education programs, including student teaching, would be abolished, and a "new social mechanism," called a training complex, would be established. After spending at least a year in a training complex, a prospective teacher would become a teaching intern for which he would be paid.

Other publications and recommended plans for teacher education could be cited. The main point to be recognized is the need for members of the teaching profession to be concerned with the continued improvement of teacher education programs so that future teachers will be able to cope adequately with the complex and increasingly difficult task of educating American youth.

It is safe to assume that rather profound changes will be made in teacher education programs, especially in the area of laboratory experiences. Education students undoubtedly will be having earlier and greater exposure to actual teaching-learning situations, and a significant portion of this exposure will be in the culturally different types of school situations [254:2]. Also, even greater use will be made of microteaching, microfilms, and video tapes to analyze teaching strengths and weaknesses [254:3].

## CERTIFICATION OF EDUCATORS

Teacher certification, otherwise known as licensure, is the process of granting legal approval to an individual to teach. Perhaps the medical profession was the first to establish licensure procedures in an attempt to protect the public from unqualified persons who might wish to practice medicine. As Stinnett points out [255:422]:

Teacher certification is the state's means of attempting to assure that only qualified persons will be permitted to teach. In this sense, certification is a privilege extended by the state and not a right. The public is then supposed to be protected from charlatans, quacks, and other unfit people in the classroom in the same way that it is protected from unqualified physicians, dentists, lawyers, pharmacists, barbers, hair-dressers, clergymen, realtors, and insurance agents. The trend is in the direction of licensing more and more occupational groups.

### Types of Teacher Certificates

In earlier days it was the practice to grant "blanket" certificates to teachers, whereby they were permitted to teach virtually all subjects in all grades. One of the positive trends in certification has been the differentiation of licenses granted for specialized grade levels and/or subject areas of instruction. Today a definite distinction is common between the certificates granted to elementary and secondary school teachers.

Secondary school certificates usually are granted on the basis of the subject areas or major fields of knowledge in which the student has studied. For instance, a teacher may be licensed to teach social studies and science rather than only history and chemistry. In time this major-area trend will decrease the odd combination of subjects that many beginning teachers often are asked to teach.

Upon meeting college and state certification requirements, a prospective teacher normally is recommended by his college to the state education department for the type of certificate for which he has prepared. Most states grant to beginning teachers some form of provisional license which specifies a limited period of validity. After this time has expired it may be renewed, provided certain conditions have been met, or it may be exchanged for a higher type of certificate. Many states grant some form of permanent certificate, usually upon evidence of a specified number of years of successful teaching and additional professional work. A permanent certificate, normally different from a life certificate, remains valid only so long as the holder teaches continuously or is not out of teaching beyond a specified number of years.

There is a trend away from the granting of life certificates to teachers. Many educators feel that the state should maintain some control over the training qualifications of its teachers. So much progress in teacher education is being made that a high standard today may easily become a

State certification laws are designed to ensure competence on the part of teachers, thereby protecting and promoting the educational welfare of youth. They also protect the competent teacher from competition with unqualified teachers. Mrs. Joan Cooney, the founder and producer of "Sesame Street," received the 1971 Gold Key award in recognition for her significant contribution to national welfare. She chose to share the award with Bud F. V. Brown of Phoenix, Arizona, in recognition of his contribution as a teacher in shaping her life. *(Photograph from the National School Public Relations Association.)*

low one within a decade. Unless some control is retained, the injurious effects of life certificates will exist long after the practice has been abolished—until the last holder of a life certificate has retired.

Some certificates expire through nonuse. Policies for renewal vary from state to state. The candidate is generally required to take some additional college work to reinstate the license.

## Present Status of Certification Standards

All the states and territories now have laws governing the certification of teachers in their respective areas. These laws in general indicate that certification is based on an applicant's having completed an approved program of teacher education, including student teaching or its equivalent, in an accredited college or university. It is not possible to describe accurately the more detailed provisions governing certification without discussing the laws of each state separately. Since certification is a state function, each state has developed its own certification requirements, resulting in considerable differences among the states in regard to the amount of training required and the types of certificates granted.

Each year Elizabeth H. Woellner and M. Aurilla Wood publish a booklet titled *Requirement for Certification of Teachers, Counselors, Librarians, Administrators for Elementary Schools, Secondary Schools, Junior Colleges* that lists the certification requirements in each state. Every three years the National Education Association publishes a report, titled *A Manual on Certification Requirements for School Personnel in the United States,* which details trends and specific data concerning certification qualifications in each state and contains the addresses of the chief state certifying officers. Information on specific certification requirements also may be obtained by writing directly to the chief state certifying officer. If a prospective teacher is attending college outside of his home state or is considering the possibilities of teaching in another geographic area, it would be wise to learn early in his training the specific certification requirements for the state or states in which he plans to teach.

A *general* idea of minimum certification requirements in states and territories in 1970 may be gained from Table 3–1. Please keep in mind, however, that certification requirements in some states may be periodically revised. For example, a bachelor's degree will be required of beginning elementary teachers in Nebraska, South Dakota, and Wisconsin in 1972. Also certain specific courses, such as state history or government, may be required. Even the general categories vary considerably in the semester hours demanded.

In 1970 the range of semester hours of necessary professional education courses ran from 8 to 36 (not including Puerto Rico), with a median of 24 for elementary and 18 for secondary teachers. Semester hours in student teaching ranged from 2 to 12, with a median of 6 for both elementary and secondary teachers. In the past, these differences have made it difficult for teachers to move freely from one state to another.

Most states have requirements for teacher certification in addition to those indicated in Table 3–1. In 1970, for instance [254:68], thirty states and territories required that applicants be citizens of the United States, twenty-one required the signing of an oath of allegiance or loyalty to the United States and to the state, ten required as a prerequisite evidence of having been hired to teach, and forty-four required a recommendation from the college in which the student did his work or from the employing official if he were already an experienced teacher. General health certificates were required in twenty-one states and territories, and chest x-rays were required in fourteen. Although twelve states specified special courses, only eight actually required special courses which could usually be secured only in an institution in that state [254:68].

Twenty-one states reported some use of proficiency examinations in

TABLE 3–1   **MINIMUM REQUIREMENTS FOR LOWEST REGULAR TEACHING CERTIFICATES***

| | Elementary School | | | Secondary School | | |
|---|---|---|---|---|---|---|
| State | Degree or number of semester hours required | Professional education required, semester hours (total) | Directed teaching required, semester hours (included in column 3) | Degree or number of semester hours required | Professional education required, semester hours (total) | Directed teaching required, semester hours (included in column 6) |
| 1 | 2 | 3 | 4 | 5 | 6 | 7 |
| Alabama | B | 27 | 6 | B | 21 | 6 |
| Alaska | B | 24 | C | B | 18 | C |
| Arizona | 5 | 24 | 6 | 5 | 22 | 6 |
| Arkansas | B | 18 | 6 | B | 18 | 6 |
| California | B | AC | AC | B | AC | AC |
| Colorado | B | AC | AC | B | AC | AC |
| Connecticut | B | 30 | 6 | B | 18 | 6 |
| Delaware | B | 30 | 6 | B | 18 | 6 |
| District of Col. | B | 15 | C | 5 | 15 | C |
| Florida | B | 20 | 6 | B | 20 | 6 |
| Georgia | B | 18 | 6 | B | 18 | 6 |
| Hawaii | B | 18 | AC | B | 18 | AC |
| Idaho | B | 24 | 6 | B | 20 | 6 |
| Illinois | B | 16 | 5 | B | 16 | 5 |
| Indiana | B | 27 | 8 | B | 18 | 6 |
| Iowa | B | 20 | 5 | B | 20 | 5 |
| Kansas | B | 24 | 5 | B | 20 | 5 |
| Kentucky | B | 24 | 8 | B | 17 | 8 |
| Louisiana | B | 24 | 4 | B | 18 | 4 |
| Maine | B | 30 | 6 | B | 18 | 6 |
| Maryland | B | 26 | 8 | B | 18 | 6 |
| Massachusetts | B | 18 | 2 | B | 12 | 2 |
| Michigan | B | 20 | 5 | B | 20 | 5 |
| Minnesota | B | 30 | 6 | B | 18 | 4 |
| Mississippi | B | 36 | 6 | B | 18 | 6 |
| Missouri | B | 18 | 5 | B | 18 | 5 |
| Montana | B | AC | AC | B | 16 | AC |
| Nebraska | 60 | 8 | 3 | B | AC | AC |
| Nevada | B | 18 | 6 | B | 20 | 6 |
| New Hampshire | B | 30 | 6 | B | 18 | 6 |
| New Jersey | B | 30 | 6 | B | 21 | 6 |
| New Mexico | B | 24 | 6 | B | 18 | 6 |

*AC means approved curriculum; B means bachelor's degree of specified preparation; 5 means bachelor's degree plus a fifth year of appropriate preparation, not necessarily completion of master's degree; C means a course.

*Source:* T. M. Stinnett, *A Manual on Certification Requirements for School Personnel in the United States,* National Education Association, National Commission on Teacher Education and Professional Standards, Washington, 1970, p. 48.

TABLE 3-1 **(Continued)**

| State | Elementary School Degree or number of semester hours required | Elementary School Professional education required, semester hours (total) | Elementary School Directed teaching required, semester hours (included in column 3) | Secondary School Degree or number of semester hours required | Secondary School Professional education required, semester hours (total) | Secondary School Directed teaching required, semester hours (included in column 6) |
|---|---|---|---|---|---|---|
| 1 | 2 | 3 | 4 | 5 | 6 | 7 |
| New York | B | 24 | C | B | 12 | C |
| North Carolina | B | 24 | 6 | B | 18 | 6 |
| North Dakota | B | 16 | 3 | B | 16 | 3 |
| Ohio | B | 28 | 6 | B | 17 | 6 |
| Oklahoma | B | 21 | 6 | B | 21 | 6 |
| Oregon | B | 20 | – | B | 14 | – |
| Pennsylvania | B | AC | 6–12 | B | AC | 6–12 |
| Puerto Rico | 68 | 53 | 6 | B | 29 | 5 |
| Rhode Island | B | 30 | 6 | B | 18 | 6 |
| South Carolina | B | 21 | 6 | B | 18 | 6 |
| South Dakota | 60 | 15 | 3 | B | 20 | 6 |
| Tennessee | B | 24 | 4 | B | 24 | 4 |
| Texas | B | 18 | 6 | B | 18 | 6 |
| Utah | B | 26 | 8 | B | 21 | 8 |
| Vermont | 90 | 18 | 6 | B | 18 | 6 |
| Virginia | B | 18 | 6 | B | 15 | 6 |
| Washington | B | AC | AC | B | AC | AC |
| West Virginia | B | 20 | 6 | B | 20 | 6 |
| Wisconsin | 64 | 26 | 5 | B | 18 | 5 |
| Wyoming | B | 23 | C | B | 20 | C |

the certification process [254:34], especially the examination prepared by the Modern Language Association, and all or part of the National Teacher Examination. Serious objections have been raised to the frequent misuse of these tests, especially the National Teacher Examination. Although the developers of the National Teacher Examination (Educational Testing Service) have never advocated that it should be used as the only test of the competency of teachers, it frequently has been used in this manner. The National Education Association, for example, maintains that "the use of examinations such as the National Teacher Examination is an undesirable method for evaluating educators in service for purposes such as salary, tenure, retention, or promotion. Such examinations should not be used as a condition of employment of an educator when the candidate is a graduate of an institution accredited by the National Council for Accreditation of Teacher Education" [169:69].

## Limited (Emergency) Certificates

Due to the extreme shortage of teachers that occurred during and following World War II, a policy of granting limited or emergency certificates was adopted in order to keep the schools open. In 1945–1946, one in seven employed teachers was on an emergency certificate [15:23]. This ratio has steadily dropped, however, to approximately one in twenty. Approximately 70 per cent of the emergency certificates involve elementary teachers.

Many of this group are actually close to meeting all requirements for certification and are good teachers. Ways and means should be provided for those who are making significant contributions to bolster their training, gain their professional certificates, and continue teaching. Those who are poor teachers should be weeded out as quickly as possible; otherwise, the teaching profession and the welfare of youth and society will suffer. The current oversupply of teachers should provide incentive for those who employ teachers to discontinue, or at least curtail, the employment of additional teachers with emergency certificates.

## Trends in the Certification Standards for Elementary Teachers

Table 3–1 indicates that an amazing amount of progress has been made in raising the certification standards for elementary teachers. In 1970, forty-six states and the District of Columbia were enforcing the minimum requirement of the bachelor's degree for the lowest regular certificate for beginning elementary school teachers [254:23]. The remaining four states and Puerto Rico were requiring that prospective elementary school teachers have at least two years of college work. Three of these states have indicated that the bachelor's degree would become a requirement by September 1972 for certification. In 1951, by way of contrast, only seventeen states required the bachelor's degree; three required at least three years; seventeen, two years; nine, one year; and two states, less than one year.

With regard to the preschool level, forty-five states, the District of Columbia, and Puerto Rico required public kindergarten teachers to hold certificates in 1970 [254:27]. Nineteen states require teachers in publicly supported nursery schools to hold certificates; whereas only nine states require such certification for private nursery school teachers [254:66]. It is highly probable that as more states support nursery school at public expense, they will require nursery school teachers to be certified.

Undoubtedly, the rapid adoption of the single-salary schedule has played a significant role in the radical increase in the requirements for elementary-school teacher certification. Also, there has been a growing understanding of the significance of early childhood and elementary education in our society and the need for well-prepared teachers at those

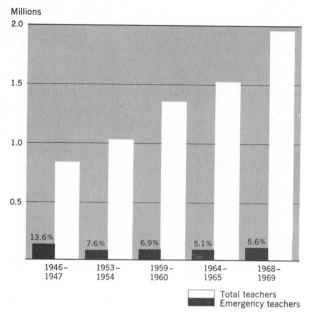

FIGURE 3-4  Percentage of teachers on emergency certificates. Although the number of teachers more than doubled between 1946 and 1968, the percentage teaching on emergency permits was reduced more than half.

levels. Many educators maintain that quality education during these early years is more critical than at any other school level since it lays the foundation for a pupil's educational career and for life. "Unless the proper foundation is laid in the lower grades, the best superstructure for future educational accomplishment cannot be erected" [215:498–499].

It is not uncommon to find people expressing concern over the rising standards for elementary teachers. They feel that this trend will tend to produce a shortage. There is considerable evidence, however, to indicate that the supply of elementary teachers will generally *increase* as standards are raised. This increasing supply-standards ratio is paralleled in other professions, e.g., law and medicine. The reasons are largely that higher standards are usually accompanied by higher salaries; both standards and salary operate to enhance the prestige of a profession. When all three factors—standards, salary, and prestige—are strengthened, the supply of potential candidates attracted to the field increases.

### Trends in the Certification Standards for Secondary Teachers

For a number of years at least, a bachelor's degree from a recognized college has been the standard requirement for high school teaching.

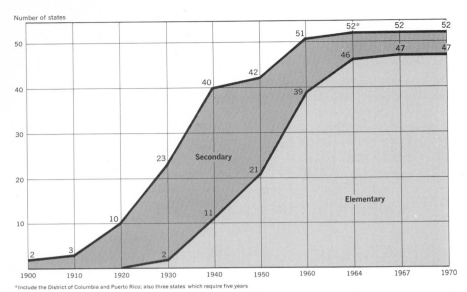

Number of states

*Include the District of Columbia and Puerto Rico; also three states which require five years

FIGURE 3–5  Number of states (including the District of Columbia and Puerto Rico) enforcing the degree requirement for lowest regular teaching certificates. A major step forward in professional standards has been the increased requirements for the preparation of beginning teachers.

Twelve states in 1970 also required the completion of the fifth year of training by the end of a specified number of years of teaching. Many educators feel that in the relatively near future five years of college training will become a common standard for the preparation of secondary teachers. A number of teacher education institutions already include a fifth year of training as a regular part of the program. Normally school systems provide higher salaries for beginning teachers who have had five years of preparation.

## Trend Toward Certification of Middle School Teachers

Some states, notably Nebraska and Kentucky, provide teacher certification specifically for the middle school. Most of the states seem to feel that existing certification arrangements for secondary school teachers are adequate for teaching at this level [80:102]. If the middle school concept continues to grow, it is highly probable that more states will establish certification patterns for teaching in middle schools.

## Certification of Teachers in Private Schools

Only twenty-six states, by either law or regulation, require teachers in private or parochial schools, at some school level or under certain conditions, to hold certificates [254:28]. Although this number may seem small, it represents an increase of nine states, in the three-year period of 1967 to 1970. The predominant practice in privately supported and controlled schools is to require certification only in the case that the school seeks accreditation by the state or to issue certificates upon the voluntary requests of teachers in the private schools.

A number of conflicting principles are involved when one considers whether or not private and church-related school teachers should meet certification requirements. Church-related schools pose the problem of separation between church and state. Should the state impose *its* definition of competence upon such a school, or does the church-related school have a right to insist upon its concept of competence? Private schools have fought for their freedom of decision in the selection of teachers in order to maintain the excellence of their institutional programs. They feel that any attempt to curtail this freedom would violate the principle of free enterprise and would handicap the development of outstandingly good educational programs. On the other hand, the state, in fulfilling its educational responsibility, has an obligation to protect all boys and girls from persons of substandard qualifications. The authors of *New Horizons for the Teaching Profession,* in viewing the problem, express the following point of view [146:153]:

Once the license represents a valid standard of competence, and once the granting of licenses is based on demonstrated competence there remains no valid argument against its application to both public and private schools—church-related, independent, and proprietary. Indeed it then becomes the moral obligation of the state to apply the standard throughout its jurisdiction.

In the years ahead the question of certification of teachers in private and church-related schools may develop into an interesting issue.

## Trends in Certification Standards of Administrators, Supervisors, and Other School Personnel

An increasing number of states are requiring school personnel such as administrators, principals, supervisors, speech and hearing therapists, audio-visual directors, librarians, psychologists, and guidance officers to hold special certificates appropriate to their respective positions. These certificates usually require some successful teaching experience in addition to college course work applicable to the specific position.

In 1970 five or more years of preparation were required for an elementary school principal certificate in forty-seven states and territories, for a secondary school principal certificate in forty-nine states, and for a superintendent of schools certificate in forty-nine states and territories [254:23]. In 1955 the certification requirement of five or more years of training was specified in nineteen states for elementary school principals, in thirty states for secondary principals, and in thirty-six states for superintendents of schools. A comparison of these requirements reveals the strong trend, during this fifteen-year period, toward increasing the requirements for administrative certificates.

Some states require that in order to qualify for a principal's or supervisor's position, a candidate also must hold a valid teacher's certificate for the level he wishes to administrate. For example, a state may specify that a person must hold an elementary teacher's certificate and complete the prescribed graduate work to be eligible for an elementary principal's or supervisor's certificate.

Trends in the certification of other school personnel, such as supervisors, counselors, psychologists, speech and hearing therapists, and guidance directors, are not so pronounced as are those for school administrators. It is inevitable that the requirements for certifying such school personnel will continue to rise. Many educators visualize a sixth year of training as necessary for the competence to perform such technical tasks.

Only eight states in 1970 were requiring some forms of licensure for subprofessionals, paraprofessionals, or teacher aides—Delaware, Illinois, Iowa, Michigan, New Jersey, New Mexico, Vermont, and Wisconsin [254:29]. Twelve states have special certification plans for adult education teachers. Special certification plans have been developed in twenty-seven states for Teacher Corps interns, and in sixteen states for Peace Corps teachers [254:29–30].

Beginning in 1969, the Missouri State Department of Education began the practice of certifying student teachers. This practice gives an air of professionalism to the student teacher, and clearly defines his legal status. Likewise, it provides a sense of security against liability for administrators and college supervisors who are involved. It is probable that this practice will spread.

## Trends in the Certification Standards for College Teachers

In 1970, there were seven states that required teachers in public-supported junior colleges to hold certificates [254:66]. In general, these were states in which the junior colleges were a part of the public-supported system and were usually maintained by the local school districts as an extension of secondary education. One state required teachers in the state teachers colleges to hold certificates.

Normally each institution of higher learning establishes its own requirements for teachers, but the requirements may vary within any one institution according to subject field. In order to secure a full-time appointment on the college level, a person normally must have at least a master's degree, with a doctor's degree being preferred. Successful public school teaching experience is almost a universal requirement for teaching professional education courses.

A number of questions have been raised regarding the desirability of developing some form of licensure for those teaching in college and graduate school. The report *New Horizons for the Teaching Profession* indicates several differences bearing on the question that are worthy of note [146:153–154]:

The freedom of the student at these levels to choose his school and to choose whether to go to school at all has bearing only insofar as the protection of the individual is concerned; it has no bearing on the state's obligation to the rest of the society.

A second, more important difference is that college and graduate students should be expected to study on their own initiative, to depend relatively little on the teacher to show them how to learn what he has to offer. Yet adults still learn more rapidly and more thoroughly from a wise and skillful teacher. And as added knowledge and techniques have to be mastered by modern specialists, the efficiency with which they learn has become vitally important for their lives and the lives entrusted to them. It may be necessary to waive the requirement of teaching qualifications for various temporary functions as lecturer, consultant, clinical demonstrator, and so on, in order to get a person with other qualifications essential for the position. Such positions, however, are the exception, and they are used to best advantage in an institution whose policy-making staff has the full range of qualifications.

Third, the candidates for full-time college and university positions can usually be chosen from a world-wide roster of experts. But this is no reason to condone the choice of a person who is below standard in any qualification requisite for the responsibility offered to him.

Fourth, the choice of personnel can be made in first-rate colleges and universities by expert judges since they are the source of the best available judgment in their fields of specialization. Yet the expertness that can be counted on is limited to one field. It does not necessarily encompass all the essential elements of competence as a teacher.

Fifth, college and university departments have a responsibility, which is far less marked in the schools, to advance human knowledge beyond what may be believed or appreciated in the surrounding society. The institution of higher education needs all the freedom necessary for this peculiar and sometimes unpopular service. But the necessary freedom does not include the freedom for inept and unskilled teaching.

Consequently, an increasing number of college and university teachers and administrators are of the opinion that somehow a minimum level of professional teaching competence should be assured throughout higher education.

In view of these differences, it has been recommended that [146:55]:

The qualifications essential for college and university teaching may not be subject to as general agreement as are those for high school teaching, or for university teaching in other countries where a candidate may be judged largely on his delivery of a lecture in his field. Before a standard can be adopted which will win assent, the elements of it will have to be hammered out by groups of specialists who have the respect of university teachers and administrators. A basic recommendation, therefore, is that such groups be brought together to define and propose the qualifications which they believe ought to be required. Only on the basis of such a proposal can there be useful talk of a license requirement in higher education.

## Influence of Professional Organizations on Certification Standards

Significant progress in the raising of standards has, as in other professions, come primarily from the efforts of members rather than from the general public. Teachers are probably in the best position to judge the standards essential for accomplishing their function. Unfortunately, in some communities selfish motives and an unwillingness to pay for teachers with high qualifications have retarded greatly the improvement of certification standards.

The National Education Association has been outstanding in its efforts to raise the certification standards for teachers. Since the turn of the century it has advocated five years of college training for high school teachers. It now stresses the importance of all public school teachers having at least five years of college preparation. Since 1946, the major efforts of the NEA in certification have been channeled through the National Commission on Teacher Education and Professional Standards.

Mention should be made of the influence of regional accrediting agencies, such as the North Central Association of Colleges and Secondary Schools. In order to become a member, which is a high honor, a secondary school must meet many relatively high standards established by the association. The association checks annually upon its members to make certain that these standards are being maintained.

## Revocation of Teacher Certificates

One obligation of any profession is to be concerned with the elimination of the incompetent and the unethical from its ranks [254:32]. Perhaps we are more aware of this obligation being exercised in the field of medicine, for example, than in the field of education. Each state, however, has laws governing the revocation of teacher certificates.

Di Nello and Hawkins [61] made a nationwide study of the existing bases for the revocation of teacher certificates and the extent of the actual application of these bases. They found that the most frequently cited bases for the possible revocation of certificates were immorality, incompetence, and violation of the law. In summarizing the study, it may be noted that [254:32]:

Other bases for possible revocation reported in state laws were abandonment of contracts (twenty-five states), unprofessional conduct (twenty-three states), and negligence (twenty states). Twenty-two states cited a variety of "other causes" for possible revocation of licenses. Among these were substantial noncompliance with school laws and regulations, inability to perform teaching duties, fraud, willful neglect of duty, misconduct in office, falsification of credentials, disloyalty to state or U.S. Constitution, dishonesty, intemperance, alcoholism and physical inability, cruelty, nonpayment of state teaching scholarships, habitual use of drugs and narcotics, commitment to a mental institution by a court, violation of rules of the board of education, revocation in another state, and voluntary revocation.

A total of 398 revocations were reported by the states for the two-year period 1967 and 1968. The most frequent causes, which accounted for approximately two-thirds of all revocations, were as follows: violation of the law (128), immorality (104), abandonment of contract (32) [254:32].

## Reciprocity in Teacher Certification

Differences in the certification requirements of the individual states have handicapped the free movement of teachers throughout the United States. For example, a teacher certified to teach in New York might not meet the specific requirement for teaching in Texas. A number of factors have accentuated this problem: rapid transportation and communication; fluctuation in teacher supply and demand; and differences in salaries, tenure, retirement benefits, etc. Thus reciprocity in teacher certification has become a national problem. Such organizations as the National Commission on Teacher Education and Professional Standards, the Association for Student Teaching, and the American Association of Colleges for Teacher Education have been quite concerned with this problem and have brought together a variety of groups who have had a logical concern for its solution. Particularly noteworthy in searching for a solution to the problem has been the National Association of State Directors of Teacher Education and Certification. Members of the association long ago agreed with leaders in the profession that the growing migration of teachers ought to be encouraged. They agreed upon the following advantages of the free movement of teachers [31:14]:

1. It tends to bring about balance between teacher supply and demand; which is essential not only to teacher welfare and prestige, but to improved educational opportunities for children.
2. It promotes national unity.
3. It tends to destroy provincialism and the inbreeding of ideas and practices in local school systems.
4. It provides a means whereby states having low standards of preparation may raise those standards to a desirable minimum.
5. It promotes teacher growth in service.

The members of the association also agreed that the following points should form the basis upon which progress in the reciprocity of teacher certification could take place [31:14]:

1. The certification of teachers is a function of the state and should never be delegated to other agencies.
2. Certification laws should grant broad general authority and not include detail which prevents flexibility in administration.
3. The baccalaureate degree should be the minimum level of preparation at which reciprocity becomes operative.
4. Only those who are graduates of teacher-education institutions approved by state

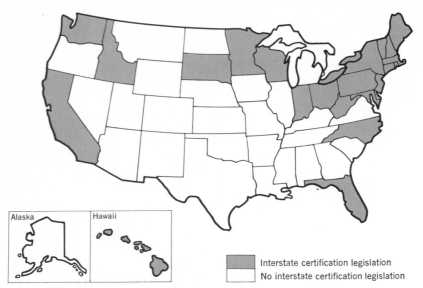

FIGURE 3–6   States that have passed interstate certification legislation. Persons who graduate from state approved programs leading to certification in one state are automatically eligible for similar certification in other states participating in legislative contractual arrangements.

departments of education and accredited by regional or national accrediting agencies should be accepted for certification by another state.
5.  The definition of a good teacher should be the same throughout the nation.
6.  The initial certificate should be issued only upon the recommendation of the head of the department of education of the teacher-preparing institution.

Regional reciprocity compacts have been established, with varying degrees of success, between states beginning as early as 1890 [255:436]. Most of the early attempts failed due to the vast differences in the specific requirements for certification. The trend toward certifying teachers upon the basis of completing institutionally approved programs of teacher education, rather than specific state departmental requirements, has given rise to the formation of new regional compact arrangements.

The most significant recent movement toward regional reciprocity of teacher certification has resulted from an Interstate Project sponsored by the New York State Education Department on a grant from the U.S. Office of Education. As a result of this project, a model bill was prepared, which became the basis for the Interstate Reciprocity Compact that has been submitted to various state legislatures. Twenty-three states already have passed an "Interstate Agreement on Qualification of Educational Personnel," enabling them to enter into contractual arrangements with other states, based on mutual acceptance of standards and procedures for teacher certification [161:14]. As a result, persons graduating from approved programs leading to certification in one state are automatically eligible for similar certification in other states participating in the contract.

The National Association of State Directors of Teacher Education and Certification adopted a recommendation in 1958 that National Council for Accreditation of Teacher Education (NCATE) accreditation should be made the basis of reciprocity among the states. In other words, graduation from an institution accredited by NCATE should be sufficient basis for reciprocity in teacher certification. Since that time considerable progress has been made in the use of NCATE accreditation as a basis for facilitating the certification of graduates from out-of-state institutions. For example, in 1970 some use of NCATE accreditation was reported by twenty-eight states—Alabama, Arizona, Colorado, Delaware, Florida, Georgia, Illinois, Indiana, Iowa, Kentucky, Maine, Maryland, Mississippi, Missouri, Nebraska, North Carolina, North Dakota, Oklahoma, Oregon, Pennsylvania, Rhode Island, South Dakota, Tennessee, Texas, Utah, Vermont, Washington, and West Virginia. In commenting upon the reciprocity of teacher certification existing between these twenty-eight states, Reisert [217:372–373] points out that:

In most states this reciprocity covers only the major field of study at the basic or probationary teaching level. A few states recognize reciprocity at the school services and administrative levels and some recognize the minor preparation as well as the major

FIGURE 3–7   States which grant some measure of reciprocity privileges in the certification of teachers to graduates of institutions accredited by the National Council for Accreditation of Teacher Education.

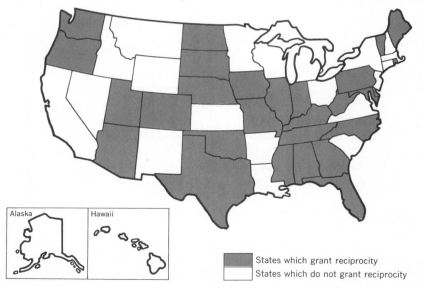

Alaska          Hawaii

States which grant reciprocity
States which do not grant reciprocity

preparation for endorsement reciprocity. One state, Oklahoma, recognizes NCATE reciprocity only from institutions in the other twenty-seven states utilizing this basis for reciprocity. Most states require graduation of the applicant subsequent to NCATE approval of the institution, while others operate on the principle, "once accredited, open to all." Institutions accredited by NCATE are listed in the council's *Annual List.*

It appears that NCATE accreditation will be the chief basis of reciprocity and that future graduates of institutions holding such accreditation (470 in 1970, which graduate approximately 80 per cent of all students prepared to teach) will not experience as much difficulty in moving from one state to another as have teachers in the past. Graduates of non-NCATE-accredited institutions are expected to meet the specific regulations of the states in which they seek certification, as has been the case in the past.

## Probable Changes in Teacher Certification

There probably has been more criticism of certification procedures and practices than of any other phase or area of teacher education. For example, as a result of his study of teacher education programs and state certification offices through the nation, Conant [51] recommended that the state should require only a baccalaureate degree  from a legitimate college or university, evidence of having performed as a student teacher under the direction of college and public school personnel in whom the state department has confidence, and a statement from the college or university indicating that the institution as a whole considers the person adequately prepared to teach in a designated field and grade level.

In reacting to Conant's position, Reisert [216:5] points out that not all preparing institutions offer quality programs, not all school boards are ethical, not all supervising teachers are master teachers, not all state departments are staffed and financed to supervise student teaching, not all college faculty members are interested in teacher education, and not all concerned parties are in agreement with the best approach. He cautions that, until such conditions exist, "we would be in a dangerous position to accept the Conant recommendations" [216:5].

An analysis of changing practices and patterns in teacher certification will reveal that decided changes have taken place, and more changes are expected in the future. Stinnett notes that "Concurrent with the rising militancy of teachers is the decided trend of states toward strengthening certification and accreditation procedures" [254:5]. In 1970, he noted that thirty-six states were making extensive use of the approved-program approach as a basis for certification, forty-two states had developed and adopted their own standards for approval, and forty states were using ad hoc professional committees for evaluating institutional programs. He foresees "state legislation putting the practitioners in a power position to bring vigorous support to the assumption of leadership roles by state education legal agencies rather than the pursuit of enforcement roles in teacher education-certification-accreditation" [254:5]. State certification authorities likewise are searching for new and better procedures for educating and certifying teachers, and professional organizations, such as the AACTE, NCTEPS, CCSSO, and NASDTEC, are "moving with vigor and determination to effect changes appropriate to new conditions" [254:1]. Furthermore, teachers and administrators in elementary and secondary schools are assuming more aggressiveness, "aimed at securing the power to alter education for all, toward higher levels of quality" [254:1]. Prospective teachers, therefore, can expect to be involved in the improvement of teacher education-certification-accreditation as they move into their teaching careers. More specifically, during the 1970s they can join forces in working toward the following ends [254:2]:

1.  A basic rationale for the free movement of qualified teachers across state lines.
2.  A simplification of the number and names of types of certificates.
3.  A universally accepted definition and design for implementation of the approved program approach.
4.  A reasonably uniform approach—in both standards or criteria and processes—to state accreditation (approval) of teacher education programs.
5.  A reasonably uniform approach to providing for democratic participation of the teaching profession in the formulation of certification requirements (through advisory councils, committees, and commissions, examining boards—whether legal or extralegal or voluntary—as well as through professional practices commissions and professional standards boards).
6.  The establishment of review boards to examine credentials and backgrounds of applicants and to advise certification authorities in cases where exceptions to the established prescriptions, as a matter of fairness and justice, may be indicated.
7.  Finding antidotes for the widely alleged defensiveness about current practices in teacher education and certification.

## NATIONAL ACCREDITATION OF TEACHER EDUCATION INSTITUTIONS

Accreditation of professional schools is a process by which a recognized voluntary agency evaluates, according to specified standards, and approves the programs and facilities of institutions preparing individuals for the profession [63:36]. Although accreditation does not guarantee quality institutions, it does tend to set basic requirements for recognition.

Perhaps the practice of national accreditation of professional schools began in the field of medicine following the publication in 1910 of the Abraham Flexner report on *Medical Education in the United States and Canada.* As a result of this report, the American Medical Association established strict standards for programs and facilities to be met by institutions preparing medical doctors if they were to be approved by the AMA. Although this act resulted in the elimination of approximately half of the medical schools at that time, it enhanced greatly the quality of medical training and the status of doctors throughout the nation [63:37].

Although state accreditation of teacher education programs has

existed for many years, we have been slow to move toward any type of
national accreditation practice—probably because education has been
considered to be so completely a prerogative of each state.

The American Association of Teachers Colleges developed some
accrediting standards as early as 1923, and began the process of national
accreditation of teacher education institutions in 1927 [255:458]. In 1948,
the AATC became a part of the newly created American Association of
Colleges for Teacher Education, which continued the function of accreditation of teacher education programs.

In a 1950 meeting of the National Commission on Teacher Education and Professional Standards, much attention was given to "evaluative
criteria for teacher education institutions," and to the establishment of a
joint council for the accreditation of teacher education that would be
broadly representative of groups interested in teacher education
[255:458]. As a result, a committee consisting of representatives from the
AACTE, National Council on Teacher Education and Professional
Standards, the Council of Chief State School Officers, and the National
School Boards Association studied the problem and recommended the
establishment of a National Council for Accreditation of Teacher Education. The recommendation was accepted, and on July 1, 1954, NCATE
assumed the national accreditation function that had been carried forward by the AACTE. The 284 institutions that had been accredited by
AACTE were automatically assumed by NCATE. Since its inception,
NCATE has accredited 186 additional institutions.

NCATE is recognized by the National Commission on Accrediting
as the only national accrediting agency for the field of teacher education.
It is a nonprofit, voluntary accrediting body that is devoted exclusively to
the evaluation and accreditation of teacher education programs [13:3].
Each institution of higher education is free to seek or not seek national
accreditation.

It would seem that there is much to be gained from national
accreditation of teacher education, since it serves at least the following
four major purposes [214:1]:

1.  To assure the public that accredited institutions offer programs for the preparation of
    teachers and other professional personnel that meet national standards of quality.
2.  To ensure that children and youth are served by well-prepared school personnel.
3.  To advance the teaching profession through the improvement of preparation pro-
    grams.
4.  To provide a practical basis for reciprocity among states in certifying professional
    school personnel.

Since its inception, NCATE has met opposition from a number of
sources that seem to be opposed to national accreditation of teacher
education. It has undergone three successive reorganizations. In spite of
these difficulties, its stature seems to be growing. In addition to placing a
quality floor under institutional programs of teacher education, it consti-

tutes a possible solution for certification officials seeking to achieve the free movement of qualified teachers across state lines [254:4].

## SUMMARY

Although considerable variation exists in the programs provided by different institutions, the preparation of teachers can be considered in terms of the following three major aspects: general education, subject-matter specialization, and professional education. Educational programs for elementary teachers tend to provide for more general and professional education, whereas secondary teachers tend to specialize in one or more subject areas and to take correspondingly less general and professional education. Professional education courses embody the specialized professional knowledge, skills, and techniques essential for successful teaching.

Performance-based teacher education programs represent a major departure in the usual pattern of preservice preparation of teachers. While there are a number of advantages to such an approach, there are a number of problems and questions that need to be considered by those concerned with teacher education.

During the past 50 years the certification requirements for teaching have increased steadily. With higher certification requirements, teaching has become more widely recognized as a profession. The function of certifying teachers has been centralized in the state department of education.

The completion of approved teacher education programs, rather than the results of teacher examinations, now forms the basis for certification. Licenses have been differentiated according to the nature of the teacher's preparation. Life licenses have been gradually abolished. The level of preparation has been raised for all types of certificates.

These advancements have come primarily through the efforts of those within the profession. Teacher education institutions, accrediting agencies, such as the National Council for Accreditation of Teacher Education, and the National Commission on Teacher Education and Professional Standards have provided outstanding leadership. Present-day graduates, especially those trained for the elementary level, generally enter the profession much better prepared than teachers already in service. Since this condition provides added incentive for experienced teachers to gain additional training, the average level of preparation possessed by all teachers is higher than it used to be. A positive relationship seems to exist between the increase in the requirements for teaching and the supply of those entering the profession.

Lack of reciprocity in teacher certification represents one of the major handicaps to the free movement of teachers throughout the United States. Regional reciprocity compacts are tending to ease this problem. It appears that NCATE accreditation will provide the chief basis of reciprocity of teacher certification. This is one of a number of reasons that would argue for some form of national accreditation of teacher education programs.

Decided changes in the preparation and certification of teachers have been made, and undoubtedly changes will be made in the future. As is already evident, elementary and secondary teachers will be playing increasingly significant roles in directing this change toward higher levels of quality education.

## QUESTIONS TO CONSIDER

1. In your opinion, what percentage of time spent in a four-year teacher education program should be devoted to general education, to specialized subject matter, and to professional education? What are the reasons for this distribution?
2. What leadership experiences with boys and girls have been of most value to you as a prospective teacher? Why? What other types of experiences should you have before you begin teaching?
3. What are the advantages and disadvantages of a teacher's taking graduate work without having had some full-time teaching experience?
4. In your opinion, what are the strengths and weaknesses of a performance-based teacher education program?
5. What suggestions would you make for the improvement of teacher education programs?
6. Do you feel that a teacher should be required to sign an oath of allegiance or loyalty to the United States? What are your reasons?
7. Should the requirements for elementary teachers be as high as, or higher than, the requirements for secondary teachers? Why?
8. For what reasons should states require elementary and secondary school principals and superintendents to have six or more years of college work for certification?
9. What are the advantages and disadvantages of granting provisional rather than life certificates to teachers?
10. What is your position with respect to requiring private and church-related school teachers to be certified? What are the reasons for your position?
11. What is your position with respect to the practice of granting emergency teaching certificates? Why?
12. For what reasons would you argue either for or against requiring some type of certification for college teachers?
13. How would you solve the problem of reciprocity in teacher certification?
14. What advantages and disadvantages do you see in national accreditation of teacher education institutions?

## PROBLEM SITUATION FOR INQUIRY

Mr. Roberts, the Winston High School Superintendent, received a letter of resignation from one of the English teachers in late August. The only application for an English teaching position which he had on file was from a Mrs. Judson.

Mrs. Judson, a resident of Winston, had decided that her life was stagnating and that she should return to a teaching career. For twenty years she had been a professor of English in various public and private colleges in the East. Her career had been distinguished. Never had she failed to arouse and inspire a class. She possessed that rare quality of being able to bring out the creative ability—no matter how small or underdeveloped—in all her students. In addition to teaching, she had written a number of books dealing with various areas of literature. Steinbeck, Hemingway, and Wilder were not only names she introduced to her classes but men with whom she was personally acquainted and perfectly capable of discussing in class.

Mrs. Judson was well qualified in her subject area as substantiated by numerous personal references and recommendations, but she was not certified to teach at the high school level. True, she had college degrees, but she had not completed the professional education courses required for certification.

Mr. Roberts was faced with a problem. Should he employ Mrs. Judson even though she was not certified, or should he attempt to locate a certified teacher at this late date? The problem was taken to the school board. The majority of the board members voted to hire Mrs. Judson, but one of them suggested that hiring a noncertified teacher might jeopardize the students and the accreditation of the high school. If Mrs. Judson were hired, formally trained and fully certified teachers may elect not to apply for positions at Winston High School in the future.

The local teachers' association, upon hearing of the impending employment of Mrs. Judson, called a meeting and passed a resolution strongly opposing the hiring of a noncertified teacher. The group expressed the opinion that the employment of noncertified teachers was a potentially dangerous practice. Teaching, they said, could never truly be a profession if noncertified personnel were employed.

The board was confronted with a dilemma. Should it hire Mrs. Judson, whose expertise as a teacher had been proven, or should it attempt to locate a certified teacher, recognizing that it might be difficult to find a highly capable certified teacher at this late date. If you were Mr. Roberts, what would you recommend to the board? Why?

## ACTIVITIES TO PURSUE

1. An increased number of educators feel that there are many common elements in the preparation of elementary and secondary teachers. Discuss with your colleagues the proposition that competency for teaching is the same, regardless of level. At what point, if any, should the preparation of elementary and secondary teachers be differentiated?
2. Some colleges and universities have developed programs in which all professional work for teachers is concentrated in the fifth year of college. Discuss with your colleagues the advantages and disadvantages of such a plan.
3. Investigate the possibilities of working with a group of children or young people in your community. Explore opportunities in scouting groups, community centers, recreation programs, church schools, and the like.
4. Examine a recent copy of Stinnett's *A Manual on Certification Requirements for School Personnel in the United States.* Note the specific requirements for teaching in the state in which you have some interest.
5. Check the requirements for teaching in a large school system in your home state to see if they exceed the minimum requirements for a teaching certificate.
6. If possible, discuss with a superintendent of schools any certification problems he has in employing teachers who attended teacher education institutions outside the state.

# 4 | OPPORTUNITIES IN EDUCATION

The teaching profession offers an enormous range of opportunities, especially for those who plan to remain in the profession. This range undoubtedly will increase as modifications are made in the organizational and instructional practices of schools, and as attempts are made to meet more adequately the educational needs of individuals of all ages. A prospective teacher's plans, therefore, should include an exploration of the many opportunities that are available.

Most educators enter the profession as teachers. As a result, you are confronted with the problem of being certain of the level and the area or areas for which you are best suited for teaching. Furthermore, the demand for teachers at some grade levels and in some subject areas is greater than in others. Teachers prepared in specialties where the demand exceeds the supply tend to receive higher salaries than do those prepared in oversupplied specialties.

No one should choose to teach a particular level or subject area solely because it holds the best promise of immediate employment. For example, it would be exceedingly unwise to prepare for elementary teaching, where the demand for teachers is stronger than it is in most high school subject areas, if you are more skilled in working with older pupils and certain that you will be happier with them.

As you read this chapter and other materials on opportunities in education and as you observe in school situations, ask yourself such questions as the following: With what age level can I work most successfully? What academic areas interest me most? Do I prefer to work with individuals rather than groups? Have I explored all the different kinds of work of educators? Would college teaching interest me? What type of work do I eventually want to do?

Population, millions

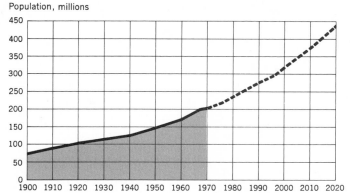

FIGURE 4–1    Past and projected increase of population in the United States by decades from 1900 to 2000.

## General Factors Affecting Supply and Demand of Teachers

Broadly conceived, the demand for teachers consists of the total number of teaching positions to be filled in a given year. Demand is created through such factors as death, retirement, disability, dismissal, resignation, and the creation of new positions. Supply is created through the completion of certification requirements and the seeking of teaching positions. Some prospective teachers complete the requirements for certification but decide not to teach. Other teachers, who have left their positions for a different type of work, wish to return to the profession. Conditions vary from one part of the country to another.

It is estimated that the number of positions vacated by teachers who leave the profession each year is equal to approximately 8 per cent of the total number of teachers. The percentage is slightly higher for secondary than for elementary school teachers [273:30]. Of those who leave each year, approximately 30 per cent are on a leave of absence, 20 per cent retire, 13 per cent assume family responsibilities or marriage, 12 per cent enter or return to another occupation, 10 per cent return to school, 6 per cent become ill, and 3 per cent either die or become incapacitated [268:120].

The mobility of teachers represents a type of demand for teachers. Approximately 10 per cent of the total teacher population move from one year to the next. Major reasons for changing the location of employment are as follows: higher salary, improved working conditions, personal reasons, change in location of husband's work, undesirable community situation, position eliminated, marriage, disagreement with school pol-

icies or the administration, and termination of contract [268:120]. Eight
out of ten of these moves are made within the state in which the teachers
are located, with a majority of the moves taking place within the school
system.

Some officials are unable to fill all their vacancies with qualified
teachers. These positions frequently are filled with teachers who hold
limited (emergency) certificates and who are not properly trained for their
positions. Positions held by these emergency teachers actually constitute
a demand for qualified teachers.

A number of people feel that one method of meeting the demand for
teachers represented by those holding limited certificates is to lower
certification standards. They likewise feel that raising certification standards will result in an increase in the number of limited certificates
issued. Neither of these feelings is substantiated by facts. In general, the
greatest shortages of qualified teachers occur in rural schools, inner-city
schools, and in states having the lowest certification standards and lowest
salaries. Most states which issue a relatively small percentage of limited
certificates not only have high standards but also pay above-average
salaries and maintain good teacher retirement systems.

Another factor which affects demand is the number of pupils assigned to a teacher. For example, if twenty rather than twenty-five pupils
were assigned to each teacher, decidedly more teachers would be needed.
Educators generally recommend no more than twenty-five pupils per
teacher. However, some research reveals that, so far as academic achievement in subject matter is concerned, the results obtained in a large class
may be just as good as those in a small one. On the other hand, modern
education assumes that the educational process must be consciously
designed to help the student (1) gain meaningful understandings, (2)
develop desirable study habits, (3) speak effectively and listen critically,
(4) build high ideals, and (5) gain respect and concern for others. In short,
education today faces a growing responsibility for the development of
habits and attitudes conducive to good adult citizenship in a local,
national, and worldwide society. In order to accomplish these aims
adequately, the number of pupils per teacher, especially on the elementary level, should be lowered.

Research studies do indicate that class size does have an effect upon
teacher morale. In small classes teachers tend to use more new practices,
give more attention to individual pupils, use a greater variety of instructional methods, and depend less on textbooks [43, RB:35].

There are great variations throughout the United States in the pupil-
teacher ratio. Generally it is lower (and therefore better) in secondary
schools than in elementary schools, lower in areas where the population
is sparse, and lower in areas where one-room schools are found.

There has been a definite trend toward the reduction of the number
of pupils assigned to a teacher. The pupil-teacher ratio in 1929–1930 was

30.1; in 1939–1940 it was 29.1; in 1949–1950 it was 27.5; in 1969–1970 it was 22.7 [212:20]. If this very desirable downward trend continues, a sizable number of new teachers will be needed. On the other hand, this trend may be reversed as a result of the increasing resistance of the general public to the mounting costs of public education.

The number of children born each year obviously has its effect on the number of teachers needed. During the late 1920s and throughout the 1930s the birthrate in the continental United States decreased. Following World War II the birthrate increased, as indicated in Figure 4–2, but has been decreasing during the past few years. Table 4–1 indicates what may be expected in kindergarten, elementary and secondary school, and college enrollments during the next few years.

A number of factors may affect population trends. For example, the increasing concern for controlling the population may cause considerable decline in the birthrate, especially if birth control devices become more available to and adopted by the lower economic groups, where the birthrate is highest [198:25]. The size of families also may be affected by

FIGURE 4–2   Birth and death rates per 1,000 population, 1910 to 1969. The birth rate has declined more than the death rate which changes the age composition of our population. In spite of the drop in the birth rate, the population of the United States may continue to grow as the post-World War II babies become parents in the 1970s.

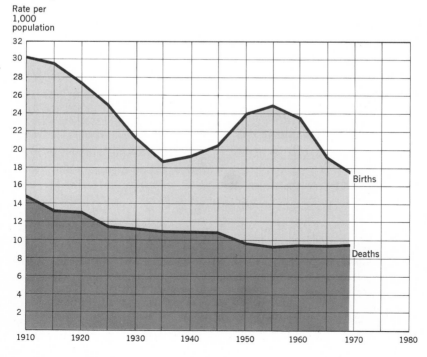

TABLE 4–1  **PROJECTIONS OF ELEMENTARY, SECONDARY, AND HIGHER EDUCATION ENROLLMENTS IN PUBLIC AND NONPUBLIC SCHOOLS 1973–1974 TO 1978–1979**

| School Year | Elementary Schools and Kindergarten (K-8) | Secondary Schools (9–12) | Institutions of Higher Education | Total |
|---|---|---|---|---|
| 1973–1974 | 35,500,000 | 16,200,000 | 9,357,000 | 61,057,000 |
| 1974–1975 | 35,300,000 | 16,500,000 | 9,796,000 | 61,596,000 |
| 1975–1976 | 35,100,000 | 16,700,000 | 10,222,000 | 62,022,000 |
| 1976–1977 | 35,100,000 | 16,800,000 | 10,617,000 | 62,517,000 |
| 1977–1978 | 35,200,000 | 16,900,000 | 10,971,000 | 63,071,000 |
| 1978–1979 | 35,500,000 | 16,800,000 | 11,325,000 | 63,625,000 |

*Source:* Kenneth A. Simon and Marie G. Fullam: *Projection of Educational Statistics to 1978–1979,* U.S. Office of Education, National Center for Educational Statistics, Washington, 1970, pp. 20–22.

economic conditions (job stability and cost of living), the increasing tendency for women to work, and the trend toward waiting to start a family.

The demand for teachers also is affected by the number of pupils who remain in school. For example, the phenomenal increase in the percentage of 14- to 17-year-olds attending secondary school has created a great demand for teachers during the past half century. The further increase in pupils attending secondary schools will make demands for additional secondary teachers. Also, as public school opportunities are extended upward to include junior college and extended downward to include kindergarten and nursery school, appreciable demands will be made for teachers qualified to teach on these levels. As evidence of the trend toward the downward extension of educational opportunities, 886,000 three- and four-year-olds were enrolled in nursery school in 1965. In 1970, the number had increased to 1,500,000 [231:2]. Undoubtedly, greater numbers of three- and four-year-olds will be enrolled in nursery schools in the 1970s.

Economic conditions affect the demands for teachers. In times of depression, fewer high-salaried positions occur outside the profession to attract teachers, more married women continue to teach, and vacancies in school systems frequently are absorbed by the remaining staffs. In times of prosperity, more teachers leave the profession to accept higher-paying positions, some married women discontinue teaching, vacancies are filled by new teachers, and new positions are often created.

As the nature of the school program changes, the demand for teachers also changes. Certainly the percentage of Latin and Greek teachers is less today than it was at the time of the Latin grammar school. In recent years new demands have been made for trade-industrial-vocational subjects, special education, Afro-American studies, school librarians, and guidance counselors.

The demands for teachers also may be affected by organizational and instructional changes that may take place in the future. As you read subsequent chapters of this book, reflect upon the extent to which such factors as the use of differentiated staffing, team teaching, computer-assisted instruction, programmed learning, and vouchering may affect the numbers and kinds of teachers needed.

The attitude of society in general toward the existing proportion of men and women within the profession has an effect upon opportunities. Although teaching in the United States has been predominantly a woman's field, especially on the elementary level, the profession presents opportunities for both sexes. Young men who ultimately wish to become school principals will do well to consider the possibilities of entering the field of elementary education, where more men are especially desired.

Federal assistance to education tends to increase the demand for teachers. As a result of federal legislation during the mid-sixties, new opportunities were generated for teachers at the preschool, elementary, and college levels.

As indicated in Chapter 1, the educational needs of adults will become increasingly greater as a result of technological and social progress. Subsequent sections of this book will emphasize some of the exciting and challenging demands that will be made of teachers at all levels and in all areas of learning.

FIGURE 4–3 Past and projected number of classroom teachers in regular public and nonpublic elementary and secondary schools.

Thousands of teachers

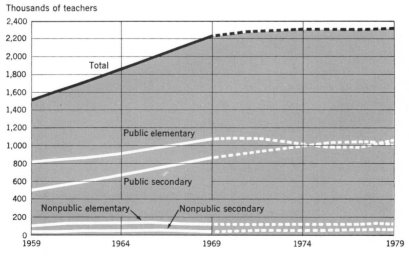

## Sources of Teacher Supply

It is extremely difficult to determine accurately the total number of certified teachers who are actively seeking teaching positions. For example, some teachers who have not taught for a number of years may desire to return to the profession. Although there is no precise way of ascertaining how many teachers for any given year will fall into this category, the rate of reentry is estimated to be 3 per cent of the total number of full-time teachers [273:28]. Furthermore, some students who have completed the requirements for teaching may never seek a teaching position or may postpone accepting a teaching position for several years.

Each year, approximately 20 per cent of the elementary teacher graduates and 30 per cent of the secondary teacher graduates are not available for teaching positions. More secondary teacher graduates who major in mathematics, physical education (women's), industrial arts, music, distributive education, library science, special education, and English tend to enter teaching than those who major in agriculture, journalism, commerce, and social studies. As might be expected, non-teaching occupations draw heavily on teachers who major in such areas as business education, chemistry, agriculture, and vocational education. Approximately 5 per cent of the secondary teacher graduates continue formal study immediately following graduation, and 3 per cent become homemakers. A number of men enter military service immediately upon graduation.

In the light of the variables indicated above, perhaps the most dependable rough indication of the supply of teachers is the number of college students completing standard certification requirements. The Research Division of the National Education Association sponsors studies that provide estimates of the number who, at the end of each school year (including summer sessions), qualify for standard teaching certificates. The results of these studies are published annually. Since some changes occur from year to year in the supply and demand for teachers, a prospective teacher should consult the most recent reports available to note any trends that may be taking place. Also, he should check with his college placement officer to see whether these national data are typical of the supply-and-demand conditions in the local area which interests him.

## Imbalance in the Demand and the Supply of Teachers

An analysis of Figure 4–4 will reveal that in some subject areas the number of qualified secondary teacher graduates exceeds the demand. On the other hand, in certain subjects the supply is not adequate. The excessive imbalance of teachers in the various fields and levels of teaching constitutes a serious problem in the minds of many educators. As a

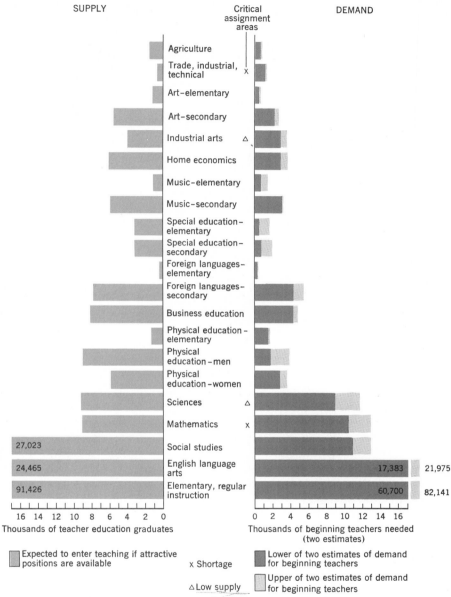

FIGURE 4–4 Supply and demand for beginning teachers according to the type of assignment for 1970. To what extent have the supply and demand conditions changed since 1970?

future professional educator you will be affected by this imbalance. How should the problem be solved? Do you feel that no planned attempt should be made to maintain a reasonable balance between the supply and demand of teachers? Do you maintain that it is undemocratic to limit, as does the medical profession, the number permitted to prepare for the profession? Do you maintain that the problem eventually will solve itself? Do you believe that, when the imbalance becomes too great, increased numbers of intelligent students preparing for secondary teaching will foresee the lack of job opportunities and therefore will not plan to teach?

Or do you feel that a definite plan should be developed to solve the problem of excessive imbalance in supply and demand? Is there no justification, so far as society is concerned, for allowing everyone to prepare for teaching who wishes to do so? Do you feel that both students and society will profit far more by guiding the less promising students into other occupations in which the probabilities of employment are much greater? Thus, many would avoid the possible bitterness of not being able to secure teaching positions and of having wasted the opportunity to prepare for something else.

A few institutions, especially in the eastern part of the United States, have attempted to limit the teacher supply by accepting only a certain number of candidates. Too often the quota plan does not give adequate attention to quality or probable fitness for teaching. Other institutions have made some attempts to control the number of graduates by raising scholastic requirements. The National Council for Accreditation of Teacher Education insists that approved colleges and universities admit to their teacher education programs only those students who have an overall grade average above that required for graduation.

In planning a career in education, it is wise to take into consideration all possible available data regarding supply and demand, especially in those areas and/or levels in which you are particularly interested. Personnel in almost all teacher education institutions today have these data available. They will be able to advise you not only in terms of the national picture but also in terms of the conditions that exist in your specific locale. Since conditions do change from time to time, it is important that you maintain close contact throughout your preparation for teaching with the teacher-employment office which your institution probably maintains.


## Analysis of Opportunities in Elementary and Secondary Schools

If the school system is to meet its responsibilities to society, the demand for thoroughly competent teachers must be met through (1) filling new positions being created to accommodate increased enrollments and to continue trends toward improved staffing; (2) replacing teachers who interrupt or terminate their careers; (3) replacing teachers who have substandard professional qualifications; (4) adding teachers in order to reduce overcrowded classes to reasonable maximum size; and (5) providing adequate staffing of new educational offerings of special instructional services, and for the reorganization of instruction [273:28–29]. What, briefly, does each demand mean as far as your opportunities for teaching are concerned?

The number of births per year foretells the approximate size of the school population in the years to come. Since the early 1960s, the birthrate has continued to decline. With the increasing attention to the problem of worldwide overpopulation, it is reasonable to assume that it may decline further in the United States, or at least remain low. Children born in the late 1950s, prior to a significant decline in birthrate, will tend to increase high school and college enrollments until the end of the 1970s [197:25].

During the ten-year period prior to 1968–1969 the number of states providing support for kindergartens increased from twenty-two to thirty-three. It seems likely that this trend will continue. Undoubtedly more school systems will be making some provisions for three- and four-year-olds.

During the 1960s the percentage of the 14-to-17 age group attending school increased significantly. This increase will not be as great in the 1970s, since the per cent enrolled is approaching the maximum limits. The leeway for increasing the holding power of the school will tend to offset some of the decrease in the elementary school enrollment in the next few years.

FIGURE 4–5   Past and projected school age population groups. What are the implications of the projected changes in the various school-age population groups for opportunities in teaching?

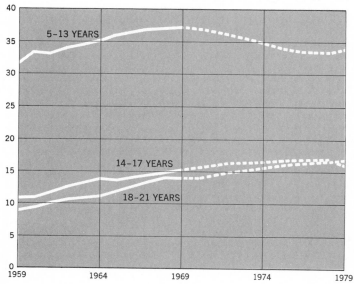

As indicated previously, the number of positions vacated by teachers who leave the profession each year equals about 8 per cent of the total number of teachers. For the fall of 1970, for example, it was estimated that 88,000 elementary and 77,300 secondary teachers were needed to fill the positions created by teacher turnover [273:31]. Approximately 7,000 elementary and 28,000 secondary teachers also were needed to fill new positions created from increased enrollments.

In addition to these two very realistic needs, others have not been met and are likely to continue. For example, in 1970 it was estimated that 10,400 elementary teachers and 9,200 secondary teachers were needed to reduce overcrowded classrooms. The problem is especially serious at the elementary school level, where both experience and mature judgment indicate that the effectiveness of the teacher falls as the 1 to 25 pupil-teacher ratio is exceeded. At the lower grade levels particularly, the immaturity of the child is such that personal attention should not be denied him. Although the number fluctuates from year to year, the U.S. Office of Education reported, in the fall of 1968, that 185,440 elementary and 131,550 secondary pupils were unable to attend normal or full-day sessions, due primarily to classroom shortages [78:22]. Unfortunately, elementary school children are less able than secondary school pupils to compensate effectively for the loss of individual attention and assistance which results from such part-time emergency measures. Any relief from these educational inequalities will demand the services of a sizable share of the graduates who annually meet elementary and secondary teacher certification requirements.

Few people would argue the fact that some teachers are not adequately prepared. There is no single answer, however, to the question "When is a person so inadequate that his removal from the classroom is justified?" Estimates of the number of teachers that fall in this category range from 10,000 to over 100,000. It could be assumed that the minimum educational requirement for qualified teachers should be the completion of the bachelor's degree, and the teachers having less than a bachelor's degree need to be upgraded or replaced. Using this criterion, it was

FIGURE 4–6  Pupils attending public elementary and secondary schools for less than a full or normal school day, according to regions, in the fall of 1969.

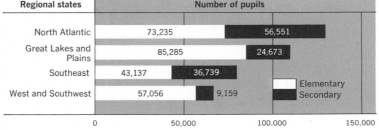

| Regional states | Number of pupils | | |
|---|---|---|---|
| North Atlantic | 73,235 | 56,551 | |
| Great Lakes and Plains | 85,285 | 24,673 | |
| Southeast | 43,137 | 36,739 | |
| West and Southwest | 57,056 | 9,159 | Elementary / Secondary |

|  | 0 | 50,000 | 100,000 | 150,000 |

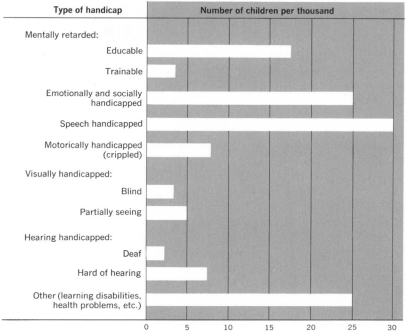

| Type of handicap | Number of children per thousand |
|---|---|

FIGURE 4–7   A general working estimate of the number of children per thousand who are sufficiently handicapped to warrant special services.

estimated that, for 1970–1971, 51,800 elementary and 8,600 secondary teachers would need to have been replaced [273:30–31]. It is gratifying to note, however, that since 1950 much improvement has been made in the level of preparation of teachers. In 1970, only 5.9 per cent of the elementary and 1.2 per cent of secondary teachers had less than a bachelor's degree [273:52].

Increasing demands are being made for the schools to provide special instructional services, enlarge the scope of educational offerings, and provide special programs for pupils having special learning needs (physically, mentally, emotionally handicapped, the educationally deprived, the culturally different, etc.). If schools are able to fulfill these functions, there will be a greater need for guidance counselors, school psychologists, librarians, social workers, vocational teachers, instructional technologists, and subject-area specialists. It is estimated that 97,350 elementary and 68,050 secondary teachers were needed in 1970 to meet this demand [273:31].

To summarize the need factors indicated above, it was estimated that, theoretically, 255,350 elementary teachers and 191,150 secondary teachers were needed in 1970 to meet the various demands. The supply of new teachers in this same year was estimated to be 133,378 elementary and 155,956 secondary teachers, resulting, theoretically, in a shortage of 121,972 elementary and 35,194 secondary teachers [273:43]. A more realistic picture of the supply and demand for teachers in 1970 may be gained from studying Figure 4–8. Obviously, the demand for teachers is affected by the financial resources available to schools.

The growing surplus of teachers is resulting primarily from increases in higher education enrollments, and in the percentage of college students preparing for teaching. The increases in college enrollments are illustrated graphically in Figure 12–10. The annual percentage of college graduates prepared to teach has increased from 26.7 per cent in 1950 to 36.2 per cent in 1971. Between 1961 and 1971 the annual supply of graduates prepared to teach increased from 129,188 to 305,711. By 1978 it is estimated that the annual number of graduates prepared to teach will be 397,000 [107:84].

The expected large surpluses of teachers in the future should not be confused with the total number of vacancies that will occur each year. In addition to former teachers reentering the profession, the 1970s promise employment for more than 100,000 qualified beginning teachers each year, which does not differ greatly from the total annual demand during the 1960s [266:72–73]. The situation does mean in general that there will be greater competition for the available positions and that school officials will be in a position to employ only the best qualified of the beginning teachers. Careful and comprehensive planning should increase one's chances of securing a position upon completion of the requirements for teaching.

FIGURE 4–8    Supply of beginning teachers expressed as a per cent of normal demand, 1952 to 1979, according to present trends. The surplus would disappear if society wanted high-quality education enough to pay for it.

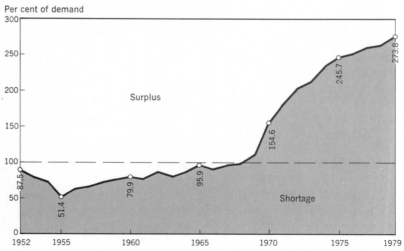

## Subject Combinations for Teaching
## in the Secondary Schools

Beginning secondary school teachers frequently are asked to teach in two or more subject areas. Even in large school systems teachers may teach in more than one subject area. Teachers in special subject areas such as agriculture, business subjects, fine arts, home economics, industrial arts, and music are more likely than other secondary teachers to teach in one subject area only.

The ease with which a prospective teacher obtains his initial appointment will depend to some degree on the extent to which the subject combination he selects is in demand. A combination that is seldom in demand, such as foreign languages and physical education, is little better than a single subject, while foreign languages with English is demanded more frequently.

Fortunately the combination of subjects tends to follow definite patterns. Unrelated combinations, such as fine arts, agriculture, physics, and English, asked by employing officials in the past, are disappearing. Small secondary schools are revising programs of study so that various courses are offered in alternate years. Many small schools are reducing the number of highly specialized subjects that are offered. Furthermore, the trend toward school consolidation, which increases the enrollment and the size of the faculty of each school, means that teachers may be assigned more nearly according to their preparation.

Many studies have been made of the combination of subjects taught by secondary teachers. Your college teacher-placement officer probably makes an annual study of the subject combinations requested by employing officials. Although almost every possible combination may be found, there are certain ones that occur more often than others. There is considerable demand for such combinations as commerce and social science and/or English; English and social science, foreign languages, or speech; mathematics and general science, social science, or English; music and English; and men's physical education and social science.

The demand for various subject combinations fluctuates from year to year and varies in different sections of the United States. For example, in some states the secondary school candidates are heavily concentrated in certain fields, while in other states they are more widely distributed. Considerable variation in the demand for subject areas may exist between school districts. Your local teacher-placement officer may be of great help in selecting the combination of subjects that seems most desirable for you and most consistent with your abilities and interests.

## Opportunities for Teaching on the College Level

A number of individuals value the opportunities that college teaching provides for writing, conducting research, and engaging in other scholarly pursuits. Some value highly the prestige that college instructors have, compared with that of public school teachers.

In some college departments, especially in the subject matter areas, a few highly selected graduates are encouraged to study immediately for higher degrees. The students usually are granted assistantships that entail some teaching, supervision of laboratories, or the like, while they continue their studies. The assistantships pay a relatively small amount of money but may provide fee exemptions for college work taken by the student. Others may receive scholarships or continue their educations at their own expense. You may wish to investigate possibilities along these lines.

A large percentage of college teachers began their teaching careers in public schools. They pursued graduate work during their summer vacations or returned for full-time study to complete their degrees. Usually they have found their public school experiences to be of great value in their college teaching. A number of years of successful elementary or secondary teaching experience is a prerequisite for securing a position for teaching education courses.

Opportunities for college teaching will be affected by the extent to which college enrollments increase. For a number of years the percentage of the group of college students 18 to 21 years old has increased approximately 1 per cent a year. This percentage recently has increased to 1½ per

FIGURE 4–9  Past and projected instructional staff positions for resident degree-credit courses in public and private colleges and universities.

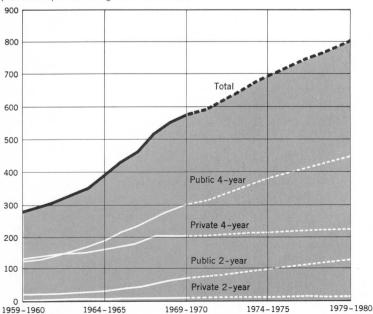

cent and may increase even more in the future. From 1950 to 1969 the percentage of high school graduates going on to college increased from 43 to 66 per cent [281:1]. Since the peak number of births in the United States occurred in 1957, the peak number of freshmen will not reach our colleges and universities until 1975. It is estimated that a peak college enrollment of 13,751,000 will occur in 1982 [281:5]—in contrast to a reported enrollment of 7,377,000 for the fall of 1970 [151:67]. In viewing these mounting numbers, several pertinent questions arise [274:11]:

1. Will junior colleges continue to be the most rapidly growing division of higher education?
2. Will the universities concentrate to a greater extent upon graduate instruction?
3. Will nonpublic institutions push their admission requirements higher, with the intent of holding enrollments at approximately the present figure?
4. Will the public universities restrict classes of entering freshmen to the top percentiles of high school graduating classes?
5. Can the small nonpublic colleges survive in the competition for really competent teachers?
6. Will there be, in fact, an open college door for all who seek admission in the years ahead?
7. Will external degree programs, which enable students to earn a college degree largely outside the confines of traditional university settings, become more prevalent?

In addition to the number of students that may be involved, another variable to be considered is the load of each teacher. It has been estimated that the nationwide student-teacher ratio in all higher-education institutions is approximately 14 to 1, although the range is great from institution to institution. In order to extend the utilization of faculty members, efforts are being made to [274:11]:

1. Thrust greater responsibility upon the individual student for his own learning.
2. Eliminate nonessential and overlapping courses, and stem the tendency toward fragmentation of subject matter into highly specialized courses.
3. Experiment further with variation in class size.
4. Make joint use of teachers by two or more institutions.
5. Use mechanical and electronic devices, including television.
6. Use nonprofessional personnel to perform nonprofessional tasks.
7. Reevaluate the committee system as a part of administrative procedure.
8. Improve the general climate and overall working conditions on the campus.
9. Clarify further the role of the college teacher as a citizen in the community.

It has been estimated that an additional 118,000 full-time instructional staff members will be needed in institutions of higher education during the six-year period 1973–1974 through 1979–1980 [247:73]. This estimate does not include a 6 per cent replacement rate for those (5 per cent) who leave employment in institutions of higher education and those (1 per cent) who die or retire. In addition to the instructional staff, it has been estimated that 24,000 additional professional staff members will be needed between 1973–1974 and 1979–1980 for general administration and service support duties. This figure does not include the number needed for replacement of staff leaving the profession [247:73]. The extent to which meeting these needs becomes a reality depends largely upon the extent to which the public is willing to finance higher education.

It is estimated that, between 1970 and 1980, the number of junior colleges will increase from 800 to 1,200 and will enroll approximately 4,000,000 students in 1980 [40:119]. Opportunities for teaching in junior colleges, therefore, may be reasonably good for those possessing at least a master's degree. Generally the doctoral degree is desired for teaching in four-year institutions and in graduate schools.

## Opportunities in Other Areas of Education

Unfortunately most people limit their concept of the opportunities in the field of education mainly to teaching in the public or private school classroom. It is true that over 80 per cent of those engaged in public school work are regular classroom teachers. On the other hand, there are specialized kinds of instruction and services to be rendered, such as counseling and guidance; research analysis; teaching speech and hearing therapy and remedial reading; teaching the mentally retarded, physically handicapped, partially seeing, hard-of-hearing, emotionally disturbed, the gifted and the culturally disadvantaged; serving as librarian; and teaching driver education and distributive education courses. Attention already has been called to the large number of superintendents, principals, supervisors, and others involved in administrative services.

It would be exceedingly interesting to analyze all the different kinds of work demanding the services of educators and to note the number involved in each. Unfortunately these data are not available. The following listing of the more common educational opportunities may be of interest to you. In no sense is the list complete.

FIGURE 4–10   Number of professional employees per 1,000 students.

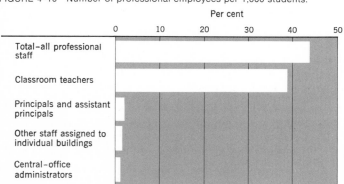

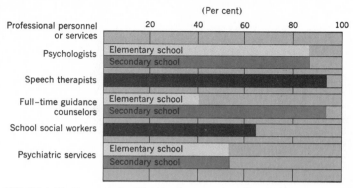

FIGURE 4–11   Per cent of public school systems, enrolling 25,000 or more pupils, having various types of special professional personnel.

I.   Preschools—nursery and kindergarten
  A.   Teachers
  B.   Supervisors
  C.   Consultant in child growth and development
  D.   Research worker in child growth and development
  E.   Director of a private nursery or kindergarten
  F.   Director of day care centers
  G.   Director of Head Start projects
  H.   Director of follow-through programs
II.   Elementary schools
  A.   Teacher for separate grades or combined grades
  B.   Teacher of special subjects such as art, music, or physical education
  C.   Teacher of a subject such as arithmetic or geography in a departmentalized school, or in a team-teaching situation
  D.   Teacher of physically handicapped, partially seeing, or hard-of-hearing children
  E.   Teacher of exceptional children—talented, mentally retarded, or emotionally disturbed, or disadvantaged
  F.   Supervising teacher in a laboratory or experimental school
  G.   General or special subject supervisor
  H.   Assistant principal
  I.   Principal
  J.   Librarian
  K.   Speech correctionist and/or hearing therapist
  L.   Visiting teacher
  M.   Child psychologist or counselor
  N.   School nurse
  O.   Curriculum consultant
  P.   Guidance counselor
III.   Secondary schools
  A.   Teacher of subjects such as English, foreign language, social studies, or music
  B.   Teaching of special subjects such as art, home economics, industrial arts and trades, music, physical education, driver education, speech and hearing therapy, Afro-American studies
  C.   Teacher of disadvantaged children
  D.   Supervising teacher in a laboratory or experimental school

       *E.*  Department head of a subject area
       *F.*  Assistant principal
       *G.*  Principal
       *H.*  Supervisor of a subject area
       *I.*  Curriculum consultant
       *J.*  Athletic coach
       *K.*  Guidance counselor
       *L.*  Librarian
       *M.*  Visiting teacher

IV.  Administrative and special services
       *A.*  Superintendent
       *B.*  Assistant superintendent—usually assigned a specific phase of work such as finance, personnel, or instruction
       *C.*  Business manager (supplies, purchasing, etc.)
       *D.*  School secretary
       *E.*  Research director
       *F.*  Attendance officer
       *G.*  Director of audio-visual materials
       *H.*  Director of school and community relations
       *I.*  School psychologist
       *J.*  School psychometrist
       *K.*  Vocational counselor and placement officer
       *L.*  School statistician
       *M.*  Clerical assistant
       *N.*  Cafeteria manager
       *O.*  Dietitian
       *P.*  School physician or dentist
       *Q.*  School nurse or health officer
       *R.*  Adult education director

V.  Junior colleges
       *A.*  Teacher of different fields (English, mathematics, science, etc.)
       *B.*  Personnel director
       *C.*  President or dean
       *D.*  Admissions officer
       *E.*  Registrar
       *F.*  Business manager
       *G.*  Health service officer
       *H.*  Director of minority group education
       *I.*  Director of vocational, technical education
       *J.*  Director of continuing education

VI.  College or university positions
       *A.*  Teacher of a subject field
       *B.*  Assistant to dean
       *C.*  Dean of a separate college such as liberal arts, education, engineering, agriculture, law, medicine, fine arts, pharmacy, social service, dentistry
       *D.*  Dean of continuing education
       *E.*  Dean of students
       *F.*  President
       *G.*  Director of programs for minority groups
       *H.*  Chairman of a department
       *I.*  Alumni secretary
       *J.*  Director of public relations
       *K.*  Registrar
       *L.*  Director of counseling

     *M.*  Business manager
     *N.*  Research worker
     *O.*  Director of research
     *P.*  Secretary and/or accountant
     *Q.*  Field worker for recruiting students
     *R.*  Field worker for carrying services of university to the people
     *S.*  Placement director
     *T.*  Health service personnel

VII.  Professional organizations such as the National Education Association, the American Federation of Teachers, the National Association for Afro-American Education, as well as state education associations
     *A.*  Director
     *B.*  Executive secretary
     *C.*  Research worker
     *D.*  Field worker
     *E.*  Writer
     *F.*  Director of publications

VIII.  State departments of education
     *A.*  State superintendent of instruction
     *B.*  Director of curriculum
     *C.*  Director of guidance
     *D.*  Director of special education
     *E.*  Special field worker

IX.  Educational directors or consultants for noneducational agencies
     *A.*  Publisher of newspapers, magazines, films
     *B.*  Manufacturing firms—job training, recreation, testing, etc.
     *C.*  Religious associations
     *D.*  Chambers of commerce
     *E.*  Aviation companies
     *F.*  Service agencies, such as state tuberculosis association
     *G.*  Minority groups

X.  Municipal, private, religious, and civic agencies
     *A.*  City recreation director
     *B.*  Boy and girl camps—director, instructor
     *C.*  Director of youth organization
        1.  Boy Scouts and Girl Scouts
        2.  4-H club
        3.  YMCA and YWCA
     *D.*  Teacher in a hospital
     *E.*  Teacher in a church or Bible school
     *F.*  Director of minority groups

XI.  Federal agencies
     *A.*  U.S. Office of Education
        1.  International education (Teacher Exchange)
        2.  Teacher Corps
     *B.*  Department of Defense
        1.  Dependent schools overseas
        2.  Military service
     *C.*  Department of Interior—Bureau of Indian Affairs
     *D.*  Department of State (Peace Corps)
     *E.*  UNESCO

XII.  Foreign countries
     *A.*  Teacher
     *B.*  Conductor of tours

C.  Consultant
D.  Research worker
E.  Defense Department appointments, military government

It should be pointed out that many of the different kinds of educational work listed above do not exist in the small schools. Furthermore, successful teaching experience normally is required for many of the positions not involving classroom teaching.

In forecasting the future, Shane [244:29–32] feels that between 1970 and 1980 a number of new assignments and specialties will materialize. The basic role of the teacher may change noticeably, to the extent that it should be more accurate to term him a "learning clinician." He explains that [244:31–32]:

In the school of the future, senior learning clinicians will be responsible for coordinating the services needed for approximately 200 to 300 children. In different instructional units (an evolution of the "team" concept) we will find paraprofessionals, teaching interns, and other learning clinicians with complementary backgrounds. Some will be well-informed in counseling, others in media, engineering, languages, evaluation, systems analysis, simulation, game theory, and individual-need analysis.

But on the whole, the learning clinician will probably not be appreciably more specialized in subject matter disciplines than he was in the 1960's except for being skilled in using educational technology. He will do more *coordinating* and *directing* of individual

The Peace Corps provides an opportunity to render service while getting travel and teaching experience. Here Judith Roberts of San Carlos, California, is shown teaching English at the College of Education in Bangkok, Thailand. *(Photograph from ACTION/Peace Corps.)*

inquiry and will engage in less 1968-style group instruction. He will be highly concerned with providing and maintaining an effective environment, skilled in interpersonal transactions, and able to work with persons of different ages and learning styles.

Ten years from now, faculties will include:

*Culture analysts ,* who make use of our growing insights into how a subculture shapes the learning style and behavior of its members.

*Media specialists,* who tailor-make local educational aids, who evaluate hardware and software and their use, and who are adept in the information sciences of automated-information storage and retrieval, and computer programming.

*Information-input specialists,* who make a career of keeping faculty and administration aware of implications for education in broad social, economic and political trends.

*Curriculum-input specialists,* who from day to day make necessary corrections and additions to memory bank tapes on which individualized instructional materials are stored.

*Biochemical therapist/pharmacists,* whose services increase as biochemical therapy and memory improvement chemicals are introduced more widely.

*Early childhood specialists,* who work in the nonschool, preschool, and minischool programs and in the preprimary continuum.

*Developmental specialists,* who determine the groups in which children and youth work and who make recommendations regarding ways of improving pupil learning.

*Community-contact personnel,* who specialize in maintaining good communication, in reducing misunderstanding or abrasions, and in placing into the life of the community the increased contributions that the schools of the 1970's will be making.

A prospective teacher should not confine his exploration of educational opportunities to the school system of the United States. New educational opportunities are continuing to develop in the business world. Industries, businesses, and labor unions all over the country need educational directors, would be glad to employ them if they were available, and would give them opportunities to make very significant contributions to education in general. The field of educational radio and television is expanding rapidly. Textbook publishers and some of the giant industries (Xerox, General Electric, Raytheon, IBM) have been uniting for the purpose of preparing instructional materials. The need for "educational engineers" is great. Also, as will be discussed later, the whole field of adult education is barely getting started in this country. There is room for thousands of new jobs in that field for men and women with sound general training, creative imagination, and drive.

For the more adventurous person, the opportunities to work in even the most remote areas of the world continue to increase. For example, over 1,000 new teachers are needed each year in the American Dependent Schools Overseas. The Peace Corps offers many opportunities to teach in a number of underdeveloped countries. You may wish to check upon the requirements and opportunities for working in schools in outlying states and areas of the United States and in schools and programs sponsored by the United States government, such as the American Dependent Schools Overseas, Teacher Exchange, Information Services, and Agency for International Development.

Preparation in the teaching profession certainly presents many

An increasing number of industries, businesses, and community agencies feel the need for educators who can counsel, and who can plan educational programs for their personnel. *(Photograph by Joe Di Dio, National Education Association.)*

different opportunities, and you can engage in the type of activity of special interest to you. If you are willing to prepare yourself well for a particular type of work, the chances of reaching your goal are good.

## SUMMARY

The teaching profession is, by a wide margin, the largest of all the professions. It provides a great variety of opportunities for anyone who wishes to prepare for, and remain in, the profession for a number of years. Most people enter the profession as public school teachers.

Many factors affect the supply and demand for teachers. In periods of economic depression the supply tends to become greater than in times of economic prosperity. Birthrates, pupil-teacher ratios, turnover, and expansion or contraction of educational services rendered by the school affect significantly the demand for teachers.

Since the birthrate has been decreasing, elementary school enrollments are expected to decline during the 1970s, and secondary school enrollments are expected to increase. Birthrates and the number of births alone do not determine entirely the demand for new teachers. Undoubtedly there will continue to be considerable downward extension of schooling during the 1970s, for which demands will be made for well-qualified early childhood teachers. The holding power of the secondary schools undoubtedly will continue to increase, although the rate may not be as great as during the 1960s. The expansion of specialized kinds of instruction and services, the changes in organizational and instructional patterns that will take place in the foreseeable future, and the increasing need for educators in business, industry, and continuing education will generate additional opportunities for teachers.

A dramatic increase in enrollments is projected for junior colleges and four-year colleges and universities, with the peak of enrollments being reached in 1982. This increase, in addition to the normal replacement rate of 6 per cent of the total instructional staff, should generate a number of opportunities for those interested in teaching at the college level—assuming that the general public will be willing to increase its financial support for higher education.

## QUESTIONS TO CONSIDER

1. Many educators feel that more men should be attracted into public school teaching, especially into the elementary schools. Do you agree or disagree? What are your reasons? By what means could this end be accomplished?
2. For what reasons should educational opportunities be extended downward at public expense? How far down should these opportunities be extended? Why?
3. For what reasons can you expect the number of fourteen- to seventeen-year-olds attending secondary schools to continue to increase?
4. What major and minor teaching combinations are in greatest demand in the area where you plan to teach? Least demand?
5. What suggestions would you make for solving the problem of excessive imbalance of teachers in the various fields and levels of teaching?
6. What sacrifices are made by pupils when they are forced to attend excessively large classes or half-day sessions?
7. As you review Chapter 1, what new opportunities do you foresee for educators?
8. What advantages and disadvantages do you see in teaching on the college level?
9. How might the growth of junior colleges affect the opportunities of secondary school teachers?
10. If you had to change your subject area or level of teaching, what would you choose? Why?
11. What are some of the opportunities that exist in adult education?
12. In your opinion, what are the frontier opportunities for teachers in industry, business, and overseas programs?

## PROBLEM SITUATION FOR INQUIRY

Mr. Harris is the principal of the elementary school in the small community of Oakwood. He has held his position for six years and has developed close relationships with the faculty and the community. Harris has an ideal situation. The students are well-behaved; there is an active PTA group in the school; he is respected in the community; and he gets strong support from the district superintendent. In essence, both Harris and his family are very happy in Oakwood.

The school board of North Crest, a wealthy suburban area, recently contacted Mr. Harris and offered him a position as principal of the North Crest Junior High School. Mr. Harris was flattered with the offer, but he requested some time to consider it before making a decision. Upon investigating the North Crest situation, he discovered many problems. He found that the students are rebellious and unconcerned about their education, and that discipline problems in the school are numerous. Principals who have previously served in the school have found it impossible to handle this large group of uninhibited youngsters. Parents are often too caught up in the community social activities to be concerned with the education of their children. These students have everything they want materially. They get bored, and try to grow up too soon.

The principalship at North Crest pays a salary of $18,000, which is considerably more than Harris's present salary in Oakwood. The new job would mean leaving the pleasant community of Oakwood in which he has a secure position. However, the new job, in addition to providing a larger salary, would offer a tremendous professional challenge. If you were Mr. Harris, what would you do? Why?

## ACTIVITIES TO PURSUE

1. Plan a number of visits to more than one school, observing various elementary and secondary school classes. Attempt to make, or further verify, an original decision regarding the subject areas and/or the level you may wish to teach.
2. Plan some leadership experiences with children of different age levels to make, or further verify, an original decision regarding elementary or secondary teacher preparation. Experience as a camp counselor, playground supervisor, boy or girl scout director, and the like should prove very valuable to you.
3. Consult your local superintendent to see if you might serve as an assistant in a school between the time public schools open in the fall and the time your college courses begin; or at some other convenient time. Attempt to gain broad experience both in the classroom and around the school. Study these experiences in terms of your fitness for teaching, the level on which you should teach, and learning significant for future courses in education.
4. Question a number of teachers whom you respect, especially those teaching on the elementary level, regarding the advantages and disadvantages of preparing for teaching in the subject areas and/or levels which they represent.
5. Visit some inner-city schools to see if teaching in such schools might interest and challenge you.
6. Consult the adviser and the teacher-placement official in your college concerning the probable supply and demand for teachers when you expect to graduate. Secure from educational literature as much data on this problem as possible.
7. If you do not plan to teach in the locale where you are attending school, secure data on teacher supply and demand for the area in which you expect to begin your work.
8. Examine the organizational setup of a large city school system to discover the different kinds of positions involved. Talk with those individuals who hold positions that may interest you. Discuss such matters as qualifications, duties, advantages, and disadvantages of the work.
9. Discuss with your college adviser any occupational plans other than teaching that you may have in the field of education. Consider specific implications that these plans may have in your preparation for teaching.

**RESOURCE
SECTION
FOR
PART 1**

## SELF-RATING SCALE FOR DETERMINING FITNESS FOR TEACHING

| | Never | Sel-dom | Some-times | Often | Al-ways |
|---|---|---|---|---|---|
| **I. Leadership ability** | | | | | |
| 1. Have you served as leader in student groups; i.e., have you held an office, taken part in programs, or led discussions? | | | | | |
| 2. Do your fellow students respect your opinions? | | | | | |
| 3. Do they regard you as a leader? | | | | | |
| 4. Do your fellow students ask you for help and advice? | | | | | |
| 5. Do you sense how others feel, i.e., whether they approve certain proposals, or like or dislike certain persons? | | | | | |
| 6. Do you try to make others happy by listening to what they say, and by being courteous, friendly, and helpful? | | | | | |
| 7. Do you succeed in getting others to follow your suggestions without creating friction or ill will? | | | | | |
| **II. Health and physical fitness** | | | | | |
| 1. Do you have good health? | | | | | |
| 2. Do you have lots of vitality? Can you stand to do hard physical tasks or nerve-racking work? | | | | | |
| 3. Can you engage in activities which others in your group customarily do? | | | | | |
| 4. Do you give others the impression that you are physically fit, well groomed and attractive in personal appearance? | | | | | |
| 5. Do you keep cheerful and even-tempered even when tired or ill? | | | | | |
| **III. Good scholarship** | | | | | |
| 1. Have you maintained a better-than-average academic record? | | | | | |
| 2. Are you interested in the subjects you have taken or are taking? | | | | | |
| 3. Do you enjoy studying and find it easy to concentrate when you do study? | | | | | |
| 4. Do you express your ideas well before a class or public group? | | | | | |
| 5. Is it easy for you to explain things so that others understand and can follow your directions? | | | | | |
| **IV. Intellectual traits and abilities** | | | | | |
| 1. Are school subjects easy for you? | | | | | |
| 2. Do you spend time finding out more about a topic discussed in class or covered in an assignment? | | | | | |

*Source:* E. E. Samuelson and others, *You'd Like Teaching,* Craftsman Press, Seattle, Wash., 1946, pp. 31–35. Materials prepared and published, and permission for use granted, by Central Washington College of Education.

## SELF-RATING SCALE FOR DETERMINING
## FITNESS FOR TEACHING (continued)

| | Never | Sel-dom | Some-times | Often | Al-ways |
|---|---|---|---|---|---|
| 3. Do you read books or magazine articles on current topics? | | | | | |
| 4. Do you like to work out ideas on your own? | | | | | |
| 5. Do you suggest new ideas or plans which can be carried out by groups? | | | | | |
| V. Emotional stability | | | | | |
| 1. Are you an even-tempered, cheerful, happy sort of person? | | | | | |
| 2. Can you "take it" without getting angry or upset? | | | | | |
| 3. Do you keep from worrying and feeling depressed? | | | | | |
| 4. Are you naturally patient with and tolerant of others? | | | | | |
| 5. Are you objectively critical of yourself? | | | | | |
| 6. Do you see the humorous side of everyday happenings even when you yourself are involved? | | | | | |
| VI. Social aspirations | | | | | |
| 1. Are you interested in the problems other people meet and do you want to help them solve them? | | | | | |
| 2. Are you interested in finding ways by which you can help improve human living? | | | | | |
| 3. Do you like people—especially children? | | | | | |
| 4. Do you set high social standards for yourself and seek to reach and maintain these standards? | | | | | |
| 5. Do you cooperate readily with other people in socially desirable activities? | | | | | |
| 6. Are you willing to make sacrifices and endure inconveniences to reach a goal you consider worthy? | | | | | |

## THE CHARACTERISTICS OF THE COMPETENT TEACHER IN
## HARFORD COUNTY

### A Statement of the Harford County Teachers' Association Bel Air, Maryland

**I. Personal Traits**

The competent teacher:

possesses adequate physical vitality.

is punctual.

is regular in attendance.

*Source:* "Evaluating Teaching Performance," *ERS Circular,* No. 3, pp. 26–28, American Association of School Administrators and the National Education Association, Educational Research Service, Washington, 1969.

is well groomed.

maintains appropriate emotional control.

has a sense of humor—laughs with people.

is trustworthy and conscientious.

fulfills responsibilities without constant supervision.

makes practical, common sense judgments.

uses tact.

can act in original situations without supervision.

is cooperative and a good team worker.

is receptive to constructive criticism and suggestion.

is self-confident.

is reasonable in self-evaluation.

is able to meet people on a courteous level of mutual self-respect.

## II. Executive Traits

The competent teacher:

completes necessary paper work promptly and accurately.

arranges to have materials at hand when they are needed.

evaluates materials and keeps only applicable material.

organizes classroom routines so children share responsibility.

creates an atmosphere that promotes learning and discourages anti-social behavior.

recognizes each child as an individual and provides for individual differences within the framework of the school program.

assumes the responsibility for disciplinary measures unless unusual factors are involved.

makes his authority understood and accepted in a gracious manner.

transmits enthusiasm for his subject.

checks assignments efficiently.

maintains a neat, clean classroom, conducive to learning.

is willing to use professional resource people within the school system.

is in firm control of his classroom at all times.

## III. Teaching Power

The competent teacher:

selects and organizes material with

definitions of aim.

compatibility with the course of study.

adaptation to pupil needs, interests, and capacities.

has intelligently prepared unit and daily lesson plans.

is aware of the importance of motivation.

uses pupil experience to enrich and give meaning to content.

uses a variety of techniques to reach desirable goals.

works to have pupils accept appropriate individual and common goals.

develops a readiness for learning.

uses pupil responses to aid his teaching.

accepts his responsibility to improve attitudes, work habits, and skills.

uses grammatically correct, precise English.

has good vocalization.

evaluates work regularly and reteaches when that is needed.

shows imagination in adapting materials for classroom use.

displays materials that stimulate children's desire to learn.

can present ideas in a clear and convincing manner.

## IV. Professional Responsibility

The competent teacher:

develops a relationship with students which is warm and inspiring and yet professional.

demonstrates a high standard of ethics in accord with the HCTA Ethics for Educators.

is proud to be a teacher and lets this pride show.

supports professional organizations, regarding this as a privilege to be able to participate in activities which advance the profession.

takes personal responsibility for individual professional growth.

contributes to the advancement of education by working effectively on committees by assuming individual responsibility for improvements for schools, by having a knowledge of legislation enacted and pending relating to education.

secures support in attracting those who should and holding those who do enter the profession.

has a professional manner as shown by reasonable dignity and appropriate personal conduct.

understands and follows county and school policies and procedures.

is loyal to co-workers, principals, and other school personnel.

respects group decisions.

respects and is discreet in using professional information.

can explain an educational point of view clearly and convincingly.

maintains a spirit of mutual respect in teacher-pupil, teacher-teacher, principal-teacher, and parent-teacher relationships.

uses thoughtful observation, inquiry, and study to learn as much as possible about the community.

## V. Scholarship

The competent teacher:

is a master of his chosen field of specialization.

maintains a continuing spirit of learning and understanding.

knows the psychology of learning and is aware of new trends in this field.

surveys recent educational periodicals and reads information pertinent to his work.

## VI. Community Relations

The competent teacher:

is informed about local problems.

participates as a citizen in local government.

understands the strengths and the problems of the school community.

realizes that the adequate support of free public schools in the community is based upon a general understanding of and respect for the educational program.

speaks and acts in all contacts in the community to support the general understanding of and respect for the educational program.

# CHECKLIST OF IMPORTANT FACTORS IN THE TEACHER'S PERSONALITY

*Directions:* Consider each of the ten divisions in this list separately. Read each statement under the major headings carefully and underline any of the qualities or traits which obviously are missing in the personality being rated. Before you proceed to the next division, look back over any of the statements you may have underlined; then place a check mark in the column that expressed your general opinion of the person with respect to the particular aspect of personality being considered.

| Suggested Standard for Traits or Qualities | Below Aver-age | Fair | Good | Excel-lent |
|---|---|---|---|---|
| 1. *Emotional stability and mental health.* Is free from fears, remorse, humiliations, and worries about trivial things; can make a realistic inventory of his mental resources; is not supersensitive to criticism; is resourceful in self- | | | | |

*Source:* Howard T. Batchelder, Maurice McGlasson, and Raleigh Schorling, *Student Teaching in Secondary Schools,* McGraw-Hill Book Company, New York, 1964, pp. 9–12.

## CHECKLIST OF IMPORTANT FACTORS IN THE TEACHER'S PERSONALITY (continued)

| Suggested Standard for Traits or Qualities | Below Average | Fair | Good | Excellent |
|---|---|---|---|---|
| entertainment; is not easily irritated; is free from excessive shyness, temper tantrums, and daydreams; meets unexpected situations well; adapts readily to changing situations; exercises self-control; is free from complexes of inferiority and superiority; has control over moods, with no sudden shifts in extremes from ups to downs; can take disappointments in life in full stride. | | | | |
| 2. *Personal appearance.* Is dressed appropriately for the occasion; is alert and well poised; is well groomed; gives appearance of being self-possessed; exercises good taste in selection of clothes; gives impression of being refined and cultured; chooses color combinations well; keeps clothes pressed and clean. | | | | |
| 3. *Health and vitality.* Shows evidence of a "driving force"; is physically and mentally alert; is enthusiastic and cheerful; looks healthy; is dynamic; is wide awake to the potential possibilities in every situation; has a happy expression; has reserve energy. | | | | |
| 4. *Honesty, character, and integrity.* Shows a good sense of values; can be expected to do the right thing under all conditions; is trustworthy and loyal; admits mistakes; keeps his word; is fair and just in his dealings with others; fulfills obligations; is intellectually honest, maintains high standards of conduct. | | | | |
| 5. *Adaptability.* Accepts gracefully and understands quickly suggestions from others; accepts responsibility for making a positive contribution to a situation; is willing to inconvenience self in helping others; is challenged by new situations; is sympathetic and patient in sharing and understanding the thoughts and difficulties of others; says what must be said with diplomacy and minimum offense; responds readily to necessary routine. | | | | |
| 6. *Cooperation.* Can work with others for attainment of a common goal; volunteers services when they are needed; fits in where most needed; welcomes suggestions and tries to improve; places welfare of the group before self; is willing to share in the "extra" tasks; is a constructive worker on a committee. | | | | |
| 7. *Voice and speech.* Shows refinement and evidence of cultural background; speaks clearly and distinctly with proper degree of inflection; has well-modulated tone, controlled, and adapted to the size of the group; has an accepted and natural accent; attracts favorable attention; is easy to understand; pronounces words correctly; is free from distracting and irritating mannerisms or defects of speech. | | | | |
| 8. *Leadership.* Commands respect; is self-confident; shows ability in planning, organization, and execution; can | | | | |

## CHECKLIST OF IMPORTANT FACTORS IN THE TEACHER'S PERSONALITY (continued)

| Suggested Standard for Traits or Qualities | Below Average | Fair | Good | Excellent |
|---|---|---|---|---|
| persuade others to a proper course of action; can act in emergencies with decision; uses good judgment; inspires others to do their best; shows mastery of a situation; exercises initiative and originality; has the ability to put into words the thinking of a group; possesses courage to support sound convictions. | | | | |
| 9. *Resourcefulness.* Has suggestions for meeting a difficulty; is discerning and quick in selection of the most promising solution; can "see around a corner"; has an abundance of reserve energy upon which to draw; knows when to take action; suggests power of mental strength, and vigor. | | | | |
| 10. *Sociability.* Knows the rules of etiquette sufficiently to avoid embarrassing, offending, or irritating others; is unselfishly interested in others; is a stimulating conversationalist with a wide range of interests; has a sympathetic point of view; puts others at ease; seeks association with others; is tolerant of the opinions of others and of community life; wins and holds friends; is a good listener; knows when to be playful and when to be serious; creates a comfortable and pleasant atmosphere; sees the humorous element in situations; is a good sport. | | | | |

## CHECKLIST FOR VOICE AND SPEECH*

There are two ways in which this checklist may be useful: (1) you may wish to ask some trained person to evaluate your teaching voice; or (2) the results may prove helpful when two or three student teachers rate each other, and later compare notes.

| Speech Factors | Needs Attention | Satisfactory or Superior |
|---|---|---|
| *Quality of voice:* Is his voice | | |
| 1. Too high-pitched? | | |
| 2. Nasal? | | |
| 3. Strained? | | |
| 4. Breathy? | | |
| 5. Varied in pitch? | | |
| 6. Clear and distinct? | | |
| 7. Rich and colorful? | | |
| 8. Adapted to the size of the listening group? | | |

*Only two columns at the right are employed in order to emphasize the items to which the teacher should give remedial attention.

*Source:* Howard T. Batchelder, Maurice McGlasson, and Raleigh Schorling, *Student Teaching in Secondary Schools,* McGraw-Hill Book Company, New York, 1964, p. 15.

## CHECKLIST FOR VOICE AND SPEECH (continued)

| Speech Factors | Needs Attention | Satisfactory or Superior |
|---|---|---|
| 9.  Well controlled and modulated? | | |
| 10. Resonant? | | |
| | | |
| *Unpleasant speech mannerisms:* Does he speak | | |
| 1.  Too fast? | | |
| 2.  In a drawling manner? | | |
| 3.  Lispingly? | | |
| 4.  Gruffly? | | |
| 5.  Too slowly? | | |
| 6.  In an uncertain, halting, or stumbling manner? | | |
| 7.  With an affected accent? | | |
| | | |
| *General speech:* Does he | | |
| 1.  Pronounce words correctly? | | |
| 2.  Enunciate carefully? | | |
| 3.  Use slang inappropriately or excessively? | | |
| 4.  Keep calm, free from anger and excitement? | | |
| 5.  Employ concepts adapted to his audience? | | |
| 6.  Adapt voice to the occasion? | | |
| 7.  Use proper inflection? | | |
| 8.  Show evidence of an adequate vocabulary? | | |

## AM I A GOOD GROUP PARTICIPANT?

1.  Do I propose new ideas, activities, and procedures? Or do I just sit and listen?
2.  Do I ask questions? Or am I shy about admitting that I do not understand?
3.  Do I share my knowledge when it will prove helpful to the problem at hand? Or do I keep it to myself?
4.  Do I speak up if I feel strongly about something? Or am I shy about giving an opinion?
5.  Do I try to bring together our ideas and activities? Or do I concentrate only on details under immediate discussion?
6.  Do I understand the goals of the group and try to direct the discussion toward them? Or do I get off the track easily?
7.  Do I ever question the practicality or the "logic" of a project, and do I evaluate afterwards? Or do I always accept unquestioningly the things we do?
8.  Do I help to arrange chairs, serve refreshments, and even clean up when the session is over? Or do I prefer to be waited on?
9.  Do I encourage my fellow group members to do well? Or am I indifferent to their efforts and achievements?
10. Do I prod the group to undertake worthy projects? Or am I happy with mediocre projects?
11. Am I a mediator and a peacemaker? Or do I allow ill feeling to develop?
12. Am I willing to compromise (except where basic issues such as truth and justice are involved)? Or do I remain inflexible?
13. Do I encourage others to participate and to give everyone else a fair chance to speak? Or do I sit by while some people hog the floor, and do I sometimes dominate it myself?

*Source:* "Am I a Good Group Participant?" *NEA Journal,* vol. 45, p. 168, National Education Association, Washington, March, 1956.

## SUGGESTED READINGS

*The number in parentheses following each suggestion denotes the chapter for which it is best suited.*

Anderson, Donald D.: "Personality Attributes of Teachers in Organizational Climates," *The Journal of Educational Research,* vol. 62, no. 10, pp. 441–443, Dembar Educational Research Services, Inc., Madison, Wis., July–August, 1969. Indicates differences in personality patterns of teachers in different organizational patterns. (2)

Blume, Robert: "Humanizing Teacher Education," *Phi Delta Kappan,* vol. 52, no. 7, pp. 411–415, Phi Delta Kappa, Bloomington, Ind., March, 1971. Stresses the role of emotions in learning and indicates suggestions for teacher education. (3)

Calisch, Richard W.: "So You Want to Be a Real Teacher," *Today's Education,* vol. 58, no. 8, pp. 49–51, National Education Association, Washington, November, 1969. Indicates some of the qualities essential to becoming an effective teacher. (2)

*Careers in Education,* National Education Association, National Commission on Teacher Education and Professional Standards, Washington, 1968. Describes a variety of opportunities in the field of education. (2 and 4)

Chambers, M. M.: "No Teacher Surplus," *Phi Delta Kappan,* vol. 52, no. 2, pp. 118–119, Phi Delta Kappa, Bloomington, Ind., October, 1970. Projects teacher needs in public schools and universities. (4)

*Do Teachers Make a Difference?,* U.S. Office of Education, Washington, 1970. A report on recent research concerning teacher effectiveness and pupil achievement. (2)

Emans, Robert: "Teacher Attitudes as a Function of Values," *The Journal of Educational Research,* vol. 62, no. 10, pp. 459–463, Dembar Educational Research Services, Inc., Madison, Wis., July–August, 1969. Indicates that teachers with extreme values have more favorable attitudes toward the curriculum than teachers with more neutral values. (2)

"Evaluating Teaching Performance," *ERS Circular,* American Association of School Administrators and Research Division, National Education Association, Washington, 1969. Indicates practices used in rating teachers in specific school systems and contains sample rating forms. (2)

Good, Thomas L., and Jere E. Brophy: "The Self-fulfilling Prophecy," *Today's Education,* vol. 60, no. 4, pp. 52–53, National Education Association, Washington, April, 1971. Reports on some research concerning the relationship of teacher expectation and level of accomplishment of pupils. (2)

Graybeal, William S.: "Teacher Surplus and Teacher Shortage," *Phi Delta Kappan,* vol. 53, no. 2, pp. 82–85, Phi Delta Kappa, Bloomington, Ind., October, 1971. Indicates that the surplus of teachers is real, but that it would disappear if society wanted high-quality education badly enough to pay for it. (4)

Greenberg, Herbert M.: *Teaching with Feeling,* The Macmillan Company, Toronto, Ontario, 1969. Stresses the fact that within the teacher's own emotional life are the forces that most powerfully affect the entire teaching process. (2)

Groner, Alex, and Carlyn Brall: "Part-Time Teachers," *Today's Education,* vol. 59, no. 1, pp. 64–65, National Education Association, Washington, January, 1970. Indicates how part-time teachers can be used effectively in school systems. (4)

Hamachek, Don: "Characteristics of Good Teachers and Implications for Teacher Education," *Phi Delta Kappan,* vol. 50, no. 6, pp. 341–344, Phi Delta Kappa, Bloomington, Ind., February, 1969. An excellent analysis of characteristics desired in teachers. (2)

Jersild, Arthur Thomas: *When Teachers Face Themselves,* Teachers College Press, Bureau of Publications, Columbia University, New York, 1967. Discusses some of the emotional strains faced by teachers. (2)

Massanari, Karl: "AACTE Explores Performance-Based Teacher Education," *Bulletin,* vol. 24, no. 1, pp. 3, 6, 8, American Association of Colleges for Teacher Education, Washington, March, 1971. Discusses the strengths and weaknesses of using performance objects as bases for teacher certification. (3)

Metzner, Seymour: "The Urban Teacher: Saint, Sinner, or Sucker?" *Phi Delta Kappan,* vol. 51, no. 9, pp. 489–492, Phi Delta Kappa, Bloomington, Ind., May, 1970. Appraises the status of urban teachers. (4)

*Milestones in Teacher Education and Professional Standards,* National Education Association, National Commission on Teacher Education and Professional Standards, Washington, 1970. Depicts progress made in the professional education of teachers. (3)

Pullias, Earl V., and James D. Young: *A Teacher Is Many Things,* Indiana University Press, Bloomington, Ind., 1969. A very interesting treatment of the many and varied roles played by a teacher. (2)

Rogers, Carl R.: *Freedom to Learn,* Charles E. Merrill Publishing Company, Columbus, Ohio, 1969. Chapter 12 is concerned with a modern approach to the valuing process. (2)

Sabine, Gordon A.: *How Students Rate Their Schools and Teachers,* National Association of Secondary School Principals, Washington, 1971. Presents what a group of students said in answer to three key questions on schools and teachers. (2)

Selkin, Sidney: *Complete Planning for College,* Harper & Row, New York, 1968. Contains many suggestions for gaining the most from the years in college. (2)

Smith, B. Othanel: *Teachers for the Real World,* American Association of Colleges for Teacher Education, Washington, 1969. Proposes major changes in the education of teachers. (3)

Stadt, Ronald, and Larry J. Kenneke: *Teacher Competencies for the Cybernated Age,* National Education Association, American Council on Industrial Arts Teacher Education, Washington, 1970. Reviews the impact of technology upon man and his world and the implications this holds for industrial arts teacher education. (3)

Stiles, Lindley J.: "State of the Art of Teacher Education," *The Journal of Educational Research,* vol. 64, no. 9, pp. 388–393, Dembar Educational Research Services, Inc., Madison, Wis., May–June, 1971. Indicates twelve emerging priorities in teacher education. (3)

Stinnett, T. M.: "Accreditation of Teacher Education Institutions and Agencies," *Phi Delta Kappan,* vol. 52, no. 1, pp. 25–31, Phi Delta Kappa, Bloomington, Ind., September, 1970. Advocates an effective coordination of state and national accreditation agencies. (3)

Stinnett, T. M.: *A Manual on Certification Requirements for School Personnel in the United States,* National Education Association, National Commission on Teacher Education and Professional Standards, Washington (latest issue). Published every three years; presents detailed information on certification requirements. (3)

Stinnett, T. M.: *Professional Problems of Teachers,* The Macmillan Company, Toronto, Ontario, 1969. Chapters 4, 18, 19, and 20 are concerned with teacher education, certification, and accreditations. Chapter 6 presents the opportunities for advancement in teaching. (3 and 4)

"Teacher Supply and Demand in Public Schools," *Research Report,* National Education Association, Research Division, Washington (latest issue). An annual, detailed report on the supply and demand for teachers. (4)

Turner, Richard L.: "Good Teaching in Its Contexts," *Phi Delta Kappan,* vol. 52, no. 3, pp. 155–158, Phi Delta Kappa, Bloomington, Ind., November, 1970. Analyzes some common characteristics of good teachers. (2)

Van Til, William: *The Year 2000: Teacher Education,* School of Education, Indiana State University, Terre Haute, Ind., 1968. Indicates changes that may need to be made in the education of teachers in order to meet educational needs in the year 2000. (3)

Walker, William J.: "Teacher Personality in Creative School Environments," *The Journal of Educational Research,* vol. 62, no. 6, pp. 243–246, Dembar Educational Research Services, Inc., Madison, Wis., February, 1969. Presents the results of a study indicating that creative teachers are more adaptive, flexible, outgoing, permissive, and nurturant. (2)

Weathersby, Rita E., Patricia R. Allen, and Alan R. Blackmer, Jr.: *New Roles for Educators,* Harvard Graduate School of Education, Cambridge, Mass., February, 1970. A sourcebook of background information for people designing unconventional careers in education. (4)

## SUGGESTED 16 mm FILMS

*The number in parentheses following each suggestion denotes the chapter for which it is best suited.*

*Abraham Kaplan* (National Educational Television, 59 min). Depicts Abraham Kaplan, professor of philosophy at the University of Michigan, explaining his own immediate background and cultural heritage, his beliefs and attitudes toward teaching, and the difference between instruction and education. (2)

*Classroom Management* (Holt, Rinehart and Winston, Inc., 18 min, color). Utilizes narration and an actual classroom situation to point out mistakes commonly made by teachers in the classroom. Suggests that awareness of these pitfalls will give the teacher more time for meaningful teaching. (2)

*I Walk Away in the Rain* (Holt, Rinehart and Winston, Inc., 10 min, color). Considers the problem of Tom, a bright youngster content with doing minimal school work. Uses an interview with Tom to present his attitude that a "C" is a passing grade and that if he does what others want, he will lose a part of himself. Asks the question, "How can students like Tom be stimulated and motivated to do better work?" (2)

*Philosophies of Education: Education for Psychological Maturity* (National Educational Television, 29 min). Quotations from Dr. Jersild's book, *When Teachers Face Themselves,* such as "Education should help children and adults to know themselves and to develop healthy attitudes of self-acceptance," set the tone for this program. Proposes that efforts to promote self-understanding should be incorporated into the nation's total educational program. (2)

*Planning for Personal and Professional Growth* (McGraw-Hill, 17 min). Shows four schoolteachers who have made certain adjustments and achieved success in their teaching, to various degrees. A middle-aged woman found teaching dull, with many frustrations; she was not aware of her problems and could not adjust satisfactorily. A science teacher made long-range plans for his growth through graduate study but found that he had to reevaluate his ambitious plans. A foreign language teacher had conflicts between family life and teaching, but by relating her teaching to life, she made a desirable adjustment. An elderly woman was enthusiastic about teaching, loved children, and found teaching a rich, rewarding experience. (2,3)

*Some Personal Learnings about Interpersonal Relationships* (University of California at Los Angeles, 33 min). Presents Carl Rogers informally lecturing about his experiences and philosophy of human interactions. Details need of people to be "heard" and to escape their self-imposed prisons. (2)

*Teach Me* (Teaching Film Custodians, 20 min, color). Uses segments of the motion picture *Up the Down Staircase* to illustrate the experiences of a novice English teacher in a New York City school. Displays the discrepancy between a beginning teacher's expectations about teaching and the practical realities of a lower-class urban school. (2)

*Who Cares about Jamie?* (Coronet Films, 17 min). Dramatizes the pressures, successes, and failures of Jamie, a first grader, at school, at home, and in his associations with adults in the community. (2)

## FIGURE CREDITS

FIGURE 3–1  (*Source:* Adapted from *Milestones in Teacher Education and Professional Standards,* National Education Association, National Commission on Teacher Education and Professional Standards, Washington, 1970, p. 6.)

FIGURE 3–3  (*Source:* "Teacher Supply and Demand in Public Schools," *Research Report 1970–R14,* National Education Association, Research Division, Washington, 1970, p. 52.)

FIGURE 3–4 (*Source: Milestones in Teacher Education and Professional Standards,* National Education Association, National Commission on Teacher Education and Professional Standards, Washington, 1970, p. 16.)

FIGURE 3–5 (*Source: Milestones in Teacher Education and Professional Standards,* National Education Association, National Commission on Teacher Education and Professional Standards, Washington, 1970, p. 19.)

FIGURE 3–6 (*Source: Milestones in Teacher Education and Professional Standards,* National Education Association, National Commission on Teacher Education and Professional Standards, Washington, 1970, p. 15.)

FIGURE 3–7 (*Source:* Data from *The Annual List, 1970–1971,* National Council for Accreditation of Teacher Education, Washington, 1970, p. 36.)

FIGURE 4–1 (*Source:* Data from *Statistical Abstract of the United States,* U.S. Department of Commerce, Bureau of the Census, Washington, 1971, p. 7.)

FIGURE 4–2 (*Source:* Data from *Statistical Abstract of the United States,* U.S. Department of Commerce, Bureau of the Census, Washington, 1971, pp. 50 and 55.)

FIGURE 4–3 (*Source:* Kenneth A. Simon and Marie G. Fullam, *Projections of Educational Statistics to 1979–80,* U.S. Office of Education, National Center for Educational Statistics, Washington, 1971, p. 6.)

FIGURE 4–4 (*Source:* "Teacher Supply and Demand in Public Schools," *Research Report 1970–R14,* National Education Association, Research Division, Washington, 1970, p. 46.)

FIGURE 4–5 (*Source:* Kenneth A. Simon and Marie G. Fullam, *Projections of Educational Statistics to 1979–80,* U.S. Office of Education, National Center for Educational Statistics, Washington, 1971, p. 8.)

FIGURE 4–6 (*Source:* Data from Richard H. Barr and Betty J. Foster, *Statistics of Public Elementary and Secondary Day Schools, Fall, 1969,* U.S. Office of Education, National Center for Educational Statistics, Washington, 1970, p. 22.)

FIGURE 4–7 (*Source:* Data adapted from Samuel Kirk, "Educating the Handicapped," *Contemporary Issues in American Education,* U.S. Office of Education, Washington, 1965, p. 89.)

FIGURE 4–8 (*Source:* Adapted from William S. Graybeal, "Teacher Surplus and Teacher Shortage," *Phi Delta Kappan,* vol. 53, no. 2, Phi Delta Kappa, Bloomington, Ind., October, 1971, p. 83.)

FIGURE 4–9 (*Source:* Kenneth A. Simon and Marie G. Fullam, *Projections of Educational Statistics to 1979–80,* U.S. Office of Education, National Center for Educational Statistics, Washington, 1971, p. 6.)

FIGURE 4–10 (*Source:* "Pupil-Staff Ratios, 1966–67," *NEA Research Bulletin,* vol. 46, no. 1, National Education Association, Research Division, Washington, March, 1968, p. 21.)

FIGURE 4–11 (*Source:* "Public School Programs and Practices," *NEA Research Bulletin,* vol. 45, no. 4, National Education Association, Research Division, Washington, December, 1967, p. 106.)

# 2 | instructional and legal concerns

One of the essential steps in becoming an effective teacher is to gain a clear perception of the duties and responsibilities that he will be likely to encounter. With this understanding, a prospective teacher can plan learning experiences, in addition to those included in a teacher education program, that will increase his competency for guiding the learning process of youth.

In order to fulfill his role, a teacher must work with many others—pupils, parents, colleagues, and community members—in situations in which legal liabilities and responsibilities are inescapable. It is important, therefore, for a teacher to have an understanding of the legal parameters that apply to his profession.

Although the role of the teacher continues to change, the first part of Chapter 5 attempts to identify some elements common to the work of all teachers. The latter part of the chapter is concerned with changing organizational and instructional patterns and procedures which may result in considerable modification in the competencies essential to the success of a teacher.

Chapter 6 indicates some of the changes and demands that may result from the increased use of educational technology. Chapter 7 contains suggestions and procedures that may be used by a prospective teacher in gaining proficiency in further understanding pupils and in guiding their educational growth. Some of the legal liabilities and responsibilities of teachers are indicated in Chapter 8.

# 5 | THE CHANGING ROLE OF THE TEACHER

What duties and responsibilities are excepted of teachers in the classroom? What does the community expect of teachers? What organizational changes are taking place that may affect instructional procedures and practices? The answers to these questions provide a major part of the framework for a teacher's professional and personal life.

This chapter will review briefly a few of the major classroom and community responsibilities of teachers, and then examine in some detail the newer organizational and instructional procedures that are bringing some dramatic changes now and promising more in the future.

## MAJOR CLASSROOM RESPONSIBILITIES OF TEACHERS

It is unlikely that any two classroom teachers would have identical responsibilities. There are great gaps between what an elementary teacher does in a one-room rural school and what a senior English teacher does in a large metropolitan high school. Likewise, conditions in public schools and communities differ considerably throughout the United States and may well change tremendously in the future. As a result, teachers' working lives vary in significant ways. Still, there are some responsibilities that are common to the work of all teachers.

### Instruction

A teacher is expected to have a thorough understanding of the subject matter and skills to be taught in his area. His main responsibility is to assist in the development of adaptable, rational, creative, and cooperative individuals who are capable of coping with the world in which they live, who are prepared to be productive citizens in the world of tomorrow, and who possess an awareness of moral, spiritual, and social values [44:13].

Elementary teachers generally have gone about the task of educating children by staying with one particular group for the greater part of the day. They have planned their lessons before and after school or during released periods when the students may be receiving instruction from itinerant specialists in music, art, or physical education.

In secondary school, teachers generally have met several different classes in each day; the variety of subjects taught by each teacher has usually been greater in small schools than in large ones. In their attempts to provide for the needs and interests of a burgeoning school population, secondary schools have added many subjects. In fact, curriculum workers view with alarm the tendency to change the secondary school program merely by adding courses. The trend they prefer to encourage is toward reducing these numbers. Curriculum workers have suggested removing courses which are outmoded or inappropriate, combining the common learning experiences of pupils in a given school around areas of living which draw upon many subjects and resources.

In attempting to assure reasonable teaching loads in member schools, the North Central Association of Colleges and Secondary Schools has recommended as one of its school accrediting policies that each teacher be assigned at least one conference and preparation period daily [194:14]. In schools operating on a six- or seven-period day, this would mean that a teacher should be assigned no more than five classes and/or study halls. In schools using eight or more periods, a teacher should be assigned not more than six classes and/or study halls.

Of course, the number of classes is only one aspect of a teacher's load. Other factors to be considered include the subject being taught, class size, length of period, administrative or supervisory duties, assignments in extraclass activities, counseling duties, and length of school day. In addition, recent innovations in teaching, such as television and other

FIGURE 5–1   How elementary and secondary school teachers divide an average work week. Noncompensated school-related activities include lesson preparation, grading papers, making reports, attending meetings, etc.

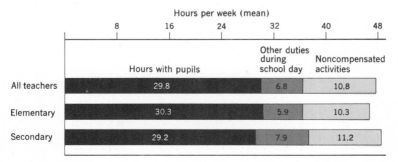

electronic aids, flexible scheduling, ungraded classrooms, team teaching, and the use of programmed material with or without machines, tend to make the "number of classes taught" a less accurate description of a teacher's day.

## Student Guidance and Counseling

A major goal of education is to develop students who are capable of and dedicated to a lifetime of learning. This means helping students define their most pressing needs and interests and problems; helping them understand themselves better; and helping them understand their families, their friends, their whole community. Out of this will emerge certain specific objectives the youngsters will consider important to achieve. The teacher's function is to guide students in formulating and appraising their objectives in terms of their value to the learners and to the community. The teacher guides the students in planning ways and means of arriving at those objectives.

In order for learning to be relevant, pupils must be able to relate the facts they have discovered to their everyday lives. This requires numerous deliberate applications and the development of generalizations which make sense to the learners—which they can use to gain better control over their future behavior. Research seems to indicate that on tests of academic achievement requiring analysis, synthesis, evaluation, and application of knowledge, the more informal group processes described here obtain better results than more formal lectures and recitations [250:20]. These are important considerations that apply in the teaching of all grades and all subjects.

The modern classroom teacher, using standardized test results, careful observations, and records of past performances, gains insight into each student's level of ability. The teacher places those of somewhat similar abilities together for certain learning experiences. However, these groupings are flexible, and as students grow in their abilities, they move from one group to another. Through careful observation, teachers are often able to select groups with similar interests. Group interests may be used to solve mutual problems or to act as a motivating force for further learning. Grouping is only one of many teaching techniques which the modern teacher uses to individualize instruction. Ungraded classrooms and flexible scheduling enable teachers to group pupils in terms of their individual needs, interests, and abilities.

Some students will need the attention of specialists who can help them with academic or emotional maladjustments; the teacher who knows the individual abilities, strengths, and weaknesses of the pupils will obviously be in a better position to render a service to students. Teachers, whose assignments make it necessary to be responsible for large numbers of students, find the teacher-guidance role more difficult.

Elementary teachers in self-contained or modified self-contained class-rooms have a distinct advantage over most secondary teachers.

## Maintaining Discipline

The traditional concept of discipline centers around order in the class-room, techniques of maintaining that order, and means of punishment. The modern concept is based on certain principles which have grown out of the findings of psychology and the viewpoints of such educators as Dewey and Kilpatrick. Sheviakov and Redl [245:9–16] listed some democratic principles which guide discipline practices in a modern conception of education:

1. Teachers use positive ways of guidance which communicate this belief in the value of each personality, rather than negative ways which undermine self-confidence and self-esteem.
2. Teachers consider each incident when discipline or order has broken down in relation to the particular persons involved, their needs and their life histories.
3. Our schools provide a climate in which mutual respect and trust are possible.
4. Teachers build understanding and communication between individuals and groups.
5. Teachers help children to understand the reasons for standards and rules and to foresee the consequences of their own behavior.
6. Schools provide for children's growth in self-government through which they share increasingly in planning their own activities.
7. Teachers study children's behavior scientifically, searching for causes and formulating hunches and hypotheses about how changes may be made.
8. Teachers help young people to understand the reasons for their own and others' behavior and to develop more effective ways of meeting common conflicts.

These principles suggest self-discipline, the internalized behavior that Kilpatrick talked about—control from within rather than control from without. The teacher assumes vastly different duties in carrying out this modern concept of discipline. Instead of assuming the authoritarian, dictatorial role, the teacher takes the part of guide and director of the learning experiences which will provide opportunities to develop self-discipline. Planning with the students and evaluating these plans becomes an important teaching technique. Children help to build their own rules and regulations within which they will operate. Prevention of behavior problems is given keen consideration by both teachers and students. Teachers help children to channel their energies and initiative into socially acceptable behavior.

Pupils learn the democratic way of life by living it. Since self-discipline is a cornerstone of the democratic way of life, the learning experiences which the school provides must foster law and order from within each individual.

In an introductory course in education, it would be premature to include an extensive discussion of the teacher's role in fostering self-discipline within students. In order to gain an adequate comprehension of this extremely important responsibility, it is essential for a prospective teacher to establish a broad base of understanding in such areas as psychology and sociology.

## Evaluating Pupil Progress

Ideally throughout each learning experience, teachers and pupils take stock of their progress to see whether their goals are being attained or whether their objectives need revising. They appraise their procedures and decide whether they are the best that can be used and whether they are being used well. They take inventory of available resources to determine whether their selection and use have been adequate and wise. These aspects of evaluation may require written reports, committee minutes, anecdotes, checklists, questionnaires, rating scales, personal documents such as diaries, projective techniques, and a variety of tests. Some of the tests will be formal and standardized, whereas others will be informal teacher-constructed instruments, both essay and objective. In either case, the administering, scoring, and interpreting of the tests will be among each teacher's important functions. Beginning teachers can receive valuable help in constructing their own evaluative instruments by turning to teacher or administrator colleagues.

## Reporting to Parents

The teacher is expected to keep parents informed about the progress of his pupils. If he does this systematically and regularly, it can prove to be one of the most fruitful avenues for bringing together the public and the schools. This should involve reviewing and summarizing the information available about each youngster, going over his activities and anecdotal records, looking into his cumulative record, observing test results of various sorts, and, finally, making an appraisal of each. This should be done in terms of each student's individual growth and development toward the stated objectives.

Unfortunately, instructional practices do not often reflect a strong goal orientation, because considered thought regarding purpose is seldom evident. Therefore, evaluation of individual student progress in terms of specific goals sought does not often take place. If this were not the case, evaluation would more often focus upon the individual and his progress—where he started and where he is now—in contrast to some other reference point. Expectations and standards would, of course, vary considerably.

Evaluation involves a negative experience for too large a number of students. It does not have to be this way. Evaluation and subsequent reporting to parents can be oriented in a positive direction: these are the ends toward which we (students and faculty) are directing our energies; this is where the student was at the beginning of instruction; here is where he is now; and, finally, here is what *we* are doing to help him achieve stated objectives. Notice the emphasis upon the individual and the supportive role of the teacher in working with students.

It is unfortunate that in most schools, particularly secondary schools, a student's accomplishment usually is determined by comparing him with other members of his class, and he is graded in terms of where he stands "on the curve." In other instances, a larger group may be used—perhaps, all the students in the school or school system at a given grade or age level. And in still other cases the reference point may be the teacher's expectation of what a student in a specific grade or subject area ought to be able to do.

All the conventional systems of grading and reporting to parents have serious limitations. Many of them fail to inform adequately, and a few actually misinform. Parents, prospective employers, college officials, even the students and the teachers are frequently confused and misled by "A-B-C" grade reports. Where numerical percentages are used, the situation is even worse. Grouping plans further complicate the picture. Does an "A" in an accelerated group mean the same as an "A" in a slow-learning section?

The most common methods of reporting to parents are report cards, parent conferences, and letters to parents. The usual parts of a report card include letter grades [218:75], attendance and tardiness records, and a checklist section on personal characteristics. In a few schools, usually on the elementary level, letter grades have been eliminated. However, even in most schools which have abandoned or supplemented the traditional report card, grades remain a part of the total evaluation of pupil progress. In view of the current emphasis on preparation for college and on college entrance requirements, it is probable that such grades will continue to be an important phase of pupil appraisal on the secondary level.

It is interesting to note that while secondary schools continue to emphasize grades, colleges and universities are now reducing such emphasis. Pass-fail grading, once an innovation in higher education, is now quite common. About two-thirds of the institutions of higher education now use some form of pass-fail grading.

Parent-teacher conferences have gained in frequency, particularly at the elementary level, and to some extent at the secondary level. Research indicates that a preference exists at the elementary school level for reporting through a combination of cards and parent conferences [219:81–82]. It is obvious that parent-teacher conferences are more easily arranged in an elementary school than in a secondary school. In an elementary school such a plan involves perhaps twenty-five to thirty-five conferences with parents. In a secondary school such a plan involves conferences with 100 to 200 parents for each report period. The latter

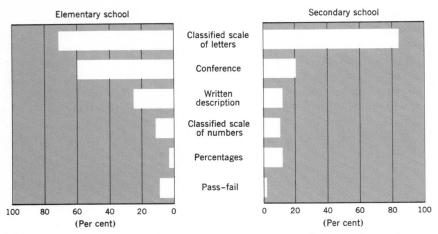

FIGURE 5–2   Methods used by public-school teachers to report pupil progress to parents.

plan is practically impossible, and other patterns have been suggested, such as parent conferences with the homeroom teacher or designated counselors. At any rate the problem is a major one at the secondary level.

Some schools have experimented with letters to parents. However, such letters are time-consuming and frequently become almost as formalized as report cards.

In the final analysis, by far the most common type of reporting remains the report card, with many schools combining it with parent-teacher conferences, and a few using letters to parents. In most schools these reports are made either four times or five times a year. In reporting to parents, new procedures and new instruments are urgently needed.

## Cocurricular Responsibilities

Most secondary and some elementary teachers have some responsibilities for cocurricular activities. Class plays, yearbook production, student government, and class organizations are typical examples of student activities which are popular with students and are capable of producing real and significant values to them.

The trend in school systems throughout the country is for teachers to receive extra compensation for cocurricular activities that demand portions of their time outside the classroom. This is justifiable, since these responsibilities are not shared equally by all teachers. However, the value a teacher may receive in experiencing a healthy new relationship with students may well outweigh any financial compensation that may be provided.

## Professional Responsibilities

Classroom teachers have many other duties of a miscellaneous nature which call for careful attention. There will be letters and professional inquiries which must be answered. Teachers are occasionally asked to answer questionnaires from other educators who are conducting research. Teachers must keep current in their own field, and one way is to plan a regular time for the reading of professional books, journals, and other materials. Some teachers spend time and effort in educational experiments and writing of their own. These things take time, but they are rewarding in terms of professional growth. New teachers will be able to receive help from experienced educators when they wish to gain information about acceptable ways of systematizing the various routine teacher tasks. However, the matter of keeping professionally alert and growing through reading and study is a highly individual matter that requires personal commitment and dedication.

## Teacher Evaluation

Every teacher should feel an obligation to review systematically the quality of his teaching. Through frequent self-analysis and appraisal a teacher gains insight with regard to ways in which his teaching may be improved.

In a very practical and informative booklet titled *Are You a Good Teacher?* Alexander [6] has prepared a list of twenty indicators of the quality of teaching. This list is located in the Resource Section for Part II for you to use in planning your career, and for checking yourself periodically after you begin teaching.

The quality of each teacher's work will be appraised by his superior, usually the principal, and this appraisal may be casual or very formal. According to a study made by the Research Division of the National Education Association [157:12–18], written ratings or evaluations are required in three-fourths of the schools for teachers not on tenure and in two-thirds for teachers who are on tenure. Beginning teachers are evaluated more often than are experienced teachers. Usually the appraisal is made as a result of observing the teacher in the classroom. Other methods of evaluating a teacher may include "gathering impressions from pupils, study of pupil achievement records and office records on each teacher, and noting what parents and other teachers say about the teacher being evaluated" [157:13].

A nationwide sample survey of public-school classroom teachers [269:70–72] indicated that most teachers think they should be evaluated. Three-fourths of the teachers felt that both probationary and tenure teachers should be evaluated regularly, and another 15 per cent felt that

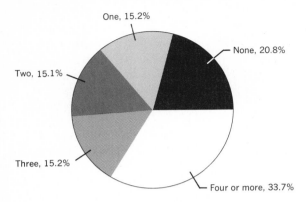

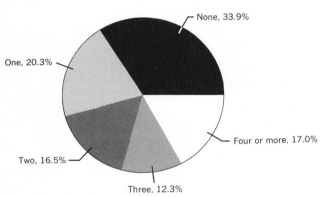

FIGURE 5–3   The results of a study of the number of times teachers were observed in their classroom work for five minutes or more, as reported by teachers.

only probationary teachers should be evaluated. The teachers agreed almost unanimously that the school principal should be responsible for teacher evaluation. The overwhelming reason why teachers wish to be evaluated is in order to improve their teaching competence.

## Relationships with Other School Personnel

Teachers have considerable freedom in fulfilling their classroom responsibilities, but they are expected to abide by and operate within the framework of school board policies in the areas of curriculum organization, teaching techniques, standard report forms, and professional behavior. In most school systems the administrator who is responsible for overseeing the detailed work of each teacher is the building principal.

The principal is responsible to the superintendent for the total educational program in his building. He works closely with the teachers, pupils, and patrons within his district. He is responsible for administering the building and school program and activities, as well as for working with teachers and other staff members to improve the instructional program. Larger school systems may employ special supervisors whose major responsibility is the improvement of classroom instruction.

All teachers have a responsibility to work cooperatively with department heads, various kinds of special teachers, teachers of the same grade or subject, health and social workers, business staff members, and custodians and clerical workers. Successful school programs depend upon all these people working enthusiastically and cooperatively.

A teacher's professional responsibilities are not limited to those things which happen in the classroom with students. School programs must gradually, but constantly, change and improve, and this improvement is the result of teachers, administrators, and other staff members setting goals and working toward attaining them. This process requires faculty meetings, committee meetings, discussions, reports, and problem-solving sessions. Every teacher is expected to help further the school's progress toward important goals by extraclass professional activities.

## COMMUNITY RESPONSIBILITIES OF TEACHERS

Teachers are expected by the community to show interest in their pupils, to be able to work effectively with them, and to be competent in their subject matter and other assignments. Additionally, teachers are expected to demonstrate certain attitudes, understandings, and behavior patterns which the community has come to associate with teachers. There is more to being a teacher than classroom instruction. A teacher's contribution is considered to be a public service paid for at public expense and influenced very decidedly by what the community wants. Despite changing views on the subject, teachers are still expected to set examples, in action and appearance, for those with whom they work and live. Teachers are considered leaders in the business of helping people grow and learn, and of helping whole communities become better places in which to live.

### Community Participation

Beginning teachers can expect to have many opportunities to assume a very active role in community affairs. Educators are eagerly sought participants in most community organizations. Religious groups, social clubs, cultural and recreational groups, and health and social-welfare organizations are usually represented by one or more professional edu-

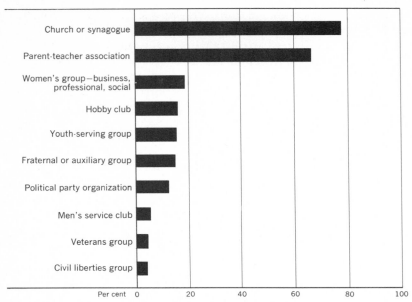

FIGURE 5–4   Percentage of teachers having membership in certain civic and community organizations.

cators. The frequency with which teachers participate in these organizations varies greatly from community to community.

Traditionally, teachers have exhibited community awareness and concern by voting. In the 1968 national election approximately 90 per cent of all teachers voted as compared to a national average of 61 per cent [210:65]. However, only a very small percentage of teachers are ever candidates for public office. In the past teachers have been discouraged from exercising their political rights and responsibilities, including such rights as campaigning for and serving in public office, because of the effect which such service might have on their tenure rights, retirement, or other job status. It is undoubtedly true that many teachers have chosen not to run for political office because it might jeopardize their teaching position. We may expect to see the number of teachers seeking public office grow. The National Education Association has taken a very strong stand [169:79] affirming the educator's right to run for and serve in public office without losing any personal or professional rights.

What is expected of any teacher depends in part upon the community where he is employed. In small schools, teachers usually have personal relationships with a relatively large percentage of the total school population. Teachers in small communities come in contact with and are known and appraised by large percentages of the people. Teachers in such communities might anticipate less liberal attitudes than those they would find in large cities. The situation may be quite different in large urban areas where a teacher may work in one section and live in another. In such instances, it is possible for the teacher to be known by a very small percentage of the total community population.

## Personal Conduct

Parents often expect teachers to be better examples for children than parents themselves are. In some communities teachers are expected not to smoke or drink alcoholic beverages in public places. Few communities frown upon such activities when practiced in moderation in private homes and parties. The teacher in many communities enjoys as much freedom in personal matters as any other professional person. As our nation adopts a more permissive attitude toward individuality in dress and behavior, teachers will share in this freedom, but will do well not to take extreme positions in controversial changes in taste.

## Public Relations

The classroom teacher helps shape public attitude toward the school. As Frasier points out [89:10]:

Good teaching is the best public relations for a school. The teacher's reputation in a community is determined largely by the children and their parents. If the teacher is doing a good job, the children are happy and bring home a positive attitude toward the teacher and the school, to their parents who transmit this feeling to their friends. When a citizen says, "We have a fine school system," he usually means that he is pleased with the type of teaching his children or his neighbor's children are receiving.

The school today needs the understanding and positive support of the public more than ever before. Many teachers engage in a variety of school and community activities that promote lay interest and participation in the schools. Teachers must be conscious of their own responsibility for developing good community relationships.

A checklist titled *How Well Are You Doing in Public Relations?* is located in the Resource Section for Part II. It will give you a good idea of the many ways in which teachers can promote positive relations between schools and communities. You may wish to use this checklist periodically after you begin teaching.

## CHANGING ORGANIZATIONAL AND INSTRUCTIONAL PATTERNS AND PROCEDURES

Changes are being called for and are taking place at all levels of the educational enterprise. Nurtured by widespread concern for instructional improvement, a search has been going on for means to make the nation's schools even better. Reforms are taking place in organizational patterns, subject content, and teaching methods.

Convincing evidence has mounted to indicate that an educational reform has begun. Throughout the country educators are formulating fresh, new approaches to learning. Education has become a field in which creativity is prized. We know that innovation includes the act of recombining old ideas into new programs as well as injecting new ideas and concepts into past practices or originating entirely new practices.

Since the late 1950s, programs designed especially for gifted pupils have been developed, guidance services have been expanded dramatically, and emphasis has been placed on new approaches in mathematics, science, modern foreign languages, and the social sciences. Educators have been trying innovative methods and formulating fresh programs to provide quality educational programs for children coming from socially and economically deprived backgrounds. Special consideration has been given to finding ways to improve the educational opportunity for minority groups. Prekindergarten educational opportunities, summer programs, and work-study projects are common today. More education and better instruction are accepted as imperative for contemporary and future living. Educators are in the forefront of the social force which is searching for solutions to the problems of environmental decay.

In 1959, the National Academy of Sciences held an important meeting at Woods Hole, Massachusetts. The conference director, Jerome Bruner [32], kindled a flame for curriculum reform in a book, *The Process of Education,* which reported the views of those attending the meeting. Bruner called for new methods of viewing content and argued convincingly for emphasis on developing understanding, as opposed to only acquiring facts, in teaching. Since 1959, curriculum reform has been going on in all the subject disciplines. Academicians have joined teachers in finding improved ways of organizing content with an emphasis on developing critical-thinking skills. What was taught a decade ago may not be taught next year. National curriculum projects in most all the disciplines have sought to organize knowledge in a sequential order and to give attention to nurturing the student's desire to learn.

As new programs have been developed, many teachers have taken additional college work or participated in workshops designed to prepare them to work in these new programs. The federal government, as well as various philanthropic foundations, have pumped vast sums of money into projects for the reeducation of teachers. With the contemporary interest in school improvement and the production of new knowledge, the modern teacher is faced with the constant problem of keeping abreast of emerging trends and new developments in the disciplines.

In 1959, the National Education Association authorized the inauguration of the NEA Project on Instructional Programs in the Public Schools. By 1963, a three-volume report of the project had been prepared.

This NEA Project wove together proposals related to content and methods of organization. Not only were recommendations made concerning what should be taught, but recommendations were set forth calling for a change in the teacher's methods of instruction and in the school's organization. Further, a series of recommendations were made for educators to consider as they planned for instruction in the years ahead. This NEA report gave attention to both expanding societal objectives for education and suggested means to achieve them. Emphasis was put on suggesting means for individualizing instruction.

While the development of improved curricular programs has been underway, attention also has been given to fresh approaches in organization for instruction. J. Lloyd Trump called for team teaching, flexible scheduling, and an improved utilization of the schools' professional and material resources. Working as director of the Commission on the Experimental Study of the Utilization of the Staff in the Secondary School, Trump stimulated studies in 100 schools of the proposals later advanced in his book *Guide to Better Schools: Focus on Change* [283]. The outcome of the Trump studies was that ways were sought to further professionalize teaching and to develop means to individualize instruction. Efforts were made to take advantage of new techniques and instructional devices resulting from our advancing technology.

In 1957, Robert Anderson, who directed the SUPRAD (School and University Program for Research and Development) project at Harvard University, pioneered the concept of team teaching at the elementary school level. His efforts received national recognition and resulted in a decided trend toward the use of team teaching in elementary schools.

## Exploring New Uses of Manpower

Much of the effort to improve the quality of schools has centered upon organizational structure and the manner in which educational manpower is utilized in the teaching-learning process. Options other than the typical one-teacher-per-twenty-five students in a self-contained elementary classroom are possible. Likewise, instruction at the secondary level need not be characterized by traditional one teacher/five period teaching assignment. It is possible to conceive roles which are neither self-contained nor departmentalized.

The innovations discussed in the sections that follow involve various attempts being made to more effectively utilize manpower resources in our schools. Although much of the experimentation in instruction is being done by individual teaching, increased strength is provided if more than one person is involved in working on program improvement. Work that is shared appears lighter, and obstacles may more easily be overcome when several people work cooperatively on a given problem. The modern teacher no longer has to work in the isolation of a single classroom but may work with others in planning and providing instruction. The contemporary professional is engaged in the continuous process of evaluation and in searching for improved methods. Education has become a developing field, seeking original solutions to the complex problems associated with individual development.

## Teacher Aides

Teacher aides, or paraprofessionals, have been used in order to increase the effectiveness of the school. By employing housewives or other nonprofessional personnel to handle noneducational tasks, the school frees the teacher to do what he was trained to do: teach. When the teacher has help for nonteaching chores and can devote his attention and time to instruction, learning products are maximized.

A national survey of the use and payment of teacher aides in public schools [265:37–39] revealed that most of the teacher aides are paid for their services, although a significant number work on a voluntary basis. The ten most widespread duties of the teacher aides receiving pay, listed in descending order of frequency, were: duplicating tests and other material; helping with classroom housekeeping; typing class materials, tests, etc.; setting up A-V equipment and other instructional materials; helping with children's clothing; supervising the playground; correcting tests, homework, workbooks, etc.; reading aloud and story telling; assisting in the school library; and collecting money from pupils [265:38].

The use of teacher aides and paraprofessionals enables a teacher to devote more attention and time to instructional responsibilities. *(Photograph by Ron Smith, Courier Tribune, Bloomington, Indiana.)*

The use of teacher aides, or paraprofessionals, is often associated with team teaching. Just as frequent, however, is the assignment of aides to teachers performing more traditional roles, i.e., self-contained or departmental roles. Always the attempt is to seek ways in which maximum use of the teacher's professional skills can be realized and the quality of education received by students enhanced. Although the teacher aide concept was introduced in Bay City, Michigan, in 1952, little progress has been made until very recently in defining the role of such personnel.

## Team Teaching

During the past decade, one of the most significant developments has been the trend toward team teaching. An alternative to the traditional self-contained and/or departmental role, professional faculty work together in teaching teams, each group being responsible for the education of a large group of students.

Just as the team approach has been used in medical clinics and business organizations, a team-teaching situation allows schools to take advantage of the individual talents, interests, and special training of teachers. While there are almost as many definitions of team teaching as there are schools that practice it, the keys to team teaching are variability, individualization, and team planning.

Most team-teaching programs feature variability or flexibility in numbers, space, and time as well as teacher variability. The objective of these variations is to provide a total school environment which encourages and accommodates individualized instruction. In a team-teaching situation teachers will work with large student groups, small groups, and individuals. Room size will vary with group size. Flexibility in length of instructional periods can be arranged to suit the needs of individuals or groups. Most experienced educators will contend that teaming must include regular team planning sessions to be successful.

Beggs [21:29–37] points out that the variety of applications of the team concept is infinite. However, some of the advantages cited for teaming are generally agreed upon. Team teaching allows one teacher to profit from the judgment and advice of his colleague(s) since all the team members plan together and work with the same pupils toward commonly designated objectives. Team teaching provides the opportunity for each member of the team to contribute his parficular strengths to the team's instruction. Teaming is intended to narrow the range of the teacher's preparation for daily class meetings. Thus, it is assumed the teacher's preparation can be sharper and more effective.

In practice the many organizational plans vary tremendously. Two teachers at a grade level may decide to "team," planning together and sharing some aspects of teaching their own classes. A teacher may have the part-time or full-time assistance of a teacher aide in order to teach fifty to sixty students. Two teachers and one aide might have the responsibility for seventy-five to one hundred students. An aide may be assigned to a team of seven teachers. Special teachers may be assigned to assist a team of classroom teachers as the need arises. All the primary grade teachers may constitute a teaching team with self-contained classes in the intermediate grades, or there also may be an intermediate team. Many of these same plans are used at the secondary level, although most secondary team plans are intradisciplinary, while elementary and middle school programs are often interdisciplinary.

Team leadership varies as does the organization. Teams of teachers may have equal rank, status, and responsibility. This was very typical of early attempts at teaming. Teams may also have differentiated rank, status, and responsibility. In this case the leadership of the team may revolve on a time basis or need basis. The leadership may be permanent, with the leader receiving a higher salary as an indication of greater responsibility. This type of leadership is usually associated with differentiated staffing, described in detail in the next section.

Typically noncertified workers may assist a team by handling all the "nonteaching" chores, such as typing, duplicating, collecting lunch money, taking attendance, etc. In many cases aides work with one or more students in a small group following the directions of the professional teacher. Aides are frequently utilized in the library or instructional materials center to help students locate and use materials.

Beginning teachers may be assigned to a teaching team led by one or more experienced teachers. With the addition of one or more student teachers, interns, and one or more aides, the adult/pupil ratio may be reduced effectively.

There are disadvantages to teaming. Not all teachers can participate effectively within a team. Many teachers are unable and unwilling to be exposed to the full view of their peers. Some teachers are unable to cope with the free exchange of ideas, suggestions, and criticisms which is necessary for a team to improve its methods of functioning.

Not all school systems adopting team teaching have provided the time for teachers to meet on a regular basis to plan, coordinate, and evaluate their efforts, and this has proven a costly error. Teaming which provides teachers with group planning periods during the student's school day is admittedly expensive, but worth it when one considers the alternative, which is the ineffective functioning of a team effort because the importance of adequate planning time was not considered.

Many team-teaching programs have failed for lack of a well-planned and well-executed public information program. Community dissatisfaction, brought on by misinformation and lack of information may doom any program to failure before it has had a chance to succeed. It also bears mentioning here that probably more consideration should be given to communicating the efforts of a team (or any innovative group) to its colleagues. Sometimes those not participating in a new effort feel resentment or reservation, which might be forestalled through some sensitive briefing.

Early advocates of teaming felt that teacher time would be saved as the special strengths, capabilities, and talents of each teacher were used, and as large groups freed several teachers for planning or study. In practice it has been found that unless there is an unusually high percentage of time devoted to large group instruction, there is no time saved at all. Even with time saved by the use of paraprofessionals, the increased need for team planning and the consideration given to meeting individual student needs require more time than is needed in non-teaming plans.

Teaming demands particular teacher characteristics. A team teacher needs self-confidence and the willingness to give and receive constructive criticism. He needs to be able to work closely and cooperatively with others. He needs to be committed to improving the broad education of students and be willing to share responsibility for the decisions of the team. The isolation and security provided by a closed classroom door is removed in teaming. The teacher who faces the prospect of teaming should examine his own feelings and attitudes before he accepts such a position.

## Differentiated Staffing

The differentiated staff concept is a natural outgrowth and a refinement of the team-teaching movement that has evolved over the past several years. Whereas most members of teaching teams had similar backgrounds (all members of the primary team were elementary majors, or all members of the high school mathematics team were mathematics majors) as well as identical teaching responsibilities, differentiated staffing emphasizes (as the name itself implies) varying background as well as responsibility in the team operation. An illustration would perhaps be helpful.

Differentiated staffing patterns allows for the many interests, abilities, and ambitions of teachers, the diversity of tasks associated with the teaching act, as well as recognizing the need for auxiliary personnel to relieve teachers of nonprofessional responsibilities. Attention to individual differences among teachers is long overdue.

The first major attempt to implement the differentiated concept took place in Temple City, California, in the fall of 1969. In addition to a desire to improve educational opportunity so that each student might more effectively develop his individual capabilities, two other factors influenced the specific changeover to differentiated staffing: (1) the desire of teachers to have a share in decision making; and (2) the desire of teachers to "shoot for top positions" without going into supervision/ administration. As a result, the Temple City Model developed as indicated in Figure 5–5. In the differentiated staff model, as described by

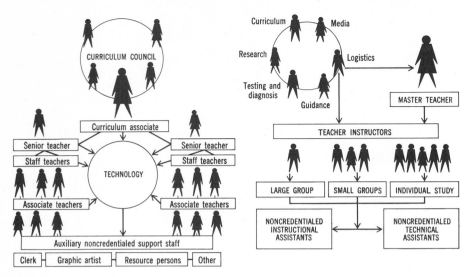

FIGURE 5–5    Two patterns for differentiated staffing. How do these patterns change the organizational structure of the school?

Olivero and Buffie [185:189–225], the master teacher is a districtwide curriculum and research specialist. His job is to keep abreast of all research in new methods, material, and content in a given field and to work with senior teachers in devising pilot projects to test new ideas. Having the equivalent of a doctorate, he teaches 25 per cent of the time and is employed for twelve months at a salary two to three times the salary of a beginning teacher [62:10–12].

A senior teacher serves as a team leader. He is an acknowledged master practitioner, a learning engineer, and a skilled diagnostician of the learning process. He devotes about 50 per cent of his time to teaching. He is responsible for program, for the employment and evaluation of paraprofessionals as well as for student teachers and/or interns, and shares with the principal the responsibility for selection and evaluation of professional colleagues. He possesses a master's degree, or its equivalent. He serves as a member of his school's Academic Senate. Earning about twice as much as a beginning teacher, senior teachers, like master teachers, do *not* have tenure. They may, however, have tenure as staff teachers.

Staff teachers are full-time classroom teachers. They comprise the bulk of the faculty. They are employed for a nine-month year and are paid according to the regular salary scale. Staff teachers must be effective in small, medium, and large group instruction. The bachelor's degree is a minimum requirement.

Associate teachers may be student or probationary teachers, or teaching interns. Their salaries fall below the range of full-time classroom teachers. Auxiliary support personnel include instructional aides and clerks. Aides work with students and teachers in resource centers, learning laboratories, and libraries. A system survey revealed that approximately one-third of the teachers' time was devoted to supervising study activities and other nonteaching tasks. Such activities are now directed by competent paraprofessionals.

The principal, whose noncertified assistant (called a "manager") reconciles the budget, orders supplies and equipment, schedules the buses, runs the cafeteria, etc., is the educational leader of the school. A catalyst, he also chairs the Academic Senate but has only one vote and no veto power.

The Academic Senate, a five-member body of four senior teachers and the principal, is the primary decision-making body in the school. All decisions affecting the school and its policies are made by this group.

Comparable decision making at the district level is made by the Academic Coordinating Council. Master teachers sit on this council, which is chaired by the superintendent. Again, he has but one vote and no veto power.

Early results of this pioneering effort reported in the spring of 1971 were very promising: 93 per cent of the students polled felt they were getting a better education; 83 per cent of the staff indicated that differentiated staffing provided a more effective way of improving instruction [261:153]. Interestingly enough only 50 per cent of the parents favored the program. Superintendent Rand commented that teachers "respond and blossom" under differentiated staffing. An evaluation of this Ford Foundation sponsored effort by the California State Department of Education's Division of Finance disclosed that: (1) staffing costs are no more under this plan; (2) capital outlays for specially constructed buildings may be a little more; and (3) flexible scheduling and supporting services costs depend upon the quality of the services provided.

Like its predecessor, team teaching, it is not likely that any single pattern of differentiated staffing will emerge in the immediate future. Because of the benefits that can be derived, we may expect a considerable amount of exploration with this concept. Dwight Allen [62:4–5] believes that differentiated staffing can produce many positive benefits. Among them:

1. When positions are identified delineating what needs to be done and are assigned on the basis of competence, there will be a basis of salary differentiation on which school boards, administrators, and teachers can agree.
2. Good teachers, who deserve as much money as administrators, will be able to afford a career in classroom teaching.
3. There will be a place for those teachers for whom no amount of money can make up for the lack of job satisfaction.
4. There will be a place for talented teachers who want only limited professional responsibility (e.g., the teaching housewife).
5. Teachers will be able to take postgraduate courses to make themselves more

competent in their specific jobs instead of taking courses on an indiscriminate units-equal-dollars basis.

6. Longevity, with all its educationally crippling effects, would cease to be a criterion for promotion.

7. Inservice teacher training could be an internal program aimed at solving problems at hand rather than problems perceived by someone once or twice removed from the school's student population.

8. Evaluation could be based on real knowledge from intimate contact and cooperation between teaching professionals.

9. Many existing problems in negotiating salaries and existing differences between professional teachers and administrators should disappear in a staff wherein status derives from performance and competence.

10. Young talent would be encouraged to grow.

11. The school would regain some control over apportioning dollars now committed to perpetuating the median rise in salary costs brought about by tenure, longevity, and automatic promotion practices.

12. Colleges could begin to focus on training teachers to handle specific responsibilities and specific teaching skills.

13. Counseling and interpersonal student-teacher relationships could be established at more profound levels of personal choice and personal relevance.

14. The best talent would be free to seek the best alternative teaching techniques, learning modes, and innovations in general through persistent liaison with colleges, universities, and other schools.

Given the changing relationship between supply and demand for teachers as well as the conservative nature of the profession, differentiated staffing is destined to become one of the hottest issues of the seventies. It poses a direct threat to two well-entrenched traditions—the self-contained classroom and the single-salary schedule.

## Flexible and Modular Scheduling

Flexible or modular scheduling is widely associated with secondary schools. This scheduling concept dictates that the frequency, duration, and instructional group size be varied depending on the particular requirements of the content. Traditional class periods are replaced by modules of 15, 20, or 30 minutes. Some classes meet fewer than five times a week. And some of the time pupils are in classes of 7 to 15 pupils; at other times they are in classes of 40 to 150 or more. In addition, pupils in schools utilizing a flexible or modular schedule usually spend part of their day working individually.

In a flexible or modular schedule, the size of each class is determined by the instructional purpose. When the teacher wants to present content, test, or use audio-visual aids, large groups are mandated. When the teacher wants pupils to discuss, verify, question, or react, small groups are scheduled. The large classes usually last no more than 40 minutes, but the small-group classes are likely to last 90 minutes. Some laboratory sessions last for several hours.

Flexible or modular scheduling encourages the use of team teaching. In some schools teachers work mostly with large groups, and in others teachers work almost entirely with small groups. This allows teachers to specialize in those aspects of instruction they can do best.

Figure 5–6 shows a flexible scheduled school. In the flexible organization, the cycle is normally a week in length. In other words, the schedule does not repeat itself for five days. In the traditionally scheduled school, the cycle is the day. Each day's activities are the same as each other day's program.

Flexible or modular scheduling has two prime objectives. First, it is intended to provide the organizational means for teachers to individualize instruction. Pupils can meet with teachers during independent study time. Also, pupils can work for blocks of time on their own or with other pupils on particular problems or projects. Pupils can be excused from content presentations when these are not contributing to their intellectual growth. In this type of scheduling, pupils can become active in discussing, verifying, and working at task-oriented projects and activities. Second, flexible scheduling allows the teacher to use both human and time resources to the advantage of pupils. If one teacher likes to and can present content better than another teacher, then the teacher with this competency can work with more pupils in this way than the traditional schedule allows. If the teacher works best in small groups, then he can spend his time working with pupils in this way.

People learn from activity—from working, discussing, constructing, and experimenting. The flexible schedule provides the opportunity for pupils to be far more active in the learning process than does a traditionally scheduled school. Teachers in the flexible-scheduled school conserve time by giving content presentations once, to a large group of pupils, rather than repeating the presentation to smaller groups. The

FIGURE 5–6   A flexible or modular secondary school schedule.

| | Module | Monday | Tuesday | Wednesday | Thursday | Friday |
|---|---|---|---|---|---|---|
| **8.30** | 1 | Mathematics | Music | Mathematics | Mathematics | Mathematics |
| | 2 | | English | English | | Music |
| | 3 | English | | | English | |
| | 4 | Social studies | Independent study | Physical education | Independent study | Physical education |
| | 5 | | | | | |
| | 6 | | | Science | | Science |
| | 7 | | Lunch | Lunch | | Lunch |
| | 8 | Lunch | Science | Health | Lunch | Independent study |
| | 9 | Science | | | | |
| | 10 | Typing | Independent study | Independent study | Science | |
| | 11 | | | | | |
| | 12 | | | | Music | |
| | 13 | Independent study | Social studies | | | Typing |
| | 14 | | Mathematics | | Social Studies | English |
| **3.30** | 15 | | | Social studies | | |

teacher's time, conserved by taking out the repetition, is used to buy the opportunity for teachers to work with individuals and with small pupil-centered groups.

Many schools using modular scheduling have developed some type of multimedia package—a course designed by the faculty. Students move through this course at individual rates. The "learning packages" are often housed in the library or laboratory.

Flexible scheduling often incorporates the concept of unscheduled or "free" student time. This requires stations or facilities in the building where students can go to relax without disturbing those who are studying. Unscheduled time is credited with creating most of the problems of modular scheduling. Vandalism, skipping, and general time-wasting are not uncommon. These problems can be attacked successfully if the school deals with the individual student violator and refrains from reacting as though all students are guilty.

Flexible schedules are often developed with the use of computers. Schedule determination is just one of the uses of the computer in modern education. Test score analyses, population studies, and other applications of computer technology are being used to provide educators with data with which more intelligent decisions can be made about pupils and the school's program. As computers become more widely available and as educators become more sophisticated in their use, flexible scheduling may become the means of providing a highly personalized, rich, and individual learning program for each student.


## Nongraded Schools

The nongraded school concept refers in part to the absence of specific grade levels, such as grades 6, 7, 8, etc. It is an attempt to eliminate, reduce, or at least minimize the effects of grade-level designations. A major purpose is to encourage teachers to view children as individuals and to abandon the idea of a predetermined lockstep curriculum that is relatively the same for all students. Still another purpose is to remove the unnecessary restrictions on depth, breadth, and rate of children's learning. As with other innovations, the motivation is to help the individual pupil achieve this maximum potential. To achieve this purpose, end expectations must vary for each student, and program accommodations must be made so that a student's progress will be continuous.

Nongradedness is said to meet the needs of individual students more effectively than the graded school does. However, examples of nongraded secondary schools that are fully implemented are rare. It has not been unusual for freshmen to take senior subjects nor for upper classmen to take freshmen or sophomore courses. Is this nongradedness? The answer is no. Eliminating or ignoring grade-level designations is not enough.

Grade level
in which
plan is used

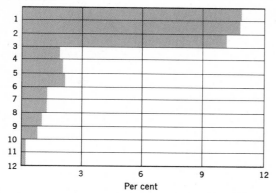

FIGURE 5–7  Percentage of school systems at each grade level using a nongraded form of organization.

The curriculum must be ungraded. Teachers and faculties who want to ungrade their programs must individualize their program and break away from the idea of covering a predetermined sequence of learning. This is a genuine obstacle in most subject-matter centered high schools staffed by specialists.

Melbourne (Florida) High School has been a pioneer in developing a nongraded program. Pupils in the Melbourne High School are not bound by curriculum guides and texts, but they are able to go into a subject with as much breadth or depth as they are able to handle. Teachers work individually with pupils to chart a course of study. Heavy emphasis is put on independent study, where pupils work on their own or with a few others.

Schools using the nongraded organization necessarily must have a wealth of instructional materials, far more than is usually found in the typical school. There is a greater need for resources in the way of specialists and librarians to assist the teacher as he encourages students to use a variety of learning sources.

## Multigrade Grouping

Certain elementary schools which wish to capitalize on the advantages of a plan that minimizes the importance of grade levels and emphasizes individualization have chosen to adopt a program that is known as multigrade grouping. In a multigrade plan the students in each class represent an equal number of first-, second-, third-graders and third-, fourth-, and fifth-graders, or some similar combination. The children of different grade levels are deliberately placed together on a random-selection basis to encourage the teachers and parents to see the students as individuals and not as fourth-graders, second-graders, etc.

Multigrading can be seen as an initial, but substantial, first step toward the development of a nongraded program. Children in a multi-graded plan retain the grade-level designations for record-keeping and report purposes. However, the groupings within the classroom are not on the basis of grade levels.

## Multiage Grouping

Another way of organizing the elementary school to encourage greater personalization of instruction is multiage grouping. This plan calls for classrooms in which children whose ages span three years are placed together on a random-selection, heterogeneous basis with no attempt being made to put students together on the basis of ability or achievement. The age groupings may overlap. There might be one or more classes of seven-, eight-, and nine-year-olds and one or more of nine-, ten-, and eleven-year-olds. This pattern allows administrators greater flexibility in moving students from group to group. The student can easily remain a member of a group for two to three years, and move on to another group which will contain some students of his own age-group. One basic hypothesis of this plan is that a student should have the opportunity, sometime in his school career, to be a member of the youngest, the middle, and the oldest age group in the room.

A multiage grouping plan undoubtedly comes the closest to approaching nongradedness of any grouping plan that has gained prominence.

## Independent Study

While secondary schools have made relatively little progress in developing nongraded programs, their success in offering students the opportunity through independent study to develop unique talents and interests has been more substantial. Nongraded in philosophy, such activity frequently involves the development of instructional materials centers.

Independent study is difficult to describe because it takes so many forms. However, there are basic guidelines which can be used in preparing and facilitating independent study.

1.   The entire faculty and staff should understand the rationale, even though particular people may have no special responsibility for the program. The understanding is necessary for the program to be supported. All teachers, administrators, and counselors should be able to explain and support the project to parents and students. Early

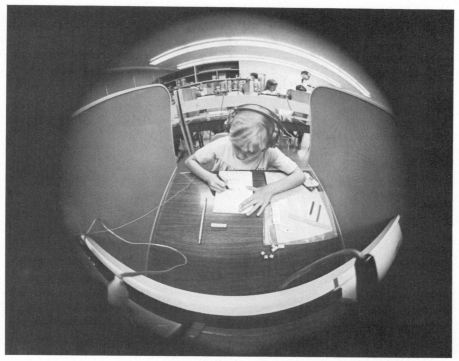

In the privacy of a study carrel, this little girl pursues her independent study project. *(Photograph by Ben Spiegel, National Education Association.)*

and deep involvement of students, parents, and other community members in the rationale of independent study is crucial to its success.

2.  Motivation must be developed. Individual, small-group, and large-group activities should be provided as a way of stimulating student interest and involvement.

3.  Independent study must be taught. Secondary students are often inclined to be overly dependent upon teachers for guidance and supervision. The teacher's objective should be to become less directive as the student's responsibility and self-direction grows. However, it is a teaching assignment and becomes part of the teacher load.

4.  The amount of time each student spends in independent study will vary.

5.  Materials, equipment, personnel, and facilities to support the program must be provided. This calls for programmed material, audio-visual hardware and software, work rooms, and instructional assistants to man workrooms and maintain records.

6.  Evaluation procedures must be developed which reflect the individual student and program goals.

## Other Individualization Plans

New, specific systems of individualized instruction are being developed through the cooperation of local school districts, universities, federal research centers, and private industry. These plans are designed:

Absorbed in the world of sound. In what ways can recordings be used to provide effective learning experiences for students? *(Photograph by Esther Bubley, National Education Association.)*

1.  To allow pupils to work at their own rate.
2.  To encourage initiative and independence.
3.  To increase the pupils' problem-solving abilities.
4.  To encourage self-evaluation.

Individually Prescribed Instruction was developed in the Pittsburgh area schools and by the fall of 1970 was serving 75,000 pupils in 264 schools throughout the country. IPI, a federally supported program, developed most of its own curriculum within the framework of detailed objectives, organization of techniques and materials to attain the objectives, individual pretesting for diagnosis and prescription, daily evaluation and guidance of each student, and constant curriculum evaluation and revision. Proponents of IPI contend that students of all school ages are working independently at different levels of achievement with little or no supervision.

Project PLAN—Program for Learning in Accordance with Needs is a project, similar to IPI, which was developed by Westinghouse Learning

Corporation and American Institutes for Research, and is the nation's second most extensive project to systematically individualize instruction. Unlike IPI, PLAN uses a computer, not to teach, but to make information available on the daily progress of each student.

Both the PLAN and IPI projects are expensive. The costs vary, but the minimum might be as much as an extra $100 per pupil per year. Some IPI projects have run well above that figure. Until the cost can be reduced, the projects will not be expanded rapidly.

## The Dual Progress Plan

The Dual Progress Plan [260:221] was started in schools in Ossining and Long Beach, New York. The theoretical base of this upper-elementary plan consists of four principal elements: (1) the concept of cultural imperatives versus cultural electives; (2) the dual progress of students based on the language arts and social studies; (3) a thorough curriculum reorganization; and (4) changes in preservice teacher education.

Children in grades 3 through 6 retain their grade-level designation in language arts, social studies, and physical education but progress through mathematics, science, music, art, recreation, and health as quickly as their interests and achievements allow. One-half the day is spent with a homeroom teacher in the basic group subjects (language arts, social studies, physical education); the other half is spent with specialists.

## Middle Schools

One current innovation which may eventually have great impact on educational planning, and which certainly seems to challenge conventional organizational patterns, is the emerging middle school program.

The middle school is defined as "a program planned for a range of older children, preadolescents and early adolescents that builds upon the elementary school programs for earlier childhood and in turn is built upon by the high school's program for adolescence" [7:5].

Current literature on the middle school is limited in quantity, and with very few exceptions, limited in its theoretical perspective of the function of middle school education. Most writers see the middle school as a transitional unit between elementary-school childhood education and high-school adolescent education.

Much of the debate concerning the middle school centers on the proper grade levels to be grouped together. This argument presupposes that grade-level designations are the sole appropriate ways of providing horizontal and vertical grouping of students. "The realities of child development defy the rigorous ordering of children's abilities and attainments into conventional graded structure." [103:3]. Boys and girls from 10 to 14 have social, physical, emotional, and mental ranges that make grade-level designations impractical in accommodating their developmental patterns. It would seem that successful middle school programs would tend to emphasize the individuality of students and deemphasize lockstep curriculum offerings.

The middle school organization is growing despite its minimal and frequently inconsistent rationale. Some boards of education are attempting to remedy overcrowding by placing students in middle schools on the basis of availability of space. Integration is a factor in some cities. Population shifts within cities have created abandoned buildings which have been converted to middle schools. The pressure to restore the four-year senior high school has prompted some middle school organization.

There are valid, educationally defensible reasons for establishing middle school programs and these reasons primarily have to do with current understanding of the growth and development of children 10- to 14-years old. The emerging adolescent:

1. is characterized by an increasing awareness of himself and his own physical and intellectual identity.
2. seeks answers about his own personal development and his relations to peer groups.
3. has an exceptional need to understand his own culture.
4. has a heightened interest in self-understanding induced by his own dramatic physical, mental, and emotional changes.

## Prekindergarten Programs

Prekindergarten education, long popular in European countries as a means of providing daytime child care for working mothers, is now being developed in the United States for a variety of reasons. Most of the reasons are closely related to the fact that there are pockets of poverty in an otherwise affluent American society, and children who grow up in the socially and economically lowest levels do not come to school with the skills and ideas that seem to be essential for formal learning. Slum homes do not provide their children with the opportunity to develop the language skills which lead to other school-valued behaviors. Since many of the slum children come from racial minorities, a high proportion of the failure-prone children are nonwhite, and the school becomes a place of failure which reinforces racial prejudice and despair.

Prekindergarten programs for deprived children are generally based on the theory that education must start at a very early age in order to minimize the lack of home orientation to formal learning. There are also those who advocate a radical change in current programs. Slum children have a viable culture, and the schools should recognize this culture and use it in the classroom.

## The Year-round School

With communities showing their impatience toward the rising cost of education, old year-round school plans are being dusted off and reexamined, and new ones are being developed. Some educator groups are turning to the year-round school as a means of providing an answer to the demands of the knowledge explosion. Whatever the reason, year-round schools are seen as a way of adding school facilities and manpower without creating new classrooms.

There is no single year-round plan. There are scores of them. They can be grouped into three basic types: the extended school year, or 11-month plan; the four-quarter plan; and the three-semester plan. Each plan has dozens of combinations.

The extended school year usually calls for a strong summer school program offered on a voluntary basis. This plan calls for little interference with regular programming.

The three-semester plan divides the calendar year into three parts. Students may elect to go two of the three semesters.

The four-quarter plan, with all its variations, is the most familiar year-round program. The school year is divided into four quarters of twelve weeks each with one week of vacation between quarters. Students attend school three quarters and vacation one quarter, giving them approximately 16 weeks of vacation per year. Teachers usually may elect to teach one, two, or three quarters of each year. Some may elect to teach four quarters occasionally.

A very interesting experiment in the use of a year-round school calendar was initiated June 30, 1970, at Romeoville, Illinois, which is a fast-growing community located 35 miles southwest of Chicago. This plan, a compulsory education system for all students in the district, calls for a 45-day (nine week) learning session followed by a 15-day (three week) student vacation [280:42]. The students are scheduled into four groups and are staggered so that only three groups attend school at any one time—reducing the enrollment at any particular time by one-fourth. Although the so-called "45–15 Plan" presents some problems for teachers, school administrators, students, and parents, it holds the promise of being used more extensively.

There are various sources of opposition to the year-round school. The vacation issue creates the most opposition. Year-round schools necessitate that some students take winter, fall, or spring vacations, rather than the traditional summer vacation, or of taking periodically short vacations throughout the year.

Additional opposition is created when it is discovered that year-round schools do not offer immediate cost savings. Year-round schools may mean better educational opportunities for students and may save a community some money by requiring fewer facilities and making better use of manpower; however, year-round schools usually are more expensive to operate on a short-term basis, since the savings in building costs are not readily apparent.

## SUMMARY

Although no two teachers will have identical responsibilities, there are some major responsibilities that are common to the work of all teachers —instruction, student guidance, maintaining discipline, evaluating pupil progress, reporting to parents, cocurricular activities, professional growth, teacher evaluation, and working effectively with other school personnel. In addition to these responsibilities, as well as many others that could have been indicated, the school community expects teachers to show interest in their pupils, to work effectively with the pupils, and to be competent in their subject matter and other assignments. They also are expected to demonstrate attitudes, understandings, and behavior patterns which the community generally has come to associate with teachers. They normally are expected to participate in various community activities, depending in part upon the types of communities in which they are located. They often are expected to serve as better examples for children than parents themselves choose to be. Teaching is an intimate social work. It is a powerful molding force. It is small wonder that those who hire teachers should scrutinize them carefully and set certain standards which they feel must be upheld. Such concern should be interpreted as a tribute and a challenge—a tribute to the significant role of teachers and a challenge to lead the community and all its people to a higher level of living.

Changes are being made in organizational and instructional patterns and procedures. Throughout the country educators are formulating fresh, new approaches to learning. Although the change throughout the nation has not been spectacular, we can expect, in the years to come, greater use of teacher aides, team teaching, differentiated staffing, flexible scheduling, nongraded classrooms, multiage grouping, independent study, and year-round school calendars. It is highly probable that the middle school will tend to replace the junior high school, and that prekindergarten programs will become accepted as an integral part of our public school system. These innovative practices undoubtedly will change the role of the teacher and hopefully will provide more efficient use of educational manpower resources.

## QUESTIONS TO CONSIDER

1. In what ways does the work of a teacher in a large school differ from the work of a teacher in a small school?

2. How might teachers be relieved of some of the time-consuming routine duties, so that they might have more time to devote to the truly professional aspects of teaching?
3. In your opinion how should the progress of pupils be evaluated?
4. What do you consider to be the best way(s) of reporting the progress of pupils to their parents?
5. Some parents (and teachers) feel that the school provides too many cocurricular activities. How do you account for this feeling? What position will you take? Why?
6. It is frequently pointed out that most teachers who lose their jobs do so not because of lack of knowledge in their teaching fields but because of lack of ability in working with others. To what extent do you feel this statement is correct and why?
7. If teachers are to be considered "professionals," to what extent are parents justified in expecting teachers to be better examples for pupils than the parents choose to be?
8. In what ways may a teacher be able to serve as a public relations agent for his school?
9. How is the role of the teacher affected in the use of each of the following practices:
   a. Teacher aides
   b. Team teaching
   c. Differentiated staffing
   d. Flexible or modular scheduling
   e. Nongraded school
   f. Independent study
10. What advantages and disadvantages do you see in the middle school?
11. What are the arguments for and against providing prekindergarten experiences for children?
12. What are the pros and cons of year-round public schools?

## PROBLEM SITUATION FOR INQUIRY

Sally Smith, an attractive first-year high school English teacher, was furious. She had just left the principal's office after receiving a lecture regarding her personal appearance in the classroom. The chief complaint, no matter how Dr. Thompson had disguised it, was that her skirts were too short and her hairdos too exotic. The principal had not criticized her teaching methods. In fact, he told her that the extra help she was giving some of the slower readers after school was commendable.

Just what *was* wrong about wearing clothes that were in style? The girls in her classes seemed pleased that they had such a "cool" teacher. And if the boys took more than an academic look at her, they kept their thoughts to themselves.

Dr. Thompson had argued that any normal, red-blooded American boy might be "turned on" by the "accentuated" dress of a very attractive young lady, and that the boys might pay more attention to her physical appearance than to what she was teaching.

But was there evidence that the boys were not learning English? Had they done worse on the departmental exams? Had anyone made a pass at her, or come up with a wolf whistle, or tried to date her?

Dr. Thompson had indicated that he was concerned over what the boys and girls might say to their parents—not that such talk would be malicious. Quite the opposite. Student comments would probably be favorable, but what would the parents think of a school which had a dress code enforced by the students which was being violated by one of the teachers?

Sally was in a real dilemma. She liked teaching at Jefferson. She liked the students, the other faculty members, and her teaching assignments. In fact, she thought she liked Dr. Thompson until this incident occurred. But she also enjoyed her freedom to wear what she pleased and to look as she pleased. She could see no harm being done. If you were Sally, what would you do? Why?

## ACTIVITIES TO PURSUE

1.  Spend as much time as you can for two or three days in succession observing the same teacher and class in school. Make a careful record of the duties the teacher performs. Try to identify those responsibilities which are most important. Examine those selected to determine whether they are of the mechanical or the leadership and human relations type.

2.  Compare the daily schedule of classes of a small high school with that of a large high school. What differences do you observe in the number and variety of offerings? Consider both the regular curriculum and the cocurricular activities. How do the educational opportunities for pupils in the two schools compare in terms of available offerings? Which areas of teaching and learning appeal to you most? Why?

3.  Become acquainted with a social or religious organization which serves children or youth in your community. Make several observations of the group at work. What relationships do you observe between the youngsters and the adult leaders of the group? Between the adult leaders and the parents of the youngsters? What similarities do you find between this situation and teaching in the public schools?

4.  Discuss the problems of discipline with various teachers. Try to ascertain the principles that guide them as they deal with the various kinds of discipline problems.

5.  Visit a number of modern classrooms and note improvements in the construction of school plants and equipment. Discuss with your colleagues how these improvements may help the teacher in meeting the educational needs of pupils today.

6.  Through the use of the checklist in the Resource Section for Part II, appraise one or more of your former teachers to see how well each fulfilled his public relations function.

7.  If possible, spend some time observing in schools that are using team teaching, differentiated staffing, flexible or modular scheduling, teaching machines, nongraded classrooms, and individually prescribed instruction. Talk with the teachers as well as students about the advantages and disadvantages of these innovative practices.

# 6 | EDUCATIONAL TECHNOLOGY, CHANGE, AND TRANSITION

Education at all levels stands on the threshold of a major technological revolution, and this revolution will affect more than the length of the school day or school year; it could transform the schools tremendously. New technology could bring about demands for a reexamination of the teaching-learning process, new visions of schools and of school construction, and totally new concepts of the role of the professional educator.

Research and careful observation have revealed that students have different learning styles; some students learn by reading, others by listening, and most by both reading and listening. Books and other visuals are needed for reading. Audio equipment is needed to develop listening skills. A combination of sight and sound materials help with reading and listening. Despite the relatively undeveloped current state of the art of technology, it can be said that the next decade will undoubtedly bring the development and deployment of expensive and inexpensive teaching tools that will encourage radical changes in education.

The aim of this new technology is not primarily to replace the teacher but to give the teacher and the student the necessary tools that will add new dimensions to learning. These new tools will allow the teacher to set up a support system of technological aids which can encourage exciting new ways of organizing for learning.

The newer technological resources now available are largely a by-product of the large expenditures that have been made for defense and for the exploration of space. Education is now in a position to profit from the research and experiences that private industry and the government have had in these areas of exploration [277:1].

It is obvious that ideas for advancement in educational technology will come from many sources. Schools will learn to make better use of the technology they currently have available and will strive to make use of new equipment and materials as they are produced. In this section we

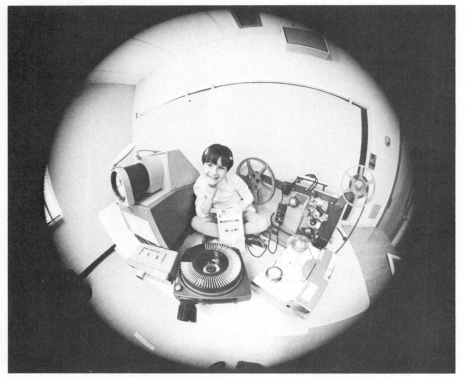

The use of a wide variety of audio-visual material enables teachers to provide more effective learning experiences for students. *(Photograph by Joe Di Dio, National Education Association.)*

will examine some of the well-established technological innovations as well as the technology of the future.

## Programmed Learning

The classroom teacher has often devised special practice materials for pupils or has selected appropriate exercises from available workbooks for pupils needing additional work. This is not new, nor is recognition of the fact that pupils need to know the immediate results of their work in order to make corrections and proceed effectively. Textbooks and workbooks with answers in the backs of the books are not new either. Having such material already prepared in a systematic way, based on principles coming from the experimental laboratories and available to the pupil to use independently, is new in the sense that machine-type instruction has now been put to wide use. Allowing students to proceed at their own pace for drill work or even original instruction from programmed material frees the teacher to do what he can do best in person: guide the educational growth of pupils.

The teaching machine, a mechanical device introduced a decade ago, is used to help the pupil learn. The machine, however, is of value only in terms of the program it contains. The learning program, housed in the teaching machine, divides organized information into small parts or frames. A user of a learning program goes from one to another related but more advanced piece of information. Immediately the pupil knows whether he has mastered the information being studied, because the learning program gives feedback on what was previously learned.

The promise of programmed learning through the use of teaching machines is greater for the future than is its current ability to help teachers. Too few programs have been developed, and to date the content of most teaching-machine programs has placed too much emphasis on factual materials.

## The Computer

As a result of Project PX, one of the best kept secrets of World War II, the modern electronic computer was born. It now became possible for man to go to the moon and beyond and to envision major breakthroughs and achievements in virtually every field of human endeavor.

Data processing, well established in business and industry since the first computer was put on the market in 1950, has begun to make its appearance on the educational scene. In addition to the use of data processing in school business offices and for class scheduling, computers are now being used as instructional tools.

An important function of educational computers of the future will be information retrieval. "An information retrieval (IR) system can be defined as a man-machine system combining human intelligence and electronic and photocopying equipment for the purpose of gathering, classifying and storing factual and textual material, and for retrieving and disseminating this information upon demand" [35:61].

Computer-based IR systems will be used in automating libraries and eliminating all cumbersome record filing. Students, teachers, administrators, counselors, as well as librarians, will eventually use IR systems in carrying a wide variety of administrative and learning tasks.

Stanford University opened the first computerized elementary school classroom at Palo Alto, California, in 1966, where first-grade students were aided in reading and in mathematics through the use of the computer. The Stanford music department has had favorable results in using the computer to teach pitch to singers. A professor at Florida State University has developed a computer-assisted instruction course to teach introductory college physics. Personnel at the University of Connecticut have developed a means of computer analysis of English compositions.

Other projects are attempting computer production of braille materials from print for blind children. These are merely a few of the examples of the vast amount of exploration that is taking place in computer technology [49:1–3].

The "talking typewriter" is the name given to a multisensory (sight, sound, touch), multimedia, fully synchronized computer-based learning system. It is designed to teach reading, writing, spelling, speech, and other language arts skills. Information is presented both by sight and sound. It has been used effectively with seriously handicapped students in special classes [67:31].

Computer-assisted instruction, whether in music, mathematics, science, reading, foreign language, or whatever, is based on the theory that a well-programmed computer can provide individualized and flexible instruction. Slow or fast students can move from one topic to another through materials that can be independently controlled for each student. The theoretical limits of the computer's ability to teach are defined only by the limits of man's creativity. However, there is one dramatic disadvantage to computer-assisted instruction that promises to limit the spread of this activity. The costs are exceedingly high. Computer hardware, installation, service, programming, and operations are costing millions today at the experimental stages. It will take, conservatively, hundreds of millions of dollars to allow all students to benefit from the advantages described for computer-assisted instruction. It is for this reason that, despite all the national publicity about computer-assisted instruction (CAI), very few teachers are actually involved with this very creative and innovative effort. Computer instruction, where it is utilized, usually takes place in large school systems, more often in the Northeast and Midwest than in the Southeast and West. Mathematics is by far the most popular subject for computer programming [182:158].

## Educational Television

Educational television (ETV) was widely proclaimed a decade ago as a panacea for education. It is apparent now that ETV is far from the total answer to educational problems, although its use is an accepted part of educational technology throughout the country and is especially strong in certain areas. "ETV enjoys a phenomenally high adoption rate in Michigan" [278:2]. ETV is so widespread throughout the nation that there are efforts to coordinate the study of its problems on a national scale. Some educators and students complain about poor programming. Hardware problems (e.g., no back-up equipment, not enough receivers, inadequate sound) have interfered with many projects. Poor coordination of content and schedules has reduced the effectiveness of many ETV projects.

ETV is a potentially good tool. Millions of dollars are being spent annually to provide better programs, to improve equipment, to train classroom teachers and television teachers, and to make good programs more accessible.

The many studies of ETV indicate that it is an effective teaching tool. When ETV is compared to face-to-face instruction, the achievement of students proves to be just as good [278:2]. In certain circumstances ETV is more effective. Some science classes use television to enlarge and project exhibits under a microscope that could not be seen by a regular class. Television is being used, on an experimental basis, in conjunction with computers. The student requests information from a central resource area, dialing the computer through a telephone network, and receives his information almost instantly on an individual television screen.

The educational potential of television has been realized most successfully by "Sesame Street." A federally supported project, this children's program, aimed primarily at preschoolers, has been shown throughout the country. A year-long study of preschool age children in many different types of environments was conducted by Educational Testing Service, an independent agency. Not only did "Sesame Street" reach its intended audience (7 million out of a potential viewing group of 12 million), but teaching and learning were effective, as represented by pre- and post-test scores relating to thirty specified objectives [235:2].

Closed circuit television is spreading in use throughout the country. Currently it is being used at all levels of education, but especially in secondary schools and in colleges and universities. Transmitting stations are set up in a single school or within a school system, and they usually link the transmission point with several classrooms. With some programs on video tape, the teacher can select the ideal time for the presentation rather than being forced to change his entire schedule to accommodate the television schedule. It is also possible to use the services of one teacher to serve students in several classrooms. Some classrooms and auditoriums are equipped with devices that enable the viewing students to relay questions to the teacher.

Satellite television programming may be used in Alaska, the first state to make such an attempt. A huge state, covering the areas of Texas, California, and Montana combined, Alaska has less than 300,000 people and is the only state without educational television. A satellite located 20,000 miles above the equator, beaming live television signals, could be used to provide commercial radio and television, telephone, computer and data-processing services, as well as educational television [131:37].

Still another variation is the use of Cable TV (CATV) in which TV programs may be transmitted from a local station over coaxial cables to classrooms, homes, hospitals, libraries, and the like [131:38]. School systems may utilize much of their own equipment; i.e., closed-circuit television cameras and video tape recorders, in developing programs to transmit over Cable TV.

The most extensive working relationship established between a local CATV operator and a school system is to be found in Long Island, New York [131:38–39]. An area educational service center SCOPE (Suffolk County Organization for the Promotion of Education) has produced a variety of special programs. To name but a few: (1) "Let's Talk Cents"—a video tape dealing with school budgets; (2) video taping of over 35 educational conferences, workshops, seminars; (3) 100 free films were video taped and sent to CATV for local showing; (4) special video taped production relating to drugs and narcotics; (5) production of student-made films, the best of which will be video taped and shown over CATV; (6) production of 20 slide-tape sets of field trips in the community.

## Other Media

It may be decades before all teachers have the assistance of a computer to aid in teaching; however, scarcely any teacher will be expected in the 1970s to rely solely on textbooks, chalkboards, and simple visual aids as teaching tools. Most beginning teachers can expect to have available a wide variety of educational films and filmstrips, audio tapes and records, individualized equipment for science instruction, special-purpose equipment for reading instruction, overhead and special purpose projectors, and even closed circuit television in addition to the more commonplace instructional television. Furthermore, it can be assumed that current audio-visual software and hardware will be redesigned and modified and adapted to specific learning strategies.

The electronic laboratory is an example of technology that has undergone much change since it was first introduced. Electronic laboratories are to be found in most secondary schools and in some elementary schools. Originally it was a simple system, which allowed a pupil to hear taped presentations and then called for him to make a response. The electronic learning laboratories were designed to be used most frequently in foreign language instruction but were also used for instruction in reading, speech, shorthand, and other areas.

The purpose of the electronic laboratory was to enable the student to go through selected content at his own pace. It provided him the opportunity to play back what he had heard previously. The repetition reinforced what he had learned.

An interesting adaptation of the electronic laboratory concept is the electronic and class piano. These spinet-sized pianos are powered electronically and connected to a teacher's console piano. Using headsets, the students hear only their own playing or instructions from the teacher. The teacher can instruct students individually, in groups, or by class. The electronic piano can be used to supplement voice training or can be used for regular keyboard instruction. The pianos never require tuning.

Students in primary school and adult education can use them. Their potential for individualized instruction is very appealing.

Many schools, especially at the secondary level, are now using a multimedia, package-approach to instruction. Learning packages prepared by teachers include sight and sound media. A science package, for example, might contain slides, 8-mm film loops or a 16-mm film, audio-tapes and/or filmstrips. The student would use the package as often as· needed in a library type carrel. Such instructional packages are becoming commonplace in science, humanities, foreign language, and social studies departments. These electronic packages are only as good as the content of the programs housed within them and that content depends upon the availability of materials and the initiative, industry, and creative planning of teachers.

To aid students and faculty in gaining immediate access to a wide variety of audio and video type materials, attempts are being made to develop and implement a plan called Dial Access Information Retrieval System. Utilizing a coaxial television cable system connecting a main center with various terminals located in individual schools, electronic switching systems will be used to bring together the student and whatever material he is seeking.

When the film comes in cartridges, young students can use a projector easily in the pursuit of their educational interests and needs. *(Photograph by Esther Bubley, National Education Association.)*

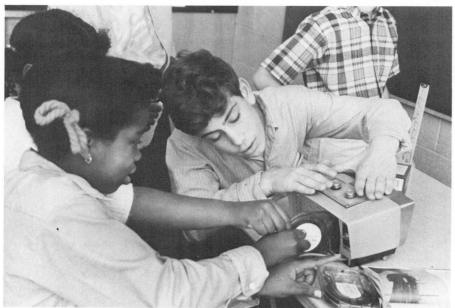

In order to use the dial-access system, a student first dials the program desired, according to the number listed in a card file. He then views and listens to the content presentation. This type of technology may be used for presentation of any programmed material for enrichment, reinforcement, or for make-up purposes, by means of which the student is able to study at his own rate and level of sophistication. *(Photograph by Esther Bubley, National Education Association.)*

Manufacturers have placed a major emphasis on developing and marketing equipment and materials, hardware and software, that can be operated and used by students of all ages with a minimum of damage and breakdown. The cassette tape recorder, which avoids the frustration of fumbling with delicate tapes and can be loaded and unloaded by very young students, offers great advantages to classroom teachers. Storage is simple, and damage can be reduced to a minimum.

Other recent developments in communication media include the use of portable video tape recorders. At the moment the recorders are used chiefly for improving professional performance, particularly that of the beginning teacher. Video-tape playbacks of the teacher-in-action can be analyzed for a variety of purposes. The potential advantages of this medium for aiding students in performance-oriented activities are great.

Rapid progress is being made in the development and use of video tape cassettes. In the foreseeable future, television sets in homes and in schools will be equipped to use cassettes. There is an enormous potential use of these cassettes for independent study, not only for the education of youth but also in the area of continuing education.

## SCHOOLS IN TRANSITION

Change in American education comes on a broken front. For example, while some schools are attempting to move from an 8–4 plan to a 6–3–3 organization, other schools are developing highly-sophisticated middle schools. Still other school districts are concentrating on the development of educational parks which will put all district schools on one site. Although the self-contained classroom still is the predominant organizational pattern in elementary schools, many educators are advocating nongraded, multiage groups, and other responsible professionals are pointing toward differentiated staffing as the best means of deploying educational manpower.

New buildings of revolutionary design are being erected in some districts—buildings designed for flexibility in space and number of students per group, and equipped to utilize the latest technological advancement. However, most new school construction has not departed radically from the familiar egg-crate design that has characterized school buildings for the past century.

The effects of desegregation attempts, urban blight, overpopulation, and demands for community control of the schools are being felt by a majority of school systems. These are important examples of the many social forces that are generating questions about the purposes of education and questions about educational practice. While few school systems are faced with all these problems, no school is completely isolated from them and the changes they foster.

Although the innovations described in this as well as in the previous chapter seem impressive, the extent to which these innovations have affected the mainstream of the educational enterprise is limited. For example, Fred T. Wilhelms, Executive Secretary of the Association for Supervision and Curriculum Development, reported in 1968 that efforts toward team teaching, despite the warnings of Anderson and Trump regarding role clarification and responsibility, had more often than not been reduced to nothing more than departmentalized teaching [205:19]. He noted further that the Trump Plan (large group, small group, independent study) had seldom been achieved in its entirety. Despite widespread development of public educational television, evidence of increased achievement on the part of students simply has not been forthcoming.

In their book, *Behind the Classroom Door,* Goodlad and Klein [104] report upon a study they had made of 67 schools in 13 states in which they evaluated 150 K–4 classrooms against 10 reasonable expectations concerning educational innovations. Among other things, these researchers hoped to find: (1) clear-cut educational objectives; (2) a wide assortment of instructional materials; (3) individualized instruction; (4)

flexible standards for evaluating and reporting student programs; and (5) expanded curricula drawing from projects in mathematics, science, and the social studies. They found that many, if not most, of the highly recommended and publicized educational innovations of the 1960s had not reached the classroom. Teachers and principals understand little regarding such innovative practices. Supporting Wilhelm's observations, they found that team teaching was too often just departmentalization; nongrading was a form of homogeneous grouping; new content was being taught by the same old methods. Teachers still focused on content—as a goal. Covering "x" amount of material, rather than helping students achieve educational objectives which are carefully specified, still appeared to be the central thrust of an "education." Lectures, recitations, textbooks, and workbooks continued to characterize instruction, which was still group-oriented rather than being individualized [130:121].

## The Problem of Change

The question may be asked, "Why have these exciting innovative practices and technological advancements not penetrated our educational structure to a greater extent than seems to be the case?" Undoubtedly there are a number of reasons, one of which is the fact that most individuals tend to resist change. Change tends to threaten or upset our sense of security. It necessitates adaptation, adjustment, and creative thought. It is so much more comfortable to continue operating in terms of well-established patterns. Although change is an inevitable component of life, few of us have been educated in such a manner which allows us to live comfortably and creatively with change—and especially with the accelerating rate of change that characterizes life in today's world.

A number of educators are concerned about the effects of rapid change upon the mental and emotional health of people—and teachers are people. In commenting upon "the premature arrival of tomorrow," Shane states that [239:191–192]:

The pressure of increasing knowledge and a growing awareness on the part of the thoughtful human that he must assume personal responsibility for the futures that are being created can be a severe strain on the individual's mental and emotional health. But perhaps an even more unsettling problem which deserves study is what the rate of change in our lives today is doing to people—especially in industrially advanced areas such as the U.S. where many new techno-, bio-, psycho-, and sociofutures are rapidly taking shape.

Let us look with care at the significance of change—at the same time keeping in mind its manifold possibilities and problems for the curriculum developer.

Suppose that one of our remote ancestors lived 50,000 years ago in the Yantze River Valley, or in the once-fertile Lake Chad area, or in a Swiss lake village cluster, or in the Dordogone Valley caves of France. If his offspring, and their children through the centuries, had lived to be 60 to 65 years old they would represent an unbroken genetic chain of 799 forebears; a chain in which a man who is 60 years old today would be the eight hundredth living link.

*In the last three decades of the 800th man's life, more changes have taken place than occurred during the previous 799¹/₂ lifetimes!*

Julius Caesar probably would have been able to understand rather quickly the lives and artifacts as they existed in the 799th man's world of 1910. However Caesar and the 799th man both would be at a loss to understand computers, the uses of atomic power, or the sophisticated technologies that are involved when man travels in space.

From an historical point of view, it seems reasonable to say that for the first time in the history of the human race man has been propelled from yesterday into tomorrow with no familiar "today" during which to become acclimated to change. We have encountered the future so rapidly, and with such violent changes in the ordered familiar patterns of our way of life, that we are suffering from what Toffler aptly called ". . . the dizzying disorientation brought on by the premature arrival of the future."

The fact that half of the biotechnical changes of the last 50,000 years have come about in the past 30 is especially important because of what this transition has done to people. Many of the changes have rendered useless the "maps" of the cultural terrain with which most persons over 30 years of age were provided by their upbringing prior to 1950.

The "dizzying disorientation" referred to by Toffler in his book *Future Shock* [282] is certainly reflected in our reactions to educational innovation. Too frequently changes in organizational structure and the use of technology may be considered to be panaceas for something that seems to be wrong or inadequate. As a result, efforts may be made to lengthen the school year; start school earlier; replace the junior high school with the middle school; go to large group/small group/ independent study patterns of instruction; try educational television; experiment with programmed materials or adopt a modern mathematics series. Yet the gap between expectations and reality remains alarmingly wide. Why?

Innovative efforts, by accident or design, have not generally centered upon people and the changing of their behavior or their roles. And the result is that relatively little success has been achieved. People are the key to change. Only people can make decisions and determine purposes. And the matter of purpose could well be the missing element in the whole enterprise.

Consider questions related to the affective/cognitive domains, or priorities related to matters of process and content. Many people believe today that the way students feel is as important as what they know or can do: how do they feel about themselves (self-concept); how do they feel and behave toward others (humanism)?

Programs focusing upon cognitive development, when viewed in its knowledge (content) and basic skill dimensions, result in certain types of programming. To predetermine a given amount and kind of content to be learned by all is a position quite different from that associated with a view that content is a means to an end, that different kinds of content can be used to help students develop an understanding of generalizations, principles, broad understandings common to all areas or topics under study.

A "basic skill" oriented program is very different from one which

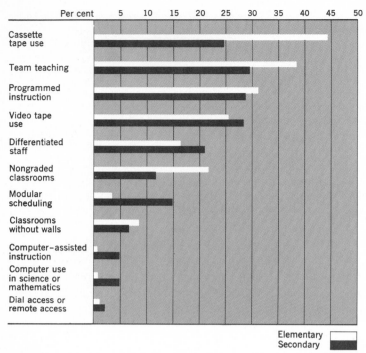

FIGURE 6–1    Per cent of elementary and secondary schools throughout the United States using newer techniques of instruction.

stresses rational development and creative thought; one which envisions tomorrow as being a quite unpredictable world—complex, and demanding of people who will deal rationally and creatively with problems unknown and undreamed of today. Such process considerations may well be expanded to include such considerations as self-evaluation and the development of personal responsibility and self-discipline for much of one's own learning.

Is it any wonder that when some form of technology, or some new organizational scheme, is put into effect, it may be dropped later? This usually occurs when there is no central purpose to sustain the effort when the going gets rough. Commitment to purpose is a primary motivating force. Significant and lasting change is *not* likely to take place without dealing with this question. Goodlad and Klein's research is very alarming in this regard, for it is all too evident that little attention, or even recognition, is given to the question—of what is worth learning and for what purpose. For the most part, education still consists of covering material, of establishing fixed standards for all, of moving through material toward those standards at a fixed rate for all.

Most of the new ideas and innovative materials have merit—*when* used to help students achieve particular kinds of purposes or objectives. Programmed learning is excellent when skill development and understanding of certain kinds of content are central to the effort. If goals related to rational development through inquiry and creative thought or something related to humanism are a concern, then programmed learning materials are not apt to be very appropriate. Ideas and materials used for inappropriate purposes result in little payoff.

Another major factor, which certainly is related to the first, is the lack of any real concern or commitment to the process of evaluation. Unless educational objectives are specified in clear-cut terms, it is virtually impossible to assess the extent to which progress is being made in achieving the objectives. All of us need to receive feedback, in reasonably objective terms, that what we are doing makes a difference, that it is worth all the time and energy that faculty and students are putting forth. Should such data not be forthcoming, then people predictably will not continue to exert much energy or try to improve.

Evaluation is also the process by which accountability can be established. The typical American teacher receives little, if any, professional criticism at any point in his professional career. Student teachers typically complain that they do not get constructive criticism from either their cooperating teachers or college supervisors; beginning and/or experienced teachers frequently indicate that they receive little of value from supervisors, consultants, etc.. As a result of ineffective supervisory practices, some of these supervisory positions, particularly in large cities, are being eliminated. Too much time and effort have been devoted to establishing and maintaining a happy social atmosphere, while tough-minded, hard-nosed assessment, which should be an integral part of one's professional activities, has been avoided.

There are growing signs that accountability can no longer be avoided. National assessment, bitterly opposed by virtually all professional organizations in the early and middle sixties, has finally become a reality. The first results began to emerge as the decade of the seventies got underway.

Interest in performance contracting is growing—a situation in which school systems contract with *business* regarding certain aspects of the school's program, i.e., reading and/or mathematics. Business *guarantees* student progress or else full payment for services rendered need not be forthcoming. Some school boards are moving toward performance contracting, which was initially funded by the federal government.

The use of educational vouchers—a situation whereby parents can enroll their children in a school of their choice by submitting a voucher to the school so that reimbursement for services rendered may be made—is still another attempt to establish some form of accountability. Should state and/or federal support of private schools become a factor, perhaps via an educational voucher system, then an alternative to public education could for the first time be universally available to the American public.

The American public is becoming increasingly sympathetic to the idea of alternative choices as is indicated by the growing number of private schools. In addition, so-called "free schools" are growing in number, particularly in Boston and San Francisco. These schools, inspired by the development of the British Infant Schools and the ideas of Jean Piaget, with their emphasis upon creativity and the development of self, numbered in the hundreds at the start of the seventies. Should events such as these show continued success, then accountability will become a reality of life with which educators must contend.

The topics of national assessment, performance contracting, and vouchering will be discussed in greater detail in later sections of this book. They are mentioned at this point primarily to indicate changes that are taking place in the American educational scene at a time when there might seem to be considerable resistance upon the part of many teachers to change, to innovate in terms of clear-cut purposes, to evaluate in terms of well-conceived performance objectives, to be genuinely concerned with the relevance and quality of education for youth today. In reading Chapter 14, which is concerned with the historical development of our schools, note what happened to the Latin Grammar Schools and the Academy when those institutions failed to be responsive to change. To what extent might some of our public schools be facing the same destiny as those earlier institutions?

## Tomorrow's Schools

Changes in the schools of the future are certain to take place. How extensive such changes will be is difficult to predict. These changes undoubtedly will reflect technological advances, organizational change, and new curricular emphases. The current emphasis on research, interest in innovative programs, and the development of new practices will make the schools significantly different, even from the most modern of today. As Locke points out [148:44]:

The most encouraging sign is that educational research is finally beginning to lead instead of follow educational experimentation. Almost all of the classroom innovations introduced in the United States after World War II—the use of audiovisual materials, language labs, educational television, and even flexible scheduling—were developed without the benefit of research into the processes of learning. Some of these ideas succeeded, but not because they rested on a foundation of research; rather because they happened to match some obvious needs. The first instructional innovation to be developed by people with a background in educational psychology and research was programmed instruction, which for that reason has more potential than many of the early developments.

Although an accurate picture of tomorrow's schools cannot be seen in detail, some obvious trends are in evidence. As examples, the school of the future will be characterized by its focus on the individual. Group teaching methods will tend to give way to personalized teaching. The teacher will become more sensitive to variations among learners, and to the educational needs of multi-ethnic groups. And the teacher's role will change. In the school of the future the teacher will tend to become a diagnostician, prescriber, and resource person, instead of a group teacher. Paraprofessionals, flexible schedules, and independent study will result in the self-contained classroom becoming less self-contained. These trends are apparent today.

School facilities will be vastly different. More space in schools will be fashioned into laboratories and individual work stations. Less space will be used for classrooms, as pupils spend increased time working on their own and meeting in small groups. Large lecture rooms will be outfitted for presentations by teachers. In these areas the appeals will be made to the pupil's sense of sight, as well as to his sense of hearing. The

FIGURE 6–2   The Valley Winds Elementary School in suburban St. Louis is an example of the innovations being made in the designing of school buildings. The school building is shaped like a snail's shell with classrooms radiating from a central core. It is air-conditioned, is carpeted throughout, and has giant-sized classrooms to accommodate the ungraded curriculum.

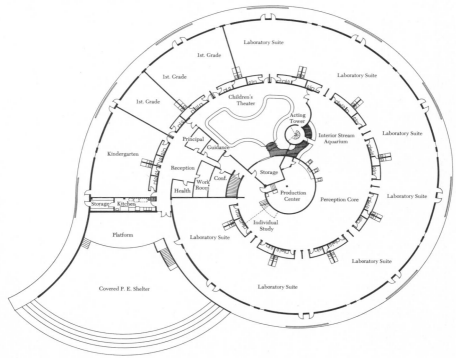

community beyond the walls of the school will offer educational facilities.

The largest area in the school will be the instructional materials center. Here all the advances of technology will be harnessed for aiding pupils. For example, dial-access systems, whereby pupils can retrieve information through a screen and earphone set, will be housed in the instructional materials center. Rich storehouses of books and booklets will be available in every school, and study carrels, small stations giving privacy on three sides, will be used by pupils as they accumulate understandings and develop skills. The length of the class period, the school day, and the school year will be varied and suited to the individual student's learning pattern. A major emphasis will be placed on developing independent learners instead of students overly dependent on teachers. Group processes will be familiar to pupils at all levels of the educational system.

New ways of financing American public education will be required in order to capitalize fully on the advantages possible through selective use of technology for well-defined purposes. Greater participation by the federal government seems likely, and such activity will necessitate a reordering of national priorities and commitment.

More and more, content will be viewed as a means to an end. A better balance between content *and* process—unique, discovery, and problem-solving activities particularly—will emerge. Independent learning and self-evaluation will also be stressed. Content emphases will focus upon broad understandings, generalizations, principles, and properties, in contrast to discrete information so often stressed today.

Public education undoubtedly will be extended past the twelfth year into post-high school vocational and junior or community/regional college programs. Programs for children below kindergarten age will be common. It is quite possible that children will start school around age three and continue studying regularly the rest of their lives.

Conditions of teaching will change substantially. In addition to increases in compensation and in insurance and retirement benefits, teachers will have more and better tools with which to work. Accompanying these improvements will be a demand for continuing in-service education. The teacher of the future will be a more highly trained and skilled professional than today's teacher. Focus in teacher education programs will be upon developing carefully specified competencies. Such competencies may quite predictably be used at some point in the future as a basis for certification. Performance-based teacher certification is already being developed in sixteen states [182:158].

Though problems of learning will continue to exist, special education classes for the retarded may gradually disappear. Although their potentialities are only beginning to be realized, developments in chemistry and biochemistry will not only extend and influence our understanding of the learning process and the mind of man but may be used to control certain hereditary deficiencies of children.

The constant for the future will be change. The continuing quest will be for improvement. Added resources for education, society's demand for fully educated people, and a developing profession will be the means for shaping the new schools of the future.

## SUMMARY

Education at all levels stands on the threshold of major technological changes that could transform educational practices, school organization, and the role of the teacher. Undoubtedly in the schools of the future, extensive use will be made of programmed learning, computer-associated instruction, computer class scheduling, closed-circuit television, cable television, cassette tape recorders, video-tape cassettes, dial-access information retrieval systems, electronic laboratories, and multimedia learning packages.

The function of this new technology is not primarily to replace the teacher, but to give the teacher and the student the necessary tools that will add new dimensions to learning. It is highly probable in the years to come that much of the kind of learning taking place in schools today will be accomplished by the students in their homes. Time spent in school will be directed more toward humanizing types of experiences—gaining skill in working together, communicating, inquiring, discovering, valuing, and developing a consistent and reasoned point of view toward life. As a result, the role of the teacher will become more truly professional— calling for a high degree of expertise in guiding the educational growth of each student.

Change in educational practices takes place on a broken front. Teachers in some school systems already are exploring the use of a number of technological resources. Many other teachers prefer to be unaffected by the possible use of these resources. With the normal human penchant for the status quo and a fondness of the "good old days," it is not at all disquieting to perceive that the educational process of change should be painfully slow. At the same time, the general public is concerned with quality education, as well as with the mounting costs of public education. Questions are being raised about educational assessment and accountability. Industry is evidencing interest in applying its expertise in the use of technology to the field of education. Undoubtedly these forces will stimulate more educators to explore the applications of technology to their work.

The rash of innovative and inventive measures for improving our educational scene during the past several years at times may have appeared to be sporadic, frenzied, disorganized, and discouraging. But this seems to be characteristic of change. The important thing is that educators are beginning to sift through the realizations of how best to proceed, and priorities are beginning to emerge.

The rapidity of change in the future will be many times that found in the past fifteen crowded years. Sharply differing instructional practices will become more evident as even newer technologies develop. Faculty deployment will become more varied and imaginative as significant attempts are made to provide greater opportunities for the teacher to help shape educational change and future planning.

The key to a better tomorrow is people—not technology, not organizational patterns. Technology and new organizational patterns are only means to an end. The question of "What shall be the proper ends of education?" will always be determined by people—and teachers play a key role in answering this question. Goal orientation with a strong philosophical base for all activity, together with the use of new technological aids, should produce an unexcelled educational era.

## QUESTIONS TO CONSIDER

1.  Within the next ten years, what uses of technology in the field of education do you foresee, and how might these uses affect your role as a professional educator?
2.  In what ways should the technological expertise of business and industry be used in the field of education? What role should the professional educator play in this involvement?
3.  What changes in educational practices and school organization do you foresee resulting from extended use of the computer?
4.  What impact might the extensive use of video tapes have upon educational practices in public schools? In what ways might the use of video tapes enhance adult education?
5.  How do you account for the slow rate of change in educational practices? What might be the consequences if teachers refuse to change their instructional practices?
6.  In what ways do you feel that teaching within the next decade will become even more interesting and challenging?

## PROBLEM SITUATION FOR INQUIRY

Miss Crone is a middle-aged high school social studies teacher. From the beginning of her teaching career, she has required students to submit written outlines and answers to questions for each chapter in the textbook which she, without examining any of the work, merely records in her gradebook. Students are graded on the basis of short-answer objective tests which she has used from year to year without change. The students invariably take a free ride on both counts, for the homework is copyable and the tests are public domain. Her discussion in class frequently involves a recounting of the events of the weekend, which are spent at her home. She feels that the students really like her as a teacher, and she points with pride at the high grades most of her students receive.

The manner in which Miss Crone conducts her classes is well known to parents. They hesitate to criticize her teaching, since they like the high grades their sons and daughters receive from her. Miss Crone is several years away from compulsory retirement, and teaching is her sole means of support.

Miss Crone steadfastly refuses to have anything to do with the innovative practices which many of her colleagues are using. Every time the principal or other teachers have encouraged her to change, she has rebuked them with the statement that "There is no substitute for good, solid academic instruction. All of that stuff is just a passing fad. I'll have no part of it, and I'll stand on the high grades my students make."

If you were chairman of the social studies department (or the principal) in this school, what would you do? Why?

## ACTIVITIES TO PURSUE

1. Spend some time in schools that have performance contracts. Try to determine how teachers and students feel with regard to this practice. How do the roles of both teachers and students change under such circumstances?
2. Examine various types of teaching machines and programmed learning materials. What strengths and weaknesses do you see in the use of these materials?
3. Interview some teachers who have used instructional television. What advantages and disadvantages do they see in the use of this medium of instruction?
4. Talk with some school administrators and teachers regarding problems involved in changing instructional practices and procedures. Try to determine what they consider to be the basic reasons for teacher resistance to change.
5. If possible, visit a school in which considerable use is being made of educational technology. Compare and contrast the role of the teacher in this kind of setting with that of a more conventional setting.

# 7 | BECOMING EFFECTIVE IN THE CLASSROOM

When a teacher first meets his class at the beginning of the school year, he begins the cycle that makes up the main portion of his responsibilities—the task of guiding the growth of his pupils. Here before him is the class waiting for—for what? As the person immediately responsible for the direction in which these young people will grow during the coming year, the teacher will have already asked himself that question, "For what?" And immediately the next question arises—"How?" Whether the pupils are first graders or high school seniors, these same questions are to be answered. *What* are the goals and how are these particular pupils to be helped to attain these goals?

Perhaps the latter question would not appear to be so troublesome if a teacher were to deal with only one pupil. But he is responsible for a number of pupils, each quite different physically, psychologically, and socially. A teacher is concerned with each pupil and his total growth. Although it would be a dull world indeed if all persons were the same, the fact that individuals within any classroom can vary to a high degree poses problems for any teacher.

The well-known axiom "Start where the pupil is" means that a teacher deals with each pupil at his present stage of educational, social, and psychological development and plans for him and with him the program that will best help him to attain the goals expected of him. This task involves depth of understanding in regard to the behavior and needs of pupils, the nature of the learning process, the selection and guidance of the learning experiences, and understanding of and skill in human relationships. Success as a beginning teacher, to a considerable degree, will depend upon the amount of understanding and skill he has regarding these matters. The rest of this chapter is devoted to an overview of some of these understandings and skills, which will be covered in greater detail in professional education courses required in most teacher preparation programs. The self-instructional plans that should emerge from this overview should make subsequent professional courses even more meaningful to the prospective teacher.

## Understanding Pupil Behavior

How may a prospective teacher become expert at understanding individual behavior? It is a process that one continues to learn throughout a lifetime. Basic courses in educational psychology, child development, and adolescent development serve to provide the general principles underlying human behavior. Early practice in applying these principles will enhance later performance when faced with the responsibility of guiding pupils toward educational goals.

Through many observations of boys and girls and discussion about their behavior, one gains greater depth of understanding of behavior, builds confidence, and achieves competence as a teacher. The immediate goal is to develop observation skills that will enable a prospective teacher to become increasingly sensitive to significant cues to behavior.

Unless observation is systematic, little useful information will be obtained. The total environment cannot be observed at one time. In a classroom context, the total environment includes not only the pupils but

Young children, especially, may reveal some of their characteristics, thoughts, and feelings through their creative activities. *(Photograph from the Audio-visual Center, Indiana University.)*

also the teacher, the materials, and the physical structure. Without an underlying system, one tends to observe whatever attracts his attention. With guides for observation formulated in advance, one can observe for specific purposes. While the experienced teacher will be able to keep several purposes in mind, a prospective teacher will probably gain more initially from observations by attempting to answer only one question, say, "What was the general response of the class to the kinds of materials used during the observation period?"

While the questions to be answered during an observation might well be posed in general purposes and in abstract terms, the answers can only be made in terms of observed behavior. In answering the question, "How is day-to-day instruction being adapted to individual differences?" for example, one might observe the teacher's behavior in terms of group management. In observing an arithmetic lesson, the question may be asked, "Are small groups made so that the wide differences within the whole group are lessened in order to meet the common needs represented by the smaller groups?" After the teacher gets the small groups started, are there one or two individuals needing special help? Does the teacher find time to help these individuals? Are instructional materials selected from various levels of difficulty, or must all pupils, regardless of present achievement level, use the same materials?

Perhaps there is a pupil who needs guidance and help because social or psychological factors are interfering with his achieving educational goals. For example, a boy may be aggressively seeking attention. He also may be interfering with the learning of other class members. Does the teacher use means that will permit him to receive attention for doing constructive instead of disruptive work?

It should be remembered that one instance is not a sufficient basis on which to make general statements. Observations must be made many times to discover the patterns of behavior which constitute the reliable signals or cues on which a teacher operates.

Opportunities for informal observation are constantly at hand. All kinds of situations may be used to observe the behavior of boys and girls. They may be observed on the street, on a playground, at church, or at a basketball game. These situations provide excellent sources for use in gaining skill in observing behavior. Classroom observation is more formal. On the other hand, it provides the context in which the teacher works. An alertness to the influence on classroom behavior of factors coming from outside the schoolroom, however, provides a better understanding of behavior observed in the classroom.

In learning to be a close observer, one should select only a few individuals and watch them in terms of only one general question. With a little practice more individuals and more questions can be included. As a help toward systematic observation, a guide sheet is presented below.

## Guide Sheet for Observing Classroom Teaching

1. What are some of the positive techniques used in working with pupils?

   _____

   _____

   _____

2. How is day-to-day instruction being adapted to individual differences?

   _____

   _____

   _____

3. What are some evidences that the teacher is alert to physical, social, and psychological needs of individual pupils?

   _____

   _____

   _____

4. What are some evidences of pupil-teacher planning?

   _____

   _____

   _____

5. What are some evidences of a rich educational environment?

   _____

   _____

   _____

6. What is the place of the teacher in the group?

   _____

   _____

   _____

7. What evidence is there to suggest that learning is taking place?

   _____

   _____

   _____

8. What questions from your observation do you wish to discuss with your college teacher?

   _____

   _____

   _____

## Understanding Pupils' Needs

The needs of youth are of several kinds. Perhaps the first that must be satisfied is that which relates to good physical condition and health. All individuals need adequate food and clothing, freedom to be active, a place and time for rest, and immunity from disease. The physical organism demands all these things. If these persistent needs are not met, individuals sometimes react in undesirable ways. Early observance of physical needs of pupils can permit early treatment and adjustment.

Mental and psychological needs are as important as physical ones. All individuals experience them—the need to feel secure in the affection of someone, the need to be a part of the group, and the need to be a creative member of society. The understanding teacher keeps these needs always in mind. He demonstrates constantly that he likes boys and girls. He finds a way for each pupil to do something well every day. He explores with them many opportunities to be creative. He plans to help each pupil find a place in the group and each group widen its circle of friendships. He knows how important it is to be one of the team.

Meeting the mental or psychological needs of pupils will help them

In what ways do these children seem to be different? In what ways do they seem to be alike? How should the school attempt to meet their differences as well as their likenesses? *(Photograph from the National Education Association.)*

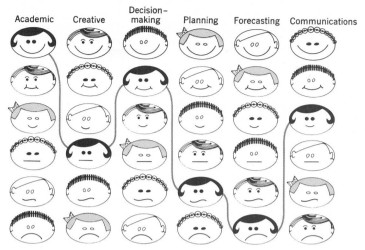

FIGURE 7–1  A teacher is confronted with the task of developing multiple talents in students by means of which they will be more successful both in and out of school.

satisfy their social needs, too. But social needs require special skills and techniques which boys and girls have to learn. They need to know how to do things, how to express themselves clearly, how to meet situations with poise, and how to win acceptance from others in the group.

Meeting individual differences does not mean that pupils must be taught one at a time. There are many occasions when it is highly desirable for the whole group to share an experience and to learn from one another. Small collective enterprises help boys and girls who have similar needs and who are of similar ability to work profitably together. Still other groups bring together pupils who have common interests but who may be at different levels of maturity. Sometimes boys and girls from several grades can cooperate on worthwhile activities. In all this interchange, individual differences come into play, and youth have opportunities to satisfy their physical, intellectual, and social needs.

## Understanding How Learning Takes Place

The word "learning" is commonplace in our language, but like the word "think," it is difficult to define precisely. A teacher observes performance rather than learning and infers from it that certain learnings have taken place. Learning involves some change or modification in the behavior of a pupil. There are times when learning becomes especially meaningful to pupils. There probably is one best time to teach everything, if teachers could only know that time. There are no magic or scientific formulas yet available for determining these exact moments when pupils should be taught. Preparation for teaching helps a prospective teacher in determining when teaching will become most significant.

Certain conditions can be cultivated or arranged which foster effective learning. From their many contacts with boys and girls teachers know that pupils learn when they are motivated by their own needs and challenged to put forth their best efforts. They know that pupils learn best when learning is closely related to and grows out of past and present experiences. They know that pupils who have opportunities to plan their activities and to select their materials under the guidance of a wise and resourceful teacher are learning far more than those who must follow the direction of a classroom autocrat. Good teachers help boys and girls to experience in a great variety of ways, to use what they are learning, to evaluate the success of their plans, and to see real progress toward a goal.

## Selecting Learning Experiences

Choosing the learning experiences which pupils should have may seem to be a big job for a young teacher. How does a teacher know in what directions to guide his pupils?

Modern teachers have many aids, one of the most important of which lies in the needs and interests of pupils. The knowledge of these needs comes from constant observation and careful study. Each activity leads the way to the next, pointing to new experiences which particular individuals need. Today's teachers, by their awareness of the community in which they live and by their understanding of the influences which affect young people, are able to help youth make wise choices.

Leaders in education tend to agree upon the kinds of experiences boys and girls need in order to participate fully in living today and in the future. These experiences include developing efficiency in the basic communication and mathematic skills, learning techniques of group planning and problem solving, making and taking responsibility for decisions, developing a knowledge of themselves and of other people that will contribute to better group living, and developing a knowledge and understanding of the environment in which all these activities take place. To these must be added participation in community activities, efforts to promote critical thinking, evaluation of experiences, building a wide range of interests that will contribute to the making of a well-balanced individual, and the development of personal and social values. (See Chapter 16.)

The teacher helps boys and girls to evaluate their group work and aids each pupil in judging his own efforts in the light of his needs and ability. In a relaxed, friendly atmosphere youth learn to face their mistakes and shortcomings frankly and make plans for improvement. Failing to reach the goal the first time merely motivates a second and better try. Pupils individually and as groups ask and seek answers to such questions as these: "Did we accomplish what we set out to do?" "What part of our work did we do well?" "Why did some of our efforts fail?" "What shall we do differently next time?" "Were all group members participating?" "Did I do my part?" "How did I feel about my part of the job?" "What new things were learned?" "How can these new ideas be used?" "What new problems came up that need to be solved?" Surely these are more important than to ask "What grade did I get?"

The teacher is concerned that each individual, whether he be working alone or in a group situation, has maximum opportunity to develop his interests and abilities. He recognizes that the strength of a democratic society is dependent upon the full development of each individual's talents. Within a group situation the development of these talents provides not only for individual self-realization but also for the enrichment of the entire group. For example, as the teacher helps a pupil develop his special abilities in science, the pupil moves toward self-realization, assumes roles of leadership within the group, and enriches the lives of others through his contributions to the group. His life, in turn, is enriched through the sharing of unique interests and abilities possessed by other members of his group.

How may teachers aid pupils in the selection of learning activities? Experiences are not of equal educative value, and pupils can engage in only as many experiences as time will allow. Teachers therefore need

Group discussion, planning, and problem solving provide opportunities not only for self-realization but also for the enrichment of the entire group. *(Photograph from TEACH ME, National Education Association.)*

some yardstick of values against which selections may be made. This yardstick consists of the values which a democratic society prizes and covets. The following summary statement of principles should aid a prospective teacher in making these choices [adapted, 101:25–27]:

1. *The experience must begin and grow out of the needs of the pupils as they see them and as society sees them.* Such needs tend to be needs which the pupils themselves recognize or can be made aware of. They may be needs for knowledge, skill, expression, the satisfaction of an interest—any one or a pattern of needs.

2. *The experience must be managed by all of the learners concerned—pupils, teachers, parents, and others—through cooperative, democratic interaction.* Experiences in the modern school frequently draw in many people who do not give full time to the school. Parents contribute in many ways, as do many civic authorities, merchants, and others.

3. *The experience must take on meaning and unity as the pupils' purposes become clearer and their work moves through one stage after another toward completion.* At times pupils may propose to do things which have relatively little meaning to them because of their meager experience, but as work progresses new understandings are added, horizons are pushed out, and the whole matter assumes new and lasting values.

4. *The experience must aid each pupil in improving his purposes and increasing his power to make intelligent choices.* Pupils' original choices may be trivial and of slight value because of their lack of experience and insight. As their work progresses, guided by a skillful and understanding teacher, the inherent values and meanings become apparent to the pupils and they proceed more and more wisely as their knowledge and insight grow. One of the major goals of all education is that of guiding the individual into ever higher and finer purposing, ever better and more worthy choices.

5. *The experience must aid each pupil to integrate past experience with present experience, making all available for future use.* Often, in the traditional school, learning has been of little permanent value because each skill or item of content was learned as a separate entity; the pupil failed to utilize past experience to solve present problems. As a result he saw little or no application of present learning to his own out-of-school experience, and the life value of the learning was negligible.

6. *The experience must increase the number and variety of interests which each pupil consciously shares with others.* One of the school's major tasks is that of opening up new and untried avenues of experience. A democratic society is one in which the genius of one individual can be utilized to enrich the entire mass and in which the level attained by the society as a whole is the aggregate of the levels attained by the interacting individuals within the society. Therefore it follows logically that the pupils need many leadership opportunities in cooperative interaction and sharing of experiences. When these shared experiences widen horizons and increase the number and variety of interests, their service is twofold.

7. *The experience must help each youngster build new meanings and refine old ones.* Real learning is forever a matter of adding new meanings and modifying old ones. If the addition and modification refine, enrich, and enlarge the total fund of meanings which the pupil possesses, they add substantially to the working material which the pupil draws upon to understand and interpret other experiences.

8. *The experience must offer opportunity for each pupil to use an ever-increasing variety of resources for learning.* Resources for learning in life outside the school include people, firsthand and vicarious experiences, books, magazines, television, radio, movies, and many other avenues. The more resources a youngster learns to use under the guidance of the school the more readily and independently he will learn in his life outside of the school.

9. *The experience must help each pupil to use a variety of learning activities which are suited to the resources he is using for learning.* Pupils need to do wide reading and intensive reading, to work alone and in groups, to learn many skills and develop many abilities, and to use those skills and abilities in many ways.

10. *The experience must aid each pupil to reconstruct his past experience creatively as the new learning situation develops.* Again, it is a matter of helping pupils to draw upon their past experience to understand their present experience and in so doing to enlarge and enrich the total concept.

11. *The experience must challenge the thinking and call forth the effort of the youngster to bring it to a satisfactory conclusion.* Any really valuable experience is broad enough in the scope of its possibilities to provide worthwhile experience for the slowest learner and still challenge the more able learner and cause him to exert himself willingly to solve the necessary problems and carry on the work. Youth enjoy work which calls for effort and energy when they feel a need for it and understand its values.

12. *The work must end with a satisfying emotional tone for each pupil.* To work hard and intensively and to reach one's goal is highly satisfying to youngsters as well as adults, and that satisfaction provides a solid foundation for future work.

How can anyone provide the kinds of experiences described here? There are no guaranteed formulas, but past experiences of teachers suggest the following: (1) Take every opportunity to build a wide background of information and experience. (2) Choose college electives with a view to broadening contacts with several areas of learning. (3) Explore different communities and try to identify the aspects of community living which will make worthwhile experiences for boys and girls. (4) Build personal interests and hobbies in areas which will contribute to effective working relationships with pupils. (5) Read widely.

## Planning with Pupils

Out of experiences with youth grows the curriculum of the modern school. From the circumstances of daily living at school and in the community come the plans which teachers and pupils make for the learning ahead. This planning is essential if pupils are to follow desirable purposes and engage in learning that is meaningful to them. The teacher must help them clarify their aims and set up their goals. "What are we trying to find out?" "Why do we need this information?" "What are the resources for finding out?" "How will we know when we have found what we are seeking?" These and other questions will be answered cooperatively by pupils and teacher.

Learning the skills of problem solving is an integral part of planning with pupils. The teacher acts as an adult resource person who, because of his experience and wider knowledge, can advise and guide pupils through the steps needed to solve a problem. Teacher-pupil planning means that pupils and teachers actually plan together. It means that they identify the problems that are pertinent to them and the questions that they need to answer. The teacher as a group leader contributes his ideas and questions. Together they apply scientific methods to the solving of problems and critical thinking to the answering of the questions. They go about this work systematically, with the teacher helping the group direct its efforts profitably. They plan how and where to locate necessary information. They exchange opinions and ideas and try to locate all the resources within the group. They organize themselves for effective work and evaluate the progress they make. The teacher encourages the reticent, helps leaders to permit others to lead sometimes, and guides those who find it difficult to assume responsibility. Pupils and teachers work through their problems to a satisfying conclusion.

Does the concept of teacher-pupil planning as indicated above seem difficult? Would it not be easier just to tell pupils what to do? As anyone explores the kinds of responsibilities which citizens of the world face today, he can see that planning is essential for schools to be relevant to the learner. Locating problems that need to be solved and knowing how to go about solving them are essential skills in a democracy.

A prospective teacher normally has many opportunities to participate in group planning experiences. These will be invaluable later, if time is taken to observe how people work together, how leadership emerges, how resources are utilized, and how conclusions are reached.

## Building Relationships with Pupils and Parents

Managing a classroom of active pupils may seem one of the biggest challenges a teacher faces. But boys and girls who are interested in following their own purposes, who are working at their own level of ability, and who see the why of what they are doing have little desire to exhibit resistive behavior. An important study of teachers and their relationships to pupils has developed some revealing phrases to describe effective and noneffective teachers. Here are some of the most telling items [adapted, 19:33–35]:

| Effective teachers | Noneffective teachers |
| --- | --- |
| Have the ability to remain self-controlled in the midst of conflicting demands. | Display an inadequacy to classroom demands, easily disturbed. |
| Are habitually quiet, poised, and courteous in relationships with children. | Are demanding, imposing, impatient in relations with children. |
| Are constructive and encouraging in comments and manner. | Resort to threats and punishments, sarcastic, cross. |
| Are enthusiastic about pupils and teaching. | Are harassed, disturbed, unsure, with no interest or enthusiasm. |
| Possess sufficient self-restraint to allow children to work through their own problems. | Impose directions and requirements upon pupils, oblivious of pupil initiative and resourcefulness. |

Skill in building good relationships with students is essential for success in teaching. *(Photograph by Carl Purcell, National Education Association.)*

| Effective teachers | Noneffective teachers |
| --- | --- |
| Are ingenious in utilizing opportunities for teaching. | Are unaware of opportunities for vitalizing classroom teaching. |
| Are careful in planning with pupils and in guiding them to successful completion of undertakings. | Expect children to know what to do and are seemingly satisfied if they keep busy. |
| Are skillful in directing pupils to evaluate their own work. | Fail to help pupils set up standards of their own. |
| Are interested in pupils as persons. | Are interested only in each child's academic progress. |

When visiting classrooms to observe teachers and pupils it may prove fruitful to identify the characteristics of the teacher who has established wholesome relationships with children. What is the teacher in the following situation building for?

"If you don't finish your arithmetic, you'll have to stay in at recess. I've warned you for the last time."

"It doesn't make any difference how you did it last year. You're in the eighth grade now, and I'm the teacher."

"I can't imagine what your mother's thinking of, to let you read such things."

"The children in this group are the most trying I've ever had. Honestly, I think I'll shut the door and never come back."

"Don't you know any better? Only stupid folks have to be told as many times as I've told you."

"If you'd put as much effort on your lessons as you do on those model planes, you'd be better off."

By contrast, how effective might the following teacher be in working with pupils?

"If your idea works out well, there's no reason why we shouldn't try it together."

"Do you feel that this is the best you can do now? What do we do next to help you improve?"

"We all make mistakes, you know. It would be a pretty dull world if everyone were perfect."

"Let's skip the spelling until tomorrow. Then you'll have time to finish planning for the assembly."

"School wouldn't be much fun without the pupils. Every day is different, new, and exciting."

Building fine relationships with pupils is easiest when teachers and parents are well acquainted. The teacher, of course, cannot know his students completely nor guide their learning experiences adequately unless he himself looks beyond the classroom to the home. How are such relationships established?

For the parent, the foremost question is, "How is my child getting along in school?" He expects the teacher to say something about the youngster, since children are the most precious possessions of parents. This concern represents a point of departure for the teacher's conversation with a parent.

It is important for the teacher to evidence a sincere and genuine interest in the welfare of the youngster. It also is important to recognize that the parent is more intimately acquainted with him than the teacher. Through the cooperative sharing of concern for the youngster, the teacher can develop a team approach that is in the best interest of the student and out of which may grow respect and understanding for the teacher.

## Creating Positive Conditions for Learning

As has been implied previously, a primary responsibility of a teacher is to create a climate in which learning can take place most effectively. In contrast to conditions that frequently exist in classrooms, Weigand [290:x–xi] points out that the following conditions should prevail:

**Freedom to explore**   The learner should have the opportunity to pursue problems by utilizing a variety of approaches. One-solution problems, questions that demand a right answer, and certain types of "busy" work all tend to deny the student the opportunity to freely explore. Examples of this denial would be the algebra teacher who demands that each student follow a certain set procedure as he attempts to solve problems even though he is able to relate other approaches to a solution; the teacher who follows set procedures in a given art activity which take away the possible creativity; and the language arts teacher who teaches a single outlining procedure and demands that each student conform to that procedure.

**Time to explore**   The thought process takes time. The amount of time necessary to explore a problem varies with the individual. A student, denied adequate time to pursue a problem, tends to give up. This tendency is readily seen in examinations where the learner may not finish in the time allowed and is penalized for the work not completed. Past research in this area tends to indicate that teachers give students with high ability an abnormally large amount of time to explore and an abnormally small amount of time to the less capable individual. If this is true, we should consciously attempt to reverse this procedure and give each individual student the time that he needs to explore.

**Acceptance and use of wrong answers**   Learning can be achieved through our mistakes and bad judgment. Many of the discoveries that have been made have come through a series of errors. The student who has his "wrong" answers rejected soon formulates a behavior of removing himself from the learning process. A teacher who assists a student in discovering his errors and in finding the "right" answers encourages a student to engage freely in the learning process.

**Less concern for closure**   Students do not learn at the same rate, and as a consequence do not arrive at closure at the same time. Nevertheless, it is common practice for teachers to pull the loose ends together and arrive at closure for all of his students. As a result, each student who is not ready for closure is discouraged from pursuing the learning that actually should take place. The student who has reached closure does not have to be told that he has arrived at that point.

**Less concern for verbalization**   It is not uncommon for teachers to rank students according to their verbal skills. The learner with low verbal ability normally recognizes his verbal weakness and tends to refrain from engaging in verbal activity in the classroom. Rather than utter words that will not receive a positive response from the teacher, he remains silent and disengages himself from the classroom activity. Teachers must recognize that low verbal ability does not mean inability to think.

In order to achieve the conditions indicated above, Weigand and his associates [290] have described eight competencies that teachers should develop, and have developed "software" materials that can be used for this purpose. A prospective teacher would profit from using the self-instructional materials that have been prepared for each competency. These competency skills are explored[1] briefly, with three of them being given special emphasis, since they have not been noted previously or in other chapters of this book.

## Developing Skills in Asking Questions

Cunningham [290:81–130] maintains that one of the most important skills for a teacher to develop is the ability to ask effective questions. Next to lecturing, teachers spend more time using questions than they do any other kind of verbal utterance. In a report of his study of primary school teachers, Floyd [86:75–76] found an overall questioning rate of nearly $3^1/_2$ questions being asked per minute. On an average, the teachers asked 348 questions daily. Questions are used to give directions, correct misbehavior, manage classroom activity, initiate instruction, create learning situations, and evaluate learning. Although the most important use of question-asking should be to stimulate critical thinking, it is the least common outcome of their question-asking.

If teachers are to be effective in their communication with pupils, they must be adept at asking questions. They must develop a questioning attitude and pose questions as they prepare for teaching. Teachers who lack this competence will have difficulty directing the learning of pupils.

Effective question-asking is not an innate talent that only a few possess. It is a skill that can be developed with knowledge of good questions and questioning procedures and practice with these procedures. Good questions and question-asking strategies go beyond the traditional purpose of finding out what pupils have learned. The question's greatest effect is the way and extent to which it causes the pupil to think critically. Research shows an almost perfect correlation between pupil's thought patterns as reflected in their verbal responses, and the questions their teachers ask. It also has been demonstrated that a teacher's questions have a strong influence on the behavior of other pupils. Effective questioning can facilitate desirable attitudes, develop and sustain interests, provide new ways of dealing with the subject matter, and give quality and purpose to evaluation.

To stimulate thinking by asking questions, it will be important to

---

[1]From manuscripts prepared by each of the authors, and edited by James Weigand, specifically for this chapter.

have knowledge of the types of questions that can be asked at different levels of thought. The simplest way to examine question types is by the two general categories of "broad" and "narrow." Narrow questions are those for which there is an expected or "best" answer. The number of possible responses is limited and usually identified with the lowest levels of thinking. In contrast, a broad question is one that permits alternative responses that are acceptable. Broad questions are "open-ended" questions that permit more thoughtful answers. A more specific way of looking at levels of questioning is to use the four sub-categories into which the two general categories of broad and narrow questions can be divided. Narrow questions can be either cognitive-memory or convergent, whereas broad questions are either divergent or evaluative.

Cognitive-memory questions are narrow questions limited to the lowest level of thinking. These questions call for answers that are reproductions of facts, definitions, naming, or other remembered information where the operations of rote-memory or recall are used. Questions that can be answered with a "Yes" or "No" are typical of this category. The following are examples of cognitive-memory questions:

"Do the words you are given fall into the category you studied?"
"How do you define the word communication?"
"What do the symbols 5, 7, 17, +, − and = mean?"
"What does the fish have which helps him to move about?"

A second and higher level of question-asking is the category of convergent-thinking. Questions classified in this category are less narrow, because the pupil may give a longer response. When answering this type of question the pupil is usually expected to give an explanation. These questions must be considered narrow because here again there is usually a one "best" or "right" answer. The person responding to the question must know certain facts, be able to associate these facts, and give an explanation. To respond to a convergent question, the pupil may use the operations of explaining, stating relationships, associating and relating, or comparing and contrasting. The following are examples of convergent questions:

"Why do plants grow toward the light?"
"What is the difference between language and communication?"
"How are the goldfish and the turtle alike or different when they move?"

Notice that the words "Why" and "How" are common to these questions. While some educators have suggested that "How" and "Why" questions are desirable, research shows that there is real danger in making children's thinking too fixed by asking convergent questions consistently. This kind of question is typical of those found in textbooks and used to review content being studied. Learning becomes more a matter of finding "right" answers rather than encouraging creativity.

A divergent question asks the person responding to organize elements into new patterns. These are thought-provoking questions. A teacher asking this kind of question allows the pupil to be original in his response as he pursues longer and more thoughtful answers.

Divergent questions may be used to create new problem-solving situations and require the pupil to synthesize ideas and construct a meaningful solution. In responding to divergent questions, the student may use the operations of predicting, hypothesizing, or inferring. Examples of these questions follow:

"How might our country be different today if we had never had slavery?"
"Suppose you could not ask a single question in a classroom; how would you communicate?"
"What would happen if you gave a turtle fins and a tail like the fish and took away his legs?"

Obviously, the preceding questions encourage responses that are more creative and imaginative. This kind of questioning stimulates interest and provides motivation. The use of divergent questions is more likely to lead to the development of insights, appreciations, and desirable attitudes. Teachers often are preoccupied with covering the content of a subject and fail to utilize this level of questioning to help pupils develop their ability to think.

The evaluative-thinking question asks the person responding to judge, value, justify a choice, or defend a position. This is the highest level of questioning because formulating a response may require the use of all the operations used at the other levels. An evaluative question causes the pupil to organize his knowledge, formulate an opinion, and take a self-selected position. This evaluative judgment, be it favorable or unfavorable, must be made on the basis of standards which either he or someone else sets. The following are examples of evaluative questions:

"What do you think is the best method by which teachers could improve their question-asking abilities?"
"The student of language might argue that both uses of the words language and communication are acceptable as long as they are understood by the group. Why would you agree (or disagree)?"
"Which animal, the fish or the turtle, do you think is better equipped to move about in the place where he lives?"

Notice that evaluative questions can often be identified by certain phrases such as:

"How did you feel about . . . ?"
"What do you think about . . . ?"
"In your opinion . . . ?"

Often the cause for ineffective question-asking can be attributed to poor phrasing. The problems related to phrasing are many. They are so numerous that it is difficult to isolate them and clearly identify the source of the problem. Some approach the ridiculous. For example, a teacher was once observed to begin questions with the word "then" and ended them with the word "then." Therefore, his questions sounded something like this: "Then this would be a rock then?" Another unique kind of phrasing problem is observed in a question such as "Did you ever not weigh anything, do you think?"

In view of the amount of time that teachers spend asking questions, how well they communicate with pupils will be greatly dependent on the way they phrase their questions. The importance of effectively phrased questions cannot be denied. Questions that are improperly phrased only confuse the pupils and hinder their learning. A teacher who fails to give careful thought to the way his questions are phrased is cheating his pupils out of the opportunity to develop thinking skills.

A question which is properly structured will contribute to clear understanding, serve as a model for the pupil's questions, and ensure accurate communication of the question's purpose. When properly phrased, a question will be clearly worded, utilize a vocabulary level suited to the group, have wording appropriate to the level of thinking sought in the question, be grammatically correct, and possess content relevant to the purpose of the question.

The true measure of a question's effectiveness is the answers it elicits. The ultimate purpose is to stimulate, direct, and extend thinking. Accomplishing this outcome not only depends on the teacher's ability to construct good questions, but on the use of suitable question-asking strategies. The measure of a good question-asker is his ability to make use of incomplete or wrong answers to enhance thinking.

In preparing for teaching, you should be conscious of different types of questions. Hopefully, you will have many opportunities to test these questions with pupils in classroom- and out-of-classroom situations. Good questioning must be planned for and developed through practice. If you are genuinely concerned with developing your own intellectual skills as well as the skills of those you will instruct, proficiency with this competency will be necessary. Research demonstrates that skill in constructing questions may be different from skill in using questions. This suggests a continuous analysis of your questioning behavior. A critical analysis of one's question-asking and its influence on learners, accompanied by appropriate changes in view of identified behaviors, is the only way it will emerge as a skill. The many self-instructional materials which Cunningham [290:81–130] has prepared should prove to be very helpful to a prospective teacher in gaining a high degree of skill in asking questions.

## Developing Skill in Interpersonal Transactions

Kurpius [290:246–305] maintains that human interaction is the most common of all personal experiences but one about which we probably know the least. How we interact, relate, and transact with others and the reciprocal impact of this phenomenon form the single most important aspect of our existence. Man's nature is such, in fact, that only through interaction with others can he become aware of his own identity. While this identity is singular, we can very quickly conceptualize a person as representing two component parts. One of the components represents the internal self, or man's attitudes, values, feelings, and beliefs; and the second component is that of the external self, or man's behavior. Another way to describe internal and external self is to think of the internal self as being observable only through man's behavior. Hence, man's internal self is only made known to others by his external self or behavior, since how one feels, for example, is made known to others only through the behavior attached to that feeling at that specific moment. Therefore, in the growth and development stages of man, his combination of and interaction between internal and external selves provide the raw material for the development of the total person. As an individual progresses through his development, he is *acquiring* new material for both his internal and external selves; he is *maintaining* selected portions of his internal and external selves; and he is experiencing the stage of *change* or *modification* in which human beings decide both consciously and unconsciously how to change or modify themselves as persons. The uniqueness of the acquisition, maintenance, and modification of self is related to the fact that only through interaction with other human beings can these three human stages be activated. Man remains dependent upon other human beings to determine his own makeup. Consequently, this process begins at infancy and continues until death for all humans.

While it sometimes appears that human interaction is quite simple, there are many times when we feel that others do not understand the real message we are communicating or intending to communicate. Within this realm, there are three elements of communication which are significant in most all human interaction. These three are the ability to listen and respond with *empathy, respect,* and *concreteness.* Each element seems so obviously important when we think of how humans interact and the impact this interaction has on our personal growth and development. However, there is universal evidence that listening (both intrapersonal and interpersonal) and responding to oneself and others are areas where most humans need assistance in developing. Often the person asking for help and understanding is not even aware of what he is asking for. Hence, it is the responsibility of the listener to aid in the process of exploring and defining the problem. Even in task meetings, such as committee meetings, and certainly in regular class meetings, there are many hurts experienced by both teacher and students which are either missed completely or misunderstood. Some are very minor, and some are quite significant. Often many minor problems collect, which if they had been responded to earlier, would not have grown into a major problem.

A simple example of a minor problem with potential for leading to a major one might develop for a student who is late for class. Lateness has very different meanings for different people. Usually the magnitude for being late for class is a function of the teacher's or professor's reaction to the situation. Occasionally, a student will quite simply oversleep and feel quite embarrassed and even guilty about coming late. If, upon the student's entering the classroom, the instructor responds from his own internal self, he may recognize only his own feelings rather than those of the student. For example, the teacher could internally experience himself as follows: (1) "No one comes late to my classes"; or (2) "The policy of the school does not allow lateness; therefore, I would look bad if I did not shape this student's behavior"; or (3) "I can't stand students interrupting me after class begins." Regardless of the internal impact, a personalized response will follow if the student's frame of reference is not considered or listened to. It is from this point that a relationship or a barrier may begin between student and teacher. If the student is "put down" for being late, a "set" is beginning between student and teacher. If the teacher recognizes the embarrassment of the student and responds from the student's internal self rather than his own, a different kind of "set" occurs, and a different and usually more positive relationship develops.

The purpose for the brief example is to suggest how what may be perceived as a very minor incident can collect into a major misunderstanding between two people. These minor occurrences are most important because they tend to set the pattern of interaction between these two people and even carry over into other relationships.

The three elements of *empathy, respect,* and *concreteness* are perhaps the most generalizable of all communication elements. If we know how the other person feels and how he is experiencing the situation (empathy), and if we know our true feeling for this person (respect), and if we can listen and respond to the whole message (concreteness), there is high probability that the outcome of that interaction will be more meaningful and productive than if the three elements were missing or being performed at a very low level. Selected programs have been designed to aid teachers, students and parents to become more effective in how they listen and respond to others. Sensitivity training programs represent one such example. These programs, which frequently are referred to as "encounter groups," "experience-based learning," "group dynamics," "awareness training," or "human relations training," have been the subject of considerable controversy. Although there are many forms of sensitivity training, it usually involves small groups of people meeting together in an attempt to gain greater insight into both the personal attitudes of group members and how the group behaves as a social entity.

Schools have used various forms of sensitivity training, with varying degrees of success, for purposes of developing a greater awareness and understanding of current problems faced by schools and school personnel. Examples of such problems are race relations, school integration, student unrest, teacher militancy, and resistance to change in general. Sensitivity training programs have been frequently conducted by persons who are not professionally qualified to engage in these activities. When this occurs, the critics feel that the programs may have an adverse effect upon the mental health of the participants. Other critics believe that sensitivity training is nothing more than brainwashing and thus is merely a Communist-inspired plot to corrupt the morals of students and teachers alike [233:45]. There is some evidence to suggest, however, that if sensitivity training programs are properly conceived and conducted by qualified professional personnel, they may serve to foster greater understanding and improved relations among individuals and among groups of individuals [233:49].

Teacher education institutions and some public school systems are giving more attention to the need for teachers to have a high degree of skill in the area of interpersonal transactions. Problems encountered in educating inner-city and minority-group students have highlighted this need. A prospective teacher can do much on his own to further his skill in this area. The self-instructional materials prepared by Kurpius [290:262–293] should prove to be quite helpful along such lines.

## Applying Self-assessment Techniques

Russell [290:306–316] feels that a teacher should seek to be as objective as possible in assessing his effectiveness in a teaching-learning situation. One technique is to use a checklist or rating scale. Such a scale may be individually prepared, provided by a school system, or found in professional periodicals or books. In the Resource Section for Part II, you will find a list of Twenty Self-rating Questions for Teachers, and Twenty Indicators of the Quality of Teaching. In the book, *Teacher Self-appraisal: A Way of Looking Over Your Own Shoulder* [9:44], you will find another very fine checklist called the Roberson Teacher Self-appraisal System.

As mentioned previously, an audio tape recording of your performance with students, whether in-school or out-of-school, may be used for studying your communication skills. A video tape recorder may be used to record both sights and sounds. Both of these systems allow the performance to be studied and restudied for analysis and comparative purposes.

An increasing number of teacher education institutions are using

Through the use of a video tape recorder, a teacher is able to study and restudy teaching-learning situations for the purpose of self-improvement. *(Photograph by Joe Di Dio, National Education Association.)*

portable video tape recorders for micro-teaching purposes. Each prospective teacher is asked to make a short presentation of a preselected topic to his classmates. The presentation is recorded on video tape and is then replayed so that it may be analyzed by the group and/or by the prospective teacher.

In recent years much research has been done in the area of interaction analysis by such educators as Flanders, Amidon, and Hunter. They have developed various scales for analyzing teacher-student verbal response behavior in a classroom. The Flanders [84] system provides for teacher-student verbal responses to be classified according to ten categories. After a tape recording has been made of an instructional situation, the teacher, or an independent observer, replays the tape so that the statements made by the teacher and the students may be classified and tallied. Various ratios can be calculated from this information, and an even more elaborate analysis of the information may be made by constructing a 10 by 10 matrix. Research studies, through the use of the Flanders system, indicate that students achieve at a higher level where teachers use "indirect" methods in contrast to "direct" or "telling" methods.

Amidon and Hunter [10] refined the system developed by Flanders by providing seventeen categories for classifying statements made by students and their teacher. Their system, which has become known as the "Verbal Interaction Category System" (VICS), provides for a high degree of precision in classifying statements. On the other hand, the system is more difficult to use.

Russell [290:310–313] provides a concise description of the systems developed by Flanders and suggests ways in which prospective teachers may improve their interactions with students.


## Sequencing Instruction

Trojcak [290:131–165] maintains that a teacher must be able to recognize where his learners are at any time (what their entry behaviors or present capabilities are) in order to be effective in sequencing instruction. Identifying the learners' entry behavior is probably one of the most important yet frequently ignored tasks of the teacher. If a teacher is unable to clearly define what he wants to accomplish or cause to happen as a result of his instruction, he will be unable to know when to conclude his instruction. On the other hand, if the teacher is able to state explicitly both the learners' entry behavior and the terminal performance he expects them to achieve, he will have established the scope or boundaries in which he can plan the instructional sequence of prerequisite or subordinate tasks. Through this threefold analysis (establishing the learners' entry behavior, defining the terminal goal, and outlining the sequence of subordinate tasks), a teacher will have a means for evaluating the effectiveness of his instruction and for determining if additional instruction is necessary. Many instructional sequences are possible. The individual teacher must develop a sequence, however, and then test, revise, and test again.

## Evaluating Educational Progress

Anderson [290:166–206] feels that many teachers and students tend to think in terms of grades or tests when the words "evaluation" or "measurement" are used in an educational setting. He maintains that these words have much broader significance and meaning. Evaluation is basically a matter of making decisions or judgments, something a teacher must do continually. A teacher's judgments about events in his classroom are important for deciding (1) what direction will be taken in future class activities and (2) what assistance should be given to individuals who are encountering difficulties, as well as for the less important but most commonly mentioned purpose of reporting (3) what educational progress has been made, through means such as grades. Thus, evaluation is a basic and continual part of a teacher's life which calls for a high degree of professional competence.

## Formulating Performance Objectives

According to Troyer [290:43–80], a performance objective is a statement which (1) specifies measurable behavior that the student will be asked to perform, (2) specifies a particular set of conditions under which the student will be asked to perform the required behavior when being evaluated, and (3) specifies the minimum level at which the student must perform the measurable behavior and still be rated acceptable. Performance objectives require that the teacher designate certain behaviors that his students must demonstrate at the conclusion of the course. As will be discussed in greater detail in Chapter 16, there are several very good reasons for developing the ability to write performance objectives. Some of the most important are: (1) a teacher is able to select, substitute, and rearrange course topics into instructional sequences which maximize learning; (2) individualization is aided by performance objectives; and (3) evaluation of instruction is greatly facilitated.

## Assessing Intellectual Development Stages

Dyrli [290:1–42] maintains that, in order to be effective in the classroom, one of the most important competencies a teacher can gain is the capability of assessing the intellectual development stages of individual students. To do this accurately and with validity, the teacher should be able to: (1) describe the major thinking characteristics of children at each level of development; (2) suggest specific tasks, problems, and techniques that may be used to determine the level of intellectual development at which a given child operates in a particular area; and (3) conduct actual diagnostic-problem interview sessions successfully. A number of the self-instructional exercises which he has prepared [290:1–42] can be used by a prospective teacher in gaining this kind of skill as he works with boys and girls in formal and informal situations.

## Recognizing and Assessing Creativity

DeVito [290:207–245] maintains that creativity is the act of drawing on all past experiences, and the act of selecting from these to yield a construct of new patterns, new ideas, or new products. It is the fusing together of knowledge gained from previous experiences for the presentation of a *new* approach to the solution of a problem or the design of a *new* technique or style for performing a previous task.

Teachers need to be highly creative in order to provide rich learning experiences for students. In this kind of climate students, in turn, gain the skills for creative living.

## SUMMARY

This chapter has been concerned with an overview of some of the understandings and skills that a prospective teacher will need to develop in order to be effective in guiding the learning process of students. With this overview in mind, a prospective teacher can formulate his own plans for gaining greater understanding and competence as a teacher and can make subsequent educational courses even more meaningful.

Every pupil has physical, psychological, and social needs. Physically, he must have sufficient food and clothing; he must have an opportunity to be active; and he must have proper rest. Psychologically, he needs to be loved, to feel he is a part of the group, and to have confidence in himself as a creative member of society. Socially, he needs to know how to do things, how to express himself clearly, how to meet situations with poise, and how to win acceptance from others in the group. A teacher needs to have a high degree of skill in observing the behavior of students in order to identify the needs of each and plan educational experiences accordingly.

It is difficult for a beginning teacher to know how to choose the learning experiences which pupils should have. To do this he must have a rich background of experience himself—experience that has taught him cooperation and helped him develop fully. The teacher must therefore read widely, have broad contacts, and build up personal interests and experiences that help him understand and promote desirable characteristics in his pupils. He must encourage pupils to cooperate with him in building a wholesome school environment, and above all, he must become a good group leader who plans with pupils and helps them clarify their aims, establish desirable goals, and devise effective ways of reaching these goals.

A number of positive conditions for learning have been suggested. The importance of developing a high degree of skill in question-asking has been emphasized, since the kinds of questions asked by teachers have a direct bearing upon the quality of learning provided for students.

The importance of interpersonal transactions in today's educational setting also has been emphasized. Teachers especially must possess a high degree of skill in interaction with others as they seek to help their students develop desirable attitudes, values, feelings, and beliefs. The great diversification of racial and ethnic groups with which teachers are confronted today necessitates a higher degree of competence in interpersonal transactions than ever before if the public schools are to fulfill their function in a democratic society.

Teachers are always confronted with the obligation of improving their professional competencies. Some self-assessment techniques have been suggested which prospective teachers may use on their own in moving toward the competencies they will need.

## QUESTIONS TO CONSIDER

1. In your opinion, how effectively are schools today meeting the physical, psychological, and social needs of students? What are some of the causes for any deficiencies you may be able to identify? What improvement should be made?
2. If a teacher can observe only performance rather than learning, what suggestions would you make for improving the manner in which education objectives are stated? Illustrate.
3. Since lack of skill in human relations precipitates many of the problems in society today, how might teachers help alleviate this problem? What basic changes in conducting teaching-learning experiences would be essential in order to achieve this end?
4. Account for the fact that many pupils lose interest in school and drop out before graduation. How might the school have failed to fulfill its function in regard to these pupils? What do you plan to do as a teacher in order to alleviate this drop-out problem?
5. What are students saying when they maintain that schools are not relevant? How will you seek to make school experiences relevant for each pupil? What competencies, not ordinarily possessed by teachers, will you need to develop? How can you, using self-improvement techniques, develop some of these competencies?
6. What criteria will you use in selecting activities or learning experiences for your pupils?
7. Account for the fact that the majority of questions asked by teachers are of the cognitive-memory type. What changes will be essential in the way teachers conceive their role before this condition will change? How can you develop skill for a higher quality of question asking?
8. How would you assess teachers in terms of their skill in interpersonal relations? In what ways might teachers improve their skill in interpersonal transactions?

## PROBLEM SITUATION FOR INQUIRY

Letter from a pupil:

I can't take your test, mainly because I haven't read the "Scarlet Letter." I am of the opinion, that no one has the right to tell someone else to read a book. I started reading the "Scarlet Letter" and I found it to be very boring. I have to be interested in a book or I can't maintain concentration. You might be thinking that, "Carl doesn't read anything because he's just lazy." Well, I am lazy but I love to read. In the last month I have read five books. Reading should be a good part of your life, not a part filled with "you will read this," and "you will read that." Maybe this is why there are so many bad readers in and out of school. Early in school, teachers handed out books and told you to read them. From that point on reading was something scary, something for the smart kids with thick glasses. Somebody gave me a mind to think with, and after reading part of the "Scarlet Letter," I don't think that I will finish the book. Maybe the book is good, but right now I don't want to read it. If I like it, I'll be more than happy to read it for you. And you won't have to give me any tests either. Because if I tell someone that I will read a book, then I will read that book. If I don't like it, I will tell you so.

I hope you're not mad at me for this, but I thought that I should state my position. If I get an "F" on my report card for not reading the book, then that's the way it will have to be.

Carl

If you received this letter, how would you handle this situation?


## ACTIVITIES TO PURSUE

1. Use the observation form and the suggestions indicated in this chapter for the purpose of gaining skill in observing the behavior of students.
2. Accompany a youngster you know well to a special event—a movie, football game, or church. Study his reactions to the various happenings. How does he identify himself with the things he sees? What does he talk about after the event? Does the presence of you as an adult seem to make a difference? Compare your knowledge of this child with descriptions which you may find in your reading.
3. Keep an anecdotal record of the successive activities and the conversation of a child whom you are able to observe unnoticed for a period of an hour or two. Try to be as objective as possible.
4. Visit an elementary classroom where children draw and paint freely. Study their artwork. Is there splash and verve or just timid daubs here and there? What differences can you see among children just from observing what they put on paper? Ask them to tell you the story of what they have painted.
5. Study the group process at work in the next group in which you participate. Who is the leader? What qualities does he exhibit? Is he a democratic or an autocratic leader? How does he motivate the group to work?
6. Work in a leadership capacity either in school or out with a group of boys and girls. Help them initiate plans for an activity, encourage them to carry out their plans, and lead them to evaluate their experiences. Analyze carefully your own part in the planning process.
7. Visit some classrooms in your community and observe:
   a. What learning seems to be taking place, based upon the behavioral performance of the pupils.
   b. How teachers are attempting to meet the psychological and social needs of pupils.
   c. How teachers are building positive (or negative) relationships with pupils. Record and classify accordingly the statements made by the teacher being observed.

    d.   How teachers are building positive (or negative) climates for learning.

    e.   What types of questions teachers ask the students. Try to classify them according to the categories discussed in this chapter.

    f.   How the students and the teacher are interacting. Speculate upon the probable effects of this interaction upon the lives of the students.

8.   Interview some high-school dropouts and attempt to determine the causes for their dropping out. Speculate upon the extent to which the school was responsible for these cases.

9.   Use some of the self-instructional materials in the book *Developing Teacher Competencies* by Weigand (ed.) for the purpose of furthering your proficiency in regard to the eight competencies discussed in the book.

# 8 | LEGAL LIABILITIES AND RESPONSIBILITIES OF TEACHERS

As we experience increases in population, in levels of educational attainment, in the complexity of society, and in concern for our health, education, and welfare, it is to be expected that lawyers and our courts will be busier than ever before. There is a tendency for the average citizen today to be more sensitive to legal affairs than he has been in the past. This tendency extends to students and their parents in their relationships with the schools.

We read frequently of lawsuits being filed against medical doctors and people in the other professions. Today teachers are sometimes the subjects of lawsuits brought by parents and other individuals. As is true in the other professions, it is highly probable that the frequency of lawsuits against teachers will increase in the future.

It is unfortunate that, as a general rule, teachers are woefully uninformed about their legal rights and responsibilities. Physicians, for example, normally receive courses in medical jurisprudence as a part of their professional education. Prospective teachers generally are not given a comparable type of instruction. It is also true that the work of a teacher, which normally does not involve the life-or-death responsibilities assumed so frequently by physicians, does not tend to stimulate an acute consciousness of the legal hazards involved in teaching. In planning a career in teaching, it is important to become familiar with the legal rights and responsibilities of teachers.

This chapter is much too brief to analyze all aspects of the law as it affects teachers. Problems of teacher contracts, tenure, strikes and collective bargaining, and retirement will be discussed in subsequent chapters. The reading list at the end of the chapter suggests numerous other resources which might be utilized for further study of these and other areas of legal concern.

An attempt is made here to provide an acquaintance with two major aspects of the law affecting teachers—*tort liability* and *pupil con-*

*trol*—since these are perhaps of more significance to teachers and prospective teachers generally than are any other legal topics.

In studying the materials concerning these two aspects, keep in mind that the courts are by no means antagonistic to teachers. Even though court decisions have gone against teachers in certain situations, they generally tend to uphold the actions of teachers so long as good judgment and common sense were used. It should be kept in mind, the cases referred to are drawn from a number of different states, and strictly speaking, precedent as established by the courts in one state may not necessarily be followed by the courts in another state. It is also important to understand that the law as it affects schools is in a period of change. The concept of tort liability is being questioned by the courts, and the area of pupil control is being affected by court extension of constitutional rights such as due process to students. The cases presented here represent the status of the law at the present time. Starting from this base, the teacher and the prospective teacher must be alert to changes which affect the legal liability and responsibility of the teacher.

## THE SOURCES OF THE LAW

You may already be familiar with three great decisions of the United States Supreme Court which have vitally affected the public schools—the 1954 decision requiring desegregation of the public schools (*Brown v. Board of Education,* 347 U.S. 438, 74 Sup. Ct. 686); the 1962 decision banning a state-prescribed prayer in the public schools (*Engel v. Vitale,* 370 U.S. 421, 82 Sup. Ct. 1261); and the 1969 decision extending constitutional protections to students during their attendance in school (*Tinker v. Des Moines Independent Community School District,* 393 U.S. 503, 89 Sup. Ct. 733). These great decisions illustrate one of the major sources of American law—the judicial process whereby a court considers a problem and arrives at a decision, thereby establishing or creating "law."

If the man on the street is asked where the law comes from, the following answers might be received: "The United States Congress passes laws," or "The state legislatures enact laws," or "The United States Constitution is the basis of all American law." All these statements are basically accurate but are superficial at best. It is true that the Congress and the various state legislatures enact *statutes,* or laws, which cover a multiplicity of subjects. It is also true that the federal and state constitutions provide the basic framework of American government. The federal Constitution is the basis for congressional authority, and the state constitutions provide limitations beyond which the state legislatures may not go. A basic source of American law, however, is to be found in the federal or state system of courts.

## The Judicial System and Precedent

One of the most important sources of law in the Anglo-American countries is the judicial, or court, system. The courts over a period of hundreds of years in England, and later in America, have been called upon to adjudicate disputes between parties arising from situations for which no legislature or constitution has made provision. In other cases the courts have been requested to interpret the meaning of portions of the various American constitutions as well as the statutes enacted by Congress or by the state legislatures.

Over the years, then, a body of court-made law has developed which has become known as *case law,* or in a broad sense, the *common law.* In developing the common law, the courts have tended to examine earlier similar court decisions and to follow *precedent,* which can be defined as an earlier court decision which furnishes an example or authority for a later decision on a similar point of law. A study of court decisions, then, can result in an understanding of how the courts are likely to rule on many questions involving teachers and the schools.

The law has been said to be an expression of public policy, whether the source is constitutional, statutory, or judicial. When the constitution and statutes are silent (as is the case in most states in the area of corporal punishment of school pupils, for example), a court is called upon actually to legislate, to formulate law, or to express public policy in deciding the dispute which is before it.

## Types of Court Action

Court action may be either *criminal* or *civil* in nature. A criminal case is initiated normally by the prosecuting attorney acting for the state against an individual who has been accused of violating the criminal statutes of the state. If guilt is proved, the penalty assessed by the court is imprisonment and/or a fine payable to the state.

A civil case is normally brought by one individual or group of individuals, known as the *plaintiff,* against another, known as the *defendant.* In a civil case, the plantiff seeks some sort of *remedy,* which may be in the form of an *injunction* (prohibiting the defendant from doing something), *mandamus* (requiring the defendant to do something), or *monetary damages* (for an injury or loss). Most cases involving teachers and the school are civil in nature.

## The Appellate Court System

Legal action is initiated in a *trial court,* or *lower court,* which may be known in the various states as "circuit courts," "superior courts," "county courts," or "district courts." Following the decision of the trial court, the loser may appeal the decision to a higher court, known as an *appellate court.* The highest appellate court in the state court system is the state supreme court. This court is known by various names. For example, the highest state court in Kentucky is known as the Court of Appeals, in Connecticut it is called the Supreme Court of Errors, and in Oregon it is termed the Supreme Court. Although the decisions of trial courts normally are not published in widely disseminated law journals and books and thus are not readily available to attorneys, the decisions of appellate courts are published and are available in any adequate law library. These published appellate court decisions form the basis for precedent and vividly portray the continuing development of the common law.

Many of the cases related to students and teachers involve the enforcement of rights found in the Constitution of the United States. Such cases usually start in a Federal District Court. Appeals go to the Court of Appeals in the circuit in which the case originated and may go ultimately to the United States Supreme Court for final decision. All the decisions of the federal courts are published and form the basis for precedent.

## TORT LIABILITY OF TEACHERS

A *tort* is a private or civil wrong which does not flow from breach of contract and which results in loss or damage to an individual or to his property. Perhaps the most common torts are negligence causing personal injury, trespass upon property belonging to another, maintenance of a nuisance, and defamation of character.

In most states, the state itself is immune from tort liability. A school district, as a subdivision of the state, therefore enjoys immunity in these states. Although there are a number of legal reasons for this type of immunity, perhaps the most frequently cited reason is to be found in the ancient doctrine that "the king can do no wrong." Since the state in the United States has replaced the sovereign, this doctrine has been modified to "the state can do no wrong." Other reasons given in support of state immunity are that school funds can only be spent for the educational benefit of pupils and cannot be used to pay damages for claims; and that school district officers can only act to carry out the bona fide purposes of the school and that they are not acting for the school district when they act negligently.

State immunity from tort liability, however, is slowly changing. In recent years several states, including Arizona, California, Illinois, New York, Washington, and Wisconsin, have abolished, either by statute or by court decision, the immunity of school districts under certain circumstances. The trend toward the abolishment of sovereign, or governmental, immunity of school districts appears to be continuing.

To the teacher the question of state immunity is of little significance. Teachers are classified as employees of school districts and do not enjoy immunity even in states where the school district is immune. Teachers are liable for their torts. This is important because the teacher has an almost constant relation with and responsibility to students. Thus the teacher is in a position where the chance of being involved in litigation arising from tort liability is ever present.

## The Standard of Negligence

The tort which results in by far the greatest number of lawsuits involving teachers is *negligence*. Negligence has been defined as conduct involving unreasonable danger to others which should be recognized by a reasonably prudent person. Since every factual situation in which an individual may be injured as the result of the actions or conduct of another is unique, the courts through the years have established the conduct of the "reasonably prudent man" as the hypothetical standard against which the actions of the person sued are measured.

A reasonably prudent man will behave differently under different circumstances. Although the courts do not expect an individual to be clairvoyant or psychic in making certain his actions do not result in injury to others, they do require the conduct of an individual in protecting others from harm to be that of the average person under similar circumstances.

The courts require teachers to exercise a greater degree of care to protect pupils from injury than they require of the ordinary person. Perhaps it would be more accurate to say that the standard of conduct demanded of a teacher is that of the "reasonably prudent teacher."

Injuries leading to litigation and sometimes to teacher liability often arise from common factual situations such as the following:

Immediately after lunch but prior to the start of afternoon classes, a senior high school student began "slap boxing" with a friend in the school gym area while waiting for classes to resume. The "slap boxing" continued for five to ten minutes while a group of thirty students gathered to watch. During the exchange of slaps, Michael was hit, fell backwards, and fractured his skull on the asphalt paving. He died later that night.

No supervision schedule had been set up for this area, and supervision had been "left to the person in the gymnasium office." While the "slap boxing" incident was in process, the teacher "in the gym office" was eating his lunch at a desk with a wall obscuring his view of the area where Michael was injured. There were no noises heard to indicate a disturbance in the gym area just before Michael fell.

Would a court be likely to find the teacher in this situation liable for negligence?

In order to answer this question, it is perhaps necessary to examine in greater detail the tort of negligence as it applies to teachers.

## Criteria for Establishing Negligence

Liability for negligence rests upon three factors: (1) a duty to act so as to protect others from unnecessary risks, (2) the failure to so act, and (3) the injury of another causing loss or damage as the result of such failure to act. A teacher may be liable either for *an act* which a reasonably prudent teacher should have realized involved an unreasonable risk of injury to another or for *failure to do an act* which the teacher was under a duty to do for the protection of another.

The major criterion used by the courts in determining negligence is *foreseeability;* that is, should the defendant as a reasonably prudent teacher have foreseen the possible harmful consequences of his action or lack of action and did he disregard these consequences? If the answer of the court is in the affirmative, liability for negligence exists.

## Liability for Pupil Injury: Classroom Activities

In order to illustrate the attitude of the courts with respect to teacher negligence resulting in injury to pupils in the classroom, court decisions from several different states are summarized in the following paragraphs.

The importance of proper instruction in dangerous activities was emphasized in a California case. A chemistry teacher during a laboratory period required pupils to perform an experiment as outlined in the textbook without giving additional instruction. A pupil used the wrong chemical and an explosion occurred, resulting in pupil injury. In finding the teacher negligent, the court in 1935 stated (*Mastrangelo v. West Side Union High School District,* 42 P.2d 634): "It is not unreasonable to assume that it is the duty of a teacher of chemistry, in the exercise of ordinary care, to *instruct* students regarding the selection, mingling, and use of ingredients with which dangerous experiments are to be accomplished, rather than to merely hand them a textbook with general instruction." (Italics added.)

Normally a teacher is not responsible for injuries occurring to pupils off the school grounds or after school hours. Under certain circumstances, however, the teacher may be held liable, since teachers apparently have the responsibility of warning pupils about dangerous practices which arise out of classroom activities.

In another California case pupils in an industrial arts class had been constructing model cannons made of bronze with wooden gun carriages. The teacher had given no warning to the pupils about the danger of firing the cannons at home, although the evidence indicated that he was aware that the pupils were taking the cannons home and firing them, using powder from shotgun shells as an explosive and ball bearings as projectiles. A pupil was permanently injured as the result of an explosion which occurred when he attempted to fire one of the model cannons at home. Since, as indicated previously, California is one of the states in which suit may be brought against the school district, the district was sued for the alleged negligence of the teacher. In 1963 the court held the teacher negligent and pointed out that, even though the injury to the pupil was incurred off the school grounds and after school hours, the teacher had failed in his duty to warn the pupils of the potential dangers of firing the model cannons (*Calandri v. Ione Unified School District,* 33 Cal. App.2d 333).

A teacher has a responsibility to be present in his assigned classroom to supervise pupils or to notify his principal that it is necessary for him to be absent. In New York, a teacher was not present to supervise his pupils during the first period of the day and had failed to notify school authorities that he would be absent. In the teacher's absence, the pupils began to engage in "horseplay," and one boy openly began to brandish a knife. After a period of time another pupil was stabbed.

The court, in 1962, found that the teacher was negligent and stated that, had the teacher been present in the classroom, it would have been his duty to take action to relieve the pupil of the knife (*Christofides v. Hellenic Eastern Orthodox Christian Church,* 227 N.Y.S.2d 946). In other words, the teacher, if present, should have foreseen and prevented the injury.

Negligence may be assessed for injuries resulting from the mismatching of pupils engaged in physical education activities. During a physical education class held in a school in New York in 1963, groups of boys were placed on each side of the gymnasium and given numbers chosen at random. When a number was called by the teacher, two boys at opposite sides of the floor would run to a soccer ball in the center of the room and attempt to kick it. A boy suffered serious injury as the result of being kicked by a taller and heavier opponent, and suit was brought against the school district on grounds of negligent supervision by the teacher. The court held that the "mismatching" of the two boys constituted negligence (*Brooks v. Board of Education,* 189 N.E.2d 497).

The element of foreseeability, previously mentioned, is a major factor in determining negligence. In 1956, a California teacher of drafting took his class out on the school lawn, with each pupil carrying his own drawing board. On the way out of the building, a boy picked up a knife and, when the pupils were seated on the lawn, began repeatedly to flip the knife into the grass. The teacher noticed this game of mumblety-peg but did nothing to halt it. The knife eventually glanced off a drawing board and struck a pupil in the eye, which caused permanent injury. The court, in holding the teacher negligent, pointed out that, since the teacher had been aware of the dangerous activity and since the activity had gone on for a period of time, the teacher should have foreseen the possible dangerous consequences and should have halted the activity (*Lilienthal v. San Leandro Unified School District,* 293 P.2d 889).

A study of the negligence cases involving teachers reveals that teachers who have supervised potentially hazardous activities over a long period of time frequently may be lulled into a false sense of security concerning the dangers to pupils. What is perhaps the most flagrant case involving teacher liability for negligence occurred in South Dakota in 1941 and illustrates this point. For a number of years it had been the practice to initiate high school male athletes into a club known as the "H" club by subjecting the candidates to an electric shock produced by batteries and run through a transformer to reduce the current. The high school coach secured permission from the school superintendent to use the gymnasium for the initiation. The transformer and batteries were not available that year; so the boys prepared a rheostat consisting of a jar of salt water and obtained current from a 120-volt light socket. Each boy, blindfolded and clad in shorts, was made to lie down with a glass of water in his hand on a series of bare copper wires connected to the circuit. The electricity was then turned on, which caused electric shock and resulted in the spilling of the water. Five candidates were in the process of being initiated. After each of the first three received his shock, the coach mopped the floor and tested the current with his hands. The fourth candidate complained that the shock was too great, after which one-half of the solution of salt water was removed from the rheostat and replaced with city water, presumably to reduce the current. The fifth boy then took his turn. When the electricity was turned on, he partially arose, gasped "Oh, my God," and fell backward. All attempts to revive the boy failed—the electric shock had resulted in a fatality.

Suit was brought by the parents of the boy against both the coach and the school superintendent. The coach was found negligent. The court pointed out that he should have known electricity was dangerous and that he had failed to observe the high degree of care he owed his pupils. The superintendent, on the other hand, was absolved from responsibility. The court held that the superintendent had performed his full duty when he permitted use of the gymnasium with the knowledge that the coach would be present [*DeGooyer v. Harkness,* 13 N.W.2d 815 (1944)].

## Liability for Pupil Injury: The Playground

Playground or outdoor athletic activities are probably inherently more physically dangerous than most classroom activities. Teachers who are charged with the responsibility for such outdoor activities should therefore make certain that pupils are warned against unreasonable hazards and should supervise these activities very carefully.

A teacher who is given playground duty, however, is not expected by the courts to protect every pupil against every possibility of injury, since the courts will use the reasonably prudent teacher as the standard measure of conduct. For example, while a Colorado teacher was supervising a playground, a pupil threw a rock which struck another pupil in the eye. The court refused to impose liability on the teacher and stated: "There is no requirement that the teacher have under constant and unremitting scrutiny the precise spots wherein every phase of play activity is being pursued; nor is there compulsion that the general supervision be continuous and direct" [*Carroll v. Fitzsimmons,* 384 P.2d 81 (1963)].

A teacher who is given responsibility for playground supervision should be on the playground rather than be "supervising" the pupils by watching through the classroom window. In New York, for example, a six-year-old pupil climbed up and fell from a fire escape which the "supervising" teacher could not see from the classroom window, since it was located around the corner of the building. The court held that the teacher was negligent [*Miller v. Board of Education,* 50 N.E.2d 529 (1943)].

The importance of adequate safety rules for playground activity was illustrated in a California case. The school principal had been aware for some time that boys on the playground were playing a game known as

What teacher liability might be involved in this situation? *(Photograph from the National Education Association.)*

"blackout." The game consisted of one boy taking a deep breath while another squeezed him tightly from behind with the object of rendering the subject unconscious. Upon being rendered unconscious, one of the boys fell, struck his head on a concrete pavement, and was fatally injured. Suit was brought against the principal, and the court found him negligent, primarily because he had known of the practice for some time and had done nothing to stop it [*Tymkowicz v. San Jose Unified School District,* 312 P.2d 388 (1957)].

## Liability for Pupil Injury: The School Patrol

Teachers are frequently required to assume general supervision of school patrol activities. When school-age pupils are called upon to shepherd other pupils across streets and highways it might be thought that the teacher selecting or supervising such patrolmen could be held liable in case of pupil injury.

Surprisingly, perhaps, there appears to be no case in courts of record dealing with teacher liability for actions of school patrolmen. Legal authorities, however, have pointed out that a teacher with the responsibility for selecting school patrolmen should make certain that the pupils selected are competent, are reliable, and are properly instructed and that the patrol activity is voluntary and engaged in with the permission of the parent (see, e.g., *Opinions of the Attorney General of Indiana,* 1929, p. 257; 1954, p. 143).

A Maryland case involving a school bus driver apparently supports the principle that the use of a school patrolman to help pupils across the street is not unreasonable. In this case the school bus driver was not found negligent when a child was injured while being escorted across a highway by a responsible older pupil who was a member of the school safety patrol. The use of a safety patrol, stated the court, was "generally regarded as a reasonable and adequate provision for the safety of school bus riders" [*Ragonese v. Hilferty,* 191 A.2d 426 (1963)].

## Liability for Pupil Injury: Errands and Field Trips

A teacher should avoid sending pupils on errands off the school grounds except in cases of real emergency. Two areas of possible liability exist: (1) injury to the pupil himself, in which case a court might be called upon to determine whether a reasonably prudent teacher would send a child on such an errand, and (2) injury or damage done by the pupil to a third party or to his property, in which case a court might hold that the pupil was acting as the agent of the teacher and that the teacher was liable.

Most educational authorities agree that field trips are desirable and should be a recognized part of the curriculum. A teacher should not

Upon being confronted with this type of situation, what should a teacher do? *(Photograph by Joe Di Dio, National Education Association.)*

hesitate to take pupils on field trips because of the possibility of liability. The teacher should, however, make certain that pupils are properly protected and that dangers are minimized. The following steps are recommended:

1. Plan the trip carefully in advance.
2. If the trip is to be a visit to an industrial plant or to some other potentially dangerous place, visit the plant in advance and discuss possible hazards with the plant manager or his representative.
3. Discuss the potential hazards with the pupils who are to make the trip. Establish safety rules for the trip and inform pupils of these.
4. Obtain the permission of the school administrator who is the immediate superior.
5. Send parental permission slips home with the pupils to be signed by the parents, and returned.
6. Provide extra supervision if this seems necessary. Parents can be utilized in this role.
7. If automobiles must be used, be certain that the drivers are properly licensed and that such drivers carry adequate liability insurance in case of an accident occurring in transit.

Keep in mind that a signed parental permission slip does not relieve the teacher of liability, since one individual (even a parent) may not sign away the right of another to sue. However, parental permission slips at least inform parents about the proposed field trip, and might be used as evidence of reasonable prudence on the part of the teacher.

Strangely, perhaps, most of the lawsuits arising out of injury to pupils on school field trips have been brought against the industrial plants in which the injuries occurred. Whether the pupil was legally a licensee or an invitee has been significant in these cases. A *licensee* can be defined as one who visits the premises of another for his own benefit; an *invitee* visits the premises of another for the benefit of the owner or for the benefit of both himself and the owner. Although a plant owner owes only a normal degree of care to protect a licensee from harm, he owes a much higher degree of care to an invitee.

In a Maryland case, a class visited the plant of a traction company. The pupils were warned of the dangerous apparatus and then told to "look around" for themselves. (The teacher in charge should have ended the visit at this point.) A pupil fell into an open vat of boiling water flush with the floor in an inadequately lighted portion of the plant, and suit was brought against the traction company. The court held that since the pupils were licensees, the plant owed them only an ordinary degree of care. The pupils had entered the plant at their own risk, and therefore the injured pupil could not recover from the traction company. The court further pointed out that if any negligence existed, "it consisted in bringing thirty-odd boys at one time to a building filled with dangerous machinery." The court obviously felt that the teacher, rather than the traction company, should have been the defendant in the lawsuit [*Benson v. Baltimore Traction Company,* 26 Atl. 973 (1893)].

In a Missouri case, the court held that a pupil injured while visiting a bakery and creamery company was an invitee. The company had advertised widely and had encouraged inspection of the plant by the public. Each year, five or six classes from the local high school visited the plant. On one such visit, a girl was seriously injured when her arm became caught in an ice crusher, which later resulted in the amputation of the arm. The court held the industrial plant liable, since the invitation to the public to visit the plant was used as a part of its advertising. As an invitee, the girl was owed a much higher degree of care than ordinarily would be required, and the plant officials had failed to properly warn her of the dangerous machinery [*Gilliland v. Bondurant,* 59 S.W.2d 679 (1933)].

## Liability Arising out of Cocurricular Activities

Teachers who supervise pupil activities of a cocurricular nature or activities which take place after school hours are held to the same standard of conduct as that required during school hours in the classroom. A teacher should exercise the same high degree of care in supervising such activities as is exercised during any other school activity.

Athletics is a particularly likely area for litigation. The problem is illustrated by a Louisiana case in which a football player died after being "denied" treatment for two hours after symptoms of heat stroke and shock had appeared. The high school football coaches were found negligent in this case. Administrators in the school were found not to be negligent, because they were not present at the practice and had no duty to be there [*Mogabgab v. Orleans Parish School Board,* 239 So.2d 456 (1970)]. Coaches need to be especially alert to their responsibility to provide for the safety and protection of student athletes.

The following statements summarize other problems and aspects of teacher liability with which teachers should be familiar:

1. A teacher probably has a responsibility to report to the proper authorities unsafe or deficient instructional or playground equipment.
2. Should a pupil be injured, the teacher probably has the responsibility to administer emergency first aid. One good rule to follow is that seriously injured pupils should not be moved until competent medical personnel arrive and take charge. In any case, the principal or appropriate supervisor should be notified immediately whenever a pupil is injured.
3. A teacher would not be expected by the courts to be able to diagnose every type of contagious disease with which pupils might become infected. Teachers therefore are unlikely to be held liable by a court in case a pupil contracts a disease in the classroom. However, teachers would be expected to utilize reasonable care in recommending the exclusion of pupils from the classroom if they are suspected of carrying an infectious disease.
4. Teachers are sometimes in the habit of dispensing medication, such as aspirin, to pupils who have a headache or who appear ill. A teacher should avoid giving medication to pupils. Ill pupils should be sent to the school nurse or to the school sickroom until parents can be notified. Good judgment should be used in such cases. If a pupil brings medication from home as prescribed by his family doctor, it is probably reasonable to permit the pupil to take such medication at prescribed times.

## Defenses against Negligence

A number of legal defenses against negligence which relieve the teacher of liability have been rather clearly defined by the courts. The first and most common defense is, of course, a denial that any negligence exists. The person bringing suit (plaintiff) must prove negligence by proving that the conduct of the defendant fell below the standard of reasonable prudence.

A Minnesota case illustrates this defense. Suit was brought against a teacher for injuries sustained by an elementary pupil during a rope-jumping activity in a physical education class. The pupil stepped on the rope as it was being rotated, and the wooden handle affixed to one end was pulled from the grasp of the teacher. The wooden handle struck the

front teeth of the pupil and caused injuries for which recovery was
sought. The plaintiff maintained that the teacher should have foreseen
the injury and could have prevented it by furnishing a longer rope or by
providing a rope without wooden handles. The court absolved the
teacher from any negligence and pointed out that the jumping rope was of
the kind normally used by children for "many years" and that the teacher
could not have reasonably anticipated the injury [*Wire v. Williams,* 133
N.W.2d 840 (1965)].


## Contributory Negligence

In most states an individual is relieved of liability if the actions of the
injured person had the effect of contributing to his own injury, and proof
by the plaintiff that he had done so is known as *contributory negligence.*
In recent years in such states as Arkansas, Georgia, Mississippi, Nebraska, South Dakota, and Wisconsin, the doctrine of *comparative negligence*
has been gaining acceptance. In states where comparative negligence is
recognized, the court seeks to "apportion the blame" between the two
parties and may assess some degree of liability to the defendant even
though the plaintiff contributed to his own injury.

An example of contributory negligence occurred in a North Carolina
case. A chemistry teacher granted a high school boy and several classmates permission to go to the chemistry laboratory to set up a specific
experiment in the absence of the instructor. Instead of performing the
experiment agreed upon, the boys made gunpowder. An explosion of the
gunpowder resulted in serious injury to one of the boys. As a result, a suit
was brought against the teacher. The court, in relieving the teacher of
liability, held that the injured boy had contributed to his own injury, and
was therefore guilty of contributory negligence. "Even an eight-year-old
would have known better," stated the court [*Moore v. Order of Minor
Conventuals,* 267 F.2d 296 (1959)].

The giving of proper instructions can be an important factor in
determining contributory negligence. In a recent case in Oregon the court
held that a student who had sustained an injury while mixing potassium
chlorate and powdered sugar could not recover from the teacher because
the student had had full knowledge of the risk (proper instructions) and
had contributed to his own injury [*Hutchinson v. Toews,* 476 P.2d 811
(1970)].

There appears to be an age below which the courts are unlikely to
assess contributory negligence. In determining whether a child is guilty
of contributing to his own injury, the court normally asks itself whether a
child of similar years and similar mental and physical ability would
reasonably be expected to protect himself from the dangers inherent in
the particular situation. As may be expected, the defense of contributory
negligence is less often successfully used in situations involving injuries

to elementary school pupils than it is in situations involving injuries to high school pupils.

The defense of contributory negligence will be weighed carefully by the courts. In the "slap boxing" case, presented previously, it might be assumed that the courts would have been influenced by the age of the students. However, despite the fact that the students were high school seniors, the court still found the teacher negligent. The court said: "Recognizing that a principal task of supervision is to anticipate and curb rash student behavior, our courts have often held that a failure to prevent injuries caused by the intentional or reckless conduct of the victim or a fellow student may constitute negligence" [*Dailey v. Los Angeles Unified School District*, 2 C.3rd 741 (1970)].

## Proximate Cause

*Causal connection* is a major factor considered by the courts in assessing whether negligence exists; there must be an unbroken "chain of causation" between the negligence of the teacher and the resultant pupil injury. In other words, the negligence of the defendant must be the *proximate cause* of the injury. A "break" in the chain of causation which results from the *intervening act* of a third party, for example, may mean that the court will conclude that the proximate cause of the injury was not the negligent conduct of the defendant and thus relieve the defendant of liability.

A sudden action by a pupil which causes injury to another pupil that could not have been foreseen by the teacher usually results in the court's absolving the teacher from liability. For example, a New Jersey teacher was standing outside the classroom door as two pupils came down the hall together. One of the pupils hit the other lightly on the arm. The teacher, believing that nothing more was likely to happen from this incident, entered the classroom. The second pupil then pushed the first through the classroom door, causing him to strike his foot against a metal desk, which resulted in an injury that eventually necessitated the amputation of the foot. Suit was brought against the teacher for negligence on the ground that he should have foreseen the action on the part of the second pupil. The court held that the first incident in the hall was not of a nature to reasonably attract the attention of the teacher, and therefore the injury to the first pupil was not *proximately caused* by the negligence of the teacher. Rather, the injury to the first pupil was the result of the *intervening act* of the second pupil [*Doktor v. Greenberg*, 155 A.2d 793 (1959)].

Although a teacher should not leave his classroom unsupervised, the courts have sometimes been lenient to teachers in this regard. For example, a Maryland teacher left her classroom for a few minutes while the class was engaged in calisthenics. The teacher had given proper instructions to the students for performing the exercise. An injury resulted when a nine-year-old boy failed to follow the instructions. His feet struck a nine-year-old girl, badly chipping two of her front teeth. The court held that the teacher was not liable because her absence from the classroom was not the proximate cause of the injury [*Segerman v. Jones,* 259 A.2d 794 (1969)].

Comparing the case just described with the earlier case in which one pupil stabbed another with a knife after brandishing it for a period of time may give further understanding of the reasoning of the courts in cases where the teacher is absent from the classroom. In the latter case, the court held that the teacher, if present, would have seen the knife and could have taken it from the pupil. In other words the teacher could have "foreseen" the possible injury. The court in the "chipped teeth" case evidently felt that the failure to follow instructions and the resulting injury could have occurred even if the teacher had been present. While the court did relieve the teacher of liability in the "chipped teeth" case, it should be remembered that a teacher runs a serious risk of liability if he leaves the classroom unsupervised.

## Assumption of Risk

An adult who knowingly engages in a dangerous occupation or activity normally is considered by the courts to have assumed the risk of the occupation. Except in the case of gross negligence of his employer or any other person, he may not recover any compensation if he should be injured. This is known as the doctrine of the *assumption of risk.* Except in cases of athletic injuries, in which the pupil and his parents know that the activity may be physically hazardous, this doctrine is seldom used as a successful defense in cases involving the schools.

## Other Reasons Assigned by Courts for Nonliability

As indicated earlier in this chapter, a court will use the reasonably prudent teacher as the standard against which the allegedly negligent conduct of a teacher is measured in a particular situation. *Proper instruction* and *due care* are terms frequently used by the courts in determining whether the teacher against whom suit is brought behaved with reasonable prudence. In New Jersey, a 14-year-old boy was injured in a physical education class while jumping over a piece of apparatus known as a "horse." The instructor had demonstrated the proper method of performing the exercise and had warned the pupils that they should not try if they felt they could not accomplish the exercise safely. The court found that the teacher had not been negligent, since he had exercised due care in warning the pupils and had properly instructed the pupils by demonstrating the exercise [*Sayers v. Ranger,* 83 A.2d 775 (1951)].

In California, an industrial arts teacher had promulgated safety rules for the automobile shop and had frequently repeated the rules to the pupils during the school year. A pupil was assigned the job of adjusting the valve tappets on an automobile. In violation of the safety rules, another pupil started the car. The vehicle, which was in gear, pinned a third pupil against the wall of the shop and caused serious injury. The evidence showed that the teacher had personally inspected the car immediately prior to the accident. The court exonerated the teacher, primarily because he had established and repeated the safety rules. Since he had used due care, he could not have foreseen the accident [*Perumean v. Wills,* 67 P.2d 96 (1937)].

Teachers should keep in mind that it is important to establish adequate *safety rules* for potentially dangerous activities.


## Defamation of Character

Another tort for which teachers occasionally are sued is *defamation of character,* which may be defined as damage to a person's reputation through communication involving ridicule, disgrace, contempt, or hatred. Written defamation is known as *libel,* and spoken defamation is known as *slander.*

Teachers are involved in possible liability for defamation of character in such activities as (1) writing letters of recommendation to or talking to prospective employers or college representatives about pupils, (2) entering comments on pupil records, (3) making comments to parents or to other teachers about pupils, or (4) making public or newspaper statements concerning pupils.


## Truth as a Defense

In many states truth is a defense against defamation-of-character lawsuits. Should the person against whom a suit is brought be able to prove the truth of his statements, no liability exists in these states.

In other states (and the number appears to be growing), truth is not a full defense unless it can be shown that spoken or written publication of the defamatory material is made without malice or with good intentions and justifiable ends.


## Privilege as a Defense

In many instances the law excuses the publication of defamatory material under the doctrines of *absolute privilege* or *qualified privilege.* Absolute privilege is based upon the proposition that in some cases a person must be completely free to speak his mind without fear of reprisals in the form of lawsuits for libel or slander. Absolute privilege is extended to comments by judges in court proceedings, statements by legislators during legislative sessions, and comments by certain executive officers of government in the exercise of their duties. Absolute privilege is not usually extended to school personnel as a defense against defamation.

Qualified (or conditional) privilege, on the other hand, is frequently used as a defense by school personnel against whom suit is brought for defamation. Qualified privilege rests upon the assumption by the courts that certain information should be given to certain individuals or agencies in the protection of the interests of the individuals, of the agencies, or of society as a whole. The existence of qualified privilege depends upon the *reason* which exists to communicate the information. If the person to whom defamatory information is communicated has a valid reason to receive such information, the communicator may be protected by qualified privilege. Recognizing the problem that school personnel have in this area, the Indiana General Assembly, in a 1965 statute, extended to counselors immunity from disclosing "privileged or confidential communication" from pupils.

## Defamation of Character: Case Examples

In California, an instructor in a teacher education institution made statements to a local newspaper that a female student was "tricky and unreliable" and "destitute of those womanly characteristics that should be the first requisite of a teacher." The court held the instructor liable for defamation of character [*Dixon v. Allen,* 11 Pac. 179 (1886)]. It is quite possible that no liability would have existed had the instructor communicated the same information to a person with *reason* to have the information, such as a prospective employer, since the teacher probably would have been protected by qualified privilege.

Teachers who report grades on school registers are normally protected so long as they report facts (or perhaps even opinions) reasonably related to the pupils' school activities. However, the limits of qualified privilege were exceeded in an Oklahoma case, where a teacher added the comment "ruined by tobacco and whisky" on the school register after the name of a pupil. The court held the teacher liable [*Dawkins v. Billingsley,* 172 Pac. 69 (1918)].

In brief, teachers have little to fear insofar as defamation of character is concerned, so long as information—even rumor or suspicion—is communicated in good faith to those having reason to possess the information. The doctrine of qualified privilege protects the teacher in such situations.

Gossip about pupils, however, is another matter. Teachers who communicate defamatory information about pupils to persons outside the school system or to other teachers who have no reason to have such information (e.g., who do not now have or who are not likely in the future to have the pupil in class) are acting imprudently, since it is possible that a successful lawsuit for defamation of character may be initiated.

## Liability Insurance and Other Protection

One means of protection against judgments resulting from tort suits is liability insurance. For a relatively modest sum a teacher may obtain a personal liability insurance policy insuring him against judgments for negligence and other torts.

As is the case with most insurance policies, tort liability insurance may be secured at a lesser cost on a group basis than on an individual basis. Many state teachers' organizations are now including liability insurance as a part of their services to members. In addition, school boards in some states are empowered by law to carry liability insurance on school employees.

There is also an increasing trend whereby state legislatures have authorized or mandated school districts to provide for the legal defense and/or pay damages for employees in claims resulting from tort liability. Such provision is known as "save harmless" legislation.

## PUPIL CONTROL

Large numbers of legal cases have been concerned with the extent to which a school board, a school administrator, or a teacher may establish rules setting limits on pupil conduct. In determining whether such rules are legally valid, the courts invariably attempt to determine the reasonableness of the rules, or whether the rules are reasonably related to the discipline, morale, or good order of the school. Regardless of the specific punishment incurred for violation of a school rule, a basic common-law principle established by the courts is that the rule itself must be reasonable.

Not only must a rule governing pupil conduct be reasonable; the punishment itself must also be reasonable. Punishment may not be excessive; excessive punishment is usually defined as punishment which results in permanent injury, is performed with immoderate severity, or is administered with malice or wicked motives.

## Reasonable Rules

Most of the general rules governing pupil conduct, such as rules dealing with pupil dress, marriage, pregnancy, leaving of school premises, pupil driving, and membership of pupils in secret societies, are established by school boards or by school administrators pursuant to authority granted by the boards rather than by the teachers. An analysis of court decisions dealing with general rules of pupil conduct will perhaps reveal the criteria used by the courts in determining reasonableness of conduct.

The reasonableness of a rule governing pupil conduct depends upon circumstances and does not exist in the abstract. This was graphically illustrated by two cases which reached the Court of Appeals of the Fifth Federal Circuit on the same day in 1966. Both involved rules forbidding students in all-black high schools in Mississippi from wearing buttons which expressed political positions. In the one case the Court of Appeals invalidated the rule [*Burnside v. Byars*, 363 F.2d 744 (1966)]. In the other case the Court of Appeals upheld the rule [*Blackwell v. Issaquena County Board of Education*, 363 F.2d 749 (1966)]. The only significant difference in the two cases was that in the latter case the rule forbidding the wearing of buttons had been made following disturbances caused by students talking in corridors, absenting themselves from classes, and attempting to pin the buttons on other students. These differences in the two situations evidently caused the Court of Appeals to reach exactly opposite judgments regarding the reasonableness of rules which were almost identical.

## Student Expression

In 1969 the Supreme Court of the United States handed down a decision of far-reaching significance regarding the free-speech rights of students. The Court invalidated a school rule forbidding the wearing of black armbands as an objection to the hostilities in Vietnam and in support of a truce. The Court ruled that the wearing of symbols such as armbands is "speech" and that students retain their rights to freedom of speech or expression while in school. Regarding the authority of schools to restrict free speech, the Court said: "undifferentiated fear or apprehension of disturbance is not enough to overcome the right to freedom of expression . . . The State must be able to show that its action was caused by something more than the desire to avoid the discomfort and unpleasantness that always accompanies an unpopular viewpoint" [*Tinker v. Des Moines Independent Community School District*, 393 U.S. 503, (1969)].

The immediacy of the free-speech issue has been demonstrated in a number of court decisions relative to the publication and distribution of student newspapers. The Court of Appeals of the Seventh Federal Circuit ruled in an Illinois case that a school could not forbid the distribution of a "literary journal" which criticized school administrators and urged other students to disregard school rules [*Scoville v. Board of Education of Joliet*, 425 F.2d 10 (1968)]. Federal courts have also held that students can distribute an underground newspaper on school grounds even though the paper is extremely critical of the school principal, so long as the distribution does not interfere with proper school activities [*Sullivan v. Houston Independent School District*, 307 F.Supp. 1328 (1969)]; that students cannot be suspended for refusing to comply with regulations that a privately printed newspaper be submitted to school administrators for approval [*Eisner v. Stamford*, 39 U.S.L.W. 2037 (1970)]; and that a school newspaper which had discussed the war in Vietnam on its editorial pages had to accept an anti-war advertisement. In the latter case the court said: "Here the school paper appears to have been open to free expression of ideas in the news and editorial columns as well as in letters to the editor. It is patently unfair in light of the free speech doctrine to close to the students the forum which they deem effective to present their ideas" [*Zucker v. Panitz*, 229 F.Supp. 102 (1969)].

The court did, in the Eisner case, recognize that students could be required to conform to reasonable regulations as to "time, exact place in school, and manner of distribution of the newspaper." That the courts are not in agreement regarding free speech and student newspapers was demonstrated by a California case in which the federal court upheld ten-day suspensions of students for distributing an off-campus newspaper containing "profanity and vulgarity" [*Baker v. Downey City Board of Education*, 307 F.Supp. 517 (1969)].

## Pupil Dress and Appearance

Most of the recent court decisions regarding the dress and appearance of pupils have dealt with rules regulating the length of student hair. The federal courts are not in agreement regarding the reasonableness of such rules. Recent cases in which the federal courts have invalidated haircut regulations include: [*Griffin v. Tatum*, 425 F.2d 201 (1970)]: [*Richards v. Thurston* 424 F.2d 1281 (1970)]: [*Danhom v. Palsifer*, 312 F.Supp. 411 (1970)]: [*Sims v. Colfax Community School District*, 307 F.Supp. 485 (1970)]. Cases in which haircut regulations have been upheld include: [*Jackson v. Dorrier*, 424 F.2d 213 (1970)]: [*Brownlee v. Bradley County, Tennessee Board of Education*, 311 F.Supp. 1360 (1970)]: [*Corley v. Daunhauer*, 312 F.Supp. 811 (1970)]: [*Stevenson v. Wheeler County Board of Education*, 426 F.2d 1154 (1970)]. These cases are representative of the numerous equally conflicting decisions handed down relative to haircut regulations.

Recent decisions have also dealt with the clothing and apparel of students. In one case the student, with the parent's permission and in violation of a school rule, was suspended from school for wearing dungarees which had been neatly cleaned and pressed. The court invalidated the rule [*Bannister v. Paradis*, 316 F.Supp. 185 (1970)]. A New York court nullified a school regulation prohibiting girls from wearing slacks. The court said school regulations were "valid only to the extent they protect the safety of the wearer or prevent disturbances that interfere with school operations" [*Scott v. Board of Education*, 305 N.Y.S. 2d 701 (1969)]. In another interesting case, a court was called upon to decide when a student could wear a hat. The court ruled that a regulation forbidding the wearing of hats in the classroom was reasonable [*Hernandez v. School District No. 1. Denver*, 315 F.Supp. 289 (1970)].

The conflicting nature of court decisions regarding the dress and appearance of students is indicative of the fact that court attitudes in this area are in a period of change and transition. It is not over-generalizing to say that courts are showing an increasing concern for student rights and are demanding that school rules and regulations be limited to those directly related to the effective operation of the school. Given this trend, it would be advisable for school personnel to reexamine rules regarding the dress and appearance of students to make certain that they are based on something other than personal preference.

## Payment for Destruction of School Property

Rules requiring pupils to make financial restitution for damage to or destruction of school property generally have not been upheld by the courts, especially if the damage is accidental or due to simple carelessness. An Indiana court held that a rule requiring such financial restitution was unreasonable, since "carelessness on the part of children is one of the most common, and yet one of the least blameworthy of their faults." The court went on to state that "in simple carelessness there is no purpose to do wrong" [*State v. Vanderbilt*, 18 N.E. 266 (1888)]. Courts in other states have held similar positions. [See, e.g., *Holman v. Trustees*, 43 N.W. 996 (Mich. 1889); *Perkins v. Independent School District*, 9 N.W. 356 (Iowa 1880).] The reasoning of these courts seems to be as follows: (1) Accidental damage to school property is not a breach of morals or discipline; (2) children from families of limited financial means may be denied an education illegally if required to make restitution; and (3) pupils are usually financially unable to make restitution, and if parents refuse to do so, pupils should not be punished for the failure or unwillingness of parents to make such a payment.

The courts do not look with favor upon willful or malicious destruction of school property. Although it is doubtful whether pupils may be required even in such case to pay for the damage, other kinds of punishment have been upheld by the courts, so long as such punishment is considered to be reasonable [*Palmyra Board of Education v. Hansen*, 153 A.2d 393 (N.J. 1959)].

## Prohibitions concerning Leaving of School Premises

School board regulations prohibiting pupils from leaving the school grounds during the noon lunch period have generally been upheld by the courts. In Virginia, a school board rule forbade pupils to leave the school campus between 9:00 A.M. and 3:35 P.M. A parent contested the rule on the ground that he wished his child to eat a hot meal at home. The court, in upholding the school board regulation, commented that it could discover no detriment to the health of pupils resulting from the eating of a cold meal at noon [*Flory v. Smith,* 134 S.E. 360 (1926)]. Similar rules have been upheld in Michigan [*Jones v. Cody,* 92 N.W. 495 (1902)], in Kentucky—where the court felt that the regulation was for the "common good" of all the children [*Casey County Board of Education v. Luster,* 282 S.W.2d 333 (1955)], and in Texas, where the board rule prohibited pupils from "taking lunch during the noon recess except from the school cafeteria or that . . . brought from home" [*Bishop v. Houston Independent School District,* 29 S.W.2d 312 (1930)].

## Pupil Driving

The increasing number of student drivers has resulted in rules by school boards prohibiting automobile driving during the noon hour. Surprisingly, perhaps, only one lawsuit bearing upon the reasonableness of such regulations has reached an appellate court in the United States.

A school board in Texas required students driving to school to park automobiles in the school parking lot in the morning and not to move the automobiles until school was dismissed in the afternoon. A girl was suspended from school for violation of the rule. The parents brought suit against the school board, contending that the board had no authority to adopt rules controlling streets and highways. The board countered with the argument that the rule had been adopted for the safety of all the pupils in the school, since there had been safety hazards created by student joyriding during the noon hour. The court upheld the school board, commenting that the rule was obviously not enacted to control traffic on streets and highways, but rather to control pupil conduct to the end that other pupils would be safe. This, according to the court, was a legitimate exercise of the power of the school board [*McLean Independent School District v. Andrews,* 33 S.W.2d 886 (1960)].

## Pupil Marriages

Numerous school boards have attempted to discourage pupil marriages either by providing for the expulsion or suspension of married pupils or by prohibiting married pupils from participating in cocurricular activities. The weight of authority seems to be that pupils may not be excluded from school solely because they are married. [See, e.g., *McLeod v. State*, 122 So. 737 (Miss. 1929); *Nutt v. Board of Education*, 278 Pac. 1065 (Kans. 1929).] A Texas court even struck down a rule which provided that upon marriage a student would be suspended for three weeks following which application for readmission could be made to the principal. The court ordered two married students readmitted for "scholastic purposes" only [*Carrollton-Farmers Branch Independent School District v. Knight*, 418 S.W.2d 535 (1967)]. The reasoning of the courts in these cases can be summarized as follows: (1) Marriage is a domestic relation highly favored by the law; therefore, pupils associating with married pupils would be benefited rather than harmed; (2) the fact that married pupils might desire to further their education is evidence in itself of character warranting favorable consideration; and (3) exclusion of married pupils denies the guarantee of free public education provided in most of the state constitutions.

Although unwilling to permit the suspension of students solely because they are married, courts did, until recently, almost uniformly hold that married pupils could be excluded from cocurricular activities. [See, e.g., *Kissick v. Garland Independent School District*, 330 S.W.2d 708 (Tex. 1959); *Cochrane v. Board of Education*, 103 N.W.2d (Mich. 1960); *State ex rel. Baker v. Stephenson*, 189 N.E.2d 181 (Ohio, 1962); *Board of Directors of Independent School District of Waterloo v. Green*, 147 N.W.2d 854 (1967).] The reasoning of these courts may be summarized as follows: (1) Pupils have no "right" to participate in cocurricular activities in the same sense that they have a right to attend school; (2) cocurricular activities are not a regular part of the school program; and (3) it is reasonable to limit the activities of married pupils to the end that they will be better able to assume the responsibilities of married life.

However, recent cases indicate a developing unwillingness by the courts to accept any restrictions placed on participation of married students in school activities. In one state, Indiana, the high school athletic association suspended enforcement of a rule excluding married students from participation in interscholastic athletics. This action was taken following several lower court decisions in which the rule was held to violate the constitutional rights of married students. It may be that the time is approaching when courts will insist that married students be permitted to attend school with the same rights and privileges as their unmarried peers.

## Pupil Pregnancy

The courts have seldom been called upon to rule on the question of the legality of the exclusion of pregnant pupils. However, there are at least two such cases on record. In a 1961 Ohio case, a board rule required pregnant pupils to withdraw from school "immediately upon knowledge of pregnancy." The purpose of the rule was clearly indicated by the board, i.e., to protect the physical well-being of the pregnant pupil. In addition, home instruction was provided to enable the pupil to maintain her school standing. The Ohio court upheld the rule of the school board under these circumstances [*State ex rel. Idle v. Chamberlain,* 175 N.E.2d 539 (1961)].

In a 1969 case in Mississippi, a federal court ruled that unwed mothers could not be excluded from high school solely on the basis that they were unwed. The court stated they could be excluded only if they "were so lacking in moral character they would taint the education of others" [*Perry v. Grenada Municipal Separate School District,* 300 F.Supp. 748 (1969)].

## Prohibition of Pupil Membership in Secret Societies

Some states have enacted statutes prohibiting membership of elementary or secondary school pupils in secret societies and permitting expulsion of pupils holding such membership in violation of school board rules. (See, e.g., *Acts 1907 Indiana,* ch. 278.) Most state legislatures, however, have remained silent on this question, and in several of these states, court cases have arisen challenging the authority of the school board to prohibit participation in cocurricular activities by pupils who hold membership in Greek letter fraternities or other similar secret societies. Courts in Arkansas [*Isgrig v. Srygley,* 197 S.W.2d 39 (1946)], Washington [*Wayland v. Board of School Directors,* 86 Pac. 642 (1906)], Oregon [*Burkitt v. School District,* 246 P.2d 566 (1952)], Ohio [*Holroyd v. Eibling,* 188 N.E.2d 797 (1962)], Illinois [*Wilson v. Board of Education,* 84 N.E. 697 (1908)], and California [*Robinson v. Sacramento City Unified School District,* 245 Cal. App.2d 278 (1966)] have upheld such rules of school boards. Missouri is one of the few states holding that a board may not take such action against pupils for membership in such organizations [*Wright v. Board of Education,* 246 S.W. 43 (1922)].

## The Teacher *in Loco Parentis*

In the eyes of the court, the school board and school administration have the right to make rules governing pupils, and the teacher may establish reasonable rules relating to the good order and discipline of pupils in his classroom, so long as such rules are not inconsistent with higher authority. [See, e.g., *Patterson v. Nutter,* 78 Me. 609 (Maine 1866); *Sheehan v. Sturges,* 53 Conn. 481 (Conn. 1885); *Russell v. Lynnfield,* 116 Mass. 365 (Mass. 1874); *Fertich v. Michener, supra.*]

A public school teacher stands in a unique legal relationship with his pupils. This relationship is known as *in loco parentis,* meaning "in the place of the parent." Under the *in loco parentis* doctrine, the teacher's authority over pupils under his supervision is substantially the same as that of a parent, but it is restricted to the limits of his jurisdiction and responsibility as a teacher.

Even parents are limited to some degree with respect to the punishment of children. Every state has enacted statutes, for example, which prohibit cruelty to children.

Although the *in loco parentis* doctrine gives teachers substantial authority in dealing with pupils, teachers should be careful not to exceed this authority. In Pennsylvania, two teachers attempted to treat the infected finger of a 10-year-old pupil by holding the finger under boiling water, even though no situation existed requiring first aid or emergency treatment. In holding the teachers liable for the resulting injury, the court made clear that the doctrine of *in loco parentis* was limited and stated:

Under the delegated parental authority implied from the relationship of teacher and pupil there is no implied delegation of authority to exercise her lay judgment, as a parent may, in the matter of treatment of injury or disease suffered by a pupil. . . . [The teachers] were not acting in an emergency. . . . Whether treatment of the infected finger was necessary was a question for the boy's parents to decide [*Guerreri v. Tyson,* 24 A.2d 468 (1942)].

## Reasonable Punishments

As indicated previously, the rules governing pupil conduct must be reasonable under the existing circumstances. In the last analysis, the courts are the determiners of the reasonableness of school rules. Not only must a rule be reasonable; the enforcement of the rule or the punishment meted for violation of the rule must also be reasonable.

There seems to be little doubt that withholding of privileges, removal from the classroom, and reasonable detention after school (where, of course, a child is not subjected to unreasonable hazards such as being required to walk home where pupil transportation is normally provided) are punishments with which it is unlikely a court would find fault. Most litigation in the area of specific punishments falls into three other categories: academic punishments for disciplinary infractions, suspension and expulsion, and corporal punishment.

## Academic Punishments for Disciplinary Infractions

In a recent case a federal court was asked to consider academic penalties which had been assessed against students as a result of absences from class resulting from suspensions related to the violation of a "dress code." The court ruled that such penalties were "unrelated to academic performance" and were "illegal and unconstitutional" (a decision in the case of *Christopher v. Smith,* United States District Court for the Northern District of Indiana filed March 10, 1971).

Denial of diplomas for violations of school rules has been declared illegal by at least two courts [*Valentine v. Independent School District,* 183 N.W. 434 (Iowa, 1921)]; [*Ryan v. Board of Education,* 257 Pac, 945 (Kans. 1927)]. From these cases, it is obvious that the courts regard academic accomplishment and school discipline to be separate and distinct, and have held that the use of such academic punishments as grade reductions or the withholding of diplomas for disciplinary infractions· is unreasonable.

## Suspension and Expulsion

Suspension can be defined as exclusion of a pupil from school for a specified brief period of time, such as a few days. Expulsion differs from suspension only in length of time. Expulsion usually involves a relatively long period of time, such as a semester or a school year.

Most authorities appear to agree that expulsion, being a more severe punishment than suspension, should involve school board rather than teacher action [see, e.g., 97]. Moreover, there is doubt as to whether even a school board may expel a pupil *permanently* [see, e.g., *Board of Education v. Helston,* 32, Ill. App. 300 (Ill. 1889)] from the public schools for disciplinary offense, since this gives the pupil no opportunity to make amends or to rehabilitate himself and would be contrary to the entire philosophy of Anglo-American law. The courts have specifically held that expulsion is not "forever" [see e.g., *Alvin Independent School District v. Cooper,* 404 S.W.2d 76 (Tex. 1966)].

In the absence of school board rules to the contrary, a principal or teacher probably has inherent authority to suspend pupils for disciplinary infractions. The following case examples illustrate the reasoning of the courts in this regard.

In Wisconsin, a school principal suspended a pupil for misconduct and refused to readmit him until he gave "sincere promise of future good conduct." The pupil declined to do so, and his parents brought suit against the principal, contending that only the school board had authority to suspend the pupil from school. The court did not agree, pointing out that a principal or teacher does not derive all of his power with respect to pupil control from the school board. Teachers, according to the court, stand *in loco parentis* to pupils and therefore are entitled to exercise authority over pupils in many "things concerning which the board may have remained silent." In upholding the principal, the court commented that, even though the law gives him the power to punish pupils corporally, this is often an inadequate punishment. If the presence of a pupil is detrimental to the school, it is "essential" that the principal or teacher have the authority to suspend the pupil from school [*State v. Burton,* 45 Wis. 150 (Wis. 1878)].

In South Carolina, pupils refused to drink milk which was in containers bearing a certain label. No cause for refusing to drink the milk was advanced. The principal called an assembly and indicated he would suspend pupils who refused to drink milk. Certain pupils were subsequently suspended. The court held that a principal has the inherent authority to suspend pupils unless deprived of that authority by board regulation [*Stanley v. Gary,* 116 S.E.2d 843 (1960)].

It should be noted that it is not a common practice on the part of teachers in the public schools to suspend pupils from school. Many school systems have established policies which limit such action to principals or other administrative officials. It is likely that such action should only be taken by an administrator in compliance with established school policy.

## Due Process

One of the most significant legal developments of the 1960s was the frequency with which due process questions involving students were brought to the courts. Very often the issue centered around the procedures used in expulsion from school. The question of due process is in an evolutionary stage, and it is difficult to identify clear legal guidelines. For example, some courts have held that a student is entitled to a hearing before expulsion [see *Dixon v. Alabama State Board of Education,* 294 F.2d 150 (1961)]. Other courts have held that no hearing is required [see *Banks v. Board of Public Instruction of Dade County,* 314 F.Supp. 285 (1970)].

An especially instructive case regarding due process occurred in Michigan. A student who had been given repeated warnings for absences was apprehended smoking in the building in violation of a school rule. Following a conference with the parents, the student was given the opportunity to appear before the school board at which time he was accompanied by his mother and counsel. He was then suspended indefinitely. The court rejected a subsequent request for a full-scale judicial hearing. The court ruled that: "The standard is whether he has been treated with fundamental fairness in the light of the total circumstances. . . . The student has been fully informed as to the offenses charged; he has been heard with respect thereto; and he has had due process in ample measure" [*Davis v. Ann Arbor Public Schools,* 313 F.Supp. 1217 (1970)].

It is possible to conclude that courts will continue to consider the due process rights of students. It may not be overly venturesome to predict that minimum due process in cases of severe student discipline eventually will lead to the following procedures: (1) a notice of the charges against the student and the nature of the evidence to support these charges; (2) a hearing; and (3) a decision based on the evidence presented in the hearing. Other issues such as the right to be represented by counsel and to cross-examine witnesses will also be litigated. While it is impossible to predict where the courts will draw the line relative to student due process, the cases already decided are indicative of a more aggressive court attitude in the protection of student rights. Teachers should understand this trend and should make every effort to comply with the standard of "fundamental fairness" in dealing with students.

## Corporal Punishment

Since 1833, there have been more than sixty cases decided in American appellate courts dealing with corporal or physical punishment of school pupils by teachers. Most of these cases were decided prior to 1900, which leads to a belief that the common law in this area is now fairly well settled.

New Jersey is the only state in which corporal punishment of public school pupils by teachers is forbidden by statute. In several states (e.g., Florida, Hawaii, Montana, New York, Vermont, Virginia, Georgia, Ohio, Michigan), corporal punishment is expressly permitted by statute. The California Education Code clearly provides that "The governing board of any school district shall adopt rules and regulations authorizing teachers, principals, and other certificated personnel to administer reasonable corporal punishment when such action is deemed an appropriate corrective measure" (California Education Code, Section 10854). It may safely be assumed that in most of the other states the right of a teacher to administer reasonable corporal punishment is protected by the common law.

## Rules of School Boards Forbidding Corporal Punishment

In some school districts, however, school board rules forbid corporal punishment of pupils. It is possible that a teacher who violates school board rules prohibiting corporal punishment might be guilty of insubordination and thus might be considered to have breached his teaching contract. However, a concurring opinion in a 1963 Indiana case may indicate a growing attitude on the part of the courts to the effect that a school board has no right to prohibit the use of corporal punishment by teachers:

. . . I have serious doubts that a teacher confronted with . . . responsibility under the law for maintaining order and a respect for authority before a classroom of pupils, can be deprived by a "rule" of the right to use physical force to eliminate . . . a disturbance. As long as teachers or parents are obligated under the law to educate, teach and train children, they may not be denied the necessary means of carrying out their responsibility as such teachers and parents [*Indiana State Personnel Board v. Jackson,* 192 N.E.2d 740 (1963)].

It should be kept in mind that the opinion stated by this judge did not represent the majority opinion of the court. Teachers who are employed in districts where corporal punishment is forbidden by school board rules should abide by such rules.

In any case, most school districts have established policies relating to procedures to be followed by teachers in administering corporal punishment, including a provision requiring witnesses. A teacher would be wise to follow closely the established corporal punishment policy of the district in which he is employed.

## Assault and Battery

Assault and battery consists of striking or threatening to strike or harm another person. Consequently, a pupil may be guilty of such a charge. An action for assault and battery may be a *criminal action,* brought by the prosecuting attorney on behalf of the state, for which conviction would result in a fine and/or imprisonment. On the other hand, it may be a *civil action* in tort, brought by the injured party, for which the penalty would be monetary damages to the injured party.

## Reasonableness of Corporal Punishment

The reasonableness of the corporal punishment administered is usually a major factor in determing the liability of the teacher. The courts normally will assume that corporal punishment which results in permanent injury is excessive or unreasonable. Corporal punishment administered with malice, which usually means with wicked motives or in anger, is also likely to be considered unreasonable. An Alabama court has listed certain guidelines which the courts tend to follow in determining whether corporal punishment is reasonable: "In determining the reasonableness of the punishment or the extent of malice, proper matters of consideration are the instrument used and the nature of the offense committed by the child, the age and physical condition of the child, and other attendant circumstances" [*Suits v. Glover,* 71 So.2d 49 (1954)].

The legality of corporal punishment of school pupils, perhaps more than any other aspect of pupil punishment, depends upon circumstances. What might be considered reasonable corporal punishment for a child of a certain age or sex might be considered unreasonable for another child of a different age or sex. Community attitudes also may affect the decision of courts. An examination of several court decisions in which action was brought against teachers for assault and battery may reveal the factors which determine reasonableness.

## Corporal Punishment: Case Examples

In Ohio, a teacher corporally punished a boy who had thrown a stone at another pupil on the way home from school and who, when questioned, had "fibbed" about it. The teacher struck the pupil six to fifteen times with a paddle of "normal" proportions, which caused vivid discoloration of the buttocks. A complicating factor in the case was the fact that the pupil was an epileptic and had suffered three seizures following the spanking. Action was brought against the teacher for criminal assault and battery. The court listed the following as "fundamental propositions of law" which should be followed when a teacher is charged criminally for assault and battery arising from the corporal punishment of a school pupil: (1) A teacher stands *in loco parentis* and is not liable for an error in judgment; (2) a teacher's authority attaches from home to home; (3) there is a presumption of correctness in the actions of the teacher; (4) there is a presumption that the teacher acts in good faith; and (5) mere excessive or severe punishment is not a crime unless it produces permanent injury or unless it is administered with malice. The court found that no permanent injury had resulted to the child and that no malice was involved. The teacher, therefore, was found to be not guilty [*State v. Lutz,* 113 N.E.2d 757 (1953)].

In Alabama, a teacher corporally punished an eight-year-old boy who was "well developed, fat and in good health" for insubordination and for "scuffling" in the hall contrary to school rules. Civil action was brought against the teacher for assault and battery. The court indicated that, according to the evidence, the boy had been struck only five times on the buttocks. The evidence conflicted as to whether the instrument used was a Ping-Pong paddle or a slat from an apple crate. In any case, no permanent injury resulted. In relieving the teacher from liability, the court stated: "To be guilty of an assault and battery, the teacher must not only inflict upon the child immoderate chastisement, but he must do so with legal malice or wicked motives or he must inflict some permanent injury" *(Suits v. Glover, supra).*

It can be inferred from the foregoing cases that teachers may be found liable for immoderate corporal punishment (1) if the punishment results in permanent injury or (2) if the punishment is administered with malice. Three cases in which teachers were held liable for excessive corporal punishment serve to further illustrate the importance of these factors.

In Pennsylvania, a teacher's corporal punishment of a child involved a blow on the pupil's right ear, which injured the eardrum and permanently impaired the hearing of the pupil. Since permanent injury had resulted, the court held the teacher liable and pointed out that, if corporal punishment were necessary, nature had "provided a part of the anatomy for chastisement" and tradition held "that chastisement should be there applied" [*Rupp v. Zintner,* 29 Pa. D. & C. 629 (1937)].

In Connecticut, a principal ordered a ten-year-old third-grade pupil to go to his office following an altercation between the pupil and a teacher. The boy refused, and the principal grabbed his wrists and tried to drag him. The boy was struggling to escape and became hysterical. The principal, who weighed 190 pounds, pushed the boy, who weighed 89 pounds, to the floor and sat on him. The boy was injured, and the court found that the principal had used "unreasonable force" [*Calmay v. Williamson,* 36 A.2d 377 (1944)].

In Louisiana, a boy who had not followed instructions in a physical education class was ordered to the sidelines. Three times he tried to return to the floor against the instructions of the teacher. As a result of the teacher using force to enforce his instructions, the student struck the floor and broke his arm. The court noted that the teacher was a foot taller and weighed twice as much as the boy and found that the teacher's actions were clearly in excess of the physical force necessary either to discipline the pupil or to protect himself [*Frank v. Orleans Parish School Board,* 195 So.2d 451 (1967)].

## SUMMARY

The most common tort involving teachers is negligence resulting in pupil injury. A teacher's actions which fall below the standard of the reasonably prudent teacher and which result in injury to pupils may make the teacher liable for negligence.

Defenses against negligence include contributory negligence, proximate cause, and assumption of risk. In spite of the existence of these legal defenses, a teacher should make every effort to foresee and to prevent pupil injury.

The importance of adequate instruction in potentially hazardous activities and the establishment of safety rules cannot be overemphasized. These two factors, in addition to the exercise of sound common sense, are vital to teachers in protecting themselves against successful negligence suits.

In addition to cases involving negligence teachers occasionally are sued for defamation of character. Written defamation is known as libel, and spoken defamation as slander. Teachers who communicate information about pupils should be certain the person to whom such information is given has a reason for having it. Teachers who follow this rule probably have little to fear from defamation-of-character lawsuits, since such communication is privileged.

School boards, administrators, and teachers have wide authority to establish rules of pupil conduct. So long as the rules are reasonable and bear reasonable relation to the welfare of the school (even though they may to some extent govern pupil conduct off the school grounds and after school hours), they are likely to be upheld by the courts. It should be remembered, however, that the courts are the final determiners of the reasonableness of a particular school rule.

Methods of enforcing school rules must also be reasonable. Such enforcement procedures as academic punishments for disciplinary infractions or the requirement that children pay for school property accidentally damaged or destroyed are likely to be struck down by the courts. Suspension and expulsion, withholding of privileges, removal from the classroom, and reasonable corporal punishment probably would be upheld.

Probably the most important trends for teachers to note are the willingness of the courts to consider legal challenges involving the reasonableness of school rules and the extent to which courts are providing protection for the constitutional freedoms of students. Courts have not removed the authority of schools to regulate the conduct of students; however, they are demanding that rules and regulations be directly related to the effective operation of the schools. There is no longer any tendency for the courts to regard the authority of the school over the student to be absolute.

## QUESTIONS TO CONSIDER

1.  How would you define the term "common law"?
2.  Why do you think the courts have established the concept of the "reasonably prudent man" as the standard for determining negligence?
3.  Why do you think the courts have established "foreseeability" as the first test of negligence?
4.  If you, as a teacher, were given the responsibility for supervising the school safety patrol, what precautions would you take?
5.  What policy do you feel a teacher should follow regarding elementary pupils who forget to bring books from home and request permission to go home after them?
6.  As a teacher, what should you do about a pupil who complains of a severe headache?
7.  What seems to be the determining factor as to the liability of a teacher for pupil injury in the classroom while the teacher is out of the room?
8.  What is the reason the courts have established "privilege" as a defense against defamation of character?
9.  What disadvantages result from a teachers' association carrying a $50,000 liability insurance policy on all members of the association?
10. What seems to be the controlling factor as to whether teachers may punish pupils for acts off the school grounds or after school hours?
11. Under what circumstances might a teacher be liable for injuries to pupils off the school grounds or after school hours?
12. As a teacher, what action should you take against a pupil who hits a baseball through a classroom window during playground activities at a school where a rule is in effect that baseball is not to be played close to the school building?

13.   Are there any circumstances under which a teacher ever suspends a pupil from school? Cite specific cases.
14.   What do you think the attitude of the courts would be toward a school rule providing for a 3 per cent grade reduction for each "unexcused" absence?
15.   Why do you think the courts have established the *in loco parentis* doctrine?
16.   Do you think it is desirable or undesirable that a school board establish a rule forbidding corporal punishment by teachers? Justify your position.
17.   In what ways will the further implementation of the "due process" concept affect the teacher's role in relationship with pupils?

## PROBLEM SITUATION FOR INQUIRY

Mr. Sennett is an instructor in biology at Russellville Junior High School. His second period class, composed of twenty-eight freshmen, was in the process of learning to dissect the clam. Because of the toughness of the muscle fibers that hold the two clam-shell halves together, the separation of these two halves can be a hazardous undertaking unless performed properly. For this reason Mr. Sennett took more time than usual to explain the dissection procedure. He placed special emphasis on the proper way to hold the clam and make the incision. He also restated the importance of reporting any injury, no matter how minor, immediately after it occurs. Having finished these instructions, he told the class to proceed with their work, while he slowly moved throughout the room to give any help he could.

Bill, one of the less conscientious students in the class, did not give his full attention to any of Mr. Sennett's opening comments. Consequently, he set to work without any significant knowledge of the possible danger involved in the task. While trying to open the shell in one swift slash, his scalpel slipped and cut a gash in the side of his left hand. The bleeding was not severe, however, and in an attempt to save himself the embarrassment of facing Mr. Sennett, he quickly wrapped a paper towel around the wound and concealed it for the remainder of the period.

That night, Bill noticed pronounced swelling around the cut area. He showed it to his parents, who, in turn, notified the family doctor. The infection resulted in a sizable medical bill. Bill's parents asked Mr. Sennett to pay this medical bill, or they would bring suit against him for negligence. If you were Mr. Sennett, what would you do? Why?

## ACTIVITIES TO PURSUE

1.   Outline the points which might have been made by the attorney for the plaintiff in the case involving the "slap-boxing" incident.
2.   Set up a mock court, including the attorney for the plaintiff, the attorney for the defendant, a judge, a bailiff, a plaintiff, a defendant, and a jury to "try" the "slap-boxing" case outlined in this chapter.
3.   Go to a courthouse law library and look up the United States Supreme Court prayer and Bible-reading cases cited in the chapter. Analyze these cases, including the facts, the issues, the decisions, and the reasons given by the Court in reaching the decisions.
4.   Analyze the 1954 desegregation decision of the Supreme Court cited in the chapter. Try to find out why the Court held that separate public school facilities for black and white pupils were "inherently" unequal.
5.   Assume that you are a school principal. Establish a set of guidelines which you might suggest that your teachers follow in order to avoid tort liability for negligence.
6.   Develop a parental permission form which might be used for pupil field trips.
7.   Develop a set of pupil safety rules for the classroom, assuming that you are an

elementary teacher (or a high school teacher of physical education, chemistry, industrial arts, or homemaking).

8.  Assume that you are a school principal. Develop a set of rules for teachers who wish to administer corporal punishment.

9.  From the references cited in the chapter and/or from your state school code, see what you can learn about the following: (*a*) Must a pupil's cumulative-record folder be shown to the parents of the pupil upon their request? (*b*) May a pupil-composed prayer be said at the noon meal in a public school cafeteria? (*c*) Do teachers have the legal right to strike? (*d*) May the King James Version of the Bible be used as a textbook in the public schools? (*e*) Under what circumstances may teachers be dismissed for unbecoming conduct after school hours? (*f*) May a person in college who will receive a teaching license in August legally contract with a school district the previous spring? (*g*) Would a school counselor likely be held liable for the suicide of a student because the counselor failed to recommend psychiatric care for the student? (*h*) What authority does the state legislature have over the public schools?

10. Discuss with a lawyer the probable effects of the further implementation of the "due process" concept upon the teacher's role in the governance of pupils.

# RESOURCE SECTION FOR PART 2

## TWENTY SELF-RATING QUESTIONS FOR TEACHERS

(These are among the characteristics of teachers the YOUTH-POLL students said they most needed and admired. Give yourself 5 points for every "yes" answer. Score 75 and you're pretty good.)

_____ Do I really care and let my students know?

_____ Do I really listen to my students and hear what they say?

_____ Am I there when my students need me—after class, after school, at home by the telephone?

_____ Do students bring their personal problems to me?

_____ Do I know all my students' names?

_____ Am I there to make any student feel important, rather than just to make myself feel powerful?

_____ Can I tell when a student is "up tight" and respond to his feelings?

_____ Do I know my subject matter well enough to welcome all questions in class?

_____ Do I get my students to think instead of merely parroting back what I say?

_____ Is there an orderly climate for learning in my classroom?

_____ Do I emphasize learning more than discipline?

_____ Do I spend time with the slow learners who really need it, rather than "copping out" by concentrating on just the bright ones?

_____ Do I keep my students from getting bored or going to sleep in my class?

_____ Do all my students participate?

_____ Do I work my students and myself hard enough so we both end the year with a sense of accomplishment rather than merely a feeling of relief?

_____ Do I grade on learning, rather than on a like-dislike basis?

_____ Can I admit my own mistakes openly?

_____ Can we still be friends if one of my students disagrees with me and proves me wrong?

_____ Do students learn from my tests, instead of merely memorizing and then forgetting?

_____ Would my students have characterized me on YOUTH-POLL as their best teacher?

Source: Gordan A. Sabine, _How Students Rate Their Schools and Teachers._ National Education Association, National Association of Secondary School Principals, Washington, 1971, pp. 75–76.

## TWENTY INDICATORS OF THE QUALITY OF TEACHING

|  | Indicating a high quality of teaching | Indicating a low quality of teaching |
|---|---|---|
| _Work with individual pupils:_ | | |
| Assignments | Varied for individuals | Uniform for all |
| Pupil-teacher relations | Friendly; personalized | Very formal or very flippant |
| Pupil-teacher conferences | Frequent, to help pupils | For disciplinary purposes only |
| Pupils' work | Carefully reviewed, promptly returned | Carelessly handled; errors not checked |
| _Planning and preparations:_ | | |
| Daily continuity | Each day built on one before | Work unrelated from day to day |
| Teacher's knowledge | Well-informed teacher supplements books pupils use | Unable to answer simple questions |
| Lesson plans | Plans on blackboard or otherwise obvious | No evidence of plans |

_Source:_ William M. Alexander, _Are You a Good Teacher?_ Holt, Rinehart and Winston, Inc., New York, 1959, p. 26.

## TWENTY INDICATORS OF THE QUALITY OF TEACHING (continued)

| | Indicating a high quality of teaching | Indicating a low quality of teaching |
|---|---|---|
| Advance arrangements | Necessary materials at hand | Necessary materials lacking |
| *Use of teaching aids:* | | |
| Use of books | Pupils know how to use books | Pupils unacquainted with special features of books they use |
| Use of library tools | Pupils use effectively card catalog, reference guides, other tools | Pupils unable to get information in the library on their own |
| Use of audio-visual aids | Aids carefully related to work of class | Little advance explanation or follow-up of aids used |
| Use of field trips | To introduce or supplement class study | Used as holiday from class |
| *Involvement of pupils in varied learning experiences:* | | |
| Types of experiences | Many different types used | Experiences mostly of one type |
| Pupil-teacher planning | As their maturities permit, pupils help in planning | Pupil participation or reaction not sought |
| Responsibilities of pupils | To prepare their own work and to help class as a whole | Only to prepare own assignments |
| Techniques of motivation | Work made interesting and important to pupils | Threats and criticisms only |
| *Active leadership of the teacher:* | | |
| Use of pupil leaders | To give leadership experiences under supervision | To rest the teacher |
| Use of play or entertainment experiences | To provide a balanced program under teacher guidance | Also to rest the teacher |
| *Active leadership of the teacher:* | | |
| Handling behavior problems | Disturbers promptly and consistently dealt with | Inconsistent leniency, harshness |
| Discussion | Genuine and general participation | Drags or dominated by a few |

## HOW WELL ARE YOU DOING IN PUBLIC RELATIONS?

*Note:* When you become a teacher you should check yourself periodically on this checklist. You will be doing very well if you can answer "yes" to all the following questions:

Do you believe that public relations activities should foster lay participation in the educational program?                                    _____

Do you really enjoy talking and working with children?                   _____

*Source:* Glen E. Robinson and Evelyn S. Bianchi, "What Does PR Mean to the Teacher?" *NEA Journal*, vol. 48, no. 4, p. 14, National Education Association, Washington, April, 1959.

Do you really enjoy talking and working with adults?                                            _____

Are you genuinely proud to be a teacher?                                                        _____

Do you believe that good public relations are your responsibility?                              _____

Do you regularly visit your pupils' homes?                                                      _____

Do you ever send newsletters home to parents?                                                   _____

Do you ever send notes to parents concerning things other than problem behavior?                _____

Do you ever send home complimentary notes concerning your pupils who are not outstanding students?

Do you encourage your pupils' parents to visit you and the school?                              _____

Do you schedule regular conferences with parents?                                               _____

Do your contacts with critical parents tend to placate them rather than increase their irritation?                                                                                    _____

Do you have a room-parent organization?                                                         _____

Does your school have a parent-teacher organization?                                            _____

Do you regularly attend parent-teacher-organization meetings?                                   _____

Does your school foster parent participation in planning class work and activities?             _____

If so, do you personally take advantage of this policy to involve parents in your classroom planning activities?                                                                       _____

Do you ever enlist the help of parents in the performance of routine clerical tasks?            _____

Would you recognize the parents of most of your pupils if you met them on the street?           _____

Do you encourage your classes to invite laymen to share their experiences with the class?       _____

Do you make an effort to bring school matters of public interest to the attention of appropriate officials or news media?                                                          _____

Do your classroom activities ever involve community problems and contacts with laymen?          _____

Do you willingly accept invitations to address groups of laymen, either on school matters or on other subjects?                                                                        _____

Do you take an active part in church, political, civic, or fraternal organizations in your community?                                                                                 _____

Do your personal actions reflect credit upon your profession?                                   _____

Do your remarks in the community tend to present a constructive view of teaching and of your local school situation?                                                                 _____

# SUGGESTED READINGS

*The number in parentheses following each suggestion denotes the chapter for which it is best suited.*

Alexander, William M. (ed.): *The High School of the Future: A Memorial to Kimball Wiles,* Charles E. Merrill Publishing Company, Columbus, Ohio, 1969. Presents the predictions and insights of a distinguished group of educators on what education may become toward the year 2000. (5,6,7)

Allen, Paul M., William D. Barnes, Jerald L. Reece, and E. Wayne Roberson: *Teacher Self-Appraisal: A Way of Looking Over Your Own Shoulder,* Charles A. Jones Publishing Company, Worthington, Ohio, 1970. Contains some excellent suggestions and rating scales for use in self-appraisal. (7)

Birnbaum, Max: "Sense About Sensitivity Training," *Saturday Review,* Saturday Review, Inc., New York, November, 1969, pp. 82–83, 96–98. Maintains that school systems will have to learn, as industry has, that not all sorts of training are functional for all personnel. (7)

Campbell, James Reed, and Cyrus W. Barnes: "Interaction Analysis—A Breakthrough?" *Phi Delta Kappan,* vol. 50, no. 10, pp. 587–590, Phi Delta Kappa, Bloomington, Ind., June, 1969. Appraises some of the research that has been done in interaction analysis. (7)

Chain, Robert H.: *Protecting Teacher Rights,* National Education Association, Washington, 1970. An excellent bulletin which summarizes judicial decisions regarding the constitutional rights of teachers. (8)

Chamberlin, Leslie J.: *Team Teaching: Organization and Administration,* Charles E. Merrill Publishing Company, Columbus, Ohio, 1969. An extensive, practical discussion of the use of team teaching. (5)

*Classroom Teachers Speak on Differentiated Teaching Assignments,* National Education Association, Association of Classroom Teachers, Washington, 1969, pp. 9–20. Contains an excellent discussion of differentiated staffing from the point of view of teachers. (5)

"Corporal Punishment: The Law," *NEA Research Bulletin,* vol. 48, no. 2, pp. 46–48, National Education Association, Research Division, Washington, May, 1970. Cites recent court decisions concerning corporal punishment. (8)

"Curriculum Change Is Taking Place," *NEA Research Bulletin,* vol. 48, no. 4, pp. 103–105, National Education Association, Research Division, Washington, December, 1970. Reports the results of a study of the types of curriculum revisions taking place. (5)

Dinkmeyer, Don: "The C-Group: Focus on Self as Instrument," *Phi Delta Kappan,* vol. 52, no. 10, pp. 617–619, Phi Delta Kappa, Bloomington, Ind., June, 1971. Emphasizes the importance of teachers studying themselves. (7)

"Discipline in the Classroom," National Education Association, Washington, 1969. A series of articles on discipline that have appeared in the *Journal of the National Education Association.* (5)

Engler, David: "Instructional Technology and the Curriculum," *Phi Delta Kappan,* vol. 51, no. 7, pp. 379–381, Phi Delta Kappa, Bloomington, Ind., March, 1970. Advocates the use of technology to further humanize education and to achieve the goals of supporters of the humanities. (6)

Flanders, Ned A.: *Analyzing Teacher Behavior,* Addison-Wesley Publishing Company, Inc., Reading, Mass., 1970. Designed to help teachers improve classroom instruction through the use of interaction analysis. (7)

Frey, George T.: "Improving School-Community Relations," *Today's Education,* vol. 60, no. 1, pp. 14–17, National Education Association, Washington, January, 1971. Describes how one junior high school tackled the problem of improving the school-community relations. (5)

Gagné, Robert M.: *The Conditions of Learning,* Holt, Rinehart and Winston, Inc., Chicago, 1965. An explanation of one of the best learning models for sequencing instruction. (7)

Goodlad, John I.: "The Future of Learning: Into the 21st Century," *Bulletin,* vol. 24, no. 1, pp. 1, 4–5, American Association of Colleges for Teacher Education, Washington, March, 1971. Discusses the changing role of teachers and of schools as we move toward the 21st century. (5)

Goodlad, John I., M. Frances Klein and Associates: *Behind the Classroom Door,* Charles A. Jones Publishing Company, Worthington, Ohio, 1970. A report on innovative practices in schools throughout the nation. (5 and 6)

Greenberg, Herbert M.: *Teaching with Feeling,* The Macmillan Company, Toronto, Canada, 1969. Points out that regardless of educational techniques, technology, and equipment or building, the humanity of the teacher is the vital ingredient if students are to learn. (5, 6, 7)

Hazard, William R.: *Education and the Law,* The Free Press, New York, 1971. Subjects covered include civil rights, religion and the schools, student and parental rights. (8)

Hillson, Maurie, and Ronald T. Hyman: *Change and Innovation in Elementary and Secondary Organization,* Holt, Rinehart and Winston, Inc., New York, 1971. Emphasizes research and descriptions of programs in action in public school organization. (5)

Holtzman, Wayne H. (ed.): *Computer-assisted Instruction, Testing and Guidance,* Harper & Row, Publishers, New York, 1970. A compilation of articles on the use of the computer in instruction, testing, and guidance. (6)

"Instructional Technology," *Today's Education,* vol. 59, no. 8, pp. 33–40, National Education Association, Washington, November, 1970. An excellent discussion of the various uses of technology in education. (6)

Joyce, Bruce R.: *Man, Media, and Machines,* National Education Association, National Commission on Teacher Education and Professional Standards, Washington, 1967. Suggests ways that teachers and technology can be brought together to create personalized programs. (6)

Kibler, Robert J., Larry L. Barker, and David T. Miles: *Behavioral Objectives and Instruction,* Allyn and Bacon, Inc., Boston, 1970. A broad coverage of cognitive, affective, and motor instructional objectives. (7)

Lake, Dale: *Perceiving and Behaving,* Teachers College Press, Columbia University, New York, 1970. Discusses the relationship between behavior and self-perception. (7)

LaMancusa, Katherine C.: *We Do Not Throw Rocks at the Teacher!* International Textbook Company, Scranton, Pa., 1969. A most interestingly written book devoted to the teacher goal of establishing classroom control and/or discipline. (5 and 7)

Levine, Sol: "The John Dewey High School Adventure," *Phi Delta Kappan,* vol. 53, no. 2, pp. 108–110, Phi Delta Kappa, Bloomington, Ind., October, 1971. Describes the radical departure made by a high school in New York City when it opened in 1969. (5)

Lewis, James, Jr.: *A Contemporary Approach to Nongraded Education,* Parker Publishing Company, West Nyack, New York, 1970. Contains many helpful suggestions for using a nongraded type of organization. (5)

Locke, Robert W.: "Has the Education Industry Lost Its Nerve?" *Saturday Review,* Saturday Review, Inc., New York, January 16, 1971, pp. 42–44, 57–58. Discusses the efforts of various corporations to apply technology in the field of education and the difficulties encountered in changing educational policies, practices, and procedures. (6)

McClure, Robert M.: "The Curriculum: Retrospect and Prospect," *The Seventieth Yearbook of the National Society for the Study of Education,* The University of Chicago Press, Chicago, 1971. Section 3 is concerned with curriculum change. (5 and 6)

Mitzel, Harold E.: "The Impending Instruction Revolution," *Phi Delta Kappan,* vol. 51, no. 8, pp. 434–439, Phi Delta Kappa, Bloomington, Ind., April, 1970. Summarizes the early stages of the revolution taking place in education and predicts its completion by the turn of the century. (5)

Oettinger, Anthony G.: *Run Computer, Run: The Mythology of Educational Innovation,* Harvard University Press, Cambridge, Mass., 1969. Warnings about the limitations of education technology. (6)

Olivero, James L. and Edward G. Buffie (eds.): *Educational Manpower From Aides to Differential Staff Patterns,* Indiana University Press, Bloomington, Ind., 1970. An excellent collection of writings on the more effective use of teachers. (5)

Punke, Harold H.: *The Teacher and the Courts,* Interstate Press, Danville, Ill., 1971. Designed primarily to assist teachers in becoming more knowledgeable in the area of law. (8)

Reichart, Sanford: *Change and the Teacher,* Thomas Y. Crowell, Inc., New York, 1969. Discusses the philosophical bases and factors affecting change. (6)

"Reporting Pupil Progress," *NEA Research Bulletin,* vol. 47, no. 3, pp. 75–82, National Education Association, Research Division, Washington, October, 1969. Reports the results of an extensive study of reporting pupil progress. (5)

Rogers, Carl R.: *Freedom to Learn,* Charles E. Merrill Publishing Company, Columbus, Ohio, 1969. Thoughts of a famous psychologist on conditions conducive to learning. (5,7)

Shank, Paul C., and Wayne McElroy: *The Paraprofessionals or Teacher Aides: Selection, Preparation, and Assignment,* Pendell Publishing Company, Midland, Mich., 1970. An excellent guide for the selection, preparation, and assignment of teacher aides. (5)

Silberman, Charles E.: *Crisis in the Classroom: The Remaking of American Education,* Random House, Inc., New York, 1970. Presents an extensive survey and condemnation of American education, and makes suggestions for reform. (5)

"The Teacher and Due Process," *NEA Research Bulletin,* vol. 48, no. 3, pp. 90–92, National Education Association, Research Division, Washington, October, 1970. Cites court decisions concerning teachers and due process. (8)

"Teaching and Learning Through Inquiry," *Today's Education,* vol. 58, no. 5, pp. 40–45, National Education Association, Washington, May, 1969. A special feature involving several educators discussing their views toward teaching and learning through the inquiry approach. (7)

"Technology in Education," *NEA Research Memo, 1969-4,* National Education Association, Research Division, Washington, February, 1969. Reviews the various ways in which technology is being used in schools. (6)

Thatcher, David A.: "Teachers vs Technicians: We Still Have a Choice," *Phi Delta Kappan,* vol. 49, no. 8, pp. 435–438, Phi Delta Kappa, Bloomington, Ind., April, 1968. Discusses the professional role that teachers must assume in working with industries involved in educating youth. (6)

Trojcak, Doris A.: *Five Stages of Instruction for Sequencing Science Activities According to Gagné's Learning Model,* Unpublished Doctoral Thesis, Indiana University, Bloomington, Ind., 1969. Good review of the literature and rationale on sequencing instruction. (7)

"TV Comes of Age in Classroom," *The Shape of Education for 1970–71,* vol. 12, pp. 50–55, National School Public Relations Association, Washington, 1970. Discusses the remarkable strides made recently in the use of TV as an instructional media. (6)

Weigand, James, (ed): *Developing Teacher Competencies,* Prentice-Hall, Inc., Englewood Cliffs, N.J., 1971. Contains excellent suggested techniques for gaining skill with respect to seven fundamental competencies for teaching. (7)

"What the Courts Are Saying about Student Rights," *NEA Research Bulletin,* vol. 47, no. 3, pp.86–89, National Education Association, Research Division, Washington, October, 1969. Indicates and discusses recent court rulings concerning student rights. (8)

Wood, Charles L.: "Modular Scheduling? Yes But—," *Journal of Secondary Education,* vol. 45, no. 1, pp. 40–41, California Association of Secondary School Administrators, Burlingame, Calif., January, 1970. Presents ten pitfalls to be avoided in initiating modular scheduling in schools. (5)

## SUGGESTED 16 MM FILMS

*The number in parentheses following each suggestion denotes the chapter for which it is best suited.*

*The Child of the Future: How He Might Learn* (McGraw-Hill, 59 min). Interviews Dr. Marshall McLuhan, University of Toronto, as he comments on educational technology. (6)

*Creating Instructional Materials* (McGraw-Hill, 15 min, color). Describes characteristic instructional materials which may be created by students in the classroom and indicates how these can most effectively contribute to instruction. Illustrates, among other things, the creation of a play, the use of a resource person, and the utilization of personal collections of materials such as slides. (5)

*Instructional Development* (Indiana University Audio-Visual Center, 17 min). Presents a systematic approach to instruction based on decisions about the learner, learning, evaluation, and the learning environment. (5,7)

*Interaction in Learning* (Indiana University Audio-Visual Center, 29 min). Presents the different types of social interaction that arise during the school years as well as the importance of this type of contact in shaping the more positive self concept. (7)

*Learning about Learning* (National Educational Television, 30 min). Outlines the work of Dr. Howard Kendler of New York University, Dr. Tracy Kendler of Barnard College, Dr. Kenneth Spence of the State University of Iowa, Dr. Harry Harlow of the University of Wisconsin, and Dr. B. F. Skinner of Harvard University in exploring the different strategies employed in developing new theoretical concepts about man's ability to learn. Shows how the work of these men has influenced methods of instruction in schools and colleges. (7)

*Learning from Visuals* (American Institute for Research, 35 min, color). Pictures four people discussing the application of the programmed approach to the design of visuals for use on educational television. Reviews principles of programmed instruction and shows how these are applied to the design of visuals. Emphasizes need for the establishing of specific objectives, active responding on the part of the students, and proper sequencing for effective learning. (6)

*The Legal Control and Discipline of Public School Pupils* (Thomas J. Barbre Productions, 40 min, color). A discussion by Robert R. Hamilton, former Dean, School of Law, University of Wyoming, on the legal aspects of pupil discipline. (8)

*Legal Liabilities of Teachers for School Accidents* (Thomas J. Barbre Productions, 40 min, color). A discussion by Robert R. Hamilton, former Dean, School of Law, University of Wyoming, on liability of teachers for pupil injuries. (8)

*Let Them Learn* (Encyclopaedia Britannica Educational Corporation, 27 min, color). Depicts how films and other audio-visual materials help to provide experiences necessary for effective language skills for students who lack these skills. Uses classroom scenes of several schools to demonstrate how teachers can foster the discovery method of teaching. (6)

*My Name Is Children* (National Educational Television, 60 min). Delineates how the Nova Elementary School at Fort Lauderdale, Florida, is using an inquiry approach to motivate students to learn. (5,7)

*A New Design for Education* (Stanford University, 28 min, color). Describes research conducted at Stanford University in relation to flexible class scheduling in high schools. Indicates how the principle of flexible scheduling has been used to adapt instruction to the abilities and interests of students. (5)

*Our Class Works Together* (Coronet Films, 11 min, color). Shows a group of children working together to build a model of a community and making pictures to show the various community helpers. Indicates that the class learns that through the sharing of ideas and cooperation, work can be done faster and better. (5)

*Perception and Communication* (Ohio State University, 32 min, color). Explains the manner in which human perceptions affect the process of communications, specifically in the teaching-learning area. Introduces two theories of perception—cognitive and transactional—and illustrates these theories in a number of sequences. (7)

*Programmed Instruction: The Development Process* (National Audio-Visual Center, 19 min, color). Illustrates the process involved in developing materials for programmed instruction. Screens a flow-chart of programming, showing the various steps involved. Offers situational examples and explanations by steps. (6)

*Programming Is a Process* (University of Illinois, 32 min, color). Uses the lecture method to present the fundamentals of programming instructional information. Provides a step-by-step exploration of the programming process. (5, 6, 7)

*Project Discovery* (Encyclopaedia Britannica Educational Corporation, 28 min, color). Describes project discovery as the many ways teachers and students use the projectors, films, and filmstrips which have been placed in the schools. Emphasizes the ready availability of the materials and indicates values in terms of learning from such materials. (6)

*Providing for Independence in Learning* (Indiana University, 30 min). Outlines the need for giving children guided opportunities to learn on their own, providing them with the skills needed to "learn what to see" and "learn to listen." (5)

*Providing for Individual Differences* (Iowa State Teachers College, 23 min). Indicates the ways in which the classroom teacher can adjust the learning environment to meet the individual differences among her pupils. Depicts a college class discussing the methods of adjustment to individual differences that they have observed on visits to an elementary school and a high school. (5,7)

*Quiet Revolution* (National Education Association, 30 min, color). Presents an overview of contemporary educational innovations via a unique framework and its effect on teaching operations. Deals with such aspects as the teaching aide, team teaching, new building designs, and the handling of students with special problems. Suggests the limitless possibilities for the future. (5,6)

*The Remarkable Schoolhouse* (McGraw-Hill, 25 min, color). Tours the Brentwood and Granada schools of California and Nova High School in Florida to show innovative educational ideas being put into practice. Surveys the experimental programs such as computer-assisted instruction, continuous progress curricula, and game methods of learning, along with new concepts of school architecture and scheduling. (5,6)

*Teaching Machines and Programmed Learning* (United World, 28 min). Presents Drs. B. F. Skinner, A. A. Lumsdaine, and Robert Glasen as each in turn discusses teaching machines and programmed learning. (6)

*Teaching Machines and Sidney Pressey* (Ohio State University, 12 min). Features Sidney Pressey, professor of psychology at Ohio State University, and the teaching machine he invented in 1925. Comments on different forms of programmed instruction with specific reference to B. F. Skinner and Norman Crowder. (6)

*Team Teaching on the Elementary Level* (Bailey Films, 13 min, color). Defines team teaching as using the staff most efficiently and to its maximum potential and reports on the establishment of team teaching at Cashmere, Washington. Indicates the need for facilities for a good instructional program. Details size of instructional groups involved and tells how the team teaching was carried out. (5)

*The Things a Teacher Sees* (International Film Bureau, 17 min). Shows the things a teacher should observe and be sensitive to in her students, such as sight, hearing, speech, dental, nutritional, and emotional problems. The results of the observant teacher's concern is the correction of many of these problems. (7)

*What Do I Know about Benny?* (Holt, Rinehart and Winston, 11 min, color). Illustrates difficulties a teacher may face in her evaluation of a student's ability and explanation of the evaluation to that student's parents. Presents problems of reconciling parents' expectations and the student's apparent ability to perform. (5)

*You and Your Classroom* (Educational Horizons, 10 min). Fourteen open-ended episodes involving classroom control and discipline are presented. After each vignette the instructions "Stop the film and discuss" are flashed on the screen. Selection of the filmed episodes was made after a survey of several hundred teachers revealed these problems to be the most prevalent in the elementary classroom. (5,7)

## FIGURE CREDITS

FIGURE 5-1. (*Source:* "The American Public-School Teacher, 1965–66," *Research Report 1967-R4,* National Education Association, Research Division, Washington, 1967, p. 27.)

FIGURE 5-2. (*Source:* "School Marks and Reporting to Parents," *NEA Research Bulletin,* vol. 48, no. 3, National Education Association, Research Division, Washington, October, 1970, p. 77.)

FIGURE 5-3. (*Source:* "Methods of Evaluating Teachers," *NEA Research Bulletin,* vol. 43, no. 1, National Education Association, Research Division, Washington, February, 1965, p. 14.)

FIGURE 5-4. (*Source:* Data from "The American Public-School Teacher, 1970–71," NEA Research Bulletin, vol. 50, no. 1, National Education Association, Research Division, Washington, 1972, p. 7.)

FIGURE 5-5. (*Source:* James L. Olivero, "The Meaning and Application of Differentiated Staffing in Teaching," *Phi Delta Kappan,* vol. 52, no. 1, Phi Delta Kappa, Bloomington, Indiana, September, 1970, pp. 38–39.)

FIGURE 5-7.   (*Source:* "Grade Organization and Nongrading Programs," *NEA Research Bulletin,* vol. 54, no. 4, National Education Association, Research Division, Washington, December, 1967, p. 119.)

FIGURE 6-1.   (*Source:* Data from "Use of New Techniques in Instruction," *NEA Research Bulletin,* vol. 49, no. 3, National Education Association, Research Division, Washington, October, 1971, p. 83.)

FIGURE 6-2.   (*Source: Shaver and Company, Architects, Salina, Kansas.)*

FIGURE 7-1.   (*Source:* Calvin W. Taylor, "Be Talent Developers," *Today's Education,* vol. 57, no. 9, National Education Association, Washington, December, 1968, p. 69.)

# 3 | professional and economic concerns

Anyone planning to become a teacher should view his role in terms of the current and the potential status of the profession. Major strides have been made in the past two decades in improving the status of teachers and in achieving professional autonomy. These gains have come primarily through the strenuous and disciplined efforts of many of its members. The continued growth of the profession, as it seeks to fulfill its monumental mission even more adequately, will come primarily from the dedicated and quality efforts of those that will enter the profession in the years to come.

Chapter 9 appraises the status of teaching as a profession, and notes some of the mechanisms and resources that may enable its membership to achieve higher levels of performance within the profession and in educating the youth of America. Chapter 10 explores the current and probable future status of teachers in public elementary and secondary schools and in colleges. Chapter 11 is concerned with such nonsalary benefits as teacher tenure, leaves of absence, group insurance, credit unions, mutual funds, tax deductions and annuities, and retirement benefits.

# 9 | THE TEACHING PROFESSION: ITS STATUS, ORGANIZATIONS, PUBLICATIONS, AND CODE OF ETHICS

What constitutes a profession? To what extent is teaching a profession? In what ways does it differ from other professions? What is the importance of the Code of Ethics of the Education Profession? What different organizations exist in the teaching profession? In what ways may these organizations benefit the individual teacher? Through what organizations can the individual teacher contribute most to the profession?

It is only as individual teachers and groups of teachers give serious consideration to questions such as these that the teaching profession can continue to advance and to assume its deserved role among the great professions.

## TEACHING AS A PROFESSION

Anyone who becomes a teacher becomes a member of a profession, with responsibility for improving the status of that chosen profession. A professional person may find it difficult at times to differentiate among his professional services in teaching, his personal life, and his work in the activities of the profession itself. Perhaps this sense of dedication is one of the distinguishing characteristics of a professional person. In this chapter teachers in preparation are asked to think carefully about their role in the profession and its organizations.

### Characteristics of a Profession

What constitutes a profession? Many scholars and many scholarly groups have given careful thought to formulating an answer to this question. The professions have studied themselves in attempts to enlighten their own members and the public concerning the characteristics and role of a profession. Although these various statements have differed in many details, there seems to be consensus concerning some of the major practices descriptive of a profession.

A profession requires that its members:

1. Commit themselves to the ideal of service to mankind rather than to personal gain.
2. Undergo relatively long periods of professional preparation to learn the concepts and principles of the specialized knowledge which earns the profession its high status.
3. Meet established qualifications for admission and keep up-to-date through in-service growth.
4. Establish and adhere to a code of ethics regarding membership, conduct, and practice.
5. Demand a high order of intellectual activity.
6. Form organizations to improve the standards of the profession, the services of the profession, self-discipline in the profession, and the economic well-being of its members.
7. Provide opportunities for advancement, specialization, and independence.
8. Regard the profession as a life career and consider membership in the profession as permanent.

Certainly there are differences among the requirements and characteristics of manual labor, skilled labor, the subprofessions, and the professions. However, in many cases it is not a simple task to differentiate between the subprofessions and the professions. The professions of medicine, law, and the ministry have long been recognized. But what of the additional groups that have sought recognition as professions—nurses, teachers, engineers, journalists, and many others? And what of recent patterns of differentiated staffing in which para-professionals and interns are used as supporting personnel in a teaching team? Does this approach to the use of various types of personnel in the total teaching situation more clearly delineate the professional person or does it further confuse the description? In addition, critics of the teaching profession sometimes charge that many teachers want to be prepared as technicians but want to be recognized and paid as professionals. Although it is obvious that at present teaching is considered a profession, it is only fair to point out that this status is challenged by many persons.

## Status of Teaching as a Profession

It is true that the requirements for entrance into the teaching profession have not always been as high as those for some other professions. It is also true that in the profession of teaching there are some members who have not lived up to desirable levels of conduct and service. Furthermore, many persons have used teaching as a stepping-stone to other professions. Finally, there are major differences between teaching and the other professions. However, these aspects of teaching and teachers do not deny to teaching its status as a profession.

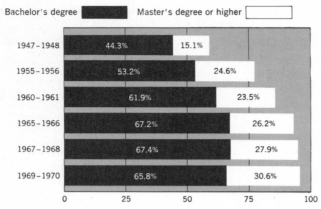

FIGURE 9–1. Change in the level of preparation of public school teachers. How may this distribution change in the future?

In what ways does teaching differ from other professions? These differences lie in the control, support, size, and the ratio of the sexes [125:66–70]. The legal control of education belongs to the public, not to the profession itself. Thus, the members of the teaching profession must work constantly to inform the public and must participate extensively in public concerns. Public school teachers are paid from tax money, which presents certain limitations and problems not inherent in other professions. Until very recent years the need for large numbers of teachers has affected the policies of recruitment and selectivity within the profession. Furthermore, the fact that women outnumber men in the teaching profession differentiates it sharply from law, medicine, and the ministry. Nevertheless, these differences should not prevent teaching from being accorded professional status.

Because of these differences between teaching and other professions, it has been said that teaching can never achieve professional autonomy; i.e., it can never become a self-managing profession. To achieve a high degree of autonomy, the members of the profession need to be clearly and firmly in charge of those aspects which are characterized as professional concerns. As Stinnett [257:12] points out, the profession should be responsible:

for determining the standards and seeing to their enforcement, for selection and admission to teacher education programs, for guidance, screening, and retention during preparation, for accreditation of teacher education institutions, for licensure and revocation of licensure, for professional growth, for working conditions, for protecting its members against unjust and capricious treatment, and for disciplining its members for unethical and unprofessional conduct.

In other words, professional autonomy means control by the profession of those standards on which it guarantees the competence of each member admitted to practice and permitted to continue in practice and through which it defines the conditions under which members will work. Perhaps the most outstanding thrust has been made through the work of the National Commission on Teacher Education and Professional Standards. This very important commission will be discussed later in this chapter.

It has been pointed out that the goal of professional autonomy is in direct conflict with our national tradition of local control of education and that "The professionalization of teachers and local, lay control of education are on a collision course" [230:333]. The 1968 Ocean Hill-Brownsville controversy in New York City is cited as an early example of this conflict. However, national opinion, according to a Louis Harris poll, apparently supports by a substantial majority the point of view that "teachers should have a bigger voice in the educational system" [176:3]. This is especially important in education today with the growing emphasis on accountability. "The teaching profession must have certain responsibilities delegated to it by the public if it is to contribute significantly to the improvement of education and to be accountable for what happens in the schools" [105:3].

What are the conditions and characteristics which support teaching as a profession? Among them are the following:

1. Most teachers are working for the sake of giving service to mankind rather than for great personal gain.
2. Teachers are required by law to complete certain requirements for certification and entrance into the profession, and these requirements are constantly being strengthened.
3. Teaching requires careful skills and understandings.
4. Teachers have professional publications to help them keep up-to-date.
5. Teachers attend summer school, extension classes, workshops, conventions, and institutes and engage in a wide variety of other in-service activities.
6. Teaching is well regarded as a life career.
7. Teachers have their standards and ethics operating through national, state, and local education associations.

## Prestige of Teachers

Occupations differ in regard to the respect or prestige generally assigned to them by members of a community. The prestige of teachers remains consistently high. For example, George Gallup, Director of the American Institute of Public Opinion, found through identical surveys that the prestige of the teaching profession had risen between 1953 and 1962 in a list of professions from a rank of seventh to a rank of third. In 1967 educators ranked fifth in a list of seventeen major professions and occupations in which the "American public places its esteem and confidence" according to a Louis Harris national poll [175:3]. They were preceded by doctors, bankers, scientists, and military leaders. They outranked such personnel as corporate heads, psychiatrists, U.S. Supreme Court Justices, local retailers, clergy, congressmen, and federal government leaders. Another Gallup poll in 1968 indicated that 62 per cent of American adults would advise young people today to take up teaching as a lifetime career. In describing the teaching profession, the people interviewed used such words as "rewarding," "creative," and "challenging" [94:B18].

What about parents' views toward teaching as a profession? Another Gallup poll in 1969 found that three-fourths of American parents would like to have their children take up teaching as a career. There were only minute differences between the opinions of white and nonwhite parents, Protestant and Roman Catholic parents, and parents thirty years of age or older. Parents under thirty years of age and Jewish parents held somewhat less positive opinions, 65 and 63 per cent respectively [91:51].

Perhaps a number of factors have contributed to this continuing high prestige of teachers. As previously indicated, the complexity of our technological and social world has placed an increasingly higher premium upon the need for education, and teachers are the chief instruments for obtaining this education. Research studies indicate that members of professions requiring extended and rigorous preparation tend to have greater prestige than those of whom little training is required. The number of years required to become a teacher has increased significantly. There is considerable evidence to support the fact that the holding power of a profession increases as the standards for entrance increase. Also, teachers are assuming an increasing role as political citizens in the life of the community, state, and nation [255:264–271]. They may feel certain that the amount of respect and prestige accorded teachers will continue to rise as professional standards, salaries, quality of members in the profession, and importance of education in everyone's life continue to rise.

FIGURE 9–2. Willingness of teachers to teach again if they were to be given the chance to start over. Teaching appears to be growing in attractiveness for both men and women. To what extent would similar results apply to other professions?

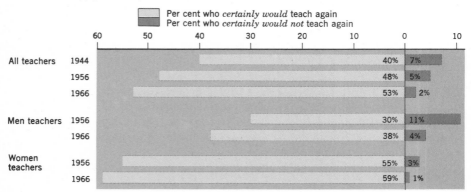

## Number in the Profession

In 1970–1971, there were more than 2,000,000 public school teachers, more than 230,000 nonpublic school teachers, approximately 13,000 superintendents, more than 121,000 principals and supervisors [151:67], and more than 97,000 other instructional personnel [76:35]. More than 830,000 faculty members were employed in public and nonpublic colleges and universities in the United States [151:67]. In addition there were many thousands employed as staff members in professional organizations, in government offices of education, and in private agencies with educational programs. The sheer size of educational endeavors in this country can be effectively summarized as follows: "If we add to the full-time students at all levels, the teachers, principals, and instructional specialists, and the cooks, bus drivers, and custodians, and the people engaged in selling or producing something for the schools, the total is 30 per cent of this country's population" [141:2].

There are conflicting forces at work and conflicting types of evidence which make it difficult to predict whether or not the number in the profession will increase substantially in the next few years. The tremendously increased number of people 5 to 17 years of age between 1950 and 1960 will move into the adult group and will then be having children. There is a growing tendency to include kindergartens, nursery schools, and junior colleges in our free public school systems, and this will increase enrollment. Also, increasing numbers of boys and girls are continuing their high school studies rather than dropping out of school. New demands for comprehensively trained personnel are being heard in many fields of instruction, and those for educational services are equally urgent. There are needs for trained counselors, specialists in remedial

FIGURE 9–3. Differences in the age distribution of men and women teachers in public schools. What changes in these distributions may take place in the future?

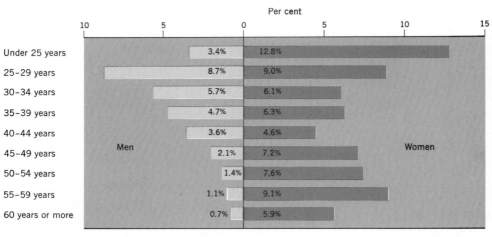

reading and speech, and instructors of the handicapped and the culturally disadvantaged, as well as for teachers in other areas not commonly
present in our school systems. Further demands are being made in the
field of adult education, since the educational needs of adults will
continue to increase. Thus, the services of the school may well extend in
many different directions.

On the other hand, the financial stringency facing many school
systems at the beginning of the decade may force a hold-the-line policy in
terms of numbers of professional persons employed. Thus, there may be
increased class sizes in some school systems, cutbacks in special services
and programs offered, and efforts to use professional personnel more
efficiently in professional tasks.

## Distribution of Men and Women

Unlike European countries, where teaching has been considered a man's
work, the United States has far more women than men teaching in its
public schools. From 1880 to 1920 the percentage of men teachers in
public schools decreased from 43 to 14 per cent. In the 20 years that
followed, the percentage of men rose to 23, but during World War II it
declined to 15 per cent of the total. Since then there has been a steady
increase; in 1970, it had reached 32.4 per cent of all public school
teachers, including 15.4 per cent of elementary teachers and 53.5 per cent
of secondary teachers [76:35].

Considerable effort is being made to attract more men into public
school teaching, especially into the elementary schools. Teachers and the
public generally feel that more men are needed in classroom teaching.
The adoption of single-salary schedules has provided added incentive for
men to consider teaching on the lower level, where the opportunities are

FIGURE 9–4.   During a half century of time, the percentage of men teachers in public schools has
increased significantly, especially in the secondary schools.

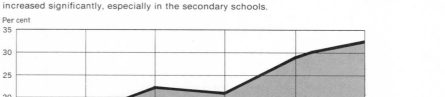

great. Higher salaries for all public school teachers should encourage more men to enter the profession on all levels.

## PROFESSIONAL ORGANIZATIONS AND PUBLICATIONS

Many years and the efforts of countless people have been involved in the development of the teaching profession in America. During this time the profession has developed a system of purposes, refined its procedures, set standards relating to training, and reduced to a definite code certain important elements in the behavior of its members.

One of the important conditions of professionalism is membership in various organizations. By sharing ideas and experiences with others through these organizations, teachers can improve the general level of their performance and exert their collective influence in bringing about more desirable conditions for work. A great portion of the improvements in education has resulted from the work of these organizations. In this world of special-interest groups, there is a very real need for teacher organizations.

In considering the services and characteristics of professional organizations, the Educational Policies Commission of the National Education Association, for many years, suggested that they should aim to do the following [202:54]:

1. Encourage members to cherish education's distinctive knowledge and insight
2. Aid in disseminating information and understanding throughout the profession
3. Promote research, support research, encourage research by members, and foster the application of research findings
4. Help improve teacher education
5. Safeguard teachers' basic freedoms
6. Meet members' personal needs
7. Improve teaching loads and school environment
8. Seek adequate salary provisions
9. Promote professional ethics
10. Inform the public
11. Take positions on issues affecting education
12. Cooperate in counseling the public
13. Influence public policy
14. Cooperate with interested lay groups

Since the organizations for teachers are considerable in number and vary in scope of membership, purpose, and procedure, a few of the more important ones should be discussed.

### Local Education Association

Local associations provide opportunities for teachers to consider matters that are of concern to the immediate community and teacher group.

Through the association, teachers are able to participate in the formulation of local school policies, to keep the community informed regarding educational matters, and to influence the policies of their state and national associations. Outside of large cities, local units are frequently formed on a countywide basis. Local groups usually are represented in their respective state associations and participate in the election of state association officials.

Local teacher organizations differ considerably in form. They may include all the school personnel within a school system, or there may be separate organizations for classroom teachers and for administrators. The number as well as the nature of the meetings held each year varies. Frequently, the organizations are very strong, and the members are vitally concerned with problems common to the group. Various subgroups may be working on such problems as reporting to parents, textbook selection, curriculum reorganization, evaluation of teachers and programs, and professional negotiations. Participation in these groups usually provides an excellent opportunity for professional stimulation and constructive work with colleagues.

## State Education Association

Educational workers are also organized at the state level. A journal is published, usually monthly, to keep teachers in the state informed on problems, trends, and events in education. Meetings of the total membership are arranged usually once or twice a year. Public schools may be dismissed for about two days, so that public school educators may attend the state convention. The state educational meetings generally are held in the capital city or in selected regional cities. Participation of many teachers and administrators is required in order to make these conventions successful and to carry on the activities of the association throughout the year. However, in many states less teacher enthusiasm for this type meeting is being exhibited, and there may well be major changes in plans for state meetings within the next few years.

The typical state education association has a headquarters building and a competent central office staff, a comprehensive organizational plan, and a constitution and bylaws. Often significant experimentation and research are centered there, and the results are communicated to the entire professional body. State teacher associations frequently know of important job opportunities within the state, and some provide placement services. Some state associations also provide for members a program of term life insurance at rates lower than normally available to an individual.

Most state organizations provide legal protection for individual teacher members against unfair or unjust practices which may arise in local situations. Few individual teachers would be able to wield much influence or stand the expense involved if such a problem should need to be carried far in the courts. It is reassuring for teachers to know that there is an organization ready and able to fight for their cause.

Since the central legal responsibility for education rests with the separate states in America, the state organization usually recommends minimum standards for teacher certification, school facilities, instructional programs, and the like. Some of the most significant laws relating to education in several states are created and promoted by the state education associations. Securing favorable legislation and improving conditions in the schools are primary functions of state education associations.

## National Education Association

Medical men have the American Medical Association to represent them. Lawyers have the American Bar Association. One of the organizations which teachers have to represent them is the National Education Association of the United States, usually referred to as the NEA, which is the oldest teacher organization in the United States. It began in 1857 when forty-three educational leaders from twelve states and the District of Columbia met in Philadelphia to establish the National Teachers Association for the purpose of elevating the character and advancing the interests of the teaching profession and promoting the cause of popular education. From 1870 to 1906 the organization was known as the National Educational Association, and the present name was adopted when the association was chartered by the Congress of the United States.

The association grew slowly at first. After World War I, teachers sought a more active role in the national organization. This was achieved through a reorganization of the association, whose control was then vested in a representative assembly made up of elected delegates from state and local teacher organizations that held membership in the NEA. At about the same time, a building in Washington, D.C., was secured to house the national headquarters. The NEA has grown in membership and influence to such a point that it approaches the status of being the official spokesman of the public school people of America (a claim likely to be disputed by the American Federation of Teachers). More than half of the public school teachers in the United States belong to the NEA. In 1970 the Association was made up of more than 1,100,000 members, and through affiliation of the local, state, and territorial associations, the NEA represented more than 1,700,000 teachers.

In 1966, the NEA merged with the 32,000 member American Teachers Association, a national organization of black educators, and also established an affiliate association composed of teachers in the schools operated by the U.S. Bureau of Indian Affairs [169:19]. However, race relations remain a problem in professional education as in many other fields, as witnessed by the expulsion of the Louisiana Teachers Association and the Mississippi Education Association by the NEA in 1970 for refusing to merge with the state's black teacher organizations [178:206].

A change in the membership qualifications provided that after August 31, 1964, eligibility for new members in the NEA would require an earned bachelor's, or higher, degree or a regular vocational or technical certificate [169:20]. If a person is not able to meet one of these qualifications, he may become an associate member without having the privilege of voting for delegates or of holding office in the organization.

The official purpose of the National Education Association is "To elevate the character and advance the interests of the profession of teaching and to promote the cause of education in the United States." At a July 6, 1970, Representative Assembly, the following goals were adopted for the Association: "an independent, united teaching profession; professional excellence; economic security for all educators; adequate financing for public education; human and civil rights for all educators and children; and leadership in solving social problems" [169:102–104].

The services performed by the NEA are of tremendous variety and scope, but in order to gain some understanding of the total program and activities these services can be listed under the following broad categories: professional growth, public relations, defense of the teaching

The many publications of professional organizations are of great benefit to educators in the improvement of educational practices. (*Photograph by Joe Di Dio, National Education Association.*)

profession, research, professional standards, teacher welfare, federal relations, curriculum and instructional development, international education, selective teacher recruitment, publications, and assistance in professional negotiations. The official journal of the NEA is *Today's Education.* The Association also provides various direct services to individual members including life and accidental death insurance, a mutual fund, a tax-sheltered annuity program, book purchase, and an auto-leasing program [169:21].

In its continuous efforts to elevate the standards of the teaching profession, the NEA provides services to local associations as well as to individual teachers. These services include various publications, consultative services, conferences, a clearing-house for ideas, and special materials to local committee chairmen. An example of one such service is that of the Research Division of the NEA. This division renders a real service to teachers, associations, and government officials by collecting and publishing nationwide data on such problems as teacher load, salaries, tenure, certification, retirement, finance, legislation, welfare, and status. These data have been of much help to teachers and teacher associations in appraising the status of local conditions in comparison with the status in the United States as a whole.

To encourage closer relationships and coordinated efforts on local, state, and national levels, the NEA has developed the unified membership plan in which teachers join all levels of associations at one time. By 1970, twenty-eight states had adopted the unified membership plan. A further attempt to strengthen local associations by bringing the services and resources of the state and national organizations closer to every teacher in Uniserv, in operation for the first time in 1970–1971. The goal is to have one staff man in the field giving direct and continuing service to every 1,200 teachers. The local, state, and national education associations pool their resources to finance each unit and to train and assist each Uniserv representative in providing service to teachers [169:22–23].

There has been much reorganization within the NEA during the past few years. For example, in 1966 there were thirty-three departments. However, in 1971, as may be noted in the organizational diagram, there were four departments, seventeen national affiliates, and twelve associated organizations. These changes represent, in most cases, a greater autonomy for the affiliates and associates. Within these various groups is an organization serving almost all levels or special interests and concerns in education.

As is indicated in the diagram, the NEA also has twenty-five commissions, committees, and councils. Illustrative of these groups, the National Commission on Teacher Education and Professional Standards has become increasingly more important since its creation in 1946. More familiarly known as the TEPS Commission, this group has evolved into a nationwide organization with parallel state commissions. As its name implies, the commission is concerned with the recruitment, selection,

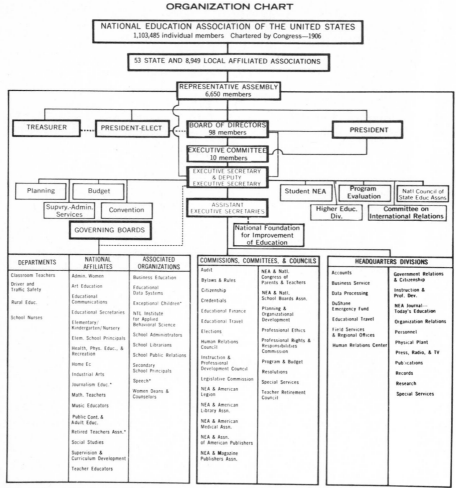

**FIGURE 9–5.** Organizational chart of the National Education Association.

preparation, and certification of teachers, and with the standards of the schools which prepare teachers.

Perhaps the greatest prominence of any NEA commission was achieved by the Educational Policies Commission, in existence from 1935 to 1969. The commission considered issues facing the teaching profession, and proposed policy for the conduct of education in this country and in its international relationships. Among its most influential publications were *The Unique Functions of Education in American Democracy* (1937), *Education for All American Children* (1948), *Moral and Spiritual Values in the Public Schools* (1951), *Manpower and Education* (1956), *The Central Purpose of American Education* (1961),

*Education and the Disadvantaged American* (1962), and *American Education and the Search for Equal Opportunity* (1965).

## Student Professional Associations

Many college students belong to the Student National Education Association, and many high school students belong to the Future Teachers of America. From 1937 to 1957 the name "Future Teachers of America" referred to both the high school and college groups. Since that time the high school organization has been known as the FTA and the college organization as the Student NEA. Student NEA is designed for college students preparing to teach, and FTA clubs are for high school students exploring teaching as a career.

In 1971 there were more than 250,000 high school students in 6,000 FTA clubs and more than 83,000 college students in 1,000 campus chapters of the Student NEA [169:118&131]. The Student NEA seeks to:

. . . develop in education students an understanding of the education profession to provide for a national student voice in matters affecting their education and their profession, to influence the conditions under which prospective teachers are prepared, and to stimulate the highest ideals of professional ethics, standards, attitudes, and training. The overall program strives to encourage its members to serve as change agents in the arena of teacher education, education more generally, society, and the profession.

Continuing SNEA programs include teacher education reform; minority education; political awareness (particularly in securing voter registration and political education); educational volunteer service, a student internship program at the NEA Center; local, state, and national programs to strengthen student governance, organizationally, in teacher education programs; and providing a national voice for education students about matters affecting them.

The FTA offers an opportunity to encourage the finest young men and women in high schools to enter the teaching profession. The official purposes of the FTA are as follows [169:130]:

To provide a means for secondary school students (a) to participate in making their education increasingly relevant to their present and future needs and (b) to engage in realistic education activities that are of assistance in making valid decisions about education careers. Among FTA's many activities are summer conferences (including the National FTA College and Career Seminar), and political and educational participation experiences.

Special attention is given to strengthening the relationship between local FTA chapters and local associations.

In 1969 the SNEA-FTA was made an NEA project with a special committee named to restudy the goals, structure, and administration of the organizations; to assess students' perceived needs; and to provide an organizational design which would provide for student self-determination. This pattern would identify mutually beneficial relationships between the student groups and the parent body [168:104]. Thus major changes in these organizations are occurring.

## American Federation of Teachers

An increasingly important organization for all levels of classroom teachers in American education is the American Federation of Teachers (AFT), an affiliate of the American Federation of Labor-Congress of Industrial Organizations. The AFT originated in 1916 and, until the merger of the AFL and the CIO in 1955, it was affiliated with the AFL. *American Teacher* is the official monthly newspaper of the AFT, and *Changing Education* is the quarterly professional journal.

The AFT has experienced an appreciable increase in membership in the past 20 years, especially in some of our biggest cities, such as New York, Chicago, Detroit, Philadelphia, Cleveland, Baltimore, Pittsburgh, Boston, and Washington, D.C. Some of the reasons behind this increase include the success of the AFT in negotiating contracts for teachers, calling for substantial salary increases and improvements in working conditions. In 1971 the total membership was nearly 250,000 in 1,000 local organizations. The membership of the AFT is centered almost entirely in the large cities and in the suburban areas which surround these cities. AFT groups are rarely found in rural areas.

The long-range objectives of the American Federation of Teachers, as stated in its constitution, are [128:10]:

(1) to bring associations of teachers into relations of mutual assistance and cooperation; (2) to obtain for them all the rights to which they are entitled; (3) to raise the standards of the teaching profession by securing the conditions essential to the best professional service; (4) to promote such a democratization of the schools as will enable them to better equip their pupils to take their places in the industrial, social, and political life of the community; and (5) to promote the welfare of the childhood of the nation by providing progressively better educational opportunity for all.

More specifically, the AFT has promoted integration within the schools, supporting the idea of equal educational opportunities for all. It has instigated special programs, such as the More Effective Schools Program in New York City, geared to providing improved educational opportunities for inner-city youth. It has opposed any form of a merit-rating salary plan as educationally unsound. More recently it has launched a national campaign against what is called "educational gimmickry" such as performance contracting, voucher plans, and differentiated staffing [179:2].

The action program of the AFT lists the following goals [97:4–11]:

*Collective bargaining goal:* Recognition of the right of teachers and other non-supervisory educational employees to negotiate written agreements with their school boards through organizations of their own choice. Such agreements should cover salaries, fringe benefits, working conditions, and all other matters of interest to teachers. They should include strong grievance procedures for enforcement of the terms of the agreement and for the elimination of inequities suffered by individuals.

*Collective action goal:* To develop techniques of collective action which give teachers the power to make collective bargaining meaningful.

*Salaries goal:* To establish fully automatic salary schedules, free from "merit" rating requirements, which adequately reflect the professional status of teachers.

*Tenure goal:* State legislation protecting teachers from discharge except for proper cause, after a limited probationary period, and establishing impartial procedures guaranteeing a fair hearing and due process of law in the event charges are made against any teacher or other professional school employee.

*Professional standards goal:* To guarantee that any person employed as a teacher meet professional standards of education, practical training, and performance ability.

*Fringe benefits goal:* To establish sick leave, health insurance and other group benefits for teachers and other nonsupervisory employees equal to those enjoyed by employees in private industry and in public employment on the state and federal levels.

*Retirement goal:* To permit teachers to retire after 25 years of service on a retirement allowance which permits them to look forward to a life of dignity and comfort.

*20/20 vision for teachers goal:* Modern, properly equipped classrooms; limitation of maximum class sizes to no more than 20 pupils (and fewer in special and "difficult" classes); no more than 20 classroom periods a week; and complete relief from nonteaching chores such as keeping clerical records, supervising buses, lunchrooms, and playgrounds.

*Handling student behavior problems goal:* To establish an orderly, cooperative climate in the school so that student behavior problems are minimal, with a clearly understood policy of support for teachers by administrators, and proper procedures and facilities for handling students with chronic behavior problems.

*Equal opportunity for all children goal:* To give every child a good education in spite of any environmental or other handicaps which may inhibit his ability and desire to learn.

*Vocational education goal:* To develop a system of trade, technical, and business education which will provide young people with new skills, or enhance their present skills, to increase their productivity, economic status, and self-esteem.

*Textbooks, teaching materials, and curriculum goal:* Full teacher participation in selection of textbooks and materials as well as in curriculum planning and revision.

*Teachers as citizens goal:* To mobilize the civic power of teachers, in cooperation with organized labor and other liberal forces, in order to bring about the social reforms necessary to eliminate poverty and build a hopeful and progressive society.

*Academic freedom goal:* To protect the rights of teachers to use their professional judgment in selecting materials to be used in their teaching, in conducting discussions of controversial issues, and in presenting the basic facts about our nation and world.

*Higher education goal:* To establish a system of free college education for all students who wish to avail themselves of the opportunity, and to ensure rights and benefits for college teachers appropriate to their professional status.

The AFT is an organization for classroom teachers only. School superintendents, principals, and other administrators at or above the rank of principal are not admitted to membership in the AFT. Within the AFT the councils on educational problems include The National Council for Effective Schools, The National Council on Teacher-Supervisory Relationships, and The National Council on Professional Standards. As in the

NEA there may be Student Federations of Teachers chartered on college or university campuses, and a similar group may be chartered in a high school through application of the sponsoring local union of the AFT [128:14].

Although affiliated with the AFL-CIO, the AFT is a legal entity in its own right. It need not join the AFL-CIO in any specific action. The AFT sees itself "first and foremost a union seeking benefits and improved working conditions for its members. But it is also an educational organization, deeply committed to improving the quality of schools at all levels. Finally, the AFT is a social force, working with other unions to improve the quality of American life" [97:11].

## International Educational Organizations

As the nations of the world grow closer together, educators find that they have many common interests. In the first place it is the desire of the free world to have peace and security. The best way to ensure this peace and security is through the development of international understanding, which is a crucial task confronting teachers throughout the world. In the second place, because of the increasing relatedness of nations today, the welfare of the teachers in any nation becomes the concern of teachers in all other nations. For these reasons efforts have been made to develop an organization for the educators of all nations.

The World Confederation of Organizations of the Teaching Profession was established in 1952 as a result of a merger of various international organizations, including the World Organization of the Teaching Profession which originally had been founded in 1946 at the invitation of the National Education Association. The organization consolidates teachers in ninety countries engaged in elementary, secondary, and higher education in order to "promote education for international understanding, material and moral rights and interests of the teaching profession, improvement of educational policy and practice, and representation of the profession in the international aspects of educational policy" [168:324].

UNESCO (United Nations Educational, Scientific, and Cultural Organization) was created in 1945 by the United Nations. According to the constitution of UNESCO, its purpose is "to contribute to peace and security by promoting collaboration among the nations through education, science, and culture in order to further universal respect for justice, for the rule of law and for the human rights and fundamental freedoms which are affirmed for the peoples of the world, without distinction of race, sex, language, or religion, by the charter of the United Nations."

Within the framework of these purposes, UNESCO has engaged in many different types of activities. Those most closely related to education have included the organizing of educational missions to assist under-developed countries, the dissemination of educational materials, the holding of international conferences and seminars, the planning of programs of fundamental education to combat illiteracy, the promotion of international understanding, and the carrying on of research in world educational problems.

## Other Education Associations

The *Education Directory,* issued regularly each year by the U.S. Office of Education, lists many national, regional, and state educational associations in addition to the few that have already been discussed. A good share of these are designed to meet the needs of various specialized groups of educators. Some of them are departments of the NEA, but many others are not.

Elementary school teachers usually become members of an association such as the Association for Childhood Education International (ACEI), which is concerned with the education of children from 2 to 12 years of age. Most elementary teachers are interested in becoming members of the American Association of Elementary-Kindergarten-Nursery Educators, a national affiliate of the NEA. Each subject area in the high school has its own national association, such as the National Council for the Social Studies, and the National Council of the Teachers of Mathematics. The NEA *Handbook* contains essential information about each of the NEA departments, such as historical background, activities, names of national officers, and the amount of regular and student dues.

Curriculum supervisors and consultants usually become members of the national association in their subject area and the Association for Supervision and Curriculum Development (ASCD). Principals and superintendents usually become members of the National Association of Elementary School Principals (NAESP), the National Association of Secondary School Principals (NASSP), or the American Association of School Administrators (AASA). College and university professors in the field of education may join various specialized groups such as the National Society for the Study of Education, The John Dewey Society, The American Educational Research Association, and the American Association of University Professors.

The associations mentioned in this section are only a few of those in the field of education. The important point is that for every position and interest, there is a professional association composed of persons holding that position and sharing that interest. Furthermore, it is the journals and yearbooks of these associations that provide much of the professional literature in education.

## Honorary Educational Associations

Professional and honorary groups in education include Pi Lambda Theta (for women) and Phi Delta Kappa (for men), or Kappa Delta Pi (for both men and women).

Pi Lambda Theta is open to undergraduate and graduate women students and women faculty members who meet the necessary qualifications. General qualifications include evidence of high professional standards, qualities of leadership, and ability to live and work with others. In addition, there are more specific requirements for both student and faculty eligibility for membership. The specific purposes are to:

recognize women of superior scholastic achievement and high potential for professional leadership; foster creativity and academic excellence at all educational levels; support, extend, and interpret the function of education in a democracy; demonstrate the power of competence in the body of knowledge unique to the profession; stimulate, conduct, and utilize research; accept responsibility for evaluation and improvement of the profession of teaching; contribute to the solution of educational, social, and cultural problems of national and international concern; and promote professional fellowship and cooperation as a means of positive action [206:i].

Membership in Phi Delta Kappa is by chapter invitation to male graduate or undergraduate students who have completed at least 90 semester hours toward the baccalaureate degree, who give promise of success in a professional career in education, and who will contribute to the purposes of Phi Delta Kappa. Additional requirements include 15 semester hours of courses in education, scholarship acceptable for admission to candidacy for a graduate degree, and commitment to a life career in educational service.

The chief purpose of Phi Delta Kappa shall be to promote free public education as an essential to the development and maintenance of a democracy, through the continuing interpretation of the ideals of research, service and leadership. It shall be the purpose of Phi Delta Kappa to translate these ideals into a program of action appropriate to the needs of public education [132:n.p.].

Membership dues in the organization includes a subscription to the *Phi Delta Kappan,* which is published monthly, October through June of each year. This journal carries many articles, reviews, and features of special interest to educators.

Kappa Delta Pi is open to both men and women and is composed of outstanding junior and senior undergraduates, graduate students, and faculty members. In addition to the functions commonly performed by honorary educational organizations, Kappa Delta Pi has contributed to the general cause of education by issuing several significant publications. These publications include *The Educational Forum, The Kappa Delta Pi Lecture Series,* and the *Kappa Delta Pi Research Publications.*

These honorary educational associations exert positive influences upon the profession. Membership is highly regarded and provides an opportunity for outstanding educators to join forces in worthy causes.

## Parent-Teacher Association

An opportunity for parents and teachers to work together effectively on both local and national levels is provided through the Parent-Teacher Association. Teachers are usually expected to take an active part in this association in those communities where it is established. All official local PTA groups are members of their state congress and of the National Congress of Parents and Teachers. The objects of this group of nearly 12 million members are as follows [184:i]:

To promote the welfare of children and youth in home, school, church, and community.

To raise the standards of home life.

To secure adequate laws for the care and protection of children and youth.

To bring into closer relation the home and the school, that parents and teachers may cooperate intelligently in the training of the child.

To develop between educators and the general public such united efforts as will secure for every child the highest advantages in physical, mental, social, and spiritual education.

In most communities the PTA takes its work seriously, studies its problems realistically, and wields tremendous power in shaping trends toward better schooling. Unfortunately, some teachers feel that PTA work requires too much of their time. Some administrators feel that it provides another unnecessary opportunity for people to meddle in school affairs.

In most PTA groups, mothers far exceed fathers in number. Many PTAs fail to reach those parents in the community when response would be most advantageous to themselves, to their children, and to the improvement of the instructional program in school. These are typical problems which, through planning, hard work, and cooperation on the part of parents and school people, have been largely solved in individual communities.

As indicated in the organizational diagram, Figure 9–5, the National Education Association recognizes the value of the PTA through a joint committee of the NEA and National Congress of Parents and Teachers. *The PTA Magazine* has won the School Bell Award of the National School Public Relations Association for distinguished service in the interpretation of education.

Within the past decade or so, in some school districts where parents and teachers have preferred not to affiliate with a national organization but have wished to retain a cooperative group that would work for better schools and in the best interest of boys and girls, the Parent-Teacher Organization (PTO) or the Parent-Teacher-Student Organization (PTSO) has replaced the PTA.

## Code of Ethics for the Teaching Profession

Besides joining and working earnestly to promote the purposes of various professional organizations, every teacher is expected to conduct himself and manage his work affairs in such ways as are approved by the profession at large. Should a teacher tutor his own students for pay? Should a teacher leave a position suddenly in the middle of a semester? Is it legitimate for a teacher to make speeches in his classroom favoring his political party?

The acceptable modes of behavior along these lines, and many others, are well established in a professional code of ethics. Medical doctors have such a code, lawyers have one, and teachers also have one. These codes are not legal enactments; nevertheless, they are definite and well understood by the great body of the profession. A prospective teacher should become well acquainted with the code of ethics of the teaching group.

The NEA has spent a great amount of time and effort in developing and revising the Code of Ethics of the Education Profession. It is designed to be acceptable to all workers in education in all parts of the nation. The first national code of ethics for teachers was adopted by the NEA in 1929 and revised in 1941, 1952, 1963, and 1968. The most recent revision is presented below [169:105–107]:

**PREAMBLE**

The educator believes in the worth and dignity of man. He recognizes the supreme importance of the pursuit of truth, devotion to excellence, and the nurture of democratic citizenship. He regards as essential to these goals the protection of freedom to learn and to teach and the guarantee of equal educational opportunity for all. The educator accepts his responsibility to practice his profession according to the highest ethical standards.

The educator recognizes the magnitude of the responsibility he has accepted in choosing a career in education, and engages himself, individually and collectively with other educators, to judge his colleagues, and to be judged by them, in accordance with the provisions of this code.

**PRINCIPLE I**

Commitment to the Student

The educator measures his success by the progress of each student toward realization of his potential as a worthy and effective citizen. The educator therefore works to stimulate the spirit of inquiry, the acquisition of knowledge and understanding, and the thoughtful formulation of worthy goals.

In fulfilling his obligation to the student, the educator—

1. Shall not without just cause restrain the student from independent action in his pursuit of learning, and shall not without just cause deny the student access to varying points of view.
2. Shall not deliberately suppress or distort subject matter for which he bears responsibility.
3. Shall make reasonable effort to protect the student from conditions harmful to learning or to health and safety.
4. Shall conduct professional business in such a way that he does not expose the student to unnecessary embarrassment or disparagement.
5. Shall not on the ground of race, color, creed, or national origin exclude any student from participation in or deny him benefits under any program, nor grant any discriminatory consideration or advantage.
6. Shall not use professional relationships with students for private advantage.
7. Shall keep in confidence information that has been obtained in the course of professional service, unless disclosure serves professional purposes or is required by law.
8. Shall not tutor for remuneration students assigned to his classes, unless no other qualified teacher is reasonably available.

**PRINCIPLE II**

Commitment to the Public

The educator believes that patriotism in its highest form requires dedication to the principles of our democratic heritage. He shares with all other citizens the responsibility for the development of sound public policy and assumes full political and citizenship responsibilities. The educator bears particular responsibility for the development of policy relating to the extension of educational opportunities for all and for interpreting educational programs and policies to the public.

In fulfilling his obligation to the public, the educator—

1. Shall not misrepresent an institution or oganization with which he is affiliated, and shall take adequate precautions to distinguish between his personal and institutional or organizational views.
2. Shall not knowingly distort or misrepresent the facts concerning educational matters in direct and indirect public expressions.
3. Shall not interfere with a colleague's exercise of political and citizenship rights and responsibilities.
4. Shall not use institutional privileges for private gain or to promote political candidates or partisan political activities.
5. Shall accept no gratuities, gifts, or favors that might impair or appear to impair professional judgment, nor offer any favor, service, or thing of value to obtain special advantage.

**PRINCIPLE III**

Commitment to the Profession

The educator believes that the quality of the services of the education profession directly influences the nation and its citizens. He therefore exerts every effort to raise professional standards, to improve his service, to promote a climate in which the exercise of professional judgment is encouraged, and to achieve conditions which attract persons worthy of the trust to careers in education. Aware of the value of united effort, he contributes actively to the support, planning, and programs of professional organizations.

In fulfilling his obligation to the profession, the educator—

1.  Shall not discriminate on the ground of race, color, creed, or national origin for membership in professional organizations, nor interfere with the free participation of colleagues in the affairs of their association.
2.  Shall accord just and equitable treatment to all members of the profession in the exercise of their professional rights and responsibilities.
3.  Shall not use coercive means or promise special treatment in order to influence professional decisions of colleagues.
4.  Shall withhold and safeguard information acquired about colleagues in the course of employment, unless disclosure serves professional purposes.
5.  Shall not refuse to participate in a professional inquiry when requested by an appropriate professional association.
6.  Shall provide upon the request of the aggrieved party a written statement of specific reason for recommendations that lead to denial of increments, significant changes in employment, or termination of employment.
7.  Shall not misrepresent his professional qualifications.
8.  Shall not knowingly distort evaluations of colleagues.

**PRINCIPLE IV**

Commitment to Professional Employment Practices

The educator regards the employment agreement as a pledge to be executed both in spirit and in fact in a manner consistent with the highest ideals of professional service. He believes that sound professional personnel relationships with governing boards are built upon personal integrity, dignity and mutual respect. The educator discourages the practice of his profession by unqualified persons.

In fulfilling his obligation to professional employment practices, the educator—

1.  Shall apply for, accept, offer, or assign a position or responsibility on the basis of professional preparation and legal qualifications.
2.  Shall apply for a specific position only when it is known to be vacant, and shall refrain from underbidding or commenting adversely about other candidates.
3.  Shall not knowingly withhold information regarding a position from an applicant, or misrepresent an assignment or conditions of employment.
4.  Shall give prompt notice to the employing agency of any change in availability of service, and the employing agent shall give prompt notice of change in availability or nature of a position.
5.  Shall adhere to the terms of a contract or appointment, unless these terms have been legally terminated, falsely represented, or substantially altered by unilateral action of the employing agency.
6.  Shall conduct professional business through channels, when available, that have been jointly approved by the professional organization and the employing agency.
7.  Shall not delegate assigned tasks to unqualified personnel.
8.  Shall permit no commercial exploitation of his professional position.
9.  Shall use time granted for the purpose for which it is intended.

## Enforcement of the Code of Ethics

Most states and local school systems have adopted the NEA code or, in some cases, have established their own codes of ethics. The Professional Ethics Committee of the NEA is responsible for the development and interpretation of the code and provides materials and assistance to the ethics committees of state and local associations in their activities and studies [70:4].

Enforcement of the code of ethics is the responsibility of the Commission on Professional Rights and Responsibilities of the NEA. It is also concerned with the defense of teachers and schools against unjust attack, development of professional personnel policies, tenure legislation, civil and human rights of the teaching profession, information regarding persons and groups criticizing and opposing education, and unethical conduct of members of the teaching profession [169:158–159]. However, serious questions have been raised about the willingness of the profession to enforce the code. Has the education profession done as good a job of policing itself as has the American Medical Association or the American Bar Association?

## Future of the Profession

Teachers and the teaching profession have come far in achieving better salaries and salary schedules, better working conditions, greater professional recognition, greater prestige and status—both locally and nationally —and improved quality of service rendered to students and communities. These accomplishments have been achieved largely through the efforts of many, many dedicated teachers working through organized groups on the local, state, and national levels.

In recent years a spirit of greater militancy has been apparent in the efforts of teachers, including those representing the NEA as well as those representing the American Federation of Teachers of the AFL-CIO. In achieving professional goals, the terms "professional negotiations," "professional sanctions," and "withdrawal of services" have come into common use within the teaching profession, just as the terms "collective bargaining" and "strike" have been associated with labor for many years and are still associated with the AFT.

It is interesting to follow the dramatic change in opinion among teachers concerning the right to strike. In the period from 1965 to 1970, the percentage of teachers answering "yes" to an Opinion-Poll question, "Do you believe public school teachers should ever strike?" rose from 53 per cent to 73 per cent [270:27]. In 1960–1961 there were three strikes, and in 1969–1970 there were 180, with a total of 500 for the ten-year period [272:69]. Both the AFT and the NEA have official statements of policy concerning "withdrawal of services" and "work stoppages."

Within the past decade "professional negotiation" and "collective bargaining" have become a way of life for educators in many, many school districts. Points of view within the profession concerning the long-range accomplishments of these procedures range from the most optimistic to severely pessimistic. The optimistic view holds that it is

only through these processes that the profession can realistically approach and solve its problems. The pessimistic view holds that short-
range gains have been achieved at the expense of community understanding of, and sympathy for, school problems; that the processes establish an
adversary relationship between teachers and administrators at a time
when unity is tremendously important; and that long-range gains will not
be any greater than they would have been without negotiations and
bargaining. In view of the time-consuming element of the processes, for
both school boards and teachers, it has been suggested that the next step
may be negotiations at the state level [170:9].

In many communities, teachers have asked to decide by vote which
group—the teachers association or the union—shall represent them
before the school board. The AFT has had its greatest comparative
success in the large cities where unionism has long been powerful,
although there are many exceptions even here. The NEA has continued to
show its great national strength in small cities, rural areas, and in entire
states, for example, Utah, Oklahoma, and Washington. The first statewide
professional negotiation law was passed in the state of Wisconsin in
1962.

A negotiation or bargaining agreement in a local school district may
be quite simple and brief, or it may be quite complicated and detailed.
The general trend is for agreements to become longer and more detailed
as they are renegotiated. At any rate a typical agreement may contain
sections on recognition and definitions, fair practices, integrated education, school calendar, class size, school day, discipline, report-card
marks, parent-teacher conferences, personnel assignments, teacher competence, substitutes, leave policy, insurance, improvement of program,
improvement of facilities, and grievance procedures [4:iv].

Principals, who are part of the management of schools but who in
most cases continue to think of themselves as teachers, have sought to
counsel both sides. For example, the National Association of Secondary
School Principals [71:11–12]:

emphasizes that discussions and decisions on purely professional problems cannot be
considered in an atmosphere characteristic of the bargaining table. It proposes instead
that such considerations take place in an atmosphere of colleagues working together as a
professional team. It welcomes the establishment of formal councils made up of
representatives chosen by teachers, principals, and supervisors. . . . Such councils can
evoke a partnership rather than an adversary relationship. They can encourage the search
for solutions rather than victories.

The National Association of Elementary School Principals at its 1970
convention adopted much the same position. They did not wish to stand
with either superintendents or teachers but to be "expert witnesses" who
will advise both sides about the "educational and management consequences of decisions under consideration" [68:201].

The achievement of professional goals and the question concerning agencies and procedures through which to achieve those goals represent a complex problem. Although there are proponents of extreme points of view, there are also those who attempt to bring about agreement, even to the extent of a merger of the NEA and the AFT. It has become obvious that the major organizational issues which have historically divided the NEA and the AFT—membership of administrators and AFT affiliation with the AFL-CIO—are no longer so divisive [145:139–140]. In fact, the two organizations have merged on the local level in Flint, Michigan (1969), and in Los Angeles, California (1970). Although many problems still exist, it seems reasonable to anticipate a national merger between the two groups.

Another major problem, alluded to earlier in this chapter, which faces the education profession today is that of accountability. A number of educators feel that "self-governance" is essential before members of the profession are held accountable for educational outcomes—for what students learn. As Bain points out [17:413]:

. . . it is pure myth that classroom teachers can ever be held accountable, with justice, under existing conditions. The classroom teacher has either too little control or no control over the factors which might render accountability either feasible or fair.

As a beginning, the teaching profession must be afforded those legal rights necessary for it to assume responsibility and accountability for its own professional destiny. At a minimum, this includes transferring to the profession the following: (1) authority over issuing, suspending, revoking, or reinstating the legal licensure of educational personnel; (2) authority to establish and administer standards of professional practice and ethics for all educational personnel; (3) authority to accredit teacher preparation institutions; and (4) authority to govern in-service and continuing education for teachers.

One approach to accountability about which both NEA and AFT are justifiably concerned is performance contracting, in which a school district contracts with a private organization to perform instructional tasks. Teacher groups fear that widespread adoption of this concept may have an adverse effect on the overall quality of educational programs and turn professional teachers into mere teaching technicians, with little or no effective voice in policy and decision making.

## SUMMARY

The advancement of teaching as a profession depends in great degree upon the vigorous work of professional organizations and their members. An individual teacher can contribute most to the profession by assuming an active role in one or more of the many organizations—striving to improve the status, conditions, and effectiveness of the profession.

Within the field of education there are professional organizations that are geographic in scope—local, state, regional, and national. There are organizations based on types of duties—teaching, counseling, super- vision, and administration. There are organizations based on subject-matter specialties, and there are organizations that are comprehensive in nature and include all these types.

Teachers need to support one. another and to work together cooperatively for the good of their schools and their pupils. Joining forces in professional organizations of various sorts, studying their purposes and procedures, and playing a responsible part in those groups is one way of accomplishing the necessary cooperation. To be effective, a teacher should take an active role in especially the local and state organizations, and at least maintain active membership in one or more national organizations that are most appropriate to his area of work.

One of the distinctive characteristics of a profession is a clearly formulated code of ethics to which its members adhere. Therefore, there is a moral obligation for a teacher to be familiar with, to respect, and to adhere to the Code of Ethics of the Teaching Profession, and to expect and insist that his colleagues do likewise. The status of the profession will grow as its membership becomes disciplined in terms of a code of ethics.

During the past several years, teachers have assumed a much more aggressive role in improving conditions within the profession. The complaints are many—inadequate salaries, few fringe benefits, heavy teaching loads, community pressures, lack of teaching materials and supplies, excessive nonteaching duties, lack of support in handling discipline problems, lack of decision-making participation in curriculum planning, arbitrary dismissals, lack of personal protection especially in inner-city situations, inadequate provision for minority groups—the list is long. This is one of the reasons why the NEA and the AFT urge teachers to become active within the profession and within the local community, state, and nation.

This is a time of critical decisions for teachers and the teaching profession. This is a time for teachers to work together in achieving greater autonomy for the profession, and in improving conditions within the profession so that the mission of our public school system may be more effectively realized. Decisions made in the next few years will determine the course of American education and the role of teaching as a profession for many years to come.

## QUESTIONS TO CONSIDER

1.  In your opinion, what should be the characteristics of a profession?
2.  How does teaching as a profession differ from other professions such as medicine and law? How are they similar?
3.  How do you account for teaching frequently not being accorded professional status? How might this condition be corrected?
4.  What are the chief differences between the NEA and the AFT with respect to policies, services, and potential contributions to the improvement of education in the United States? In what ways are they similar? How would you justify joining one or the other?

5. Why should a teacher be expected to give some of his time to the profession itself?
6. Should teachers be required to join one or more professional organizations? Why?
7. There are many opportunities today for teaching abroad. What values usually come to the teacher who participates in such a program? What special responsibilities does he have?
8. Why do you suppose the Parent-Teacher Association has usually been more successful at the elementary level than at the secondary level?
9. What are the differences between professional negotiation and collective bargaining and between sanctions and strikes?
10. What procedures may the teaching profession ethically use in attempting to gain higher salaries and better working conditions?
11. What should be the role of teachers, principals, superintendents, and school boards in professional negotiation as well as in collective bargaining?
12. What are the values of a code of ethics for you as a teacher?
13. Consider the teachers whom you have had. To what extent did they seem to be aware of a code of ethics? To what extent did they seem to practice the provisions of this code?
14. Who should speak for the profession of teaching? Why?
15. How can you reconcile autonomy for the teaching profession and local control of schools?
16. What kind of provisions should the NEA and the AFT make to assure active involvement of racial and ethnic groups?
17. What are the pros and cons of teacher strikes?

## PROBLEM SITUATION FOR INQUIRY

When the time came for salary negotiations, it became obvious that the school board was going to ask the teachers to "hold the line" for another year. But the teachers had already held the line for two straight years, and therefore it seemed that a work stoppage or strike was imminent. Phil Jones had strong reservations about the ethics of teacher strikes. He was aware of the need for salary increases because his personal budget was being taxed by inflation as much as anyone else's. He also was aware of his responsibility to the teaching profession, realizing that higher salaries might attract better teachers and encourage experienced teachers to decline lucrative offers outside teaching. Furthermore, he felt the need for supporting his fellow teachers. Still, Phil felt a deep responsibility to the pupils in his classes. Striking and closing the schools, he believed, would hinder the educational progress of the students. Since teacher strikes are illegal in the state in which Phil teaches, he also felt that breaking the law would set a poor example for his students.

If you were Phil, what would you do? Why?

## ACTIVITIES TO PURSUE

1. Attend one or more local and state teachers' meetings. Make a careful study of the problems discussed and the values gained by teachers as a result of these meetings.
2. Learn about your campus chapter of the Student National Education Association. Secure information concerning its major purposes and its program.
3. Arrange a panel to discuss the meaning and value of a professional code of ethics. If possible include on the panel a clergyman, a medical doctor, a lawyer, an engineer, and a school superintendent.
4. Have a superintendent of schools or a principal discuss infractions of the Code of Ethics of the Teaching Profession which he has observed. Discuss with him how such infractions might be avoided in the future.

5.  Watch the newspapers for a month for all NEA and AFT news releases. Try to classify the items as to types and purposes.
6.  Invite representatives of various honorary groups in the teaching profession to explain the purposes and programs of their organizations.
7.  Spend some time in the library examining the journals published by the various professional organizations. Make a list of those that may prove to be especially helpful to you when you begin teaching.
8.  Discuss with a legislator how teachers might be more effective in improving conditions confronting teachers.
9.  Formulate a plan of action on how you will proceed to enhance the teaching profession.

# 10 | SALARIES OF EDUCATORS

How high a salary can a beginning teacher expect? How do beginning salaries in teaching compare with those in other professions requiring comparable preparation? To what extent are salaries related to years of experience and additional preparation? What kinds of salaries are paid to teachers in differentiated staffing situations, and to other personnel, such as principals, supervisors, superintendents, counselors, librarians, special education, special fields, and college teachers? Are there sources of other income for teachers? These are important questions to consider in planning a career in education.

The salary status of teachers, especially since World War II, has been a matter of concern both nationally and locally. Since teachers require the same basic necessities of life and have the same desires as all other normal people, it is not possible for them to render maximum service, regardless of ability and preparation, if their income is not sufficient for them to feel economically secure.

Progress has been and is being made to increase the salaries of teachers. Data on salaries for any one year, therefore, may be obsolete the following year. Furthermore, in interpreting salaries, it should be remembered that the mere number of dollars earned per year does not take into account other factors such as a variation in overhead expenses between those in the teaching profession and those in certain other professions.

## Standards of Living Maintained by Teachers

Salaries need to be considered in terms of general standards of living fixed by society for different occupations. For example, professional people are expected to maintain higher standards of living than are unskilled laborers. A teacher needs a salary adequate to continue his professional study, to travel, and to provide for his cultural, recreational, and civic needs in order to bring to the classroom increasingly richer experiences.

Unfortunately, the American public has never been too clear in its thinking as to whether the teacher belongs to the wage earner or the professional class of workers. From a study of the historical development of education in America, it is easy to understand why there has been confusion as to the status of teachers. The work of national, state, and local teacher organizations, however, is contributing much to the establishment of teaching as a profession in the minds of the general public. It is reasonable to believe that the teacher will be accorded higher status and therefore will be expected to maintain the standard of living generally associated with professional people.

## Relationship Between Income and Standard of Living

The money required to maintain a certain standard of living varies with respect to the community in which one lives. The incomes of people in a given area largely determine the local standards of living and the standards that will be expected of teachers. In a very wealthy community, a teacher will be expected to maintain better housing facilities and to do more entertaining than in a rural section where a more simple mode of living is practiced. Generally speaking, the cost of rent and services is less in rural areas. A beginning salary in a nonurban community may be

FIGURE 10–1.    Average annual salaries of instructional staff in public schools for the period 1929–1930 to 1970–1971.

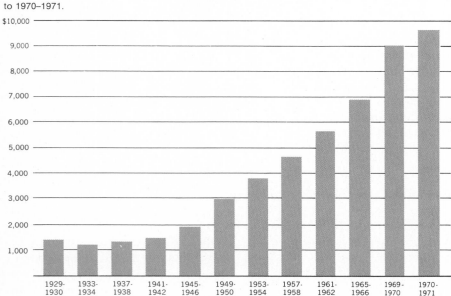

Per cent

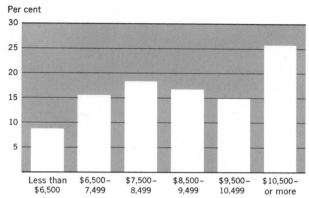

FIGURE 10–2. Percentage distribution of public-school teachers' salaries in 1970–71. What changes in this distribution may take place by 1980?

more favorable economically than an appreciably higher salary in a city, and a lower salary in one section of the United States may be equivalent to a higher salary in a similar community in another section.

## Salary Trends in Teaching and Other Occupations

The average income reported for any vocation may not give a true picture of the situation. For a number of reasons, this is particularly true of teaching. Only a relatively small percentage of teachers have made teaching a life career. As a result, a large number of the teachers are either beginners or those with limited amounts of experience. Obviously these salaries are low. Furthermore, some teachers, especially in the elementary schools, have less than four years of preparation, since they earned life certificates a number of years ago, when standards for certification were relatively low. These teachers are paid appreciably lower salaries. In other words, the heterogeneous background of teaching personnel makes it unwise to compare their average income with incomes in other occupations, such as law and medicine, where the professional background is more homogeneous. Also, the beginning teacher today is generally better trained than his predecessors and consequently has a greater earning capacity. It is difficult to indicate accurately, for a number of reasons, the salary trends in many occupations. Only scattered information is available. We do know that since World War II, there has been a considerable change in earnings, especially of unionized labor and professional workers who are not on regular salaries. Furthermore, wages in some occupations fluctuate rapidly according to the cost-of-living index, whereas other occupations remain relatively constant in earning power. There is however, much information upon salaries and salary trends for teachers. The average salary of public school teachers in

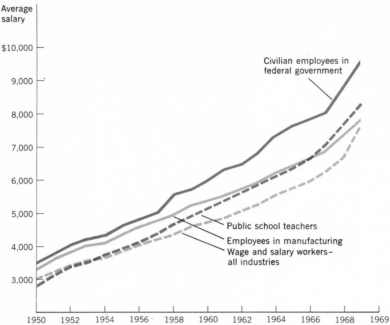

FIGURE 10-3.  Average annual salary of public school teachers compared with salaries for certain other occupational groups. Is it reasonable to assume that the trend since 1950 will continue?

1970–1971 was estimated to be $9,265 [77:49]. The average salary of elementary school teachers was $9,025 and of secondary school teachers was $9,540. The average beginning salary for teachers with a bachelor's degree in large school systems was $7,165, as compared to $2,603 in 1950–1951—an increase of 175.3 per cent [22:83].

Since the earnings of all persons working for wages and salaries establish the movement of wages in the economy as a whole, it is important to compare the gains of teachers with those of all employed persons. From 1950 to 1969 (calendar year), the average salary of teachers increased from $2,823 to $8,180 (189.8 per cent). During this same period of time the average earnings of all wage and salary workers increased from $3,008 to $7,655 (154.4 per cent) [77:49]; average earnings of employees in manufacturing increased from $3,300 to $7,768 (135.5 per cent); and average earnings of civilian employees of the federal government increased from $3,503 to $9,445 (169.6 per cent). Disregarding losses due to price changes, the earnings of all wage earners increased 48.3 per cent from 1950 to 1969, as compared to 63.5 per cent for teachers. This differential in increases represents a potentially higher standard of living for teachers.

A number of studies have been made comparing the salaries of teachers with those in other professions. The Research Division of the

National Education Association, for example, compared the mean starting salaries of teachers and other selected graduates with bachelor's degrees in 1970–1971. The results of the comparison are indicated in Figure 10–4. Specifically, it was found that male graduates in the other professions were employed at an average starting salary that was 36.7 per cent higher than the average beginning salary for teachers. The beginning salaries paid female graduates were lower than the average salaries paid to men graduates, but were higher in each of the selected areas than the average for beginning teachers [228:75–77].

FIGURE 10–4. Mean starting salaries of teachers and other graduates with bachelor's degrees, 1970–1971.

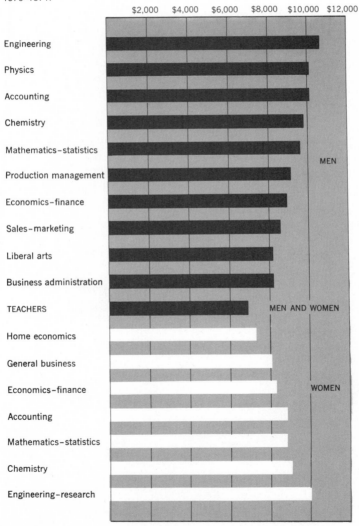

In the resolutions proposed in 1971, the National Education Association expressed the belief that salaries of educators should compare favorably with income in other professions and occupations requiring comparable preparation and responsibility.

A salary schedule should provide a starting salary of $12,500 for a qualified beginning teacher with a bachelor's degree. Advancement to $25,000 with a master's degree or state certification equivalency, and to $31,250 or more with two years' advanced preparation beyond the master's degree should be attainable in no more than 10 years [169:84].

## Trends in Teachers' Salaries in Various States

Figure 10–5 indicates the great range in average salaries paid in the various states. It should be remembered, however, that the average state salaries are subject to all the weaknesses indicated previously. The extreme range shown in this figure points up a very crucial problem in education. Differences in the cost of providing the basic necessities of life for teachers cannot account for the variation in average salaries. As will be explained more fully in Chapters 13 and 18, the differences result more from the lack of taxable resources for financing schools than from the willingness of the states to pay for education. The inequalities are so great that there seems to be little hope of rectifying them without some form of federal assistance. Generally speaking, the Northern and Western states, where there are greater financial resources, have higher average

FIGURE 10–5.   The range in the average annual salaries of instructional staff in the public schools in 1970–1971. The average salary for each state is more meaningful than an average salary for the United States.

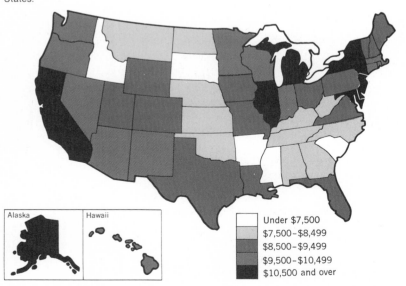

salaries than the Southern states, where the financial resources are more limited. There is a trend, however, toward narrowing the range in salaries, especially with respect to the schools in the Southeastern states.

Teachers, like individuals in other occupations, tend to gravitate toward areas in which high salaries are paid. Many of the able teachers leave the poorly paying states and find teaching positions elsewhere. Wealthier states can demand better professional training, and many large school systems have well-organized personnel divisions which select incoming teachers very carefully. Thus, the states having low teachers' salaries tend to be left with fewer well-qualified teachers.

## Trends in the Salaries of Various Types of School Employees

Throughout the history of education, elementary teachers have received less salary than have secondary school teachers. For example, in 1970–1971 the average annual salary for elementary teachers was estimated to be 94.6 per cent of the corresponding figure for secondary school teachers, which represented a narrowing of the gap of approximately 9 per cent in a 15-year period [77:49]. The narrowing difference between elementary and secondary school teacher salaries may be the result of several factors: (1) increased preparation of elementary school teachers, (2) a shortage of good elementary school teachers, especially during the 1950s and 1960s, (3) longer periods of service, and (4) improved status in the position of elementary school teachers.

As early as 1918, however, cities began to establish single-salary schedules. This kind of schedule specifies the same salary to teachers, regardless of sex, with equal training and experience when assigned to regular positions in elementary, junior high, and senior high schools. Progress at first in the adoption of single-salary schedules was slow, even though it had been urged by the National Education Association as early as 1920. As late as 1940–1941 only 31.3 per cent of the schedules were of the single-salary type, but today this type of schedule is almost universally used. It is interesting to note that the Soviet Union, in September, 1966, adopted a single-salary schedule for teachers in rural and urban elementary, middle, and higher grades [174:4].

If the practice of differentiated staffing and, to some extent, team teaching should be used more extensively in schools, adaptations would need to be made in the single-salary schedule concept. As indicated in Chapter 5, salary adjustments are made according to the levels of leadership exercised by teachers in a differentiated teaching situation. This type of situation has the advantage of providing an opportunity for a teacher to move to a decidedly higher salary level without having to assume a supervisory or administrative position.

A superintendent of schools typically is employed on a contract basis, with the number of years and the salary being specified in the contract. The range is quite great, since the amount usually is related to the size of the school district.

The older practice of determining the salaries of principals usually involved a dollar differential, a fixed sum of money above the amount the principal would receive if he were a classroom teacher. For example, an elementary school principal might receive $1,000 more than the teaching maximum for his level of preparation, plus $500 for each year of administrative experience up to four years. In recent years, there seems to be a definite trend toward relating the salary of principals to the salary of teachers by means of an index or ratio differential. In other words, the salary that a principal receives is stated as a ratio of salary he would receive if he were classified as a classroom teacher. For example, an elementary principal may receive 138 per cent of the maximum salary for a master's degree on the teachers' salary schedule. This method of computing the salaries of principals would seem to have definite merit. It is highly probable that it will be used increasingly in determining the salaries of other central administrative officers, such as supervisors, consultants, directors, and coordinators. The practice of using the same salary schedule for elementary and secondary school principals in a school system still is rare. This situation is understandable since elementary schools tend to be smaller and elementary school principals frequently are paid for fewer months of service than secondary school principals.

FIGURE 10–6.   Comparison of salaries paid public school professional employees using an index of 1.00 for salaries paid to teachers.

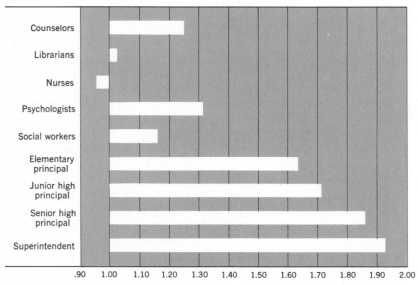

As early as 1904, regulations regarding the minimum salaries to be paid to teachers were enacted by several school systems. In 1970, public school teachers in thirty-one states were employed under minimum-salary laws [163:1–2]. These laws differ greatly in requirements as well as in the amount of salary. Some states only guarantee a flat-rate minimum. Other states specify only minimum salaries for beginning teachers, according to the amount of preparation, whereas still other states specify a minimum salary both for beginning teachers and for teachers who have had a specified number of years of teaching experience.

There are a number of advantages in having minimum-salary laws. For example, they protect children against boards of education which would be willing to employ poorly qualified teachers at low rates of pay. Some boards of education have been willing to sacrifice quality in order to keep the local school budget as low as possible. Minimum-salary laws also improve ethics in the employment of teachers. Heretofore, a process of salary bargaining was in practice, especially for teachers in over-crowded subject areas. Wherever a minimum salary is stated, both the employee and the employer are operating on a higher professional plane. A state's adoption of a minimum-salary law in no way threatens local control of the school, and a community is free to pay teachers above the minimum to whatever extent it is able and desires.

## Trend Toward Definite Salary Schedules

If teachers' salaries are to be placed on a professional basis it is necessary to establish a definite classification of them with respect to minimum salaries, yearly increments, and maximum salaries.

A definite salary schedule is desirable for a number of reasons. When a teacher is able to determine definitely the income that he will receive during and at the end of the next 10 or 20 years, he is able to do long-range financial planning. A teacher is relieved of trying to get as much money as possible, sometimes having to resort to unethical practices; an administrator is not tempted to pay a teacher as little as possible. The tensions between teachers are relieved, since the initial salaries and the yearly increases are known to all. The administrator cannot be accused of playing favorites by giving unwarranted raises. Administrators and school board members can calculate budget needs more easily when a definite salary schedule is at their disposal.

Superintendents of schools normally are happy to provide prospective teachers with salary schedules. Some state departments of education publish the salary data of the major school systems in the state. The placement officer in your college will probably have copies of such schedules for various school systems. Study them and try to discover the strengths and weaknesses of each.

A salary schedule usually contains from two to four columns, representing various levels of preparation, such as the bachelor's, master's, sixth-year, and doctor's degree; and from 11 to 15 steps representing annual increments for each year of experience. The size and the number of increments that are provided are important factors to consider. For teachers having a bachelor's degree, the typical number of increments is 12, with relatively few schedules providing fewer than 9 or more than 16. The number of increments usually is greater for teachers who have more than the bachelor's degree. The basic weakness in the use of salary increments is that the increment is not primarily a reward for increased efficiency or competence on the part of the teacher. No provision is made for merit raises because of outstanding work. If the increments do not extend over a long period of time, a teacher reaches a maximum salary early in his career and faces the prospect of 20 or more years of service with little chance of a raise unless he is able to obtain another type of position as a teacher, or becomes a supervisor or an administrator. On the other hand, if the teacher is delayed too long in reaching a maximum salary, he may experience great hardships in the early part of his career as his dependency responsibilities expand. A few schools have followed the practice of granting large increases during the first few years of a teacher's service and smaller increments in the remaining period until the maximum is reached.

An increasing number of school districts have been using an index or ratio to determine the salaries of teachers. This kind of schedule typically

FIGURE 10–7.  Hypothetical index salary schedule.

**Base: $ _ _ _ _ _ _ ←——————— Base amount to be reviewed annually**

| | Salary step | Bachelor's degree | Master's degree | Sixth year M.A. 30 | Doctor's degree | |
|---|---|---|---|---|---|---|
| Uniform increments; 6 per cent of the bachelor's degree minimum | 1 | 1.00 | 1.10 | 1.20 | 1.35 | 10 per cent above base for each additional year of professional preparation; 15 per cent for doctor's degree |
| | 2 | 1.06 | 1.16 | 1.26 | 1.41 | |
| | 3 | 1.12 | 1.22 | 1.32 | 1.47 | |
| | 4 | 1.18 | 1.28 | 1.38 | 1.53 | |
| | 5 | 1.24 | 1.34 | 1.44 | 1.59 | |
| | 6 | 1.30 | 1.40 | 1.50 | 1.65 | |
| | 7 | 1.36 | 1.46 | 1.56 | 1.71 | |
| 12 increments for bachelor's degree class and 13 for master's degree class; typical of present practice | 8 | 1.42 | 1.52 | 1.62 | 1.77 | |
| | 9 | 1.48 | 1.58 | 1.68 | 1.83 | |
| | 10 | 1.54 | 1.64 | 1.74 | 1.89 | |
| | 11 | 1.60 | 1.70 | 1.80 | 1.96 | |
| | 12 | 1.66 | 1.76 | 1.86 | 2.02 | Twice the bachelor's degree minimum |
| | 13 | 1.72 | 1.82 | 1.92 | 2.08 | |
| | 14 | | 1.88 | 1.98 | 2.14 | |
| | 15 | | | | 2.20 | |

uses the bachelor's degree with no experience as its base of 100 or 1.00. Increments for years of experience and for additional preparation beyond the bachelor's degree are calculated as percentages of the base. For example, the annual increment may be 6 per cent of the base, and an inexperienced teacher with a master's degree may receive a salary 10 per cent above the base. The index schedule has the advantage of establishing salary-step relationships that remain constant even though the dollar amounts change. If the base salary is raised, the increments increase, and the relative distance between the minimum and maximum salaries is not reduced.

## Professional Growth Requirements

In order to advance vertically on the salary schedule, approximately one fourth of the school systems [201:1] require their teachers to show evidence, after a specified number of years, that they have engaged in one or more kinds of professional growth activities. In order to meet this requirement, many teachers take additional college courses. Others meet the requirement through travel, outside work experience, committee work, curriculum development, publications, and research. In view of the urgency for continued professional growth, it is highly likely that an increasing number of school systems will relate evidence of professional growth to salary schedule advancement.

## Merit Rating and Salary Schedules

One of the very thorny problems with which teachers and school administrators are confronted involves rewards and penalties for quality of service. A salary schedule based entirely upon the amount of training and years of experience does not reward the teacher who is doing superior work or penalize the teacher who is doing an inferior job. Much of the pressure to alter this situation comes from those outside the teaching profession.

Some of the arguments in favor of merit rating are as follows [14:2-5]:

1. It has been used successfully by business and industry.
2. It will attract and keep highly competent teachers.
3. The public will be willing to pay higher salaries for outstanding teachers.
4. It will lead to a general increase in the professional and social status of teachers in the community.
5. Teachers will have added incentive to improve their competence.
6. It will provide recognition for excellence of performance in the most meaningful way—financially.
7. A combination of rating devices, rankings, and records can be used successfully in evaluating the competence of teachers.

8. The present system of relating salaries solely to training and experience rewards unequal work equally.

## Those opposed to merit rating maintain that [14:2–5]:

1. Teachers do not start with the same quality or amount of raw material as do those in an industry or business, not do they produce a product that lends itself to easy and precise measurement. Teachers produce people, not things. No individual teacher is the sole cause of pupil success. Merit rating in the business world has shown distinct limitations, especially in rating management and executive personnel.
2. Higher salaries are not assured for superior teachers. Therefore, merit rating will not increase the supply of teachers.
3. By giving higher salaries to a few, the salary level of most teachers will be kept at a low level.
4. The only way in which status equivalent to that of other professional groups in the community can be assured is by raising the salaries of all teachers rather than by stressing the merit of a few.
5. Merit rating will foster conformity to the administrator's ideals, precepts, and concepts and destroy teacher creativity, originality, and initiative.
6. Good human relations between teachers and administrators, supervisors, and consultants will be destroyed.
7. The intangibles in teacher performance resist accurate measurement. Furthermore, the great range of specialization in the modern school system militates against objectivity of evaluating teacher performance.
8. School systems already dismiss incompetent teachers by not placing them on tenure.
9. Relationships between the public and the school will deteriorate, since parents will exert much pressure for their children to be placed in classes of teachers with higher ranks.

Both the National Education Association and the American Federation of Teachers have strongly opposed merit rating. The Association of Classroom Teachers of the National Education Association, for example, passed a resolution in 1969 vigorously opposing merit rating for determining salaries. "It maintains that experience shows that the evaluation of individuals for merit rating destroys professional relationships and morale; creates strife and discord; impedes the cooperative improvement of education by classroom teachers, supervisors and administrators; and leads to deterioration in the quality of education of children" [195:5].

The National Education Association conducted a nationwide teachers' poll to determine how individual teachers view the issue of merit pay. The results indicated that 40.3 per cent strongly oppose, 32.5 per cent tend to oppose, 20.3 per cent tend to favor, and 6.9 per cent strongly favor merit pay. Secondary school teachers are more inclined to favor such a plan than are elementary teachers [291:31].

Since a number of the school systems have tried merit systems and have abandoned them, the National Education Association wrote to ninety-one of these school systems asking why it had been abandoned. The reasons listed included the following: the evaluation of teacher performance was unsatisfactory; dissension was created among the teachers; ratings were really not based on merit; a sense of injustice was created; the plan was opposed by the teachers organizations; it placed a heavy burden on the raters; it damaged the service of the principal [296:17].

It is estimated that approximately 7 per cent of the school systems make some provision for additional compensation for superior teachers [156:1]. The most frequently used plan provides for merit supplements to be granted either shortly before or after the regularly scheduled maximum has been reached. In some school systems provision is made for accelerating the progress of outstanding teachers on the regular schedule by granting double increments. Higher salaries paid to master teachers in differentiated staffing situations, in a sense, constitute another method of recognizing merit.

The controversy over merit rating and merit pay will continue in the future. It would seem that any attempt along such lines should involve the following criteria developed by Edmund Thorne, superintendent of schools in West Hartford, Connecticut, where a merit-pay plan was initiated in 1953 (adapted):

1. The prime principle underlying the plan should be the improvement of instruction—to help teachers succeed and improve in their work.
2. Merit awards should be based upon predetermined criteria and not on percentage quotas.
3. A good professional salary schedule should already exist in the school system.
4. A merit-salary program should not be adopted until after it has had sufficient study and been accepted by a substantial majority of the staff.
5. The plan should be adapted to local conditions.
6. The plan should have the complete understanding and support of the administrative personnel, the board, and the public.
7. All personnel in the school system, including administrators, should be rated.
8. There should be well-defined standards of evaluation agreed to and understood by those who are to be evaluated.
9. There should be ample opportunity for evaluation.
10. Only those teachers who request it should be evaluated for merit-pay purposes, and conversely, teachers should be allowed to withdraw from the procedure if they so desire.
11. Merit awards should be commensurate with the value placed upon superior service.
12. Teachers must have confidence in those who are responsible for evaluating them.
13. Sufficient personnel should be provided to ensure adequate time for evaluation.
14. Final selection of merit teachers should be entrusted to more than one individual.
15. Individuals should be given the right to appeal.
16. An adequate budget should be established to provide continuity of program from one year to the next.
17. The plan should be continuously reevaluated in the light of new experience.
18. Provision should be made for informing new and potential staff members regarding the plan.

## Trends in the Salaries of Men and Women Teachers

Statistics on average salaries indicate that men teachers receive higher salaries than do women teachers. It should be pointed out, however, that the discrimination against women teachers may not be as great as it may seem. Approximately 6 per cent of the women in the elementary schools still have less than a college degree. The great majority of men, however, teach on the high school level, where a degree is required. Furthermore, a high percentage of the administrative positions are filled by men. The fact that men have more training, for which a higher salary is paid, and that they fill a majority of the administrative positions may give the impression of higher discrimination against women than actually exists in the teaching profession. Studies show that there is less inequality between men and women in teaching than in other professions [81:53].

The battle for equal pay for those with the same training and experience, especially on the college level, is not over. Basically, almost all would agree that the theory is sound, based on the assumption that teachers with the same amount of training and experience are making the same contributions to society. Furthermore, the idea is in harmony with democratic concepts. Any policy that fosters discrimination among a group of individuals who are equals is undemocratic. Teachers, above all, need to demonstrate concepts of democracy.

The advocates of a dual-salary schedule in regard to sex, however, feel that there should be more men teachers, especially in the elementary school, than there are at present. Since the opportunities for men in industry are greater than those for women, schools should pay higher salaries to men in order to attract them to teaching. Advocates of the dual schedule also feel that equal pay provokes undue hardships on men teachers, who generally have more dependents than women. A few school systems have solved the problem of dependents partially by adopting a policy similar to one used in computing income tax; that is, all teachers are given allowances for the number of dependents [74:52–54].

## Period of Time Teachers Receive Pay

The predominant practice in paying teachers is to distribute their salaries monthly over the period in which school is in session. A small percentage of school systems have adopted the policy of paying teachers semi-monthly.

There seems to be a trend, however, for schools to distribute the pay of teachers over a 12-month period for services rendered while school is in session. This helps teachers to budget their salaries throughout the year. Otherwise they often find it necessary to borrow money during the summer vacation.

An increasing number of school systems are adopting a policy of expanding the period in which teachers are employed during the year. Some states—Florida, for example—employ teachers for an extra month of work. This enables the school staff to plan before schools open in the fall and after they close in the spring, providing a much-needed time for teachers to work together to improve their teaching.

Some school systems hire teachers on a year-round basis and adjust the work accordingly. The school usually is organized so that teachers work in the classroom for the traditional nine to ten months. During the summer they may prepare teaching materials, revise curricula, attend workshops to improve teaching techniques, work in recreational programs, or study and then have one month's vacation with pay. Advocates of the year-round employment plan maintain that [73:7]:

Teaching has changed from a part-time to a full-time profession.

Orientation programs give new teachers the opportunity to do a more effective job.

Time for workshops and committee meetings is available, which gives opportunities for greater teacher growth in service.

Teachers are doing during the summer those things for which they are trained. Thus the school system is making better use of both its personnel and physical facilities.

Teachers can do things, such as prepare teaching materials and revise curriculum, that time limits or even prohibits during the regular year.

The total staff—teachers, counselors, and administrators—have the opportunity to develop a better perspective of the total school program because of the opportunities they have to work toward the mutual solution of problems.

Most superintendents and a large percentage of principals are employed on a year-round basis, which accounts in part for their salaries being higher than those of classroom teachers.

As indicated in Chapter 1, increasingly greater demands will be made of school personnel in the future, especially for adult education and recreational services. Undoubtedly these demands will tend to extend the year-round contract idea. In the meantime, the employment of teachers by the school system during the summer probably will take more nearly the form of a greatly expanded summer school.

## Extra Earnings of Teachers

"Extra pay," "additive salaries," "off-schedule salaries," or "compensation for irregularities" are terms used to identify provisions for paying teachers for assignments beyond the regular school day or term. The most common activities that fall within the range of the definition are coaching athletics, directing bands, directing choirs, directing dramatics, and sponsoring school publications.

A study conducted by the Research Division of the National Education Association revealed that a scale of flat rates usually was provided in salary schedules as extra pay for specific coaching duties or other supervisory assignments outside of school hours. The amount varied somewhat according to the size of the school. The highest pay was reported for head football coaches, whose extra compensation ranged

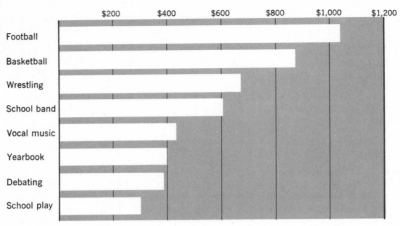

FIGURE 10–8. Median maximum annual supplemental pay for directing selected co-curricular activities, 1969–1970.

from $248 to $5,000 [229:5]. Head basketball coaches were the next highest paid, followed by track, cross country, baseball, golf, tennis, and wrestling. Extra compensation for supervisory assignments involving band, dramatics, newspaper, yearbook, and vocal music ranged from $25 to $2,000.

A number of educators feel that the total educational program is undermined by extra-pay policies which encourage teachers to assume duties requiring time that should be devoted to teaching responsibilities. Some feel that it is a type of exploitation, since it would cost far more to employ enough teachers to do the extra work. There is no question that limited budgets and teacher shortages are forcing many school districts to depend upon extra-pay practices in order to provide for these extra duties.

Other types of extra-pay activities involve a wide range of jobs in which teachers engage outside the school hours. During the school year these jobs usually relate in some way to the specialized field of the teacher, such as giving private music lessons, teaching adult education classes, driving a school bus, giving public lectures, sewing, and serving as a consultant to a business. A number of school districts impose limitations on the employment of teachers outside school. The most common requirements are that outside employment must not interfere with teaching duties and that approval of the board, superintendent, or other administrative officer must be secured.

During the summer months teachers engage in a wide variety of jobs. Some of these jobs are in keeping with the professional preparation of teachers (such as teaching in summer school, serving as camp counselors, and supervising summer recreational activities) and many are not. Many teachers feel that they can enhance their classroom teaching by "rubbing shoulders" with the outside world, thus not only keeping abreast of

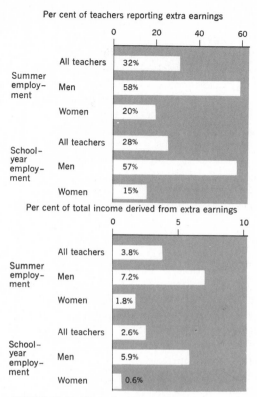

Per cent of teachers reporting extra earnings

Per cent of total income derived from extra earnings

FIGURE 10–9.   The extent to which teachers supplement their teaching salary.

technical advances, but also helping form closer ties between the schools and the community.

As more schools offer summer school programs, more teachers will have opportunities to increase their annual earnings. It is probable that more than 50 per cent of all pupils will be attending summer sessions as we approach 1980.

## Trends in Salaries for College Teachers

It is more difficult to present precise salary schedules for college teachers than for public school teachers because of the fluctuation of college salaries based on the supply and demand for instructional personnel. Approximately one-half of the colleges and universities have clearly defined salary schedules with designated increments. It is apparent, however, that improvements in college salary practices have lagged behind those in the public schools.

The most common type of college salary schedule utilizes minimum and maximum salaries according to rank, i.e., instructor, assistant professor, associate professor, and full professor. The limits as well as the average salaries within each of these ranks vary considerably among institutions as well as among departments within institutions. For example, the average salary received by a full professor in a small private college may be more than the salary received by a teacher of comparable rank in a large university, or vice versa. Also, the full professor in the English department of a large university may be receiving a lower salary than a full professor in the law college. The teachers in the college, school, or department of education in larger institutions generally receive slightly higher salaries than other college personnel in all ranks because of the amount of public school experience required and competing salaries in public school work.

Table 10-1 indicates the 1969–1970 median salaries according to rank for nine months of full-time teaching in all colleges and universities having at least four-year programs. It also indicates the percentage of increase for a period of two years.

The salary range for each of the ranks was wide. For example, one-fourth of those holding the rank of professor had a salary of $19,442 or greater, and one-fourth earned salaries of $14,656 or less [227:9]. The highest median salaries for professors were paid in the larger nonpublic universities, followed by the larger state universities, the smaller nonpublic universities, public universities having enrollments of 5,000 to 9,999, state colleges, and the larger nonpublic colleges. In terms of geographic regions, the median salaries for all full-time college teachers were highest in the Far West, followed by Mideast, New England, Great Lakes, Southwest, Plains, Rocky Mountains, and Southeast in the order named.

The median salary for nine months of full-time teaching in public

Table 10–1  **MEDIAN SALARIES FOR NINE MONTHS OF FULL-TIME TEACHING IN ALL COLLEGES AND UNIVERSITIES, 1967–1968 AND 1969–1970**

| Rank | Median Salaries | | Increase, Per Cent |
|------|-----------|-----------|-----------|
|  | 1967–1968 | 1969–1970 |  |
| Professor | $14,713 | $16,799 | 14.2 |
| Associate professor | 11,393 | 12,985 | 14.0 |
| Assistant professor | 9,472 | 10,698 | 12.9 |
| Instructor | 7,496 | 8,416 | 12.2 |

*Source:* Adapted from *Salaries in Higher Education,* 1969–1970 Research Report 1970-R6, National Education Association, Research Division, Washington, 1970, p. 11.

junior colleges in 1969–1970 was $10,626 [227:65], which was higher than the median salary in nonpublic junior colleges ($8,190).

In addition to the actual salaries paid, almost all institutions provide various types of fringe benefits such as health, accident, and life insurance and contributions to retirement funds. Although the range is considerable, these benefits may be equivalent to approximately 11 per cent of the actual salaries paid.

Practically all multipurpose institutions, state colleges, and teachers colleges have summer instruction programs in which approximately one-half of the regular full-time teachers have an opportunity to supplement their salaries by teaching courses [227:39]. Some college teachers are able to earn an appreciable amount of money by writing for publication or by serving as consultants in school systems, in businesses, or in industries.

## Standards for Professional Salaries

The National Education Association has fought vigorously for many years for higher salaries for teachers. As a policy statement, the Association believes that [169:73–74]:

The salary policy of any school system should be based on clearly defined factors which are applicable to salaries for all professional services including summer school, after-school activities, federally supported programs, and research and writing assignments. Teachers shall not be required to perform extra duties within the school day. No professional group should be overlooked in the establishment of such policies.

The Association believes that salary scales for principals, other building supervisors, and central-office administrators should be related to the salary schedule for teachers by ratios which reflect differences in assigned responsibilities and length of contract year. Said ratios should be developed and applied in such manner as to grant equal salary differentials for equal amount of advanced preparation.

The Association believes that a professional salary schedule for teachers should—

a. Be based upon preparation, teaching experience, and professional growth.
b. Have structural continuity through the use of an index or percentage guide.
c. Be revised by methods that prevent deterioration in the ratios of maximum salaries, experience increments, and preparational differentials.
d. Provide scheduled minimum salaries which are competitive with beginning salaries paid to college graduates entering business and industry.
e. Provide a differential of 15 per cent or more between the scheduled minimum salaries for the bachelor's degree and master's degree scales.
f. Have automatic annual increments for experience which are in no case less than 7 per cent of the bachelor's degree minimum.
g. Provide for doubling the bachelor's degree minimum in the master's degree class and for advancing at least to a ratio of 2.5 times the bachelor's degree minimum with advanced preparation beyond the master's degree class.
h. Establish salary credit for intermediate preparation levels between full-year classes to encourage academic advancement beyond the bachelor's degree.
i. Permit no discrimination as to grade or subject taught, residence, creed, race, sex, marital status, or number of dependents.

j.  Place newly appointed teachers on step according to their teaching experience, allowing full credit for all previous service outside the district.
k.  Be applied in actual practice in an equitable manner so that teachers are not penalized in changing assignments.
l.  Be developed through the process of professional negotiation.

It is encouraging to note the amount of progress that is being made in school systems throughout the nation in their efforts to prepare salary schedules based on the principles recommended by the National Education Association. As continued changes are made toward the achievement of these minimum- and maximum-salary recommendations, teachers certainly will gain greater professional status.

## Teachers' Responsibilities for Improving Salaries

Low teachers' salaries in the past have been excused somewhat upon the grounds that teachers love their work and therefore are willing to receive low salaries. This thesis is no longer acceptable, and teachers have a responsibility for correcting this outmoded philosophy.

A nationwide Gallup poll of the public's attitude toward teachers' salaries revealed that 43 per cent felt that the salaries were "just about right," 2 per cent maintained they were "too high," 33 per cent indicated they were "too low," and 22 per cent did not express any opinion [91:53]. It would appear from this survey that much work will need to be done in order to raise the salaries of teachers to the levels recommended previously in this chapter.

It is thoroughly respectable for a professional group to work ethically toward the improvement of salaries. The public must realize that, as is true of virtually everything in life, there is a direct relationship between quality and price. Quality education is expensive. On the other hand, in this day and age, poor education is even more expensive in terms of the welfare of our society. This the public must understand, and teachers have an obligation to help the public gain this understanding.

Through their professional associations teachers are assuming increasingly significant roles in the determination of salary schedules. As this trend continues, teachers assume greater responsibilities for participating intelligently in this process. As a result [255:153–154], teachers will need to possess a basic understanding of economics and be well informed on general economic problems and conditions. They also will need to be well informed about school finance and financing. In other words, they will need to know what they are talking about when they discuss the need for salary increases if they wish to be heard, respected, and effective in their efforts. Furthermore they will need to be able to work cooperatively in the decision-making process—being able to reconcile their differences, and abiding by the decisions made by the group.

Teachers have a responsibility to work ethically toward the improvement of their salaries. *(Photograph from the National Education Association.)*

## SUMMARY

Any average salary listed must be interpreted carefully in the light of all factors that enter into the establishment of an average. Teaching should be viewed in terms of existing and probable future salary schedules for beginning teachers.

Although some very definite improvements have been made during the past several years, the average salaries of teachers are low compared with those of other professions requiring comparable training.

There is positive evidence that the general public is concerned about the economic welfare of teachers. Because of the organized efforts of educators and others, the prospects of continued improvement of teachers' salaries look promising.

Some positive trends are to be noted in the scheduling of teachers' salaries: the establishment of minimum salaries for beginning teachers, definite yearly salary increments, the same pay for men and women who have equal training and experience, and a single-salary schedule for elementary and secondary teachers. Unfortunately, the practice of having salary schedules on the college level has lagged behind that of the public schools.

Improvements in the scheduling of salaries should encourage competent teachers to remain in the profession for a longer period of time, attract more people with promise into the profession, and enable educators to be more selective of those who are prepared, certified, and employed as teachers. As these factors operate, the level of the teaching profession will be raised; this, in turn, will tend to raise salaries.

## QUESTIONS TO CONSIDER

1. What factors should be kept in mind as you interpret average salaries of teachers?
2. Can you think of any teachers who are being overpaid? If so, upon what grounds do you base your judgment? What should the school board do about these situations?
3. How do you account for the fact that public school teachers are not as well paid as members of other professions? What should be done in order to obtain salaries comparable to those received in the other professions?
4. What are the advantages and disadvantages of a salary schedule that is based entirely upon the amount of training and experience of teachers?
5. In your opinion, how should superior teachers be rewarded?
6. In contrast to the single-salary concept, what advantages and disadvantages do you see in the emerging policies for the payment of teachers in differentiated staffing situations?
7. Should teachers in inner-city schools be paid higher salaries than those paid in suburban schools? Why?
8. To what extent do you feel that teachers should be given salary allowances for the number of dependents they have?
9. Are you in favor of the trend for schools to distribute the pay of teachers over a 12-month period for services rendered during a 9- or 10-month school year? Why?
10. What advantages and disadvantages do you see in the year-round employment plan for teachers? Should schools be operated on a 12-month plan?
11. For what extra duties should a teacher be paid? What should be the basis for the amount of pay? Discuss these questions with your colleagues.
12. Some teachers work on jobs during after-school hours and on weekends. Do you favor such practices? Upon what grounds might a school board specify that teachers are not to engage in such practices?
13. How can you account for the wide range in the salaries of college teachers? To what extent and by what means should these salaries be made more equitable? What effect might the women's liberation movement have upon the salaries of women college teachers?
14. How might you work positively toward the improvement of salaries for teachers?

## PROBLEM SITUATION FOR INQUIRY

As a physics teacher in a public high school, Jack Sullivan was not earning enough money to support his wife and three children at a middle-class standard of living. As a result, Jack began working evenings and weekends in the laboratory of a local chemical industry. However, as the year progressed, Jack spent increasingly more time on his part-time job and less time in preparation for his teaching. One student complained to the principal that "Mr. Sullivan simply refused" to give her help on an assignment after school.

Jack has taken much more sick leave this year than he has in the past. Although he may have been working at the laboratory on some of the days he was absent from school, his physical appearance suggests that he might well have been ill.

Jack Sullivan's effectiveness as a teacher has declined since he began moonlighting. He also has failed to fulfill some of the responsibilities of a good teacher—such as helping students with special problems and grading and returning daily assignments. However, Jack's family has been more financially secure than they have at any time during the previous five years.

If you were the principal in Jack's school, what would you do? Why?

## ACTIVITIES TO PURSUE

1.  Consult your hometown superintendent of schools regarding the bases upon which his teachers are paid. Discuss with him the problems of salary schedules.
2.  Secure information on the salary schedules for all school systems in which you might like to have a position. Compare them in terms of minimums, maximums, number and size of increments, credit for previous teaching experience, credit for advanced professional work, provisions for recognition of outstanding work, and the like.
3.  Compare the salary schedules of school systems in various types of communities, sections of the United States, and foreign countries.
4.  Make a careful study of different kinds of occupations to discover the extent to which the salaries or wages of men differ from those of women who possess equal training and experience.
5.  Discuss teachers' salaries with community members in various types of work to determine how they feel about the subject.
6.  Discuss with lawyers, doctors, dentists, engineers, and other professional workers the satisfactions they receive from their work and earnings. Have them compare and contrast the work and the earnings of teachers with their professions. Consult the latest issues of *Economic Status of Teachers,* National Education Association, Research Division, to determine how teachers' salaries compare with salaries in other occupations. Report your findings to your colleagues.
7.  Read some articles in current professional magazines regarding the advantages and disadvantages of merit raises. Report your findings to your colleagues.
8.  Set up a teachers' salary schedule for a school system based upon the NEA salary recommendations.
9.  Organize a panel to discuss the controversial issue of federal aid for teachers' salaries.
10. Write to the United Negro College Fund, New York City, and secure data on salaries paid black professors in black colleges. Compare these salaries with salaries in higher education cited in this chapter.

# 11 | OTHER ECONOMIC BENEFITS

Practically everyone is interested in becoming economically secure. This means more than earning a good salary. It means being reasonably certain of steady employment; of not losing a job unjustifiably. It means being able to turn to various financial sources in time of adversity—illness, medical operations, disability, or other personal calamities. It means being able to assume heavier financial obligations with marriage, dependents, and home responsibilities. It also means being able to retire in comfort and dignity, even though that time may seem irrelevant at this time. All these factors are to be taken into consideration in planning a career in education.

## TEACHER TENURE

The term "teacher tenure" refers to the prospects that a competent teacher has of remaining in a position without being dismissed for unjustifiable reasons. It refers to the amount of protection a teacher has against losing his job.

### Reasons for Teacher Tenure

For a number of years the general public has recognized that civil employees need protection against prejudice and pressure groups if they are to do their jobs effectively. In government work this protection is provided through civil service appointments. The public now realizes more thoroughly the importance of the job of the teacher in our society and his need for position security because of the peculiar nature of teaching. The teacher has the task of transmitting and professionally refining the culture and of promoting understanding of the problems and purposes of modern group living. In order to accomplish this task the teacher must be protected from vacillating public opinion and unjustified dismissal; otherwise children suffer in the long run, and the schools are no longer instruments of *all* the people.

Professional organizations have been successful in securing considerable legislation for the protection of teachers. On the assumption that a better teacher means a better school and that the betterment of teaching depends in part on the improvement of teaching conditions, the Committee on Tenure and Academic Freedom of the NEA has set forth the following reasons for tenure [11:6–7]:

1. To protect classroom teachers and other members of the teaching profession against unjust dismissal of any kind—political, religious or personal.
2. To prevent the management or domination of the schools by political or non-educational groups for selfish and other improper purposes.
3. To secure for the teacher employment conditions which will encourage him to grow in the full practice of his profession, unharried by constant pressure and fear.
4. To encourage competent, independent thinkers to enter and to remain in the teaching profession.
5. To encourage school management, which might have to sacrifice the welfare of the schools to fear and favor, to devote itself to the cause of education.
6. To set up honest, orderly, and definite procedures by which undesirable people may be removed from the teaching profession.
7. To protect educators in their efforts to promote the financial and educational interests of public school children.
8. To protect teachers in the exercise of their rights and duties of American citizenship.
9. To enable teachers, in spite of reactionary minorities, to prepare children for life in a democracy under changing conditions.

## Kinds of Tenure Provided for Teachers

An analysis of contracts and tenure laws reveals many differences in the degree of security provided for teachers. These differences are understandable when it is realized that in the beginning each school system was largely responsible for developing its own policies. Through the work of professional organizations and state legislation, however, policies have become more standardized.

Generally speaking, tenure provisions for teachers may be classified into the following types: annual contracts, contracts that extend for a definite number of years, continuing contracts with spring notification, protective continuing contracts, and permanent tenure. The general provisions of the various types of contracts and laws indicated above should be understood, since they may have a significant influence upon where you accept a teaching position.

**Annual contracts** A beginning teacher usually is given a contract which gives him a legal right to teach in a school system for one year only. A school year generally is considered to be that period of time between the opening of school in the fall and the closing date in the spring or summer. The teacher cannot be dismissed by the board of education during this period without justifiable cause. In some states, the bases for dismissal are written into the contracts given to the teacher, and in some they are found in the state statutes governing schools. The term "justifiable cause" generally involves incompetence, inefficiency, immorality, insubordination, neglect of duty, unprofessional conduct, and physical or mental disability. Some laws specifically include intoxication, dishonesty, and commission of a felony. A few states require that the causes for dismissal be indicated in writing. The teacher may have a right to contest a dismissal, either in court or through the professional organizations.

In return for the protection that the annual contract provides, the teacher has an obligation to the employing officials. As Stinnett points out, "The truly ethical person takes great pride in strict observance of a written agreement or oral pledge" [259:328]. Furthermore, it is often difficult to find a competent teacher to replace one who decides to discontinue teaching. In order to protect the welfare of the children in the school, the teacher who wishes to terminate his services usually is required to give 30 days' notice of his intention to resign, whether that resignation is before the beginning of school or during the school year, and to secure the consent of the board of education. It is true that there is nothing to prevent a teacher from just quitting his position. If he does this, however, his certificate for teaching probably would be revoked by the state board of education, in which case he would be unable to secure another position in that state.

**Contracts for a definite number of years**   In the states of Georgia, Mississippi, South Carolina, Vermont, and Utah it is permissible by law to issue contracts for more than one year upon the initial assignment of a teacher. These contracts definitely specify the maximum term of employment. They usually extend for only a reasonable period of time beyond the term of office of the employing officials. They may be renewed for another definite number of years.

**Continuing contracts with spring notification**   A teacher employed on an annual contract might not know whether he is to be reappointed until it is too late in the year to find a position elsewhere. In order to improve this situation, a number of states have what is called the "spring notification type of continuing-contract law." This type of contract provides for a teacher to be automatically reemployed for the next year unless notified of dismissal before a specified date. The date, such as April 15, is early enough for the teacher to find a position elsewhere, if necessary. Usually there is no obligation on the part of the school board to renew any contract. In reality, the typical continuing-contract law offers only a limited amount of protection to teachers.

**Protective continuing contracts**  Some of the states have a protective type of continuing contract. With this type of contract a teacher is employed from year to year without being dismissed except by a prescribed procedure to be followed by the board of education in regard to the notice, the statement of charges, and the right to a hearing. This type of contract gives teachers virtually as much protection as a true tenure law. A probationary period of three years normally is required before a teacher is granted this type of contract. During this probationary period, the teacher's annual contract is not renewed if he does not measure up to the standards held by the school system. This probationary period protects the school from becoming overloaded with incompetent teachers.

Many school officials follow the practice of warning the teacher who has a protective-type continuing contract that his contract will not be continued unless certain conditions are improved. This practice seems to be in harmony with good school administration. The teacher is given the added assurance that he will not lose his position without having a chance to improve any unsatisfactory aspects of his work.

In order to dismiss a teacher who is employed on a protective-type continuing contract, the board of education must notify the teacher at an early date of its intentions and must state the reasons for dismissal. The teacher is provided an opportunity for defending himself if he so desires.

**Permanent tenure**  The greatest amount of tenure that a teacher may be able to gain will be in a situation that provides for what is commonly called "permanent tenure." After serving a probationary period ranging from one to five years, the continuous employment of a teacher is assured, provided he renders efficient service and shows appropriate conduct.

The procedure for dismissing a teacher on permanent tenure is very similar to that required by the protective-type continuing contract. The employing officials must establish good cause for dismissal with higher authorities. Usually the bases upon which teachers can be dismissed are written into the tenure laws. A teacher has the right to request a formal review or trial of the case before a special committee or court, provided he feels that inadequate reasons for his dismissal can be shown. Permanent tenure differs primarily from tenure under continuing contracts in that under the former arrangement the case normally is not tried before the employing officials. Many teachers feel that the teacher who is to be dismissed is at an unfair advantage if he has to appeal his case to employing officials who serve as both accusers and judges.

## Status of Teacher Tenure

Figure 11-1 presents a fairly accurate picture of the status of state tenure or contract provisions in the various states. Thirty-seven states, and the

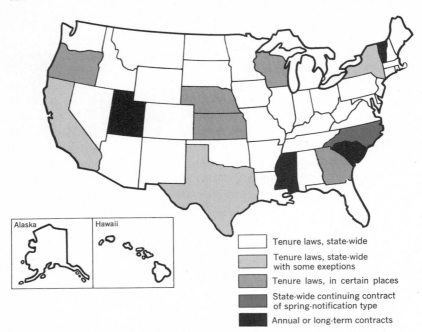

FIGURE 11–1.   Types of state tenure or contract provisions in effect in various states.

District of Columbia, have state-wide tenure laws without any exceptions [276:7]. An additional eight states have tenure laws with exceptions. For example, tenure is optional in California districts with average daily attendance under 250 pupils. Certain rural districts in New York are not covered by a tenure law. All school districts in Texas have the option of coming under the tenure provisions. Only certain places are covered by state tenure provisions in Georgia, Kansas, Nebraska, Oregon, and Wisconsin. Annual or long-term contracts, or continuing-contracts of the spring notification type are provided for the other school districts within these states. North Carolina has a state-wide law providing for continuing contracts of the spring notification type. Laws in Mississippi, South Carolina, Utah, and Vermont provide for annual or long-term contracts [276:7].

In general, the tenure laws include supervisors, principals, teachers, and other school personnel. The types of employees covered are specifically mentioned in many tenure laws. A few laws extend tenure status to classroom teachers alone or only to teachers and principals.

A number of states grant school superintendents contracts that extend for three, four, or five years. The recognized head of a school system is especially vulnerable to the shifting attitudes and reactions of community members; hence, it is felt that he should be granted more protection than is afforded in a one-year contract. This type of information also may be gained by writing to the department of education of the particular state in which a teacher may be interested.

## Characteristics of Good Tenure Laws

The provisions in state tenure laws differ considerably. The following characteristics of a good tenure law may be used to appraise the provisions made in any state [Adapted 275:9–11]:

1. A teacher should be employed on a probationary basis for a definite number of years—possibly a three-year period. The law should specify whether this employment is to be on an annual- or a spring-notification type of continuing contract and should indicate the conditions and procedures regarding dismissal that are contained in the contract.
2. After the teacher has successfully completed the probationary period the law should specify that the superintendent is required to recommend the teacher for tenure status.
3. The law should establish definite, orderly, legal procedures for dismissing unsatisfactory teachers by requiring that there be:
   a. Adequate notice given to the teacher.
   b. Charges stated in writing and including a record of criticism and aid offered.
   c. A hearing before the entire board, either private or public as the teacher may request.
   d. Benefit of counsel and witnesses.
   e. Safeguard of salary rights during suspension.
   f. Final appeal to higher educational authorities or to the courts.
4. In cases of demotion or suspension, the law should make virtually the same provisions as for a dismissal case.
5. The tenure law should apply to all teachers, whether in rural, village, or city schools and without regard for race or color. Any less comprehensive law is discriminatory and divisive.
6. In cases of economic emergencies or depletion of school enrollments, a tenure law should provide for the fair and systematic dismissal of teachers along the following lines:
   a. A qualified tenure teacher should replace a probationary teacher.
   b. Tenure teachers should be dismissed in reverse order of seniority.
   c. Dismissed teachers should be reemployed in order of length of service and tenure status.
7. The law should define the status of the temporary teacher.

## Tenure in Institutions of Higher Education

Colleges and universities generally have been free to develop their own policies regarding tenure. As a result, considerable variation exists among the institutions. The continuing contract seems to be the favored type of tenure. The college teacher who is new to an institution usually serves a probationary period before he is granted tenure status. The length of the probationary period varies among, as well as within, institutions. Variations within are governed largely by the rank of the teacher. The instructor serves approximately five years before being placed on tenure; whereas the assistant, associate, and full professors serve respectively shorter periods.

The American Association of University Professors acts as a board of appeals for a college teacher who is in danger of being dismissed. An investigation is conducted by an appointed committee of the AAUP. If, in the judgment of the committee, the college or university is using unjustifiable procedures in dismissing staff members, the association usually places it on its censure-list until such procedures are changed. The censuring of an institution gives it unfavorable publicity with the general public and weakens its standing among other colleges. College teachers are hesitant to accept positions in such institutions. As a result, a college or university does not wish to incur the disfavor of the association.

## Objections to Teacher Tenure

There have been some objections raised by community members and some school officials to placing teachers on tenure. The fact that ten states still do not have tenure laws indicates that, even though great strides have been made, the battle for tenure laws is far from won. In fact some state legislatures are giving serious consideration to the elimination of tenure for teachers.

It is maintained by some that competent teachers do not need tenure protection. The argument is true, no doubt, for a vast majority of teachers. The relations of schools and communities in some sections, however, may not have reached a level at which the "spirit of the law may function without the law." For example, in some cases the employing officials, particularly those in small schools, follow the practice of never permitting teachers to gain permanent-tenure status, and in this way they avoid problems of having to dismiss tenure teachers. They have the feeling that it is too difficult to collect objective evidence to show incompetence and that unpleasant publicity might result from having to dismiss a tenure teacher. As a result, they fail to reemploy a teacher just prior to the time that tenure status would be granted. Hence, these teachers expect to remain in a school system no longer than the probationary period, regardless of their competency.

Before accepting a position, it is wise to investigate the practices used by a specific district in placing teachers on tenure. The chief sources of information will be the employing officials, teachers already in the school system, college instructors, teacher-placement personnel, and the state office of the state education association.

Many maintain that incompetent teachers on tenure are too difficult to dismiss. This argument is advanced especially against permanent tenure. Perhaps the basic weakness lies in the administration of the tenure law rather than in the law itself.

It is claimed that a teacher on tenure has little or no incentive to grow professionally. Undoubtedly, there are far too many tenure teachers for whom this objection is justified. Some school systems counteract this tendency by requiring teachers every five or more years to show evidence of professional growth. Reviews of a teacher's work should be made periodically. If the teacher has made no improvement, he should be placed on probation for a period of time adequate for the situation to be corrected. If he fails to make the desired improvement, he should be dismissed. All teachers must assume the obligation of continuing to grow in order to be deserving of tenure privileges. It should be remembered that tenure is a privilege rather than a built-in right of a teacher.

## Due Process Rights of Nontenured Teachers

Two court decisions handed down in 1970 by the U.S. District Court for the Western District of Wisconsin may have significance for nontenured teachers whose contracts are not renewed. The first case involved a professor in a public university [*Roth v. Board of Regents of State Colleges,* 310 F. Supp. 972]. In the second case [*Gouge v. Joint School District,* No. 1 at 991], the court ruled that "a teacher in a public elementary or secondary school is protected by the due process clause of the Fourteenth Amendment against a nonrenewal situation which is wholly without basis in fact and also against a decision which is wholly unreasoned, as well as a decision which is impermissibly based (such as race, religion, or exercise of First Amendment rights)" [276:6]. This court held further that a nontenured teacher is "entitled to a fair procedure to determine whether legitimate grounds for nonrenewal exists; and that minimum requirements of procedural due process include a statement of reasons for considering nonrenewal, adequate notice of hearing at which the teacher may respond to the stated reasons, and an actual hearing if the teacher appears at the appointed time and place, at which he must have a reasonable opportunity to submit evidence relevant to the stated reasons" [276:6].

## LEAVES OF ABSENCE

Everyone faces the possibility and probability of having his work interrupted because of illness or family emergencies such as sickness and death. In order to promote professional growth, it also is essential for a teacher to attend professional meetings, visit other schools, and engage in various projects which will enrich his work in the classroom. These kinds of absences from regular classroom duties may be classified as temporary or as sabbatical leaves.

## Provisions for Temporary Leaves

Teachers generally enjoy good health, and the job is less hazardous, from the standpoint of accidents, than many other types of work. However, they occasionally do become ill or have other reasons for being absent from work. If the teacher who is ill is encouraged to work in order to avoid loss of pay, he endangers the welfare of the pupils through both his inefficiency and his poor health. Thus, sick leaves are granted by school systems more frequently than leaves for any other cause. There are, however, a number of other reasons widely accepted for absence from the classroom. They have been classified under the following three headings [267:2]:

A.  Personal and Family
    1.  Personal illness or injury
    2.  Maternity
    3.  Religious holidays
    4.  Death in immediate family
    5.  Illness in immediate family (including quarantine)
    6.  Wedding or birth in immediate family
    7.  Moving from one domicile to another
    8.  Emergencies
B.  Professional
    1.  Attending or participating in educational meetings
    2.  Visiting other schools
    3.  Studying at colleges and universities
    4.  Traveling for professional improvement
    5.  Exchange teaching
    6.  Joining the Peace Corps
    7.  Serving the organized teaching profession through a local, state, or national education association as an officer, committee member, speaker, or legislative agent
C.  Civic
    1.  Answering a court summons
    2.  Serving on a jury
    3.  Voting; serving as an election official
    4.  Serving in an elective office
    5.  Participating in community-sponsored projects (fund drives, civic celebrations, etc.)
    6.  Military duty

Short-term leaves of absence are granted by a majority of the larger school systems so that a teacher will not lose pay when an emergency or other compelling circumstance not involving personal illness requires him to be away from his job for a brief period of time. Short-term leaves may be granted in such cases as death in the immediate family, illness in the immediate family, attendance at professional meetings, answering a court summons, jury duty, professional organization work, visits to other schools, military reserve duty, religious holidays, and personal business. Plans for granting short-term leaves vary greatly. Provisions are made for a teacher to be absent for a certain number of days at full pay or part pay each year.

The laws of thirty-two states and the District of Columbia make statutory provisions for teachers' sick leaves [252:43–44]. Almost all modern school systems grant sick leaves, with ten days' full pay for sick leave per year being the most common [252:43]. It is unfortunate that practices in rural sections have lagged behind those in cities. A few states provide for sick leave on an annual basis, with no carry-over being allowed. The more typical plan, however, calls for an accumulation of unused leave from year to year, up to a specified total amount usually ranging from 20 to 250 days. On the other hand, Alaska, California, District of Columbia, Hawaii, New Jersey, Pennsylvania, and Tennessee do not place any limit upon the amount that may be accumulated. There is a definite trend in favor of the accumulation of leave time, up to a maximum, since it provides teachers with greater protection during extended periods of illness.

As is the case in any occupational group, a few individuals are inclined to abuse provisions that have been made for such matters as sick leave. For this reason, some school officials require teachers to provide written statements declaring that personal illness necessitated their absence from teaching. Usually a doctor's statement is required if the illness extends over a period of two or more days [252:4]. In a few school systems teachers upon retirement are paid for unused accumulated sick leave. In at least six states (California, Indiana, Ohio, Oregon, Virginia, and West Virginia) legislative provisions have been made for sick leave accumulated in one school district to be transferred to another school district within the same state [142:5–15].

Provision for maternity leave is not quite as common as provision for sick leave, but it is being provided in an increasing number of school districts. This provision enables married women to live normal lives without fear of endangering their positions. As a general rule, such leaves are without pay, but they assure teachers the right to return to their positions after a stated period of time.

School boards generally require teachers to apply for maternity leaves four to six months prior to the anticipated birth of the child. Usually an application for maternity leave must be accompanied by a physician's statement confirming the expected date of birth. The period of leave granted after the birth of the child ranges from three to twelve months.

In addition to maternity leaves, extended leaves of absence for classroom teachers are being granted in an increasing number of school systems for such purposes as military service, professional study (other than sabbatical), exchange teaching abroad, restoration of health, work in professional organizations, government service such as the Peace Corps, Department of Defense schools, travel, research, exchange teaching in the

United States, election to a political office, and work experience [143:2]. An extended leave enables a teacher to leave his classroom for a semester or more without losing his job or salary status. A policy of granting extended leaves helps to encourage professional improvement, keeps good teachers in the profession, and improves the educational program in general. As one might expect, policies governing extended leaves vary considerably from school system to school system.

It is fairly common to grant extended leaves without pay to public school teachers who wish to continue their studies toward advanced degrees. By receiving the advanced degree, the teacher may place himself in a higher salary bracket, and although he suffers a temporary loss in salary, he is able to gain financially in the future. The teacher who is granted an extended leave of absence also has the assurance of his position upon his return.

Provisions for temporary leaves in colleges and universities tend to be less formal than in public schools. It is generally assumed that the college teacher will occasionally be absent in order to attend professional meetings, lecture, consult with public school teachers, and the like. By virtue of the nature of the work, it is easier to provide for the temporary absence of college teachers than for that of public school teachers.

Teachers for whom temporary leaves are provided are more fortunate than many other types of workers. Doctors and lawyers, for example, lose their fees and possibly some of their clientele when they are absent from their offices. When a person's income depends upon the amount of work he performs, he does not enjoy the same protection that teachers do when on temporary leave.

## Provisions for Sabbatical Leave

The granting of sabbatical leave is a very common practice on the college level of teaching. The term originated from the practice of granting an extended leave to teachers every seventh year, and the seven-year period of service is usually a requirement today for sabbatical-leave eligibility. The purpose of the leave is to provide an opportunity for the teacher to improve himself professionally. The amount of time granted varies among institutions from a semester to a full year. The salary received on leave varies from full pay in a few cases to a fraction (usually one-half) of the teacher's regular earnings.

The practice of granting sabbatical leave in colleges and universities probably has had some influence on granting extended leaves to public school teachers. A growing number of public school systems provide for sabbatical leave. Twenty states and the District of Columbia have statutory provisions for sabbatical leaves for public school teachers [142:2]. Many of the larger school systems throughout the United States have made provisions for paid sabbatical leaves. The amount of pay varies from the full amount of the regular salary to none at all, with the great majority allowing one-half salary to the teacher on sabbatical leave. In some cases the teacher receives the difference between the cost of a substitute and his regular salary.

## INSURANCE PROVISIONS

Group insurance programs are rapidly becoming available to teachers at all levels. The major types of insurance of importance to teachers are life insurance, hospital insurance, medical-surgical insurance, major medical insurance, disability insurance, and accidental death and dismemberment insurance.

Group life insurance is a low-cost protection in the event of death. Usually it is of the "term" variety, which provides for no cash or paid-up value over the years. The National Education Association sponsors four basic plans that are available to its members. Most state teachers' associations offer one or more life insurance plans.

Group hospitalization insurance provides protection for all or part of the hospital expenses incurred by the insuree. Generally, provision is made for room and board, incidental hospital expenses, and maternity care.

Group medical-surgical insurance provides for the payment for all or part of the expenses of surgery, generally on the basis of a schedule of allowances for specific operations. It frequently includes allowances for obstetrical services. It may cover visits made in the hospital, in the doctor's office, and in the patient's home.

Group major medical insurance provides protection from the cost of extraordinary illnesses and accidents. While hospitalization and medical-surgical plans provide for the basic costs of medical care, major medical insurance plans may provide in some cases for as much as $50,000 of medical care.

Group disability insurance, sometimes called income protection insurance, is designed to provide for all or a portion of the salary lost by a teacher who is temporarily absent from work because of illness or accident. Some policies pay beginning with the first or second day of total disability; others pay after the amount of accumulated paid sick leave has become exhausted [109:49].

Accidental death and dismemberment insurance is a relatively new type of insurance that has become available to educators. For example, the National Education Association has designed specifically a travel-accident insurance policy that offers coverage on a 24-hour basis wherever the insuree may be. It is available at a very low yearly cost to any member of the association.

Many states have workmen's compensation laws that help offset the loss of pay resulting from accidents and illnesses contracted on or as a result of an individual's work. Public school teachers usually are included in these benefits, which represent another type of disability insurance.

A school district may cooperate in providing group insurance in one or more forms, such as payroll deduction for premiums paid partly or entirely by the employees, sponsorship of the insurance plan, payment of part or all of the cost of the premiums for the coverage of the employee, and payment of part or all of the cost of the premiums for the coverage of the employee's dependents. Generally, the larger school systems are more likely than the small systems to cooperate in providing the various types of group insurance [109:49].

Usually, when the national or state teachers' association is the sponsor of the insurance plan, such as life insurance, the teacher pays the whole cost of the premiums. When the school district is the sponsor, it often pays part or all of the cost. The trend is very definitely toward the school district's assuming part or all of the cost [109:49].

## CREDIT UNIONS

Many teachers have found credit unions to be exceedingly helpful to them in managing their salaries and in meeting financial obligations. This fact is reflected in the growth of the number of credit unions.

A teachers' credit union is a cooperative savings and loan organization that is owned and operated by and for its members. The federal government has legalized the establishment of teachers' credit unions. In order to form a credit union, a charter must be obtained which limits the operation to the members of the group. Its records and operations are subject to annual examination by either state or federal authorities. Its management is under the direction of a board of directors chosen from the members of the group. In order to become a member of a credit union, a teacher must pay an entrance fee (usually 25 cents) and purchase at least one share of stock (usually costing $5). Only members can borrow from a credit union.

Credit unions offer several advantages to teachers. About half of the unions provide for payroll deductions, which make it easier for teachers to save. The savings are invested in loans to members, in United States bonds, or in other investments of a trust-fund type. The dividend rate compares very favorably with the cash return from many other types of investments. More than three-fourths of the teachers' credit unions carry life insurance for each member, which represents a substantial addition to the annual dividend. Loans are made to credit-union members so that they can pay cash for needed items rather than resort to an installment plan which usually is decidedly more expensive. Personal counseling on economic problems is provided to members.

## INCOME TAX DEDUCTIONS

In filing income tax reports, teachers are allowed to deduct justifiable business expenses. These expenses include membership dues in professional organizations as well as expenses incurred in attending classes, workshops, and other educational meetings in order to improve their professional skills or to retain their salary, status, or employment. Stinnett [259:282] points out, however, that expenses incurred for the following are not deductible: "(1) to prepare for the profession (that is pre-service education), (2) to meet minimum qualifications for a position, (3) to obtain a promotion, (4) to fulfill his general educational aspirations, or (5) to satisfy any other personal purpose." Since you may have difficulty in interpreting some of the business expenses you will incur, you may wish to consult a tax expert in regard to the exact meaning of the law.

## TAX-DEFERRED ANNUITIES

Since 1961, teachers and other school employees have been eligible for tax-deferred annuities under federal tax laws [264:94]. The employee pays no federal tax during the current year on the amount of his salary used to pay premiums for the annuity. Although the employee must pay taxes on the benefits received from the annuity at retirement, this payment will occur at a time when his income is lower, and therefore, the amount will be less than it would have been during his work years. The money earns interest while it is in the annuity account. If the member should die, his beneficiary receives the full amount of the annuity.

Tax-sheltered annuities are available to teachers through commercial insurance companies, and in nearly every state through the NEA plan. Because the program is nationwide, a member may continue to build his annuity even if he changes positions and moves from one state to another. To be eligible, a teacher must be a member of the NEA and his state education association.

## TEACHER RETIREMENT

An increasing concern through the years has been shown by the general public for the old-age welfare of all people. The most monumental evidence of this concern is to be found in the federal Social Security Act passed by Congress in 1935. Another recent evidence of this concern is to be found in the provision of Medicare which became effective July, 1966.

An increasing number of young people are planning to make teaching their life career. Since the age span is increasing, and people are tending to retire at an earlier age, financial security during the period of retirement assumes even greater significance to anyone planning a career.

A sound retirement system for teachers has the following advantages [271:1]:

1. It provides a dignified exit from active service after usefulness has diminished seriously through age or permanent disability.
2. It gives children the advantage of instruction from younger and more efficient teachers.
3. It increases the health and efficiency of teachers by removing worry and fear of a destitute old age.
4. It keeps good teachers in service.
5. It attracts capable, foresighted young people into the teaching profession.

## Extent of Teacher Retirement Systems

Since 1946 all states and territories of the United States have had at least one law providing retirement benefits for teachers who have reached a stated age or have served for a stated length of time. There is considerable variation in the provisions of the laws. A complete analysis of each of the laws would be of little interest. A general idea of their provisions, however, may be gained from a study of materials periodically published by the Research Division of the National Education Association. Details regarding provisions in any particular state may be secured from its department of education.

In spite of the decided trend toward statewide retirement programs, a number of cities have their own plans. The local systems are confined mainly to large cities, such as New York and Chicago, where the programs operate independently of the statewide program or under permissive legislation of the state concerned.

## Provision of Funds for Retirement

Each state has some form of a retirement allowance to which both the teacher and the state or school system contribute. It is commonly referred to as a "joint-contributory plan." From his active salary, the teacher contributes a flat rate or a given percentage (usually 5 or 6 per cent) to the retirement fund, and this amount is usually matched by the local school system and/or the state. Unlike a pension plan, the courts have held that in a joint-contributory retirement plan, retirement allowance *must* be paid to the retired teacher or his beneficiary.

Colleges and universities may belong to the retirement system provided by the state for public school teachers, may have their own system of retirement, may belong to an association such as the Teachers Insurance and Annuity Association, or may have no provisions at all for retirement. Virtually all the larger colleges and universities provide for the retirement of their staff members, although the plans differ greatly.

Some critics of retirement systems maintain that the teacher really pays for all the retirement benefits, that the amount which the state or local school system pays is rightfully a part of the teacher's salary. They fear that such an arrangement encourages teachers to accept lower salaries than they would otherwise. Statistics regarding teacher salaries and retirement benefits fail to substantiate this fear but, rather, indicate that an increase in one tends to accompany an increase in the other.

## Trends in Providing Retirement Benefits

Although the provisions for retirement vary considerably among the states, there seem to be certain trends in evidence. For example, many states have established plans whereby a teacher may retire voluntarily without meeting the full requirements and receive proportionately less retirement benefits. In some cases the teacher may retire voluntarily at an early date and receive full retirement benefits by paying the total amount that he and the state would have paid had he met the regular requirements for retirement.

The retirement laws in a majority of states specify the age when a teacher is compelled to retire from full-time teaching, regardless of the amount of time the teacher has taught. This age usually ranges between 60 and 70.

When the requirements for retirement have been met, most systems now specify a formula for computing the allowance available to the teacher. The allowance is computed as a total amount usually, but not always, as a percentage or fraction of the final average salary multiplied by the total years of service credit. Normally, the yearly retirement allowance is approximately one-half of the average salary, payable until the recipient's death. Attempts are being made to increase the retirement allowance to provide a more comfortable living for the teacher during his retirement.

Although the practice is still rare, an increasing number of school systems are granting *severance* pay to teachers and 12-month employees when they terminate their services [236:102]. The purpose of severance pay is "to provide teachers, who have given services to the school system, with financial security during the period of transition to a new position or to retirement" [111:7]. The guidelines to fringe benefits developed by the NEA recommends that teachers with five or more years of service be paid an "additional salary upon termination of employment at the rate of one day's pay per year of service in the system" [111:7].

Approximately two-thirds of the systems having such policies, however, use accumulated sick leave to figure severance pay [236:103]. Annuity plans, as indicated previously, are being explored by retirement systems as a way to protect retirement benefits against the erosion of inflation.

Virtually all states now require all new teachers to participate in a retirement program. This procedure seems justifiable since otherwise many teachers would delay making adequate provisions for their retirement and the welfare of children would be jeopardized.

Almost all retirement systems provide some sort of credit for service in the Armed Forces. In order to gain credit, however, the teacher usually must serve during a time of war or national emergency or be drafted or called as a reservist. Few systems provide retirement credit for overseas teaching unless the teacher is on exchange and is being paid by his American employer.

Many retirement plans are expanding the optional benefits for the retiring teacher so he may choose the method of payment of benefits best suited to him.

All states except Iowa make provision for disability retirement if the teacher becomes permanently disabled prior to normal retirement. Most of the laws, however, state that the teacher must have a specified minimum number of years of service, such as 10 years, before he is eligible for disability benefits. The amount of benefit to be received depends on the amount of service that the teacher has given or on a fixed sum specified by policy or law.

## Withdrawal after Limited Service

A teacher normally is entitled to a percentage of the amount of money which he has contributed toward retirement if he withdraws from teaching prior to the minimum time required for retirement. This percentage increases with the length of service. Usually after ten years of service, a teacher will be refunded 100 per cent of the amount he has contributed. A few systems refund the total amount regardless of when a teacher withdraws. In many cases a teacher will not be forced to withdraw his money if he leaves the profession. The capital usually accumulates at a fair rate of interest. Furthermore, if he returns to teaching, he has to his credit the money contributed during the previous years of service.

Death of the teacher concerned naturally constitutes a withdrawal from teaching. In this case, the amount of money due would be paid to beneficiaries. Death benefits vary greatly from one state to another.

## Transfers from One State to Another

There is a very strong possibility, in this highly mobile society, that a teacher will start his career in one state and finish it in another. If he crosses state lines, he may jeopardize his accumulated retirement interests unless the law of the state he leaves provides for full vesting of his retirement rights.

Most of the states have provisions for vesting retirement rights and the payment of a deferred retirement allowance to a teacher who ceases to teach in a state and leaves his contribution in the retirement system. As a result, he becomes entitled at a later time to receive an annuity which is derived from his own contribution as well as from public funds contributed by the state and/or the local school district. Payment of the allowance usually starts at age sixty [220:106].

There is considerable variation among the states in the age and service requirements for vesting of retirement rights and in the age at which the deferred benefits become available. Fewer than one-fourth of the states, however, measure up to the resolution of the National Education Association, which urges full vesting of retirement rights after no more than five years of service [169:86]. It is highly probable that an increasing number of retirement systems will move in the direction of this resolution in order to make more liberal provisions for teachers who move from one state to another.

At least twenty-seven states grant service credit toward retirement for teaching performed outside their boundaries [220:106]. In most cases, the transfer teacher has to purchase the amount of credit he wishes to have, which usually may not exceed 10 years. A few states will not allow service credit to be purchased if a teacher is receiving or is entitled to receive retirement benefits from another state.

## Social Security Benefits for Teachers

In 1954, Congress extended greatly the benefits to be derived from the Social Security Act and also made it possible for public employees to obtain social security benefits without abandoning any existing public employee retirement system. As a result, government employees, as of January 1, 1955, could become eligible for social security benefits if the members, after having had 90 days' notice of the referendum, voted in favor of it. The teachers in a number of states took advantage of this opportunity.

The states that have adopted social security have used various formulas for accomplishing this purpose. In some states, teachers have social security coverage in addition to their retirement benefits. In other cases the social security benefits are coordinated or are integrated with the retirement benefits.

Social security has certain advantages that are not present in many teacher retirement laws. Since it is nationwide in scope, a teacher does not run as much danger of losing his benefits in moving from one state to another as he does in the case of state retirement plans. There is no compulsory retirement age in the federal plan, although there is a limitation on the amount an individual can earn between the ages of 65 and 72 and yet draw full social security benefits during those years. If a man wishes, he may retire as early as 62, but the benefits per year are less. A wife, if 65 or more years old, receives an additional one-half of her husband's benefits (or less if she wishes to begin receiving benefits at age 62), while the husband collects the full amount. Survivors' benefits are provided for widows over 62, children under 18, and widows of any age caring for the deceased's children.

The NEA maintains that "If retirement systems are supplemented by participation in the federal Social Security program, such participation should be wholly in addition to, and not in place of, retirement benefits previously guaranteed by law; must be without impairment of the financial soundness of the existing system; and must be approved in advance by a majority of the active members of the existing system" [169:75].

## SUMMARY

In this chapter, some of the important factors other than salary that affect the economic security of teachers have been examined. Although practices and provisions vary throughout the United States, much progress has been made in providing security through tenure for the competent teacher by means of which he is better able to fulfill his professional responsibilities to youth. The reasons for, the kinds, the present status, and the characteristics of good tenure laws were examined. Increasingly liberal provisions for leaves of absence are being developed. As is the case in business and industry, school officials are showing increasing concern for hospitalization and life insurance protection for their employees. Many teachers are finding credit unions to be exceedingly helpful to them in managing their salaries and in meeting financial obligations. The need for teacher retirement, and the extent, provisions, and trends in regard to retirement systems were carefully examined. Social Security benefits for teachers were also described.

These added benefits to teachers have come primarily through the concerted efforts of various local, state, and national professional teacher organizations in an attempt to place careers in the field of education on a truly professional level. Continued efforts on the part of all should bring about even further benefits.

## QUESTIONS TO CONSIDER

1. What are the advantages and disadvantages of tenure as it relates to annual contracts, contracts extending for a definite number of years, continuing contracts, and protective continuing contracts?
2. What is the least desirable type of teacher tenure? The most desirable? Why?
3. In what ways may permanent tenure be misused professionally?
4. How may teachers on tenure be encouraged to continue their professional growth?
5. What are the advantages and disadvantages of superintendents' not having permanent tenure?
6. What leave-of-absence provisions should a school system make for teachers?
7. To what extent should school districts sponsor group insurance programs for teachers?
8. What are the arguments for and against teachers' belonging to credit unions?

9.  What advantages do tax-deferred annuities have for teachers?
10. Why is a joint-contributory retirement plan more desirable than a pension plan?
11. Why should teachers be encouraged to invest in a mutual fund, such as the one sponsored by the NEA?
12. How can teachers safeguard their retirement benefits against erosion that may result from inflation?
13. What, in your opinion, is the most desirable retirement plan which will prevent the migratory teacher from being penalized?
14. What are the advantages and disadvantages of a law which compels teachers to retire upon reaching a certain age?
15. Do you feel that all teachers should be eligible for Social Security benefits? Why?

## PROBLEM SITUATION FOR INQUIRY

Mr. Michael was fired from his teaching position at Westview High School at the February school board meeting for allegedly "corrupting the morals of his students." The official dismissal letter indicted Michael for distributing literature in his American Problems class dealing with the subject of abortion. The board cited this material as "not in the best interest" of students, while Michael explained he thought the material was very pertinent to the class objectives—to study American problems.

The material traced the evolution of abortion laws in the United States and indicated that the American public has drastically modified its attitude toward abortions in the last five years. The material also outlined procedures for obtaining a legal abortion in the United States. "The purpose of the article," Michael said, "was to draw the attention of students to a controversial issue which exists in society today. I handed the paper out to a class of thirty-eight students who were divided into pro and con groups to argue for or against the merits of legalized abortion." The lesson was designed, Michael said, "to enable students to intelligently examine the opposing viewpoints on the subject of abortion."

Michael has taught at Westview for two years and is not on tenure. Even though not on tenure, can the Westview School Board legally take the action which it did? Could the Board have taken similar action if Michael were a tenured teacher? If you were Michael, what would you do? Why?

## ACTIVITIES TO PURSUE

1.  If you were a superintendent of schools, what would you do if parents reported one of your teachers on permanent tenure as incompetent in the classroom?
2.  Study as many occupations as possible in terms of the provisions preventing an individual from losing his job unfairly. Compare and contrast these occupations with teaching.
3.  If you know of a teacher on permanent tenure who seems to be shirking his job responsibilities, analyze the personal factors or values that may be involved.
4.  Study in detail the retirement plans in three or more states in which you may be interested in teaching.
5.  Investigate the amount of Social Security benefits you might receive upon retirement.
6.  Investigate various occupations in terms of provisions for emergency leaves. Compare and contrast these provisions with those in your home school system.
7.  Compare the rates for group insurance plans for teachers with those of commercial concerns.
8.  Assume you wish to borrow money to buy a new automobile. How would the total cost of the automobile, if financed through a credit union such as the teachers' credit union, compare with its cost if financed through a regular loan company?
9.  Investigate the fringe benefits for teachers in a large and in a small school system. What differences, if any, exist?

# RESOURCE SECTION FOR PART 3

Checklist for Appraising a Teacher
Salary Schedule

Suggested Readings

Figure Credits

# CHECKLIST FOR APPRAISING A TEACHER SALARY SCHEDULE

If you can answer "yes" to each of the following questions, you may be certain that the salary schedule is a good one.

| Item | Yes | No |
| --- | --- | --- |

*Rules and regulations*

1. Are the following requirements for employment specified: a degree; graduation from an institution accredited for teacher education; full professional certification?
2. Are safeguards provided against arbitrary denial or withdrawal of increments?
3. If "professional growth" requirements are utilized, are increases based on clearly defined qualifications which can be reasonably expected of all teachers?
4. Is the application clear and equitable with regard to: credit for prior service outside the district; credit for military service; placing teachers on steps; advance warning and follow-up supervisory help if increments are denied?
5. Is discretionary initial step placement prohibited?

*Starting salaries*

1. Is the B.A. minimum competitive in respect to beginning salaries offered to college graduates?
2. Does this minimum make it possible for teachers to invest in advanced preparation?
3. Does this minimum permit a professional living standard?

*Experience increments*

1. Is each increment at least 5 per cent of the B.A. minimum?
2. Does the B.A. scale have less than 12 steps (11 increments)?
3. Is the increment structure devised to reduce teacher turnover and to promote in-service growth?

*Training differentials*

1. Is the extent of recognition sufficient to include:
   a. A class for the master's degree?
   b. A class for sixth year of college preparation?
   c. A class for the doctor's degree or a seventh-year preparation level as a substitute for the doctoral class?
   d. Intermediate preparation levels for at least each half-year of graduate credit?
2. Are differentials adequate in amounts so as to:
   a. Be an incentive for voluntary professional growth?
   b. Allow teachers with advanced preparation and professional growth credits a salary potential at least $1,000 above the regular B.A. scale?
   c. Reimburse teachers within a reasonable period (not more than 10 years) for their investments in advanced preparation?

*Maximum salaries*

1. Excepting super-maximums, are they attainable in a reasonable number of years (10 to 15)?
2. Is the B.A. maximum at least 60 per cent above the B.A. minimum?

*Extra compensation*

1. Are higher salaries based on differences in qualifications, avoiding such discriminatory practices as sex differentials and subject or grade-level differentials?

*Source:* Eula May Taylor and Erwin L. Coons, "Salary-scheduling Check List," *NEA Journal*, vol. 49, no. 7, p. 33, National Education Association, Washington, October, 1960.

## CHECKLIST FOR APPRAISING A TEACHER SALARY SCHEDULE
## (continued)

| Item | Yes | No |
|---|---|---|

2. Are salary differentials allowed for work beyond normal load?
3. If extra pay is granted, is a schedule of payments included in the salary policy or personnel policies?
4. Has "extra pay" been abolished in favor of a balanced load for all teachers?

*Other considerations related to quality*
1. Is the schedule a "booster" rather than a "buster" of teacher morale?
2. Does the schedule enhance the professional standing of the teaching staff?
3. Does the schedule generally provide freedom from financial worry?
4. Does the schedule indicate that teachers are to devote full time to teaching?
5. Are teacher-supervisor relations for improvement of instruction kept on a high plane of co-operation?
6. Are irregularities which tend to tear down teachers' prestige, self-confidence, and status avoided?

## SUGGESTED READINGS

*The number in parentheses following each suggestion denotes the chapter for which it is best suited.*

Barker, Kenneth: "International Education and the Professional Associations," *Phi Delta Kappan,* vol. 51, no. 5, pp. 244–246, Phi Delta Kappa, Bloomington, Ind., January, 1970. Indicates the need for professional associations to emphasize the international aspects of education. (9)

Broudy, Harry S.: "Teaching—Craft or Profession?" in *Contemporary American Education* by Stan Dropkin, Harold Full, and Ernest Schwarcz, pp. 421–432, The Macmillan Company, Toronto, Ontario, 1970. Raises the question as to whether teachers should be classified as craftsmen or as professionals. (9)

Chanin, Robert H.: *Protecting Teacher Rights,* National Education Association, Washington, 1970. An up-to-date summary of judicial decisions regarding the constitutional rights of educators. (9)

Darland, D. D.: "The Profession's Quest for Responsibility and Accountability," *Phi Delta Kappan,* vol. 52, no. 1, pp. 41–44, Phi Delta Kappa, Bloomington, Ind., September, 1970. Maintains that the teaching profession is systematically moving toward self-governance machinery and processes necessary for accountability. (9)

"Differentiated Staffing Stirs Debate," *The Shape of Education for 1970-71,* vol. 12, pp. 30–33, National School Public Relations Association, Washington, 1970. Indicates that differentiated staffing may end the single-salary schedule. (10)

"Discrimination and Professional Ethics," *Today's Education,* vol. 60, no. 3, pp. 34–35, National Education Association, Washington, March, 1971. Discusses the problem of discrimination from the standpoint of professional ethics. (9)

"Economic Status of the Teaching Profession," *Research Report,* National Education Association, Research Division, Washington (latest issue). An annual publication containing excellent information on teacher salaries. (10)

*Enforcement of the Code of Ethics of the Education Profession,* National Education Association, Committee on Professional Ethics, Washington, 1969. Discusses the procedures for the national enforcement of the Code of Ethics. (9)

"Family Illness and Bereavement Leaves in Negotiation Agreement," *NEA Research*

*Bulletin,* vol. 49, no. 1, pp. 5–7, National Education Association, Research Division, Washington, March, 1971. Presents the results of a nationwide study of provisions for family illness and bereavement leaves of absence. (11)

*Goals of the American Federation of Teachers AFL-CIO,* American Federation of Teachers, AFL-CIO, Washington, n.d. A concise statement of the goals of the American Federation of Teachers. (9)

*Guidelines to Fringe Benefits for Members of the Teaching Profession,* National Education Association, Washington, 1969. A statement of recommendations regarding fringe benefits for the teaching profession and procedures for securing them. (11)

*How to Negotiate: A Handbook for Local Teacher Associations,* National Education Association, Division of Field Services, Washington, 1969. Contains some excellent suggestions on procedures to be followed in teacher negotiation at the local level. (9)

"Leaves of Absence Provisions for Teachers, 1968-69," *NEA Research Memo 1969-22,* National Education Association, Research Division, Washington, October, 1969. Presents the results of a national survey of leave of absence provisions for teachers. (11)

"Merit Provisions in Teachers' Salary Schedules, 1969–70," *NEA Research Memo 1970-7,* National Education Association, Research Division, Washington, April 1970. Contains information on school systems that make provisions for merit salary increases. (10)

*Milestones in Teacher Education and Professional Standards,* National Education Association, National Commission on Teacher Education and Professional Standards, Washington, 1970. Graphically presents much data on status of teaching as a profession. (9)

*NEA Handbook for Local, State and National Associations,* National Education Association, Washington (latest edition). An annual publication containing abundant information about the NEA. (9)

Perry, Charles R.: *The Impact of Negotiations in Public Education: The Evidence from the Schools,* Charles A. Jones Publishing Company, Worthington, Ohio, 1970. Analyzes the results of negotiations in terms of improvements in school situations. (9)

"Professional Growth Requirements Specified in 1968–1969 Salary Schedules (Reporting School Systems with Enrollments of 6,000 or more)," *NEA Research Memo 1969-10,* National Education Association, Research Division, Washington, April, 1969. Presents the results of a study of local professional growth requirements for vertical advancement on the salary schedule. (10)

"Professional Negotiation," *Today's Education,* vol. 59, no. 2, pp. 33–40, National Education Association, Washington, February, 1970. A special feature in which various educators discuss problems encountered in professional negotiations. (9)

"Salaries in Higher Education," *Research Report,* National Education Association, Research Division, Washington (latest issue). A detailed report on salaries in higher education is published annually. (10)

"Salary Schedule Supplements for Extra Duties, 1969–70," *Research Report 1970-R4,* National Education Association, Research Division, Washington, 1970. Presents the results of a comprehensive study of supplemental pay for extra duties in public schools. (10)

Sanstead, Wayne: "Are you Politically Involved?" *Today's Education,* vol. 59, no. 9, pp. 44–45, National Education Association, Washington, December, 1970. Indicates how teachers can and should be politically involved. (9)

"Teacher Strikes," *NEA Research Bulletin,* vol. 48, no. 3, pp. 69–72, National Education Association, Research Division, Washington, October, 1970. Analyzes teacher strikes occurring over a 10-year period. (9)

"Teacher Tenure and Contracts," *Research Report, 1971-R3,* National Education Association, Research Division, Washington, 1971. Contains a state-by-state summary of statutory tenure provisions relating to teachers and other professional school personnel. (11)

"Trends in Salaries Scheduled for Teachers," *NEA Research Bulletin,* vol. 49, no. 1, pp. 10–13, National Education Association, Research Division, Washington, March, 1971. Identifies trends in salary schedules for teachers. (10)

"What's New in Teacher Retirement Systems," *NEA Research Bulletin,* vol. 48, no. 4, pp. 108–113, National Education Association, Research Division, Washington, December, 1970. Indicates recent legislative changes in statewide teacher retirement systems. (11)

Williams, Lois: "Governance Is Integral to Accountability," *Today's Education,* vol. 60, no. 4, pp. 59–60, National Education Association, Washington, April, 1971. Emphasizes the importance of professional autonomy as a component of accountability. (9)

"Your Personal Finances," *Today's Education,* vol. 59, no. 8, pp. 49–52, National Education Association,Washington, November, 1970. Analyzes the various kinds of insurance needs of teachers. (11)

## FIGURE CREDITS

FIGURE 9-1. (*Source: Milestones in Teacher Education and Professional Standards,* National Education Association, National Commission on Teacher Education and Professional Standards, Washington, 1970, p. 9, and data from "Highest Degrees Held by Teachers," *NEA Research Bulletin,* vol. 49, no. 2, National Education Association, Research Division, Washington, May, 1971, p. 56.)

FIGURE 9-2. (*Source:* "Profile of the American Public School Teacher, 1966," *NEA Journal,* vol. 56, no. 5, National Education Association, Washington, May, 1967, p. 15.)

FIGURE 9-3. (*Source:* "Profile of the American Public School Teacher, 1966," *NEA Journal,* vol. 56, no. 5, National Education Association, Washington, May, 1967, p. 12.)

FIGURE 9-4. (*Source:* Data from *Milestones in Teacher Education and Professional Standards,* National Education Association, National Commission on Teacher Education and Professional Standards, Washington, 1970, p. 27.)

FIGURE 9-5. (*Source: NEA Handbook for Local, State, and National Associations,* National Education Association, Washington, September, 1971, p. 18.)

FIGURE 10-1. (*Source:* Adapted from "Facts on American Education," *NEA Research Bulletin,* vol. 49, no. 2, National Education Association, Research Division, Washington, May, 1971, p. 50.)

FIGURE 10-2. (*Source:* "Facts on American Education," *NEA Research Bulletin,* vol. 49, no. 2, National Education Association, Research Division, Washington, May, 1971, p. 49.)

FIGURE 10-3. (*Source:* "Economic Status of the Teaching Profession, 1970-1971," *Research Report 1971-R4,* National Education Association, Research Division, Washington, 1971, p. 48.)

FIGURE 10-4. (*Source:* "Salaries of Beginning Teachers and Beginners in Other Professions," *NEA Research Bulletin,* vol. 49, no. 3, National Education Association, Research Division, Washington, October, 1971, p. 74.)

FIGURE 10-5. (*Source:* Data from *Financial Status of the Public Schools,* National Education Association, Committee on Educational Finance, Washington, 1971, p. 14.)

FIGURE 10-6. (*Source:* Data from "Salaries Paid Public-School Professional Employees," *NEA Research Bulletin,* vol. 47, no. 3, National Education Association, Research Division, Washington, October, 1969, p. 79.)

FIGURE 10-7. (*Source:* "Index Salary Schedules for Teachers," *NEA Research Bulletin,* vol. 39, no. 4, National Education Association, Research Division, Washington, December, 1961, p. 111.)

FIGURE 10-8.  (*Source:* "Salary Supplements for Extra Duties," *NEA Research Bulletin,* vol. 48, no. 2, National Education Association, Research Division, Washington, May, 1970, p. 42.)

FIGURE 10-9.  (*Source:* "Profile of the American Public School Teacher, 1966," *NEA Journal,* vol. 56, no. 5, National Education Association, Washington, May, 1967, p. 15.)

FIGURE 11-1.  (*Source:* Data from "Teacher Tenure and Contracts," *Research Report 1971-R3,* National Education Association, Research Division, Washington, 1971, p. 7.)

# 4 | organizational, administrative, and financial concerns

Prospective teachers frequently ask, "Why must we study school organization, administration, and finance? These topics are not relevant to the preparation of teachers and should be reserved for prospective administrators." These comments were probably justified in an earlier era when administrators and school board members independently and arbitrarily made all decisions relating to the operation of the schools.

We are in the midst of a period of change. Teachers are engaged in a minor power struggle with administrators and school board members. As a result, teachers are becoming more actively involved in the decision-making process. But power is a peculiar phenomenon. Many seek it, but few are competent in its exercise. Effective and responsible participation of teachers in decision-making activities is dependent upon a basic understanding of all major aspects of the school operation.

The "activism" of students and young adults is widely recognized. The involvement of the vast majority of individuals in this movement has grown out of a sincere desire to improve our social institutions, including our schools. A careful analysis of these activities reveals that the most successful attempts—those which have resulted in responsible and effective change—have been produced by individuals who have developed a basic comprehension of the structure of our social institutions.

An understanding of how schools are organized, administered, and financed, as discussed in Chapters 12 and 13, will place beginning teachers in a better position to make critical analyses of present conditions, to successfully participate in the decision-making process, to exert more positive influence in gaining community support for schools, and to aid in the improvement of learning opportunities for young people.

# 12 | ORGANIZATION AND ADMINISTRATION OF SCHOOLS

How is the system of education in the United States organized and administered? What are the functions of local, state, and national levels of school organization? How do teachers fit into this complex organizational structure? What changes in the organization and administration of schools may be expected in the future? What opportunities and responsibilities will teachers have in determining changes that will take place?

Questions and issues examined in this chapter are of profound importance in the work of a teacher. The various individuals and bodies of government which have a voice in the organization and operation of schools determine, to some extent, such matters as (1) the curriculum of the school, (2) the relationship between teachers and other school personnel, (3) the criteria utilized for employing, retaining, and dismissing teachers, (4) the basis upon which teachers will be certified, (5) the legality of teacher strikes, and (6) what constitutes academic freedom.

In a very real sense, teachers have always performed major administrative and organizational functions within the classroom. For example, teachers have made decisions about what concepts or units were to be taught, what textbooks or other media were to be used, what groupings of students were necessary, the methods by which the progress of students was to be measured, and the standards of performance that were to be expected of students. But teachers and teacher groups are now beginning to influence the development of school policies outside the realm of the individual classroom. School administrators are increasingly seeking the advice and creative thinking of teachers in making decisions.

Professional education organizations are gaining strength, and their influence on legislation related to educational matters is being felt. Not only have educators learned to recognize the realities of politics, but legislators and congressmen are also being more receptive to professional advice and information available through professional education associations.

In order to be effective in the classroom and help the school accomplish its mission, a teacher needs to have breadth as well as depth of understanding with respect to the organization and administration of the school system throughout the United States. To assist the prospective teacher in gaining this understanding, this chapter has been organized into two parts: (1) the relationship of governmental levels to education, and (2) the organization and administration of schools according to levels. An understanding of the legal basis of public education, first of all, will help provide a perspective for a consideration of these two parts.

## Legal Basis of Public Education

Unlike many other countries, the United States does not have a national system of public education in which power over schools is concentrated at the national level of government. Since the United States Constitution does not mention education and since court decisions throughout the history of the United States have consistently upheld the states' responsibility for maintaining free public education, there is no legal basis for a national system.

The constitution of each state provides for the organization and operation of a system of public schools. In reality we have a collection of fifty state systems of education which may be spoken of as the American systems of education rather than as a national system.

Although education is legally a state function in the United States, each state relies upon both the local school district and the federal government to play a role in the development and operation of public education, In effect, public education is a shared responsibility of local, state, and federal governments—the local unit usually operates schools; the state is legally responsible for provision of an educational system; and the federal government is an agent of support and change that encourages the extension and improvement of education in the fifty state systems. As an agent of change, the federal government, through such agencies as the U.S. Office of Education, the Office of Economic Opportunity, and the Department of Labor, senses national manpower and social needs and offers state governments so-called "incentive moneys" to develop new and/or better instructional programs. The states then voluntarily accept or reject such opportunities to work with the federal government in such educational affairs. Details of this and other types of federal financial assistance will be discussed in Chapters 13 and 18.

## Conceptions of Organization and Administration

An educational program requires goals, a plan to realize the goals, and an organizational structure for implementing the plan. Organization is the means of effectively concentrating the efforts of a group of people on the

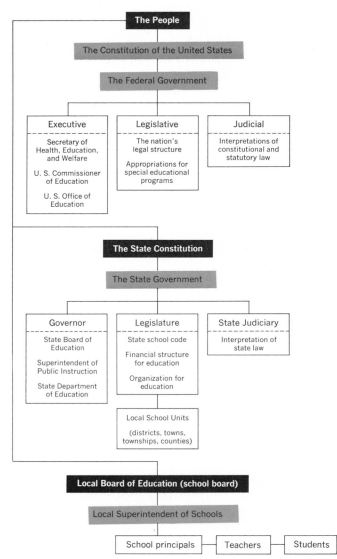

The People

The Constitution of the United States

The Federal Government

| Executive | Legislative | Judicial |
|---|---|---|
| Secretary of Health, Education, and Welfare | The nation's legal structure | Interpretations of constitutional and statutory law |
| U. S. Commissioner of Education | Appropriations for special educational programs | |
| U. S. Office of Education | | |

The State Constitution

The State Government

| Governor | Legislature | State Judiciary |
|---|---|---|
| State Board of Education | State school code | Interpretation of state law |
| Superintendent of Public Instruction | Financial structure for education | |
| State Department of Education | Organization for education | |

Local School Units

(districts, towns, townships, counties)

Local Board of Education (school board)

Local Superintendent of Schools

| School principals | Teachers | Students |
|---|---|---|

FIGURE 12–1.  Structure of the organization of education in the United States.

attainment of common goals, and the prime role of administration is to facilitate the attainment of these goals. A school organizational structure does not exist as an end in itself, but rather as a means to an end. In the United States, the primary goal of the schools is the educational development of students for effective living in a democratic society. Thus, the efforts of all school personnel should be geared to the realization of this goal. Although the numerous local school systems share a common goal, they differ in the ways they are organized and administered.

Programs or organizational goals represent but one side of the educational coin. The community, individual teachers, students, and other school personnel also have goals which may or may not be consistent with the goals of the organization. Ideally, a teacher, in the process of facilitating the attainment of the organizational goals, would also satisfy his personal goals. But the degree to which this ideal may be realized is partially dependent upon the manner in which the school system employing the teacher is organized and administered.

Although there are many diverse conceptions of organization, for our purposes they can be grouped into two broad categories: (1) traditional bureaucratic, and (2) modern pluralistic.

The traditional concept of organization is built upon a framework of command, line of authority, control, and hierarchy. It may be pictured as a pyramid, with the power for making decisions flowing from the top down to the subordinates on the lower echelons. A precise division of labor is essential in this form of organization. Each member of the organization has an assigned task. Higher-echelon personnel, such as administrators, are expected to provide leadership. Individuals in lower echelons, such as teachers, are expected to follow the leaders. If followers (i.e., teachers) attempt to exercise leadership, they may be branded as trouble-makers. Tight control, so essential to the success of the traditional organizational structure, is achieved through such processes as reporting, inspecting, and commanding. Participation in the formulation of goals, policies, programs, and the evaluation of results is limited to individuals in the upper echelons. Since great emphasis is placed upon "going through channels" in the traditional organization, communication within this organization is restricted, especially from the lower to the upper echelons.

The modern concept of organization, a modification of the traditional concept, provides for a pluralistic sharing of power. This organization is loosely structured when compared to the traditional structure, and places less emphasis on a precise definition of duties and responsibilities. It is highly decentralized; thus, leadership is not confined to those who hold status positions in the organization. All members of the organization have the opportunity to exercise leadership; therefore, authority and leadership are situation-oriented rather than position-oriented. The communication channels are open and readily accessible to all persons in the modern concept of organization. There is broad participation in the formulation of goals, policies, and programs, and in the evaluation of results [164:83–118].

What are the implications for teachers working in school systems structured along traditional versus modern organizational lines? Which structure holds the greater promise for both realizing the goals of the organization and for enabling teachers to realize their personal goals? Which structure is more likely to encourage individual initiative and creative approaches to teaching? Is one structure more likely to involve teachers in curriculum planning and textbook selection than the other? Which structure provides the greater job security for teachers? Do both structures place a high priority on the professional growth of teachers? Is one structure more vulnerable to teacher strikes than the other? Which type organization has the stronger potential to be innovative and to adopt new approaches such as nongraded schools and independent study programs? Would teacher morale be higher in one type of organization than in the other? Which structure is more likely to encourage competition among teachers?

The traditional pattern of organization and administration has been dominant in school systems throughout the United States. There is, however, strong evidence to suggest that many systems are gradually shifting toward the modern organizational structure. A prospective teacher may want to examine carefully the organizational structure of an individual school district before accepting a position, using this information to decide if the district structure will permit the individual to realize his personal goals. It should be recognized that school systems are not likely to fall neatly into either the traditional or modern category, for in reality these two categories should be viewed as opposite ends of a continuum.

## RELATIONSHIP OF GOVERNMENTAL LEVELS TO EDUCATION

Since education in the United States is a state function, each state legislature is responsible for establishing and maintaining a public system of education, subject only to the limitations of the state and federal constitutions, federal laws, and state statutes. The state may create or abolish school districts either with or without the consent of the people living within the districts. It may vest the educational authority in any local body it chooses, or it may operate the schools itself.

Even though the states and the federal government play important roles in education, the tradition of local operation of schools still prevails in the United States. This tradition of maintaining close contact with the local citizenry is consistent with the democratic form of government. In reality, the public education system in the United States is composed of approximately 18,000 semiautonomous local school districts. The federal-state-local structural relation with respect to public education may then be described as a federal interest in the local operation of a state function.

### The Role of the Federal Government in Education

The federal government, throughout its history, has shown an interest in the educational welfare of the nation. This interest has increased sharply in recent years. Furthermore, the role of the federal government is undergoing change.

Federal involvement in education is centered around the Constitution, the Congress, and the Supreme Court. The Constitution contains clauses which direct the Congress to concern itself with the defense and general welfare of the citizens. Because of the vagueness of these clauses, the Supreme Court is frequently called upon to interpret laws and rule on their constitutionality. The passage of the National Defense Education Act in 1958 provides a good example of Congress acting in the interest of the country's defense. The Elementary and Secondary Education Act, which was passed in 1965, demonstrates congressional interest in the general welfare of the country. And recent rulings of the Supreme Court on desegregation of schools illustrate the impact which this judicial body has had on public education.

The realities of the relationship between politics and education should not be overlooked. The federal government has a sincere interest in education, but this interest is intensified when congressmen find it politically expedient to support education. For example, the mid 1960s saw tremendous emphasis being placed upon education because of its inherent relationship to the "Great Society" program of the Johnson administration. Consequently, the Elementary and Secondary Education Act overcame great obstacles to become Public Law 89–10. Another factor which may have had some bearing upon passage of this act was the desire to pour money into and thus stimulate a sluggish economy.

Educators have, until recent years, either ignored or failed to comprehend the political realities of Washington. The U.S. Office of Education (USOE) has only recently become an important political force in terms of drafting and lobbying for education measures before the Congress. Francis Keppel, U.S. Commissioner of Education in the Kennedy administration, was largely responsible for this transition of the USOE. Keppel was a close friend of President Kennedy and apparently understood how to circumvent the red tape of the massive federal bureaucracy. Professional educational organizations have also begun to recognize that, collectively, they have tremendous lobbying power. While profitmaking enterprises have long lobbied for legislation which favored their interests, educators are only now beginning to recognize and employ their political clout in a similar fashion.

## U.S. Office of Education (USOE)

The USOE was established in 1867 and was then known as the Department of Education. Henry Barnard, an outstanding educator of his day, was appointed by the President as the first Commissioner of Education. The department was initially charged with the responsibility for:

collecting such statistics and facts as shall show the condition and progress of education in the several states and territories, and of diffusing such information respecting the organization and management of schools and school systems, and methods of teaching, as shall aid the people of the United States in the establishment and maintenance of efficient school systems, and otherwise promote the cause of education throughout the country.

The U.S. Department of Education operated as an independent agency until 1869, when it became an office attached to the Department of the Interior. In 1870 the title was changed from Office of Education to Bureau of Education, but its former title was restored in 1929. In 1939 the Federal Security Agency was created and the Office of Education was placed under its jurisdiction, and in 1953 the Office of Education became one of the units in the Department of Health, Education, and Welfare, which replaced the Federal Security Agency.

Thus, in its early years, the USOE was chiefly concerned with the collection and dissemination of data. It still performs these functions, but its role has been greatly expanded. Today, the office is engaged in conducting educational research, providing educational services to schools, and fostering change in education throughout the United States. To assist it in performing its various functions, the USOE employs specialists to provide consultative services and general leadership in their respective areas in addition to conducting research.

The U.S. Commissioner of Education, as an officer in the Department of Health, Education, and Welfare, is the chief education officer of the federal government and is responsible for formulating educational policy and coordinating educational activities at the national level. The Commissioner is appointed by the President, by and with the advice and consent of the Senate. He is responsible for the operation of the Office of Education, for the administration of educational legislation, and for the performance of other functions assigned by Congress and the Executive Office of the President.

## Teachers and the Federal Government

Teachers benefit from federal interest in education in numerous ways but chiefly through the promotion of curriculum change by various federal agencies. The best example of this is found in the work of the National Science Foundation. This foundation, established by Public Law 507 in 1950, has been highly successful in initiating and supporting programs to strengthen research in mathematics, and in the physical and biological sciences. Much of the new science and mathematics curricula has been developed under the sponsorship of this foundation. More recently, other curriculum areas, including foreign languages and the humanities, have received the attention of federal agencies. Although the USOE and other federal agencies have not realized their full potential as change agents, they have proven that adequately financed federal programs can successfully foster curriculum change.

The National Science Foundation and the National Defense Education Act have provided thousands of teachers and prospective teachers with grants, loans, and fellowships. They have also sponsored summer and year-long institutes designed to help established teachers to improve their teaching skills.

Teachers also indirectly benefit from other educational research activities of the federal government. Various research and development centers have been established throughout the country for purposes of conducting and coordinating research in specific areas such as reading. A network of regional laboratories has been funded and is designed to work closely with individual school districts in an attempt to utilize .the findings of research in the improvement of instruction.

## Trends in the Relationship of the Federal Government to Education

Although federal involvement in education has been the subject of numerous controversies, few people today are questioning the legality or merit of this involvement. Instead, the focus is upon determining the appropriate role of the federal government in relation to both state and local educational agencies.

There are some discernible trends in the relation of the federal government to education, such as the following:

1. Selected educational activities, such as research and curriculum development, may be coordinated increasingly at the federal level. Local and state education agencies generally lack the financial and personnel resources to successfully pursue these activities on the large-scale essential to the improvement of education. This is not to imply, however, that local and state personnel should be excluded from participating in these activities.
2. Because of population mobility and the interdependence of the states, there is growing awareness that equality of educational opportunity is in the national interest. Some state and local school systems are either unable or reluctant to provide a quality educational program for all youth. As a result, the federal government may assume greater responsibility in this area.
3. There may be a consolidation of the many different federal agencies, in addition to the U.S. Office of Education, that administer federal education programs.
4. An even greater utilization of education as an instrumentality to attack some of the social problems of the country is likely to occur, especially in the large urban complexes.
5. Undoubtedly there will be increased federal spending for education due to the limited ability of local and state governments to adequately finance education. As early as 1971, the U.S. Commissioner of Education was advocating that the federal government should be paying 25 per cent of the cost of public education instead of the 6.9 per cent that was being provided [152:143].

## Federal Government and Education at the International Level

Since the welfare of our nation is affected by the welfare of all other nations, and since international education is inextricably related to international relations and the social and economic growth of other countries, the people of the United States must be concerned with the education of people throughout the world. Congress has passed numerous bills related to the subject, including the International Education Act whose goal was to internationalize education within the United States by making American education a part of a world system of education. The goal of this International Education Act has never been realized because of inadequate funding, but the potential remains.

The United Nations adopted a resolution designating the year 1970 as the first International Education Year. UNESCO established a special unit to stimulate and coordinate action for this event. Member nations were encouraged to generate a number of programs such as: designing research studies, assessing the existing situation with respect to education throughout the world, eliminating all forms of discrimination, fostering equality of educational opportunity, and studying ways to increase the financial support for educational development.

Previous efforts in the realm of international education have included studying educational policies and practices in other nations, providing financial and technical assistance to aid in the development of educational systems in emerging nations, exchanging students and teachers, sharing various instructional materials and procedures with other nations, arranging cultural exchange programs, and providing educational tours to other countries. These and other international education programs will undoubtedly broaden and deepen mutual understanding and appreciation among the various peoples participating and will eventually affect teaching and learning in schools throughout the United States.

## State-Federal Compact for Education

In 1964 Dr. James B. Conant, president emeritus of Harvard University, expressed a need for a new kind of intermediate unit between the fifty states and the federal government, a so-called "compact for education," designed to improve education throughout the United States [52:109–123]. The Compact for education became a reality through the leadership of North Carolina's former Governor Terry Sanford, who believed that state governors should be the leaders in implementing Conant's idea, and through financial assistance from the Carnegie Corporation and the Danforth Foundation. By 1970, more than forty states had voluntarily elected to join the Compact. Purposes of the Compact are [48:3]:

1. To establish and maintain close cooperation and understanding among executive, legislative, professional, educational, and lay leadership on a nationwide basis at the state and local levels
2. To provide a forum for the discussion, development, crystallization and recommendation of public policy alternatives in the field of education
3. To provide a clearing house of information on matters relating to educational problems and how they are being met in different places throughout the nation, so that the executive and legislative branches of state government and of local communities may have ready access to the experience and record of the entire country, and so that both groups in the field of education may have additional avenues for the sharing of experience and the interchange of ideas in the formation of public policy in education
4. To facilitate the improvement of state and local educational systems so that all of them will be able to meet adequate and desirable goals in a society which requires continuous qualitative and quantitative advance in educational opportunities, methods and facilities

The Compact has been further described as a partnership between educational leadership and political leadership for the advancement of education, which is intended to present a coordinated nationwide voice of the states in dialogue with the federal government.

The governing body of the Compact organization is the Educational Commission of the States. Membership consists of seven representatives from each state: the governor, two legislators (one from each house), and four others from all levels of education. In addition, there are ten nonvoting commissioners who represent national education organizations.

The Compact has been interpreted by some authorities as a counterthrust action of the states to the growing federal involvement in education. The quick response of state governments to the Compact idea tends to support this notion. Many states apparently viewed the Compact as a means of slowing or halting the gravitation of educational control from a state base to a federal base.

The Compact has experienced some difficulty in determining its mission. Initially the group decided to study problems of mutual statewide interest, such as educational finance, vocational education, and community colleges. The emphasis was later shifted away from conducting studies toward providing a forum for the discussion of federal-state relations in education. Has the Compact realized the potential envisioned for it by Conant and Sanford? This question is a current subject of debate.

## The Role of the State Government in Education

The state constitution, which is an expression of the people, directs the state government to provide a system of public education. The state legislature enacts laws relating to education and delegates the responsibility for their execution to a state department of education. State courts are frequently called upon to interpret these laws and rule upon their constitutionality.

## State Department of Education

Each state has a state department of education or state education agency consisting of a chief state school officer and a professional staff. The functions and activities of the state department are broad and varied. Attempts are made to provide comprehensive plans for a total state program of education and to coordinate all educational efforts within the state for the purpose of promoting unity and encouraging proper balance in education. The department suggests educational measures for the consideration of the state legislature and executes those laws which have been enacted. It distributes state moneys for the support of local school units, usually on the basis of student attendance in the same schools. The state department also establishes certain minimum standards and regulations relating to such matters as certification of teachers, building construction, health and safety factors, and programs of instruction. The department frequently prepares and issues courses of study, syllabi, and other instructional materials, which usually take the form of suggestions rather than prescriptions.

The functions of the state department of education may be divided into four broad categories: regulation, leadership, service, and operation. Regulatory functions are designed to insure that local school systems are adhering to the laws and policies established by the state and that at least the minimum prescribed educational opportunities are available in every community. Leadership functions include long-range planning, conducting research, promoting public relations, and serving as a change agent. In performing a leadership function, efforts are made to inform the public of the educational needs and the progress which is being made toward the fulfillment of these needs. Furthermore, the public is encouraged to participate in the formulation of educational policy. Service activities include consulting with local school systems, disseminating research findings, and preparing curriculum guides. Some state departments are also directly responsible for operating certain schools, such as area vocational schools and schools for the blind.

It is widely recognized that strong steps must be taken to strengthen state departments of education. These departments have historically failed to provide strong leadership. Most efforts have been concentrated on the regulatory functions to the neglect of leadership and service responsibilities. There are, however, notable exceptions to this pattern.

The weakness of many state departments may be attributed to several factors, the most important of which is a lack of money. Some state departments are too closely tied to politics, and many have failed to employ creative solutions to the educational problems of their state. The combination of these factors has often made it difficult to attract and hold top-quality personnel. Several states, however, have taken positive steps to remove or alleviate these conditions.

Title V of the 1965 Elementary and Secondary Education Act was designed to enhance the effectiveness of state departments of education. There is some evidence to suggest that this act has influenced vast changes in state departments. Staff sizes and operating budgets have been increased, new programs have been developed, and existing programs strengthened. Nevertheless, performing regulatory functions still dominates the efforts of many state departments of education. Federal funds have also made the states more dependent upon the federal government. In a rapidly changing society marked by massive social upheaval, problems involved in providing adequate finance, equality of educational opportunity, and relevant curricula cannot all be resolved in Washington. Thus, there is an urgent need for a strong educational partnership between federal, state, and local levels of government. This partnership will maximize its success potential if all partners are healthy and strong.

## State Board of Education

The chief function of the state board of education is to interpret educational needs, practices, and trends to the people of the state and to develop the policies of education which the citizens seem to desire. These policies are usually administered by executive officers and other professional staff members. Thus, the function of the state board of education, and the relationship between this board and the chief state school officer, are similar to those of the local school board and the local superintendent of schools. The state board serves as a policymaking body, while the state superintendent serves as the board's executive officer, administering the policies established by the state board.

State boards of education vary in many ways. In four states (Florida, Idaho, Montana, and New York), the state board of education has general supervision of institutions of higher education as well as of the public schools. In size, state boards range from three to twenty-three members, with forty-four of the state boards having a membership ranging from five to fifteen. The usual term of office is six years, although the range is from two years to life. In eight states, state board members are elected by popular vote, and there are some indications that the number of states electing board members in this way may increase. In the other states, the board members usually are appointed by the governor of the state. In many states, educators are excluded from serving as members of state boards of education. In other states, a specified percentage of the members must be practicing educators.

## Chief State School Officer

The chief state school officer in the various states is known by different titles, such as superintendent, commissioner, or director. There is a definite trend toward having the state board of education appoint the chief state school officer rather than having him appointed by the governor or elected by the people. This trend has also resulted in more attractive salaries and higher qualifications for the position. The officer's term is typically four years, though in a few states it is indefinite as long as the work of the officer is acceptable to the board.

The chief state school officer, as the executive officer of the state board of education, is responsible for general supervision of the public schools. Theoretically, this person administers the board's policies, but in reality, many of the state board's policies will be based upon recommendations proposed by the chief state school officer.

In essence, the chief state school officer is the state educational leader, and, therefore, represents the most important educational position in the state. In addition to making recommendations to the state board, he also interprets the state's educational needs to the legislature, to the governor, and to the people. As a result, the position should be filled by the most competent educator available. As the position is removed from partisan politics and salaries become more attractive, the recruitment and retention of qualified chief state school officers will be enhanced.

## Teachers and State Government

The activities of the state government in general and the state department of education in particular may have a great impact upon the work of a teacher. Regulations and laws concerning teacher tenure, certification standards, teacher retirement plans, minimum salaries, teacher-school board negotiations, emergency and sick leave policies, to name just a few, all emanate from the state. Thus, teachers have a tremendous stake in the activities of the state government. For example, there are now elderly retired teachers in some states who receive less than $100 per month in retirement benefits. This amount would hardly pay the rent, much less provide for other necessities. It is in the interest of teachers to make their desires known concerning state educational matters, especially those which relate to teacher welfare. Teachers cannot solely rely upon state officials to protect their interests.

The curriculum is another phase of education which may bring the state and the classroom teacher close together. State departments frequently employ subject-area specialists who may be called upon to consult with teachers to help design experimental programs or to develop new approaches to the teaching of a particular subject. The results of experimental approaches may then be disseminated to other teachers throughout the state. In-service education programs sponsored and conducted by the state can enable teachers to learn of new developments in their subject areas.

Teachers and teacher organizations are becoming more aware that they can and should participate responsibly in guiding the educational activities of a state. Teachers belonging to state or local teacher organizations are more frequently becoming involved in the preparation of proposed legislation and in working to get legislation favorable to education passed at the state level.

## Intermediate School Administrative Unit

An intermediate school district is an area comprising the territory of two or more basic administrative units and having a board or officer, or both, responsible for performing stipulated services for the basic administrative units or for supervising their fiscal, administrative, or educational functions. Historically, the unit has served as an intermediary between the local school district or unit and the state educational agency.

When states were first organized in the United States, the county was established as a local unit of government and was regarded as an appropriate area for the general promotion and supervision of public education as well as for other governmental services. Thus, the origin of the intermediate unit was on a county basis, and its primary concern was with county rural and village schools. As the villages became cities and experienced a rapid growth of population, they were eventually empowered to operate schools that were independent from the rural schools and from the intermediate district. As a result, the intermediate district offered leadership predominantly to rural schools.

Today, an intermediate school administration unit generally serves the following functions [150:97]:

(a) to aid the state central office in exercising general supervision over schools; (b) to provide an organization whereby special supplementary services can be made available on a pooled basis to local districts which, because of small population or other reasons, cannot administer them alone economically; (c) to have responsibility for special phases of the educational program, such as certain vocational training, classes for handicapped children, and so on; and (d) to provide a program of education for post-high school youth who do not attend college.

A number of intermediate units provide excellent services to basic school units, particularly in the state of California. The establishment of a supplementary educational center and service units as forms of intermediate units will undoubtedly be a national trend through encouragement of federal funding under Title III of the Elementary and Secondary Education Act of 1965. The difference between a poor and a good school could be the resulting services in special instruction in science, language, music, and the arts; counseling and guidance, health and social work; and access to resources such as art galleries, museums, and theaters.

## Relation of Teachers to Intermediate Units

The intermediate unit concept is attractive to teachers because it enables small school districts to consolidate into larger units for specific purposes. For example, only the large school districts can afford to provide services and personnel such as: (1) effective in-service programs for teachers, (2) subject-area specialists to aid teachers in curriculum development and to help teachers keep abreast of trends and developments in their subject-area, (3) specialists in educational research and development, and (4) a well-equipped instructional materials resource center staffed with professionals trained to assist teachers in the selection and development of instructional materials and teaching aids.

If small school districts were reorganized into larger districts, individual school districts could assume many of the functions now being performed by intermediate units. However, school reorganization is a slow process and is often not feasible in sparsely populated areas. Therefore, in the interim, the intermediate unit represents possibly the best approach to providing those services and programs for teachers and students which small school districts are not capable of providing.

## The Role of Local Government in Education

Historically, education in America has been mainly a matter of local concern. Although it is true that local educational governing bodies typically spend considerable time and money in administering state educational policy, much emphasis is given to what is termed "local leeway for diversity," or discretionary power in matters of establishing schools, raising money, erecting buildings, providing materials and supplies, employing professional personnel, and supervising pupil admission and attendance. They also regulate in essential detail such matters of curriculum and teaching as actually determine the kind of school experiences students will have. In most school affairs, the local community is almost completely independent. In fact, this tenacious regard for local autonomy among smaller and sparsely settled communities is one of the main hindrances to school district reorganization designed to provide better educational opportunities for the youngsters in those areas.

The local school administrative district consists of an area in which a single board or officer has the immediate responsibility for the direct administration of all schools located therein. It is a subordinate unit of the state, performing the duties of the state in the conduct and maintenance of the public schools. It is *not* a subordinate unit of the local civil government, which performs the duties related to police and fire protection, street construction and maintenance, and other services. Historically, school government has been separated from civil government for many reasons, including an attempt to divorce the school administration from highly partisan local politics often found in civil affairs and to give special attention to the unique problems involved in educational matters.

The number of school districts in the United States reached a peak of about 125,000 in 1933. Through reorganization and consolidation, the number has been reduced drastically. In 1971 there were only 17,896 school districts as compared to 40,520 in 1960–1961 [77:52]. Even this number falls far short of the recommendation by the President's Commission on National Goals that individual states pass laws making reorganization mandatory under the direction of each state department of education and that the number of local school districts be reduced to 10,000 by 1970 [200:95].

Reorganization has eliminated many of the small high schools, primarily those enrolling fewer than 100 students. This is viewed by educators as a step toward improving educational programs because it is

FIGURE 12-2. The number of school districts in the United States continues to decline as a result of reorganization laws, the consolidation of small districts, and the elimination of nonoperating school districts.

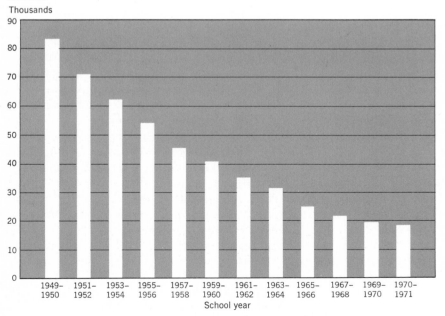

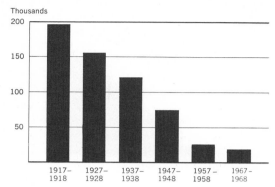

Thousands

FIGURE 12–3.   The number of one-teacher schools has decreased from 196,037 in 1917–1918 to 4,146 in 1967–1968.

difficult and expensive for small schools to offer a broad curriculum and provide the equipment, facilities, and student services essential to a good quality educational program.

Attracting and keeping teachers in small districts has been a problem in the past for several reasons: (1) rural areas often have little to offer the young, single teacher in the form of an active social life; (2) instructional programs typically have not been as innovation-oriented as have the programs in suburban areas; (3) teachers often are expected to teach four or five different subjects; (4) salaries generally are below the state average; and (5) small districts can rarely afford the specialized personnel and material resources needed to support and facilitate the work of the classroom teacher.

While emphasis is being placed upon district consolidation in rural areas, efforts are being made to decentralize the control of large-city school systems. The community control movement is being fostered by parents who feel they are losing effective contact with their schools. This trend is especially noticeable in ghetto areas where parents feel that existing large-city systems have not been responsive to the needs of their children and their community.

Most large-city districts have long practiced a form of decentralization such as placing district superintendents throughout the city in an effort to maintain contact with the people. But the community-control concept differs from the decentralization concept, according to Rhody McCoy, controversial unit administrator of New York City's Ocean Hill-Brownsville Demonstration Project (an experiment in community control). McCoy believes that the central school system still should retain strong control under most decentralization plans. Therefore, he favors the establishment of local community school boards with the power to control budgets, curriculum, personnel, and school construction. Given these broad powers, McCoy feels that community control can then be realized [47:13].

## Local Professional Staff

In districts of adequate size (preferably 2,000 pupils or more) there are typically four kinds of professional personnel: These are first, top-level managers (superintendents) who, along with the policy-making board, are responsible and accountable for the direction of the organization's affairs; second, supervisors (principals and/or department heads) who direct and evaluate the work of teachers; third, the frontline workers, or teachers, who provide direct instructional service to the pupil population; and finally, a central staff of specialists who provide the highly technical services (reading, audio-visual, special education, etc.) as requested by teachers and/or supervisors. A fifth level of personnel might be added—that of nonprofessional personnel, such as typists, book-keepers, cooks, and custodians. The first, second, and fourth types of personnel designated above ideally have supportive roles to play relative to facilitating the work of teachers.

    The superintendent serves as the chief executive officer of the board of education and is responsible for administering all phases of the educational program. His duties include long-range program planning, evaluation, budget preparation, personnel selection, building operation and maintenance, and public relations.

    The principal is the chief administrative officer and instructional leader of a building or attendance unit in a school system. He works closely with the superintendent of schools in securing staff, materials, and facilities for a building program and is responsible for the day-by-day operation of a school unit. Areas of major concern to the competent principal are developing individual pupil programs, allocating work and assigning responsibility to professional and nonprofessional staff, managing differences of opinion regarding educational issues, planning and conducting in-service activities, and developing educational programs. There is a trend to employ competent instructional leaders as principals and to give them authority concerning the improvement of instruction. Since effective teachers are demanding competent building leadership, this trend is likely to continue.

## Local School Board

Each district or unit has its own board of education, which is responsible for policy making and supervision of the schools. Members are also referred to as trustees, directors, or committeemen. Most board memebers are elected by popular vote in nonpartisan elections; others are appointed by local officials. They usually serve without salary.

    School boards are responsible for levying taxes, maintaining buildings, contracting for the construction of school buildings, purchasing

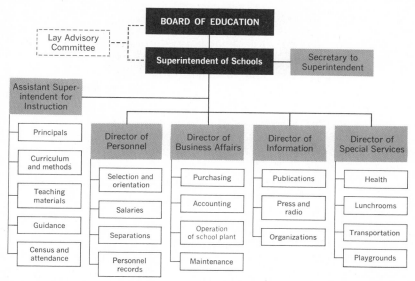

FIGURE 12–4. Organization of the superintendency in a middle-sized school system. A position assigned to a director in this figure might be filled in a smaller system on a part-time basis by a classroom teacher or principal, who is relieved of other duties for part of each day. In a larger system such a position might be assigned to an assistant superintendent.

supplies and equipment, employing the local administrative head of the school, approving salary schedules, and establishing policies in regard to the employment of school personnel and the content of the curriculum. In fulfilling their responsibilities, boards of education comply with the regulations established by the legislature and the educational agencies of the state in which the district is located. Each state generally sets the minimum standards which all local school districts are required to meet.

It is not the function of the board of education to administer the schools. The board selects a competent administrator who, as superintendent, serves as chief executive officer of the board and is responsible for administering policies formulated by the board. A board has the power to make and to enforce reasonable policies, rules, and regulations. Board action, in order to be valid, must be taken in an official meeting of the board, which is usually a public meeting. Board members have no official authority in school matters as individuals, since the laws vest power to act in the board as a body.

Theoretically school boards make policy, and superintendents administer policy. In reality, the development of policy is frequently based upon the recommendations of the superintendent and other school personnel. Teachers and teacher groups are beginning to play a more active role in policy formulation, especially in those cases where policy has a direct bearing upon the welfare and working conditions of teachers.

## Relation of Teachers to the Local District

Because schools in the United States are decentralized and subject to strong local control, the teacher has a much closer working relation with this level than with either the state or federal levels. The teacher and the local school system are in a superior position to have a mutual impact upon each other.

In a very real sense, local teacher organizations are becoming an increasingly important part of the local school structure. These organizations have long been in existence, but until recent years, their efforts were largely directed toward providing social activities for their members. Their attention has now turned to educational matters, especially those relating to the welfare and working conditions of teachers. These organizations are accomplishing collectively what individual teachers were unable to achieve. The efforts of local teacher groups to attain higher salaries and improved working conditions for their members are well-publicized. Less noted, but equally important, are the steps which these organizations have taken to improve the total instructional program. The New York City teachers organization, for example, has been successful in gaining support for the *More Effective Schools* program, which attempts to provide an improved educational opportunity for inner-city youth. Inadequate provisions for instructional materials centers, kindergartens, and teacher aides have also been the subject of teacher-school board negotiations. Consequently, the teacher, both individually and collectively, is becoming a more integral part of the local school system. Teachers are beginning to say: "Look, we are full-fledged members of this system; therefore, we want a voice in its operation." The evidence suggests that administrators and board members are listening.

## ORGANIZATION AND ADMINISTRATION OF SCHOOL LEVELS

Local school districts in the United States have traditionally been organized in one of four basic grade patterns: 6–3–3, 6–2–4, 6–6, or 8–4. For example, a 6–3–3 district organization has an instructional pattern of six elementary grades, three junior high school grades, and three high school grades.

The four basic grade patterns have been altered in recent years to reflect the growing popularity of the nursery school, kindergarten, middle school, junior college, and/or community college. Those elementary schools which have added a nursery school and/or kindergarten have gone to an N–6 or K–6 grade organization plan. Where school districts have adopted the middle school concept, a switch has been made to a 5–3–4 or 4–4–4 grade pattern. The result is four or five elementary grades, followed by three or four middle school grades, and then four high school grades. Where junior or community colleges are considered part of a regular school district, another school level including grades 13 and 14 has been added to traditional grade patterns.

A study conducted by the Educational Research Service found that approximately two-thirds of the school districts examined were organized on a 6–3–3 plan; about one-fifth are equally divided between the 6–2–4 and 8–4 plans; and nearly one-twentieth use a 5–3–4 plan. Following these in order of popularity are the 6–6 and 7–5 plans [106:2].

FIGURE 12–5.   The structure of education in the United States.

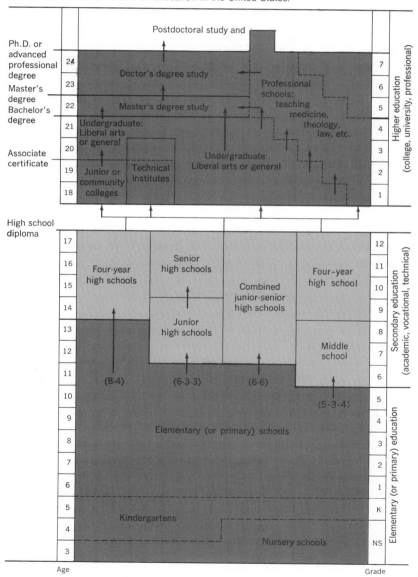

It is apparent that no single plan of organization has received unanimous acceptance in the United States. Local conditions still largely determine the organization of schools. Certain advantages and disadvantages are claimed for the many different plans. Factors which tend to influence the organization of a particular school or school system include the following: established practices, available buildings, financial support, educational leadership, equipment, and transportation.

The issue of the ideal grade pattern is further clouded by innovative approaches to the utilization of school staffs and nongraded schools. As a result, the dividing lines between existing school levels may be modified. Robert H. Anderson believes that the various school levels will eventually overlap, with each existing school level providing some of the educational and social opportunities now present in the school level both preceding and following it [12:24–25]. If Anderson is correct, then grade and school levels may eventually disappear entirely in favor of a totally nongraded school structure.

## Nursery School and Kindergarten

Enrollments in these segments of the total educational program have gradually increased throughout the years, with a particularly sharp increase beginning in the mid-sixties. According to a study published in 1969 by the U.S. Office of Education, approximately 8 per cent of the three-year-olds, 23 per cent of the four-year-olds, and 66 per cent of the five-year-olds sampled were enrolled in either kindergarten or prekindergarten programs [199:7]. In 1970–1971 over 56 per cent of the public school systems had kindergartens [77:53].

Unlike elementary and secondary education, all states do not provide financial support for nursery school and kindergarten programs. However, the fact that nearly two-thirds of the states now provide some support for these programs attests to the growing recognition that they should be an integral part of the total educational program.

The attempt to attract inner-city youth to a formal education program at an earlier age has met with a large measure of success. Among inner-city youth, 9 per cent of the three-year-olds, 28 per cent of the four-year-olds and 71 per cent of the five-year-olds were enrolled in nursery school or kindergarten [199:4–5]. Statistics also show that for the first time, nearly as many eligible nonwhite children are enrolled in nursery schools or kindergartens as are eligible white children (31.9 per cent nonwhite and 33.2 per cent white). This is a significant increase over 1965 when 27.9 per cent white and 23.3 per cent nonwhite children were enrolled [199:2].

A type of kindergarten which merits consideration is the Montessori system. It is utilized more frequently in private kindergartens than in public ones, but has received considerable attention and parental enthu-

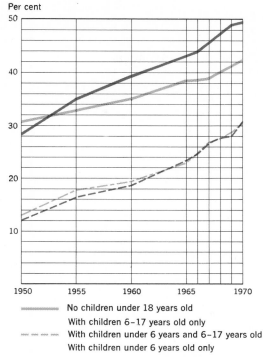

Per cent

No children under 18 years old
With children 6-17 years old only
With children under 6 years and 6-17 years old
With children under 6 years old only

FIGURE 12–6. Married women in the labor force and living with husbands. Between 1950 and 1970 the percentage of women with no children under 18 years of age increased only a third, but the percentage with children under 18 years of age more than doubled. If this trend continues, what are the educational implications?

siasm because of its promise of quick and early learning. The system was developed in the early 1900s by Marie Montessori, an Italian physician, primarily to help slum children learn to follow directions, to keep themselves and their surroundings clean and in order, to recognize the shapes and sounds of letters. Emphasis is placed upon the child mastering a task for which there is only one correct way of performing—even if it involves hand washing, desk scrubbing, or shoe polishing. "Children prepare to learn to read by learning the alphabet through a combination of tactual, auditory, and visual experiences. They spend hours fingering sandpaper letters, looking at them, and saying the letter names and sounds. Some become familiar with the letters, and some learn to put the letters together" [25:36]. But, as Beyer points out, many children have no need for this step and are bored by these preliminary exercises. Furthermore, children who are not ready to read find this type of experience meaningless and monotonous drudgery. Little opportunity is given for social interaction and for dramatic play as a release of tensions and as a means of learning through identification and creative role playing.

Dreyer and Rigler, in investigating the cognitive performance of

Montessori and other nursery school children, found that the two groups did not differ with respect to traditional achievement scores but did differ on the time they took to accomplish the task. The Montessori children were more highly task-oriented than other nursery school children. They speculated that the difference between the two groups would have been more easily discernible if economically disadvantaged rather than homogeneous middle-class children had been involved in the research [64:415].

Now that nursery school and kindergarten programs are gaining wide acceptance, what is the next logical step? How far down can and should the formal education program be extended? Some educators have proposed starting while the child is still in the crib stage, while others have contended that formal education should begin during the prenatal care period. Do these proposals sound unreasonable? Perhaps not when one considers, for instance, that the effect of nutrition in the fetal and infant stages upon future mental abilities has now been carefully documented. As knowledge concerning the development of children increases, there is a growing realization that even nursery school may be too late [123:42–45].

## Elementary School

This segment of the educational pattern is important both in terms of the total number of students who attend elementary schools (over 27 million in 1970) and in terms of its task of laying the foundation for further education [151:67].

The six-year elementary school is still the prevailing pattern in the United States. However, this pattern is being slightly modified in some school districts through the addition of nursery schools and/or kindergartens, and through the transfer of grades five and/or six to middle schools.

The majority of elementary schools have retained the self-contained, one-teacher-per-classroom-type organization. There is a trend, especially in the upper elementary grades, to break from this tradition. A growing number of elementary schools have adopted a semi-departmentalized structure, while others are utilizing team teaching and time-block programs.

More attention is being focused upon the elementary school. As new knowledge is discovered concerning child growth and development, educators are becoming more conscious of the tremendous task which is thrust upon the elementary phase of education.

The elementary school has a major responsibility for helping youngsters get a good start in their lifelong pursuit of education. In fulfilling this responsibility, the elementary school attempts to establish a foundation for future intellectual development by concentrating its efforts on the basic skills. But this school level also strives to foster the development of attitudes, interests, individual creativity, and realistic self-concepts. Therefore, in addition to intellectual development, the elementary school is also concerned with the social, emotional, and physical development of children.

Many problems which develop later in a child's life frequently may be traced to the elementary school years or earlier. For example, a large number of students still drop out of school prior to high school graduation. Factors contributing to early termination of education include poor reading ability, general lack of academic success in school, poor attitude toward school, and unrealistic self-concepts. These factors don't suddenly appear when students reach age 16. Instead, they develop over a span of time. This should not be construed as a criticism of the elementary schools. It merely emphasizes the important role which the elementary school plays in the total development of young people.

## Grouping of Elementary School Pupils

Increased interest is being expressed in the desirability of assigning children to work in groups upon the basis of ability. A number of reports have called attention to the fact that our brightest youngsters may not be challenged according to their abilities and that, as a result of this waste of human talent, our nation's defense and future are being weakened.

Diverse grouping plans have been suggested, initiated, discarded, revised, and in some cases used again. Some of the plans are described as follows:

*Chronological age grouping.* Children of a specific age are placed in a grade group and one teacher works with them. For example, six-year-old children are placed in a first-grade group and seven-year-old children in a second-grade group.

*Heterogeneous grouping.* Children in a grade group are taught by one teacher irrespective of their intelligence and achievement.

*Homogeneous grouping.* This is known as "ability grouping." Determinants of classroom placement include intelligence, readiness, and achievement test data.

*Winnetka plan grouping.* This is a form of heterogeneous grouping, but provision is made for use of self-instructional materials. Individual goal cards encourage optimum academic growth by each child.

Other grouping plans have been termed XYZ grouping, Dalton plan grouping, platoon grouping, organismic age grouping, intraclassroom grouping, interclassroom grouping, opportunity room, self-realization room, and ungraded primary or intermediate [241:1–11].

The merits of grouping have been debated throughout the history of education and the practice has been the subject of numerous research studies. The results of these studies have been mixed; thus, a dichotomy of opinion still exists with regard to the advantages and disadvantages of any practice. There is, however, a growing recognition that even though pupils are grouped according to a specific criteria, such as ability, a wide range of individual differences still exists within the group. Grouping reduces the range of pupil differences but fails to eliminate entirely those differences.

Many elementary schools have demonstrated an interest in the ungraded or nongraded concept. This concept, which may be interpreted as a form of ability grouping, is designed to permit pupils to progress at their own individual rate. Thus, pupils move vertically according to their own readiness. The terms ungraded or nongraded refer to the absence of grade levels, such as grade 1, 2, etc., and do not imply that letter or numerical grades are omitted.

In the ungraded school, boys and girls are assigned to primary, intermediate, junior high school, or senior high school program blocks. Pupils spend two, three, or four years working within each program block. The pupil who is able to progress rapidly in all areas of the curriculum and whose physical and social maturity indicates readiness for advanced work is placed in the next school block. Thus, he may finish a primary block in a two-year period instead of a normal three-year period and then be placed in an intermediate block. Conversely, a pupil who progresses slowly may spend four years instead of a normal three years in a block. The pupil under these conditions is not faced with failure in his first-grade work and retention in the same grade the following year. Rather, he remains in the primary block during his second year in school, and his academic work is a continuation from the point to which he progressed the previous year. In the mean time, he has social and academic experiences with children of his age group.

The most frequently mentioned reasons for having nongraded groups are [191:167]: "(a) Learning should be continuous; (b) children grow and learn at different rates and each should have the opportunity to achieve at his own rate; (c) school programs should be flexible so as to meet varying developmental needs and growth patterns of individual children; and (d) greater achievement will result when children experience success in school."

The multiunit school plan, an outgrowth of the federally funded Wisconsin Research and Development Center for Cognitive Learning, is an organizational pattern that attempts to replace the conventional classroom with nongraded "instructional and research units." Each unit contains from 100 to 150 children within four age groups, such as 4–6, 6–9, 8–11, 10–12. A master teacher, two or three staff teachers, a teaching intern, and one or more teacher aides usually are assigned to each unit. The master teacher of each unit and the principal of the school are members of an "instructional improvement committee" that is responsible for articulating and improving the work of the units within the school. The plan seems to be gaining favor throughout the nation and may constitute a significant change in the organizational pattern of elementary schools.

## Secondary School Organization

What constitutes the secondary phase of education? It is difficult to respond to this question because the term defies precise definition. Secondary education follows elementary school and precedes college. It is designed to build upon the foundation established in the elementary school. For some students, it serves to prepare them for further education; for others, it is a terminal institution.

Historically, this phase of education has included both the high school and junior high school. But with the introduction of the middle school concept, this tradition has taken on a new meaning. Most educators favor including the middle school in the secondary education category. Other changes in secondary education also make it difficult to define. More innovative practices have been introduced into the secondary school during the past ten years than occurred during the previous fifty years.

## Middle School

This new concept in the school organizational pattern is beginning to challenge the traditional junior high school. The middle school usually serves the age group of 10 to 14 and includes grades five or six through eight. In 1971 it was estimated that there were over 2,000 middle schools [160:133] existing in the United States, which represented approximately twice the number found through a survey conducted by Alexander in 1967–1968 [8:355]. Part of the increased interest in the middle school may be attributed to noneducational reasons, such as building expediency, attempts to correct racial imbalance, or economy moves. Many have, however, grown out of a desire to find an alternative to the junior high school.

Proponents of the middle school cite a number of reasons in support of this concept: (1) Evidence suggests that children are maturing earlier; the sixth grader today is more physically, emotionally, socially, and intellectually like the seventh grader of past years.(2) There will be less of a tendency to copy the high school academic, athletic, and social pattern. The result will be a shift from a subject-centered curriculum to a child-centered approach, based on the unique and changing needs of this age group. (3) The change will facilitate the introduction of new programs, therefore providing optimum individualization of instruction. (4) When the middle school becomes established as a distinct unit, separate from both the elementary and secondary school, teachers may then be trained specifically for the purpose of teaching in this school unit.

Those opposing the middle school contend that: (1) Mixing fifth and/or sixth graders with older students will only enhance the trend toward earlier sophistication. (2) Adding a grade or two to the junior high school and changing its name will not necessarily result in an improved educational program. (3) The plan may result in a downward extension of the departmentalized structure. (4) Adoption of the middle school plan merely results in change for the sake of change and is tantamount to bandwagon-hopping.

Alexander reports [160:133] that middle schools are acquiring certain common characteristics, which include flexible scheduling, team teaching, individualized instructional systems, and a home base and teacher for each student for purposes of counseling and guidance. He feels that the middle schools are now becoming distinctive in character rather than being just warmed-over junior high schools.

Will the middle school eventually replace the traditional junior high school? The answer is dependent upon the ability of this innovation to provide a superior educational program for pre- and early adolescent youth. Thus, in the final analysis, results based upon careful evaluation and research will determine the ultimate success of the middle school.

## Junior High School

The junior high segment of the school program is closely related to both the elementary and high school, but it also has purposes which are separate and distinct from these two units. The junior high school has evolved as an institution to meet the unique physical, social, emotional, and intellectual needs of the pre- and early adolescent. Where separate junior high schools have been established, the most popular form of organization has been the 6–3–3 plan. Therefore, the majority of junior high schools contain grades 7, 8, and 9.

The junior high school has been charged with the responsibility of performing a number of functions including the following:

1. Continue and extend the general education program started in the elementary school.
2. Provide opportunities for students to explore, discover, and pursue personal interests.
3. Further develop basic learning skills such as those associated with critical thinking and reasoning.
4. Facilitate continuous progress and smooth articulation between the elementary and high school.
5. Introduce new subjects.
6. Provide opportunities for students to integrate the knowledge and experiences they have gained from multiple sources.
7. Facilitate greater depth and specialization within basic subject areas.
8. Provide opportunities which assist and guide the physical, emotional, and social development of students.

Numerous other functions could be added to the list and probably will be as the role of the junior high school is continually evaluated. Societal changes and new knowledge about the nature of the youth which the junior high school serves may also dictate other changes in this segment of the educational program.

The interests of junior high youth may be changing. Students in this age group are demonstrating an increased awareness of, and assuming active participation in, social problems such as water and air pollution and social justice. This may be viewed as a good sign. However, the increased desire of these youth to experiment with harmful drugs is a very disturbing sign. These trends present unique challenges for the junior high school. If this school unit is to meet these challenges and provide an educational opportunity which is relevant, then the total junior high program must be subjected to continual evaluation.

## Senior High School

One of the unique aspects of the American public education system is the comprehensive high school which provides educational opportunities for all the youth in a community, regardless of their economic status, sex, family background, education, and vocational ambitions. About 80 per cent of the high schools in the United States are reported by their principals to be comprehensive high schools [120:40]. The United States stands alone among the nations of the world in making a high school education available to virtually all youth. Many educators from other countries, including England, annually visit the United States to study the American comprehensive high school with the hope of making adaptations of it in their countries.

Environmental studies provide relevant and vital curriculum content for students of all ages. (*Photograph by Joe Di Dio, National Education Association.*)

At a hearing before the Subcommittee of the Committee on Appropriations in the House of Representatives during the Eighty-sixth Congress, Dr. Lawrence G. Derthick, who was then U.S. Commissioner of Education, presented a dramatic contrast to the comprehensive high school in the following manner [221:11]:

What would it be like to have the traditional European system? At approximately age 11, your child would take a series of national achievement tests, and his performance on these tests would largely determine his future track or specialized secondary school, if any. His whole future might well depend on these tests. Think of your own experience back in the fifth grade of elementary school. What marks were on your report card? Would you have been placed in the classical high school for collegebound professionals or would you have been placed in another school where your education might have ended at the age of 14? Would you have been happy to have somebody else determine what your future would be by deciding what type of education you should have after the age of 11 or 12?

Let us ask, too, why have the rigid class barriers of many Western European nations been maintained? Why have most class barriers in this country been removed?

More than 50 years ago American parents decided that they would not give any person the right to close any doors to the future for their 11-year-old children. They made this decision with a full knowledge of the system of education used in Europe —and of the social consequences of this system.

The comprehensive high school is designed to meet the needs of all youth in attendance. It strives to prepare some students for future education while serving as a terminal institution for others. While offerings most frequently include general education, college preparatory, and vocational curricula, students normally have the option to pursue the curricula of their choice and are not requried to take entrance or qualifying exams as is the case in some countries. The programs are usually flexible enough to meet the changing needs of students and the desires of parents. Thus, students starting in one curriculum may switch to another.

State departments of public instruction and the local school districts establish standards and requirements for the subjects to be taught, the number of years they are to be studied, the number of years of required pupil attendance, the minimum graduation requirements, and the requirement of textbooks and other instructional materials. Ordinarily, states have statutes or regulations mandating instruction which represent approximately 50 per cent of the requirements for high school graduation. The local school districts have discretionary powers concerning the remaining 50 per cent of the requirements. Teachers are increasingly becoming involved in reviewing standards and requirements that apply to the school in which they teach and in recommending changes that should be made.

The diversified offerings and the flexibility of the comprehensive high school in meeting the changing needs of pupils account in part for the increased enrollments and holding power of the schools. The American high schools enroll over 93 per cent of the boys and girls who are 14 to 17 years of age [253:108], whereas in 1890 the number of pupils attending high schools was only 7 per cent of the 14 to 17 age group. More than 78 of every 100 youths of this age group are now graduating from high school [211:28]; approximately 40 per cent of these graduates are entering college on a full-time basis; and an additional 9 per cent enter college on a part-time basis.

An example of the increased holding power of the American elementary and secondary school is indicated by the fact that of 1,000 fifth graders enrolled in school in 1932, only 455, or 45.5 per cent, were graduated from high school in 1940; whereas, of the 1,000 fifth graders enrolled in 1962, 752, or 75.2 per cent, were graduated from high school in 1970 [253:125].

The data concerning the improved holding power of schools is encouraging, but the drop-out problem has not been solved. A high percentage of dropouts list lack of success in studies or lack of interest in school as their reason for terminating their education prior to graduation from high school. In essence, these students may be saying that the high school curriculum is not meaningful and relevant for them. This has some important implications for the educational program. The bulk of the curriculum development efforts in recent years have been directed toward college preparatory programs. Only recently has considerable interest been shown in improving curricula for those students who elect not to attend college.

The drop-out problem is especially critical in the large inner-city areas. In some cases this condition is due to a reluctance to break from traditional curriculum programs, while in other cases it may be a failure

FIGURE 12-7. Survival rates of groups of 1,000 pupils entering the fifth grade in 1932 and in 1962—a 30-year period. What factors have contributed to the fact that the drop-out rate has continued to decrease?

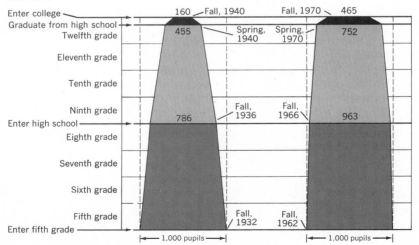

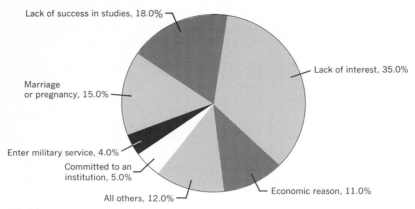

FIGURE 12–8.   Reasons given by pupils in one state for dropping out of high school.

to commit resources to provide quality education, or the absence of curricula built on inner-city community needs, or a lack of involvement of the community in the education of their children, or a combination of these and other factors. Difficult as it may be, it is a national problem which demands our immediate attention.

## Trends in Secondary Education

Several trends in secondary education are in evidence as attempts are made to meet the needs of increasingly greater numbers of young people. These trends may be summarized in the following manner:

1. Approaches which depart from the traditional organization of the school day, such as flexible or modular scheduling, are being used as it becomes apparent that not all courses require the same length of class period.
2. Instructional methods which emphasize problem-solving and the development of the ability to inquire independently into a subject are being favored over the "telling" type lecture approach.
3. A wide variety of instructional media, such as television, programmed learning materials, and computer-assisted instruction, are being utilized.
4. The traditional classroom setting is giving way to plans which emphasize large and small group instruction and independent study.
5. Curriculum programs aimed at the below average student are now being developed by national organizations as they were for the above average student in recent years.
6. Remedial classes in English and arithmetic for pupils who are deficient in the basic skills of reading, writing, and computation are being provided.
7. Teachers are being assisted by specialists in materials preparation, community resources, and diagnostic evaluations.
8. Principals and/or directors of instruction are playing a more active role in the improvement of instruction.
9. Increasing attention is being devoted to program results.
10. Instructional objectives are increasingly being stated in terms of the performance or behavior expected of students.

11. Students are beginning to assume a more important role in the development of school policies and regulations which have a direct bearing upon them.
12. The concern over dress and grooming codes is diminishing, and more attention is being directed toward the development of an educational program which is relevant and meaningful for young people.

The new content, media, and learning theory are aimed at individualizing instruction at the secondary level. It is through flexible scheduling, as explained in Chapter 5, that a principal and his staff can probably best arrange a program whereby an individual pupil is able to assume a greater degree of responsibility for his own learning.

The building principal is the key person in the secondary school to effect changes and has the prime responsibility of working with the faculty in improving the instructional program. His development of an organization and his style of administration are important variables in the determination of professional opportunities for teachers.

## Summer School Programs

During the past few years more school districts have been providing summer sessions. They have been doing so largely because they have a new concept of the scope of the summer program and they wish to use school facilities more extensively. The emphasis in summer school is shifting from helping only the slow student to that of providing the opportunity for all students to attend summer school for enrichment purposes, for acceleration, or for the early completion of their secondary school work. In many schools, advanced or highly talented students may take more advanced courses in such areas as mathematics and science that cannot be offered economically during the regular school year. The length of the summer school programs at both the elementary and secondary levels ranges from four to ten weeks. The usual length of the school day is four hours.

There is considerable variation in the manner in which summer schools are financed. State aid is available for summer schools in fourteen states [144:31]. Very frequently tuition is charged those who wish to attend. Funds from the Economic Opportunity Act may be used for summer schools, especially for courses for migrant workers and dropouts and for courses in vocational, technical, and adult basic education.

There is also growing interest in extended school year programs. Enrollments and construction costs are rising, and the general public is becoming less willing to vote in favor of tax increases for school support. Therefore, the three-month summer vacation is increasingly being viewed as a waste except in those school districts which have a large summer enrollment. Only a few districts have moved to the 12-month school plan, the most notable being the 45–15 plan being used at Romeoville, Illinois, as described in Chapter 5, and the four-quarters plan being used in the Atlanta, Georgia school system. In the Atlanta plan, which began in 1968–1969, a student may elect to attend any three of the four quarters, or he may attend the full year [133:61].

## Associations of Secondary Schools and Colleges

Many of the secondary schools throughout the United States belong to associations of secondary schools and colleges. These are quasi-legal, voluntary associations. There are six such regional associations. The states included in each of the respective associations are indicated in Figure 12–9.

The primary purposes of these associations include the improvement of instruction at each level, closer articulation between levels, and the accrediting of schools. The New England and the Western associations are exceptions in that they do not accredit schools. The North Central association has been the most conspicuous of the group in size, activity, and influence. The Southern association has engaged in noteworthy experimentation and exploration in education.

Accreditation by a regional association means that the school concerned meets, in general, the pattern of standards set by the association. In that case, pupils in accredited schools are assured of more adequate educational opportunities; they have easier access to other institutions at the same or at a higher level. Both pupils and institutions gain some

FIGURE 12–9. Regional areas of the association of colleges and secondary schools in the United States. To which association do your college and your secondary school belong?

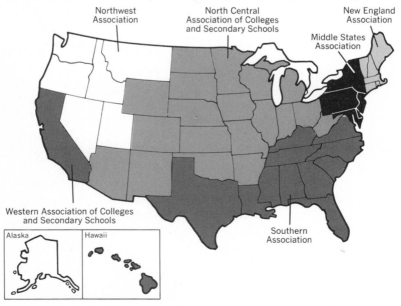

measure of prestige. Very careful surveys of local educational situations are made by the regional associations, and significant improvements are often effected as a result of their work.

## Specialized Schools

Besides those divisions which are ordinarily considered in our present educational system, there are many other schools, the majority of which are privately supported. Religion-affiliated schools will be discussed in the next chapter. In addition to these, there are schools organized as military academies, boarding schools, college preparatory schools, finishing schools, and the like. A great number of specialized schools are almost purely vocational in character, such as the large technical schools, the very specialized High School of Fashion Industries, the Juilliard and Eastman Schools of Music, and various schools of nursing, commerce, business, electronics, or flying. Such schools as the Bronx High School of Science in New York and the Boston Latin School cater to students with special abilities and may even require rigid entrance examinations. Other kinds of specialized schools include those for the handicapped in sight, hearing, or muscular coordination. Many of these schools are state-supported. Special schools also are available for the mentally retarded and the emotionally disturbed. For any prospective teacher who has interest in teaching in any of these types of schools, the opportunities are great.

## Higher Education

Higher education includes those educational programs which require for admission approximately 12 years of previous schooling or the equivalent. There are approximately 2,500 higher education institutions in the country, which represents an increase of 500 since 1960 [151:67]. The majority of these institutions are financed by private sources, but more than 40 per cent are now supported by public funds. Approximately 70 per cent of the enrollees in colleges and universities are studying in publicly supported institutions, as indicated in Figure 12–10, and it is anticipated that this figure will reach 85 per cent by 1985 [281:1].

A considerable amount of progress has been made in increasing the number of private and public black colleges granting the four-year degree, as well as in improving the quality of instruction within these colleges. The United Negro College Fund and the Office for the Advancement of Public Negro Colleges have contributed much in recent years to improve the faculties, study programs, and research programs in black colleges. Quality programs are to be found in such black colleges as Bethune-Cookman College, Daytona Beach, Florida; Moorhouse College and Spelman College, Atlanta, Georgia; Fisk University, Nashville, Tennessee; Southern University, Baton Rouge, Louisiana; Hampton Institute, Hampton, Virginia; Bennett College, Greensboro, North Carolina; and North Carolina Central University, Durham, North Carolina.

Junior and/or community colleges represent the fastest growing segment of higher education. It is estimated that 1,000 junior colleges existed in 1970 with an enrollment of nearly 2 million students. The majority of these junior and/or community colleges are publicly supported. These colleges normally offer higher education at a nominal cost to students within commuting distance. Most offer a program of general education and courses that prepare students for occupations requiring less preparation than a four-year degree program.

## Adult Education

For many years, some public schools and institutions of higher learning have felt a responsibility for meeting some of the educational needs of adults. For example, in 1883 a law was passed in Massachusetts compel-

FIGURE 12–10.   Past and projected enrollments in public and private institutions of higher education. In 1951 slightly less than half of all students attending colleges and universities were in publicly supported institutions. In 1969, three-fourths of the students were attending publicly assisted institutions. If this trend continues, more than 85 per cent of all higher education students in 1985 may be attending publicly assisted institutions.

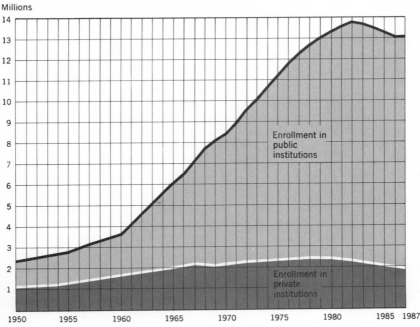

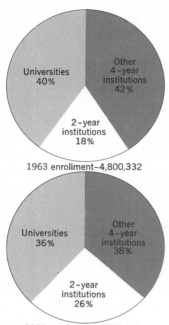

1963 enrollment–4,800,332

1969 enrollment–7,978,408

FIGURE 12–11.   Comparison between Fall, 1963, and Fall, 1969 of enrollments in higher education and the percentage distribution of enrollments according to institutions. An increasingly higher percentage of students are enrolled in two-year institutions.

ling cities of over 10,000 population to establish public elementary evening classes [167:1–2]. As a result of the low educational level of enlisted men, as revealed in World War I, the federal government and a number of state legislatures enacted various laws and grants of aid to meet vocational education needs of adults. During the depression of the 1930s, adult education programs were dropped by many school districts in order to conserve resources. Since World War II, adult education has become an increasingly greater responsibility of the public schools.

New York and California are two states that are relatively advanced in providing state aid, supervision, and control for adult education programs. An idea of the scope of their programs may be gained by studying the following list of fields included in their programs [167:12]:

Agriculture
Americanization
Arts and crafts
Business and distributive
Civic and public affairs
Elementary
Engineering and technology
General academic

Health and physical education
Homemaking
Industrial and trade
Miscellaneous
Music
Parent and family life
Remedial
Safety and driver education

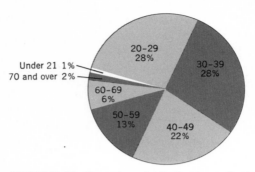

FIGURE 12–12.   Percentage distribution, according to age, of participants in adult education. How should society attempt to meet the imperative need for more adult education?

It has been estimated that approximately 25 million American adults participate in some form of learning activity, and that over 17 million adults are enrolled in courses on a part-time basis [135:1]. The participants are divided almost equally between men and women. Typically, they are under 40 years of age, are married and are parents, enjoy above-average incomes, and live in an urban area [75:2]. The programs attract larger numbers from professional, managerial, and skilled occupations than from laborers, operatives, service workers, and persons engaged in agriculture.

An adult education administrator has greater difficulty in developing educational programs than do elementary and secondary school principals, since adult programs are based upon the diverse needs of people within a community. Furthermore, the programs may be held in churches or synagogues, business buildings, factories, and community buildings, in addition to the public school buildings. Regardless of where the programs are held, the public school's program should provide consultative services to nonschool institutions so that these programs may be a part of a coordinated adult program in a community. It would seem that the adult education administrator should have a parallel position with those responsible for elementary and secondary school programs and should report directly to the superintendent of schools. As a result, the total educational activities within a community would be coordinated by the superintendent as the executive officer of a board of education.

The Adult Education Act of 1966 provides for a program of basic education for adults so they may increase their employability. The program is implemented by local public schools, according to a state plan. Through this program, adults have the opportunity to gain an eighth-grade level of reading and comprehension. Approximately 455,700 individuals were enrolled in this program during fiscal year 1968 [2:1].

Continuing education programs for adults are growing in popularity.

Several factors have contributed to the growth of these programs. Reduced work-weeks, earlier retirements, and increased life expectancy have all created additional leisure time. The expansion of knowledge and vast technological developments have made it an economic necessity for persons in selected occupations to upgrade their skills and knowledge. The sheer desire of the general public to become involved in stimulating educational acitvities has also led to further development of adult education programs. Finally, the improvement and expansion of adult education programs themselves have served to attract an increased number of the adult population.

## SUMMARY

As teachers become more involved in the decision-making aspects of schools, their stake in the organization and administration of these schools increases. A basic understanding of the organization and administration of schools serves to provide: (1) the foundation for responsible involvement in the decision-making process, and (2) a springboard for improvement. The patterns of school organization have been many and varied, depending upon the needs of different communities. With the passing decades, conditions have changed so markedly that these elements of organization have undergone considerable change.

Sincere efforts are being made to improve the organization of our schools. Very impressive strides are being made to consolidate certain districts in order to provide better school facilities, better teachers, and better education programs. School programs are being reorganized to provide greater continuity and educational effectiveness.

Traditionally and constitutionally, education in the United States is a state responsibility. Each state delegates such responsibilities to its local communities and encourages them to use a large measure of initiative, support, and control. However, in order to bring about greater equality of educational opportunity and to spread knowledge, understanding, and fellowship abroad in the world, the federal government and even international organizations have assumed increasingly greater roles of leadership.

Attention has been given to the various organizational levels of education. Present practices, trends, and recommendations for improvements have been noted. Throughout the chapter it is evident that the organization and administration of our schools are changing. The future will undoubtedly see more changes being made as educators and others work together to provide the best setting possible for the education of future generations. Teachers have an opportunity to provide leadership in this great endeavor.

## QUESTIONS TO CONSIDER

1. How are the work and professional relationships of the teacher affected by each of the two conceptions of school organization and administration indicated in this chapter?
2. What advantages and disadvantages do you see in having local communities responsible for providing educational facilities for their children?
3. What role does the board of education play in your home community? What are the occupational backgrounds of the board members? How representative are they of the entire community? What qualifications should a school board member have?
4. Many countries have ministries of education that exercise great control over the educational systems in their respective countries. What advantages and disadvantages do you see in having the U.S. Office of Education exert a greater role of leadership?
5. What are the advantages of having a state superintendent of schools appointed by a state board of education rather than having him elected by popular vote? What are the disadvantages?
6. How do you account for the tremendous decrease in the number of school districts in the United States? Why has there been so much resistance to reorganization of school districts?
7. What advantages and disadvantages do you see in the self-contained classroom in the elementary school?
8. What advantages and disadvantages do you see in the nongraded type of organization? How does this type of organization change the teacher's work?
9. What advantages and disadvantages do you see in flexible scheduling for secondary school pupils? How will this type of scheduling change the design of school buildings?
10. What behavior patterns are characteristic of junior high and middle school pupils? What special provisions should be made in the school's program for such pupils?
11. Does the middle school provide a viable alternative to the junior high school, or is it a mere fad?
12. What do you consider to be the unique characteristics of the comprehensive high school?
13. How can the holding power of the secondary school be further increased?
14. What advantages do you see in regional associations of secondary schools and colleges? Do the regional associations encroach upon the legal rights of local school districts?
15. What effects has the Elementary and Secondary Education Act of 1965 had upon elementary and secondary schools?
16. Define the term "community control." What are the advantages and disadvantages of community control as you define it?

## PROBLEM SITUATION FOR INQUIRY

For nine years Mr. Turk had served as Student Government Sponsor at West Junior High School. During this time he had spent hundreds of extra-duty hours in its development.

In the last five years the Student Government had matured into an active, responsible organization which had been invaluable in the development of school policies related to student activities. The staff of West Junior High, the school administration, and the central district office personnel had come to respect and appreciate the growing tradition and helpfulness of the organization.

The Student Government, with the advice of Mr. Turk, had developed an excellent planning and approval procedure for student activities. When major activities were planned, the appropriate committee prepared an outline of essential information, including the date, and submitted it to the school principal for his initial approval. Upon receiving this approval, the committee developed the complete proposal with all necessary information, and returned it to the principal for his final approval. The proposal was then sent to the Assistant Superintendent for Student and Community Services who, upon approval, placed it on the master calendar for student functions.

Mr. Turk was holding a final meeting with the Social Committee for the annual All-School Party to make certain that everything was in order. As the meeting neared adjournment, Mr. Gott, the new principal at West, made a rare appearance with the following announcement: "All students attending the All-School Party on Friday evening will be expected to dress as follows: girls, formal or semi-formal dresses with hose; boys, suits or dress jackets with ties. Anyone not properly attired will be refused admission."

The All-School Party was one of the major activities of the year at West. Since approval had been gained two months in advance, and had specified informal dress, the announcement fell like a bomb. Mr. Turk and the committee members knew full well that most students had purchased new, informal outfits especially for the party. To further complicate matters, it was now ten minutes until dismissal time on Thursday, and the party was scheduled for Friday evening.

Mr. Turk turned and faced the Social Committee members with shocked surprise evident in his expression. He wondered what he could say. Almost oblivious to their sponsor, the committee members sat in mute thoughtfulness.

If you were in Mr. Turk's position, what would you do? Why?

## ACTIVITIES TO PURSUE

1. Investigate and share with your colleagues specific details relating to the organization and support of the high school from which you were graduated.
2. Investigate how school board members in your home community are selected. Discuss with two or three of the members, if possible, what they consider to be their responsibilities and duties. Compare their views with those of the superintendent of schools.
3. Invite a school superintendent to discuss with your class the administrative organizational problems of his schools.
4. Discuss with various school officials methods they use in grouping pupils. What are the advantages and disadvantages of each method?
5. How does your community provide for the education of youngsters who are deaf or blind or paralyzed to some extent? How does it provide for those who are extremely slow to learn or those who are unusually gifted? Describe the specialized school situations available for such persons.
6. Select a large-city school system and study the drop-out rates. At what grade levels do most students drop out of school? Do more boys drop out of school than girls? Why? What are the drop-out rates for white and nonwhite students? How can the holding power of the secondary school be increased?
7. Prepare a display of publications issued by the U.S. Office of Education and share the display with your colleagues.
8. Attend a meeting or talk with an official of a citizen's community action group in a large city which favors breaking the big-city school structure into several smaller independent school units.
9. Identify a school district which has recently shifted from an organizational plan which included junior high schools to one which includes middle schools. Talk with the principal of a middle school concerning the rationale behind the change.
10. Examine a selected school system and attempt to determine the provisions which are made for teacher-involvement in the decision-making process.

# 13 | FINANCING OUR SCHOOLS

Education is big business as evidenced by the approximately $70 billion devoted to the support of both public and private elementary, secondary, and college education programs in the United States during the 1970–1971 school year. The size of local school budgets is further illustrated by the fact that the local school system represents the largest single employer in many communities.

Securing adequate finances for the operation of quality educational programs in this multi-billion dollar enterprise is increasingly becoming an acute problem. While financial support for public schools has increased annually in recent years, inflation has consumed a major portion of the additional money. The taxpaying public, burdened by heavy property taxes, is beginning to react unfavorably to requests for additional education funds and is demanding verifiable proof that teachers are securing results. Consequently, a record number of requests for school bonds and additional taxes to support education were defeated at the polls in the late 1960s and early 1970s. Concomitantly, a growing segment of the general public has demonstrated a sincere interest in accountability, the relationship between money spent for education (input) and results (output).

In the past, many teachers have demonstrated a lack of interest in school money matters, preferring that superintendents and school business managers handle these affairs. Is this stance justifiable in view of the problems which schools face in securing adequate funds? The answer to this question depends upon how one views the role of the teacher. To what extent do teachers have a responsibility for being well informed about matters concerning school finance? Are they in turn responsible for keeping others, such as parents and other members of the community, abreast of school finance problems and their possible solutions? If a school district takes a bond issue or request for tax increase to the voters, should teachers remain neutral or should they actively seek support for

FUNCTION

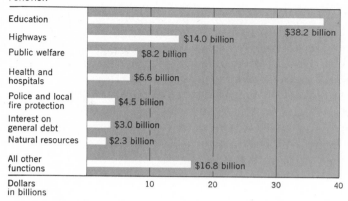

FIGURE 13–1. Direct general expenditures of state and local governments in 1966–1967 according to functions. Normally more than 40 cents out of every dollar spent by state and local governments goes for education.

passage of these measures? Should teachers participate individually and collectively through their teacher associations in activities designed to influence legislation which would provide additional funds for education? Answers to these and other similar questions should be of vital concern to a teacher. Obviously, improvements in salaries, facilities, equipment, instructional materials, and other factors affecting the welfare of teachers and pupils are dependent upon increased funds. In view of the taxpayer revolts that have already occurred in some communities, it is likely that administrators and school boards will need the help of all available resources if adequate financial support for schools is to be

FIGURE 13–2. Past and projected total expenditures by regular elementary and secondary day schools in the United States.

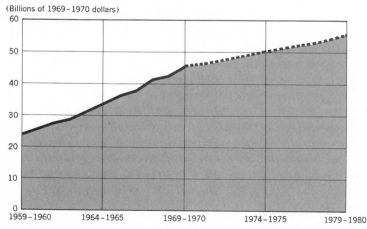

(Billions of 1969–1970 dollars)

secured. Administrators need more than sympathetic understanding; they need teachers who are committed to the goals of education and who are willing to work for the attainment of those goals.

In an effort to help prospective teachers gain greater insight into the broad area of school finance, this chapter will examine the bases of some of the current school finance problems and discuss the modes of providing local, state, and federal financial support for public elementary and secondary schools.

## BASES OF CURRENT SCHOOL FINANCE PROBLEMS

The states' responsibility for maintaining and operating the American public school systems necessarily includes the obligation of each state to make provisions for financing its school system. Generally, the states have relied chiefly upon local financial support for public schools. At the turn of the twentieth century only 17 per cent of school funds were provided by the states. Since the economic depression in the 1930s, however, the amount of state funds to aid local school district support has increased significantly. For the 1970–1971 school year, 41.1 per cent of the total school revenue in the United States was derived from state sources, 52.0 per cent from local sources, and 6.9 per cent from federal sources [77:53]. The share from federal receipts was fairly constant through 1964–1965, but by 1966–1967 it had nearly doubled because of several new and expanded federal programs.

The development of the public schools during the twentieth century has not been the same in all states, partly because each state has had different goals at different times. Other reasons for the variations in the development of public school programs among states include differences in tax systems, economic conditions, centralization of local school districts, political beliefs, fear of change, and willingness to provide funds for education [18:93–94].

As our nation has moved through the industrial revolution and into a scientific revolution, the educational system in each state has had to

FIGURE 13–3. Comparison of the cost of education with other expenditures in 1970. How much can we afford to pay for education?

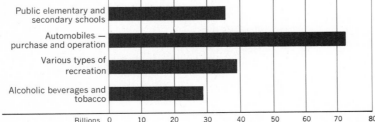
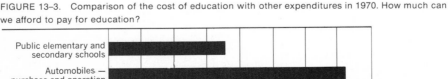

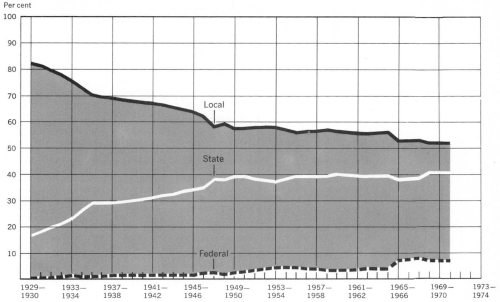

FIGURE 13-4. Trends in school support represented by the percentage of revenue for education derived from federal, state, and local sources.

undergo varying adaptations to the changing economic and social conditions in order to best serve the educational needs of individuals and of society. Basic and intermediate school administrative units have not always been able to cope adequately with financial problems, partially because of constitutional and organizational limitations. Constitutional limitations have included debt limits and tax limits as well as provision for earmarked taxes. Although earmarked taxes have assured districts of a definite source of income, educational services have been generally limited because local educational revenues have been tied to a yield from a tax whose rate has been difficult to increase. Small administrative units have often lacked an adequate tax base and sufficient pupil population to provide a quality educational program.

In addition to the above factors, school finance problems are the result of six major forces: (1) record increases in school enrollment, (2) demand for greater quality in education, (3) rise in educational costs due to inflation, (4) extension of educational services, (5) backlog of school construction, and (6) priority claims on federal funds. Each of these forces will be discussed in the following paragraphs.

## School Enrollment Increases

The extent of increase in public school enrollments is indicated by the fact that in the decade of 1960 to 1970, there were over 11 million additional students in public elementary and secondary schools, repre-

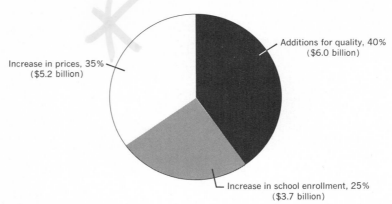

FIGURE 13–5. Factors that have accounted for an increase of $14.9 billion in school expenditures between 1958 and 1969.

senting a 30 per cent increase for the decade [76:37]. This enrollment rise was basically due to two factors: (1) the school-age population had increased, and (2) students were remaining in school for longer periods of time. In 1969 the average adult had completed 12.1 years of education, compared with only 10.5 years in 1960 [76:39]. Population statistics, however, indicate that the annual rate of growth in elementary and secondary school populations during the 1970s may not continue to increase so rapidly. It is estimated that during the period between 1968 and 1978, public secondary school enrollment will increase 11 per cent, while public elementary school enrollments will decline five per cent; thus, the enrollments in 1975 will approximate those of 1970 [246:2].

Institutions of higher education, however, face large enrollment increases in the period between 1970 and 1982. The college student population was 4.8 million in 1965, and it had increased to 7.4 million students by 1970–1971 [151:67]. This growth pattern is expected to continue, and it is estimated that over 11 million students will be enrolled in institutions of higher education by 1979 [247:9].

## Quality of Education

Our system of government, our economy, our position of world leadership, and our exploration of space have combined to bring education into national focus with emphasis upon the goal of quality education. Educational research is greatly concerned with the problem of relating the cost of education and educational quality. One of the most ambitious research projects of this type has been the Quality Measurement Project of the New York State Education Department, in which 70,000 youngsters participated in a mass testing program over a three-year period as they moved from grade to grade. In this project it has been found that there is evidence of a positive relationship between the level of school expenditure and both the achievement test scores of pupils and the holding power of the school. However, the low correlation indicates that good quality of education is not assured by high expenditures alone. The relative effectiveness of schools may vary according to pupil IQ, socioeconomic-level classification, subject-matter classification, or sex. Few schools are universally good or bad but are mosaics of specific strengths and weaknesses [293:87].

Another comprehensive research project, conducted by Professor Kreitlow of Wisconsin, concerned the effects of school district organization upon the quality of education. This longitudinal study was involved with a study of youngsters who were in the first grade in five newly reorganized school districts and in five matched control communities. The effects of reorganization in terms of educational opportunities, achievement, cost, and social impact were measured at first, sixth, ninth, and twelfth grades, and follow-ups were made for a five-year period after pupils had graduated from high school. Results of the study indicated that both boys and girls in reorganized districts were ahead in twenty-one of twenty-two measures of achievement. In the ninth grade, boys of reorganized districts were ahead in eight of eleven measures, and girls were ahead in all eleven. Conclusions drawn from the study are as follows: (1) Boys and girls in reorganized districts had greater educational opportunities; (2) reorganized districts produced higher academic achievement as shown by standardized achievement tests; and (3) instruction in reorganized districts cost $12 more per elementary pupil per year [140:47–48].

Rajpol [209:57–59] made a study of the relation between various measures of educational quality and expenditures in 459 public high school districts of Iowa, in which the influence of the school district size was held constant. Upon the basis of his study, he concluded that the "higher expenditure per pupil usually results in higher educational quality. More money invested generally means higher return" [209:59]. He also found that the expenditure per pupil in small school districts has to be substantially higher than in districts with larger enrollments in order to achieve the same quality measures of education, and that larger administrative units can be associated with increases in quality measures, reduced expenditure levels, or both.

A number of curriculum revisions have been taking place in numerous school districts. Our affluent society has been taking stock of its values, and quality education is emerging as a vital want and need. Herein lies the basic reason for the mounting interest in national assessment, accountability, and the voucher system. As is true of almost everything else in life, quality products and programs cost more money. However, taxpayers have sometimes been reluctant to pay for the quality which they desire in their schools. This has been especially true in those communities where the local property tax has become exceptionally high.

Potential sources of additional money for the support of education exist at both the federal and state level. However, if the level of support for education is to be increased, at least three things must occur: (1) priorities must be realigned to a point whereby the amount of support which education receives is more congruent with the value placed upon education by the American public, (2) the method of supporting education must be revised in a manner which reduces (or possibly eliminates) the burden on the local property tax, and (3) educators and school boards must vividly demonstrate to the general public that wise and efficient use is being made of moneys now provided.

## Inflation

Money available for the support of education has been increasing, but the inflationary spiral of the past few years has absorbed the bulk of the increased funds. For example, the average cost of educating a student in the public elementary and secondary schools was $776 in 1970–1971. This represented an increase of $103, or 15 per cent over the 1969–1970 school year. It has been estimated that nearly 60 per cent of the additional money made available for the support of education since 1957 has been consumed by inflation [55:10–15]. Thus, if inflation continues, vast amounts of new money will be required for education simply to maintain the status quo.

## Extension of Educational Services

In the previous chapter, attention was given to the tendency to extend formal education both upward and downward. Publicly supported programs are rapidly being developed for three-, four-, and five-year-old youngsters, and higher education is being made available to a larger segment of the population. In addition, the public schools have instituted several new programs and services and expanded others, such as guidance services, adult education, special education, vocational education, and "compensatory" education. These programs and services have largely resulted from three major developments, which are both national and international in scope—the urgency of scientific progress in order that the United States can compete satisfactorily with other socioeconomic systems, the changing educational requirements for employment, and the nation's commitment to a war against poverty and pollution. Frequently the demands for these additional educational programs and services have been made without providing the necessary means to finance them.

## School Construction

Comparatively few new school buildings were erected during the years from 1930 through 1950 because of the national depression and war emergencies. By 1950 a backlog of needed construction, plus needed remodeling, faced many school communities. The problem was intensified by the postwar inflation which materially increased the cost of construction. The fact that 44 per cent of the nation's classrooms available in 1961 were built during the 1950–1960 decade is evidence of the school construction boom of the 1950s. It is anticipated that an average of 70,000 classrooms will be built annually during the next few years to replace abandoned classrooms and to accommodate additional enrollments [247:97]. This will mean an outlay of approximately $5.2 billion annually, depending upon construction costs.

The mounting cost of construction has caused some school districts to delay their building programs; thus, there were fewer schools and additions built in 1970 than at any time during the previous fifteen years. In the period between 1960 and 1970, the cost of building a new school rose more than 40 per cent [54:15].

The systems approach to school construction, such as that used in the School Construction Systems Development project, may tend to lessen delays, due to increasing costs, in building construction. This approach to building employs the efficiency of modern industrial mass production

FIGURE 13–6. Public elementary and secondary classrooms constructed between 1942–1943 and 1969–1970. What demands for the construction of classrooms will be made in the future?

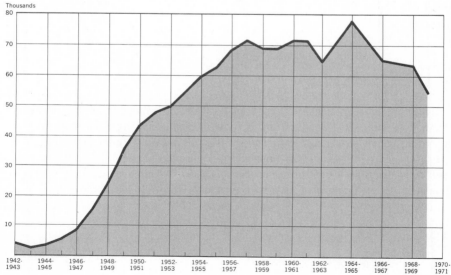

with respect to selected components of the school facility. Preliminary results indicate that where this approach has been used, school facilities have been constructed in less time and at lower cost than in districts utilizing conventional building programs [23:9–10].

## Priority Claims on Federal Funds

Federal financial support for public schools reached a peak of approximately 8 per cent of total expenditures for education in the late 1960s. However, by 1970, the federal contribution had been reduced to approximately 6 per cent. Spending for defense programs has had top priority on the federal dollar; as a result, expenditures for nondefense programs such as education have been deferred. Many educators believe that if substantial increases in funds for education are to become a reality, they will have to come from the federal government. Local and state governments, they reason, are simply not in a position to provide money in sufficient quantities to maintain and improve existing educational programs. However, even if defense spending were to be sharply curtailed, there is no guarantee that education would receive sizable increases in federal contributions. Other groups and programs, such as poverty and pollution, will no doubt attempt to lay claim to any surplus federal funds. Thus, if education is to receive a portion of these funds, it is up to educators to clearly demonstrate their needs.

## THE SCHOOL BUDGET

In order to cope intelligently with financial problems created by forces such as those cited above, local school districts prepare long-term and annual school budgets. Effective school administrators and boards of education are planning educational programs and anticipating revenue needs for 10 to 20 years in the future. Long-term projections of pupil enrollments are made on the basis of each annual school census; long-term financing is exemplified by cumulative building levies which provide funds so that educational facilities can be partially paid for on an installment plan in advance of the actual construction of the facilities. For various reasons, such as population shifts and changes in birthrates, long-range budget plans must be considered highly tentative.

## The Annual Budget

The annual budget presented in a teacher's school district each spring should be of interest to him since it reflects teacher salary increases and other rewards for his professional efforts. A teacher may have an opportunity to work with a committee of teachers, administrators, and school board members on salary problems.

The annual budget, generally prepared for a fiscal year of July 1 to June 30, is a financial plan for attaining the objectives of the educational program. The three aspects of budget making are the educational plan, the spending plan, and the revenue plan.

The educational plan, consisting of service, materials, and activities, is determined principally by the school administration, the teaching and nonteaching staff, and the school board members. The plan prescribes the educational program that is to be provided for the pupils in the district. Lay citizen groups often participate in expressing and accumulating opinion concerning the educational program. Factors to be considered include pupil population, teacher-pupil ratio, curriculum, the program scope (i.e., kindergarten through junior college), state department directives, parental aspirations, the impact of technological changes upon teaching methods, and teacher quality.

In the spending plan, expenditures are determined by translating the accepted educational plan into costs. Expenditures are ordinarily classified to show the amount which will be spent for each educational function. Classifications generally include instruction; administration; fixed charges (rent and insurance); operation and maintenance of physical plant; services such as health, transportation, and school lunch; summer school; community college; capital outlay; and debt service. Typical percentages of expenditures for the various functions are shown in Figure 13–7.

Unfortunately, many school systems do not allocate an appropriate amount of their annual operating budget for research, experimentation, and innovation. It has been recommended that each school system provide not less than 1 per cent of the annual budget for teachers "to participate in curriculum planning, research, evaluation, and other activi-

FIGURE 13–7. How the current school dollar is spent.

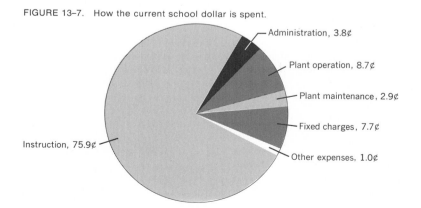

Administration, 3.8¢

Plant operation, 8.7¢

Plant maintenance, 2.9¢

Fixed charges, 7.7¢

Instruction, 75.9¢

Other expenses, 1.0¢

ties designed to improve the instructional program" [232:22]. In contrast with even this modest recommendation, approximately 3 per cent of our gross national product is spent for research and development purposes [248:120].

The revenue plan involves a listing of the sources of funds and the estimated amount of revenue to be received from each source. For example, state school authorities ordinarily let the local school administrators know how much money they can expect to receive from the state government. In addition, the local school administrator anticipates receipts from the federal government as well as from tuition fees or other charges. Local property and/or nonproperty tax rates necessary to raise the balance of funds needed are then computed and either levied by the board or put to a vote by the people in that district.

After the budget has been approved, the chief school administrator and the board defend the budget at public hearings conducted by local and state tax commissioners. Such a system of checks and balances forces the school administration to review the allocation of resources for varied phases of the educational program at least once annually. Funds are then committed for expenditure, as defined by the spending plan, for the ensuing budget year.

## Relation of Teachers to School Budgets

Compared to the teachers of a few decades ago, today's teachers are becoming more knowledgeable about budgetary affairs; and they are beginning to exert more influence with regard to certain provisions of the budget. Teachers have ideas about how the education dollar should be spent, and administrators and school boards are increasingly seeking faculty advice on these matters. Budget allocations are frequently the subject of negotiations between teacher groups and school boards. Teachers are obviously concerned about the amount of money allocated for faculty salaries; but other items, such as allocations for instructional materials and special programs, have also been the subject of negotiations.

The annual budget may reveal the extent to which a school district's actions are consistent with its beliefs. A candidate for a teaching position may want to examine a school district's budget to determine what the district really deems most important, and then, examine the written philosophy and objectives of the district to determine if the budget is in accord with the stated philosophy and objectives.

The budget of a school district may be further analyzed by comparing the budgetary allocations of the district with those of the average school district in the United States. This information is available in the

Cost of Education Index, which is published annually by *School Management* magazine.

## STATE SCHOOL FINANCE PROGRAMS

Since there are fifty state systems of education in the United States, there are fifty different systems of state school finance. The amount of state support, for example, ranges from 10 per cent in New Hampshire to 89 per cent in Hawaii. A few states, such as Hawaii, Delaware, Alaska, and North Carolina, provide most of their school funds from state tax sources. The majority of states have favored a partnership plan of state and local support, with only minor support coming from the federal government [212:49].

State funds have been used in our nation's history to (1) help communities establish the operation of a school system; (2) afford relief to those districts unable to provide sufficient local funds; (3) encourage new programs (such as special education, audio-visual communications, and transportation) and support services (such as new buildings, salaries, textbooks, and pupil transportation); (4) provide emergency aid, such as in the 1930s, by relieving the tax burden on the property holder; (5) provide payments in lieu of taxes through property lost by local districts to new state parks or to new industry which received tax exemptions for a period of years; and (6) provide general support for schools through a foundation program.

As is evident, much of the state school aid has been provided to meet financial crises and to serve as an incentive for local districts to add new educational services. Such aid has been piecemeal and has not been made within the framework of a comprehensive and systematic state school support program.

### Distribution of State Aid

State money is disbursed to local school districts according to a state distribution formula. Many states make flat grants to schools on the basis of student enrollment, number of teachers, number of classrooms, or some other criteria. Thus, each local district receives a fixed sum of money from the state for each student enrolled or teacher employed. Other states, in lieu of or in addition to flat grants, distribute money to local districts on the basis of the wealth of the district. Thus, poor districts—those less able to support schools through local tax sources —receive more state aid than do those districts which are wealthy. The relative wealth of a school district may be determined by dividing the total assessed valuation of the property in the district by the number of students enrolled in the district's schools; the result is the school district's assessed valuation per pupil.

## State Foundation Programs

More than forty states have developed what are termed "state foundation programs." Such a program designates the amount that must be made available to all administrative units in the state to support the basic instructional program considered to be essential for all youngsters in the state. Thus, state foundation programs are based on the premise that the state should guarantee all students in the state a respectable education regardless of the local district's ability to support its schools.

The steps in the development of a state foundation program include the following:

1. Definition of the educational program.
2. Translation of the educational program into costs necessary to provide the essential educational services.
3. Determination of the local district's share of cost according to measures of fiscal capacity. The tendency is for programs to require that wealthier districts pay a greater local share than districts of less wealth and, conversely, that they receive less state aid than the poorer districts. This equalization concept is typical of many foundation programs.
4. Determination of the total state share to each district.

A state foundation program normally includes expenditures for current operation, school facilities, transportation, and special education. The scope of the program in some states includes nursery school through

FIGURE 13–8. A hypothetical example of state and local cooperation in financing a foundation program of support in all school districts of a state.

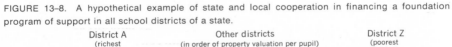
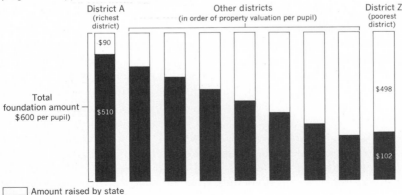

the junior college. Most of the existing programs provide funds for elementary and secondary schools enrolling grades 1 through 12.

The effectiveness of a state foundation program depends on the adequacy of a state's tax system and the extent to which the program has been periodically reviewed to ensure that the money provided is sufficient to support a quality educational program. The inability of some foundation programs to keep pace with current costs of education has been a problem in recent periods of inflation.

## State Tax Systems

Each state has its own system of taxes with different types of taxes, different items included in the tax base, and different rates of taxation. In addition, each state gives local units within its boundaries certain taxing privileges, which often differ from those enjoyed by similar local units in adjoining states.

The reason for these great differences is that our present tax system has developed a little at a time. As changes occur in our economy and in the distribution and form of sources available for taxation, the old taxes become less effective and new ones must be added to the old to provide the necessary funds for governmental activities. The history of taxation indicates that a tax, once it is imposed, is rarely repealed.

Most states rely upon sales and income taxes to finance state obligations. The general sales tax is the best single source of state tax revenue. It yields over 25 per cent of the total state tax revenue in the nation. The general sales tax plus selective sales taxes, that is, taxes on motors, fuels, alcoholic beverages, and tobacco products, constitute approximately 60 per cent of the total state tax collections.

A majority of states have an individual income tax. The advantage of the individual income and the general sales tax is that they have a broad tax base and have a capacity for producing a large amount of revenue at a relatively low rate. Both, however, are tied directly to the economy. If the economy is high, revenue from these sources is high, and vice versa.

## Local School District Taxes

Most school districts in the United States have relied heavily upon the local property tax for support. Property taxes have accounted for 98 per cent of all taxes collected from local sources by school districts. Property taxes originally developed as "ability to pay" taxes. It was assumed that the ability of an individual to pay taxes was evidenced by his wealth, which in turn was evidenced by the amount of property an individual owned. In the early days of the United States, real property constituted 75

Example of the per cent of revenue from their three sources: 52 (local)
41 **(state)**
7 (federal)

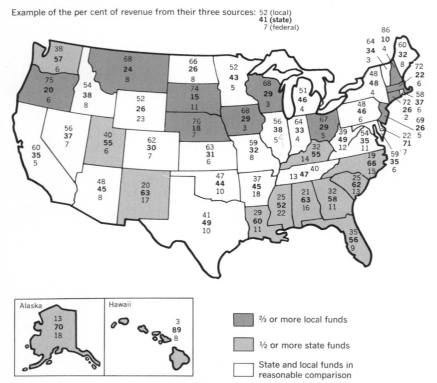

| | ⅔ or more local funds |
| | ½ or more state funds |
| | State and local funds in reasonable comparison |

FIGURE 13–9. Percentages of public school revenue in each state derived from local, state, and federal tax sources. Note the wide diversity of the sources of school revenue. What do you consider to be the most desirable distribution?

per cent of the wealth. However, it is estimated today that real property constitutes only 25 per cent of the wealth. The property tax is therefore considered by many to be a regressive tax because, in relation to wealth, it places the heaviest tax burden upon low-income families.

Since the advent of the industrial revolution in the United States and the resultant change in economic and social conditions, financial experts have been seeking new taxes to replace the property tax. This trend was accelerated particularly during the depression years of the 1930s, when many property owners were unable to pay their taxes. Many states are increasing state sales and/or income taxes in an effort to ease the local property tax burden. In the state of Illinois, for example, the Constitutional Convention voted to eliminate the personal property tax on businesses and individuals as of 1979.

Opposition to high property taxes has been demonstrated in recent years by the number of tax referendums (requests for increases in the local property tax rate) and bond issues (requests for money to construct or remodel buildings) which have been defeated by the voters. Approximately 55 per cent of the dollars requested for school construction in 1968–1969 were vetoed by the voters compared to a failure rate of only 20 per cent in 1964–1965. This display of opposition may be a voter expression of displeasure with regard to the total local, state, and federal tax load rather than specific opposition to taxes for the operation and construction of schools. School tax elections represent one of the few opportunities which voters have in most states to express directly their opinions on the matter of tax increases. It is apparent that voters are increasingly taking advantage of this opportunity by voting "no" at the ballot box [54:21].

One advantage of the property tax is that it provides residual tax support for local services. Other taxes are established at a fixed rate, such as 3 per cent, whereas the property tax rate is adjusted to each budget to provide that part of expenditures not covered by other receipts. Thus, a property tax rate might be $3.65 per $100 of assessed valuation one year and $3.95 the following year in order to provide the balance of funds needed in each case.

Local school district property tax rates are usually expressed in terms of dollars per $100 of assessed valuation, or in terms of mills per dollar of assessed valuation. If a home, for example, is assessed at a valuation of $12,000 and the local school tax rate is $6.00 per $100 of valuation, the annual school tax would equal $6.00 × 120, or a total of $720.00.

Suggestions for improving the administration of the property tax include the following: (1) Assessment districts in most states should be enlarged, and assessors should be trained to effect uniform assessments; (2) the personal property tax, which has been a negotiated tax, should be replaced, or personal property should be assessed according to a state classification of "book values"; (3) property tax exemptions should be reviewed, since such exemptions result in higher tax rates to offset the exemption or to shift tax responsibility, sometimes unfairly; (4) the law pertaining to assessments should either be applied to all taxpayers or be changed.

Two separate court cases, one in California [*Serrano v. Priest,* 5 California 34d. 584, 1971] and one in Minnesota [*Van Dusartz v. Hatfield,* Cause #3-71 Civ. 243, dated October 12, 1971], may have far-reaching implications upon the extent to which school systems depend upon local property taxes as a primary source of revenue. The courts found the entire public school financing systems in California and in Minnesota, based largely on the local property tax, to be unconstitutional because they produced inequalities in the financial ability of individual school districts. The Minnesota court, for example, said that the question was whether students have a right to have money spent on them "unaffected by variations in the taxable wealth of their school districts or their parents." The court answered by saying: "This court concludes that such a right exists." It is highly probable that a number of other states will have similar court cases in response to concern over

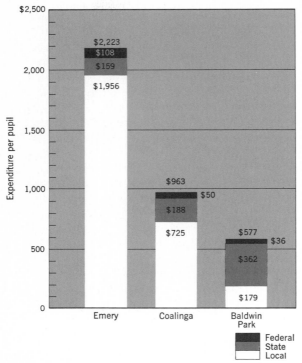

FIGURE 13–10.  Per pupil expenditures in three school systems in California in 1968–1969 showing patterns of inequality. Emery had a tax rate of $2.57 for an assessed value per average daily attendance of $100,187, as compared to a tax rate of $5.48 for an assessed value per average daily attendance of $3,706 for Baldwin Park.

highly local property taxes and the inequalities in educational opportunities that result from dependence upon local property taxes as a primary source of school revenue.

## Local Nonproperty Taxes

States may give permission for local governments to levy nonproperty taxes, such as taxes on gasoline, tobacco, alcoholic beverages, and income. However, local school districts in the United States have not generally been given the authority to levy nonproperty taxes. Administration of nonproperty taxes would not be practical in the typical small school district because of relatively high administrative costs. Local nonproperty taxes can be practically administered, however, in large urban or metropolitan areas or in a combination of small school districts.

## FEDERAL SUPPORT FOR EDUCATION

Although education in the United States may be characterized as the local operation of a state function, the federal government has maintained an interest in education and assisted in terms of financing and programming for nearly 200 years.

The statement given in Section 101 of Public Law 85–864, commonly known as the National Defense Education Act (NDEA) of 1958, represents a typical congressional expression of interest in education:

The Congress hereby finds and declares that the security of the Nation requires the fullest development of the mental resources and technical skills of its young men and women. The present emergency demands that additional and more adequate educational opportunities be made available. The defense of this Nation depends upon the mastery of modern techniques developed from complex scientific principles. It depends as well upon the discovery and development of new principles, new techniques, and new knowledge. . . .

We must increase our efforts to identify and educate more of the talent of our Nation. . . .

The Congress reaffirms the principle and declares that the States and local communities have and must retain control over and primary responsibility for public education. The national interest requires, however, that the Federal Government give assistance to education for programs which are important to our defense.

### Types of Federal Assistance for Education

Federal financial assistance to states for public education may be classified under four categories: (1) unconditional land grants, (2) conditional grants for advanced education, (3) conditional grants for secondary education, and (4) emergency grants.

Although federal assistance to education actually began in 1785 when Congress adopted an ordinance relative to the Northwest Territory, assistance to specific states began with the Ohio Enabling Act of 1802, when the federal government unconditionally granted one section or more of land to the new state for the use of schools. Money from the sale of these lands totaled approximately a half billion dollars. The federal government never officially questioned the states concerning school-land policies, and there was no federal control over expenditures.

Conditional grants of land for advanced education began under terms of the Morrill Act in 1862. Beginning with the second Morrill Act, passed in 1890, and continuing with supplemental acts, land-grant colleges or universities have received federal appropriations.

The Morrill Act and the supplemental acts, which are examples of conditional grants for advanced education, introduced the following changes in federal educational policy: (1) some control by specifying programs (land-grant institutions were to include agriculture and mechanical arts in their curriculum as well as military science and tactics); (2) annual appropriations for programs in addition to the original land grants; (3) reimbursement of the state after federal authorities were reassured that money had been spent for the purposes designated by law.

Conditional federal grants for secondary schools is illustrated by the Smith-Hughes Act of 1917, followed by supplemental acts, which provides appropriations annually for vocational education at the secondary school level. Under the Smith-Hughes Act, the federal appropriations are matched dollar for dollar by the states. The Vocational Education Act of 1963 represents the first federal act to provide comprehensive vocational education programs at the secondary school level.

A fourth type of federal support was in operation during the depression years of the 1930s when the federal government provided several hundred million dollars annually during the emergency period to aid distressed school districts. This aid also included assistance for needy secondary, college, and university students so that they might continue their education during the depression, as well as provisions for nursery schools, literacy classes, correspondence instruction on both secondary and college levels, vocational education, parent education, work for unemployed teachers, and funds for school buildings.

Public Law 874 approved contributions, beginning in 1950, toward the "maintenance and operation" of school districts which suffered a financial burden due to the provision of educational services for children whose parents are employed on federal property or to sudden substantial increases in enrollments because of federal activities. During the 1950s, also, Congress began appropriating funds under Public Law 815 for assistance in the construction of minimum school facilities for federally connected children. Minimum facilities include instructional and auxiliary rooms and initial equipment, but do not include auditoriums and gymnasiums.

Another program of federal support for education in an emergency period is exemplified by the National Defense Education Act (NDEA) of 1958, which was amended in 1963 and in 1964 and extended through 1971. Use of funds is specified by the act, and the states are required to match the federal funds. Funds have been provided for loans and fellowships to students; strengthening instruction in mathematics, science, foreign languages, civics, history, geography, and reading; guidance counseling and testing; area vocational education; research in uses of television, radio, and movies; science information service; and improving statistical service. This act touches levels of education from the elementary schools through the graduate schools, both public and private.

The NDEA represents an expression of the federal government's concern over the fact that the long struggle of the free world against communism could be won or lost in the classrooms. Particular interest was shown first in improving mathematics, science, and foreign language instruction and then extending the work to civics, history, geography, and reading. Thus, the federal government encouraged improvement in these and other educational areas by offering financial incentives to the states.

## Major Federal Education Acts

The following are brief descriptions of the major education acts passed by the U.S. Congress in the mid-1960s and the early 1970s:

Elementary and Secondary Education Act (ESEA): provided, since its inception, over $5 billion for special educational programs for children from low-income families; school library resources, textbooks, and other instructional materials; supplementary educational centers and services; strengthening state departments of education; and expanding educational research. ESEA was enacted in 1965 and has since been amended and extended. Recent amendments provide funds for drop-out prevention and bilingual education programs, and for aid to handicapped children. ESEA, for example, provided approximately $1.2 billion during the 1969–1970 school year to strengthen and improve the quality of educational programs in elementary and secondary schools. Passage of ESEA signified a major accomplishment in the drive for federal support to education, because it represented the largest single commitment by the federal government to the nation's schools.

Higher Education Facilities Act: initially enacted in 1963, this act authorizes grants and loans to public junior colleges and public technical institutes and to public and nonpublic colleges and universities.

Economic Opportunity Act of 1964 [PL 88–452]: provides, through its education sections, for setting up a Job Corps for unemployed youth, for community action programs to combat poverty, for work-experience demonstration projects, and for the setting up of Volunteers in Service to America (VISTA), modeled after the Peace Corps. Preschool and high school projects are included in the community action program.

Civil Rights Act of 1964: provides for technical assistance, grants, and training institutes to help communities prepare for school desegregation (Title IV). This act also authorizes withholding of federal funds to school districts maintaining segregated schools (Title VI).

Vocational Education Act of 1968: provides for aid to support area vocational schools, consumer and homemaking education, work-study programs, curriculum improvement in vocational education, and the Neighborhood Youth Corps. A minimum of one-third of the funds provided under this act are reserved for economically depressed communities or for areas with high rates of unemployment.

Education Professions Development Act (EPDA): serves to consolidate existing programs, such as, the Teacher Corps, NDEA summer institutes, and the Experienced Teacher Fellowship Program. The largest segment of money—$80 million—has been allocated for training and retraining teachers and teacher aides. Special emphasis is placed upon the preparation of personnel to serve both handicapped children and children from low-income families.

## The Issue of Federal Aid to Education

The question of federal aid and federal involvement in education has long been the subject of heated debate. Only a few short years ago, numerous school districts refused to accept any form of federal aid, fearing that acceptance would eventually lead to federal control. These fears have proven to be unfounded, and federal aid has become a universal reality. Thus, the issue today is not one of accepting or rejecting federal aid, but one of determining the appropriate form and function of federal financial support to the nation's schools.

The issue of categorical versus general federal aid is a current subject of debate. Categorical aid refers to support for a specific purpose, such as aid for the construction of higher education facilities or aid for the purchase of library materials. Most federal legislation in recent years has been in the form of categorical aid. General aid allows the individual states and local school districts to determine the purposes for which the federal money will be used.

The federal government has tended to favor the categorical aid approach. Since education is a state function, Congress has viewed its role as one of supporting selected segments of the educational program rather than one of supplementing the general aid provided by state and local governments. Congress attempts to identify and provide for needs which are not or cannot be met at the local or state level. This role of the federal government is characterized by congressional support of educational research and curriculum development activities. Congress has also enacted education legislation which is deemed in the best interests of the country. Thus, the National Defense Education Act (NDEA), which provided support for improvement in the teaching of science and mathematics, was passed in the interest of the defense of the United States. In addition to the above arguments, the political realities of elected office favor categorical aid because it permits congressmen running for reelection to point to specific accomplishments such as Head Start or the Higher Education Facilities Act.

Educators have been the chief proponents of general federal aid to education. They feel that this approach minimizes federal control and permits schools to adapt the use of federal funds to local needs. Educators contend that school officials on the local level are in a better position than Congress to determine local needs, and can therefore make better use of federal funds if these funds are in the form of general aid.

Another justification for general support to education by the federal government is based upon the need to equalize educational opportunity in the United States, a need evidenced by the great range in the amount spent per student and the capabilities of the fifty states to support an adequate educational program. Universal education, long a dream in the United States, has now become a reality. But the battle for equality of educational opportunity has only begun. Students who attend school in the ghetto areas of large cities, in small rural areas, and in economically depressed sectors of the country have not enjoyed the same educational opportunity as their counterparts who happen to live outside these areas. Differences in amounts spent per student in average daily attendance, however, do not necessarily indicate differences in the willingness of the states to support education. Instead, in many cases they represent differences in the resources available. Some states with low personal incomes actually spend more, in proportion to personal income, to support schools than do states having high personal incomes.

Since the areas of the country where inequality exists seem to have little immediate prospect of increasing expenditures through state and local funds, a number of educators advocate additional federal assistance to these areas. The California and Minnesota court cases mentioned previously may add support to this position. Also, it must be recognized that equal funds may not ensure equal educational opportunity. Due to

FIGURE 13–11. Estimated current expenditures for public elementary and secondary schools per pupil in average daily attendance in 1970–1971.

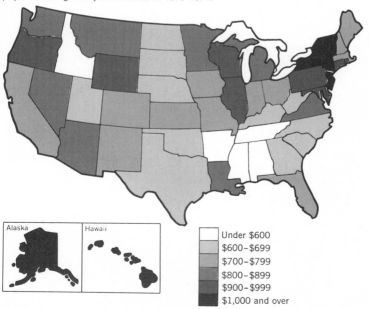

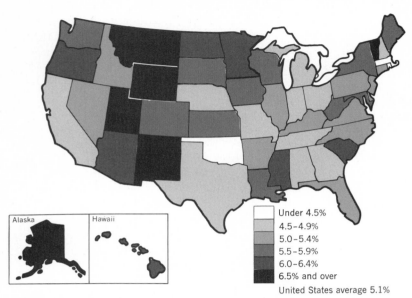

Under 4.5%
4.5–4.9%
5.0–5.4%
5.5–5.9%
6.0–6.4%
6.5% and over
United States average 5.1%

FIGURE 13–12.   Relative financial effort made to support public schools in 1969–1970 expressed as a percentage of personal income in 1969. Compare the relative efforts of each state with the amount of per-pupil expenditure in each state. What do these differences mean, and what are the implications for the future financing of public education?

past neglect and the severity of the problem, massive unequal funds may be needed if any degree of equality is to be achieved. In the world's wealthiest nation, where the importance of state and regional boundaries have been minimized by rapid transportation and a vast system of mass communication, and where population mobility has become a way of life, continued educational inequality becomes increasingly difficult to justify. The battle, however, is not likely to be easily won. Universal education became a reality only after a long struggle, and the evidence suggests that the realization of equal educational opportunity faces a similar struggle.

The issues listed below represent those aspects of federal aid to education which are most frequently the subject of debate [adapted, 46:15–16]:

### Typical Pro and Con Arguments on Federal Aid to Education

| Pro | Con |
|---|---|
| 1.  *Education is a federal problem.* | |
| Federal assistance has been an accepted part of our tradition from the Land Ordinance of 1785 through the Elementary and Secondary Education Act of 1965. | Local governments can best determine the needs of their schools, and the several states are responsible for education. Federal control would likely follow federal aid. |

|                    Pro                    |                    Con                    |

2. *Classroom shortage is critical.*

There is a continuing building shortage requiring double sessions and classes in obsolete, overcrowded, defective, and temporary facilities. Too many high schools lack funds to provide laboratories for chemistry, physics, and foreign languages and to provide adequate libraries.

State and local agencies have done much to meet the needs for new school construction. The rate of increase of enrollment is expected to taper off, so that new construction can eliminate the backlog soon.

3. *Teachers' salaries are very inadequate.*

Many teachers who leave the profession for other occupations cite their low pay as a principal reason.

The average teacher's salary has risen at a faster rate than per capita income generally. Higher salaries will not guarantee better teachers. Federal money for teachers' salaries on an emergency basis would be dangerous and difficult to discontinue.

4. *More money for public education is essential.*

The most pressing problems of public education can be traced to lack of money. State and local sources cannot keep up even with present needs.

The real problem of the schools is not more money but inadequate use of manpower and facilities.

5. *Federal taxation is best source of additional funds for education.*

The federal government already collects two-thirds of all tax moneys and can most effectively tax personal and corporate income. The federal government can put the money in areas where needs are greatest.

The federal government has only the tax resources of the fifty states, and if it takes a larger tax bite, this leaves even less for state and local governments. Most states are not as debt-ridden as the federal government and are not asking for federal aid to education.

6. *Federal control of public education is not a real danger.*

The federal government has been aiding education for almost two centuries without any real evidence of federal control.

The federal government imposes policies on state and local school authorities and can exercise indirect control by threatening to withhold funds.

7. *Federal aid facilitates racial integration.*

Money and technical assistance can be provided to help racially segregated schools develop plans which will lead to orderly progress toward integration.

The federal government fails to understand local problems. Federal involvement in this matter infringes upon the rights of the individual states.

8. *Equality of educational opportunity is dependent upon federal aid.*

The strength of the Nation may only be insured if each child has the same opportunity for a quality education. Because of

Inequalities exist in some cases because different segments of the country make a greater effort to support education than do

| Pro | Con |
|---|---|
| existing differences in the ability of various areas of the country to provide this opportunity, the federal government must assume a greater role in this endeavor. | other segments. Granted, substandard programs do exist in some areas because of inadequate funds, but the people in the wealthy sectors of the country cannot realistically be expected to subsidize less fortunate areas in addition to providing a quality educational program in their own area. |

The National Education Association seeks federal support of public education in line with the following principles [168:71–72]:

1. That federal programs comply with current civil rights statutes and judicial decisions.
2. That there be substantial general federal support of the whole of public education.
3. That present federal programs of specific aids be continued, expanded, and improved by consolidation and simplification of administration, and modified so that all federal monies for elementary and secondary education, educational goods and services either direct or indirect, shall be expended solely for the support of public schools. The federal government must be responsible for the added costs of educating youth whose presence in the local district is due to federally connected jobs or programs.
4. That further expansion of federal support to education be general in nature, and that these funds be allocated without federal control for expenditure and sub-allocation by state education agencies.
5. That the amount of aid be generally predictable for long-range planning and specifically predictable for year-to-year planning.
6. That legislation be consistent with the constitutional provision respecting an establishment of religion and with the tradition of separation of church and state with no division of federal funds, goods or services to nonpublic elementary and secondary schools.
7. That the legislation contain provision for judicial review as to its constitutionality.
8. That all federally supported educational programs, including those now assigned to other federal agencies (except those programs designed to train armed forces personnel), be administered by the U.S. Office of Education.

## PUBLIC FUNDS AND THE NONPUBLIC SCHOOLS

Nonpublic or private schools are not part of the state school systems but are under the immediate operational control of a private individual or organization. The state, under its police power (i.e., the state's power to safeguard the health, morals, and safety of its citizens), may regulate and supervise nonpublic schools for the purpose of ensuring each child an education equivalent to the education offered in public schools.

It is the established right of parents and guardians in the United States to send their children to nonpublic schools. Approximately 11 per cent of the total number of elementary and secondary students in 1970 were enrolled in nonpublic schools, a reduction of 3 per cent since 1965. The reduction is largely attributed to the closing of 1,000 Catholic elementary and secondary schools between the years 1965 and 1970, resulting in a Catholic school enrollment drop from 6 to 5 million students [38:24].

## Parochiaid—A Critical Problem

An issue since the establishment of the American public school system is whether or not public financial aid, particularly federal aid, can be provided for the support of sectarian schools—schools which account for over 90 per cent of the nonpublic education institutions. The constitutional provisions separating church and state prevent direct aid to sectarian schools. However, the main point of the issue is whether or not indirect public financial aid can be provided.

Proponents of general federal aid to sectarian elementary and secondary schools argue that public funds are used to finance fire, police, and other governmental services to people of all religious sects and that aid to sectarian schools is analogous. Opponents of general federal aid to sectarian schools are fearful that such assistance would lead to the eventual destruction of the public school system.

Provision is included in the new federal educational acts for participation of children and teachers from private nonprofit schools. A U.S. Office of Education *Manual for Project Applicants* under Title III of the Elementary and Secondary Education Act includes the following [189:18].

All project proposals should include provisions for children enrolled in nonprofit schools in the geographical area to be served whose educational needs are of the type which the project proposes to meet, so that they may benefit from innovative and exemplary programs through participation, observation, visitation or dissemination of information. . . . It is clear that the benefits must be extended to individuals, the ultimate beneficiaries, and not to the institution concerned.

The Elementary and Secondary Education Act clearly provides that all personnel employed in any capacity in an approved project must be employed as public employees, and the title to all equipment must be retained by a public local educational agency.

Participation of children and teachers under the Elementary and Secondary Education Act and other federal legislation is justified under the child- or individual-benefit theory. Without this justification and allowance for participation, it is likely that such important educational legislation would not have been approved by Congress because of opposition by powerful lobbies.

Starting with the Cochran case in 1930, the Supreme Court of the United States approved the provision of textbooks to students attending private schools. This type of assistance was considered to be constitutional on the theory that it was aid to students and not to the religious institutions they attended [*Cochran v. Louisiana State Board of Educa-*

*tion,* 50 S. Ct. 335 (1930)]. A 1947 court case extended the student benefit theory to the transportation of students [*Everson v. Board of Education,* 67 S. Ct. 504 (1947)]. A 1968 case reaffirmed the earlier decision relative to the provision of textbooks to private school students [*Board of Education v. Allen,* 88 S. Ct. 1923 (1968)].

As financial problems have become severe, states have also looked for ways to provide financial help to parochial and private schools. Rhode Island implemented a plan by which the state would pay a portion of the salaries of nonpublic school teachers, and Pennsylvania developed procedures calling for the state to "purchase secular services" from private and parochial schools. In 1971 the Supreme Court handed down precedent-setting decisions invalidating both the Rhode Island and Pennsylvania plans upon the grounds that they violate the First Amendment of the Constitution [*Lemon v. Kurtzman,* 91 S. Ct. 2105 (1971)]. In the light of this decision, religious leaders have expressed doubt that parochial schools can survive in the face of increasing school costs, which will result in forced transfers to public schools and a corresponding increase in cost to the public for elementary and secondary education. Some states are considering the adoption of a semipublic school plan. Under this plan, the curriculum would be divided into public and parochial segments, with lay teachers teaching the secular portion and church-employed teachers teaching the religion-oriented subjects. The school would receive state aid to support the secular portion of the curriculum with the remaining subjects being financed by the church.

One other effect of the 1971 Supreme Court decision has been to

FIGURE 13-13. Trends in public and nonpublic (parochial and nonsectarian) school enrollments. During the ten-year period (1959–1960 to 1969–1970), public school enrollments increased nearly 10 million as compared to an increase of 100,000 for nonpublic schools. Between 1969–1970 and 1970–1980 total enrollments in public schools are expected to increase slightly, with enrollments in nonpublic schools decreasing approximately 300,000.

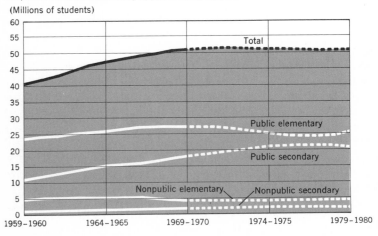

arouse interest in the voucher plan for aiding private schools. In theory the voucher plan works as follows: School districts issue "vouchers" to parents equal in dollars to a single child's per-pupil share of annual school district expenditures. Parents are then free to use the voucher to "buy" a year of schooling at any school—public or private—participating in the plan [289:2].

The Office of Economic Opportunity has championed the voucher plan in the belief that public schools have failed poverty children—thus necessitating new methods being used to break the poverty cycle. However, such organizations as the National Education Association and the American Association of School Administrators are vigorously opposed to the plan. The AASA views the plan with "grave alarm" believing it could "remove the schools from public to private control, carry decentralization to absurdity and create a massive bureaucracy to enforce safeguards and regulations" [1:139].

If the voucher plan does not develop into a major vehicle for support of nonpublic education, the search for other methods to provide such support will continue. Teachers in both public and nonpublic schools should be aware of the various aid programs which are being proposed. Such aid could come at the expense of public education. At the same time teachers in nonpublic schools need to be concerned that aid does not come at the expense of the freedom which is the major characteristic of private school education.

## Higher Education

Colleges and universities in the United States have not escaped the massive financial problems which have beset educational institutions at all levels during the late 1960s and early 1970s. In some respects, funding problems confronting institutions of higher education are more critical than those faced by public elementary and secondary schools. While it is projected that elementary school enrollments in the next eight years will decline, it is anticipated that the number of students attending colleges and universities will increase from approximately 7.4 million students in 1970–1971 to 10.3 million by 1978. These enrollment figures do not include the increasingly large number of persons enrolled in college and university sponsored continuing education programs, such as adult education classes, independent study courses, and short-term workshops and institutes. Increased enrollments represent only one of the reasons for the financial crisis facing higher education. The problem of securing adequate financial support has been compounded by inflation and the public demand for improved services. In essence, costs have risen more rapidly than have enrollments.

While expenditures for higher education have been substantially increased during the past decade, they have not kept pace with the needs.

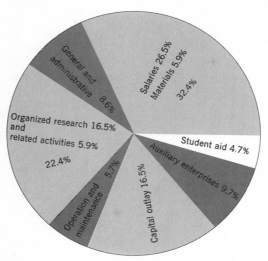

FIGURE 13–14. Distribution of the costs of higher education.

The total amount of money spent for higher education, including both current expenditures and capital outlay, was $8.9 billion in 1959–1960 [247:88]. By 1969–1970, the amount had risen to an estimated $24.9 billion. It is projected that expenditures for the support of higher education will rise to $42.2 billion, excluding capital outlay by 1979–1980 [247:89].

Four sources of financial support for institutions of higher learning are of major importance: endowments, gifts and grants, student fees, and appropriations from governments. Appropriations from local, state, and federal governments provide over 60 per cent of the funds for public higher education.

It is expected that support for higher education will increase from

FIGURE 13–15. Past and projected total expenditures by institutions of higher education in the United States.

(Billions of 1969–1970 dollars)

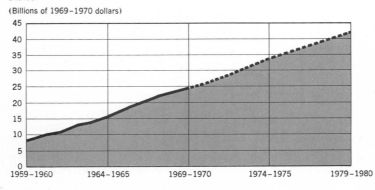

existing sources in the years ahead. The major unanswered questions are: (1) will the level of support keep pace with the needs resulting from expanded enrollments, inflation, and the demand for increased services; (2) will there be new forms of state and federal aid for public higher education; and (3) will an increased amount of public funds be used to support private institutions? A fourth question concerns the form that higher education will take in the future. If some of the proposed alternatives to the present structure become widespread realities, such as independent study, credit-by-examination and external degrees—alternatives which permit students to earn all or part of the credits required for graduation without entering a regular classroom—all projections concerning higher education finances may need to be revised.

## SCHOOL FINANCE IN THE 1970s

School financial reform is sorely needed and long overdue in the United States. Several school districts in recent years have been forced to extend vacations or shorten the school year due to insufficient operating funds. Other districts have been able to operate only through the use of borrowed funds. Numerous districts have cancelled or postponed needed building programs. In view of these conditions, dramatic changes in educational finance may be expected in the 1970s. Given the multiple of variables involved, predictions on this subject are always risky, especially in periods of radical change.

It is generally accepted in the United States that the free public school is obligated to provide every person with an educational opportunity enabling him to be an intelligent and responsible citizen. The system of financing public education, which in 1971 provided $1,325 per child per year for the operation of schools in some school districts while providing as little as $241 per child per year in other districts, renders the attainment of this objective difficult if not impossible. The condition of the national economy may have some impact on needed changes in educational finance; but in the final analysis, the attitude of the citizenry will perhaps have the greatest influence. This does not suggest, however, that the impact of the education profession itself on the level and kind of support which education is to receive should be discounted. There is strong evidence to suggest that the collective action of educators and other citizens has resulted in higher levels of funding for education. Higher salaries, improved programs for inner-city youth, the expansion of kindergartens, and the addition of libraries in many elementary schools serve as vivid examples of the success which collective professional effort has realized [55:13].

As indicated in Figure 13–16, the per cent of the Gross National Product (GNP) devoted to education in the United States, except during the World War II period, has gradually increased since 1929. Whether or

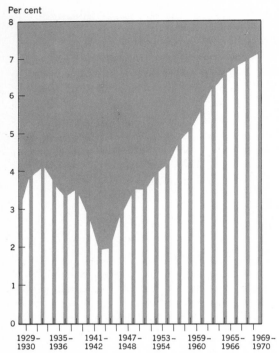

FIGURE 13–16. Total expenditures for education expressed as a percentage of Gross National Product. Educational expenditures were relatively high in the mid 1930s, declining to a low point of 1.8 per cent in 1943–1944. Since the end of World War II, there has been a steady increase in the proportion of the GNP spent for education.

not this gradual increase may be attributed to a higher priority being assigned to education by the American public, to increased collective activity on the part of the profession, or to other factors is open to speculation. Looking toward the prospects for the future, James Heald and Samuel Moore make the following observation concerning emerging societal goals:

Man would seem to be disposed to a continuing support for his social institutions. Probably at no other time has the system of public education, one of man's social institutions, been more important to the aspirations of man. In an earlier year, the school was seen as a possible aid to achieving higher status and greater prosperity. Today, the system is looked upon as utterly essential for man if he is to be able to cope with new knowledge and new technology and their impact upon mankind [117:33].

These remarks suggest that education may be assigned an even higher priority by the American public in the future. If their reasoning proves accurate, may we expect an even higher percentage of the GNP to be devoted to education in the future?

## Predicted Trends in School Finance

Predicting future courses of action in school finance is made difficult by such uncertainties as the continuation of conflicts in various sections of the world, the condition of the U.S. economy, and the attitude of the general public toward education. However, various indicators suggest that the following trends are distinct possibilities in the 1970s:

1. Greater emphasis will be placed upon the process and concept of accountability; thus, the focus will be upon results or evidence of educational productivity.
2. Performance contracts with private industry for the operation of all or part of a school system will become more prevalent. Many of these contracts will provide that the private corporation will get paid only if predetermined results are produced, such as raising a child's reading level 1.0 years in a given period of time. This same performance concept may carry over into the area of teacher salaries. If so, teachers may receive a monetary bonus or merit increase based on the progress which their students make toward the attainment of the established educational objectives. Dollar inputs may be rearranged whereby a smaller percentage of the educational budget is devoted to teacher salaries with a larger share being devoted to instructional materials, equipment, and facilities.
3. We may see the beginnings of a competitive school system. Parents may be given tuition vouchers to be used to send their children to the school of their choice, either public or private.
4. There will be general recognition that unequal dollars are needed to provide equal educational opportunity.
5. An increasing number of private legal suits, similar to those in California and Minnesota, will be filed in the courts, charging that state school aid distribution formulas have served to shortchange specific groups of children, thereby denying them an equal educational opportunity.
6. Continued efforts will be made to provide some form of indirect support from public funds for private and parochial schools.
7. Competition for funds between higher education institutions and public elementary-secondary schools will continue.
8. The taxpayer's revolt resulting from high real estate property taxes will ease as a higher percentage of educational funds come from the state and federal governments and less from local sources.
9. Greater attention will be given to federal revenue-sharing plans whereby individual states would share in federal income tax receipts with no-strings-attached. The amounts allocated to the states would be based on each state's share of the national population with a premium being paid to those states with the greatest need.
10. Present features of state school finance programs which help perpetuate small and poorly organized school districts will be partially eliminated.

## SUMMARY

Approximately 7 per cent of the annual Gross National Product, or $70 billion was spent for the operation of schools in the United States during the 1970–1971 school year. Thus, in terms of dollar expenditures, education is the largest single nondefense government enterprise.

Because each state has its own school financial system, it is to be expected that there is considerable variation among the states in the manner of financing education. However, each state delegates a large measure of responsibility for education to its local communities and encourages them to use a large amount of initiative, support, and control. In order to provide a greater amount of equality of educational opportunities, state governments have had to provide increasing amounts of support. The federal government, since the Ordinance of 1785, has continued to exercise a definite interest in education and has greatly increased its financial support as a result of major education legislation in the mid-1960s.

Securing adequate funds for the support of America's schools represents a crucial problem which has already reached crisis proportions. A sluggish economy, inflation, an antiquated tax structure, dwindling public confidence in the schools, and the general public's perception of student activism, among other things, have contributed to the crisis. Maintaining the status quo may be difficult, but if the demands for extending and improving education at all levels are to be met, a massive effort will be required.

The demands and desires of the public, including educators, for a quality educational program are inconsistent with the unwillingness of the public to provide the finances necessary to attain the level of quality desired. This dilemma obviously cannot be resolved until the public understands the need for additional school revenues as well as more equitable state financing plans for public schools. Teachers may help resolve this problem by interpreting the needs of schools to the general public.

## QUESTIONS TO CONSIDER

1. Why has the amount of state funds to aid local school districts increased significantly since the depression in the 1930s? Will this trend continue?
2. What was the cost of public education per pupil in average daily attendance in your state last year? How does this expenditure compare with that of other states and with the national average?
3. What are the sources of school revenue in your home community?
4. To what extent are federal moneys used for education in your home town? What percentage of total school costs are met by federal support? What specific school affairs does the federal program support?
5. Is your home community able to support a quality program of public education, or do you believe that more financial assistance should be provided by the state?
6. Of what significance are the Quality Measurement Project of the New York State Education Department and the comprehensive research project being conducted by Professor Kreitlow?
7. As you see it, what are the arguments for and against the use of public tax money to support nonpublic schools?
8. What solutions can you propose for financing higher education within the next decade?
9. What are the advantages and disadvantages of the "voucher" plan?
10. What steps should be taken to facilitate equality of educational opportunity in small, rural, poor, and inner-city schools throughout the United States?

11. What approach should teachers use in an effort to interpret the needs of education to the general public?

12. In your opinion, will performance contracts with private industry for the operation of all or part of a school program substantially reduce the cost of education?

13. What outcome may be expected to result from the current emphasis on "accountability?"

14. The idea of free public elementary and secondary schools has long been accepted by the public. Why has this same concept not been totally applied to public colleges and universities?

## PROBLEM SITUATION FOR INQUIRY

Assume that you are a member of the state legislative body in a state where the majority of the support for public schools is derived from local property taxes. Within the state there are some school districts which spend as little as $200 per year to educate each student in the district. Other districts in the state spend as much as $1,200 per year per child for education. In some instances, the disparity among expenditures for education in the state is due to the wealth of the district—those districts which have a high assessed property valuation per child spend more than those districts which have a relatively low assessed valuation per child. In other cases, the disparity is due to the limited effort which the district makes to support education. Some districts with only an average assessed valuation are spending $1,200 per year per child for education, because the community places great emphasis upon a good quality educational program. In other cases, very wealthy districts have elected to spend less for education than they could actually afford to spend. In an effort to provide a quality educational program for all children in the state, regardless of where they live, what proposal for change would you submit to the state legislature?

## ACTIVITIES TO PURSUE

1. Determine the amount of money your home state spends for public school education in one year. If possible, compare this amount with expenditures for tobacco and liquor products.

2. Analyze a local school district budget and prepare a bar graph indicating the percentage of the budget devoted to each educational function, such as administration, instruction, and maintenance.

3. List several ways of determining your state's ability to pay for education. How does your state's effort to support education compare with its ability?

4. Analyze the budget of a local community action program committee and determine the percentage of funds expended for various education functions.

5. Invite a school superintendent to discuss with your class the financial problems of his school district.

6. Organize a panel to debate the appropriate role of federal aid to education.

7. Make a study of the various grants for research in education being made by the U.S. Office of Education. In what ways may these grants improve educational practices?

8. Write a skit to portray the personalities who are striving to cut taxes in your home community. Analyze the values these people seem to hold.

9. Study the various countries in the world for the purpose of determining any relationship that may exist in regard to average amount of education and percapita income.

10. Devise a plan of action for purposes of securing a favorable vote on a school bond issue or school tax referendum.

11. Debate the issue of public aid to parochial schools.

12. Make a comparative study of the tax base of an inner-city and a suburban community. What do your findings reveal?

## SOME IMPORTANT DATES IN THE ORGANIZATION OF PUBLIC ELEMENTARY EDUCATION IN THE UNITED STATES

| Approximate date | |
|---|---|
| 1848 | First graded school in America established at the Quincy Grammar School of Boston. |
| 1860 | The graded school system became widespread throughout the United States. |
| 1870 | Efforts made to reorganize the graded school to overcome some of its deficiencies (such as overageness, dropouts, and nonpromotions). |
| 1893 | Cogswell originated the Cambridge Plan, forerunner of the multilevel track system, in one of the early attempts to provide for individualization of instruction. |
| 1900 | Departmentalization of upper grades began in New York City and the platoon plan began in all the grades in Bluffton, Indiana. |
| 1919 | Individualized instruction emphasized in graded schools as shown by the Winnetka and Dalton experiments. |
| 1920 | Intelligence test scores first applied on a wide scale to ability groups in Detroit, Michigan. |
| 1930 | Hosic's Co-operative Group Plan, forerunner of team teaching, began. |
| 1942 | The ungraded primary unit emerged in Milwaukee, Wisconsin. |
| 1947–1955 | The ungraded plan appeared in various places. |
| 1955–1959 | Multigrade classes, ungraded classes, team teaching, team learning, TV teaching, and combinations of graded and ungraded classes continue to be under experimentation. |

*Source:* Rose Koury, *Elementary School Organization . . .What Direction Shall It Take?* U.S. Office of Education, Education Briefs, no. 37, Washington, January, 1960, p. 15.


## SUGGESTED READINGS

*The number in parentheses following each suggestion denotes the chapter for which it is best suited.*

Alexander, William M.: "The New School in the Middle," *Phi Delta Kappan,* vol. 50, no. 6, pp. 355–357, Phi Delta Kappa, Bloomington, Ind., February, 1969. Presents the results of a survey of the status of the middle school throughout the nation. (12)

Anderson, Robert H.: "How Organization Can Make the School More Humanistic," *The National Elementary Principal,* vol. 49, no. 3, pp. 6–13, National Education Association, Department of Elementary School Principals, Washington, January, 1970. Suggestions by an outstanding educator on how the schools may become more humanistic through changes in organizational structure. (12)

"Are Courts Running the Schools?" *The Shape of Education for 1970–71,* vol. 12, pp. 40–44, National School Public Relations Association, Washington, 1970. Discusses the effect that recent court decisions have had upon the operation of schools. (12)

Brownell, S. M.: "Desirable Characteristics of Decentralized School Systems," *Phi Delta Kappan,* vol. 52, no. 5, pp. 286–288, Phi Delta Kappa, Bloomington, Ind., January, 1971. Suggests ways of improving the organization of our school system. (12)

Calkins, Hugh: "Financing Education in the 70's," *Today's Education,* vol. 60, no. 2, pp. 30–32, National Education Association, Washington, February, 1971. Suggests means by which 20 per cent of our population, currently excluded from the mainstream of American life, can acquire the educational level they must achieve to enter it. (13)

"Catholic Schools Face Crisis," *The Shape of Education for 1970–71,* vol. 12, pp. 24–29, National School Public Relations Association, Washington, 1970. Discusses problems confronting Catholic schools as they face the seventies. (13)

"Decentralization and Community Involvement in Local School Systems," *NEA Research Bulletin,* vol. 48, no. 1, pp. 3–6, National Education Association, Research Division,

Washington, March, 1970. Analyzes the process of administrative decentralization and community participation in 32 school systems. (12)

"The $$ Challenge: Time for Reform?" *The Shape of Education for 1970–71,* vol. 12, pp. 34–39, National School Public Relations Association, Washington, 1970. Indicates that many educators agree that the time has arrived for radical reforms in the way school districts are financed. (13)

"Early Childhood Education," *Today's Education,* vol. 59, no. 4, pp. 34–42, National Education Association, Washington, April, 1970. A special feature in which prominent educators discuss various aspects of childhood education. (12)

"Estimates of School Statistics," *Research Report,* National Education Association, Research Division, Washington (latest issue). An annual publication containing excellent information on school organization and administration as well as instructional staff and school finance. (12 and 13)

*Financial Status of the Public Schools,* National Education Association, Committee on Educational Finance, Washington (latest report). An annual publication presenting a wide range of statistical information upon the financial status of education. (13)

Furno, Orlando F.: "Planning Programming Budgeting Systems: Boon or Bane?" *Phi Delta Kappan,* vol. 51, no. 3, pp. 142–144, Phi Delta Kappa, Bloomington, Ind., November, 1969. Discusses the merits and weaknesses of a planning, programming, budgeting system. (12)

Hamilton, Norman K., and J. Galen Saylor: *Humanizing the Secondary School,* National Education Association, Association for Supervision and Curriculum Development, Washington, 1969. Suggests some characteristics of a humane secondary school. (12)

Havighurst, Robert J.: "The Reorganization of Education in Metropolitan Areas," *Phi Delta Kappan,* vol. 52, no. 6, pp. 354–358, Phi Delta Kappa, Bloomington, Ind., February, 1971. Describes the role that the central administration office should play in the operation of school systems. (12)

Heald, James E., and Samuel A. Moore, II: *The Teacher and Administrative Relationships in School Systems,* The Macmillan Company, Toronto, Canada, 1968. An excellent treatment of the leadership role that teachers may play in the administration of schools. (12)

"How Early Should Education Start?" *The Shape of Education for 1969–70,* vol. 11, pp. 42–45, National School Public Relations Association, Washington, 1969. Indicates that some authorities believe early education should begin with prenatal care. (12)

"Kindergarten Education in Public Schools, 1967–68," *Research Report 1969–R6,* National Education Association, Research Division, Washington, 1969. Presents the results of a nationwide survey of kindergarten programs in public schools. (12)

McLure, William P.: "The Urgent Need for Education Finance Reform in the Seventies," *Phi Delta Kappan,* vol. 51, no. 3, pp. 160–162, Phi Delta Kappa, Bloomington, Ind., November, 1969. Indicates some imperative changes that need to be made in educational financing. (13)

"The New Trend: Year-round Schools," *U.S. News and World Report,* vol. 71, no. 4, pp. 35–37, U.S. News and World Report, Inc., Washington, July 26, 1971. Discusses trends toward the use of the summer months and the controversy that is caused. (12)

Rajpol, Puran L.: "Relationship between Expenditures and Quality Characteristics of Education in Public Schools," *The Journal of Educational Research,* vol. 63, no. 2, pp. 57–59, Dembar Educational Research Services, Inc., Madison, Wis., October, 1969. Presents statistical data indicating that higher expenditures per pupil usually results in higher educational quality. (13)

"Ranking of the States," *Research Report,* National Education Association, Research Division, Washington (latest issue). An annual publication presenting excellent data on school finance. (13)

*The Realities of School Finance,* American Association of School Administrators, Washington, n.d. Contains some excellent graphs on school finance. (13)

Rogers, Carl R.: *Freedom to Learn,* Charles E. Merrill Publishing Company, Columbus,

Ohio, 1969. A famous psychologist presents "Some Thoughts about Educational Administration" in chapter 10, and "A Plan for Self-Directed Change in an Educational System" in chapter 15. (12)

"Total Cost of Higher Education Continues to Rise," *College Management,* vol. 6, no. 1, pp. 9–12, CCM Professional Magazines, Inc., Greenwich, Conn., January, 1971. Indicates how costs have risen in a ten-year period and the financial crisis which higher education faces. (13)

Unruh, Glenys G., and William M. Alexander: *Innovations in Secondary Education,* Holt, Rinehart and Winston, Inc., New York, 1970. Explains the forces that necessitate innovations at the secondary school level, emphasizes the role and power of innovations in educational changes, and discusses various innovations which have taken place and will likely take place in secondary schools. (12)

"Vouchers: Reform or Catastrophe," *The Shape of Education for 1971–72,* vol. 13, pp. 56–59, National School Public Relations Association, Washington, 1971. Analyzes the pros and cons of the voucher system. (13)

"What Is a Programming Planning Budgeting System?" *NEA Research Bulletin,* vol. 46, no. 4, pp. 112–113, National Education Association, Research Division, Washington, December, 1968. Explains the meaning of a PPB system. (13)

Wrightstone, J. Wayne: "Ability Grouping and the Average Child," *NEA Journal,* vol. 57, no. 1, pp. 9–11, 58, National Education Association, Washington, January, 1968. An outstanding authority discusses the pros and cons of ability grouping. (12)

## SUGGESTED 16 MM FILMS

*The number in parentheses following each suggestion denotes the chapter for which it is best suited.*

*A Chance to Learn* (NBC Educational Enterprises, 21 min, color). Shows black dissatisfaction in the school and contrasts black and white demand for local control in New York City and in Little Rock, Arkansas. (12)

*The Difference Between Us* (National Educational Television, 60 min). Compares the secondary school education system in England and the United States. Discusses the differences in both approaches to advanced education. (12)

*The Dropout* (International Film Bureau, 28 min). Depicts various factors and their origins that stimulate teenagers to drop out of school, using several case histories for illustrations. Lists various reasons for dropping out, such as academic failure, need for money, and lack of being part of a group. Illustrates the feeling of a need to grow up on the part of the dropouts as they try to assume an adult role. (12)

*The Dropout* (Mental Health Film Board, Inc., 28 min). Presents one of the millions of youngsters who leave high school without graduating. Shows how a community, through remedial reading programs, work experience programs, and other educational activities may tackle the problem of underachievement. (12)

*Education* (National Educational Television, 29 min). Presents a discussion of educational problems including "Whom shall we educate, how, and for what?" Proposes early testing for abilities, special training, more creative teaching, less administrative and clerical burdens on the part of the teacher and the evaluation of new teaching techniques. (12)

*Next Year Is Now* (Modern Talking Picture Service, 28 min). Points out the serious problems encountered in higher education today, such as overcrowding of the colleges and the rising cost of education. (13)

*No Reason to Stay* (Encyclopaedia Britannica Educational Corporation, 25 min). Dramatizes some of the classroom procedures and administrative indifferences which contribute to the lack of interest on the part of students and which can lead to their dropping out of school. (12)

*Portrait of the Inner-city School: A Place to Learn* (McGraw-Hill, 18 min). Deals with problems of learning in an inner-city school. Points up the sharp areas of conflict between school practices and the cultural patterns of the pupils. Indicates positive attitudes which will help to facilitate adjustments in such schools. (12)

*A Way of Life* (International Harvester Co., 25 min, color). Presents the story of a school at Beaverton, Michigan, and how the problem of finance for educational purposes was solved, providing broader educational opportunities for the young and new ideas and better living for the whole community. (13)

## FIGURE CREDITS

FIGURE 12-1. (*Source:* Edward J. Power, *Education for American Democracy: An Introduction to Education,* McGraw-Hill Book Company, New York, 1958, p. 80.)

FIGURE 12-2. (*Source:* Kenneth A. Simon and W. Vance Grant, *Digest of Educational Statistics,* U.S. Office of Education, National Center for Educational Statistics, Washington, 1970, p. 43.)

FIGURE 12-3. (*Source:* "One-teacher Schools Today," *Research Monograph 1960–M1,* National Education Association, Research Division, Washington, June, 1960, p. 9; and "Facts on American Education," *NEA Research Bulletin,* vol. 49, no. 2, National Education Association, Research Division, Washington, May, 1971, p. 53.)

FIGURE 12-4. (*Source: The American School Superintendency,* Thirteenth Yearbook of the American Association of School Administrators, Washington, 1952, p. 88.)

FIGURE 12-5. (*Source:* With a modification from Kenneth A. Simon and W. Vance Grant, *Digest of Educational Statistics,* U.S. Office of Education, National Center for Educational Statistics, Washington, 1970, p. xii—modified to show the middle school.)

FIGURE 12-6. (*Source:* Data from *Statistical Abstract of the United States,* U.S. Department of Commerce, Bureau of the Census, Washington, 1971, p. 213.)

FIGURE 12-7. (*Source:* Data from *Statistical Abstract of the United States,* 1971, U.S. Department of Commerce, Bureau of the Census, Washington, 1971, p. 125.)

FIGURE 12-8. (*Source: Education: An Investment in People,* Chamber of Commerce of the United States, Education Department, Washington, 1964, p. 23.)

FIGURE 12-10. (*Source:* Ronald B. Thompson, *Projections of Enrollments, Public and Private Colleges and Universities, 1970–1987,* American Association of Collegiate Registrars and Admission Officers, Washington, December, 1970, p. ix.)

FIGURE 12-11. (*Source:* George H. Wade, *Opening Fall Enrollments in Higher Education,* U.S. Office of Education, Washington, 1970, p. 7.)

FIGURE 12-12. (*Source:* Data from John W. C. Johnstone and Ramon J. Rivera, *Volunteers for Learning,* Aldine Publishing Company, Chicago, 1965, p. 73.)

FIGURE 13-1. (*Source:* Kenneth A. Simon and W. Vance Grant, *Digest of Educational Statistics,* U.S. Office of Education, National Center for Educational Statistics, Washington, 1969, p. 19.)

FIGURE 13-2. (*Source:* Kenneth A. Simon and Marie G. Fullam, *Projections of Educational Statistics to 1979–80,* U.S. Office of Education, National Center for Educational Statistics, Washington, 1971, p. 7.)

FIGURE 13-3. (*Source:* Data from "Personal Consumption Expenditures, by Type of Product," *Survey of Current Business,* vol. 51, no. 7, U.S. Department of Commerce, Office of Business Economics, Washington, July, 1971, p. 24, and "Magnitude of the American Establishment," *Saturday Review,* Saturday Review, Inc., New York, Sept. 19, 1970, p. 67.)

FIGURE 13-4. (*Source:* Clayton D. Hutchins and Dolores A. Steinhelber, *Trends in Financing Public Education, 1929–30 to 1959–60,* U.S. Office of Education Circular 666, 1961, p. 39; and "Estimates of School Statistics," *Research Reports,* National Education Association, Research Division, Washington, various years.)

FIGURE 13-5. (*Source: What Everyone Should Know About Financing Our Schools,* National Education Association, Washington, 1968, p. 12.)

FIGURE 13-6. (*Source: Education: An Investment in People,* Chamber of Commerce of the United States, Education Department, Washington, 1964, p. 51, and "The Cost of Building in 1969–70: Out of Sight," *School Management,* vol. 14, no. 7, CCM Professional Magazines, Inc., Greenwich, Conn., July, 1970, p. 21.)

FIGURE 13-7. (*Source:* Data from "Cost of Education Index 1970–1971," *School Management,* vol. 15, no. 1, CCM Professional Magazines, Inc., Greenwich, Conn., January, 1971, p. 15.)

FIGURE 13-8. (*Source: What Everyone Should Know About Financing Our Schools,* National Education Association, Washington, 1968, p. 42.)

FIGURE 13-9. (*Source:* Data from "Estimates of School Statistics, 1970–71," *Research Report 1970–R15,* National Education Association, Research Division, Washington, 1970, p. 35.)

FIGURE 13-10. (*Source:* Arthur E. Wise, "Financing Schools: Property Tax Is Obsolete—The California Doctrine," *Saturday Review,* Saturday Review, Inc., New York, Nov. 20, 1971, p. 83.)

FIGURE 13-11. (*Source:* Data from "Estimates of School Statistics, 1970–71," *Research Report 1970–R15,* National Education Association, Research Division, Washington, 1970, p. 37.)

FIGURE 13-12. (*Source:* Data from "Ranking of the States, 1971," *Research Report 1971–R1,* National Education Association, Research Division, Washington, 1971, p. 47.)

FIGURE 13-13. (*Source:* Kenneth A. Simon and Marie G. Fullam, *Projections of Educational Statistics to 1979–80,* U.S. Office of Education, National Center for Educational Statistics, Washington, 1971, p. 4.)

FIGURE 13-14. (*Source:* "The Total Cost of Higher Education," *College Management,* vol. 6, no. 1, CCM Professional Magazines, Inc., Greenwich, Conn., January, 1971, p. 1.)

FIGURE 13-15. (*Source:* Kenneth A. Simon and Marie G. Fullam, *Projections of Educational Statistics to 1979–80,* U.S. Office of Education, National Center for Educational Statistics, Washington, 1971, p. 7.)

FIGURE 13-16. (*Source:* Kenneth A. Simon and W. Vance Grant, *Digest of Educational Statistics,* U.S. Office of Education, National Center for Educational Statistics, Washington, 1970, p. 20.)

# 5 | historical and philosophical concerns

The extent to which a teacher is able to assess accurately the present status of education will depend in part upon how thoroughly he understands the historical development of schools in America. As the distinguished Winston Churchill advised, "We cannot say 'the past is past' without surrendering the future." Thus, a good understanding of how our schools have developed will enable a teacher to be more effective in improving school practices and procedures today and to perceive more clearly the role that the school must play in the future.

Chapter 14 is designed to acquaint a prospective teacher with the major developments in the American school system as they have occurred during four rather clearly defined time periods. Chapter 15 briefly explores the historical development of some modern concepts of education. An understanding of the contributions of various educators—both past and present—should enable a prospective teacher to assess more clearly current conceptions of educational functions, practices, and procedures. Chapter 16 is a straightforward presentation of the broad purposes that seem to shape the design of American education, as well as statements of objectives that seem to provide a framework for educational practices and procedures at each school level.

# 14 | HISTORICAL DEVELOPMENT OF OUR SCHOOLS

The American school system is the expression of the hopes, desires, ambitions, and values held by those who have made our nation what it is today. It represents, in fact, one of the most noble and visionary experiments ever attempted by mankind. The story of how it came into being and developed through the years is a unique and fascinating one.

Furthermore, it is a story that has no foreseeable ending. Our school system is continuing to change at "a breath-taking pace and there is much unfinished business before us. We are still striving toward our ideals of liberty and opportunity for all. In many ways, these goals are still to be reached" [153:4]. Any teacher has the opportunity to help write a new chapter in this ongoing story.

Unfortunately, Americans are not inclined to be historically minded. Too frequently, they tend to make the same mistakes over and over again. There are critics of American education today who would have the schools return to purposes and practices that long ago were found to be undesirable in fulfilling democratic ideals. Likewise, there are educators who make claims for some of the so-called innovations in education, such as teaching machines and programmed learning, that are similar to the claims made for workbooks over 40 years ago.

Although futuristic thinking is a desirable characteristic of American educators, this type of thinking needs to be coupled with a sound understanding of where we have been and of our mistakes as well as successes. As the learned Santayana once said, "Those who won't study the mistakes of history are doomed to repeat them." Thus, a really competent educator has a good understanding of how our schools have developed, understands what influenced them to develop, and is aware of the "constant interplay between challenge and response, new needs and new ideas to meet them" [153:4]. He is able to identify proposed solutions to current problems that may have been tried in the past and have failed and probably would fail again. He uses the past for possible clues to the effective solutions of today's problems.

In reading this chapter, one should apply the understandings he has gained from courses he has taken in high school and in college that have been concerned with the development of the United States. These understandings, accompanied by brief descriptions of religious, social, economic, and political forces and factors, should help anyone in studying the major periods in the development of our schools. By continuing to study and work in the field of education, a deeper understanding of the historical backgrounds of education may be obtained  Through such efforts an educator is less likely to repeat yesterday's mistakes and be more able to attain tomorrow's aspirations.

## EDUCATION DURING THE COLONIAL PERIOD (1620–1791)

The early settlers in the New World brought with them their respective political traditions, religions, styles of architecture, and social customs. When they were faced with problems, it was natural for them to do the same thing that men have done throughout the ages—they drew upon the experiences with which they were familiar. As a consequence, the first institutions in the New World were built on the foundation of the life and customs of the Old World. Essentially, it was a process of transplantation. Early schools, therefore, were patterned in the European tradition, and the attitudes toward education followed European beliefs.

It should be pointed out that European education had been influenced greatly by the Greek and Roman concepts of the cultured man. Education primarily was a process of cultivating the intellect and the character of those destined to be of the ruling class. A classical curriculum seemed to be proper for the education of these people.

A rigid class structure was mirrored in European education. It was a stratified society in which each individual, generally at birth, found his role in life assigned to him [37:110]. Emphasis was placed upon the stability and maintenance of the society, and it was rare indeed to find any individual advancing through this stratification to a higher class status. Apprenticeship training was considered to be adequate for the lower classes, who were to serve the elite.

European education also was affected by a concept developed by the ancient Hebrews. They believed [187:7], "For the good life to be lived and salvation attained, one had to be acquainted with religious truths. These truths, divinely inspired and transcribed in the sacred literature, were to be studied, understood, and memorized. Unless one possessed a deep understanding of the truths contained in the scripture, neither the good life nor salvation was possible." As a result, formal education and religion were linked together to form a tradition that would be carried to America by the Puritans.

During the Protestant Reformation in the sixteenth century, Martin Luther gave further impetus to the ancient Hebrew concept of relating education and religion. "Education, literacy, religion, and salvation became inseparably linked and culturally interacting elements. For the American colonist this religious sanction for education was of prime importance" [187:10].

In addition to the religious sanction for education, many of the early settlers brought with them the concept of a direct relationship between the state and the church. This feeling was so strong that various laws were enacted establishing religions for such colonies as Connecticut, Massachusetts, New Hampshire, and Virginia. These laws were in conflict with the religious freedom sought by many of the early settlers and in a short time presented major sources of conflict. The influence of the church upon education in colonial days can scarcely be overestimated.

Since the groups of early settlers came from different countries in Europe, their language, customs, and religion differed, and so did their views on education. As a result, various patterns of education developed in the Colonies. It is possible to identify three different approaches to education centered in three loosely defined areas—New England Colonies (primarily Massachusetts, Rhode Island, Connecticut, and New Hampshire), Middle Atlantic Colonies (principally New York, New Jersey, Delaware, and Pennsylvania), and Southern Colonies (mainly Virginia, Maryland, Georgia, North Carolina, and South Carolina). These attitudes provided bases from which the ultimate structure of our educational system grew.

## The New England Colonies

The early New England settlers made their journey to the New World primarily to achieve religious and political freedom. They wanted to create a new kind of society, devoid of the caste system, in which men would be free to govern themselves.

In order to achieve the religious freedom they desired, it would be necessary for each individual to be able to read and understand the word of God as set forth in the Bible. Therefore, the New England colonists felt a distinct obligation to teach their children to read, so that they could take the first step toward saving their souls. Their strong religious attitude was well set forth in a quotation from a pamphlet titled *New England's First Fruits* [171:242]:

After God had carried us safe to New England, and wee had builded our houses, provided necessaries for our liveli-hood, rear'd convenient places for God's worship, and settled the civill government: One of the next things we longed for and looked after was to advance learning and perpetuate it to posterity; dreading to leave an illiterate ministry to the churches, when our present ministers shall lie in the dust.

Another motivating force in the development of education in New England was that a number of the early settlers were highly educated. Estimates have been made which indicate that approximately 3 per cent of the adult men were university graduates. Without a doubt they were highly influential in promoting interest in education. This influence can be appreciated when we consider the fact that by 1635 the Pilgrims, who landed at Plymouth Rock in 1620, had established the Boston Latin School.

**The Latin grammar school** The Boston Latin School was the first successfully organized school of any kind in America. It was a so-called Latin grammar school, copied directly from the type developed in England. Its central purpose was to prepare boys for college. Because colleges were concerned primarily with the preparation of ministers, the curriculum consisted chiefly of Latin, Greek, and theology. Pupils entered usually at age seven or eight, having previously learned to read and write. They completed the course in about seven years.

The Latin grammar school provided the framework of secondary schools in America. Although it was essentially a select school—reserved for the wealthy and elite and aimed solely at preparation for college—it had some occasional public financial support. This type of school spread slowly throughout New England and further along the coast. There is some evidence that such a school was planned by the Virginia Company in 1621, but the colony was wiped out by the Indian massacre of 1622.

The Latin grammar school was prominent until the Revolutionary War, when it was challenged by another type of secondary school, but some of its influences are still to be found in public schools. The classical emphasis in many high school programs, the persistence of Latin as a part of the curriculum, the rigid graduation specifications, which are so often pointed toward college preparation, the emphasis upon logical order per se and rote learning—these are some of the conspicuous influences of the Latin grammar school which have persisted in many public secondary schools to this day.

It should be kept in mind that the Latin grammar school was a private school which charged tuition. This fact alone made it impossible for many boys to attend grammar school in order to prepare for college. Furthermore, practically no relationship existed between what might be called colonial elementary schools and grammar schools. The educational ladder which is so distinctly a part of the American school system had not yet come into being.

**Dame school** In the early days of New England it was felt that each family should bear the responsibility for the elementary schooling of its children. Many families, not feeling equal to this responsibility, sent their children to the famous "dame schools" or to private tutors. The dame school was simply a private home where a group of children met under the leadership of a housewife or mother and where opportunities were provided for the children to learn their ABC's, the catechism, and at times a little simple arithmetic. The teacher usually charged tuition for her services. Occasionally a group of parents would engage a schoolmaster to give the same type of instruction which the dame school provided.

**Massachusetts school laws**   It soon became evident that the dame schools and the private tutors did not guarantee that all children would attain the basic requirements of literacy which the Puritan societies required. By 1642 there had grown a deep concern about "the great neglect of many parents and masters in training up their children in learning and labor." This condition prompted the Massachusetts Bay Colony to enact the Massachusetts School Law of 1642. The law charged the local magistrates in each town with "the care and redress of this evil." These local officials were to take note periodically of what had been done in educating the children, and if their education had been neglected, the magistrates could require that the children be sent to school. Actually this law did not provide for the establishment of schools but, through fines, attempted to enforce upon parents their responsibilities for having their children learn to read.

As Marshall pointed out, "Here was the first modest step toward two characteristics of our modern educational system—universal education and compulsory education. For the first time, a government had declared that all children should be taught to read and had made its purpose enforceable under law" [153:7].

During the five years following the enactment of the 1642 legislation, it became evident that the law was not being strictly enforced. The feeling grew that government must do more than merely *insist* upon education. It must *make provisions* for education, if children were to be properly educated. Thus in 1647 Massachusetts passed a new law which became known as the "Old Deluder Satan Law." As the name implies, the Massachusetts Law of 1647 reveals a definite church influence. An excerpt (in modernized spelling) follows:

It being one chief object of that old deluder, Satan, to keep men from the knowledge of the Scriptures, as in former times, by keeping them in unknown tongue, so in these latter times by persuading from the use of tongues, that so at least the true sense and meaning of the original might be clouded by false glosses of saint-seeming deceivers, that learning may not be buried in the grave of our fathers in the church and Commonwealth, the Lord assisting our endeavors. . . .

This "mother of all school laws" required that each town of fifty families provide a teacher to instruct the children sent to him. The teacher was to be paid by the parents, by the church, or by the inhabitants in general, as those who managed the affairs of the community might decide. The law also stipulated that every town of 100 families should provide a grammar school to prepare boys for college. This law, therefore, established a common school to teach the rudiments of learning and a preparatory school to qualify young boys for college.

Another part of the law of 1647 stated that any town would be subject to an annual penalty of 5 pounds if it neglected to establish these schools. Unfortunately some localities found it cheaper to pay the penalty than to observe the stipulations of the law.

New England, in general, was unique in the fact that its governments were the first in the New World to accept any responsibility for educating the young. No such effort was put forth in the other colonies along the Atlantic seaboard. As the first serious attempt to establish schools by legislation, the law of 1647 was the cornerstone of our free public school system. This unprecedented concept was carried to other parts of the country as many of the New England colonists migrated westward.

Remarkable though the New England achievement was, it would be erroneous to believe that the Massachusetts schools were comparable with the American schools as we know them today. The former were substantially parochial schools, even though they operated under the authority of the state rather than of the church. It is well to remember that the religious motive was very strong in the establishment of education in the New England Colonies and that what the church wanted could easily be enacted into law.

FIGURE 14–1.   Various types of schools predominated in the development of our educational system.

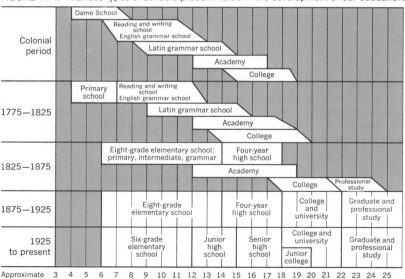

## The Middle Atlantic Colonies

The development of education in the Middle Atlantic or Middle Colonies differed considerably from that in the other colonies. There were the Dutch in New York, the Swedes along the Delaware River, and the English Quakers in Pennsylvania. These people came to the New World with different ideals and customs, different languages, different styles of architecture, and different types of Christianity.

Of these groups, possibly the Dutch in what is now New York were the most advanced in their educational thinking. By the 1630s there was some evidence that they had established schools under the authority and the supervision of the government. It is to be remembered, however, that all schools in that day were vitally interested in teaching religion. With all the ethnic and religious differences to be found in the Middle Colonies, the only solution to the educational problem was to have each church organize its own school and teach its own beliefs, rather than depend upon the local civil government.

The typical school of the Middle Colonies, then, was the parochial school—the school of the church parish. Parents were expected to pay tuition for their children, but, if they could not pay, the church sometimes permitted the child to attend nonetheless. In later years, the more common custom was for local authorities to pay tuition for poor children out of the "poor fund."

When the English took over New Amsterdam (New York) in 1664, they added to the complications already in existence. The English, at this time, were more backward than the Dutch in matters of education. Historians agree that in the later colonial period schools in and around New York deteriorated under English rule.

With the heterogeneity of cultural backgrounds and religious beliefs represented in the Middle Colonies, attempts to weld such great differences into a sound educational pattern presented a baffling problem.

## The Southern Colonies

Virginia was the most important of the Southern Colonies, and the development of education here was fairly representative of the colonies in this area. The Virginia settlers, who were mainly Englishmen, came to the New World not primarily because of discontent with the social, religious, and political system of the home country but to better their fortunes. They had no particular quarrel with the English way of doing things. The English had developed an aristocratic society whose government took little or no interest in education.

The South was characterized by large plantations, rather than small communities, in which class distinctions existed between the wealthy and the indentured servants and slaves who worked for them [153:6].

Education was not considered to be a function of the government. Rather, parents were expected to attend to the education of their own children. As a result, schooling in the Southern Colonies was almost entirely the private-tutor type. A few schools were established, but these were mainly for youngsters of wealthy plantation owners. Many of the sons of these plantation owners were sent back to England for a large part of their formal schooling. Those who could not afford to do this had very little opportunity to secure an education.

There were, however, several free schools in the Virginia Colony, which were established through the private contributions of public-spirited citizens. In order to send their children to these free schools, families had to declare themselves publicly to be paupers. The schools became known as "pauper schools." Many parents who could not pay the rates charged by the private schools and who refused to advertise themselves as paupers had no alternative but to keep their children out of school. Thus a large proportion of young people grew up illiterate.

Virginia, like many of the other colonies, followed the European custom of apprenticing orphans and the sons and daughters of very poor families. The law, which constituted a form of compulsory education, provided that the local magistrate could apprentice such a child to a master craftsman, who would teach the child his trade, give him board and lodging, and provide instruction in reading, writing, and religion. The child in turn agreed to help his master unquestioningly in his work. From reports of this type of vocational education, it was found that far too often the masters were more interested in the services which their apprentices could render than in providing good basic learnings for the child.

## Separation of Church and State

As indicated previously, the New England colonists soon found that the direct relationship between church and state conflicted with the religious freedom they sought. They had come to this new continent to escape the state's dictating the religious beliefs of its subjects. Additional groups of colonists brought greater diversification in religious beliefs. Through the leadership of Roger Williams, primarily, the charter of 1663 for Rhode Island granted religious freedom to the people of that colony. In 1682, William Penn was successful in getting a law passed in Pennsylvania granting religious freedom to the people. Gradually, as church and state separated throughout the colonies, the state supplanted the church in the educational field until, ultimately, the principle of state obligation and state sovereignty was born. The full implementation of this principle, however, has presented a problem throughout the development of education in America, and has been the basis of a number of court decisions in recent years.

## Early Elementary Schools

Educational practices in the early colonial period provided little in the way of an organized pattern of elementary education. Dame schools, early parochial schools, private tutors, apprenticeships, and pauper schools developed quite independently of one another. This condition was due in part to the fact that parents were expected to care for the rudimentary education of their children.

**The common school**  Gradually, various systems were developed for teaching the three R's to youngsters. There were reading schools and writing schools, and often the two were combined into one. The pupils could attend one school in the morning and the other in the afternoon. These became the common schools that spread first through the New England area. There were no rigid regulations about entrance or attendance or withdrawal. The common schools served the masses of youngsters, most of whom did not attend the Latin grammar school or college.

Life in and around these early schools was very different from that in our modern public schools. It is very difficult to visualize the conditions under which colonial settlers struggled to obtain an education. In place of the modern, large, well-lighted, and heated building, they had a single, bare, unattractive room. The room typically was a rough log structure. A few of the better school buildings had glazed windows. In structures which were designated solely for the use of education, the usual practice

The typical early American schoolroom was a far cry from the attractive well-heated and well-ventilated classrooms of today. (*Photograph from the Library of Congress.*)

The hornbook takes its name from the thick sheet of transparent horn used to protect the paper from dirt. (*Photograph from Ruth Strickland.*)

was to leave a log out of one side of the building in order to provide both light and ventilation.

More often than not a rough plank served as the teacher's desk. Long, rough, backless benches were provided for the pupils. Often the feet of the young children did not touch the floor. Equipment was quite meager. Along one side of the room, there would occasionally be a long shelf where students would practice such activities as penmanship, using quill pens. A great stone fireplace furnished the only heat by which the children could keep warm. As with many a present-day fireplace, those who were close to its blazing hearth were likely to get scorched while those farthest away shivered with the cold. Considering many reports of complaints which were recorded and passed down to posterity, it was evident that most of these rooms and buildings were in sad need of repair.

It was in this kind of atmosphere that the hornbook was used. This aid to learning consisted of a piece of wood shaped like a paddle to give a convenient handle. Fastened to the thin board was a sheet of paper on which was printed the alphabet, some syllables, and usually the Lord's Prayer. Various primers were used along with the hornbook.

**The New England Primer**   This first appeared in 1690 and was one of the more famous primers. During a period of more than a hundred years, this book dominated the curriculum of the elementary schools and 3 million copies were sold. The primer was a crudely printed 90-page booklet, with pages about one-fourth the size of those in our present textbooks. The primer contained the alphabet, syllables, and a few spelling lists. The alphabet was learned through the use of rhymes beginning with "In Adam's fall, We sinned all." A large part of its contents consisted of two catechisms: John Cotton's *Spiritual Milk for Boston Babes . . . Drawn Out of the Breasts of Both Testaments for Their Souls' Nourishment* and the *Westminster Shorter Catechism.* This reading material was made of doleful admonitions such as the following:

> Tho' I am young, yet I may die,
> And hasten to eternity;
> There is a dreadful fiery Hell,
> Where wicked ones must always dwell;
> There is a heaven full of joy,
> Where Godly ones must always stay;
> To one of these my soul must fly,
> As in a moment when I die.

Teaching methods and materials in these early schools were almost as crude as the buildings in which they were housed. Except for the spelldowns, each pupil was called before the teacher and recited individually. This practice was largely necessitated by the lack of books, writing paper, pens, and ink. It was common for some of the smaller children to receive only 15 to 20 minutes of individual attention from the teacher during a school day of six to eight hours. During the remainder of the time they were expected to sit quietly on their rough, uncomfortable benches. Slow children might take as long as three terms to master the alphabet. Since arithmetic books were rare, pupils made copy books and sum books by folding sheets of rough paper and sewing them along one edge.

Crude, poorly lighted and heated structures, limited teaching methods, and a dearth of teaching materials were all typical of our early elementary schools. Yet in these schools, while engaged in the consuming task of building a new world, our forefathers preserved the rudiments of learning.

As the population continued to increase, people began moving away from the towns to develop new farming areas. Their children had to travel longer and longer distances to attend school until it became quite difficult for them to get there at all. In some instances school would be held in one part of the township during one term and in another during the next term. This rotation of schools gave rise to the famous "moving school" of early New England days.

Because of the limitations of educational facilities, people in outlying districts organized their own schools, one for each extended neighborhood. Thus were born the "district schools," a term not uncommonly used today. Here there was usually one teacher, often with as many as fifty pupils or more. The counterpart of the district school persists to this day all over the nation.

## The Academy

At about the time of the Revolutionary War, there was a strong demand for a more practical kind of education beyond the three R's. Men who tilled the soil, fought Indians, sailed ships, developed commerce, and started industries in America began to question the appropriateness of the narrow and rigid college preparatory curriculum of the grammar school to train youngsters for a practical world. Such men were led by Benjamin Franklin, who established the first public academy in Philadelphia in 1751.

This academy was essentially a private tuition school, though some academies gained public support and eventually became public schools. In the academy, English as a language was emphaiszed; girls were admitted to study; school libraries were established; American history and natural science were introduced; mathematics, especially algebra, navigation, and astronomy, was emphasized; and logic, ethics, and psychology, as well as commerce, surveying, debating, dramatics, and athletics, were given attention. The academy movement led to deeper concern for human progress and higher respect for human worth. It stimulated better teaching in the elementary school and provided good educational opportunity for the emerging middle class in America—the substantial farmers, businessmen, tradesmen, and government workers. The movement spread rapidly over the United States.

The academy started out with three particular curricula: the English, the Latin, and the mathematical. A fourth was soon added—the philosophical. The teachings of the Latin and philosophical divisions were geared to prepare youngsters for college. Eventually the college preparatory aspects of the academy involved more and more of the time and energy of teachers and pupils alike. By the turn of the nineteenth century, the academy acquired most of the characteristics of the Latin grammar school against which it originally protested. It became narrow, rigid, select, essentially classical, and college preparatory in nature.

The academy movement enjoyed wide prosperity, reaching a peak at about the time of the Civil War. Although the number of Latin grammar schools never grew large, there were over 6,000 academies in the United States by 1850. Many of these are still in existence and hold a distinctive position among private college preparatory schools. Some academies, such as Franklin's original one, which became the University of Pennsylvania, have contributed significantly to higher education.

| Present Name | Date | Religious Affiliation |
|---|---|---|
| Harvard University | 1636 | Congregational |
| College of William and Mary | 1693 | Episcopal |
| Yale University | 1701 | Congregational |
| Princeton University | 1746 | Presbyterian |
| University of Pennsylvania | 1753 | None |
| Columbia University | 1754 | Episcopal |
| Brown University | 1764 | Baptist |
| Rutgers University | 1766 | Dutch Reformed |
| Dartmouth University | 1769 | Congregational |
| Washington College | 1782 | Episcopal |
| Washington and Lee University | 1782 | Presbyterian |
| Hampton-Sidney College | 1783 | Presbyterian |
| Transylvania College | 1783 | Presbyterian |
| Dickinson College | 1783 | Presbyterian |
| St. John's College | 1784 | Episcopal |
| University of Georgia | 1785 | None |
| College of Charleston | 1785 | Episcopal |
| Georgetown University | 1786 | Catholic |
| Franklin and Marshall College | 1787 | German Reformed |
| University of North Carolina | 1789 | None |
| University of Vermont | 1791 | None |
| Williams College | 1793 | Congregational |
| Bowdoin College | 1794 | Congregational |
| Tusculum College | 1794 | Presbyterian |
| University of Tennessee | 1794 | Presbyterian |
| Union University | 1795 | Presbyterian |

Source: Edward J. Power, *Education for American Democracy: An Introduction to Education,* McGraw-Hill Book Company, New York, 1958, p. 201. Used by permission.

## Higher Education

The religious influences and English collegiate tradition imported from abroad were dominant factors in the establishment of our first colleges. Harvard University, founded in 1636, was a copy of Emmanuel College, Cambridge University, England. Practically all our early American colleges were developed under the auspices of some church in order to provide means for perpetuating a literate ministry for their churches. It was not until the establishment of the University of Pennsylvania in 1753 that an institution of higher learning was sponsored by a civil group instead of the church. Growth of universities was slow during the colonial period. As you may note from the above table, only nine universities had been established by 1775.

## Education and the Constitution

The principles of freedom and the equality of mankind were emphasized in the writing and adoption of the Declaration of Independence in 1776.

"We hold these truths to be self-evident: that all men are created equal; that they are endowed by their Creator with certain unalienable rights; that among these are life, liberty and the pursuit of happiness; that to secure these rights, governments are instituted among men, deriving their just powers from the consent of the governed."

Although there was little evidence throughout the Colonies of equality of educational opportunities, the principle has been of tremendous importance in shaping the development of our public school system. Problems still remain, however, in fully implementing the principle, as you will note in Chapters 13 and 18.

Education was a major concern of those attending the Constitutional Convention of 1787. Such leaders as Washington and Jefferson were strong advocates of a centralized system of education in order to preserve liberty and to enable mankind to govern himself. Washington felt so keenly that there should be a federally sponsored national university that he left a part of his estate to endow such a university, but the institution was never established. In 1779, Jefferson clearly expressed his concern for free education in his "Bill for the More General Diffusion of Knowledge" in the following manner [87:221]:

And whereas it is generally true that the people will be happiest whose laws are best, and are best administered, and that laws will be wisely formed, and honestly administered, in proportion as those who form and administer them are wise and honest; whence it becomes expedient for promoting the publick happiness that those persons, whom nature hath endowed with genius and virtue, should be rendered by liberal education worthy to receive, and able to guard the sacred deposit of the rights and liberties of their fellow citizens, and that they should be called to that charge without regard to wealth, birth, or other accidental condition or circumstance; but the indigence of the greater number disabling them from so educating, at their own expence, those of their children whom nature hath fitly formed and disposed to become useful instruments for the publick, it is better that such should be sought for and educated at the common expence of all, than that the happiness of all should be confined to the weak or wicked.

Some of those attending the Constitutional Convention had reservations about the government being responsible for education. As a result, the writers of the constitution made no specific provision for the promotion of education. In reflecting upon this fact, Burrup [34:42] makes the following comment:

There appear to be at least three important reasons why education was thus neglected: (1) solution to problems of education did not seem to be so necessary and urgent at that particular time as many others which the new country faced; (2) consideration of the role of education contained the possibility of stirring up more dissension among the 13 states; (3) several of the original colonies already had some semblance of state educational systems. In the light of all the problems extant at this particular crucial time in American history, perhaps it is fortunate that the important question of the relationship of education to government was left until a later time when more consideration could be given to its solution.

Although the Constitution did not specifically mention education,

Article 1, Section 8 specified that Congress was to have power for the general welfare of the people. This expression formed the basis for federal support of education. In 1785, Congress adopted an ordinance relative to the Northwest Territory to the effect that "there shall be reserved the lot number sixteen of every township for the maintenance of public schools within the said township," and in 1787 the following important statement appeared in the famous Northwest Ordinance of 1787: "Religion, morality, and knowledge being necessary to good government and the happiness of mankind, schools and the means of education shall be forever encouraged." These documents, as well as the thinking of a number of outstanding leaders, did much to lay the foundation for more rapid educational developments to follow.

The Bill of Rights, ratified in 1791, defined the role of education more clearly than did the Constitution. The First Amendment of this bill strengthened the principle of the separation of the church and state by forbidding the establishment of a national or state religion and by guaranteeing religious liberty to all. The Tenth Amendment declared that "the powers not delegated to the United States by Constitution, nor prohibited by it to the States, are reserved to the States respectively, or to the people." As a result, education in the United States was destined to develop as a state function in contrast to the single educational system typical of other nations throughout the world. The federal government was to be confined to a supportive, grants-in-aid type of role.

## Education of Minority Groups

The opportunity to engage in a program of formal education was almost nonexistent for members of minority groups during the Colonial era. For blacks, most of whom were slaves, formal education was generally discouraged or forbidden by the slave-holders. For the American Indian, who was struggling for survival and who was frequently in conflict with white settlers over land ownership, formal education was of little immediate concern.

There were some limited attempts on the part of church-related groups and colleges to provide for the educational needs of minority group members. The Quakers, for example, established programs of education for blacks and American Indians. Indian charity schools were established by other groups, primarily in the Middle and New England colonies. Both Harvard and Dartmouth expressed a desire to educate the youth of Indian tribes. The College of William and Mary, chartered in 1693, declared that one of its purposes was to teach Indian boys religion and the 3 R's.

The Society for the Propagation of the Gospel, which was originated in England, sent 300 missionaries to the Southern colonies in 1701 to teach blacks and American Indians to read and write. In addition to basic education, the Society was also concerned with the religious education of these two minority groups. The work of the Society was viewed by some states as an invasion of the internal affairs of the state and thus was often met with strong opposition. South Carolina, for example, enacted legislation which prohibited the teaching of writing to slaves [223:29].

Although some church-groups and colleges made efforts to provide some type of formal educational experiences for members of minority groups, only a small number of those eligible were allowed to participate. This was at a time in history when a majority of the Anglo-American children were enrolled in the equivalent of an elementary school.


## EDUCATION IN EARLY AMERICA (1792–1865)

The development of an organized system of education received relatively little attention for several years following the Revolutionary War. This was a period of transition in which the thoughts and energies of people were concerned primarily with such matters as the formulation of a constitution, the establishment and operation of an organized system of states, and the fighting of the War of 1812.

At first, other factors tended to push education into the background. The rapid development of industry in America encouraged many children to work in mills, stores, and shops rather than to attend schools. Many families, especially immigrant families, were so poor that they needed whatever money their children could earn. The need for earning a living in order to survive was so great that education tended to be considered a luxury. Also, the extreme mobility of settlers who continued to push westward made the task of establishing permanent schools difficult. There was little time for education in the rugged life of the pioneer. Teachers were scarce. Churches, sod houses, and log cabins often were used as schoolhouses. The sparse settlements across the land were not conducive to the establishment of school districts.

During this critical time, however, new meanings and values were emerging in the minds of people. Greater attention was being given to concepts of democracy, freedom, equality, individual rights, and faith in the common man.

By approximately 1825 our nation had achieved a certain amount of national stability and had begun to develop rapidly. The population was increasing, with much of the increase coming from the large streams of immigrants arriving in America. Industry was growing rapidly, and labor associations were beginning to be formed. The economic and social status of the common man was beginning to improve.

## The Fight for Free Schools

Prior to the 1820s, the idea that state and local governments should provide schools for all children through public taxation was slow in being accepted outside of New England. In the Middle states, the concept of education being the responsibility of the church and of private agencies continued to exist. Education in the Southern states was still considered to be largely a responsibility of parents. Voting privileges in a number of states had been limited to those who owned property, and many of the property owners felt that they should not be forced to pay for the education of other people's children.

When voting rights were extended to all men of legal age, the need for universal education became more apparent. Labor groups, likewise, began to demand more educational opportunities for children. Greater concern was being expressed for the equality of man and the need for free, nonsectarian, public schools.

Public school societies were organized in various cities. Public-spirited citizens became members of these societies, contributing sums of money annually to carry forward the educational program. The most famous and probably the most efficient of these organizations was the New York Public School Society, which for 40 years was New York City's chief agency for educating the children of the poorer classes.

A number of outstanding leaders emerged to help fight the battle for free schools. Particularly noted among them were Horace Mann of Massachusetts, who became known as "the father of the American free public school," Henry Barnard of Connecticut, Thaddeus Stevens of Pennsylvania, John D. Pierce of Michigan, Caleb Mills of Indiana, Robert J. Breckinridge of Kentucky, Ninian Edwards of Illinois, and Lyman Rucker and Calvin Stowe of Ohio. In general it was maintained that these common schools should be: (1) free and open to all since no other system, least of all the dual system used in Europe, was acceptable for a democracy; (2) of such excellent quality that all parents would be willing to send their children to them; (3) common in the sense that all children would attend and that it would serve as a unifying force to weld communities together; (4) publicly supported through taxation of the whole community; (5) publicly controlled through elected or appointed public officials responsible to the whole community and not to any particular political, economic, or religious group; (6) nonsectarian in character; and should (7) provide the basic knowledge and skills essential to enable students of diverse backgrounds to assume responsibilities of citizenship in the young Republic [adapted, 37:127–128].

The men who fought for public schools marshaled their arguments along the following lines [adapted, 37:128]:

1.  Suffrage had been extended to include all men, and if men were going to vote they had to be educated.

2. Pauper schools and the private and religious schools were inadequate because (a) the pauper schools had a social stigma which kept many children from attending, (b) fees charged by private schools kept some children from attending school, and (c) religious schools might force certain religious teachings upon children.
3. Education was essential to preserve the well-being of the state by preventing pauperism and crime and by reducing poverty and distress.
4. Schools would help prevent a class society from forming.
5. Education served to increase productivity.
6. Education is the God-given right of all children.

By 1865 the concept of providing common-school education for all children at public expense had gained considerable acceptance. A number of states, especially in New England and in some of the Middle states, had enacted laws compelling local communities to support through taxation what would be considered public elementary schools.

Although less intense, the battle for free public schools has continued through the years. Even today there are some who question the right of the government to tax everyone for the support of schools. The issue often becomes very conspicuous when kindergartens and junior colleges are proposed to be a part of local public school systems.

## The Lancastrian System

In the early 1800s, the financing of schools enrolling several thousands of children presented a problem of staggering proportions. Fortunately, a new plan of school organization and management was introduced from England to New York City in 1806, which tremendously reduced the cost of educating a child. Most of the society schools rapidly adopted this new plan. It was known as the Lancastrian system, named after its founder, Joseph Lancaster, an English schoolmaster. In this system, one teacher, by using his brightest pupils as monitors to teach about ten pupils each, might himself be in charge of from 200 to 600 pupils. The schoolmaster taught the monitors, who in turn taught their groups. Everything was rigidly organized in a somewhat military fashion. Each group was marched to its station along the wall of a large classroom, where the monitor presented the lesson. Lancaster himself thought that a real master teacher could take care of 1,000 pupils. With such a high pupil-teacher ratio, it was reported that the per capita cost of operating a school was reduced to $1.25 per year per pupil.

Because of the great public service the school societies were rendering, they felt justified in asking the government for aid in carrying out their program. In some instances this was given. Both the state and city governments in New York regularly contributed substantial sums to the New York society to help support its schools. New York City in 1832 was the first city to establish free public elementary schools. Gradually the public mind became accustomed to the idea of governmental support of schools, and the low cost of the Lancastrian system began to suggest that this way of supporting schools might not be prohibitive. While the system passed away within a few decades, it did much to advance the cause of free public education.

Some modified remnants of the Lancastrian concept can be found in educational circles today—the manner in which teacher aides frequently are used, some aspects of differentiated staffing, pupil-assisted instruction, the use of large lecture and small discussion sections on the college level, and the use of student tutors. As public schools, colleges, and universities face mounting financial costs, it is possible that further extensions of the basic concept may be explored and practiced. In fact, an opinion survey on "What Will the Schools Become?" indicates that "the use of student tutors (for example, 11-year-olds working with six-year-olds in reading) will be commonplace if not a standard procedure by the early 1980's" [243:597].

## The Kindergarten

Although an infants' school was established in Boston as early as 1816, the kindergarten as conceived by Friedrich Froebel, its founder, was not introduced into America until 1855. In that year, Mrs. Carl Schurz, a strong disciple of Froebel, established a private kindergarten in Watertown, Wisconsin.

During the next 15 years about ten private kindergartens were organized in German-speaking communities. In 1860 the first English-speaking private kindergarten was opened in Boston, and eight years later a teacher training course for kindergarten teachers was established in Boston. Under the auspices of Superintendent William T. Harris of St. Louis, the first public school kindergarten in the United States was opened there in 1873.

There has been considerable misunderstanding regarding the role of the kindergarten in our educational system. Many people feel that what the kindergarten features in its program is already included in a good primary school program. Since the kindergarten is a relatively new rung in our educational ladder, it has had to compete with other schools for public support. As a result of these attitudes and forces, the establishment of kindergartens as an integral part of public schools throughout the United States has been greatly retarded—so much so that many of our children still do not attend a kindergarten.

## The Primary School

In 1818 another school was introduced in Boston which became known as the "primary school." Children of ages four through seven were admitted to this school. At first the primary schools were distinctly separate from other schools in the city. They were open all year and prepared children for admission to the city schools, which by this time were known as "English grammar schools." The primary schools had their own buildings and teachers and were quite different from the dame schools, which had previously prepared the pupils for entrance to the grammar schools.

It was not until the latter half of the nineteenth century that primary schools were made a part of the general school system. It often has been pointed out that this origin of the lower grades led to a distinction between primary and grammar grades—a distinction which may be found even today.

## Changes in Elementary School Practices and Building Construction

As social and economic advancements were made, the educational needs of boys and girls expanded. As a result, the curriculum of the elementary school was expanded beyond the teaching of reading, spelling, arithmetic, and religious instruction, which characterized the early elementary schools.

Pupils originally were not grouped into grades as they usually are today. In approximately 1848, a rudimentary type of grading was attempted in the large schools by roughly dividing the pupils into age groups and assigning the groups to different teachers.

The graded-school concept spread rapidly and froze the vertical organization of schools into a pattern that has persisted since its inception. The concept was based upon three main assumptions: "(1) Elementary . . . schools should 'cover' a specific body of subject matter; (2) this subject matter should be identified and rigorously prescribed; and (3) individual differences merely determine one's chances of success in the race to cover the prescribed material" [232:79–80]. If a child was unable to master the prescribed material, he was retained in the grade. The motto was "If at first you don't succeed, try, try, again."

It has been pointed out that [232:80]:

In spite of its firm hold on our educational system, the graded system has been under criticism almost from the beginning. The mold had scarcely stiffened before some educators began to question it, contending that the graded "lock-step" denied individuality, stifled initiative, and unjustly punished the willing but slow. Many experimental plans to modify grade-by-grade progression were conceived, but most of them grew and died without reproducing their kind. The graded system, efficient for classifying large numbers of students, became standard practice.

The graded type of school organization suggested the desirability of having a room for each group and led to a new type of school building designed in 1848. It was three stories high, and on each story—except for the top one, which was one large assembly room—there were four separate rooms designed to accommodate approximately fifty children each. Cloakrooms were substituted for the usual small recitation chambers which adjoined the large room. This type of building became standard for a large part of the country. In almost any city established prior to the twentieth century, school buildings constructed on this general plan can still be found.

## The Early Public High School

One of the important lessons for educators to learn from a study of the history of education is the fact that the public starts searching for alternative systems whenever the existing schools fail to meet the educational needs of that society. An example is to be found in the dissatisfaction that grew over the academy, even though it represented certain important improvements over the Latin grammar school. People whose children had completed the common schools but could not or would not attend the expensive aristocratic private academies insisted increasingly upon more education of a practical sort at public expense. Their efforts bore fruit in 1821, with the establishment of the Boston English Classical School, the first high school in the United States. The name was soon changed to the English High School because of the emphasis given to the teaching of English rather than the classics.

This type of high school, however, developed slowly. In 1840 there were no more than fifty. Except for the omission of Greek and Latin, the programs offered by these high schools were at first very similar to those of the original academy. Pupils were admitted upon examination at the age of 12 for a three-year course. The high school was free to all the pupils.

## Strengthening of State Departments of Education

During the first part of the nineteenth century a number of people became concerned over the great variation among communities in the extent to which they provided for the education of the young. It was felt that if a local school district were left free to provide a poor education or no education at all for its children, the welfare of the state would suffer. Furthermore, these children would be denied their birthright to an education that would prepare them for effective citizenship.

There was a gradual growth in the feeling that each state must exert more authority to ensure educational opportunities for all of its children. As a result, New York State created the office of state superintendent of schools in 1812. Massachusetts established a state board of education in 1837 with the distinguished Horace Mann serving as secretary. Henry Barnard became the first secretary of the state board of education estab-

Horace Mann (1796–1859) gave up a brilliant career in law and politics in order to campaign vigorously for better schools and better teachers. Among his many contributions, he helped establish the first normal school for teachers in Lexington, Massachusetts. (*Photograph from the Library of Congress.*)

lished in Connecticut in 1839. Other states followed. As Butts [36:38] pointed out in his excellent article, "Search for Freedom":

These state agencies could then set minimum standards for all the schools of the state. Meanwhile, the direct management of schools would be left in the hands of locally elected school boards, local superintendents, and locally appointed teachers. Local management served the cause of flexibility, diversity, and freedom.

This arrangement was designed to assure that schools would serve the whole *public* and would be controlled by the *public* through special boards of education, not through the regular agencies of the state or local governments. This is why in America we use the term public schools, not simply state schools or government schools, as they are often called in those countries that have centralized systems of education.

## Developments in Higher Education

In order to meet the growing needs of a young nation and to provide an educational outlet for the liberalism which developed during the revolutionary period, more colleges and universities were established. Twenty-six, having a combined enrollment of 2,000 students, had been established by 1800, and the number continued to increase. Little opposition to these new colleges was encountered in those sections where colleges had not already been established. However, when some of the older states attempted to turn the already existing colleges into nonsectarian state universities, friction resulted. The climax was reached in the famous Dartmouth College Case in 1819. The decision, which was handed down by the United States Supreme Court under Chief Justice John Marshall, specified that states could not modify the charter of a college without the consent of the institution's authorities. Although this decision terminated the attempts of a number of states to transform private colleges into public ones, it did provide the stimulus for the establishment of state universities and more private colleges. Since then, private and denominational institutions have undergone many changes, so that in many ways it is difficult at the present time to distinguish them from state or public institutions.

In 1862 the Morrill Act was passed by Congress and signed by President Lincoln; it led to the establishment of land-grant colleges. This legislation gave 30,000 acres of public land to each state for every representative and senator the state had in Congress. This land and the proceeds from its sale were to be used to endow colleges or universities which would teach agriculture and the mechanical arts in such a manner as the legislatures of the respective states prescribed. Scientific and classical studies and military tactics were not to be excluded from the curriculum. In general, the states were to promote the liberal and practical education of the industrial classes. To date, a total of almost 11,400,000 acres of public land has been given for endowment of these colleges by the federal government. When the centennial celebration was held for the signing of the Morrill Act, there were sixty-nine land-grant colleges and universities in the United States. Many of these institutions were originally named agricultural and mechanical colleges, but most of them have since changed their names to state universities.

Prior to 1860 higher education in our country was dominantly the concern of denominational and private colleges; after 1860 the land-grant colleges and universities increased rapidly in number, size, and influence. As this happened, the character of many of the private and denominational schools changed markedly and the pattern of higher education as we know it today began to evolve.

## Teacher Education Institutions

The first institutions to undertake the preparation of teachers in our country were the academies. Although there were a few sporadic efforts to train teachers for special assignments, such as the infants' school and the kindergarten, these were isolated attempts and did not foster the whole idea of teacher preparation. Although teacher training was not one of the more important functions of the academy, it provided some of the initial impetus to the movement. Actually, the academy provided preparation only in the subject-matter fields. Methods, techniques, observation, and student teaching were not included in the curriculum.

Before the establishment of the first public normal school in America at Lexington, Massachusetts, in 1839, teachers' seminaries existed in Germany, where they offered a rich background in subject matter and courses in the professional preparation of teachers. There is considerable controversy among historians of education as to whether the concept of teacher preparation had originated from these German seminaries or was indigenous to America, but some of the features of the American normal school were definitely unique. It should be noted, however, that the American normal schools and the German seminaries both had as their point of origin an extension of the academy. Regardless of the exact origin, normal schools were the most influential type of American teacher training institutions for almost a hundred years.

The teacher training programs of the early normal schools were usually one year in length. Gradually this practice gave way to a two-year course of study, and, shortly before the teachers college development, a few normal schools had developed strong four-year programs. In addition to a review of the common branch subjects—reading, writing, arithmetic, spelling, and grammar—the normal school also taught the science and art of teaching and classroom management. Often there were opportunities to do practice teaching in a "model" school.

## Education of Minority Groups

When compared with the condition which existed in the Colonial era, provision of formal educational opportunities for members of minority groups, such as the blacks, American Indian, Mexican American and Chinese, showed little improvement during this period of history. These groups were frequently struggling to provide themselves with the basic necessities of life—food and shelter. In some cases, they were also fighting to retain land which they believed rightfully belonged to them. As a result, formal education was necessarily a low priority item for many minority group members. Those who sought education were often discouraged. Slave-holders generally provided no education for blacks, thereby perpetuating ignorance and dependence. In some states, teaching blacks to read was illegal. The educational opportunities for blacks living in the Northern states were superior to conditions in the South, but only a small percentage of the black population lived outside the South. The minimal education programs which did exist, principally for blacks and American Indians, ignored the cultural heritage of these groups and concentrated on conformity to the mores of white society.

Blacks were not solely dependent upon the "white majority" for education in this period of history. There are several recorded instances where groups of blacks attempted to provide for their educational needs. In 1807, a group of former slaves built the first schoolhouse for blacks in the District of Columbia. The curriculum in this school consisted of reading, writing, arithmetic, and English grammar. In 1810, blacks in Charleston, South Carolina, organized the "Minor Society" which established and supported a school for blacks. A group of Baltimore blacks established a school for adult blacks in 1820. By the middle of the nineteenth century, blacks in Philadelphia were operating schools and had established a system of Lyceums and debating clubs. The self-educating efforts of blacks were highly significant because they gave blacks a sense of pride and accomplishment, enhanced their self-image, and contributed toward self-sufficiency [149:353].

## EDUCATION IN THE POST CIVIL WAR PERIOD (1865–1918)

Following the Civil War, rapid progress was made in the industrialization of America. This progress was fostered through advancements in science and technology. More power became available; new machines were invented; and transportation facilities were improved. Through the application of mass production and specialization, America was destined to become an industrial giant.

Industrialization brought about the formation of corporations, new methods of management, and an increased amount of urbanization. With these changes, the demands for more and better education arose. Progress in medicine and sanitation reduced the rate of infant mortality and increased the life-span. Immigrants continued to stream to our shores. As a result more children needed to be educated. More and better teachers had to be trained. More and better schools had to be built. More educational opportunities at the higher levels had to be provided. During this time segment the foundation for the system of education which now exists in this country largely became established. The concept of free public high schools for all youth gained acceptance, both the junior high school and the junior college were conceived, vocational education gained support in the secondary school curriculum, and programs for the preparation of teachers were altered and expanded.

### Secondary Education

Initially, the progress of the free public high school (English high school) was slow because many people considered it unnecessary and maintained that it would be too costly for the government. Many were unwilling to pay additional taxes when they had no children in school. A test case of public-supported high schools developed in Kalamazoo, Michigan, in 1874. The state supreme court ruled that, upon the consent of the citizens, a city could levy taxes to support free public secondary schools. Similar decisions and laws followed rapidly in other states, resulting in the legal establishment of the high school as an integral part of our free public school system. Once the concept of free, publicly supported high schools was established, the academies declined in popularity, and the die was cast for a comprehensive high school which would serve the needs of all youth, offering both terminal and college preparatory work. The comprehensive high school distinguished the free American public high school from the dual system of secondary education which existed in Europe. As a result, free public high schools began to prosper, and by the turn of the century they enrolled approximately one-half million students.

Although the foundation for the comprehensive public high school had been established, the concept failed to fully materialize until following World War I. Due to the rapid growth in both the number of students and schools, organizational problems became acute in the late 1800s. Colleges expressed concern about the wide diversity which existed in high school programs. Given the lack of standards or guideposts, the instructional hours devoted to a given subject, such as chemistry, varied from the equivalent of one hour per day for 12 weeks in one school, to the equivalent of one hour per day for 30 weeks in another school. Colleges were also disturbed by the excessive duplication of the elementary school curriculum at the secondary school level. The instructional program in grades seven and eight was often a repetition of programs existing in earlier grades. Various national committees studied the problems and made specific recommendations which led to the establishment of the Carnegie Unit and a rigid college preparatory program for the public secondary schools. As a result, the comprehensive high school concept was temporarily shelved in favor of a single, narrow curriculum for all students, which allowed for little or no elective courses.

The college preparatory pattern dominated the secondary school curriculum until 1918 when the Commission on the Reorganization of Secondary Education issued its momentous report entitled the *Cardinal Principles of Secondary Education.* This report served to reorient people to the central purposes of education in a free society. In essence, the findings and recommendations of this Commission amounted to an emancipation of secondary education in the United States. Following the issuance of this report, secondary schools gradually became more comprehensive in nature, thus, better serving the needs of all who sought entrance.

## The Junior High School

The junior high school represents a fairly new development in American education. Several eminent educators had become dissatisfied with the graded elementary school as it was set up during the 1840s and 1850s. Their dissatisfaction was called to the public's attention by an address delivered by President C. W. Eliot of Harvard University in a meeting of the Department of Superintendents of the National Education Association in 1888. Shortly after this address, several committees were appointed by the NEA and they began to study the situation. One of the more famous of these groups, the Committee of Ten, made specific recommendations concerning problems affecting elementary, secondary, and higher education. Early reports from this and similar committees favored a 6-6 plan, i.e., six years of elementary education and six years of secondary education. Numerous subsequent reports suggested that the secondary school be divided into two separate institutions—one to be known as the junior high school and the other as the senior high school, i.e., the 6-3-3 plan.

In 1909, junior high schools were established at Columbus, Ohio, and Berkeley, California; there has always been considerable controversy as to which one was first established. Principles upon which the junior high school was founded include [183:4]:

1. Articulation—helping children to go from elementary school through junior high school into senior high school with as little difficulty as possible
2. Exploration—giving young teen-agers a chance to find out through brief experiences what some of the high school courses were like, with the expectation that this would help them to choose their senior high school courses more wisely
3. Educational guidance—helping pupils to choose from among elective subjects offered in the junior and later in the senior high school
4. Vocational guidance—helping pupils to make decisions about jobs and careers
5. Activity—providing social and athletic experiences and giving the students a chance to participate in administration and control of the school

## Junior College

During the latter part of the nineteenth century considerable demand was being made to extend public secondary school programs into the thirteenth and fourteenth grades. A few private junior colleges already had been organized. For example, New London Seminary in New Hampshire, founded in 1837, became Colby Junior College. Decatur Baptist College, founded in Texas in 1891, was reorganized into a private junior college in 1898.

Through the encouragement of President William Rainey Harper of the University of Chicago, the public high schools of Joliet, Illinois, established a separate educational unit in 1902 that included grades 13 and 14. This became the first public junior college in America. President Harper agreed that the University of Chicago would accept any credits earned by students attending this junior college. He reorganized the program at the University junior and senior college with the hope that the University eventually would not need to provide freshman and sophomore course work.

At first, junior colleges attempted to offer the same courses as those offered during the freshman and sophomore years of regular colleges and universities. Later a number of the junior colleges began to adapt their programs to the needs of their respective communities and were called "community colleges." Regardless of whether or not students planned to transfer to a regular college or university, these colleges provided terminal programs, designed to prepare students for occupations primarily in their communities. Frequently late-afternoon and evening courses were offered especially to serve the needs of adult members of the community.

## Vocational Education

Although the college preparatory program dominated high school curricula during the post Civil War period, some attempts were made to include "manual training" in both elementary and secondary schools. In a few cases, in selected high schools specifically designated as manual training schools, college preparatory courses were omitted from the curriculum.

Vocational education was greatly enhanced in the early part of the twentieth century through the passage of the Smith-Hughes Act. This federal legislation provided aid for vocational teachers' salaries and for teacher training programs geared to the preparation of vocational teachers.

## Teacher Preparation

As the normal school movement gradually gave way to the teachers college movement, the number of students in teacher education institutions increased enormously. These institutions eventually became degree-granting colleges beginning in the early 1890s. Several states, however, did not require a four-year college degree for certification, and as a result, many teachers were certified after completing a preparation program of two or fewer years in duration.

In-service education programs for teachers, usually in the form of teacher institutes, also became a popular means of upgrading the skills of teachers during this period. Frequently, two or three days were reserved during the school year for these institutes. During this period, teachers would travel to a central location to listen to speeches, to participate in discussions, and to view exhibits of instructional materials prepared by participating school districts and textbook publishers. These programs were generally sponsored by professional organizations, such as the National Education Association or state teacher associations, and in some cases by state departments of public instruction or local school districts.

## Education of Minority Groups

Numerous attempts to improve the educational opportunities for members of minority groups in the United States were made in the period immediately following the Civil War. Blacks in the South had been freed from the bonds of slavery and were in desperate need of education to become self-sufficient and truly free. The federal government recognized the need to provide basic education programs for American Indians and began to assume this responsibility. Interest in providing formal education programs for Mexican Americans and Chinese also grew during this era. All levels of government, foundations, religious groups, philanthropists, and the National Education Association seemingly developed an awareness of the need to provide at least a program of basic education for members of minority groups.

Efforts to aid blacks resulted in congressional creation of the Freedmen's Bureau in 1865. This bureau, which was staffed primarily by white teachers from the North, was established to provide basic education programs for blacks in the South and to help them in their transition from slavery to freedom. The Freedmen's Bureau was moderately successful in helping many blacks develop basic skills and improve their self-concept; however, it did not accomplish its goal of preparing blacks to enter the mainstream of life in the United States.

Later in this time period individual Southern states made provisions in their constitutions for the support of black schools. Although the support represented a significant improvement over previous conditions, it was inferior to that provided for schools enrolling "white" students.

In addition to the efforts of governmental bodies, religious and charitable groups and private foundations also promoted programs of education for blacks in the South. These groups provided funds, established programs, aided in the preparation of teachers, and assisted in the construction of physical facilities. For example, in 1867, George Peabody, a wealthy philanthropist, contributed substantial funds for improving the preparation of black teachers in the South.

One of the early leaders of education for blacks was Booker T. Washington, a black graduate of Virginia's Hampton Institute. Washington advocated a program of reading, writing, and industrial education for blacks as a means of preparing them for useful and gainful employment. In an effort to place his ideas into practice, Washington founded Tuskegee Institute in 1881. The curriculum in this Alabama school for blacks emphasized practical and useful subjects, but was also concerned with improving the self-concept of the black. Although Washington is credited with providing significant leadership in the cause of black education, he was not without his critics. W. E. B. DuBois, a black scholar, for example, contended that a curriculum stressing vocational training was too narrow in scope. He wanted blacks to have a liberal education background. He believed that blacks should have a broad choice of programs, thereby enabling them to prepare for any and all types of employment. He feared that vocational preparation would perpetuate blacks as second-class citizens and deny them equal opportunity [286:193–194].

Educational provisions for American Indians were significantly different from those for other minority groups because the federal government, in negotiating treaties with various Indian tribes, guaranteed that it would provide for the formal educational needs of the American Indian. In the late 1800s, the federal government chose to meet this responsibility by providing funds to various religious groups for the operation of Indian mission schools rather than operate these schools itself. However, this practice was discontinued when the public protested the use of federal moneys for the support of religious-oriented schools. As a result, a system of federally operated schools for American Indians developed.

The primary educational thrust during this period of history with regard to members of minority groups was to provide the masses with a program of basic education to assist them to be self-sufficient, participating members of a democratic society. Woodson and Wesley, however, maintained that "The education of the Negro, therefore, has been largely a process of telling the Negro what someone else wants him to say or do and watching him do it in automation fashion" [300:572]. This task was a formidable one because of the minimal efforts which had been made prior to the Civil War. To a much lesser extent, emphasis was also placed upon school integration. But the fight for integrated schools received a strong setback when in 1896 the U.S. Supreme Court ruled in the Plessy v. Ferguson [163 US 537, 16 Sup. Ct. 1138] case that separate but equal treatment of minority groups was legal. The interpretation of this ruling meant, in essence, that segregated schools were legal. As stressed in Chapter 17, this ruling was specifically made in terms of travel accommodations but was immediately applied to all facilities provided blacks [26:294–296]. Three factors, which have been overlooked, are historically important about this decision: (1) the Court did not declare that segregation should be permitted where equal facilities are provided; (2) the Court did not give criteria for equality, and never enforced its decision; (3) the Court did not specify proper judicial remedies where equal facilities did not exist.

## CONTEMPORARY AMERICAN EDUCATION (1918 to the present)

Growth and development in education during this era dwarfed all previous periods of the history of education in the United States. Change and the complexity of problems resulting from rapid industrial progress, the expansion of knowledge, and the changing nature of society, in addition to a multitude of other factors, fostered the development of new thoughts and practices in education. The ideas of men like Rousseau, Pestalozzi, Froebel, G. S. Hall, William James, and John Dewey exerted strong influence upon schools in the first half of the twentieth century. Later, names such as Bruner, Conant, Piaget, B. Frank Brown, and J. Lloyd Trump were associated with significant innovations in education.

The scope and magnitude of the educational establishment was vastly expanded during this period. Curricula were overhauled and enlarged. Enrollments skyrocketed. Teaching methods were modified. Teacher education programs were redesigned. A building boom resulting in improved school facilities occurred. Major federal aid to education bills were passed by Congress. The per cent of the Gross National Product devoted to education increased seven-fold. These massive changes may be attributed to numerous factors, foremost of which were the citizens' demands for improved educational programs for youth in an effort to meet the growing demands and increasing complexity of life.

Several of these changes, discussed in other parts of this book and therefore not reexamined here, were changes in the curriculum, teaching methods, and ways of organizing for instruction (Chapters 5 and 6), and federal participation in education (Chapters 12, 13, and 18).

## Nursery and Kindergartens

Interest in nursery and kindergarten education has grown rapidly in recent years due to research findings which demonstrated the importance of early school learning experiences for children, especially those from socioeconomically disadvantaged homes. Growth in this sector of education is typical of the manner in which educational programs and services have been expanded and extended in recent years. As the economy in the United States has grown and the standard of living improved, increased resources have become available for the support of programs such as these.

## Elementary Schools

Significant changes have occurred at the elementary school level primarily in three areas: (1) the curriculum, (2) the manner in which instruction is organized, and (3) the expansion of services. Although the curriculum reform movement first focused on the secondary school, important modifications have been made at the elementary level.

Modern approaches to the teaching and learning of mathematics, and the expansion of science programs are indicative of recent elementary school curriculum revisions. The compartmentalized classroom organizational pattern has been replaced in many instances by semi- and total departmentalization in the upper elementary grades. Team teaching and nongraded programs have become common at this school level. Finally, materials resource centers and guidance services have been incorporated into several elementary school programs.

## Junior High and Middle Schools

The junior high school movement spread rapidly from the time of its inception, and today there are several thousand of these school units in existence. The junior high school has evolved as an institution to meet the unique physical, social, emotional, and intellectual needs of early adolescent and preadolescent youth.

Many of the purposes which the early advocates of this movement visualized have not been fully realized. Consequently, several school districts have shifted away from the junior high form of school organization to the middle school concept. Part of the increased interest in the middle school may be attributed to noneducational reasons, such as building expediency, attempts to correct racial imbalance, or economy moves. However, a substantial portion of shifts to the middle school have resulted from the attempt to devise alternatives to the traditional junior high school.

## High Schools

Expansion in both enrollments and in the curriculum represents the two most important changes which have taken place in the high schools during the post World War I period. Fewer than three million students, or one-third of the 14- to 17-year-olds, were enrolled in the secondary schools in 1918. The enrollment had increased to approximately nine million by 1970–1971, representing over 90 per cent of those in the high school age group. Thus, by 1970, universal secondary education had become a reality in the United States [151:67].

Dramatic changes in the curriculum and in the manner in which the instructional program is organized have been made in the high school during the twentieth century, especially since World War II. Course offerings have been expanded with the addition of a variety of new courses to the curriculum, such as calculus, Russian, Black studies, and electronics. Greater emphasis has been placed upon the process of education including inquiry and discovery approaches to learning. New ways of organizing for instruction including team teaching, independent study, modular scheduling, and nongraded programs have become prevalent.

Numerous factors have contributed to these changes in the high schools, among which have been the following:

1. Dissatisfaction with the status quo in view of important societal changes which were taking place.
2. New research information concerning how students learn.
3. The expansion of knowledge, which led to greater emphasis upon the structure of disciplines.

4. School reorganization resulting in the consolidation of small high schools into larger units, thereby making the offering of a broad curriculum more feasible.
5. Tests given to military personnel during World War II and the Russian launch of Sputnik I in 1957, both of which suggested that curricular weaknesses existed in the areas of science and mathematics.
6. The increased involvement of students and teachers in curriculum planning and development.

## Junior Colleges

The junior college grew slowly at first, but since World War I it has been the fastest growing segment of higher education. Both private and public junior colleges have been established, with the great majority of them being publicly controlled institutions which derive their support primarily from local and state taxes. Most junior colleges have been designed to serve a specific community or geographic area, thereby making it possible for students to commute to classes. The growth of the junior college represents another example of how education in the United States has expanded to meet the changing needs of society.

FIGURE 14–2. Past and projected degree-credit enrollments in 2-year institutions of higher education.

Enrollment, thousands

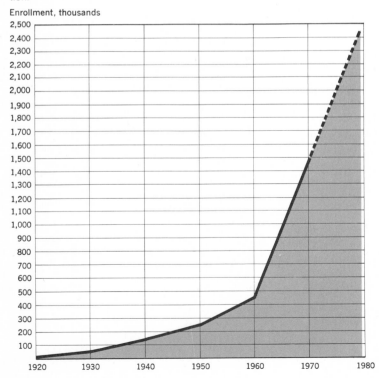

## Higher Education

Enrollments in colleges and universities gradually increased during the first half of this century, followed by a spectacular influx of new students during the past 20 years. Approximately 600,000 students attended higher education institutions in 1919–1920, and by 1970–1971 nearly 7.4 million were enrolled [151:67]. By way of comparison there were more graduate students (800,000) enrolled in 1969–1970 than were enrolled in all levels of higher education in 1919–1920 (600,000) [248:2].

Several factors contributed to the enrollment boom. The explosion of knowledge and the great industrial growth experienced in this era made a college education more essential. For many vocations which previously required relatively little formal education, a college education became imperative. Furthermore, scientific and technological advancements created a vast number of new jobs requiring advanced training. Finally, economic growth in the country and the GI Bill, which supported the further education of veterans, made it financially feasible for more persons to attend college.

Many of the same factors which caused the enrollment boom contributed to an expansion of college curricula. New courses and area majors, such as computer science, Afro-American studies, and electronics, began to appear in the curriculum. An increasing number of elementary and secondary school teachers returned to the universities in the summer to pursue graduate courses in advanced teaching methods, guidance, and audio-visual aids, in addition to other courses leading to advanced degrees. Recently, universities have enlarged the scope of their operations through the expansion of continuing education programs, thereby providing educational opportunities for persons outside the realm of the traditional campus setting.

Historically, colleges and universities have demonstrated the ability to both lead and adjust to cultural and societal changes. Much of the scientific and technological progress achieved in the United States stems directly from research activities on the college and university campuses. The impact of these research results upon society has frequently been followed by a corresponding impact upon both the curriculum and the enrollments in higher education institutions.

## Teacher Preparation

Changes which took place in educational programs during the past 50 years have been reflected in teacher preparation programs. Normal schools disappeared entirely to be replaced by four-year degree granting institutions, many of which added a fifth-year program leading to the master's degree. The knowledge explosion has resulted in an expansion of both the general education and subject-area–teaching-field phases of the teacher education program. Elementary teaching candidates often have developed an area of subject specialization in addition to or in place of concentrating on all elementary subjects. Prospective teachers have been introduced to new curricular approaches and contemporary instructional methods in various undergraduate and graduate courses. Finally, specialized programs for students preparing to teach in inner-city schools have been developed in many universities.

In-service programs for teachers and other professional personnel have markedly increased in the past 50 years. Statewide teacher institutes have become less popular in favor of regional and district-wide in-service programs. Numerous colleges and universities began offering short-term summer workshops as a form of in-service training. The summer and year-long institutes supported by the National Defense Education Act and the National Science Foundation also have strongly contributed to the upgrading of teacher competencies relative to the teaching of revised curricula in the areas of science, mathematics, and foreign languages.

Although the picture is not perfect, as indicated in Chapter 3, much progress has been made in the improvement of the status of teacher education on college and university campuses. Much of this improvement has come from the growing realization, upon the part of university personnel, that the quality of university education is directly related to the quality of instruction received by pupils in the public schools, that the security of our nation depends upon a high quality of instruction being promoted in the public schools, that the behavioral sciences are integrally involved in the preparation of teachers, and that a major portion of our colleges and universities must be involved in the enormous task of preparing teachers for the nation's public schools. In order to receive NCATE accreditation of its teacher education program, a university must show evidence that teacher education is considered a function of the total university.


## Education of Minority Groups

The right of minority-group students to attend public schools had been clearly established by 1918. Although a significant battle had been fought and won, the struggle for quality educational programs for members of minority groups had just begun in earnest. Schools for blacks, Mexican Americans, American Indians, and Puerto Ricans were still largely segregated and programs were of relatively poor quality. De jure, or intentional, segregation still existed in many parts of the country. De facto segregation, or segregation resulting primarily from housing patterns, existed in other parts of the country. As a result, the vast majority of minority-group members attending school in 1918 were enrolled in segregated schools.

Curricula were primarily white, middle-class oriented, virtually ignoring the rich cultural heritage of minority groups. American Indians, Mexican Americans, and Puerto Ricans were restrained from using their native language in the public schools. Religious practices peculiar to minority groups were ignored. American Indians were discouraged from identifying with specific tribes such as the Cherokee or Navajo. Traditional behavioral patterns of minority groups were largely ignored. Instructional materials were often culturally biased in favor of the white middle class. In essence, members of minority groups were compelled to adapt to the system, a system often foreign and frightening to them. Their backgrounds, needs, and interests were often overlooked.

Indian school programs were modified as a result of the Meriam Report in 1928 and the Indian Reorganization Act in 1934. These changes were designed to better serve the needs and interests of American Indians and to place increased emphasis on their cultural heritage [90:54–55].

Educational programs and physical facilities for American Indians were dramatically expanded in the 1950s and 1960s under the auspices of the Federal Bureau of Indian Affairs. Between 1959 and 1967 enrollments doubled. Today, approximately one-half of the Indian children attending school are enrolled in schools sponsored by the Bureau of Indian Affairs, an agency of the U.S. Department of Interior [90:56–57].

Near mid-century, the National Association for the Advancement of Colored People (NAACP) began its long series of legal battles against segregation in the public schools. A significant milestone was attained when the U.S. Supreme Court ruled in 1954 that separate but equal schools were "inherently unequal." Several other court cases also had an impact upon segregation, among which were the 1947 Mendez case in which the California courts ruled that segregation of Mexican Americans was a violation of the U.S. Constitution, and the 1950 decision by the U.S. Supreme Court that Herman Sweatt, a black, must be admitted to the University of Texas Law School. It should be noted, however, that some local school districts, both in the South and the North, voluntarily integrated their schools. The Louisville, Kentucky school system, for example, integrated its schools long before it was popular or legally mandatory to do so. Other such examples were in evidence throughout the country [119:47].

In the late 1960s and early 1970s numerous efforts were made by Congress, the federal court system, and local school districts to integrate schools and to improve the quality of education for members of minority groups. A number of those efforts will be discussed in Chapter 17. Numerous school districts in all parts of the country were required by the federal government to submit plans for racially mixing their schools. Congress appropriated funds to aid local school districts in the implementation of school integration plans. Finally, in 1971, the U.S. Supreme Court ruled that schools must be racially integrated even if students must be bussed to accomplish this end.

The massive push for integrated schools was not without problems.

Members of minority groups were often ostracized in previously all-white schools and were sometimes placed in segregated classes. Black schools have generally been closed and black students sent to white schools. Hundreds of black administrators and teachers lost their jobs following integration. In some communities, "whites" responded to integration orders by opening private, all-white academies, resulting in public school systems which were largely attended by blacks. Some black leaders, having second thoughts about the merits of integration, began advocating community control of schools whose enrollments were predominately black in an effort to improve the quality of the educational programs in these schools.

By the 1970s, educational opportunities for members of minority groups were better than at any time in history. Many barriers preventing equal educational opportunity had been removed through voluntary action, legislation, court decisions, and nonviolent protests. Segregated schools, especially of an intentional nature, were clearly illegal. With regard to educational programs for minority-group members, there has been a growing emphasis on a multi-ethnic curriculum, one that teaches the knowledge and skills essential to success in a modern, democratic society, but which also emphasizes respect for the cultural heritage of minority groups.

It is evident, however, that much still needs to be accomplished if all persons in the United States are to enjoy equality of educational opportunity. Schools which enroll primarily members of minority groups are frequently inferior to schools, often in the same school district, in which the enrollment is made up largely or totally of white pupils. Due to housing patterns and slow acceptance of the idea of total integration, segregated schools still exist in virtually all parts of the country. Nevertheless, to deny that progress has been made toward the attainment of equal educational opportunity for all is to ignore existing evidence.

## SUMMARY

During the early colonial period in America, many and varied educational attempts were made in the quest for literacy and learning. Basically a dual school system developed, in which the common or district schools, offering the three R's, attempted to serve the educational needs of the masses and the grammar schools were reserved for the wealthy, the select, the elite. Actually the development of the grammar school preceded the development of the common school. Completion of the common school in the early period did not lead to entrance into the grammar school but marked the end of the educational career of the common-school pupil.

Academies arose in order to meet the demand for a more practical type of education than was being provided in Latin grammar schools. Public high schools were established when the curriculum of the academies failed to meet adequately the needs of the people, when large numbers of children wanted to extend their education, and when the concept of governmentally supported schools became a part of the thinking of the general public.

During the nineteenth century and in the early part of the twentieth, many improvements were made. The various units of our educational system were welded into a definite pattern. The kindergarten, the junior high school, and the junior college came into being. Professional education for teachers was initiated in normal schools, colleges, and universities. Educators began to appraise their efforts critically, to experiment, and to bring about desirable changes and improvements.

Education in the United States experienced its greatest period of growth and development during the past 50 years. During this period school enrollments dramatically increased, the curriculum was expanded, new teaching strategies were developed and replaced by modern centers for learning. The growing demands and increasing complexity of life dictated improved educational programs for youth. Nursery schools became increasingly popular, kindergartens grew in numbers, the middle school arrived on the scene, and the junior colleges experienced phenomenal growth. Significant progress was made in bringing about some equalization of educational opportunity throughout the United States and in giving serious attention to the educational needs of minority groups. The complexion of education changed more during this period than in all previous periods of history combined in the United States.

It would be erroneous to assume that the educational system which our forefathers bequeathed to us has reached its fullest and last stage of development. Our American public school system derives part of its dynamic character from the concept of continuous evolution and progress.

## QUESTIONS TO CONSIDER

1. Why does the American school system represent one of the most ambitious experiments ever attempted by mankind?
2. How do you account for discipline and punishment being so severe in colonial schools?
3. What basic issues led to the separation of church and state? What current evidences can you find that this issue is not completely settled?
4. In order to become a craftsman in a number of trades today, an individual first must serve a period of apprenticeship. Where did this practice originate?
5. What elements in the typical high school of today reflect back to (a) the Latin grammar school, (b) the academy?
6. If a school is to survive, it must meet the changing needs and demands of the public. What historical evidence can you give that supports this statement?
7. How do you account for the fact that free, public, tax-supported schools developed first in the New England Colonies?
8. Do you know of any individuals today who question the right for everyone to be taxed for the support of schools? What seem to be their reasons?

9.  Why was the idea of a dual system of education, similar to the pattern used in Europe, rejected in the United States?
10. Why did teacher education programs start in normal schools rather than in colleges and universities?
11. What were some of the reasons for organizing elementary schools by grades, beginning approximately 1848, and why are some educators today advocating ungraded elementary schools?
12. What are the major effects of industrialization on education? How does educational advancement affect industrialization?
13. What were some of the reasons for the appearance and development of the junior high school?
14. How do you account for the fact that a large number of school districts have shifted away from the junior high school form of school organization to the middle school concept?
15. If such a decision as the Dartmouth College Case in 1819 had never been made, how might the development of colleges in America have been affected?
16. Why has the growth of the junior college been so great in recent years? Do you feel that this growth will continue? Why?
17. How do you account for the fact that most teachers colleges have changed their names to state colleges?
18. What contributions have church or denominational colleges made to American education?
19. How do you account for educators being so slow in recognizing the educational needs of such minority groups as blacks, American Indians, Mexicans, and Puerto Ricans?
20. What improvements need to be made in multi-ethnic education?

## PROBLEM SITUATION FOR INQUIRY

The city of Merville has two relatively small high schools. The student body and teaching staff in the Northside High School is composed largely of members of minority groups including blacks, Mexican Americans, and Puerto Ricans, while both teachers and students in the Southside High School are nearly all Caucasian. Since both of the school buildings are relatively new,the school board has decided to achieve integration by assigning all students in grades 9 and 10 to the Northside building, and all students in grades 11 and 12 to the Southside facility. The majority of the residents in the community are in favor of the move since they feel that it will result in an expanded curricular program at a lower per pupil cost. Some residents, however, feel that the identity and pride of the various minority groups may tend to be lost and that educational programs will become less relevant to especially the minority groups of students.

Historically, what problems have accompanied attempts to racially integrate schools? What factors and conditions are generally present in successful integration attempts? In your opinion, what can the City of Merville do in an effort to help guarantee the successful integration of its two high schools?

## ACTIVITIES TO PURSUE

1.  Imagine that you are a student in one of the American common schools in the eighteenth century. Develop a detailed account of a day in your school.
2.  Analyze the various types of schools which attempted elementary education in early days and show how they became part of the present elementary school.
3.  See what you can learn about the early history of your local high school.

4. Compile a list of historical bases to justify the federal government's taking an active role in supporting education today. In your opinion, has the federal government been justified in playing such an important role in education?
5. Consult a directory of colleges and universities and identify some institutions that were established under the Morrill Act of 1862. How do these institutions differ from other colleges or universities?
6. Make an intensive study of the contributions that outstanding black educators have made in the improvement of public education and report your findings to your colleagues.
7. Talk with individuals of various university groups and compile a list of their suggestions for improving public education in the United States. Discuss this list with your colleagues.

# 15 | THE DEVELOPMENT OF MODERN CONCEPTS OF EDUCATION

Education in any subject field, whether it be physics, English, or mathematics, consists primarily of learning, clarifying, and organizing the key concepts of that discipline. The discipline that is especially concerned with criticizing, clarifying, and systematically ordering the concepts involved in the study of education (in all the various meanings of this word) is known as *philosophy of education*. And when someone clarifies and orders concepts in such a way that it enables others to gain a systematic understanding of education, this arrangement of ideas and meanings is usually called a *philosophy of education*. If someone asks "What is your philosophy of education?"—as is frequently done during an interview for a position—he generally means "How are your ideas about education organized so as to enable you to understand and intelligently to criticize and to make suggestions about education?"

Over the years some of the world's greatest philosophers and other scholars have contributed to our understanding of education, and some have developed the kind of systematic arrangement of ideas that are called philosophies of education. Some of these philosophies will be indicated later.

To be effective in the classroom, it is important for a prospective teacher to develop a clear understanding of *modern* concepts of education and to know how they differ from older ones. The development of a thoroughly reasoned understanding of the school's function and the teacher's role in achieving this function is a major task in planning for a career in education.

Even for the student who is not planning a career as a teacher, it would be useful to understand modern concepts of education and be able to recognize variations on these concepts displayed by the instructional behavior of his professors. One of the most common difficulties encountered by students as they move from class to class is that they are unable to cope with the differing teaching styles that are found in today's colleges and universities. For the most part college instructors are primarily scholars in their respective subject matter fields, and they may or may not have given critical attention to their own concepts of education. Students should find it both interesting and useful to "try out" what they learn from reading this chapter by seeing to what extent they can identify the concepts of education that seem to lie behind the teaching behavior of the various instructors encountered.

In the following summary some of the men and movements of Western civilization that have influenced the development of certain important concepts in education will be identified.

## CONTRIBUTIONS OF SOME EARLY OUTSTANDING THINKERS

### Socrates (469–399 B.C.)

Socrates lived during a period of transition in Greek thought and education. He felt that "the unexamined life was not worth living." Above all, in his opinion, the individual should seek to "know thyself." He felt that ignorance was the root of evil and that no man would deliberately choose evil if he knew how to recognize and obtain something good.

Socrates attempted to improve moral life in Athens by roaming through the streets of the city and talking with people who seemed to need help in their thinking. Instead of "telling," Socrates used a question-and-answer, or inquiry, approach to teaching. Upon the pretense that he knew nothing of the subject, Socrates would ask questions of an individual until the individual exposed his ignorance of fallacies in thinking. Through further questioning, Socrates assisted the individual in developing a more consistent and more adequate set of concepts. Or, at the least, he would help the person see that much that had been taken for granted or accepted uncritically was neither very sure nor very clear.

Socrates' method of teaching, which became known as the *Socratic method,* was in opposition to the formal lecture method used by the Sophists of his day. The object was to enable the individual to arrive at truth through a thinking process. The purpose of the teacher, as Socrates saw it, was to stimulate, promote, and guide this thinking process rather than to impart only knowledge to the pupil.

The impact of Socrates upon education is felt even today. An increasing number of the textbooks used in elementary and secondary schools utilize the inquiry approach to learning. This approach casts the teacher in a decidedly different role from the lecturer, or the "drill-master" role he has served in the past.

## Plato (428–347 B.C.)

Over 2,000 years ago, Plato, in his writings about a utopian society, stated that the role of education is "the drawing and leading of children to the rule which has been pronounced right by the voice of the law, and approved as truly right by the concordant experiences of the best and oldest men." Why is it that Plato would have such an idea about education? It has been said that Plato's ideas were greatly influenced by his master teacher, Socrates.

But Socrates lived in a society more of transition than of conflict, while Plato grew up in a chaotic period when the great struggles between Athens and Sparta had become full blown and were dividing the loyalties of men throughout the Greek world. Plato had been impressed by the military superiority of Sparta and by the excessive individualism that prevailed in Athens. Therefore it was no great wonder than when Plato wrote his *Republic,* he was dreaming of setting up an ideal state that would do away with factional conflict.

In his desire to set up an ideal state, Plato believed that every individual should be strictly subordinated to the welfare of the republic. If the state were to be well ordered and efficient, it must reflect in its organization the different levels of competence and ability that existed among human beings. Believing that there were essentially three levels or types of human competence, he maintained that there should be three types of citizens: (1) the leaders, guardians, or statesmen (sometimes called philosopher kings), (2) the administrators and soldiers, and (3) the artisans. Plato was opposed to an aristocracy based upon birth or heritage, so he needed some plan for ensuring that each individual, regardless of birth or the status of his parents, would find his way into his own appropriate place in society so that his duties and responsibilities would be commensurate with his ability and competence. Plato saw that a well-designed system of public education might be the answer.

In the schools envisioned by Plato there would be no compulsory attendance. With a curriculum that progressed very gradually from the simple to the complex and from the concrete and particular to the abstract and universal, he believed that each student would remain in school as long as he found the lessons understandable and relevant to his own interests and abilities. Those who became bored and restless after only a few years of study would leave school and enter into the various arts and crafts necessary to sustain the life of the community. Others would remain to equip themselves to fill various military and administrative positions. A few would persevere to the very end of the schooling provided and then, after a period of service in the army, would (at age 35) begin a study of philosophy and prepare themselves for the responsibility of leadership. Only after they thus became "the best and oldest men," were they to be charged with making or improving the laws. And, incidentally, in order that these leaders would never be tempted to place personal gain above the security and justice of the state, they were to be required to forego all personal ownership of property and all identifiable parenthood.

Plato was the first to show that a system of education is integral with the welfare of the state. Over the years his utopian ideas have been the source of both insight and controversy. Equalitarians have, of course, always objected to Plato's "anti-democratic" assumptions, but some scholars believe that the history of education shows, for the most part, a series of unsuccessful attempts to accomplish the ends that Plato had in mind without the boldness to adopt the radical controls that he saw as necessary means. The educational proposals made by Thomas Jefferson, who believed in an "aristocracy of talent," were plainly influenced by Plato's *Republic.*

### Aristotle (384–322 B.C.)

Aristotle, like Plato, had no particular loyalty to democracy. Aristotle felt that a good monarchy or a good aristocracy which could promote to the highest degree the welfare of the state in question was just as acceptable as a good democracy. His basic thesis was that man was a "political animal."

In one sense, however, Aristotle favored democracy over anarchy or dictatorship. In an attempt to work out guidelines for the virtues (wisdom, courage, justice, and temperance) with which the Greeks were much concerned at this time, Aristotle developed the concept of the golden mean. In the golden mean, Aristotle maintained that to each virtue there are attached two vices: the vice of excess and the vice of defect. With the virtue of courage, you find foolhardiness (when one has too much courage) and cowardliness (when one has too little courage). Virtue is thus seen as the mean between two extremes.

To evaluate one form of government over another, Aristotle added the notion that governments should provide their citizens with both freedom and security. Since democracy had "the better character," it made "the better government." For him an anarchy was characterized by too much freedom and too little security. An oligarchy or a dictatorship, conversely, was characterized by too little freedom and too much security. For example, if everyone were "free" in an anarchy, then everyone would be at the mercy of everyone else. As a result, there would be little if any security. In a dictatorship, everyone was secure only if he did not openly disagree. One's security depended upon his toeing the line. He was not free to disobey. The democratic ideal, however, was seen to entrust certain powers to the people so that the government did not become too powerful—thus avoiding a dictatorship—while it also entrusted power to the government so that the individual did not run rampant as in the case of anarchy. Democracy provided a system whereby checks and balances could be maintained in regard to an individual's freedom and security.

To Aristotle, education was the development of the well-rounded individual divorced from the mechanical, practical areas of vocational or professional training. Further, Aristotle held that the highest form of virtue was speculation, contemplation, and the exercise of intellectual ability. In this scale of reasoning, man as a knower was higher in the scale of worthy citizenship than was man as a practical citizen.

In Aristotle's day, a liberal education was the education that was deemed best suited to Greek free men. Aristotle, like Plato, did not advocate the same education for all people. Rather, there was a general education for the citizenry, additional education for the warriors, *and* an even higher education for the leaders. Rediscovered during the time of the Renaissance, both Aristotle's and Plato's concepts of education provided much of the basis for the classical tradition in education. As mentioned in Chapter 14, our early colonial forefathers imported this tradition from abroad. In fact, many aspects of the educational practices in our American public schools today can be traced to this classical tradition. Why has vocational education in the past been accorded such a low status in the American school system? To what extent is the "track system" used in many schools today consistent with Aristotle's ideas?

## Vergerius (1349–1420)

A fifteenth-century humanist, Pierre Paolo Vergerius, formulated certain goals for education and set forth a basic theory of formal discipline to which many people today still adhere. He wrote as follows [99:126]:

We call those studies liberal which are worthy of a free man; those studies by which we obtain and practice virtue and wisdom; that education which calls forth, trains, and develops those highest gifts of body and mind which ennoble men and which are rightly judged to rank next in dignity to virtue only, for to a vulgar temper gain and pleasure are the one aim of existence, to a lofty nature, moral worth and fame.

Vergerius was the proponent of a doctrine of a *limited* body of subject matter, which he felt had some special power to train the mind. Evidences of this doctrine can still be found in American schools today.

## Locke (1632–1704)

Three hundred years after Vergerius formulated his theory of formal discipline, John Locke further developed the theory. John Locke introduced a new element at this point, his concept of the nature of the learner. This is commonly known as the *tabula rasa* doctrine, which held the mind, at birth, to be like a smooth tablet upon which nothing yet had been written. Locke put great emphasis on educational methods that would develop all of the senses of the child, not merely through reading, but through the senses of sight, taste, smell, touch, and hearing. In line with this point of view, Locke laid great stress on the importance of the physical development of the body. He felt that education, through sense impressions, should supply all the data used in thinking, as well as provide training in thinking. He advocated difficult intellectual exercises for disciplining the mind and severe tasks for disciplining the body. He saw education as a great power to make men good. But what are the factors that would cause Locke to view education as a great power?

Since this was the period of Newtonian physics, the scientists and mathematicians were prominent in expanding the horizons of knowledge. Knowledge made evident by the sciences and mathematics was a knowledge that was empirically observable. In the biological sciences, an enormous mass of facts was gathered; and the status of the social sciences began to improve in this eighteenth century. Even historical documents began to be treated as though they were scientific data to be gathered, classified, and criticized. This was the time of Voltaire and his Encyclopedists. The job of the Encyclopedists was to simplify knowledge into factual statements that could be recorded in encyclopedia form; they worked for freedom of thought, reform of harsh and unjust laws, elimination of poverty, disease, slavery, and war. These were just a few of the influences that gave John Locke theoretical justification for sense realism in education. It would appear that he, like Plato and Aristotle, viewed education in terms of a select group of people only. His humanistic doctrine and advocacy of the formal-discipline theory gave further impetus to these conceptions of education.

## CONTRIBUTIONS OF SOME EARLY CONCEPTS OF MIND AND BODY

Out of the past fraught with myth and superstition, various theories developed concerning the soul, mind, and body of man, which influenced early concepts of education. Although these superstitions and theories have been largely cast aside as the result of scientific investigations, they still seem to have some influence upon present-day practices in education.

### Faculty Psychology

Various theories concerning the mind and body of man have played enormously significant roles in educational practices. According to early theories, mind and body were in sharp contrast. Mind was considered to have spontaneity, initiative, and independence of action. Body was considered inert and passive.

Out of this dualistic theory of mind and body grew a type of psychology which became known as "faculty psychology." This theory was based upon the hypothesis that the mind was composed of many mental faculties, such as reasoning and memory, and that these faculties were localized in the cerebral hemisphere. It was further theorized that the faculties could be strengthened through exercise, like muscles. Since the more difficult subjects, such as classical language and mathematics, were supposed to provide the best type of exercise for the mind, these subjects were looked upon with great favor. Rote memorization became a favorite technique, for it provided the necessary exercise of the faculty of memory. With this doctrine no justification for learning needed to be given other than the training of the mind.

Certain types of subject matter were included in textbooks to exercise the powers of reasoning. This typical problem found in an old arithmetic book demonstrates this kind of teaching material:

A man went into an orchard which had seven gates and there took a certain number of apples. When he left the orchard, he gave the first guard half the apples that he had and one apple more. To the second, he gave his remaining apples and one apple more. He did the same in the case of each of the remaining five guards and left the orchard with one apple. How many apples did he gather in the orchard?

How did an education which trained the mind prepare students for life outside the school? Faculty psychologists explained this through the theory of the transfer of training. This theory postulated that, if the faculty of memory or reasoning was trained by such subjects as foreign language or mathematics, you would be able to remember or reason in every situation in which you encountered such activities.

According to this concept, educators need be concerned only with a limited curriculum. Those few subjects which best train the faculties prepare the student for any eventuality. Teachers do not have to be concerned with teaching methods and techniques which integrate knowledge and understanding. This integration automatically takes place from one subject to another, one situation to another, and one skill to another. A prime example of this kind of teaching is found in the area of arithmetic, where number computations are learned and practiced in isolation. These skills are then supposed to transfer automatically to the solving of verbal arithmetic problems.

The field of educational psychology has produced experimental evidence which raises many questions about the validity of a general transfer of training. Yet many educational practices are based upon this theory.

It would seem that casual observations might raise some questions about this general transfer-of-training theory. How would you explain a situation in which a person with a prodigious memory for dates and names in history cannot remember the names of people he meets? Or how would you explain the situation of the great theoretical mathematician who could not balance his checkbook? Through these and many other casual observations this theory seems to break down.

## SOME IMPLICATIONS OF EARLY CONCEPTS OF EDUCATION

In studying these early concepts of education and early theories about the mind, many questions come into focus. What are the implications of the classical tradition, the humanistic viewpoint, and the doctrine of faculty psychology for educational practices?

### Meaning of Education

According to the classical tradition, knowledge (acquiring facts) is education. On the basis of this concept of education, teaching becomes a matter of acquiring the techniques of getting pupils to learn established content. The business of the teacher, according to this viewpoint, is to teach the subjects of the curriculum, generally by assigning pages in a textbook, by hearing a recitation consisting of the answers to the teacher's questions, and by grading papers and examinations in which boys and girls reveal their mastery of the formal content of the subject. The teacher also needs to learn the methods by which law and order are preserved in a classroom, so that academic learning may be accomplished.

To those who hold this viewpoint, the student who acquires the most knowledge is the student who is best educated. Where knowledge becomes the end rather than the means to an end, students must learn great masses of material. Isolated, factual information becomes important because it increases the learner's reservoir of knowledge. Page-by-page assignments in textbooks lend themselves well to this concept of education. Little concern is felt about how the students learn as long as they can "parrot" back what they have read or heard. Here the mark of a cultured person is the knowledge which he has concerning his own culture and the cultures of the past.

### Preparation For Life

Early thinkers generally considered children as miniature adults. Young minds were like Locke's "smooth tablets," upon which an education must be imprinted as a preparation for life. Where preparation becomes the major emphasis in education, certain practices seem to follow. The teacher attempts to get boys and girls to learn something because it will help them when they "grow up." Since the teacher is not necessarily appealing to children's interests, he must resort to ways of getting the work done. Artificial techniques, such as gold stars as rewards, threats in the form of demerits, and additional assignments as punishment, are some of the more familiar techniques which teachers use. Competition between pupils is one of the procedures used by many teachers to stimulate pupils to learn. Since competition supposedly exists at a rather high level in adult life, teachers feel that they should provide competitive experiences which will prepare their students for adult society. Some of the more familiar kinds of competition are spelldowns, oratorical contests, and speed drills in arithmetic. Competition is carried into the realm of evaluation, where students compete for grades on examinations and on their report cards.

With the emphasis on preparation, most of the materials of instruction are slanted toward adult problems. Textbooks use adult situations as the context within which children work. It was believed that the more difficult these materials and problems, the better prepared students would be to face the realities of adult life.

Preparation for the future has been a dominating concept of education throughout history. Have teachers ever been known to say that they must prepare their boys and girls for the next grade? An underlying theory which pervades many a school system is that the elementary school prepares for the high school and that the high school prepares for college. This theory is in contrast to the one stated so aptly by Dewey: "The future which grows out of the present is surely taken care of" [59:65].

## Training the Mind

Under the doctrine of faculty psychologists, *exercise* of the different faculties of the mind was of major importance in teaching. Thus, the harder the subjects were for the pupils, the better they fulfilled this purpose. Teachers chose not only hard subjects but also the most difficult subject matter within each subject. After the material was chosen, drill techniques were used. The teacher's purpose for constant drill and the resulting rote memorization was not to facilitate understanding of the material studied but rather to exercise the faculty of memory. Long lists of historical dates, names of presidents and vice presidents, and names of state capitals were favorite drill exercises. Are there teachers today who seem to operate in terms of this concept of learning?

## CONTRIBUTIONS OF LATER OUTSTANDING THINKERS

As early as the sixteenth century, there were rumblings of disagreement and dissent over educational practices. Great thinkers began to question existing theories and to formulate different concepts of education.

## Comenius (1592–1670)

John Amos Comenius (of Nivnitz, Moravia, which is now part of Czechoslovakia) made his education contribution in the seventeenth century, which was a period when many cultural forces were striving for the loyalties of man. This was a time of great religious conflict between Catholic and Protestant churches and a time of new outlook characterized by science and the scientific method. In this setting, a two-track system of universal education emerged. Because of the class structure of society, which was deeply ingrained in all the countries of Europe, differences were made in the amount and kind of education provided for the various classes. The upper classes received a classical secondary education, whereas the lower classes received a vernacular elementary education.

In a book called *The Great Didactic,* Comenius stated his views on education. Many of his ideas are to be found in schools today. He believed that children should be taught practical things and that learning should progress step-by-step from the familiar to the less familiar, from the less difficult to the more difficult. He was the first to prepare profusely illustrated textbooks for children, the first of which was called *Orbis Pictus.* He felt that there should be four levels in the organization of a school system. The mother should teach the child from birth to age six. From six to twelve, he should attend the vernacular school, followed by six years in the gymnasium or Latin school, and then six years in the university.

Comenius was a strong advocate of general universal education. At the time, this idea was in sharp contrast to the views of other educators. But Comenius felt that all children, rather than a select few, should have an opportunity to learn. He also believed that education is a natural process and that educational practices should therefore be in harmony with the nature of the learner. He expressed a desire for a "kindlier" discipline which would be consistent with his view of the natural process of education. He was a deeply religious man and was a prolific writer on both religion and education.

Because of the religious and political turmoil in Europe at this time, Comenius' ideas on education were not recognized until approximately 200 years after he proposed them.

## Rousseau (1712–1778)

Jean Jacques Rousseau was an extreme critic of the humanist formal-discipline theories of education. He believed in the child's right to freedom in development, and his concept of education was based on the premise that it should be according to the nature of children. Rousseau has been termed by many as an anti-institutionalist. He believed that man was basically good and that it was only under the influence of evil institutions that man became corrupt. The first sentence of his famous work *Emile* (1762) vividly makes this point: "Everything is good as it comes from the hand of the Author of Nature; everything degenerates in the hand of man."

The description of a mythical school in *Emile* set forth several principles which have heavily influenced modern concepts of education, such as the idea that the curriculum and teaching methods should be planned in terms of the needs of the pupil, that authority should be replaced by reason and investigation, and that the natural interests, curiosity, and activities of children should be used in their education.

Rousseau was one of the first to propose a "child-centered" school. He would not accept the notion that the child is a miniature adult, but conceived the child as a growing, developing organism. From Rousseau's contributions it is possible to catch the first glimmerings of the study of child development.

Rousseau's concepts of child development may have caused some educators, particularly during the 1930s, to take an extreme point of view toward the meaning of the "child-centered school"—that children should be permitted to do whatever they want to do. Even today, some educators mistakenly place this same interpretation upon the term "progressive education" as well as on the concepts proposed by John Dewey.

## Pestalozzi (1746–1827)

Johann Heinrich Pestalozzi was a Swiss educator who became interested in Rousseau's methods of teaching children and attempted to practice them. Although he found a number of weaknesses, the experimentation provided the basis for writing his famous book *Leonard and Gertrude.* Pestalozzi felt that children should be treated like human beings, educated in terms of their needs, and learn through the full use of their senses. His "doctrine of interest" to provide the motivation for learning caused a great deal of furor in his time. He insisted that "learning should be a pleasant experience." Other educators felt that this would eliminate the distastefulness of school and might be bad for character development.

Pestalozzi put his ideas into practice in five different schools in Switzerland, the most famous of these being his Neuhof School. Neuhof was actually an orphanage, as was his school at Stanz. These schools were for poor children whose fathers had been killed in the wars. Since most of the children enrolled were children of broken homes, Pestalozzi tried to recapture the ideals of a sound family life, with emphasis being given to mild discipline, loving care for children, and religious and moral inspiration. It is said that he "lived like a beggar in order to learn how to make beggars [orphans] live like men."

Pestalozzi's greatest contribution to education was in the area of

A statue of Johann Heinich Pestalozzi has been erected at Aargon, Switzerland, in commemoration of his efforts to discover more effective methods of teaching. The experimental schools he established were instrumental in bringing about early educational reforms in elementary schools in America. (*Photograph from the Library of Congress.*)

teacher training. He may well be called "the father of normal schools." During the last 20 years of his life, he conducted an experimental school and teachers institute at Yverdon. He achieved an international reputation for his innovative ideas and practices. Pestalozzi is regarded as a national hero in his native country, as attested by the erection of statues of him in many of the cities.

The work in his schools emphasized learning from objects and practical experiences. This and his analysis of various teaching methods may be considered the foundation upon which the scientific investigation of similar educational problems has since been undertaken.

## Froebel (1782–1852)

Friedrich Froebel taught with Pestalozzi and conducted his own schools in Switzerland and Germany. Froebel was very impressed with Pestalozzi's sense of realism, but he also leaned heavily upon the idealistic philosophy of his day. Froebel looked on the world as a great unity, where there was no division between the realm of what was spiritual and what was natural or between the individual and society. In his opinion all things found their unity and their essence in God and His will unfolded on earth.

Froebel looked upon the child as an agency for the realization of God's will in human nature. It was through education that the child's spirit became linked with the spiritual unity of God. Froebel believed that the child had latent powers that were to be unfolded as he entered into the spiritual union with God. Education, then, would be a process of spiritual acitivity, a process that was creative and morally good.

Since the educative process was so dedicated to the development of the child, Froebel felt that his process should start with the small child of three or four years. He called his new school the kindergarten, a garden where children grow. In his garden, Froebel introduced a new method of teaching that was designated the method of play activity. Froebel felt that play was a natural and appropriate activity for small children, and therefore he wanted to capitalize on the child's interest in play activity. This activity, however, was structured and involved drawing, clay modeling, painting and coloring, singing, dancing, telling dramatic stories, manipulating blocks and paper and cardboard objects, balls, and other objects. As the children played, Froebel tried to teach symbolic meaning in the objects with which they were playing, such as the ball meaning perfect unity in matter.

In America there was much debate about the mystical ideas of Froebel and the symbolic attachment that his theories gave to play activity, sitting in a circle, and the like. Nevertheless, his emphasis on respect for the child, for his individuality, for the active qualities of learning, became influential in American education. As the kindergarten movement spread, a foundation was laid for the child-centered emphasis in the elementary school.

## Herbart (1776–1841)

Whereas the European men who preceded Herbart had greatly influenced elementary and preschool education, Johann Herbart's theories found acceptance largely among secondary school and university teachers. In keeping with his times and with his societal emphasis, Herbart laid great stress upon the social and moral character of education. To this end, he insisted that education should be primarily moral in its outlook and intent. To Herbart, morality was not necessarily religious in character but was a matter of relevance to a particular society.

Herbart was greatly concerned that the individual be well adjusted to his society. He believed that the school should be concerned with historical and literary studies and that all other studies should be correlated with them. Herbart stressed the learning theory termed "associationism," in which great stress was placed upon the development of clear ideas in students. All qualities of man were considered to be secondary to that of the association of ideas in the mind. To guarantee the best association of ideas, Herbart developed the four formal steps of learning and teaching: (1) clearness in presenting new ideas; (2) association, or relating of new ideas to compatible old ideas; (3) system, or arrangement of associated ideas in logical order; and (4) method, or application of new ideas to some specific problem or new situation. Two of Herbart's followers, Prof. Tuiskon Ziller of Leipzig and Prof. Wilhelm Rein of Jena [20:149–150], renamed the above and added a fifth, so that the now popularized five Herbartian formal steps are given as follows: (1) preparation, (2) presentation, (3) association, (4) generalization, and (5) application.

These steps were introduced at a time when reading, memory, and recitation were the principal methods of teaching. Because of the emphasis that society was placing upon scientific and mathematical developments, these steps in the teaching-learning process became vastly popular. Herbart's "formula" for teaching spread rapidly through elementary and secondary schools in both Europe and the United States. It became the standard in the normal schools of the time, and students preparing to become teachers were taught to develop lesson plans involving these five steps.

It would be difficult to overestimate the influence of Herbartianism in American educational practices. It was certainly the dominant theory until the twentieth century, and as late as World War II the official training program of the armed forces was based on a modification of these steps, that is: (1) preparation, (2) presentation, (3) demonstration, (4) application, (5) examination. Even today many would agree that this is an effective procedure for *training,* as distinct from *education.* Moreover, two of Herbart's basic ideas, associationism and formal steps in teaching-learning, have been very influential in the recent development of programmed instruction.

## Parker (1837–1902)

Francis Parker, a teacher and an administrator who has been called a leader of the progressive education movement in America, ranked high among the pioneers. His theories were geared toward making the school less artificial and conventional. He advocated field trips in science and geography. He felt that children should come into closer relationship with their natural environment.

As principal of the Cook County Normal School at Chicago, Parker trained many teachers. These teachers became disciples of his ideas and spread them throughout America. It has been said that his teachings, his writings, and his speeches laid the groundwork for a large part of John Dewey's concepts of education.

## William James (1842–1910)

James holds a number of distinctions. First, he is recognized as the father of American psychology. His two-volume *Principles of Psychology,* consisting of 1400 pages, was 12 years in the writing, and it remains today one of the most instructive in the field. Second, James serves as a good example of an integration and culmination of intellectual concerns. He was trained first as an M.D. (received at Harvard in 1870) and then taught anatomy and physiology while he developed his competence in the area of psychology. He likewise distinguished himself in philosophy. Third, he came from an interesting family. His father was a Swedenborgian mystic, and his brother Henry distinguished himself as a writer. In fact it is said of the brothers William and Henry that "William wrote psychology like fiction, while Henry wrote fiction like psychology." Fourth, his *Principles of Psychology* had a far-reaching effect on the thinking of John Dewey. Dewey had been a Hegelian idealist until he read James's psychology books. These works so impressed and influenced his thinking that Dewey shifted from the idealists' camp to that of the experimentalists, or pragmatists, or progressivists (these labels have been used interchangeably, for the most part depending on the author being read).

## Dewey (1859–1952)

Many people who are acquainted with John Dewey's work in education recognize that, in formulating his point of view, Dewey drew upon three centuries of educational thought. This fact should in no way detract from his significant contributions to modern education. His knitting together of a consistent point of view, based upon a critical examination of ideas advanced by his predecessors, is in itself a prodigious undertaking. In fact, his work stands as an excellent example of the kind of theory that he advocated; namely, that creative and seminal ideas do not appear magically out of the blue but as hypotheses formed on the basis of critical thinking and imaginative reconstruction of prior experience. He defined

Many of the concepts of education today have resulted from the thinking and writings of John Dewey.
(*Photograph from Teachers College, Columbia University.*)

education as that reorganization or reconstruction of experience that adds to the meaning of experience and increases control over the course of subsequent experience [59:89–90].

Dewey early established a laboratory school in Chicago. Here teachers were encouraged to experiment. This was a testing ground for the concepts of child development advanced by Rousseau and for the direct investigation of actual objects as a method of teaching, which had been advocated by Comenius and Parker. As a result of this experimentation, better teaching methods were developed. The experimental attitude found in his school spread to hundreds of teacher training institutions.

While at the University of Chicago, Dewey published *School and Society,* which is about education suitable for a democratic society. He pointed out the importance of the individual within the context of a democracy, placing emphasis on the school's role in developing self-discipline for true democratic participation. Throughout the years this book has had a marked effect upon the functions of the American public school. Some of the books which followed his first publication include

*Interest and Effort, Democracy and Education,* and *Experience and Education.*

To John Dewey, the learner rather than the subject matter was the prime concern in the educational process. An understanding and appreciation of logically organized subject matter was a desirable goal, but the activities and experiences of the learner became the focal point of emphasis instead of books and verbalisms. Dewey considered the teacher a guide to the learner rather than a "walking encyclopedia." He believed that schooling should illustrate the practical value of careful thinking and the advantages of using the distilled experience of the human race (that is, logically organized subject matter) in an attack upon present concrete problems accepted as real and important in the life of the learner. Education should thus become a process of continual reconstruction of experience whereby further intellectual growth and development might be realized, rather than merely an end in itself, largely disconnected from the ongoing life of the individual and his society. Two passages from his *Democracy and Education* (a "classic" written in 1916) will illustrate:

Education means the enterprise of supplying the conditions which insure growth, or adequacy of life, irrespective of age [59:61].

Since in reality there is nothing to which growth is relative save more growth, there is nothing to which education is subordinate save more education . . . the purpose of school education is to insure the continuation of education by organizing the powers that insure growth. The inclination to learn from life itself and to make the conditions of life such that all will learn in the process of living is the finest product of schooling [59:60].

Thus, Dewey favored the attainment of ends which had a direct, vital appeal to the learner and which would serve as further steppingstones to something beyond, rather than have learning become the acquisition of isolated skills and techniques through drill. That is, "ends," were viewed as "new beginnings"! He felt that pupils should make the most of the opportunites of their present life as the best way to prepare for the future. Dewey, like Rousseau, saw a negative consequence in viewing childhood or immaturity as primarily the absence of maturity. As a result, Dewey added a new dimension by maintaining that the *ability* of children to grow and develop is a *positive* aspect rather than a negative one. He maintained that childhood or immaturity should be viewed intrinsically rather than comparatively.

Unfortunately, it is impossible to present a complete expression of John Dewey's philosophy in this brief description of his contribution. In fact, many people today form different interpretations of his writings and of his thinking concerning education. Even more unfortunate, however, is the fact that it is said of Dewey that "he is the *most criticized* and *least read* of any educator." It would indeed be desirable to read one or more of his books (most are available in inexpensive paperbacks) and seek firsthand information regarding his philosophy of education.

## Kilpatrick (1871–1965)

William Heard Kilpatrick was one of the leaders in the progressive movement who attempted to interpret the work of John Dewey. In addition to being a philosopher of education in his own right, Kilpatrick made a significant contribution to modern conceptions of education by his interpretation of Dewey's thinking. The "project" method of teaching is one of Kilpatrick's many contributions to education. Like Dewey and Pestalozzi, he developed schools where his ideas could be tested. His work with these schools and as a professor of education at Teachers College, Columbia University, convinced Kilpatrick that "pupil purposes" are the key to pupil learning. He set forth the idea that pupils might learn to behave in certain ways without any real changes taking place. As a consequence, he became very much concerned about the development of character through education.

In his work at Columbia University, Kilpatrick influenced the thinking of thousands of elementary and secondary school teachers who attended his classes. This influence has been reflected in the practices which his students have used in their own schools. In addition, through his books *The Project Method, Foundations of Method,* and *Source Book of Philosophy,* Kilpatrick reinforced the concept of instruction through life activities and placed emphasis upon methodologies which use the concept of living as learning.

## Bagley (1874–1946)

The concepts of education expressed by Dewey and Kilpatrick were vigorously opposed by some of their contemporaries. One of their most notable opponents was William C. Bagley, who took a conservative point of view with respect to the role of the school in society. As an essentialist, he believed that the school should teach only certain tried and true aspects of our cultural heritage. What similarity is there between this point of view and the thinking of Plato?

Bagley maintained that the school should be society- rather than child-centered. In contrast to an experimental institution that may foster change, the school should help pupils adjust to the existing society. The school should seek to equip the pupil with the knowledge and skills which would enable him to compete with others. The curriculum would contain the known essentials derived from a study of what human beings do in an adult-approved society. Emphasis would be placed upon memorization and drill so that the pupil would acquire the knowledge and skills considered to be essential. His success in school would be determined through the use of tests designed to measure mastery of the specific facts and skills prescribed in the curriculum. Bagley would oppose elective courses being a part of the school's curriculum. For him, education was the hard process of imparting facts, involving a relatively narrow range of studies that were considered to be essential to effective living.

Shortly before his death he summarized his views on essentialism in the following manner [16:202]:

1.  Gripping and enduring interests frequently. . . . grow out of initial learning efforts that are not intrinsically appealing or attractive. Man is the only animal that can sustain effort in the face of immediate desire. To deny to the young the benefits that may be theirs by the exercise of this unique human prerogative would be a gross injustice.

2.  The control, direction, and guidance of the immature by the mature is inherent in the prolonged period of infancy or necessary dependence peculiar to the human species.

3.  While the capacity for self-discipline should be the goal, imposed discipline is a necessary means to this end. Among individuals, as among nations, true freedom is always a conquest, never a gift.

4.  The freedom of the immature learner to choose what he shall learn is not at all to be compared with his later freedom from want, fraud, fear, superstition, error, and oppression—and the price of this later freedom is the effortful and systematic mastery of what has been winnowed and refined through long struggle of mankind upward from the savage—and a mastery, that, for most learners, must be under guidance of competent and sympathetic but firm and exacting teachers.

5.  Essentialism provides a strong theory of education; its competing school (progressivism) offers a weak theory. If there has been a question in the past as to the kind of educational theory that the few remaining democracies of the world need, there can be no question today.

There are those today who hold educational positions somewhat similar to that of Bagley. For example, those belonging to the Council on Basic Education would tend to share this point of view. Vice-Admiral H. G. Rickover, in a scathing article entitled "The World of the Uneducated," written in 1959 [222:8], indicated that educators should throw out modern concepts of education and return to the traditional task of the school and the process of teaching. Arthur Bestor [192:35–46] maintains that there are certain subject areas that can best equip the student, and these include the sciences and humanities—history, language, and literature. He would have every citizen be concerned that everyone be carried as far along the line of intellectual discipline as his abilities would enable him to go. In his opinion, the public should insist that our schools engage in serious intellectual discipline and not be concerned with the development of various vocational skills. In a number of ways the concepts of education expressed by James B. Conant [50] are similar to those of Bagley.

## CONTRIBUTIONS OF SOME CONTEMPORARY EDUCATORS

An analysis of current educational articles in daily newspapers and in periodicals and books will reveal that a variety of concepts concerning education exist today. Many of them are similar to, or are a mixture of, those that have been described in this chapter. The views of only a few prominent current educators will be discussed.

## James B. Conant (1893–    )

Conant, a former President of Harvard University and a well-respected scientist, has had considerable impact upon American education through the publication of his report titled *The American High School Today* [50]. Early in his report he set up three things that are necessary in order to have a good high school: first, a school board that is composed of intelligent citizens who can make the distinction between policy making and administration; second, a first-rate superintendent; and third, a good principal.

Conant does not endorse the grouped "tracks" system that categorizes the "vocational," "commerical," and other curriculum plans. Rather, he feels that each pupil should have an individualized program that is carefully supervised and guided. He stresses the importance of such basic subjects as English, social studies, American problems or government, mathematics, and science. An individualized program automatically gives special consideration to gifted and exceptional boys and girls. He feels that, above all, the schools must provide top-quality programs that utilize our manpower and brainpower.

## Robert M. Hutchins (1899–    )

Hutchins is most commonly associated with the phrase: "Since men are everywhere and always the same, education should be everywhere and always the same." He is labeled a Neo-Thomist (to be treated later in this chapter), and he serves as a good example of how Thomistic philosophy has developed from Aristotle. One of Aristotle's many definitions of man was that he was a "rational animal." The Neo-Thomists have taken this trait, deemphasized the animal aspect, and stressed the *rational* character of man. What they see as essential about this quality is that it is common to all men. Hutchins has written of this trait [126:68]:

Every man has a function as a man. The function of a citizen or a subject may vary from society to society, and the system of training, or adaptation, or instruction, or meeting immediate needs may vary with it. But the function of a man as man is the same in every age and in every society, since it results from his nature as a man. The aim of an educational system is the same in every age and in every society where such a system can exist: it is to improve man as man.

What this means for education is that specific attention should be given to the training of the intellect. (It was in this vein that Hutchins criticized all nonintellectual activities which took place in schools, and, in this same vein, he put his theory into practice when, as chancellor of the University of Chicago, he removed their intercollegiate football program.) Such functions as "preparing for life adjustment," "meeting the needs of youth," "preparation for democratic citizenship," and "reforming the social order" are not proper functions of Hutchins's schools; such competencies, if desired, should be left to the home, church, television, Boy Scouts, and others. The school's task is solely the training of the intellect, everywhere and always.

## Jerome S. Bruner (1915–    )

Bruner [32] has contributed to education with his examination of concept formation in children as well as in adults. This research, along with other sources of related principles involving methods of scientific inquiry, has assisted the educator attempting to build a detailed analysis of scientific method.

Bruner's *The Process of Education* grew out of a 10-day conference of thirty-four scholars, scientists, and educators (at Woods Hole on Cape Cod, September, 1959) who met to discuss how education in science might be improved in our elementary and secondary schools. The following four themes are treated in the book:

First, the role of structure in learning and how it may be made central in teaching. Here the dominant view is that an understanding of "the fundamental structure" of any subject is a minimum requirement for using knowledge inside as well as outside the classroom.

Second, readiness for learning. Here the consensus is that "the foundations of any subject may be taught to anybody at any age in some form."

Third, the nature of intuition, i.e., the intellectual technique of arriving at plausible but tentative formulations without going through the analytic steps by which such formulations would be found to be valid or invalid conclusions. Here it was agreed that more should be done in investigating (and possibly in training or developing) "hunches," "shrewd guesses," "fertile hypotheses," and "courageous leaps to tentative conclusions"—all of which are invaluable to the thinker at work.

Fourth, the desire to learn and how such desire may be stimulated. Here the hope was that the subject matter itself would be the best stimulus to learning, rather than gold stars, grades, or later competitive advantage. A look into teacher training, the nature of school examinations, and the quality of any given curriculum shows that all are found to be related to this fourth problem.

More recently, in a book titled *Toward a Theory of Instruction* Bruner has written [33:71]: "If a curriculum is to be effective in the classroom it must contain different ways of activating children, different ways of presenting sequences, different opportunities for some children to 'skip' parts while others work their way through, different ways of putting things. A curriculum, in short, must contain many tracks leading to the same general goal."

In brief, Bruner is concerned with "how best to aid the teacher in the task of instruction." His book *The Process of Education* is concerned primarily with scientific inquiry and analysis of method.

## Jean Piaget (1896– )

Piaget has presented to educators new understandings in the area of developmental psychology. His theories of cognitive development are currently moving child psychology in entirely new directions. It is Piaget's finding that growth is genetically controlled and limits the ability of the individual to internalize (assimilate) and react logically to (accommodate) certain learnings before others have occurred.

In the sensorimotor level (birth to age two), the child is concurrently developing a concept of reality of both himself and his surroundings; instinctive, cognitive, and affective aspects of perception; and coordinated sensorimotor intelligence, or intuitions, about the organization of his actions for purposeful results. Overlapping this level (from ages one to two) is the perceptual or preoperational level. Now the child begins to develop perceptual constancies or the concept of functional relationships and cause and effect relationships. The third level (from three to ages six to seven) is called "semiotic" of symbolic functions. At this level the child incorporates imitative play, uses drawings to symbolize his realities, develops image memories, uses symbolic role play and also language in building his store of methods for relating to his environment.

The educator is urged (and also the parent) to make available to the child many varied experiences and materials (toys, books, etc.) so that more of the world may be realized and internalized. Contrary to popular thought, Piaget makes no age limitations or definite time limitations on these developmental levels, but rather, stresses that the individual's genetic structure, combined with his exposure to either limited or widely varied experiences, will determine his rate of growth. Flavell, Piaget's bestknown interpreter in the United States, has placed strict age limits on these levels, but in his latest publication *Psychology and the Child* (193), Piaget defines these given ages as "always average and approximate." Thus, Piaget attempts to discourage the concept of a definite change in modes of operation at a definite age.

At approximately the age of six to seven, the normal child is able to relate to education as it is found in most schools. Piaget calls this the level of concrete operations. The child now develops the ability to construct reality mentally rather than just instinctively. The child gradually becomes able to seriate or handle numerical relationships, to classify invariant structures, and to relate to number, space, time, and speed. He also begins to have social and affective interactions with many persons and realizes moral feelings and judgments toward duty. In other words, he develops a conscience.

Finally, the pre- or early adolescent (ages 11 to 13) may enter the level of formal operations once he has been able to reverse the concrete operations. Formal operations are basically abstract mental operations not dependent on visible or manual cues. Proportions, notions of probability, propositional and hypothetical thinking take place as a totally mental process.

Piaget's research and writings have much to say to educators in regard to their often unrealistic expectations for accomplishment, in regard to the scope and sequence of what is taught, and in regard to the experiences and activities to be included in the individual teaching areas. His findings have done much to encourage individualization of instruction, to foster new criteria for evaluation of the child's learning, and to urge more actual participation by children in the learning activities. Piaget's concepts of child development, already widely incorporated into these areas of concern, will surely influence educational change even further in the next decades.

### Robert M. Gagné (1916–        )

Gagné is another child psychologist who has had tremendous impact on designs for better education through his findings in the field of cognitive development. Gagné is much more structured and theoretical in his research than is Piaget, and he approaches development from the stimulus-response point of view.

Eight conditions of learning are identified by Gagné as occurring in a very specific and unchangeable sequence. These conditions are similar in concept to Piaget's levels or stages of development. Unlike Piaget, Gagné views no overlapping or concurrent appearance of two or more of these conditions of learning. This is not to say, however, that lower conditions no longer function once the higher ones are achieved by the individual, but that the individual having achieved all eight conditions will then select and use the condition most appropriate for the particular learning or experience required.

The first learning condition, called signal learning, is the initial form of cognitive development in the infant, and is the learning of an adequate response to a given cue or signal. This is a general, emotional, or diffuse response of an almost involuntary nature. Stimulus-response learning is the second condition, involving precise, controlled, and voluntarily selected responses appropriate to the given stimulus. This learning condition is primarily associated with motor rather than mental responses and indicates instinctive selection rather than cognitive selection of a response.

Chaining, the third condition, is an extension of condition two to include two or more appropriate responses in sequence. This stage may also include the understanding of the prior learned separate links which form the appropriate response. Condition four concerns verbal associations, or the ability to form an association between an object and a word or, finally, a chain of words. Multiple discrimination is the fifth condition, and implies the now added ability to perform complex chaining, selective identification and classification of many stimuli, both verbal and environmental. By Gagné's own terms, this seems to be a "rote memory" type of mental development, and seems not to depend on the prior learning of individual chains of response.

Condition six, concept learning, is the ability to put together discriminated sets of information in order to arrive at a generalization or concept about these sets of information. Several stimuli are, in other words, related to a single appropriate response. Concepts, taken together as sets, are used to form the principles of condition seven. Principle learning, then, is the relating of one complete concept to several other subconcepts, forming principles, as in a physics formula. The final learning condition, the eighth, is problem solving. The definition of principles is now embedded in problem form, requiring solution by the application of a set of principles. No age limitations are defined for these eight conditions.

Gagné's greatest contribution has been in the area of programmed instruction. His theories have provided the basis for programming effectively and sequentially. One can easily discern the progression of the later conditions in all well-developed programs. Like Piaget, Gagné promises to offer much to education in future years, as technology enables us to create programs which will release the teacher from the routines of teaching basic skills through the use of individualized programmed instruction. Gagné's tenets may also enable us to look more carefully at the sequencing of all learning experiences so that the child may benefit from instruction based more realistically upon his individual level of ability.

## Benjamin S. Bloom (1913–     )

Bloom, in conjunction with several other authors, has published two "taxonomies" of educational objectives. The purpose of the taxonomies has been to compile the theories of many eminent child psychologists and experts in child growth and development and to integrate their findings in a structure that would be meaningful to the educator. This has been done in both the cognitive and the affective domains. Objectives in each of these domains will be discussed in greater length in Chapter 16.

There is much for the educator to gain from Bloom's work, for much is offered which will further better teaching. However, this area perhaps more than others will involve great effort and concentration from the educator if he is to internalize the concepts and use them effectively with his pupils. Those educators incorporating Bloom's levels and structures at the present time have found them very helpful in their self-improvement. It can be said that, at the least, a more precise and stimulating experience is available for both teacher and pupils when Bloom's taxonomies are put to use in the classroom.

## SOME CONTRASTING PHILOSOPHIES OF EDUCATION

In reading about the concepts of education held by men of the past as well as the present, you probably have noted a number of similarities and differences. Many writers have noted these similarities and differences, and one approach to the study of philosophy of education is to classify persons according to their basic philosophic orientation and then compare their recommendations for education. Categories such as Idealism, Realism, Pragmatism, Existentialism are sometimes used for this purpose. A number of books have attempted this task, although there is considerable variation in the categories used. But Smith [251:19–20] has pointed out that there are many dangers and shortcomings in attempting to attach philosophic labels to individuals and to their recommendations for education. More important than labels, which may often become substitutes for thought rather than tools for thinking, is the effort to understand the key ideas of a person in relation to *educational problems,* regardless of how the person might be classified in terms of general philosophy.

It also is important to remember that within any one school of thought, such as realism, vast differences of opinion may be found. For instance, people who are called realists may seem to differ more than realism and idealism differ. So long as it is recognized that labels are not so concise as we are inclined to suppose, we can avoid many of the hazards involved in studying educational theories.

Gruber, in his book *Modern Philosophies of Education,* has analyzed some of the current educational theories in terms of purposes, curriculum, methodology, position of pupil, position of teacher, and evaluation. One or more of the leading proponents of each theory also is indicated. His analysis,[1] which is indicated below in a modified form, with the theory of reconstructionism having been added to his list, may prove to be helpful to anyone preparing to teach—recognizing the limitations of such an analysis.

---

[1]Reprinted by permission of the publisher from Frederick C. Gruber, *Foundations for a Philosophy of Education,* Copyright © 1961 by Thomas Y. Crowell Company, pp. 302–303.

*Idealism*
   *Proponent:* Socrates, Plato, J. Donald Butler.
   *Objectives—Aims—Purposes:* Based on tradition, what has withstood the test of time, the cultural heritage. Aim to attain the good life of the spirit. Largely intellectual; to form an intellectual elite. Aims are distant and individualistic and are in terms of knowledge.
   *Subject matter—curriculum:* Accumulated heritage of the race. The finest in literature, art, music, and ethics.
   *Method:* Physical, mental, moral discipline. Reading, textbook, lecture, drill, memorization, recitation, controlled discussion.
   *Position of the pupil:* A plastic mind to be molded. Much attention is given to the child and to individual differences.
   *Position of the teacher:* All important, the purveyor of all culture.
   *Evaluation:* In terms of how nearly the pupil has attained the ideal standards established by the best work, achievement, and tradition of the past and the specific standards set by the instructor.

*Natural realism—Naturalism*
   *Proponent:* Horace Kallen.
   *Objectives—Aims—Purposes:* The natural development of the child (presentism).
   *Subject matter—Curriculum:* What the child does or wants to do and know.
   *Method:* Children living together.
   *Position of the pupil:* All important—an individual to be allowed (encouraged) to enjoy present-day life.
   *Position of the teacher:* A servant of the learner.
   *Evaluation:* In terms of the child's freedom and happiness.

*Catholic supernatural realism—Thomism*
   *Proponents:* Jacques Maritain, Fulton Sheen.
   *Objectives—Aims—Purposes:* To cooperate with Divine Grace to form the true and perfect Christian (Catholic).
   *Subject matter—Curriculum:* The Catholic religion and its application to all phases of life. The Catholic Church possesses the Truth and is the representative of God on earth.
   *Method:* Conditioning the individual through precept, example, memorization, and drill to live the Catholic life.
   *Position of the pupil:* A soul to be saved.
   *Position of the teacher:* An instrument of God to work through the church.
   *Evaluation:* Degree to which pupil exhibits conformity to the ideal of the Catholic ideology.

*Rational realism—Neo-Scholasticism—Classical humanism—Perennialism*
   *Proponents:* Aristotle, Robert Maynard Hutchins, Mortimer J. Adler, Mark Van Doren.
   *Obejctives—Aims—Purposes:* To develop the rational powers of man: to reason, to judge, to discriminate. Reason differentiates man from the lower animals. To perfect man through the development of his intellect and through humanistic endeavors. To form an intellectual elite.
   *Subject matter—Curriculum:* The great moments of thought. A study of philosophy, especially logic, and of the classics. (For Hutchins it is a study of the "great books.") Content of the curriculum should be the same for everyone.
   *Method:* Disciplined exercise of the mind in logical processes. Memorization.
   *Position of the pupil:* A mind to be trained and to be filled with enduring facts, truths, and principles.
   *Position of the teacher:* The umpire between true and false logic.
   *Evaluation:* Profundity of knowledge. Skill in logical analysis and in abstract thinking.

*New realism—Essentialism*
   *Proponents:* Harry S. Broudy, William C. Bagley, Arthur Bestor, Admiral Hyman G. Rickover, James B. Conant.
   *Objectives—Aims—Purposes:* To equip man with the exact knowledge and skills which will enable him to compete with the world in which he lives. Based upon demonstrable facts—what people do. Impersonal, objective adjustment of the individual to society.
   *Subject matter—Curriculum:* What human beings do—the essentials. Adult-approved behavior. Known facts about natural phenomena.
   *Method:* Memorization and drill for the acquisition of facts, skills, and principles.
   *Position of the pupil:* A machine to be conditioned.
   *Position of the teacher:* A servant of nature and of society.
   *Evaluation:* Measurement of the achievement of the learner as compared with objective norms of standardized tests and of scientific measuring instruments.

*Pragmatism—Experimentalism*
   *Proponents:* Rousseau, Pestalozzi, Comenius, James, Parker, Dewey, Kilpatrick.
   *Objectives—Aims—Purposes:* Based upon the activities and goals of members of society and the interest of the learner. Objectives: to help the individual become a socially efficient member of a democratic society.
   *Subject matter—Curriculum:* Socially desirable activities. Knowledge and skills of interest and use to the learner.
   *Method:* Activity, mental, manual, physical, appreciative, social. Any method which motivates the learner and catches his imagination. A problem-solving approach which has its setting in the context of circumstances of the immediate or near future.
   *Position of the pupil:* The learner is an individual who grows or develops from within through activity in a social setting and through the use of intelligence.
   *Position of the teacher:* A guide who serves to stimulate pupils and to assist them in focusing on the issues involved in the areas under consideration.
   *Evaluation:* Progress of the learner in terms of his native ability to master the facts, skills, and attitudes demanded by the social group of which he is a part. The degree to which pupils grasp crucial concepts, problems, or values, which have been, are, or should be operating in today's society.

*Reconstructionism*
   *Proponents:* George S. Counts, Harold Rugg, Theodore Brameld.
   *Objectives—Aims—Purposes:* To build a new social order that is consistent with current social and economic forces and is democratic in nature. To foster "frontier thinking," and the organization of "action groups" in schools, labor, politics, and in other phases of life. Move toward a planned democratic society.
   *Subject matter—Curriculum:* Socially oriented. Future objectives take precedence over immediate interests or goals. Stress placed upon the development of social concerns, the anticipation of future needs, and leadership qualities.
   *Method:* Any method which instills a sense of concern and responsibility in the learners for the direction of societal evolution or change.
   *Position of the pupil:* A social member potentially capable of actively participating in the realization of future social objectives.
   *Position of the teacher:* To direct and assist pupils in the acquisition of sensitivities and competencies necessary for social participation and leadership. To act as a stimulus in effecting directed social change.
   *Evaluation:* Degree to which one becomes aware of, involved in, and committed to his responsibilities for reconstructing his society.

Some educators combine or draw, in a piecemeal fashion, from various theories of education. These educators may be called eclectics.

They feel that one cannot develop a unified or consistent pattern of beliefs. Such an approach, the eclectic maintains, is the only philosophically honest approach to the problem. This approach causes many to insist that eclecticism does not constitute a "school" of educational thought in the strictest sense of the term. There are those, however, who feel that an eclectic may have a consistent theory of education, although it may not agree with any one of the commonly accepted theories of education. The assumption upon which his theory is based may differ to some degree from those of other theories of education. In preparing, for teaching, the formulation of a consistent theory of education should be an item of first priority.

## SUMMARY

The influences of outstanding men briefly discussed in the preceding paragraphs have had a profound effect on the concepts and practices of education in the United States. Several different concepts of education have been noted in the development of educational theory.

The conventional concept of education centers upon formalism and routine procedure. It views the education process as that of "keeping school." According to this view, the materials of the curriculum have been selected, classified, graded, and organized into a program of subject matter and classes. The business of the school is to see to it that boys and girls acquire the content of this predetermined curriculum to train the mind, gain knowledge, and prepare for adult life. The master teacher is the one who can encourage, cajole, and drive the inherited content of the course into the minds of the pupils. Idealism, realism, and Neo-Thomism share certain commonalities in this respect.

The modern concept has grown out of attempts to free the school of its formalism, tradition, and selectivity. It centers its attention on the student rather than on subject matter—on stimulating and organizing the pupil's experiences so that his interests and needs may be used to facilitate learning. Units, projects, and activities are made a framework for learning, and the readiness of the pupil for a new kind of educational experience is carefully studied. Since, in a very real sense, students are viewed as having crucial uniquenesses, a variety of teaching techniques and materials attempt to provide for these individual differences. Internalized behavior is promoted through experiences in self-discipline and self-responsibility. Critical and diligent study of the most desirable forms of social life are undertaken to determine which skills, attitudes, and abilities should be built into the lives of the young. According to this concept, subject matter and the development of skills become means to an end rather than ends in themselves. Strains from Socrates, Plato, Aristotle, Rousseau, Pestalozzi, Locke, Comenius, William James, and Dewey, to name but a few, have all contributed to this approach.

Exponents of schools of thought which hold these convictions have been identified as the experimentalists, pragmatists, and reconstructionists.

In connection with all the above, an outline of the unique characteristics of some of the current conflicting theories of education has been presented within the precautionary framework of certain deceptive features of labeling and of notions of differences within as well as among groups. These are but some of the fundamental problems confronting all who try to develop a theory of education systematically.

Still more important, however, the history and philosophy of education are included in the professional preparation of teachers to enable prospective teachers to develop an understanding of educational problems in historical and philosophical perspective. Problems concerning the nature and aims of education, the curriculum, the organization and administration of a school system, and the process of teaching and learning can be studied with respect to their historical development and the philosophical issues to which they are related. It is hoped that through this introduction into the field of "The Development of Modern Concepts of Education" a foundation has been laid for continuous interest in such a professional understanding of the problems of education.

## QUESTIONS TO CONSIDER

1.  In what ways have early concepts of education influenced educational practices today?
2.  What different concepts of discipline exist in homes and in schools today? What is your concept of discipline?
3.  What do educators mean when they talk about the "whole child" attending school? What are the implications of this concept for you as a teacher?
4.  What differences exist between training a dog and educating a child? Are there any similarities? Explain.
5.  Which of the men mentioned in this chapter would you judge to have been ahead of their times? Explain.
6.  In view of Piaget's research, what suggestions for educating children would you make to parents, teachers, and textbook authors?
7.  What weaknesses do you find in each of the philosophies of education indicated in this chapter?
8.  Which philosophy of education seems to be most consistent with your thinking? Why?

## PROBLEM SITUATION FOR INQUIRY

J. W. Morris, a high school social studies teacher, has carefully developed a personal philosophy of education which he attempts to practice in his teaching activities. He maintains an informal atmosphere in his classroom; occasionally conducting class with the students sitting in a circle on the floor; permitting students to participate in planning the learning activities; viewing himself as a learning facilitator; and placing major emphasis upon problem-solving actvities, demonstrations, and individual and group projects. He develops good personal relationships with his students and involves them in the formulation of rules and regulations designed to govern class activities and student conduct.

The school administrators hold to a philosophy of education which differs from that of Mr. Morris. They believe that classrooms should be conducted in a highly organized, systematic, and businesslike manner. Emphasis, they feel, should be placed upon rote memorization of facts and information, book reports, and student recitations. They believe that student-teacher relationships should be formal and impersonal. They expect each teacher to establish rules and regulations to govern the classroom behavior of students, and they expect students to adhere to these established procedures.

As might be expected, Joe Morris finds himself in conflict with the school administrators. Morris has been advised by the administrators that they are displeased with the manner in which he performs his duties. If you were Joe Morris, what would you do? Why?

## ACTIVITIES TO PURSUE

1. Construct a historical calendar of outstanding thinkers and indicate their contributions to education.
2. Contrast the concepts of *(a)* man, *(b)* learning, and *(c)* subject matter used by some of the early thinkers as opposed to those of educators today.
3. Visit psychological laboratories, testing bureaus, and any similar facilities in order to see what contributions they make toward improving educational practices.
4. List some of the ways in which educational practice has lagged behind educational thinking today.
5. Prepare a summary or abstract of the personal life of one or more of the thinkers who lived before 1800.
6. Make a list of modern critics of education and indicate the points of criticism of each.
7. Analyze a number of your professors and secondary school teachers in terms of the philosophies of education to which they seem to subscribe.
8. Discuss with your colleagues the various current philosophies of education. Which seems to be the most defensible?

# 16 | PURPOSES OF EDUCATION IN AMERICAN DEMOCRACY

In the period of the rise of the common school in America, the chief concern of the teacher was to provide a standard curriculum which would make possible the task of teaching the large numbers of pupils who came into the public school. In this era of school expansion it was altogether natural that specific subjects should be established as the content of education. With large classes, many poorly prepared teachers, and a highly complex and confused social scene, the schools needed a curriculum that could be taught formally. The school was also influenced to be selective and to prepare for college those who had the academic, social, and economic advantages necessary for higher education.

The changing conditions in the American scene necessitated that schools be free of the rigid formalism, tradition, and selectivity of pupils. Youth were graduating or withdrawing from school and meeting community conditions to which the school program had not been relevant. A new, positive educational program was needed.

## Considering the Schools Today

Although the schools have made considerable progress in developing programs that are responsive to the needs of youth as well as to the requirements of modern society, much yet remains to be done. Criticisms of the nature of the programs in many of our schools suggest that some basic assumptions are being *uncritically* followed. Too frequently we assume (1) that the child goes to school for the sole purpose of acquiring mastery of *prescribed bodies* of knowledge and that the mastery of this knowledge will ensure effective citizenship, (2) that if the child does not at first succeed in mastering the prescribed bodies of knowledge, he should try, and try again, (3) that education is preparation for life and has no particular significance for living while it is being acquired, (4) that children feel the same needs for acquiring subject matter as adults feel, (5) that learning is primarily a passive rather than an active process, (6) that it is more important for the teacher to transmit knowledge than it is for him to help pupils learn how to learn, (7) that one of the most important tasks of the teacher is to have the pupils "cover the book" in the time prescribed, (8) that obtaining the correct answer to a problem is more important than knowing how to solve the problem, (9) that all boys and girls in a grade or class must meet the same grade standards in order to be promoted, (10) that learning devoid of purpose or interest provides good discipline, (11) that it is more important to measure what has been learned than it is to learn, (12) that youth has no part to play in conceiving, planning, and appraising the educative processes, (13) that standardized intelligence and achievement tests provide accurate information on the intellectual and creative capacities of *all* pupils, including the economically and culturally deprived, (14) that some pupils are destined to drop out of school because they lack interest in education, and (15) that the school's curriculum consists of a rigid, predetermined content to be mastered by the pupils.

These beliefs are of such long standing and are so thoroughly built into our thinking by tradition that they frequently are not recognized. Furthermore prospective teachers, by virtue of having attended elementary and secondary schools operating in terms of these beliefs, may be inclined to perpetuate them when they become teachers.

Thoughtful educators today are more and more concerned with the discrepancy between the conditions of modern life and the assumptions upon which the schools have, in general, been operating. Prospective teachers, while in the process of planning to teach, may find it beneficial to, first, examine the extent to which many educational practices continue to lag behind the salient characteristics of modern culture, and then second, develop the habit of thinking critically about the steps which teachers, both individually and collectively, may take to close this gap.

If an integral relationship between society and education is to be maintained, educators cannot ignore the current social context in which formal education occurs. Therefore, prospective teachers are encouraged to ferret out information concerning (1) what is done in schools, (2) the common assumptions upon which these actions rest, (3) the state of the current culture which the school is to serve, (4) the ways in which the educational process should change in order to better fulfill its function in the group. These activities present vital, relevant, and serious content for anyone interested in teaching.

## Formulating Some Principles Basic to Public Education

What, then, are the principles or new assumptions which should underlie any move to bring the program of the schools up to date and to vitalize their function? Pursuit of an answer to this question becomes, in a complex and rapidly changing society, a lifelong task of educators. Consider the following ten statements of educational principles to determine whether or not they are more adequate than the usual assumptions underlying educational practices:

1. *The child goes to school in order to acquire behavior patterns which will enable him to meet the problems of his time and to grow in ability to handle them successfully.* In this basic principle it is maintained that the function of the school is far more than the acquisition of existing bodies of academic subject matter; it is to guide youngsters in their ability to behave in certain ways. As such, everything that goes on in a school is an active part of the curriculum. The basic business of the teacher is to channel this behavior which is built into the character of the pupil.

Not only should school experiences be provided in terms of the problems of the contemporary community, but they should also be provided in terms of individual behavior patterns—patterns which encourage the youngster's abilities to handle the problems he faces. It is the business of the teacher to study the behavior patterns that are being built, in an attempt to encourage those which are more fruitful and to remove those which are less likely to lead to successful problem solving.

2. *The growth of youth toward constructive citizenship is a continuous process with which the school is primarily concerned.* Teachers must be constantly concerned with behavior that promotes good citizenship and behavior which may detract from it. The future calls for citizens with broad perspectives, who have a critical and constructive approach to life and standards of value by which they can live effectively and constructively. There is a desperate need for citizens who have the ability to think, to communicate, to make valid judgments, and to evaluate moral situations. Also, there is a need for citizens who have a deep sense of responsibility for their fellow men, who are concerned with moral and spiritual values, and who do not shape their philosophy of life entirely in terms of materialistic considerations. Furthermore, citizens are needed who realize that the democratic way of life not only cherishes freedom but entails obligations and sacrifices for its preservation. Finally, citizens are needed who are capable of making creative, constructive adaptations to the inevitable changes that will take place in our technological and social world.

3. *The democratic way of life provides a sound basis for the continuous direction of educational activities.* Teachers are charged with building and employing a clear conception of the democratic process. Boys and girls must learn to distinguish at all points between behavior patterns which have the quality of democracy and those which are fundamentally autocratic, totalitarian, and anarchistic. This means that educators must become increasingly more competent students of the democratic way of life and must interpret democracy in more than its

superficial and partial aspects. Specifically, boys and girls must be helped to develop depth of understanding of, and deep-seated convictions in, such basic aspects of democratic life as respect for the dignity and worth of each human being, the principle of human equality and brotherhood, freedom of speech and of group discussion, the ideals of honesty and fair-mindedness, the supremacy of the common good, the obligation and right to work, and the need to be informed and concerned about the affairs of society.

In all the activities of the school, the characteristics of the democratic way of life should be at work giving youth educational direction and guidance. Teachers should ensure that full and free participation is provided in all learning experiences. Boys and girls should be helped to solve problems on the basis of democratic action and the free play of intelligence as opposed to methods of coercion and dogmatic acceptance of belief. Members of a group should be encouraged to accept each individual as a contributing member. Large variations among students should be welcomed as an opportunity for teaching basic democratic values, such as the precious worth of an individual, whose own way of saying, thinking, and doing contributes to the welfare of all. Teachers should show students how to distinguish between bigotry and intolerance, on the one hand, and freedom of inquiry and the use of minority dissent on the other.

4. *Through careful study of modern society and ideal conceptions of democratic living, teachers may become leaders in building a democratic society which can meet the test of our troubled times.* Not only are teachers constantly concerned with building democratic behavior in youth, but they are attentive to the community's needs for democratic leadership in meeting its problems. Because teachers need to be careful and thorough students of the conditions of the modern community as well as interpreters of the meaning of democracy today, they should be able to interpret crucial problems to students and provide democratic processes for solving them. Thus, teachers are key figures in leading the culture toward a fulfillment of its democratic values.

This does not mean that teachers should become militant authorities, striking out blindly for what they may deem desirable from their point of view. Nor does it mean that teachers working together should establish a cut-and-dried program for community living and seek to impose it upon others. It does mean that teachers should carefully and critically study current economic, social, and political problems, appraise existing conditions in terms of the democratic values, and seek to help the community to appraise its effects upon youth. This calls for an expertness in social action which teachers in general have still to achieve. It is one of the challenges to the educational profession in modern times, the response to which will determine whether teachers become a fully professional group or merely "keepers of schools."

Wherever totalitarianism has gained power, one of the first acts of the

dictators has been that of capturing the educational process for indoctrination of their form of tyranny. Therefore, in today's society, it is more
imperative than ever that teachers foster the democratic life, not only
within the school program but also within the total life of the community.
As teachers perform a social leadership function, they will help the
learning within the school to become effective in the real life of the
neighborhood and the nation.

5. *The modern concept of educational leadership affords teachers the
best opportunity to study human development in all its aspects.* The
teacher should feel a great responsibility for providing learning experiences appropriate to the maturity level of the learner. However, teachers
need a fundamental concept of their role in the social process in order to
determine what direction the content of education ought to take. As has
been indicated, direction may be inferred from a careful study of the
democratic way of life.

The modern concept of educational leadership, then, means that
there is no real opposition between education geared to the needs and
requirements of the young and education devoted to the study and
leadership of society. A child-centered school and a community-centered
school are not in conflict. Only as both these aspects of the teacher's
business become related can any adequate sense be made out of either.

6. *Youth, adults, and teachers have a part to play in conceiving,
planning, and appraising the educative processes.* As noted in the
preceding sections, the function of the school is not one that is dis-
charged wholly within the walls of an academic building. The real
business of the school goes on within the total life of a community. This
means that teachers operating by themselves, without including pupils
and the lay members of the community, may not hope to fulfill the
functions of social leadership and guidance of human growth.

There are many instances in which schools that have failed to
establish adequate working relationships with their communities have
been unable to carry on programs designed to meet the current needs of
young people. The school which fails to interpret its endeavors to the
public finds itself out of step with the thinking and activities of the
community. For this reason it is particularly important that teachers
include the layman in their educational planning.

But there are reasons other than this practical one for the participation of the lay community in the educational process. Only as parents and
adults understand the function of the modern teacher can they help
achieve his purposes by providing out-of-school experiences and learnings which will support the school program. If the learning within the
school program is rendered ineffective by the informal educational
process, it can hardly be expected to succeed in producing a democratic
life for all.

The teacher in today's school should not overlook the fact that in
almost every community there are quite able people who can serve as

good resource persons if they are properly approached. It is important to recognize and utilize these people in planning and in providing quality educational programs. It is impossible for the teacher to possess all the skills and knowledge that are demanded in meeting the intellectual needs of youth today. It is shortsighted of any teacher if he fails to utilize these talents. Furthermore, the frank and happy use of the abilities and qualifications of community members may do more to establish the teacher and enhance the school in the community than any amount of social propagandizing about the values and dignity of the profession.

7. *An education for democratic citizenship includes disciplined effort for mastery of subject matter.* Teachers genuinely interested in educating youngsters to meet modern social conditions will recognize

Education for democratic citizenship includes the development of skill in working together in the pursuit of knowledge and in the solution of problems. *(Photograph by Joe Di Dio, National Education Association.)*

that this type of education is not achieved by letting students "do their own thing" to the exclusion of discipline and persistent work to achieve desired objectives. To meet the conditions of contemporary society, a disciplined system is necessary; but this does not mean that students will not know what they are doing or will have no part in determining what they shall learn. Nor does it mean merely the development of a disciplined mind by sharpening it on a whetstone of formal subject matter. Rather, the disciplined effort needed to meet modern requirements is one in which boys and girls organize their efforts carefully over a period of time and persist in their endeavors in the face of difficulties and discouragements. This disciplined effort is fundamentally social in quality. It results from working together on common concerns in which each individual finds his appropriate place. It means the ability of an individual to subordinate his immediate and personal liking for an eventual outcome that will benefit everybody.

8. *Human relations and the ways that people work together are worthy subject matter.* As has been repeatedly emphasized, learning for democratic citizenship is essentially a humanizing process. In this process, youth must work together in groups, large and small, and must feed their own individual efforts into the work of the group. Such a process demands skills and abilities which are learned primarily from experience with other people rather than from books. The meaning of participation with others should be studied, evaluated, and re-created in the democratic tradition. The skills and techniques of group participation are vital learnings which may be achieved only through a disciplined effort equal to that normally applied to the formal subject matter. This means that teachers should become experts in guiding human relationships and developing the skills of participation in social undertakings. At the same time, provision must be made for self-realization upon the part of each.

9. *Teaching skills should be related to the broader functions of the school in a democratic society.* It is essential that professional skills be related to the basic aims and purposes of the learning process. Thus, teaching techniques should not become ends in themselves, but should be continuously adapted to the basic objectives of the teacher's function as social leader in a democratic society. As a result, teaching becomes more than a matter of studying the techniques of other teachers and adopting them. It is not primarily a matter of employing what works in one situation as a technique in another. Rather, the function of the teacher is to study the particular educational situation and, with a broad background of skills, to devise and use those techniques which will most effectively bring about a desirable outcome.

10. *The ability to think for oneself and the willingness to inquire critically into all problems are as important as the acquisition of special knowledge.* If the democratic way of life is to meet today's critical social

situation, an effort must be made to create more effectively than ever before the citizen who knows how to think for himself, who is willing to do so, who is committed to the results of his thinking. Teachers must be increasingly effective in showing students how they may work creatively at the solutions of problems and how they may test the results of their thinking. It is particularly important in our complex and interrelated society to help each individual build behavior patterns that will enable him to isolate problems, to determine the facts which are pertinent to them, to create with imagination possible solutions, and to test the consequences of these solutions.

Perhaps most central in a teacher's thinking about the basic function of the school is the belief about the place of the school within a changing society. Some teachers believe that the school does not influence the nature of society to any appreciable extent. "Education does not, strictly speaking, have an effect upon culture at all; *it is a part of it.* . . . It is not people who control their culture through education; it is rather the other way around; *education is what culture is doing to people* . . . determining how they shall think, feel, and behave" [294:241].

On the other hand, one may believe that "education is the fundamental method of social progress and reform" and that "it is the business of every one interested in education to insist upon the school as the primary and most effective instrument of social progress and reform . . ." [60:15–16]. To what extent do you feel the school should assume a positive role of leadership in shaping the culture of the future?

## OBJECTIVES OF EDUCATION

The preceding ten statements of educational principles place a different meaning upon the term "education" than the fifteen uncritical basic assumptions listed at the beginning of the chapter. The meaning which a teacher gives to the term has an enormous impact upon the general and specific objectives which he will seek to achieve with his pupils.

Education has been defined as:

(1) The aggregate of all the processes by means of which a person develops abilities, attitudes, and other forms of behavior of positive value in the society in which he lives; (2) the social process by which people are subjected to the influence of a selected and controlled environment (especially that of the school) so that they may obtain social competence and optimum individual development [98:191].

Stated in another manner, education is a process of changing behavior —the way people think, feel, and act. These changes should be in the direction of the fundamental values, ideals, and aspirations that our society accepts as desirable, as is indicated in the following quotation [5:132–133]:

The purpose of the school cannot be determined apart from the purposes of the society which maintains the school. The purposes of any society are determined by the life values which the people prize. As a nation we have been striving always for those values which constitute the American way of life. Our people prize individual human personality above everything else. We are convinced that the form of social organization called democracy promotes, better than any other, the development of worth and dignity in men and women. It follows, therefore, that the *chief purpose of education in the United States should be to preserve, promote, and refine the way of life in which we as a people believe.*

## Determining the Objectives of Education

Who actually determines the objectives of education? At first it might appear to be the sole function of educators, since they are supposed to be the authorities in this field. But in the final analysis, the objectives or purposes of education in a democratic society are determined by the people. The right of the people to perform this function is a part of our democratic heritage.

The people are provided with a variety of avenues for expressing their thoughts, both individually and collectively, concerning the purposes which the educational institutions in the United States are to achieve. Elected and appointed governmental officials, such as congressmen, state legislators, state superintendents of public instruction, and local school board members, constitute important spokesmen concerning educational purposes. Various organizations and special interest groups, such as the Chamber of Commerce, American Legion, Students for Democratic Action, various groups of blacks, labor unions, private foundations, professional organizations, business and parent groups, provide strong inputs into the determination of educational goals. In fact, it is difficult to find a major organized group of people that does not have some concern for the functions of our educational institutions.

It is safe to say, however, that the many professional education associations at the local, state, and national levels provide leadership in clarifying, formulating and expressing the general objectives of education and the objectives for each level of our educational enterprise. In the final analysis it is the teacher in the classroom who determines what educational objectives will become functional in the learning experiences of his pupils. For this reason, the individual teacher needs to be clear in his understanding of the broad as well as the immediate objectives that he should seek to accomplish in his pupils.

## General Objectives of Education

One of the most significant statements of educational objectives was formulated in 1938 by the Educational Policies Commission of the National Education Association [207]. Over a thousand educators collaborated in the development of these objectives. The members of the commission identified four major objectives (each related to the others) and analyzed each in terms of the specific behavior patterns that should characterize an educated person. Because of the wide acceptance of these objectives, they are indicated below in outline form.[1]

### The objectives of self-realization

*The inquiring mind.* The educated person has an appetite for learning.

*Speech.* The educated person can speak the mother tongue clearly.

*Reading.* The educated person reads the mother tongue efficiently.

*Writing.* The educated person writes the mother tongue effectively.

*Number.* The educated person solves his problems of counting and calculating.

*Sight and hearing.* The educated person is skilled in listening and observing.

*Health knowledge.* The educated person understands the basic facts concerning health and disease.

*Health habits.* The educated person protects his own health and that of his dependents.

*Public health.* The educated person works to improve the health of the community.

*Recreation.* The educated person is participant and spectator in many sports and other pastimes.

*Intellectual interests.* The educated person has mental resources for the use of leisure time.

*Aesthetic interest.* The educated person appreciates beauty.

*Character.* The educated person gives responsible directions to his own life.

### The objectives of human relationships

*Respect for humanity.* The educated person puts human relationships first.

*Friendships.* The educated person enjoys a rich, sincere, and varied social life.

*Cooperation.* The educated person can work and play with others.

*Courtesy.* The educated person observes the amenities of social behavior.

*Appreciation of the home.* The educated person appreciates the family as a social institution.

*Conservation of the home.* The educated person conserves family ideals.

*Homemaking.* The educated person is skilled in homemaking.

*Democracy in the home.* The educated person maintains democratic family relationships.

### The objectives of economic efficiency

*Work.* The educated producer knows the satisfaction of good workmanship.

*Occupational information.* The educated producer understands the requirements and opportunities for various jobs.

*Occupational choice.* The educated producer has *selected* his occupation.

*Occupational efficiency.* The educated producer succeeds in his chosen vocation.

*Occupational adjustment.* The educated producer maintains and improves his efficiency.

*Occupational appreciation.* The educated producer appreciates the social value of his work.

*Personal economics.* The educated consumer plans the economics of his own life.

*Consumer judgment.* The educated consumer develops standards for guiding his expenditures.

*Efficiency in buying.* The educated consumer is an informed and skillful buyer.

[1]For a more thorough study of these objectives, read the publication of the Educational Policies Commission in which they appeared and were interpreted [207:50, 72, 90, 108].

*Consumer protection.* The educated consumer takes appropriate measures to safeguard his interests.

### The objectives of civic responsibility

*Social justice.* The educated citizen is sensitive to the disparities of human circumstance.

*Social activity.* The educated citizen acts to correct unsatisfactory conditions.

*Social understanding.* The educated citizen seeks to understand social structures and social processes.

*Critical judgment.* The educated citizen has defenses against propaganda.

*Tolerance.* The educated citizen respects honest differences of opinion.

*Conservation.* The educated citizen has a regard for the nation's resources.

*Social applications of science.* The educated citizen measures scientific advance by its contribution to the general welfare.

*World citizenship.* The educated citizen is a cooperating member of the world community.

*Law observance.* The educated citizen respects the law.

*Economic literacy.* The educated citizen is economically literate.

*Political citizenship.* The educated citizen accepts his civic duties.

*Devotion to democracy.* The educated citizen acts upon an unswerving loyalty to democratic ideals.

These objectives provide a framework for educational activities on all school levels. They not only describe the kind of person which the school should seek to develop for society, but they also constitute guideposts for the development of learning experiences for pupils.

In 1961, a committee under the auspices of the Educational Policies Commission issued a statement regarding the central purpose of American education [39:1–21]. The committee recognized that the American school must be concerned with all the objectives indicated in the 1938 statement of the Educational Policies Commission if it is to fulfill its function. On the other hand, these objectives place upon the school an immense, if not impossible, task. Neither the schools nor the pupils have sufficient time or energy to engage in activities that will enable pupils to achieve fully all these goals by the time these pupils graduate from high school. Furthermore, education does not cease when pupils graduate. As a result, the committee expressed the feeling that a guiding principle was needed so that the school would be able to identify its necessary and appropriate contributions to individual development and the needs of society.

The members of the committee maintained that the development of the individual's ability to think should undergird the statement of objectives published by the Educational Policies Commission in 1938. For example, each of the school's traditional objectives, such as teaching the so-called "fundamental processes," can be better achieved as pupils develop the ability to think and as they learn to apply reflective thinking to all the problems that face them. Developing the rational powers of the human mind, therefore, constitutes the central purpose of the school.

In 1966, the American Association of School Administrators published the results of a two-year study made by a special commission of the association [127]. The members of the committee had focused their attention upon the major educational imperatives that should be at the forefront as curricula are modified, instructional methods revised, and organizational patterns reshaped to meet the educational needs of this country. Although the imperatives identified in the document *Imperatives in Education* are not intended to be educational goals, they do represent points at which the program may need to be revised and reshaped in order to meet the needs of the times. Since these nine imperatives may have considerable impact upon the thinking of school administrators and other educators, they are listed below and are accompanied with very brief discussions as well as suggestions for the improvement of our public schools.

1. *To make urban life rewarding and satisfying.* Urbanization is one of the most pronounced phenomena of the times. People in great numbers are coming to large cities, seeking better jobs, better education for their children, and a better way of life. They come on the crest of a rising wave of human aspirations. If these aspirations are to be realized—

    All schools must have the best available instructional materials and equipment.

    School plants must be designed and equipped to give pupils and teachers full opportunity for efficient and effective work.

    Overcrowded classrooms and teacher shortages must be eliminated.

    The instructional program must be extended downward to include kindergarten and prekindergarten-age children.

    The educational program must be vitally related to the life of the community.

    In-service education programs for teachers must be greatly expanded.

    Financial support must be greatly increased to provide the special services and the additional facilities necessary to meet the educational needs of great groups of children who have recently migrated to the cities.

2. *To prepare people for the world of work.* Appropriate education stands squarely between the individual and the job he expects to get. At a time when the gross national product is at an all-time high and when demands for skilled workmen are increasing in many fields, thousands of young people ready to enter the labor market cannot find jobs because they lack the necessary qualifications. If this educational deficit is to be erased—

    Every child, youth, and adult must have as much education and as broad an education as his capacity will permit.

    High priority must be given to developing the knowledge essential for supporting economic enterprise and meeting manpower needs.

    Opportunities for technical and vocational training must be greatly extended and updated.

    Appropriate training in simple occupations must be provided for less-gifted students.

    The schools must take leadership in maintaining training and retraining programs for adults.

    Programs of vocational guidance must be extended and improved.

3. *To discover and nurture creative talent.* Individually and collectively the people of this country are looking to the schools for a great contribution toward developing the reservoir of creative power needed to meet and deal with challenges arising on the forefront of cultural change. To develop this potential—

The educational objective of self-realization includes the development of aesthetic interests and talents. *(Photograph by Joe Di Dio, National Education Association.)*

Every useful talent must be discovered and nurtured.

Schools must lay the ground work, kindle the curiosity, provide the skills, and create the incentives that motivate continued learning year after year.

Pupil-teacher ratios must be maintained which permit teachers to meet the unique needs of every child.

Every capable student must continue his formal education beyond the twelfth grade in an appropriate institution.

Instruction in science, mathematics, and languages must begin in the elementary school and be continued and extended to the fullest degree student capacities will permit.

Greater emphasis must be given to the humanities and the arts in the instructional program as a way to further develop the creative capacities of all students.

4. *To strengthen the moral fabric of society.* The basic values which undergird the American way of life and which have guided the actions of people for centuries are being put to a severe test in an era of rapid technological change, social readjustment, and population expansion. The results of this test are most visible where they apply to children and youth. If the schools are to be successful in helping young people develop values that will give them a sense of direction—

The dignity of each individual must be recognized and enhanced through the instructional program and the organization and operation of the school.

High priority in the instructional program must be given to the development of moral, spiritual, and ethical values.

Every child must be led to fully understand that freedom and responsibility go hand in hand.

All pupils must acquire a sense of values that will enable them to make intelligent decisions between right and wrong.

Commitment to common purposes above and beyond immediate selfish interests must be developed.

The true meaning of fair play, personal honor, and social justice must be exemplified in every facet of the school's operation.

5. *To deal constructively with psychological tensions.* Psychological tensions have been accentuated by, if they are not an actual outgrowth of, cultural change—change that has placed children and youth in new and vastly different situations. In unfortunate circumstances, these tensions have exploded into violent action; in less visible but equally important instances, they have impaired learning and blemished personalities. If the school is to help young people develop behavior patterns that will enable them to live without undue stress or conflict—

Children and youth must learn to meet and cope with social change.

A firm working alliance between the school and the home must be established.

Counseling and other supporting educational services must be provided to meet the needs of each student.

Every school must institute a continuing program of health education, multidisciplinary in nature and reaching pupils at every grade level, to develop the highest level of health attainable. The school plant must provide an environment for pupils and teachers that is healthful, convenient, comfortable, and inspiring.

6. *To keep democracy working.* The basic purpose of the school is to develop in all people the skills, understandings, beliefs, and commitments necessary for government of and by the people. This is in essence the responsibility for teaching citizenship—but teaching citizenship under a set of circumstances perhaps more trying than in former years. These circumstances are characterized by urbanization, powerful pressure groups, controversies over civil rights, and increasing interdependence between different parts of the country. To prepare a generation of young people for effective citizenship in these circumstances—

Every child must have proficiency in reading, writing, and the use of numbers.

Everyone must be led to recognize his privileges and to accept his responsibilities as an American citizen.

The schools must aid in developing the understandings, the skills, and the points of view essential for resolving broad cultural problems through reason and considered judgment.

The schools must not be dominated and unduly influenced by special interest groups and the changing tides of political pressures.

All forms of discrimination and racial and group prejudices must be eliminated from the schools.

Everyone must have an understanding of the basic principles of democracy and a commitment to uphold and to support them.

7. *To make intelligent use of natural resources.* In keeping with the basic tenets of democracy, the control and use of natural resources have been entrusted to all the people. The question that now confronts everybody, and the schools in particular, is whether control of natural resources can continue to be left with the people or whether, because of dramatic increases in their use and misuse, regulatory measures will have to be imposed. The answer to this important question will depend in large measure upon whether—

All people—young children, adolescents, and adults—know and believe that natural resources are not inexhaustible.

Conservation is viewed as intelligent planning for efficient use, and not merely as saving.

Conservation is regarded as a problem based upon scientific principles firmly established in the laws of nature.

Extravagant use and waste leading to depletion of natural resources are eliminated.

Understandings and skills needed to deal with problems relative to the use of natural resources through community action and the processes of government are developed.

Students are involved in activities that will lead them to develop a sense of order among all things and to form concepts relative to the use of natural resources.

8. *To make the best use of leisure time.* Leisure time was once a luxury for the few. Now it has become a privilege for the many. With each passing decade the amount of leisure time increases through shorter work weeks, unemployment, a longer life-span, labor-saving devices, and customs and legislative action that cause many people to retire while their minds are still active and their bodies still vigorous. If this leisure time is to be used for cultural betterment—

The schools must develop creative and imaginative programs to change the boredom of idle hours into fruitful and satisfying experiences.

Public libraries must cooperate with the schools in providing books and encouraging reading.

The schools must remain open until the late hours of the evening and throughout the summer months.

Creative writing, drama, art, music, and modern dance must be emphasized throughout the elementary and secondary grades.

Children must be taught how to relax in the out-of-doors and to appreciate and enjoy the beauty and wonders of nature.

Community choruses, orchestras, and little theater groups must be encouraged and supported.

Young people must be given opportunities to develop the leadership abilities and sense the satisfactions that come from participation in community service programs.

9. *To work with other peoples of the world for human betterment.* Through historical circumstances, a world leadership role has been thrust upon the United States. The hopes of people in other lands are kindled by the ideals and concepts that undergird the American way of life. Because of its strong commitments to maintaining peace; safeguarding the rights of freedom-loving people; and reducing poverty, ignorance, famine, and disease, it becomes increasingly important that the people of this country become familiar with the cultures of other lands and learn how to work in a fruitful manner with people whose customs, values, and traditions differ from their own. To meet this responsibility—

Every American must be led to support his country in its efforts to achieve its supreme goal of peace with freedom.

Students must become sensitive to the problems and circumstances prevailing in. other nations and know the historical backgrounds of the people, their religious beliefs, their forms of government, and the problems they face.

Ways must be found to teach children how to respect deep-seated cultural values of other people without losing or diminishing in any degree their confidence, respect, and commitments to the ideals, values, and customs of their own country.

Instruction in foreign languages must be strengthened and extended [127:165–173].

# EDUCATIONAL OBJECTIVES ACCORDING TO SCHOOL LEVELS

Although the objectives of education that have been presented provide the broad framework within which the school's contribution is made, teachers and administrators need objectives appropriate for the particular school level in which they work. These objectives must take into consideration the maturity levels of children in the various stages of their development. How can these maturity levels be identified?

Havighurst has formulated a list of developmental tasks with which an individual is confronted during certain periods of his life. Since his list has had considerable impact upon the formulation of educational objectives at various school levels, you may wish to become familiar with an outline of these tasks [116:chaps. 2, 4, 9, 10, 16–18].

### Developmental tasks of early childhood

Learning to walk
Learning to take solid foods
Learning to talk
Learning to control the elimination of body wastes
Learning sex differences and sexual modesty
Learning physiological stability
Forming simple concepts of social and physical reality
Learning to relate oneself emotionally to parents, siblings, and other people
Learning to distinguish right from wrong and developing a conscience

### Developmental tasks of middle childhood

Learning physical skills necessary for ordinary games
Building wholesome attitudes toward oneself as a growing organism
Learning to get along with age-mates
Learning an appropriate masculine or feminine social role
Developing fundamental skills in reading, writing, and calculating
Developing concepts necessary for everyday living
Developing conscience, morality, and a scale of values
Achieving personal independence
Developing attitudes toward social groups and institutions

### Developmental tasks of adolescence

Achieving new and more mature relations with age-mates of both sexes
Achieving a masculine or feminine social role
Accepting one's physique and using the body effectively
Achieving emotional independence of parents and other adults
Achieving assurance of economic independence
Selecting and preparing for an occupation
Preparing for marriage and family life
Developing intellectual skills and concepts necessary for civic competence
Desiring and achieving socially responsible behavior
Acquiring a set of values and an ethical system as a guide to behavior

### Developmental tasks of early adulthood

Selecting a mate
Learning to live with a marriage partner
Starting a family
Rearing children
Managing a home
Getting started in an occupation
Taking on civic responsibility
Finding a congenial social group

### Developmental tasks of middle age

Achieving adult civic and social responsibility
Establishing and maintaining an economic standard of living
Assisting teen-age children to become responsible and happy adults
Developing adult leisure-time activities
Relating oneself to one's spouse as a person
Accepting and adjusting to the physiological changes of middle age
Adjusting to aging parents

### Developmental tasks of later maturity

Adjusting to decreasing physical strength and health
Adjusting to retirement and reduced income
Adjusting to death of spouse
Establishing an explicit affiliation with one's age group
Meeting social and civic obligations
Establishing satisfactory physical living arrangements

You may wish to keep these developmental tasks in mind as you examine purposes and selected statements of objectives for each of the commonly recognized school levels.

While Havighurst has described stages of maturity, objectives for a given school level or age-group must also consider the stages of intellectual development which students go through as they progress through life.

According to the theories of Jean Piaget, a child progresses through a series of periods and subperiods of intellectual development beginning at birth and continuing through adolescence. Passage through each stage of development lays the foundation for subsequent stages. The stages of intellectual development as conceived by Piaget were discussed in Chapter 15.

If the notion is accepted that the development of educational objectives for specific school and age levels must start with the nature of the student, then the theories of Havighurst and Piaget must be considered by curriculum planners.

## Prenursery School

The relatively recent attention which our society has given to the plight of disadvantaged children has resulted in revelations of the critical importance of education during the first few years of a child's life. Research evidence growing out of Project Head Start indicate that the IQ's of youngsters can be raised through a good learning environment. There is substantial evidence that poor diet during these first few years may have a permanent crippling effect upon a child's future educational development. There also is evidence to indicate that some juvenile delinquency, many nervous breakdowns, and certain adult psychoses may be traced to maladjustments which could have been prevented or corrected in early childhood. Some educators are looking to a future where concern for the learning environment of the child begins in prenatal care [123:42].

An increasing number of parents feel that the home training of their young children needs to be supplemented by more constructive or better-planned learning experiences. Many factors contribute to this feeling. Some parents believe that they are unable to provide the best kind of guidance for their children at this age. Also, an increasing number of mothers find it necessary to work outside the home, and their children need to be placed in a healthy, happy, and constructive learning environ-

Children playacting in a Project Head Start program. Such activities help them in developing imagination, clarifying concepts, and expressing their feelings. *(Photograph from the National Education Association.)*

ment for at least part of the day. As a result, agencies within many communities are providing day nurseries for very young children.

Another evidence of the concern for the education of the very young is to be found in public television programs. Perhaps the best example of this kind of program is the highly successful "Sesame Street." Although this program focuses on both cognitive and affective objectives for culturally deprived three-, four-, and five-year olds, it attracts audiences of children from all types of homes and in every sector of the country.

## Nursery School

In contrast with the "child-care center" which is concerned mainly with the physical well-being of a child, the nursery school has the characteristics of a nursery and a school. In a sense, it is a downward extension of the kindergarten, and is designed to provide valuable educational and social experiences for children.

Moustakas and Berson of the famous Merrill-Palmer School indicate the objectives of a good nursery school in the following statement [165:17–18]:

We see the nursery school as an educational center that furthers the full development of

FIGURE 16-1   Primary goals of nursery school education indicated by a study of 141 school systems.

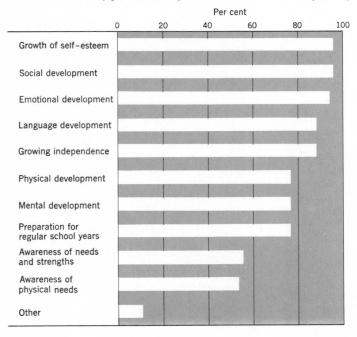

the young child and the successful functioning of a group of young children. Its goal is to maintain a balance between spontaneous behavior and conformity to society's standards. It is concerned with the feelings and attitudes of young children and their developmental skills. It seeks to help children realize their potential and at the same time aids them to accept the limits of life in a democractic society.

The nursery school recognizes how important it is for young children to learn routine health habits. Activities are planned to strengthen and facilitate the use of their large and small muscles, build coordination, and develop sound, strong bodies.

The nursery school guides the child in experiencing the stimulation and enjoyment that come from the association with persons both younger and older than himself, as well as with those of the same age. It offers many opportunities for sharing and cooperating and helps children learn when and how to share.

The encouragement of rational thinking, fair play, self-reliance, and individual freedom and responsibility are all part of the nursery school's value. . . .

The nursery school must be concerned with the enhancement of the child's individuality, and the development of attitudes, interests, understandings, and beliefs which will enable the child to be a happy, secure, contributing member of society. To reach these goals the nursery school must have an emotionally warm, friendly, relaxed atmosphere.

## Kindergarten

The kindergarten experiences of children are somewhat similar to those of the nursery school except that they are adapted to the maturity level of five-year-olds. The kindergarten provides a transition between home and school or between nursery school and formal school. Provision is made for rich experiences that will help prepare children for further schooling, although such formal training as instruction in actual reading normally is limited.

In 1970, the Los Angeles City School System published an instructional bulletin titled *Guidelines for the Kindergarten* [110:2]. The bulletin specifies that: The Kindergarten teacher should provide experiences and materials that will help each child to:

1. Develop a positive self-concept, independence, acceptance of himself and others, and an increasingly better way of doing things.
2. Gain security and feelings of success early in his school career.
3. Learn to work and to play individually and in various groups.
4. Develop perceptual-motor skills, and good health habits.
5. Learn how to think for himself in various situations.
6. Perceive and understand the world around him.
7. Learn language and its usage as a satisfying means of communication and expression.
8. Enjoy aesthetic experiences that induce creative self-expression.
9. Acquire social skills within the school community.
10. Learn to adjust emotionally to the "give-and-take" of group activities.
11. Begin to make critical observations of the experiences, activities, and materials in his environment.
12. Progress at his own rate through the initial levels of language, reading, writing, and mathematics.

Each of these broad objectives is broken into more specific objectives, accompanied by suggested methods and procedures to be used by the teacher in assisting each child in achieving the objective.

## Elementary School

An outstanding formulation of objectives for the elementary school was prepared by the Mid-century Committee on Outcomes in Elementary Education [136:35–40]. The committee assumed that the elementary school should attempt to bring about behavior changes that are desirable in a democratic society. It also attempted to identify the objectives in such a manner that they might be susceptible to measurement, evaluation, and critical philosophical analysis.

The committee identified nine broad areas of elementary school learning: (1) physical development, health, and body care, (2) individual social and emotional development, (3) ethical behavior, standards, values, (4) social relations, (5) the social world, (6) the physical world, (7) aesthetic development, (8) communication, and (9) quantitative relationships. As a child learns in these areas, changes should take place in his knowledge and understanding, his skill and competence, his attitudes and interests, and his action patterns (broad generalized ways of behaving, such as response to problems through the use of intelligence, good work habits, and scientific methods of thinking).

As may be noted in the graphic presentation of elementary school objectives (Figure 16–2), the committee felt that a fifth column, titled

FIGURE 16-2    Elementary school objectives. The behavior continuum - broad curriculum areas intersecting major behavior categories.

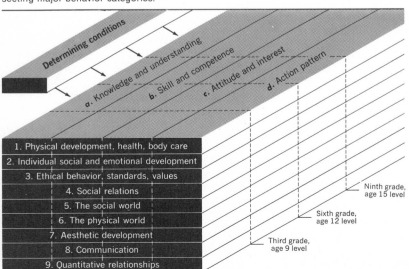

"Determining conditions," should be added to account for the many forces, in addition to the school, that mold or limit the young learner. These conditions, more than anything else, represent the biological and sociological context in which children and schools carry on together.

The committee chose to visualize the objectives by means of a grid arrangement to convey the idea that growth, development, maturation, and learning are continuous in all the subdivisions. Similarly, they chose to consider outcomes in terms of the range of abilities within a group of children or of the traits in one child at each of three levels.

## Secondary Education

Since the founding of the Boston Latin School in 1635, designed to prepare the intellectually elite boys for college, the objectives of secondary education have undergone many changes.

In response to considerable criticism of secondary schools, the National Education Association appointed the Commission on Reorganization of Secondary Education in 1913 for the purpose of studying desirable objectives for secondary schools. The report of this commission in 1918 was instrumental in expanding greatly the objectives of secondary education. The following, which have become known as the "seven cardinal principles," were recommended: (1) health, (2) command of fundamental processes, (3) worthy home membership, (4) vocation, (5) civic education, (6) worthy use of leisure time, and (7) ethical character.

For many years these objectives exerted considerable influence upon educators in the development of the secondary school curriculum. A number of educators, however, became increasingly concerned over the extent to which the secondary school curriculum was dominated by college entrance requirements. They felt that a good high school should serve the needs of both college-bound pupils and those who would not go to college. In response to this feeling, the Progressive Education Association conducted an experimental study during the period of 1933 to 1941, in which thirty school systems were freed from the traditional college entrance requirements. These schools were asked to provide the best total educational programs possible for all their pupils, so that the progress of those who would attend college could be studied. Upon entrance into college, the graduates of the experimental schools did as well academically and substantially better in student leadership positions than did the graduates from the other schools [5]. As a result of this study, objectives of secondary education were designed more in terms of meeting the life needs of all youth attending the secondary school.

Davis formulated the following statement of objectives for secondary education, which seems to have gained general acceptance [57:55–57]:

1. Secondary education should provide for the development of each personality to the fullest realization of inborn capacities.

2. Secondary education should provide for the maximum development of each student's intellect.
3. Secondary education should provide for the development of good citizenship on the part of students.
4. Secondary education should provide for the development of understanding and knowledge about life that will lead to good physical and mental health.
5. Secondary education should provide for the desirable moral development of its students.
6. Secondary education should provide education in family living.
7. Secondary education should provide educational experiences that will help students equip themselves with the skills, knowledge, understandings, and attitudes necessary for earning their own living.
8. Secondary education should help students live a better, more enriched, enjoyable life.

It should be emphasized that these major objectives of secondary education apply to both the junior and senior high school, and to some degree to the middle school. Because of differences in the maturity levels of students, the more specific objectives for the middle school and junior high school differ in some respects from those for the senior high school. Actually, the goals of the middle school and junior high school tend to overlap those of both the elementary and the senior high school. This is to be expected since, from an organizational standpoint, the middle school and junior high school provide for the transition of students from the elementary school to the senior high school. For example, Alexander and his associates state that the aims of the emerging middle school are [7:9]:

1. To serve the educational needs of the "in-between-agers" (older children, preadolescents, early adolescents) in a school bridging the elementary school for childhood and the high school for adolescence.
2. To provide optimum individualization of curriculum and instruction for a population characterized by great variability.
3. In relation to the foregoing aims, to plan, implement, evaluate and modify, in a continuing curriculum development program, a curriculum which includes provision for: (a) a planned sequence of concepts in the general education areas; (b) major emphasis on the interests and skills for continued learning; (c) a balanced program of exploratory experiences and other activities and services for personal development; and (d) appropriate attention to the development of values.
4. To promote continuous progress through and smooth articulation between the several phases and levels of the total educational program.
5. To facilitate the optimum use of personnel and facilities available for continuing improvement of schooling.

Bossing and Cramer [30:52–53] formulated the following objectives for the junior high school:

1. To develop within students their abilities to observe, listen, read, calculate, think, speak, and write with purpose and comprehension
2. To offer assistance and direction to students in the resolution of their problems so they may effectively cope with their fears, anxieties, and frustrations
3. To create learning opportunities which will permit the intellectual capacity of the early adolescent to grow and develop to its maximum

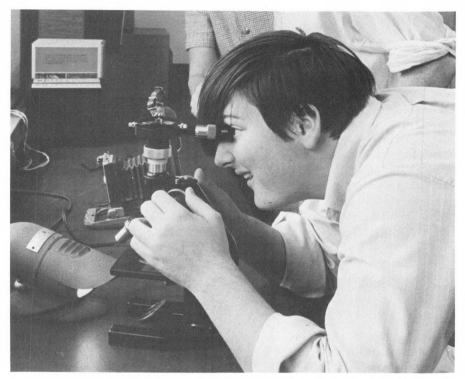

When the microscope is adjusted, a new world appears, new discoveries are made, and the thirst for new knowledge is cultivated. *(Photograph by Esther Bubley, National Education Association.)*

4. To plan situations and activities that will provide typical experiences for students which will best accommodate their social and emotional needs
5. To expand and enrich the progression of learning begun within the general educational framework of the elementary school
6. To institute learning situations which will assist early adolescents in the healthful advancement from childhood orientation to one of later adolescence or beginning adulthood
7. To make available sufficient personal interest explorations to initiate a clear understanding of the industry and culture of the adult world
8. To provide experiences designed to develop appropriate attitudes and values necessary for living in a democracy as an individual member and as a contributor to the common good
9. To establish effective resources for developing the health and physical fitness of all students
10. To organize experience opportunities which will assure a smoother transition from the elementary school to the junior high school, and on to the senior high school

## Junior College

Three types of junior colleges can be rather definitely identified: (1) the community junior college, which attempts to serve any local community needs which are not being served by other institutions of the community; (2) the special junior college, which attempts to excel in a few areas of instruction and admittedly neglects certain other community needs; (3) the junior college that attempts to offer the first two years of a senior college curriculum.

Among these three types, the community junior college concept is the prevailing pattern in the United States today. The popularity of this plan is due to its flexibility in meeting the post-high school educational needs of the community which it services. As the desire for additional education increases, and as enrollments in the large state universities reach practical limits, the importance of the community junior college is likely to be enhanced.

The community junior college, which establishes its function in terms of the needs of the geographic area in which it is located, has the following major objectives:

1. To provide for the extension of education designed to meet the added requirements of life and work
2. To provide preparation for further college study to students who will be transferring to a senior college
3. To provide opportunities for individuals to continue, on a part-time basis, their education as the need and interest arise
4. To relieve the pressure of enrollments increasingly experienced by regular colleges and universities
5. To provide a center for adult education activities

In the book, *The Two-Year College: A Social Synthesis,* Blocker, et al. [27: 268–284] discuss the still emergent nature of, and problems associated with, the character and role of junior colleges. They point out that, as this relatively recent innovation in higher education develops, increasing clarification will be gained with regard to such factors as: (1) the differentiation of its mission as a part of higher education, (2) the quality of instruction provided, (3) issues of control, (4) financial support, and (5) role in adult education.

## Higher Education

Institutions of higher education have four interlocking types of programs to offer: liberal or general education, professional or vocational education, graduate study and research, and public services. Colleges and universities differ greatly throughout the United States in the extent to which they emphasize each of these four offerings.

The modern world requires that highly skilled technicians be prepared to perform the necessary services to society in such areas as education, medicine, law, business, engineering, communication, and transportation. For this reason a large percentage of the students attending college are preparing for a profession. In addition to the vocational competencies required for their respective vocations, these students also need to acquire a general educational background that will assist them in being effective citizens.

In addition to instructional obligations, higher-education institutions have the responsibility to society of contributing new knowledge through research. For this reason the larger institutions, especially those having good financial resources, often have graduate schools and research facilities to provide for training above the baccalaureate level in almost all fields of learning. Although various independent research agencies have been developed in such fields as science, business, and agriculture, institutions of higher education continue to contribute a very substantial amount of the findings.

Colleges and universities have become centers of information and trained ability to which society can bring its problems. Increasing demands for assistance in almost every area of human endeavor are being made upon college and university staff members. Through such activities institutions of higher education assume a leadership role.

In making a study of university goals and academic power, Gross and Grambach identified a number of goals that were consistent with the functional imperatives of social systems and modified them to apply to a university. A partial listing of these goals follows [108:13–14]:

*Student-expressive* goals involve the attempt to change the student's identity or character in some fundamental way.
1. Produce a student who, whatever else may be done to him, has had his intellect cultivated to the maximum.
2. Produce a well-rounded student, that is, one whose physical, social, moral, intellectual, and esthetic potentialities have all been cultivated.
3. Make sure the student is permanently affected (in mind and spirit) by the great ideas of the great minds of history.
4. Assist students to develop objectivity about themselves and their beliefs and hence examine those beliefs critically.
5. Develop the inner character of students so that they can make sound, correct, moral choices.

*Student-instrumental* goals involve the student's being equipped to do something specific for the society which he will be entering or to operate in a specific way in that society.
6. Prepare students specifically for useful careers.
7. Provide the student with skills, attitudes, contacts, and experiences which maximize the likelihood of his occupying a high status in life and a position of leadership in society.
8. Train students in methods of scholarship and/or scientific research and/or creative endeavor.
9. Make a good consumer of the student—a person who is elevated culturally, has good taste, and can make good consumer choices.
10. Produce a student who is able to perform his citizenship responsibilities effectively.

*Research goals* involve the production of new knowledge or the solution of problems.
11. Carry on pure research.
12. Carry on applied research.

*Direct service* goals involve the direct and continuing provision of services to the population outside the university (that is not faculty, full-time students, or staff). These services are provided because the university as an organization is better equipped than any other organization to provide them.

13. Provide special training for part-time adult students, through extension courses, special short courses, correspondence courses, etc.
14. Assist citizens directly through extension programs, advice, consultation, and the provision of useful or needed facilities and services other than teaching.
15. Provide cultural leadership for the community through university-sponsored programs in the arts, public lectures by distinguished persons, athletic events, and other performances, displays, or celebrations which present the best of culture, popular or not.
16. Serve as a center for the dissemination of new ideas that will change the society, whether those ideas are in science, literature, the arts, or politics.
17. Serve as a center for the preservation of the cultural heritage.

It should be emphasized that these output goals apply primarily to universities. The emphasis which each goal receives will vary from one university to another.


## Continuing or Adult Education

Since adulthood involves a large part of life, some major goals of adult education include (1) helping the (adult) learner achieve a degree of happiness and meaning in life, (2) helping the learner understand himself, his talents and limitations, and his relationships with other persons, (3) helping adults recognize and understand the need for life-long learning [24:30–31].

Adult education is broad and diverse in its nature. Too frequently it seems to consist merely of courses of instruction taught in a school building, but more than 90 per cent of all the education of adults carried on in America is done outside the school building. Other types of adult education take place through such media as newspapers, group discussions, magazines, radio, television, books, forums, speeches, advertisements, movies, and pictures and cartoons.

It is important to remember that adults must be convinced of the need to learn. They generally want the type of learning that is both useful and down to earth. Most adults find little meaning in abstract goals, regardless of how essential they are to the advancement of civilization, unless they can see the specific relationships between these goals and ideas that are already familiar to them. However, as mature people have the opportunity to participate in the development of concrete ideas, even the more abstract goals become meaningful and acceptable to them. As a result, adults are stimulated to expand their intellectual horizons and their competencies as useful citizens in a democratic society.

Members of the Adult Education Association of the United States maintain that our concept of adult education must change from an optional to an imperative activity in our society. They feel that, if adult education is to fulfill its new mission as "an imperative of our times," the following conditions must be met [3:14–15]:

1. There must be a *national perception,* especially on the part of those who control educational policy, of the essential role of continuing education in preventing human obsolescence and in preserving and further developing the American society.
2. The education of children and youth must be reoriented to a *conception of learning as a lifelong process.* Teachers in schools and colleges must learn to teach youth so that they leave formal schooling (*a*) with an insatiable curiosity, (*b*) with a mastery of the tools of learning, and (*c*) with a commitment to continue learning through the rest of their life span.
3. *The agencies of adult education must clarify their respective tasks* of establishing between themselves orderly working arrangements and interrelated planning and to ensure that the resources of adult education are used effectively in meeting the adult educational needs of individuals, institutions, and communities.
4. A *coherent curriculum* of adult education must be developed that provides for the sequential development of the knowledge, understanding, skills, attitudes, and values required to maintain one's effectiveness in a changing social order.
5. The *corps of leaders and teachers* of adults must be enlarged and provided with the knowledge and skills required for them to help adults learn efficiently.
6. A special responsibility is placed on the universities of the country to expand the resources available for *research and advanced professional training* in adult education.
7. Community agencies of adult education, especially schools and colleges, must upgrade the *standards of professional competence* required of those guiding adult learning, and employ personnel with these competencies.
8. There must be a *national commitment* to provide the resources and moral support necessary for the development of lifelong learning as an integral element of the American way of life.

## TRENDS IN THE DEVELOPMENT OF EDUCATIONAL OBJECTIVES

An analysis of the preceding lists of objectives for the various school levels will reveal considerable variation in the manner in which they are stated. Some of them are so general, all-inclusive, and high sounding that a teacher may have difficulty in planning learning experiences in terms of which these objectives may be accomplished. Furthermore, it may be equally difficult for a teacher to determine the extent to which his pupils had achieved a given set of objectives. It is encouraging to note that considerable attention is being given to the nature and formulation of objectives.

### Taxonomy of Objectives

In 1948, Benjamin S. Bloom served as a leader of a meeting of psychologists who were attempting to establish a common frame of reference for describing the human behavior characteristics which they were attempting to appraise through achievement tests. As a result of this meeting, a taxonomy of educational objectives eventually was developed. The objectives were divided into three major categories or domains: cognitive, affective, and psychomotor. These three types of educational objectives are described by the committee as follows:

1.  Cognitive: Objectives which emphasize remembering or reproducing something which has presumably been learned, as well as objectives which involve the solving of some intellective task for which the individual has to determine the essential problem and then reorder given material or combine it with ideas, methods, or procedures previously learned. Cognitive objectives vary from simple recall of material learned to highly original and creative ways of combining and synthesizing new ideas and materials. We found that the largest proportion of educational objectives fell into this domain.
2.  Affective: Objectives which emphasize a feeling tone, an emotion, or a degree of acceptance or rejection. Affective objectives vary from simple attention to selected phenomena to complex but internally consistent qualities of character and conscience. We found a large number of such objectives in the literature expressed as interests, attitudes, appreciations, values, and emotional sets or biases.
3.  Psychomotor: Objectives which emphasize some muscular or motor skill, some manipulation of material and objects, or some act which requires a neuromuscular co-ordination. We found few such objectives in the literature. When found, they were most frequently related to handwriting and speech and to physical education, trade, and technical courses [138:6–7].

Those objectives which fall into the cognitive domain have dominated the curriculum in the past. And, within this domain, considerable emphasis has been placed upon relatively low-level forms of learning such as memorization and simple factual recall. However, an increasing amount of attention is being devoted to higher levels of learning, such as application, analysis, synthesis, and evaluation.

Support for the increased emphasis upon those objectives which fall into the affective domain is growing rapidly. For example, science courses which have emphasized primarily the cognitive aspects of science are placing greater stress upon the relationship between science and the quality of the physical environment in which we live.

The lack of demonstrated interest in affective types of objectives may be attributed to several factors. First, affective objectives are much more difficult to evaluate. Sophisticated appraisal techniques to serve these purposes have not been developed. Conversely, most cognitive objectives are relatively easy to measure, particularly at the lower levels of cognition. Second, affective objectives are not easily approached through conventional verbal teaching methods such as the lecture approach. Approaches for dealing with the affective domain in the classroom have yet to be fully developed and refined. Third, the speed with which results may be attained is much slower when dealing with affective objectives as compared to cognitive objectives. Certain kinds of information may be quickly learned; thus, immediate results may be demonstrated. But the development of attitudes, interests, values, and appreciations is a relatively slow process; thus, the results are less visible and immediate.

While affective objectives have been traditionally stressed in some subject areas, such as art and music, there is growing concern that they be stressed in other subjects. The world is faced with massive problems, such as environmental pollution, overpopulation, hunger, poverty, peaceful coexistence, and the responsible utilization of natural resources. Knowledge concerning these subjects is abundant. But the solution of these problems basically hinges upon the affective domain—the values, attitudes, appreciations, and interests held by those who possess the knowledge.

## Performance or Behavioral Objectives

During the 1930s there was considerable concern for stating educational objectives in terms of behavior, based upon the assumption that an educational experience should result in a change in the behavior of the pupil. The 1938 statement of general objectives of education indicated previously reflected this concern.

Since the mid 1960s there has been renewed interest in stating educational objectives in terms of the behavior or performance expected in the learner. Undoubtedly the accountability concept in education will give further impetus to this trend. Proponents of behavioral objectives believe that objectives stated in this manner are more definitive because they describe a student's behavior or performance upon successful achievement of the stated objective. Thus, it becomes easier to evaluate the learning successes and the learning deficiencies of students. For example, the extent to which a student attains objectives stated in general and vague terms such as "to learn to type" or "to learn the basic fundamentals of chemistry" is difficult to evaluate. However, when stated in behavioral or performance terms such as "to type at the rate of fifty words per minute with no more than five errors on a ten-minute timed writing," or "to recognize the name and symbol for each chemical element," it becomes relatively easy to evaluate a student's progress toward the attainment of these objectives. Those who advocate greater use of behavioral objectives believe that grandiose statements of objectives of the past should be replaced by statements which define how students are behaving or performing upon successful completion of the objective. A paperback book by Robert F. Mager titled *Preparing Instructional Objectives* provides an excellent description of the nature and value of behavioral or performance objectives.

Haberman, in an excellent article on "Behavioral Objectives: Bandwagon or Breakthrough," indicates that behavioral objectives have the following benefits [112:91–92]:

1. Teachers and pupils have clear purposes. Teacher planning is facilitated, and the pupils know clearly what to do.
2. Broad content is broken down into manageable, meaningful pieces.
3. Organizing content into sequences and hierarchies is facilitated.
4. Evaluation is simplified.
5. Teacher training is facilitated. Teachers gain skill in identifying particular strategies for moving particular pupils to demonstrate particular objectives.
6. Selection of materials is clarified. The teachers know precisely what outcomes are expected of students; it is much easier to determine the materials and equipment needed, and the procedures to be used.

Haberman also indicates the following dangers or limitations in the use of behavioral objectives [112:92]:

1. Too great an emphasis may be placed upon content. The most powerful element in the process of schooling is social interaction, not content. A mastery of content is only a part of the total task of educating youngsters.
2. Too great a stress may be placed upon scope, sequence, and hierarchy. Pupils organize content psychologically as well as logically.
3. Too great an emphasis may be placed upon the development of skills. Teachers may tend to stress those aspects of content that can be expressed in behavioral terms, and will tend to neglect the more intangible components such as appreciation, interpretation, valuing, and enthusiasm or thirst for learning.

So long as teachers keep in mind the limitations of behavioral objectives in fulfilling their total educational obligation to students, it would seem that the use of behavioral objectives is to be highly desired.

## SUMMARY

In the first part of this chapter, attention was given to several *uncritical* basic assumptions which operate in some schools today. The validity of these assumptions in fulfilling the school's function for today's youth was questioned. Ten statements of educational principles and their implications for educational practice were submitted on the assumption that the school provides the primary means of social progress. Governed by these principles, teaching becomes a most challenging and adventuresome profession.

Teachers are responsible for providing a most vital function—directing the experiences of youth in such a manner that fosters individual development as well as enhancing the welfare of the group. The future of democracy depends upon the resourcefulness, insight, and courage with which teachers accept this basic social responsibility.

In the second part of the chapter, attention was focused upon the objectives of education as they pertain to education in general and to the various levels ranging from preelementary to adult education. Educational objectives grow out of the life values which people prize. They are essential in order to provide direction to the planning and appraisal of educational activities.

The general objectives prepared by the Educational Policies Commission in 1938, as well as the statement of central purpose of American education issued in 1961, provide a broad frame of reference within which each level of our educational system makes its particular contribution in terms of the maturity of the learner. A clear understanding of the general objectives of education in addition to the objectives for the particular level upon which the prospective teacher plans to teach will give direction to the candidate's professional preparation and work as a teacher.

Two relatively recent trends were noted—namely, to view objectives in terms of a taxonomy, and to state objectives in terms of behavior or performance. These trends should result in decided improvements in the planning and evaluation of learning experiences for pupils.

## QUESTIONS TO CONSIDER

1. What are the so-called "broader" functions of the school?
2. What values in our society should the school seek to preserve, promote, and refine?
3. In what ways do the objectives of education in our American democracy specifically differ from those in a totalitarian country?
4. Under what conditions would it be possible for a political interest group to seize control of the schools and dictate the purposes which the schools will serve, such as occurred in Germany during the Hitler era?
5. What impact have groups such as the SDS and the Black Panther Party had upon the purposes which the schools in the United States serve?
6. If you assume that pupils go to school in order to acquire desirable behavior patterns, how will you attempt to evaluate the progress made by your pupils? What instruments and techniques will you use?
7. What is meant by the statement that a more rigorous and a more disciplined kind of education is necessary in order to meet the conditions of contemporary society? What are the implications of this statement for you as a teacher?
8. To what extent do the four objectives developed by the Educational Policies Commission adequately describe the kind of person schools should seek to develop for our society?
9. How do the objectives of nursery and kindergarten differ from those of elementary education?
10. How have the objectives of the secondary school changed during the past 50 years?
11. What does the 1961 statement on the central purpose of education add to the statements of objectives published by the Educational Policies Commission in 1938?
12. How, if at all, do the objectives of education in a rural community differ from those in a large metropolitan community?
13. What is meant by a community-centered school or college?
14. In what ways may you as a teacher serve as a key figure in leading the community toward a fulfillment of its democratic values?
15. What responsibilities do the public schools have for meeting adult education needs?
16. What difficulties might a teacher encounter in preparing performance objectives that involve the affective domain?

## PROBLEM SITUATION FOR INQUIRY

You are employed to teach world history in the West Lake High School beginning next September. During the summer you are given a copy of the text to be used in your classes and are given a copy of the class schedule. The principal suggests that you contact the chairman of the Social Studies Department if you have any other questions. You talk to the departmental chairman, and he explains that the school does not have any curriculum guides or course outlines for the course which you are to teach. You inquire about the objectives which have been established for the world history course and are told that none exist. This disturbs you because you view course objectives as a means of guiding your lesson planning and as a method of determining both the success of your students and yourself. You express this opinion to the department head, and he agrees. He asks you to develop a plan for establishing the objectives for the world history course. How would you approach this task? What plan would you recommend to the department chariman?

## ACTIVITIES TO PURSUE

1. Appraise the public school experiences you had in light of the function of the school as presented in this chapter. In other words, how adequately were the schools you attended fulfilling their purpose as herein defined?
2. Make a list of the competencies for teaching which the content of this chapter suggests.
3. Review the fifteen uncritical assumptions which seem to characterize the way some of our schools operate. Discuss with your colleagues the extent to which these assumptions seem to be sound.
4. Match the "Developmental tasks of early childhood" with the objectives of education for each school level. Do they seem to be compatible?
5. List ways in which you will attempt to help your pupils achieve the objective of human relationships, as formulated by the Educational Policies Commission. Repeat the process in connection with the other three objectives.
6. Perhaps you have heard people express the feeling that certain school subjects were good for disciplining the mind. Discuss this point of view with your colleagues and explore its educational implications. As you engage in this activity, attempt to describe the behavior characteristics of a well-disciplined democratic citizen.
7. School superintendents frequently question candidates for teaching positions regarding their views toward education. Write on two or three sheets of paper what you consider the school's function to be. Compare what you write with the opinions of your colleagues.
8. Many school systems distribute bulletins to teachers and parents containing statements of the school's function. Collect one or more of these bulletins and critically appraise the statements made.
9. Select a school system that seems to be fulfilling the function of the school as described in this chapter. Plan with the superintendent, or some other school official, to make several classroom observations. Discuss these observations with your colleagues, your college instructor, and, if possible, the classroom teachers whom you observe.
10. Have some of your public school teacher friends show you examples of the day-to-day as well as the more ultimate objectives which they use in planning suitable classroom activities. What relationship do these objectives have with the general objectives of education discussed in this chapter?
11. Talk with a labor union leader and a chamber of commerce representative to determine the position of these groups concerning the objectives which the schools should strive to attain.

**RESOURCE SECTION FOR PART 5**

## CALENDAR OF SOME IMPORTANT EVENTS IN EDUCATION

As you can sense from these chapters, a number of important events have occurred in the development of education in America. It may prove helpful to organize several in chronological order, so that you may get a bird's-eye view of them. For this reason the following calendar of events is presented.

| | |
|---|---|
| 1635 | Founding of the Boston Latin School, first college preparatory school |
| 1636 | Founding of Harvard, first permanent college in English North America |
| 1647 | Massachusetts Act ("Old Deluder Act," which followed the 1642 law ordering that children be taught to read)—first general school law in America |
| 1693 | Founding of College of William and Mary, first permanent college in the South |
| 1751 | Chartering of Benjamin Franklin's Academy, representing the transition between Latin schools and a more practical curriculum |
| 1785, 1787 | Northwest Ordinances, the beginnings of national aid for education |
| 1819 | Famous Dartmouth College Decision of the U.S. Supreme Court, which established the inviolability of a college's charter |
| 1821 | First high school in the United States, in Boston |
| 1839 | Founding of the first state normal school, Lexington, Massachusetts |
| 1848 | First graded school in America, established at the Quincy Grammar School of Boston |
| 1852 | Enactment of the first compulsory school law, Massachusetts |
| 1857 | Founding of the National Teachers' Association, now the National Education Association |
| 1862 | Passage by Congress of Morrill Bill, which became the basis of land-grant colleges |
| 1867 | Federal agency now known as the U.S. Office of Education created by Congress |
| 1873 | First public kindergarten in the United States in St. Louis |
| 1874 | Kalamazoo Decision by Michigan Supreme Court, which established a state's legal right to public funds for high schools |
| 1881 | Tuskegee Institute established by Booker T. Washington |
| 1890 | Passage of the second Morrill Act, which provided for money grants to institutions of higher education |
| 1893 | Significant report of NEA Committee of Ten, first of a series of NEA reports with far-reaching effects on curriculum and standards |
| 1897 | Founding of the organization now known as National Congress of Parents and Teachers |
| 1902 | First junior college in the United States, in Joliet, Illinois |
| 1909 | First junior high schools, established at Berkeley, California, and Columbus, Ohio |
| 1914 | Smith-Lever Act, providing for extension work in agriculture and home economics |
| 1917 | Smith-Hughes Act, providing federal assistance for vocational education in public schools |
| 1918 | Publication of the Report on Reorganization of Secondary Education—"Cardinal Principles of Secondary Education" |
| 1919 | First public nursery school established in the nation |
| 1920 | Compulsory education became effective in all states |
| 1923 | Formation of World Federation of Education Associations, forerunner of the present World Confederation of Organizations of the Teaching Profession |
| 1933 | Federal government began aid to schools operating nonprofit school lunch programs |

| | |
|---|---|
| 1937 | Enactment of the George-Dean Act, which provided federal aid for vocational education and distributive education |
| 1941 | Publication of the Eight-year Study by the Progressive Education Association |
| 1944, 1952 | Enactment of GI Bill of Rights for World War II (Public Law 346) and Korean veterans |
| 1945 | Creation of United Nations Education, Scientific, and Cultural Organization (UNESCO) |
| 1949 | Organization of National Citizens' Commission for the Public Schools—a nonprofit organization designed to improve education |
| 1950 | National Science Foundation Act passed by Congress to promote basic research and education in the sciences |
| 1952 | Extension of the GI Bill of Rights to include those serving between June 27, 1950, and January 31, 1955 (Public Law 550) |
| | Ruling of the U.S. Supreme Court on released time for religious instruction |
| 1954 | Ruling of U.S. Supreme Court on nonsegregation in the public schools |
| 1955 | White House Conference on problems of school housing, finance, personnel, and organization |
| 1958 | Enactment by Congress of the National Defense Education Act, providing federal funds for the improvement of instruction in various subject areas and for guidance, audio-visual aids, and student loans and fellowships |
| 1960 | Golden Anniversary White House Conference on Children and Youth called by the President |
| 1961 | Establishment of the Peace Corps |
| 1962 | Ruling of U.S. Supreme Court on prescribed prayers being required of pupils |
| | Manpower Developmental and Training Act passed by Congress to facilitate the retraining of laborers |
| 1963 | Higher Education Facilities Act passed by Congress to provide loans and grants for the construction of academic facilities for graduate schools, colleges, and technical institutes |
| | United States Supreme Court ruled that the reading of the Bible in public schools was unconstitutional |
| 1964 | Economic Opportunity Act passed by Congress |
| | Civil Rights Act (Public Law 88–352) provided for the U.S. Commissioner of Education to grant *on request* financial and technical assistance to public school systems having problems of desegregation |
| 1965 | Elementary-Secondary Education Act (Public Law 89–10) greatly expanded the federal role in financing public education Project Head Start, under the auspices of the Economic Opportunity Act |
| | Higher Education Act passed by Congress, providing for community services and continuing education programs, assistance to libraries, student assistance, strengthening developing institutions, establishment of a National Teachers Corps, and assistance for the purchase of special equipment for undergraduate institutions |
| 1966 | Extension of the GI Bill of Rights to all veterans discharged since 1955, except those who enlisted for a six-month period (Public Law 358) |
| 1967 | Education Professions Development Act provided for broad training programs for education personnel |
| 1967 | Public Broadcasting Act created a public television corporation |
| 1968 | Handicapped Children's Early Education Assistance Act provided for experimentation that would produce successful teaching approaches and prototype programs for the handicapped child of preschool age |
| 1970 | Ruling of the U.S. Supreme Court that the "one man, one vote" principle applies to the election of school board members |

1971   Beginning of experimental, federally funded projects in the use of voucher plans in public and private elementary and secondary schools

     Ruling of the U.S. Supreme Court that the use of public money to pay the salaries of teachers in private schools, and the purchase of similar services from private schools are unconstitutional

     Ruling of the U.S. Supreme Court that federal courts may order bussing of children in public schools as a means of desegregating schools

     California Supreme Court rendered unconstitutional the entire public school financing system of the state, based largely on the local property tax, since the system unfairly discriminates against the poor

## SUGGESTED READINGS

*The number in parentheses following each suggestion denotes the chapter for which it is best suited.*

Alexander, William M. (ed.): *The High School of the Future: A Memorial to Kimball Wiles,* Charles E. Merrill Publishing Company, Columbus, Ohio, 1969. Provides the predictions and insights of a distinguished group of educators on what education may become toward the year 2000. (16)

Blaustein, Albert P., and Robert L. Zangrando (ed.): *Civil Rights and The American Negro,* Trident Press, New York, 1968. An excellent analysis of civil rights as they relate to the Negro. (14)

Bloom, Benjamin S. (ed.): *Taxonomy of Educational Objectives Handbook I: Cognitive Domain,* David McKay, New York, 1967. A thorough explanation of six cognitive levels with numerous examples. (16)

Borton, Terry: "What's Left When School's Forgotten?" *Saturday Review,* Saturday Review, Inc., New York April 18, 1970, pp. 69–71, 79–80. Discusses a new kind of curriculum that cuts across subject areas and is designed to develop an individual as a productive thinker. (16)

Brown, L. M.: *Aims of Education,* Teachers College Press, Columbia University, New York, 1970. An excellent discussion of the aims of education in a democratic society. (16)

Bruner, Jerome S.: "The Process of Education Revisited," *Phi Delta Kappan,* vol. 53, no. 1, pp. 18–21, Phi Delta Kappa, Bloomington, Ind., September, 1971. Indicates changes in the author's thinking since writing the book by the same name in 1961. (15)

Bruner, Jerome S.: "The Skill of Relevance or the Relevance of Skills," *Saturday Review,* Saturday Review, Inc., New York, Apr. 18, 1970, pp. 66–68, 78–80. Emphasizes the need to help youth develop the skills that will enable them to solve the problems of society. (16)

Buetow, Harold A.: *Of Singular Benefit,* The Macmillan Company, Toronto, Ontario, 1970. An historical account of Catholic education in the United States. (14)

Buford, Thomas O.: *Toward a Philosophy of Education,* Holt, Rinehart and Winston, Inc., New York, 1969. Contains helpful suggestions for formulating a philosophy of education. (15)

Crosby, Muriel: "Who Changes the Curriculum and How?" *Phi Delta Kappan,* vol. 51, no. 7, pp. 385–389, Phi Delta Kappa, Bloomington, Ind., March, 1970. Emphasizes the need for professional educators to exert leadership in making curricular changes. (16)

*The Development and Evaluation of Behavioral Objectives,* Charles A. Jones Publishing Company, Worthington, Ohio, 1970. An excellent reference for gaining skill in the development of behavioral objectives. (16)

Diederich, Paul B.: "Progressive Education Should Continue," *Today's Education,* vol. 58, no. 3, pp. 12–19, National Education Association, Washington, March, 1969. Discusses the relevance of progressive education for today's schools. (15)

Dropkin, Stan, Harold Full, and Earnest Schwarcz: *Contemporary American Education,* The Macmillan Company, Toronto, Ontario, 1970. Sections 2 and 3 are concerned with the historical background and the aims and purposes of American education. (14 & 16)

"Environmental Education: A New 'Must'," *The Shape of Education for 1970–71,* vol. 12, pp. 56–61, National School Public Relations Association, Washington, 1970. Indicates how schools are developing effective environmental education programs. (16)

Fantini, Mario D., and Milton A. Young: *Designing Education for Tomorrow's Cities,* Holt, Rinehart and Winston, Inc., New York, 1970. Discusses strategies for reforming city schools and refers to a case study concerning the development of the Fort Lincoln New Town school system located in a model city just outside Washington, D.C. (16)

Furth, Hans G.: *Piaget for Teachers,* Prentice-Hall, Inc., Englewood Cliffs, N.J., 1970. An excellent presentation of Piaget's concepts. (15)

Gagné, Robert M.: "Some New Views of Learning and Instruction," *Phi Delta Kappan,* vol. 51, no. 9, pp. 468–472, Phi Delta Kappa, Bloomington, Ind., May, 1970. Discusses new theories of learning and explains their experimental bases. (15)

Gordon, Ira J.: "The Beginnings of the Self: The Problem of the Nurturing Environment," *Phi Delta Kappan,* vol. 50, no. 7, pp. 375–378, Phi Delta Kappa, Bloomington, Ind., March, 1969. Examines the significance of early childhood years for subsequent education. (16)

Gronlund, Norman E.: *Stating Behavioral Objectives for Classroom Instructions,* The Macmillan Company, Toronto, Ontario, 1970. A practical guide on preparing instructional objectives for teaching and testing. (16)

Gutek, Gerald Lee: *An Historical Introduction to American Education,* Thomas Y. Crowell Company, New York, 1970. An excellent historical treatment of American education. (14)

Handlin, Oscar, and Mary F. Handlin: *The American College and American Culture,* McGraw-Hill Book Company, Inc., New York, 1970. Discusses the changing nature of colleges and universities from colonial times to the present. (14)

*Historical Highlights in the Education of Black Americans,* National Education Association, Washington, n.d. An excellent booklet showing the continuity, from 1619 to the present, of movements in the education of black people in the United States. (14)

Holt, John C.: *The Underachieving School,* Pitman Publishing Corporation, New York, 1969. Indicates how schools fail to help students develop to their potentialities. (16)

Howson, Geoffrey, (ed.): *Children at School: Primary Education in Britain Today,* Teachers College Press, Columbia University, New York, 1970. Deals with policy and curriculum areas which have not been considered central to primary education. (16)

Johnson, Clifton: *Old-Time Schools and School-Books,* Dover Publications, Inc., New York, 1963. A very interesting history of very early American education with many excellent pictorial illustrations. (14)

Inlow, Gail M.: *Education: Mirror and Agent of Change,* Holt, Rinehart and Winston, Inc., New York, 1970. Part One examines the role of education in a changing society and Part Three discusses the purposes of education at all school levels, elementary through higher education. (16)

Junell, Joseph S.: "Can Our Schools Teach Moral Commitment?" *Phi Delta Kappan,* vol. 50, no. 8, pp. 447–451, Phi Delta Kappa, Bloomington, Ind., April, 1969. Advocates that schools assume greater responsibility for helping youth develop desirable moral values. (16)

Manning, Duane: *Toward a Humanities Curriculum,* Harper and Row Publishers, New York, 1971. Contains many excellent suggestions for humanizing the school experiences of students. (16)

Metcalf, Lawrence E., and Maurice P. Hunt: "Relevance and the Curriculum," *Phi Delta Kappan,* vol. 51, no. 7, Phi Delta Kappa, Bloomington, Ind., March, 1970. Maintains that a curriculum must assist young people in an examination of their own basic assumptions about society and its improvements. (16)

Perkinson, Henry J.: *The Imperfect Panacea: American Faith in Education, 1865–1965,* Randon House, Inc., New York, 1968. Traces the role of the school in the development of American society. (14)

Rich, John Martin: *Education and Human Values,* Addison-Wesley Publishing Company,

Reading, Mass., 1968. Focuses on the critical value conflicts confronting American education today. (16)

Rosen, F. Bruce: *Philosophic Systems and Education,* Charles E. Merrill Publishing Company, Columbus, Ohio, 1968. An excellent, concise booklet on different philosophies of education. (15)

Rubin, Louis J. (ed.): *Life Skills in School and Society,* National Education Association, Association for Supervision and Curriculum Development, Washington, 1969. Examines our changing times, speculates about the capacities mankind will need, and converts the resulting ideas into practical implications for the school. (16)

Schrag, Peter: "End of the Impossible Dream," *Saturday Review,* Saturday Review, Inc., New York, Sept. 19, 1970, pp. 68–70, 92–95. Indicates ways in which schools have failed to achieve their function in a democratic society. (14 & 16)

Schwartz, Lita Linzer: *American Education: A Problem-centered Approach,* Holbrook Press, Inc., Boston, 1969. Chapter 3 contains an excellent discussion of idealism, realism, pragmatism, essentialism, and existentialism. (15)

Silberman, Charles E.: *Crisis in the Classroom: The Remaking of American Education,* Random House, Inc., New York, 1970. Presents an extensive survey and condemnation of American education, and makes suggestions for reform. (16)

*To Nurture Humaneness: Commitment for the '70's,* National Education Association, Association for Supervision and Curriculum Development, Washington, 1970. Stresses the need for new goals in society as well as more humane purposes in school. (16)

Toffler, Alvin: *Future Shock,* Random House, New York, 1970. Chapter 18 is concerned with "Education in the Future Tense," although the entire book has implications for the function of education. (16)

Woodson, Carter Godwin, and Charles H. Wesley: *The Negro in Our History,* Associated Publishers, Washington, 1962. An excellent history of the Negro in America. (14)

## SUGGESTED 16 MM FILMS

*The number in parentheses following each suggestion denotes the chapter for which it is best suited.*

*America's Crises: The Individual* (National Educational Television, 59 min). Examines the problem of the individual in a complex society by looking at various areas of American life in relation to man's needs for self-identification. Probes the effects of government planning in agriculture on individual initiative and community identification. (16)

*America's Crises: Marked for Failure* (National Educational Television, 59 min). Discusses American education and examines the profound handicaps to learning that affect children from depressed areas. Describes a number of proposed solutions. Focuses on a prenursery pilot program in New York City schools. (16)

*America's Crises: The Parents* (National Educational Television, 59 min). Presents a documentary report on the changing problems of America's parents today and their attempts to find identity, meaning, and purpose in their lives. Features frank interviews with parents and children. Shows the effects of rural-urban-suburban social change and presents interviews with Benjamin Spock, Betty Friedan, and Paul Popenoe. (16)

*America's Crises: The Young Americans* (National Educational Television, 59 min). Discusses the problems of American youth and examines who they are, what they want, where they fit in, how they affect society, and what they believe in and why. Features individual and group interviews with students in colleges, high schools, beach areas, and resort towns. Presents a frank questioning of traditional views on sex and youth's confused struggle to find a new morality. Looks at youth minority groups, such as the Peace Corps and the hippies, who attempt to define themselves and their beliefs, in contrast to the majority of youths, who are uncommitted. (16)

*American Teacher* (March of Time, 15 min). Presents some pros and cons of the progressive education movement and points out the citizen's responsibility toward the schools; also gives a brief history of education in the United States, including the present emphasis upon psychology. (15)

*Black History: Lost, Stolen or Strayed* (Bailey Film Associates, 53 min, color). Compares the real history of the black American with the prejudiced and subverted history; cites some black historical figures never mentioned in usual history texts. (14)

*Children of Change* (International Film Bureau, 30 min). Discusses the problems faced by working mothers in caring for their children during working hours and also the problems and activities of the children in day-care centers. (16)

*Colonial America in the Eighteenth Century* (McGraw-Hill, 17 min, color). Presents an overview of the geography of the American colonies in the eighteenth century, showing boundaries, areas settled by various nationalities, and typical family and community life of the period. Discusses the reasons for immigration and indicates the influence of each major group on the colonies. Describes geographical differences among the Southern, Middle, and New England Colonies. (14)

*The Dropout* (McGraw-Hill, 11 min). Focuses upon a boy who drops out of school in the tenth grade; dramatically portrays the conditions and events leading to a typical high school dropout. Depicts the influence of the environment and his peers on the dropout. Interviews the dropout, his mother, teachers, and school officials in an effort to determine the cause of the boy's leaving school. (16)

*Education* (National Educational Television, 29 min). Presents a discussion of educational problems including "whom shall we educate, how, and for what?" Proposes early testing for abilities, special training, more creative teaching, less administrative and clerical burdens on the part of a teacher, and the evaluation of new teaching techniques. (16)

*Education: The Public Schools* (National Educational Television, 29 min). Indicates the forces which have influenced the form of our public schools. (16)

*Education in America: The Nineteenth Century* (Coronet, 16 min, color). Describes significant historical developments and the changing character of American education in the nineteenth century. Points out contributing factors of change, such as the establishment of the first high school, problems growing out of the Civil War, the teachings of Horace Mann, compulsory laws, the trend toward uniformity under state regulations, and the beginning of teacher training schools. (14)

*Education in America: The Seventeenth and Eighteenth Centuries* (Coronet, 16 min, color). Gives historical background to the early developments in American education—in New England, the South, and the Middle Colonies. Relates the character of the different schools—dame, Latin grammar, private, parochial, pauper, academy, and college—to prevailing social, economic, and cultural conditions. (14)

*Education in America: Twentieth-century Developments* (Coronet, 16 min, color). Reviews significant developments in American education in the twentieth century and relates these developments to the social, economic, and cultural life of the nation. Considers the influences of outstanding educators, educational theories and movements, and major trends and problems. (14)

*Horace Mann* (Emerson Films, 19 min). Portrays important episodes in the life of Horace Mann, "the father of the common schools"; reviews his activities as teacher, lawyer, state senator, board of education member, and college president; emphasizes his work in pointing up the need for well-built schools, good textbooks, democratic methods of learning, schools for teachers, and universal education in the United States. (14)

*Learning for Life* (National Education Association, 28 min, color). Gives overview of adult education as a new force in public schools through which people can learn to live for themselves and their communities. Explains the reasons for having adult education programs and shows how critically they are needed in the face of the future challenges facing society. A brief historical treatment is given emphasizing the social changes in our country. (16)

*The Meaning of Democracy* (Republic Steel Corporation, 19 min). Depicts democratic concepts on which our government is based, political morality in a democracy, and the role of partisanship in a democracy. Contrasts the characteristics of a democracy and dictatorship, defines the goals of a democracy, and examines the exercise of political power by the individual in a democracy. (16)

*Our Problems in Education* (National Educational Television, 29 min). Discusses the problems facing American education. Dr. Mark Van Doren and Dr. William Hocking are questioned on what should be taught in America's schools and who should be educated and for what purpose. (16)

*Philosophies of Education: A Catholic Philosophy of Education* (National Educational Television, 29 min). Points out that the realities of God and of Jesus Christ, the guidance, teaching, and influence of the Church, and the ideals of the Christian life are constantly presupposed. Within this integral framework all physical and intellectual disciplines have their place. (15)

*Philosophies of Education: The Classical Realist Approach to Education* (National Educational Television, 29 min). Defines "classical realism," putting special emphasis on definitions of each of the two words. Explains the theory's basis in the "natural law" and the theory's application to modern educational problems. Answers objections and comments on a filmed physics class discussion in which the teacher uses the classical realist approach. (15)

*Philosophies of Education: Education for Cultural Reconstruction* (National Educational Television, 29 min). States that reconstructionism is, above all, a goal-centered, future-oriented philosophy of education. It is one of the fundamental assumptions of reconstructionists that education has unprecedented tasks that would not exist in a more normal, less revolutionary, or less dangerous time. (15)

*Philosophies of Education: Education as Intellectual Discipline* (National Educational Television, 29 min). Comments on the importance of a disciplined mind and outlines the methods of obtaining intellectual discipline in a democratic society. Answers objections and comments on a filmed illustration. (15)

*Philosophies of Education: An Experimentalist Approach to Education* (National Educational Television, 29 min). Defines experimentalism as a systematic theory of education stemming from the work of John Dewey. States that the experimentalist turns *to* experience rather than *away* from it. Indicates that intelligence, operating in quite human ways in relation to quite human problems, will give the answers that are needed to bring the newly born infant to maturity. Elucidates the experimentalist viewpoint, answers objections, and comments on a film sequence of a "progressive" classroom. (15)

*Philosophies of Education: A Protestant Philosophy of Education* (National Educational Television, 29 min). Explains that diversity is part of the Protestant tradition and belief. States that although there is no single Protestant view, it is the Protestant heritage to drive toward excellence in education. Notes that any Protestant view holds that some appropriate way must be found of teaching in schools that man does not live by bread alone and that God exists and is sovereign. (15)

*Piaget's Developmental Theory: Classification* (Davidson Films, 16 min, color). Describes the first two stages in Piaget's development theory of classification—preoperational and concrete. Shows children's thinking processes concerning logical, multiple, and hierarchical classification at different stages of development. (15)

*Piaget's Development Theory: Conservation* (Davidson Films, 28 min, color). Describes three stages in the development of logical intelligence—preoperational, concrete, and the beginning of formal operations. Suggests that teaching programs can help children make the transition from one stage to the next. (15)

*The School (Two Thousand Years Ago)* (Gaumont-British, 15 min). Portrays the educational methods used by the Jewish people of Palestine at the time of Christ. Shows the techniques practiced in the instruction of boys in the formal temple schools and shows the girls in their informal learning at home, where their mothers were primarily responsible for the instruction. Stresses that most learning was based on reading, memorizing, and discussing the laws and the writings of the prophets. (14)

*Schools and Learning: Learning Is My Job* (McGraw-Hill, 11 min, color). Presents a child as he explains to his grandmother how he is taught and given the responsibility to learn. Reviews the methods employed—reading, experimenting, solving problems, and reconstructing what has already been done. (16)

*Section Sixteen* (Westinghouse Broadcasting Company, 14 min). Describes the historical development of free, compulsory public education in the United States. Uses realistic settings and costumes to portray the character and spirit of the changing public school. Points out important legislation contributing to educational progress and observes other influences of major historical events upon education. Focuses attention upon the problems confronting public education today. (14)

## FIGURE CREDITS

FIGURE 14–1 (*Source:* Calvin Grieder, and Stephen Romine, *American Public Education: An Introduction,* The Ronald Press Company, New York, 1955, p. 97.)

FIGURE 14–2 (*Source:* Data from Kenneth A. Simon, and Marie G. Fullam, *Projections of Educational Statistics to 1979–80,* U.S. Office of Education, National Center for Educational Statistics, Washington, 1971, p. 25.)

FIGURE 16–1 (*Source:* "Nursery School Education," *NEA Research Bulletin,* vol. 46, no. 2, National Education Association, Research Division, Washington, May, 1968, p. 55.)

FIGURE 16–2 (*Source:* Nolan C. Kearney, *Elementary School Objectives,* Russell Sage Foundation, New York, 1953, p. 38.)

# 6 | current and future concerns

The field of education has more than enough problems and issues to challenge anyone who wishes to become a part of the profession. Many of them are of long standing. Others are more temporal in nature. New ones are certain to emerge as we encounter an enormous amount of change in the social, economic, and technological aspects of life in the years to come.

Some of these major issues and problems have been discussed somewhat at length in preceding chapters of this book. Others have been only mentioned. The purpose of Part VI is to bring into sharp focus some major issues and problems that previously have not been discussed adequately.

Chapter 17 is devoted to some of the problems and issues with which educators have been confronted for many years, and which will require attention in the years to come. Chapter 18 contains a variety of relatively new problems and issues that have emerged from major social, economic, and technological changes that have taken place in recent years. In planning your career in education, it is hoped you will weigh carefully ways in which you can contribute effectively to the solution of these problems and issues, and to the fuller realization of the school's function.

# 17 | RECURRING CONTROVERSIAL ISSUES AND PROBLEMS IN EDUCATION

No major improvement takes place in society without attendant problems. Difficulties are certain to be present whenever changes in the thinking and behavior of people are involved. This is true in the field of education as well as in any other major field of endeavor.

This chapter is concerned primarily with some of the educational issues and problems that have confronted educators for many years. For example, schools have been criticized as long as they have existed, and will continue to be criticized. There is abundant evidence of a communication gap between the general public and the school system. The relationship between the public schools and our religious institutions has been a basic issue since not long after this country was founded. Freedom to teach has been a long-time goal of teachers. The 1954 desegregation decision made the schools the continuing battleground for efforts to eliminate the vestiges of segregation in our society. Meanwhile the issue of what the schools should teach and the importance of academic versus vocational training continue to be debated.

In the following pages these recurring issues are examined in some detail.

## Why Do Schools Continue to Be Criticized?

There probably has never been a time when the public schools were so besieged by criticism from so many diverse and varied sources.

What are the reasons for the attacks? Are they due in part to the increased amount of education which each succeeding generation has gained? As people become more educated, they tend to place a higher value upon schooling and to become increasingly critical of educational practices. Have the two major opposing ideologies in the world today contributed to an outburst of concern for the education of the young? Are these attacks due to an increasing awareness upon the part of the general public of the importance of education as a means of preserving and promoting democratic living? Are these attacks sincere efforts designed to improve the education of the young, or are they motivated by desires to weaken our schools, curtail educational costs, or spread seeds of suspicion? To what extent do these attacks represent differences in opinion or confusion in regard to the school's function in a democratic society? To what extent are the attackers misinformed or unaware of valid research findings in terms of which modifications have been made in educational practices? These are only a few of the questions to keep in mind in appraising criticisms of the public schools.

The public has a right, in fact an obligation, to prescribe policies by which the public schools shall abide and to appraise the extent to which these policies have been fulfilled. Furthermore, the public for many years has exercised the right to criticize educational endeavors. Aristotle in 384 B.C. wrote the following: "There are doubts concerning the business of education, since all people do not agree in those things they would have a child taught." Some of the people at that time, and even earlier, complained that the children preferred sitting around chatting to participating in athletic activities, had bad manners, were disrespectful of their elders, and ruled the household. Confucius, approximately 2,500 years ago, noted: "The teachers of today just go on repeating things in a rigmarole fashion, annoy the students with constant questions, and repeat the same things over and over again. They do not try to find out what the students' natural inclinations are so that the students are forced to pretend to like their studies, nor do they try to bring out the best in their talents" [188:1].

Horace Mann, in his report of 1838, stated:

I have devoted special pains to learn, with some degree of numerical accuracy, how far the reading, in our schools, is an exercise of the mind in thinking and feeling, and how far it is a barren action of the organs of speech upon the atmosphere. . . . The result is, that more than eleven-twelfths of all the children in the reading classes, in our schools, do not understand the meaning of the words they read; that they do not master the sense of the reading lessons, and that the ideas and feelings intended by the author to be conveyed to, and excited in, the reader's mind, still rest in the author's intention, never having yet reached the place of their destination.

In 1845 the Grammar School Committee of Boston, after having administered various tests to the pupils, reported that:

They [tests administered] show beyond all doubt that a large proportion of the scholars in our first classes, boys and girls of 14 and 15 years of age, when called on to write simple sentences, to express their thoughts on common subjects, without the aid of a dictionary or a master, cannot write, without such errors in grammar, in spelling, and in punctuation, as we should blush to see in a letter from a son or daughter of their age.

John Erskine, in *My Life as a Teacher,* said, regarding his teaching at

Amherst in 1903, "A large proportion of my first Amherst freshmen were unable to spell."

Do these statements have a familiar ring, even though some of them were made over 2,000 years ago?

Older people often appraise present conditions and practices in terms of "the good old days." There seems to be a human tendency to glamorize and "haloize" days past. Furthermore, there is a tendency to resist change and to impose an element of rightness to our own past experience. These tendencies may operate as older people appraise the products of today's schools.

How do children in present-day schools compare with the products of an earlier system? It is difficult to find meaningful comparisons except in quantitative measures. However, data that are available would indicate that schools have performed and continue to perform a tremendous job with reasonable competency. In 1900, 11.3 per cent of the population 15-years-old and older was illiterate. By 1930 the percentage had dropped to 4.8 per cent of the population 14 years and older, and by 1960 the percentage was down to 2.4. Tentative 1970 census data indicate that the percentage has dropped below 1.0.

The median number of years of school completed by adults 25-years of age or older has increased continuously. The data are as follows [76:39]:

| Year | Median Years of School |
|------|------------------------|
| 1940 | 8.6 |
| 1950 | 9.3 |
| 1960 | 10.5 |
| 1969 | 12.1 |

These statistics are reinforced by the fact that the number of public high school graduates in 1970 was estimated at 2,640,338, which was an increase of 61.7 per cent over 1960 [76:37].

These data indicate the increasingly important role the school is playing in the lives of Americans—which may have resulted in more attention being given to the effectiveness of schools. The expanded use of the public schools has contributed to increased costs, which, in turn, have tended to produce increasingly negative public reactions. During the ten-year period of the sixties, for example, the cost of public elementary and secondary schools more than doubled—going from $15.6 billion in 1959–1960 to $39.5 billion in 1969–1970 [76:40].

In the "Third Annual Survey of the Public's Attitude Toward the Public Schools, 1971" [93], an effort was made to determine what the public believes is right about public schools. To the question: "In your own opinion, in what ways are your local public schools particularly good?" The significant factors identified by respondents were: Teachers—21 per cent; Curriculum—15 per cent; Facilities—9 per cent; and

Up-to-date teaching methods—5 per cent. The only other response which exceeded 5 per cent was from the 7 per cent who indicated they could find nothing good to list [93:37].

The same poll gave the respondents the opportunity to list the biggest problems relative to the public schools in their communities. The five major problems cited and the percentage of respondents identifying each problem were [93:37]:

| Problem | Percentage |
| --- | --- |
| Finances | 23 |
| Integration/Segregation | 21 |
| Discipline | 14 |
| Facilities | 13 |
| Dope/Drugs | 12 |

A survey finding of equal significance may be the fact that 68 per cent of those surveyed indicated the high schools place too much emphasis on "preparing students for college" and not enough emphasis on "preparing students for occupations that do not require a college degree" [93:42].

Regardless of the strengths or weaknesses of American public education, criticism is present today in many quarters and probably will continue. There is no reason to assume that the schools will ever be free of criticism, public discussion, and controversy. Few would argue that such criticism and discussion are undesirable. Constructive criticism is at the heart of the democratic process, and improvements in American public education undoubtedly can continue to be made.

Unfortunately not all the criticism seems to be constructive by intent. Finn points out that [82:31]:

Books that have good things to say about our society do not sell very well; very few orders for pamphlets and reprints are received when the pamphlets and reprints have something worthwhile to say in favor of a person or institution. It's small consolation, but the last best seller that sang praises was probably the Book of Psalms.

At the moment, there's money, prestige and almost sure publication without much chance of getting slapped back awaiting anyone willing to kick an educationist in the stomach. Aggressions are also relieved. By creating a new minority group (the educationists) to push around, most of the critics . . . (but not all critics) have discovered a form of therapy that brings wonderful release . . . and money.

As teachers are confronted in the future with criticisms of the schools, they will need to examine the apparent motives behind the author, as well as the accuracy, objectivity, logic, and depth of understanding with which he writes or speaks. Teachers need to be prepared to react positively to criticism which is well intentioned and based on fact, willing to defend education against that which is not, and enlightened enough to distinguish between the two.

## How Can the Communication Between the General
## Public and the Schools Be Improved?

Many of the attacks upon public schools, mentioned previously, are caused by a lack of understanding and facts. The results of a Gallup Poll illustrate the problem faced by the American schools relative to public information. To the direct question, "How much do you know about the local schools?" 18 per cent responded that they knew "Quite a lot," 40 per cent felt that they knew "Some," and 42 per cent indicated that they knew "Very little" [91:27, 36, 37]. Additional questions and responses were as follows:

| Question | Percentages | |
| --- | --- | --- |
| | Yes | No |
| Do you happen to know the name of the superintendent of schools? | 56 | 44 |
| During the last year, have you received any newsletter, pamphlet, or other material telling what the local schools are doing? | 35 | 61 |
| During the last month, have you read any articles in the newspapers about local schools? | 60 | 34 |
| Have you heard anything about local schools on radio during this period? | 36 | 58 |
| Have you heard anything about local schools on television during this period? | 35 | 59 |

While these responses are not particularly encouraging, a heartening fact was the indication that two-thirds of those surveyed wanted and would appreciate more information about the public schools [91:39].

The necessity for developing an informed public is indicated by the response to a question asked in a 1971 Gallup Survey: "Suppose the local public schools said they needed much more money. As you feel at this time, would you vote to raise taxes for this purpose, or would you vote against raising taxes for this purpose?" [93:33]. A total of 40 per cent responded affirmatively to this question, but a majority of 52 per cent indicated they would not vote to raise taxes to provide money for schools. Since a public school system is dependent upon tax dollars, the survey responses clearly indicate the need for increased attention to programs of public information [93:33].

In general, it is difficult to convey to the public the economic value of education to the individual and to society. It is not possible to translate into dollars and cents the exact capital gains that accrue from having studied American literature for one year or music in the third grade.

When asked to pay more taxes for schools, however, the American public tends to ask such questions as "Will we get our money's worth?" or "Can we afford better schools?"

Chapter 13 indicated the staggering costs of education with which the public will be confronted if future generations are to be at least as well educated as children are today. Actually, the quality of education must be improved if future generations are to be prepared to deal adequately with the increasing complex social, economic, and technological problems. Somehow the general public must remember an old saying that may be paraphrased as follows: "We cannot use yesterday's tools for educating youth to do the job today and expect to be in business tomorrow."

There are a number of activities at the community level that are being used, and perhaps could be used even more effectively, to acquaint the general public with the activities, purposes, and outcomes of schools. These include such activities as participation in parent-teacher groups and various educational associations; the observance of special days and weeks devoted to education; wide use of television, radio, and newspapers; the formation of study groups, local conferences, board-appointed lay advisory committees, counsel groups, and scheduled individual parent-teacher conferences; work on school newspapers; community use of school buildings; cocurricular activities; preparation of illustrated annual reports by school boards; class reunions; student participation in community activities; teacher participation in community affairs.

One aspect of public relations has generally been neglected in most of America's school systems. Although we teach pupils about local, state, and national government in "government," "civics," or other social studies classes, very few school systems have ever made any attempt to

FIGURE 17-1   The percentage of teachers who use various public relations techniques who consider these techniques to be effective. Are there other techniques that should be used?

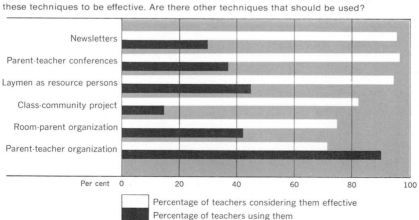

Per cent

Newsletters
Parent-teacher conferences
Laymen as resource persons
Class-community project
Room-parent organization
Parent-teacher organization

0    20    40    60    80    100

☐ Percentage of teachers considering them effective
■ Percentage of teachers using them

educate pupils with respect to local school government or to help them understand and appreciate the American educational system as an expression of our society. Yet teachers and school administrators apparently expect pupils in later life to become effective school board members and informed school patrons and to financially support the public schools through tax levies and bond issues, even though they have little knowledge of the public school as a legal and social institution. Some thought should be given to the advantages which might accrue on a long-range basis to any school district which attempts to provide instruction to pupils in such areas of local school government as school purposes, school board authority, local taxation for schools, and state authority.

Many of the suggestions already given require action by the school board, administration, or the organizations which represent teachers. This should not be taken to minimize the role which the individual teacher can and should play in improving the public image of the schools. That which the teacher does behind the closed classroom door remains the most effective means the school has for communicating with the community it serves. The major impact of the school comes in the intrapersonal relationships which parents, students, and concerned community residents have with school personnel. An effective and formal school information program can help to build a base of community approval and support. However, it cannot replace or overcome weaknesses in the best communication device—effective teaching.

## What Should Be the Relationship Between Religion and the Public Schools?

Any discussion of the relationship between religion and public education must, at least initially, be approached from a historical base. As indicated in Chapter 14 many of America's early colonists came to the New World to escape religious persecution in Europe. These early settlers had lived in European countries where a certain church or churches were given sanction or approval by the government and where religious freedom as we know it today did not exist.

When many of these early colonists arrived in America, they made provision for an established church sanctioned by the colonial government and began to persecute religious dissenters at least as vigorously as they themselves had been persecuted in Europe. In fact, in many of the American Colonies dissenters such as Baptists, Roman Catholics, Quakers, and Jews were denied the right to assemble and to worship publicly, and punishments for violation of these early religious laws ranged from a fine or imprisonment to, in some cases, death.

During the years prior to the American Revolution, opposition to the practice of persecution of religious minorities grew, and by the time the federal Constitution was drafted, colonial leaders such as Jefferson and Madison were firm in their determination that never again would government in America sanction or support a particular religion or prohibit any religious faith from public worship or from expressing publicly its beliefs.

Out of the reaction against governmental involvement in religion grew the First Amendment to the federal Constitution. This amendment provides, in part, that "Congress shall make no law respecting an establishment of religion, or prohibiting the free exercise thereof."

The First Amendment originally applied only to Congress or the federal government. Following the Civil War, however, the Fourteenth Amendment was enacted, which guaranteed to citizens of all states the basic rights protected by the federal Constitution. In recent years, the United States Supreme Court has interpreted the Fourteenth Amendment to mean that the First Amendment applies not only to Congress but also to the states. The First Amendment, as interpreted today, means, then, that neither Congress nor a state may establish a religion or prohibit the free exercise of a religion.

The public schools are a part of state government. In fact, a local school district is a legal subdivision of the state, and the members of local boards of education are state officers. Since a state may not establish a religion, neither may a local school district, because such a district is a state entity. This legal concept has been the basis for many of the most significant and critical court decisions involving the schools which have been decided by American courts in recent years.

The McCollum case, decided by the United States Supreme Court in 1948, was one of the first wherein this concept was tested. It involved a situation common to many schools of the day—that of *released time,* which was a practice whereby public school pupils were released from their normal classes to attend religious classes held in the same public school building and taught by church school teachers who came from outside the school. Suit was brought to prevent the continuation of such a program of religious instruction in the public schools of Champaign, Illinois, primarily on the grounds that such a program violated the "establishment of religion" clause of the First Amendment.

The Supreme Court declared that the Champaign religious education program violated the First Amendment and ordered the program discontinued. The practice of permitting outside religious teachers to conduct religious classes on public school property during the school day constituted "too great" a cooperation between government and religion and thus amounted to an establishment of religion by government, according to the Court (*McCollum v. Board of Education,* 333 U.S. 203, 68 Sup. Ct. 461).

For some four years, religious educators in America were in a quandary. Did the McCollum decision mean that released time programs were prohibited entirely? Could such programs be conducted off school grounds rather than within public school facilities? Did the decision mean that the Supreme Court was antagonistic toward any religious teaching of public school youngsters?

In 1952, another case reached the Court, which at least in part answered these questions. This case, known as the Zorach case, involved a challenge brought by parents in New York City against a public school practice which permitted pupils to be released from classes to attend religious instruction off the school grounds. This practice differed from the McCollum case in that the religious instruction was not given in the public school buildings.

In upholding the release of pupils to attend religious classes held away from the public school buildings, the Supreme Court made it clear that, although the government was compelled to remain "neutral" in religious matters, this by no means meant that the government was "hostile" to religion. According to the Court, cooperation between government and religion, such as releasing pupils for off-school religious classes, was permissible under the First Amendment (*Zorach v. Clauson*, 343 U.S. 306, 72 Sup. Ct. 670).

Many questions involving the public schools and religion remained, however. In nineteenth-century American public schools, teachers were expected to impart to pupils religious and "moral" training, including use of the Holy Bible as a text, as a moral guide, and as a basis for classroom "devotions." Pupils were also expected to participate in prayer in many public school classrooms. Vestiges of these religious practices remained in American public schools as late as 1962.

In 1962, challenge of a prayer adopted by the New York Board of Regents (the state board of education) reached the Supreme Court (*Engel v. Vitale*, 370 U.S. 421, 82 Sup. Ct. 1261). The prayer, developed by representatives of several religious faiths and designed to be interdenominational, had been recommended by the Board of Regents for use in the public schools of New York.

After lengthy consideration, the Supreme Court held that the use of a governmentally composed prayer in the public schools violated the establishment clause of the First Amendment—in other words, the government of New York was establishing a state-approved religion. Even the fact that children might be excused from the classroom during the saying of the prayer made no difference. According to the Court, the mere existence and use of a state-approved prayer constituted an establishment of religion by the state. Mr. Justice Black, speaking for the majority of the Court, stated (370 U.S. 424, 82 Sup. Ct. 1263):

We think that by using its public school system to encourage recitation of the Regents' prayer, the State of New York has adopted a practice wholly inconsistent with the Establishment Clause. There can, of course, be no doubt that New York's program of daily classroom invocation of God's blessings as prescribed in the Regent's prayer is a religious activity. It is a solemn avowal of divine faith and supplication for the blessings of the Almighty. The nature of such a prayer has always been religious.

Justice Black went on to say (370 U.S.429, 82 Sup. Ct. 1266):

The First Amendment was added to the Constitution to stand as a guarantee that neither the power nor the prestige of the Federal Government would be used to control, support or influence the kinds of prayer the American people can say, that the people's religions must not be subjected to the pressures of government for change each time a new political administration is elected to office. Under that Amendment's prohibition against governmental establishment of religion, as reinforced by the provisions of the Fourteenth Amendment, government in this country, be it state or federal, is without power to prescribe by law any particular form of prayer which is to be used as an official prayer in carrying on any program of governmentally sponsored religious activity.

In 1963, the Court was faced with another decision of far-reaching importance to American public education. At this time, two cases, known as the Schempp and Murray cases, which dealt primarily with the legality of devotional use of the Holy Bible in the public schools, reached the Court (*School District of Abington Township v. Schempp; Murray v. Curlett,* 374 U.S. 203, 83 Sup. Ct. 1560).

In the Schempp case, suit was brought to prevent enforcement of a Pennsylvania law which required that at least ten verses from the Holy Bible be read without comment at the opening of each school day in the public schools of that state. In the Murray case, a rule of the Baltimore school board provided that opening exercises in the public schools of that city consist of the reading, without comment, of a chapter from the Holy Bible and/or the use of the Lord's Prayer.

The Supreme Court handed down a single opinion dealing with both cases, holding that both the Pennsylvania law and the Baltimore school board rule were unconstitutional. In reaching this decision, the Court pointed out that the religious exercises were a "prescribed part of the curriculum" and were "held in the school buildings under the supervision and with the participation of teachers" and therefore constituted a state sanction or establishment of religion. The Court made clear, however, that although devotional use of the Bible was prohibited, use of the Bible as a literary or historical document was permissible.

Mr. Justice Brennan, speaking for the Court, stated (374 U.S. 283, 83 Sup. Ct. 1603):

There are persons in every community—often deeply devout—to whom any version of the Judaeo-Christian Bible is offensive. There are others whose reverence for the Holy Scriptures demands private study or reflection and to whom public reading or recitation is sacrilegious. . . . To such persons it is not the fact of using the Bible in the public schools, nor the content of any particular version that is offensive, but only the manner in which it is used.

Justice Brennan went on to outline the position of the Court on the relationship between religion and government (374 U.S. 294, 83 Sup. Ct. 1609):

I believe that the line we must draw between the permissible and the impermissible is one which accords with history and faithfully reflects the understanding of the Founding Fathers. It is a line which the Court has consistently sought to mark in its decisions expounding the religious guarantees of the First Amendment. What the Framers meant to foreclose, and what our decisions under the Establishment Clause have forbidden, are those involvements of religious with secular institutions which (*a*) serve the essentially religious activities of religious institutions; (*b*) employ the organs of government for essentially religious purposes; or (*c*) use essentially religious means to serve governmental ends, where secular means would suffice. When the secular and religious institutions become involved in such a manner, there inhere in the relationship precisely those dangers—as much to church as to state—which the Framers feared would subvert religious liberty and the strength of a system of secular government.

A recent ruling, added to the earlier decisions, appears to have settled the question of prayer. A teacher in a classroom in Illinois had her students repeat the following verse before going to the cafeteria:

> Thank you for the world so sweet,
> Thank you for the food we eat,
> Thank you for the birds that sing,
> Thank you for everything.

How do recent decisions of the Supreme Court affect the use of prayer in public schools? What guidelines should a teacher follow in regard to this matter? *(Photograph from the National Education Association.)*

The court ruled that even this kind of nondenominational prayer violated the First Amendment to the Constitution [*DeSpain v. DeKalb County Community School District,* 384 F 2d 836 (1967)].

In considering court rulings on the prayer issue, teachers should remember that what the Supreme Court has barred is religious exercises. It has not barred, but rather has encouraged, teaching about religion. While teachers and schools cannot and should not promote any single religion or creed, the historical aspect of religion can and should be communicated to students.

## How Can Freedom to Teach and to Learn Be Assured?

Freedom to think, speak, and write as reason and conscience dictate is basic to the survival of a democratic society. Our forefathers recognized this fact as they formulated the First Amendment to the Constitution of the United States. It would seem, therefore, that the development of skill in thinking and expression constitutes one of the very important tasks to which the school should give attention. The development of this skill takes place most effectively in an environment where individuals feel free and are encouraged to think and express themselves, one which offers opportunities for young people to come to grips with problems of real concern to them. Many such problems will be of a controversial nature.

Academic freedom refers to the freedom of teachers to seek and to present the truth on problems and issues without fear of interference from school boards, governmental authorities, or pressure groups. From a learner's standpoint it refers to the opportunity to study all points of view in regard to a problem or an issue and to arrive at reasoned conclusions. The teacher does not have a right to tell pupils what to think, nor does he have the right to advocate one theory only. The teacher's concern is the development of skill in thinking, expression, and problem solving on the part of his pupils. Unless both teachers and pupils feel free to examine, discuss, think, and arrive at reasoned conclusions on issues affecting their daily lives, the school is handicapped greatly in fulfilling its function in a democratic society.

Do teachers and pupils today feel free to teach and to learn? Teachers in some communities feel that they would run considerable risk of losing their jobs if they permitted students to examine all sides of issues concerning trade unions. In some sections of the country it would be extremely hazardous to encourage free inquiry and discussion of the racial problem. The discussion of sex education is questionable in some school systems. Certain textbooks in some communities have been censored. A number of teachers have been accused of being Communists if they permit pupils to learn *about* communism. These and many other instances which could be cited indicate that teachers and pupils are not entirely free to teach and to learn.

Yet the picture seems to be changing. Materials prepared by the U.S. Office of Education and other agencies pertaining to teaching *about* communism and other controversial subjects are becoming plentiful. Surveys of school administrators have indicated that these leaders increasingly favor teaching about controversial issues, and the teaching of such issues appears to be more accepted today than ever before. The National Education Association believes that academic and professional freedom is essential to the teaching profession.

Controversial issues should be a part of instructional programs when judgment of the professional staff deems the issues appropriate to the curriculum and to the maturity level of the student. Academic freedom is the right of the learner and his teachers to explore, present, and discuss divergent points of view in the quest for knowledge and truth.

Professional freedom includes the teacher's right to evaluate, to criticize, and to advocate his personal point of view concerning the policies and programs of the schools. The teacher also has the right to assist colleagues when their academic or professional freedom is violated [169:79].

Recent Supreme Court decisions have expanded teachers' constitutional rights of self-expression. In 1969 the Court observed that neither "teachers or students shed their constitutional freedoms at the schoolhouse gate" [*Tinker v. Des Moines Independent Community School District,* 89 S. Ct. 733 (1969)]. In an earlier decision the Court had protected a teacher's right to comment upon his conditions of employment and to speak critically of his school board [*Pickering v. Board of Education of Township High School District,* 88 S. Ct. 1731 (1968)]. These decisions are sufficiently extensive to justify the conclusion that courts will provide protection to teachers in the reasonable exercise of academic freedom.

The exercise of academic freedom also places a substantial responsibility upon the teacher. It is important for teachers to remember that academic freedom should never be used as a protective device in terms of which society suffers. Teachers in our democratic society have a basic responsibility to their pupils and to their communities to promote freedom of thought, freedom of expression, and the pursuit of truth. Society, in turn, has an obligation to provide and to promote these conditions.

## How Can Problems of Discrimination and Segregation Be Resolved?

In addition to the financial inequalities that have existed within the American school system, educators also have been confronted with problems arising from racial discrimination and segregation. These problems are precipitated when attempts are made to provide equal educational opportunities for boys and girls regardless of race, color, and religion. Although much progress has been made since 1954 in lessening the amount of discrimination and segregation, problems still remain. Teachers are confronted with the task of helping resolve these very complex problems.

From the study of social problems, it is obvious that there are varying degrees of prejudice and discrimination existing throughout the United States wherever minority groups are involved. Race, color, and religion affect to some degree job opportunities, housing, churches, labor unions, clubs, and political groups. In various parts of the country definite discriminatory practices still exist with respect to such minority groups as Jews, Orientals, Latin Americans, and blacks. As an example, the large influx of Puerto Ricans in New York City presents a major problem of integration.

As Thayer indicates [279:479–480], court decisions affecting the education of blacks, oddly enough, date back to a decision of a Massachusetts court in 1849 [*Roberts v. the City of Boston,* 5 Cush. 198, 206]. In this particular case a black child claimed the right to attend the school nearest her home rather than the one to which she had been assigned, since the Massachusetts constitution stated that all persons are equal before the law without distinction of age or sex, birth or color, origin or condition. In denying this right, the court maintained that,

when the great principle (of equality) comes to be applied to the actual and various conditions of persons in society, it will not warrant the assertion, that men are legally clothed with the same civil and political powers, and that children and adults are legally to have the same functions and be subject to the same treatment; but only that the rights of all, as they are settled and regulated by law, are equally entitled to the paternal consideration and protection of the law, and their maintenance.

Following the termination of the Civil War, Congress took steps to ensure the equality of blacks and whites. As a result, the Thirteenth, Fourteenth, and Fifteenth Amendments were added to the Constitution. Furthermore, states applying for statehood were required to include in their constitutions provisions for the establishment and maintenance of free public schools [279:479].

In meeting their educational obligations, the Southern states segregated blacks upon grounds that they would be provided with equal facilities. This action was upheld in various courts, using as a precedent the "separate but equal" decision that had been pronounced by the Massachusetts court in 1849. In 1896 the United States Supreme Court, in the famous case *Plessy v. Ferguson* [163 U.S. 537, 16 Sup. Ct. 1138], validated the "separate but equal" practice of dealing with blacks. Although the actual case involved segregation on a railroad engaged in interstate commerce, in a number of states the policy was subsequently applied to public facilities, such as parks, beaches, and golf courses, and eventually to public schools.

After the turn of the century, a number of decisions rendered by federal courts began to weaken the rigid tradition and state laws regarding segregation. In 1915 the Court declared that the grandfather clause was a violation of the Fifteenth Amendment [*Guinn v. United States*, 238 U.S. 347, 35 Sup. Ct. 926]. Subsequent cases, involving such matters as housing and seating on buses, further weakened the legality of segregation practices. In 1950, a black student sought admission to the Law School at the University of Texas. The Court [*Sweatt v. Painter*, 339 v. 629, 70 Sup. Ct. 859] ruled that he must be admitted. In May, 1954, the Supreme Court [*Brown v. Board of Education of Topeka*, 347 U.S. 483, 74 Sup. Ct. 686], interpreted the Constitution to mean that compulsory segregation is unconstitutional. In the words of Chief Justice Warren, the decision was as follows:

Today, education is perhaps the most important function of state and local governments. Compulsory attendance laws and the great expenditures for education both demonstrate our recognition of the importance of education to our democratic society. It is required in the performance of our most basic public responsibilities, even service in the armed forces. It is the very foundation of good citizenship. Today it is a principal instrument in awakening the child to cultural values, in preparing him for later professional training, and in helping him to adjust normally to his environment. In these days, it is doubtful that any child may reasonably be expected to succeed in life if he is denied the opportunity of an education. Such an opportunity, where the state has undertaken to provide it, is a right which must be made available to all on equal terms.

We come then to the question presented: Does segregation of children in public schools solely on basis of race, even though the physical facilities and other "tangible" factors may be equal, deprive the children of the minority group of equal education opportunities? We believe that it does. . . .

We conclude that in the field of public education the doctrine of "separate but equal" has no place. Separate educational facilities are inherently unequal. Therefore, we hold that the plaintiffs and others similarly situated for whom the actions have been brought are, by reason of the segregation complained of, deprived of the equal protection of the laws guaranteed by the Fourteenth Amendment.

Teachers are generally familiar with some of the problems encountered in the implementation of this decision. In a great many cases, as was indicated in Chapter 14, the integration of the races in the public schools has been without difficulty. In some cases, however, efforts to implement the ruling have met with defiance and subterfuge. Obviously, it takes time to implement such a ruling, since in a number of cases it strikes deep into the heart of tradition, feelings, and emotions. Legislation does not quickly change such factors.

In 1964, however, a significant attempt to reduce segregation legislatively occurred when the federal Congress enacted the Civil Rights Act. Title IV of this act provides for a cutoff of federal funds to any school district which maintains a segregated system. It is anticipated that this type of federal legislation may hasten the day when all school districts are fully integrated.

There also is evidence that the Supreme Court will insist upon compliance with its 1954 decision. In a 1969 case, the Court emphasized the responsibility of local school boards and the immediacy of the problem by stating that: "The burden on a school board today is to come forward with a plan that promises realistically to work now . . . until it is clear that state-imposed segregation has been completely removed" [*Green v. County School Board,* 88 S. Ct. 1689 (1969)]. In a 1971 decision the Court further stated that [*Swann v. Charlotte-Mecklenberg Board of Education,* 91 S. Ct. 1267 (1971)]: "Today's objective is to eliminate from the public schools all vestiges of state-imposed segregation that was held violative of equal protection guarantees by *Brown v. Board of Education.*" In this decision, the Court referred to the "broad powers" which lower federal courts have "to fashion a remedy" to end segregation. The Court also recognized that court ordered bussing could be "one tool of desegregation" and was within the power of the courts to order.

The involvement of the individual teacher also extends beyond the responsibility of providing equal and nondiscriminatory treatment for students. In the years immediately following the Brown decision of 1954, the courts were occupied with students and gave little attention to faculty desegregation. However, beginning in 1965, the courts began to require simultaneous staff and student desegregation. In the Swann case of 1967 the Supreme Court referred to faculty desegregation and specifically pointed to its approval of a lower court plan which required the ratio of black and white teachers in each school in a given school corporation to approximate the ratio of black and white teachers in the total corporation.

The courts are distinguishing between *de facto* and *de jure* segregation in relation to the integration of schools. Intentional maintenance of segregation, as prohibited by the 1954 decision of the Supreme Court, is known as *de jure* segregation. Any school board which consciously maintains segregated schools, through gerrymandering of school attendance zones so as to promote segregation, for example, is guilty of furthering *de jure* segregation and may be required by a court to end such segregation. Since the 1954 Supreme Court decision clearly prohibits *de jure* segregation, it is reasonable to suppose that it will finally be eliminated in American schools.

As *de jure* segregation recedes, another problem relating to segregation has taken its place—*de facto* segregation. *De facto* segregation can be defined as segregation of school pupils which results primarily from the housing patterns in many of America's large cities. Blacks and other racial minority groups tend to congregate in certain areas of such cities, owing perhaps in part to discrimination in matters of housing, and thus the neighborhood schools which serve such areas tend to become almost entirely populated by members of the minority race.

From an educational standpoint, teachers are responsible for understanding the problems of discrimination and segregation in evidence in all aspects of life and for relating these problems to the basic tenets of a democratic society. A teacher has the opportunity to help pupils as well as adults to identify these inconsistencies in our society and to formulate ways for effectively resolving them.

Without doubt, teachers have played a very significant role in the progress that has been made over the years. Teachers work primarily with younger people, who tend to be more tolerant than their elders. Furthermore, research indicates that people tend to become more tolerant as they become better educated.

A careful examination of countries throughout the world will reveal that problems of segregation and discrimination are not unique to the United States. They exist in every society. In many countries they are of much greater magnitude than they are here. Furthermore, in some countries the problems are becoming decidedly more acute. Teachers have a responsibility for understanding these problems as they exist on a worldwide basis and for aiding in the resolution of them. Most of all, teachers should do everything possible to foster progress in the solution of these problems in the United States, so that our country may be increasingly effective in demonstrating to the world a better way of life.

## To What Extent Should the Public School Provide Vocational Education?

As indicated in Chapter 1, the modern world is changing so rapidly that many of today's pupils will be working in jobs that do not exist at present. M. J. Rathbone, chairman of the board and chief executive officer of Standard Oil Company of New Jersey, points out that approximately 70 per cent of the skilled trades in American manufacturing in the year 1900 do not exist today and that "a large proportion of today's skills will become obsolete in the shorter period between now and the year 2000, which is a period shorter than the average man's working lifetime" [213:8].

This era of rapid change poses a dilemma for the public schools. Can or should the public schools attempt to specifically prepare pupils for the world of work? The problem is made more acute by the fact that of every ten pupils presently in elementary school, two will not finish high school and only five will continue their education beyond high school.

The report of the Project on Instruction of the National Education Association states that competence in basic understandings and skills is still the best contribution of the elementary schools to future workers, but that the schools should also help pupils to learn more about the world of work. The report suggests that high schools offer some direct vocational education to pupils who do not plan to continue their formal schooling beyond the secondary school, with special programs being provided for the physically handicapped and the culturally deprived [232:112]. The importance of adequate vocational guidance programs in high schools, including testing programs and the providing of information to pupils about opportunities in the various occupations, has been cited as a special need for American high schools by many authorities.

All too often when a need is discovered in American education, a crash program is quickly developed to meet the need. There are those today who feel that such a program is needed in vocational education. Harris [115:365], however, points out that the essential purpose of American education is to train citizens rather than workers and that such crash programs are not defensible. Harris also feels that separating pupils into two different kinds of high schools, one academic and the other vocational, is not the answer to the need for vocational education. Rather than have this type of separation, Harris suggests post-high school education of at least one or two years' duration for the majority of American youth and cites the community junior college as the best answer to the problem.

The American Association of School Administrators [127:24] points out another aspect of the problem of vocational education. The more specific the vocational training of an individual becomes, the more vulnerable he is to changes in employment opportunities over which he

The objective of economic efficiency highlights the need for secondary schools to be concerned with the vocational interests and needs of students. In what forms should this concern be expressed? (Photograph by Joe Di Dio, National Education Association.)

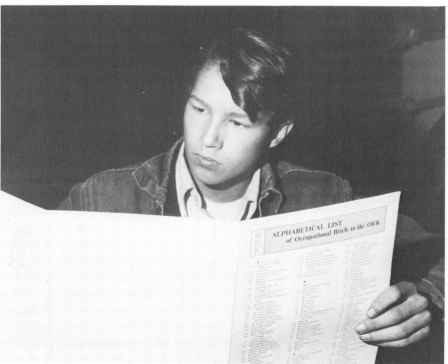

has little or no control. The association suggests that the vocational education program be directed toward "general vocational excellence" in "broad occupational areas," leaving to the specific industry or craft the training of workers for particular assignments.

In 1969 the National Advisory Council on Vocational Education reported to the Secretary of Health, Education, and Welfare that 25 per cent of the young men and women who turn 18 each year are not educated to "a level of employability." The Council cited this condition as an important cause of the unrest and violence prevalent in the country. The Council maintained that: "At the very heart of the problem is a national attitude that says vocational education is designed for somebody else's children." The Council deplored this attitude as "snobbish, undemocratic, and a revelation of why schools fail so many students." The Council further charged that local school districts concentrate on college preparatory students in "reckless disregard of the fact that for 60 per cent of our young people high school is still the only transition to the world of work" [190:11].

While the Council saw the provision of additional federal financial support as a solution to the problem, it is clear that the charges, if true, impose a significant responsibility upon teachers. Teachers are in a position to diagnose the ability and potential of students; to help them understand their potential; and to assist them in coming to realistic decisions relative to career choices. Not all students are suited for college training, and the economy does offer many opportunities for noncollege-bound students who develop employable skills. The preparation of students for diverse kinds of employment is a responsibility of schools and teachers.

## SUMMARY

This chapter has been concerned with some of the problems and issues with which educators have been confronted for many years. Teachers moving into the profession will encounter these problems and can play a vital role in determining how successful the schools may move toward their solution.

Prospective teachers should be aware of the kinds of criticisms directed at the school, and understand their underlying causes and assess the validity of the criticisms. Undoubtedly much of it springs from a lack of understanding of what the schools are doing. Teachers can do much to develop this understanding. They are in direct contact with students and parents, and much of the community reaction to the schools is based upon the interactions they have. It is also likely that some of the criticisms directed at the schools are valid and require positive responses.

Some of the criticism of the schools also can be attributed to problems concerning discrimination and segregation. Courts are now demanding that desegregation plans give promise of immediate results and that faculty and student desegregation occur simultaneously.

Freedom to think, to speak, and to write as reason and conscience dictate is basic to the survival of a democratic society. The development of skill in this regard constitutes one of the very important tasks to which teachers and schools must give attention. The restraints placed on teachers in determining what the instructional program will be have been eased as the courts have shown an increasing tendency to protect teachers in the exercise of academic freedom. Having this freedom also places a grave responsibility upon teachers to be certain that the experiences they provide for boys and girls contribute to the development of skills necessary for effective living in a democratic society.

Continuing attention must also be given to what the schools should teach. Prospective teachers should study the function of the school in promoting moral growth and character without providing instruction in particular religious faiths and doctrines.

The extent to which the public schools should provide vocational education will continue to be a major issue, especially in view of the changes in occupational requirements resulting from the rapid advance of technology. Undoubtedly problems resulting from unemployment, the quest for relevance in education, the demands of industry, the increasing concern of government for education, and a host of other factors will thrust educators into major roles of leadership in determining the public school's function in meeting the vocational needs of youth.

## QUESTIONS TO CONSIDER

1.  What, in your opinion, are the reasons for so much criticism being made of public schools today? How do you plan to handle these criticisms when you become a teacher?
2.  When you begin teaching, how will you attempt to lessen the communication gap between the general public and the schools?
3.  What responsibilities do you feel a teacher has for promoting a high level of support for schools in any given community and in what ways should this be accomplished?
4.  In what ways will you attempt to promote moral and spiritual values in your pupils?
5.  A number of people feel that an amendment should be written into the Constitution proclaiming the United States to be a "Christian nation and giving full legal sanction to religious expressions in public schools and other governmental activities." What would be your reaction to such a proposal? Why?
6.  Do you feel the Bible can be used effectively in public schools as a historical document? As literature? If so, how would you determine which version of the Bible to use? What are some of the problems a teacher would face in attempting to use the Bible as history or literature?
7.  How might teachers misuse academic freedom?
8.  Are there any controversial issues that should not be discussed in public schools? Explain.
9.  Do you feel a teacher should be able to take a public stand on any issue without fear of reprisal? How would you justify your position?

10. What suggestions do you have for resolving the problem of discrimination and segregation in schools?
11. What should be the function of the public schools with respect to vocational education?

## PROBLEM SITUATION FOR INQUIRY

Mr. Ward had taught social sciences for three years in a large city high school before he and his wife moved to Milford Center, a small conservative community, over a year ago. He was very popular with students because of his robust physical appearance, his liberal, relaxed class presentations, and his vibrant out-of-class personality. The students came to look to him as an authority on things beyond their rural community and state. He was unanimously chosen as the faculty advisor to the senior class.

Mr. Ward's teaching was above average, and his students scored high on achievement tests in the subject areas for which he was responsible. In essence, he performed all his school-oriented duties in a highly satisfactory manner.

Mr. Ward had strong feelings about war and did not hesitate to make his feelings known in his classes. Upon learning that the local American Legion would have a military parade on Veteran's Day, for which school was to be dismissed, Mr. Ward suggested and organized a student march protesting a recent decision of Congress to extend military assistance to a foreign country at war. The student march caused some disruption of the parade of the American Legion. A large segment of the citizens of Milford Center were angered, and demanded that, unless Mr. Ward were fired, they would withdraw their sons and daughters from his "unsavory and subversive influence."

If you were Mr. Ward's principal, what would you do? Why?

## ACTIVITIES TO PURSUE

1. Construct a list of key questions that would reflect an individual's feelings toward schools and teachers. Use these questions in conducting a representative community survey. To what extent are their criticisms typical of those reported in educational literature? How do you account for the criticisms they express?
2. Have a group of your colleagues visit one or more of the modern schools and one or more of the very traditional schools. Compare and contrast the learnings gained by the pupils. Which type of school is helping pupils the most in terms of effective democratic living?
3. Discuss with your college or university admissions officer the question of whether college freshmen are better prepared for college today than they were a decade ago. You might ask him to speak to your class on this subject.
4. Question some teachers and school administrators on how they attempt to bridge the communication gap between the general public and the schools. When you begin teaching how will you attempt to communicate effectively with the general public?
5. Arrange for a public school official, such as a superintendent of schools, to discuss with your class the ways in which schools develop moral and spiritual values in boys and girls. You may wish to discuss this matter with several teachers.
6. Conduct some research on how many different versions of the Holy Bible are in existence, some of the differences between the versions, and the faiths which subscribe to each version.
7. Have a group of students talk with their former public school teachers regarding the extent to which the latter feel they have academic freedom. Compile a list of any restrictions which they note.

8. Spend some time in one or more ghetto schools talking with teachers, administrators, and students regarding problems of discrimination and segregation. Upon the basis of your findings, what suggestions would you make for resolving this problem?

9. Investigate the area of vocational education through reading, research, and conferences with educators and laymen. Upon the basis of your findings, prepare a philosophical statement which indicates the role of public schools in meeting the occupational needs of students.

# 18 | CURRENT CONTROVERSIAL ISSUES AND PROBLEMS IN EDUCATION

The traditional problems and issues which schools and teachers have faced are joined today by a series of relatively new problems, many of which are rooted to a very considerable extent in the rapid social, economic, and technological changes that are taking place. Students, especially in the secondary schools and in colleges, are demanding changes in educational practices and in conduct. The public is seeking evidences of quality education in our schools and of practices for assuring this quality. Increased pressure is being placed upon schools and teachers to deal more adequately with various disadvantaged groups of students and with the problem of racism. These problems are explored in the remaining sections of this chapter.

## STUDENT DEMANDS FOR RELEVANCE, RECOGNITION, AND CHANGE

As students become increasingly aware of the complex problems of society which they will face in the future, they frequently feel frustrated. They may experience difficulty in finding channels open to discuss their problems, concerns, fears, and frustrations. These feelings may lead to the desire to protest various conditions with which they are confronted. Hence, it was not alarming to find that 18 per cent of all the nation's high schools had faced a serious student protest in the 1968–1969 school year. The major issues of protest were "disciplinary rules, dress codes, school services and facilities, and curriculum policy" [234:145]. The most popular forms of protest were sit-ins in smaller schools and the use of underground newspapers in the larger schools.

 In the years to come, it is reasonable to assume that students will continue to seek change through the use of organized protests, although the issues and the forms of protest may differ. Teachers and school administrators are confronted with the task of trying to understand the sources of student concerns and frustrations. They should listen to students, talk with them as human beings who have individual and unique problems and concerns, and encourage them to get together intellectually for open discussion on controversial issues [292:407]. By recognizing and dealing with students on these bases, teachers may be able to lessen the undesirable causes of student protests, and at the same time, provide more positive learning experiences.

## How Can Schools Become More Relevant?

One of the most common areas of concern to students involves the relevance of the school curriculum. In discussing the relationship of "relevance" to student protest groups, Shaffer maintains that the crusade toward a more relevant education involves the provision of courses and the reform of instructional programs to bring them more closely into line with student interests [238:647].

The striving for relevance has taken many forms, one aspect of which has been the request for educational experiences which are of immediate value and significance. Use of school time for protest against governmental activities, the demand for a "black studies" program, and sugges-

Youth today want to have the opportunity to discuss their problems, concerns, fears, and frustrations. They want to participate increasingly and more meaningfully in shaping their school experiences. *(Photograph by Joe Di Dio, National Education Association.)*

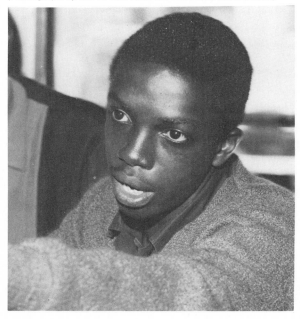

tions that grading be eliminated are representative of proposed changes advanced as part of the thrust for relevant education.

Van Til believes that much of the content taught in schools is unrelated to the lives of the learners. He identifies the problem faced by the teacher in the following manner [288:14, 16]:

Classes do exist in your community and mine in which an uninterrupted academic content bores young people. Classes do exist where subject matter is quite unrelated to the dilemmas and struggles and aspirations of many prospective learners.

The teacher who realizes that his content of instruction isn't meaningful has two viable alternatives. He can change his content from irrelevant to the relevant. Or, if he cannot change the required content, he can teach it in such a way as to give it relevance.

Yes, a third possibility does exist. One can continue with the meaningless content, break his heart trying to teach, and achieve very little.

The alternatives listed by Van Til may oversimplify the problem. Obviously teachers cannot give to elementary and secondary school students the responsibility for deciding what education is relevant and should be retained. This is a professional responsibility for which the mature, adult teacher is specifically prepared. Yet, the students' reactions should not be ignored. As the one most affected, the student can be a valuable source in aiding teachers in determining the relevance of curricular offerings.

The phenomenal expansion of technological knowledge and skills creates new demands in the education of youth. Relevance today includes familiarity with, and at least minimal skill in the use of, computers. *(Photograph by Joe Di Dio, National Education Association.)*

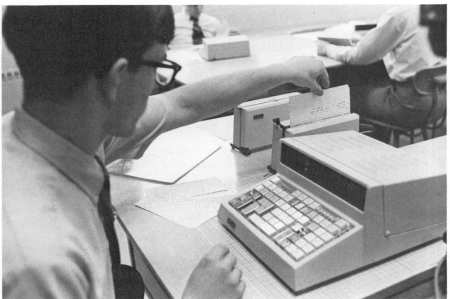

In all likelihood most school programs are more relevant than critics of the schools would have us believe and less relevant than school personnel would like them to be. Teachers are in the best position to assess course offerings, to gauge student reaction, and to continuously "tune" the curricular offerings so that they will be designed to meet changing student needs.

## What Is the Role of Students in School Government?

Student protests, the demand for relevance in education, and a general awareness of the problems and concerns of young people have helped to produce demands for a greater role for students in the governance of the schools they attend. The reduction of the voting age in federal and in most state elections, as well as military service for 18 year olds, has added incentive and logic to this trend. High school graduates go into the world as adults with the responsibility and authority to become practicing members of a democratic society. If they are to be ready for this role, the preparation must come in the experiences students have as they move through school. The need for graduate students who are ready to participate in government is a powerful argument for student participation in school governance.

Surprisingly the school board members who have the authority for directing the schools appear to agree with the need for greater participation by students. When asked to give their views on student participation, a group of school board members made the following comments [29:27–28]:

Anybody enlightened enough to take a seat on a school board ought to recognize readily "that our youth, for numerous reasons, are capable of responsible thinking and should be given the opportunity to express the logic of their opinions." Students should and do have excellent ideas for improving policies that govern their education. I think they should be encouraged to develop these ideas systematically; to research them as to legality, possibility of accomplishing anticipated results, and effect on the school system. They should take part in discussions prior to the vote of the school board and be willing to assume some of the responsibilities of implementing policies.

Santa Barbara, California, for example, has a student board of education that assists the "senior" school board in making policy. The student board, which meets on the day preceding the "senior" board meeting, considers the agenda to be taken up by the "senior" board and reports its actions to the "senior" board during its regular meeting [162:29].

The attitude of students toward their own role in school government was indicated in a survey in Ohio in which 90 per cent of the students interviewed expressed a desire to be involved in the decisions that affected them, specifically "curriculum planning, dress codes, and rules

Student councils should provide excellent opportunities for students to assume meaningful roles in the goveranance of schools. *(Photograph by Carolyn Salisbury, National Education Association.)*

of conduct." The students in the survey expressed the opinion that a major problem in schools was the lack of communication between "themselves and school administrators and teachers" [186:85].

As in other areas relating to students, the teacher's role is extremely significant. While much of the discussion and writing relative to student participation in school government is concerned with the school board and administrative structure, the fact remains that students spend most of their school hours in direct contact with teachers. This relationship offers much of the opportunity for effective student involvement in school government. Teachers should recognize that students have ideas, and that they want to be involved. The primary responsibility for directing the schools should remain with administrators and teachers. However, carrying out this responsibility will be easier if the views of students are actively sought and considered.

## Can the School Curriculum Be Adapted to Changing Needs?

The traditional school curriculum has undergone many changes in recent years. In addition to changes being made in the usual subject areas, the schools have attempted to adjust the curricula to meet the new and changing problems of society. Two of the most significant areas of curriculum expansion have been in sex education and drug education.

The growth in the number of family life and sex education programs in the schools has, according to one authority, been a reaction to the increasing number of premarital pregnancies, forced marriages, early divorces, abortions, and an increased veneral disease rate [237:3]. These problems have demonstrated the need for students to have factual knowledge of and an orientation to sexuality. That students have not received the necessary information from nonschool sources was shown in a Purdue University poll in which 53 per cent of the boys and 43 per cent of the girls stated that they "got the word" from their friends. Another 15 per cent "pieced things together" from a variety of sources. Only 15 per cent of the boys and 35 per cent of the girls received sex information from their parents [237:3].

While the public has generally favored school efforts to fill the need for responsible sex education programs, there are those who believe that schools should not be involved in such programs. Organizations have been formed to fight the spread of sex education programs in schools, and individual parents have become actively concerned. There is a tendency on the part of some school people to feel that these reactions come from right-wing radicals. However, even the proponents of sex education agree that this is not necessarily the case. As one writer indicates ". . . there are nevertheless many astute parents who recoil from something as psychologically important as sex being taught by teachers who may have few or no qualifications for such a job and may have sexual hang-ups of their own" [129:2].

The effort to provide drug education also has been a response to current problems. In 1970 the Drug Abuse Education Act was passed by Congress providing money for state departments of education to use in planning and carrying out drug abuse education programs [173:77]. Enactment of this program followed a report that drug use by students was extensive in half of the nation's urban schools and in 30 per cent of the rural schools. The report indicated that there were 100,000 heroin addicts in New York City's high schools alone [287:7].

The challenge involved in providing drug education may be summarized as follows [65:9]:

The urgent need for drug education in our schools goes beyond the task of conveying the facts of drug use and abuse—at best a difficult and sensitive job. It challenges the very meaning and methods of education.

The challenge comes in answers to the fundamental question: Why do students use drugs? Ignorance, curiosity, peer pressure, the desire to rebel are all considered factors in stimulating drug use by high school students—and increasingly by elementary school pupils. Students also use drugs because they enjoy them. But equally significant motives for student drug use are described as loneliness, unhappiness with one's self or one's family, and lack of fulfillment.

This challenge to the schools has produced many kinds of reactions including the development of courses of study in the problems of drug addiction, insertion of units on drugs in teacher preparation courses, and the distribution of pamphlets and materials designed to acquaint students with the dangers of drug abuse. Hope that the problems of drug abuse can be dealt with is heightened by a Purdue University poll indicating that high school students are "cautious" in their outlook on drugs. Only 11 per cent of those surveyed favored legalizing the sale of marihuana, and a majority indicated they would not try drugs even if the threats of addiction or arrest were absent [177:26].

The efforts of schools to react to drug and sex problems are probably a forerunner of more active school involvement in the problems of our society. This trend places a heavier responsibility upon teachers and administrators. It means they will often be at the center of controversy, since the issues involved and the solutions are seldom uniformly clear. School involvement in current issues also reemphasizes the importance of continuing education for teachers and other adults. Remaining up-to-date on the drug problem alone is a challenging responsibility. Adding to the school's curriculum also creates the problem of finding room in an already crowded program.

## CONCERNS FOR THE QUALITY OF THE EDUCATIONAL PRODUCT

A second set of current problems and issues centers upon the quality of the educational product. The public has become more "results-oriented," and they are talking in terms of benefits derived from dollars spent, or cost-benefits analysis. Taxpayers are increasingly demanding that schools and school personnel be held "accountable" for educational results. One of the more controversial responses to this demand has been the use of "performance contracting" in an attempt to guarantee a specified level of pupil achievement. Educational results vary widely throughout the country, and many parents rightfully contend that their children are the victims of unequal educational opportunity. All this activity, the criticisms and the reactions, has been focused in demands for the institution of a program of national assessment.

### Can the Process of Education Be Made Accountable?

A growing number of individuals concerned with education have become convinced that it is possible to hold schools responsible for the results of their activity. The emphasis on accountability is not upon the teacher or the teaching process. Rather it is upon results as reflected by the degree to which students actually develop the knowledge and skills which are the objectives of instruction.

The search for accountability has taken many forms. Descriptive terms, such as educational engineering, management by objectives, systems analysis, and performance contracting, have become a part of the vocabulary of education. Regardless of the terms used, it is apparent that the idea of holding schools responsible for achievement is popular with those outside the field of education.

A survey taken by a professional polling firm in the early 1970s asked the adult public to respond to the question: "Would you like to see students in the local schools be given national tests so that their educational achievement could be compared with students in other communities?" A total of 70 per cent responded favorably to this question [93:33]. In one Gallup Survey, the following question, dealing directly with the concept of accountability, was asked: "Would you favor or oppose a system that would hold teachers and administrators more accountable for the progress of students?" In response to this question, 67 per cent responded in favor, 21 per cent were opposed, and the remaining 12 per cent had no opinion [92:101]. In response to the question "Should each teacher be paid on the basis of the quality of work or should all teachers be paid on a standard scale basis?" 58 per cent favored a "quality of work" base as compared to 36 per cent favoring "a standard scale basis" [92:101].

While enthusiasm within the field of education relative to "accountability" has not matched that of the general public, a number of school systems are moving in this direction. For example, the New York City Schools have employed the Educational Testing Service at a cost of "not more than $100,000" to develop a systemwide plan for accountability [181:134]. Given this kind of impetus and the favorable public reaction, it is probable that the search for accountability will be of long duration.

## Can Performance Contracting Guarantee Pupil Achievement?

One of the chief devices used in attempts to provide accountability has been that of performance contracting. A major thrust in this direction occurred in 1969 when the Texarkana school district entered into a contract by which a private business firm took over the operation of a part of the instructional program. The firm guaranteed to produce specific instructional results in the areas of reading and mathematics with payment under the contract conditioned on the success the company realized in raising student achievement to the guaranteed levels.

Other school systems have ventured into the field of performance contracting with encouragement and financial assistance being provided by the U.S. Office of Education. For example, in 1970 the Gary, Indiana School Board received a four-year federal grant in excess of $2,000,000 to experiment with performance contracting in an attempt to overcome the "gross underachievement" of Gary's children [203:39]. A private firm was given the management and instructional responsibility for an all-black elementary school. The company agreed to refund the approximately $800 it received for teaching a pupil if, at the end of the instructional period, the pupil's achievement was not up to national norms on tests administered by an independent evaluator.

Whether performance contracting will develop into a basic part of the instructional program of the public schools is uncertain and will depend, in part, upon the degree to which early efforts are successful.

Certainly the development of performance contracting has its share of critics and skeptics. The National Education Association has taken an attitude of extreme caution in advising affiliates "not to become parties to a performance contract without careful prior planning and consultation" [180:86]. Among the conditions which the NEA believes should be present are: involvement of teachers in every phase of planning from contracting to evaluation; use of professionally trained and certificated personnel; and compliance which the negotiated agreements already in effect between school boards and teacher groups [180:86]. There are also legal problems to be considered. Many of the early performance contracts have required temporary suspension of statutory regulations and administrative rules in areas such as class size and teacher certification. Almost certainly some of these contracts have involved the delegation of school board authority in ways which can be considered extra-legal. If performance contracting is to flourish, a firm legal basis will have to be provided.

Despite the problems already encountered, performance contracting is not likely to go away. Education is big business, and many private firms are looking toward the instruction of public school pupils as a promising source of productive investment. Also, the public is receptive to the idea of "guaranteed results." These conditions present a challenge to teachers to attempt to provide within the public schools the type of innovation and experimentation that would have even greater appeal to the public than performance contracting. At the same time, teachers need to be alert to the techniques used by private firms so that those which prove successful can be integrated into the public school program.

## How Can Educational Opportunity Be Equalized?

The emphasis on accountability in education has given new significance to a fundamental ideal in the American school system: equal educational opportunity for all children. Since early colonial days, considerable progress has been made, but much yet remains to be done. One factor in limiting the progress which has been made has been the seeming inability to provide a sound financial base for all schools. Inequalities in financial support of public schools among the various states and communities are a basic fact of educational life.

In recent years those working to guarantee equal educational opportunity have turned to the courts in an attempt to gain improved state programs of school financing. Early efforts were unsuccessful. In a typical Illinois case the court held that the "equal opportunity" controversy could not be adjudicated because there were "no discoverable and manageable standards by which the court can determine when the Constitution is satisfied and when it is violated" [*McInnis v. Shapiro,* 293 F. Supp. 327 (1968)]. However, more recent efforts have met with a success which many believe could lead to alteration of state finance programs throughout the country. The California and the Minnesota court cases of 1971, as described in Chapter 13, found the public school state financing systems, and in particular the local property tax, to be in violation of the "equal protection clause" of the 14th Amendment because they produced inequalities in the financial ability of individual school districts. While these decisions were concerned with state plans, those who argue in favor of federal aid to education believe the reasoning used by the courts supports their contention that only the federal government is in a position to equalize educational opportunity throughout the United States through provision of funds to needy states and school districts.

Another type of education inequality involves the educationally deprived. In considering the objective of equal educational opportunity, Kirp maintains that [137:635]:

While educators have long spoken of equality of educational opportunity, it has been tacitly understood for at least as long that the quality of education that a school child received depended in large part on the community in which he happened to grow up. Suburban towns have had sufficient financial resources to afford the finest facilities and the best qualified teachers; their students have come almost exclusively from upper middle-class backgrounds. In contrast, at least since World War II, the big cities have been poor cities, poor both in money available to spend for facilities and teachers, and in vitally important human resources.

The educationally deprived youngster is often poverty-stricken and frequently lives either in a depressed rural area, on an Indian reservation, or in one of the ghettos of large cities. He comes from a family which typically exists on a low economic and educational level and which is likely to place little value on formal education. His family tends to be mobile, moving in an attempt to find a better life. But this mobility seldom solves the family's problem. Unable to achieve success in one location, the family frequently is also unable to establish a better living standard elsewhere, primarily because of the inadequacy of its cultural and educational background. It is easy to see that the problems of educating a child from such a family are tremendous.

In 1965, the Congress moved to provide better educational opportunities for the educationally deprived through passage of two of the most significant legislative acts dealing with public education that have ever been passed. The first of these, the Economic Opportunity Act, established Project Head Start, providing for preschool experiences for educationally deprived children. The second act, the Elementary and Secondary Education Act, bases much of its financial support to school districts upon the economic level of families living within each district and requires that those school districts which seek to take advantage of the act make provision for special programs for disadvantaged children.

The explosion of technology has resulted in a demand for workers and technicians possessing more training than ever before. This situation is likely to become even more critical in the years ahead. The educationally deprived child is therefore less and less likely to become a productive member of society when he reaches adulthood. Not only must we find ways to finance a more adequate educational program for this child, but educators must be willing to make whatever changes in our traditional school programs are necessary to meet his unique needs.

Teachers need to study the background of efforts to provide equal educational opportunities and see the relevance of current attempts to remedy inequities. To do this it will be necessary to study carefully and critically the current legislation and the agencies and forces which are at work to promote or defeat this imperative need in our time.

In the face of the great differences that exist in educational opportunities, it is difficult to help young and old alike maintain their faith in democracy despite its limitations in American life. Teachers have to teach youngsters and adults the actual state of affairs today, at the same time fostering a belief in the American ideal of equality for all and a democratic respect for the uniqueness of the individual. This is a task of a political nature, a task of statesmanship, and one of the most important aspects of the role of the teacher today.

## Will National Assessment Answer the Critics?

In 1969 a program of "national assessment" was initiated. The program resulted from many years of discussion and six years of planning and preparation, dating from 1963 when the Carnegie Foundation asked a group of educators to explore the feasibility of making a "national assessment" of education.

From the very beginning the concept of assessment on a national basis has been surrounded by controversy. Proponents believe that:

1. The program will give the nation as a whole a better understanding of the strengths and weaknesses of the educational system.
2. Information secured from a national testing program will be invaluable to educational leaders in planning for innovation and change in educational practices.
3. It is unrealistic to expect Congress and the state legislatures to continue to increase educational expenditures without having some tangible measurement of results.

Those opposing a national assessment program contend that:

1. A national testing program is the first step in what could develop as a federal system of education and could be the basis for federal coercion of local school systems.
2. No test or series of tests can measure all the varied outcomes of education or take into account different state and local educational aspirations and objectives.
3. A national testing program will result in teaching for the "tests" and will stifle curriculum development, innovation, and change.

While the controversy continues, the program of national assessment is underway. It started in 1969 under the direction of the Education Commission of the States, with the testing of 9- 13- and 17-year olds and young adults in the 26–35 age group in the areas of citizenship, science, and writing. Testing followed the next year in the areas of reading and literature, and the following year in music and social studies. Additional testing areas are mathematics, art, and vocational education. Tests are to be repeated on a cyclical basis so that progressive comparisons can be made. The testing is being carried out by private contractors. Results are reported using the following subdivisions: male and female; four geographic regions (Northeast, Southeast, Central, and West); different types of communities (large city, urban, fringe, middle-sized city, and rural-small town); race (black, white, and other) and two socioeconomic levels [124:13].

The early results are so tentative and a basis for comparison so lacking that they cannot be used to judge the assessment process itself. Sample conclusions based on the first round of testing include the following [42:72]:

1. Large percentages of the nation's school-age youngsters and young adults don't understand or value some basic Constitutional rights.
2. The least understood or valued right is the freedom to express controversial or unpopular opinions.
3. Fifty-four per cent of the 17-year-olds and 61 per cent of the young adults believe they can personally influence government.
4. A total of 50 per cent of the 17-year-olds, compared with only 38 per cent of the young adults, can write an acceptable description of an automobile accident after studying a conventional accident diagram.
5. Only 28 per cent of the 9-year-olds can include all the information needed to address an envelope correctly.

As testing continues, information of the kind illustrated by the above conclusions and findings will be voluminous, and proponents hope that it will become highly significant as future testing enables comparisons and measurement of progress.

Almost certainly national assessment will continue. Prior to 1970, the federal government has spent $3.9 million on the program, and additional expenditures of $4.5 million were scheduled for 1971 [83:234]. The Education Commission of the States also has volunteered to aid states in setting up their own assessment programs, and Florida has become the first to accept the opportunity. A statewide assessment program costing the State of Florida as much as \$12 million per year is underway [166:229].

The evidence of potential controversy continues to surround the assessment concept. The National Education Association included the following among its 1971 resolutions [169:89]:

The National Education Association notes that the first report of the National Assessment of Educational Progress on writing, citizenship and science has been issued.

The Association will continue to resist any attempt to transform national assessment results into a national testing program that would seek to measure all students or school districts by a single standard, and thereby impose upon them a single program rather than providing opportunities for multiple programs and objectives.

The cautious attitude expressed in the second paragraph of the resolution is representative of the views of those who continue to view national assessment with concern. Whether such fears will prove groundless may be determined as annual testing continues, data accumulate, and results are interpreted.

## CONCERNS OVER DEPRIVATION AND RACISM[1]

American society is a mixture of national origins and social classes. In some schools as many as fifty nationalities are represented in the pupil body. Because of local conditions and pressures to integrate the schools, children of the poor and the wealthy, the illiterate and the educated, are sometimes found in the same school. But in the inner city the Negroes and the Puerto Ricans are forced by circumstance to live off by themselves, and thus their children attend schools in which there is less variation of cultural background and wealth. The same observation can be made about the children who live in rural poverty, or in Mexican communities, or on Indian reservations. Such variety among communities and pupils demands that all educational personnel be prepared to cope with problems arising from all kinds of social circumstances.

Even where the children come from apparently similar social and racial situations, as in suburbia or the black ghettos, a teacher ought to have a broad background, not only better to understand a child's situation but to direct him in his search for broader experiences. For example, a teacher who knows that use of a dialect is in itself no indication of shallowness of thought or feeling may be able to relate to the child by showing an understanding of the depth and vigor of that dialect. From

[1]This section has been reproduced from *Teachers for the Real World,* pp. 11–20, 1969, written by B. Othanel Smith and others, with permission granted by the American Association of Colleges for Teacher Education, Washington.

this the teacher may expand the ability of the child to use language in a way that helps him maintain respect for both his old and new manners of speech. To extend his language habits is to expand the child's possibilities of human associations. . . .

Should teachers for culturally deprived children be given some special type of training as are the teachers of the blind or mentally handicapped? One answer to this question is that the special motivations, attitudes, language system, and conduct of disadvantaged children require that their teachers be trained in methods different from teachers of middle-class children. Another answer is that under-privileged children learn in the same way as other children and that their teachers need no special training. This latter is the view taken here. The problem of preparing teachers adequately for the disadvantaged is the same as the problem of preparing teachers adequately for all children. We do not need special teachers for the children of different ethnic and social groups. Rather, we need teachers who are able to work effectively with children regardless of race or social situation, but mindful of what that is in each case.

The special circumstances from which children come cannot, indeed, be ignored in the preparation of teachers. On the contrary, teachers should be trained to work with the cultural and racial background of each child. A child's cultural heritage should be considered by his teacher to be the basis for his education, not a stumbling block. A child should learn because of what he already knows, not in spite of it. "Culturally deprived" is not an accurate term. No one is lacking in culture whether he be from the vast ranks of the poor, or the middle or upper class, or from differing areas of the country. The poor are not lacking in culture; theirs is as different from that of the middle class as the Southern culture is different from the New England culture. For example, one of the authors of *The Disadvantaged: Challenge to Education* speaks of interesting an eighth grade class in poetry. The teacher presented them a poem by Langston Hughes written in a dialect close to their own and known in Hughes' time as "jive." The class came alive and participated as any good teacher dreams of his class doing, illustrating "an approach to nonstandard dialect in such a way that the pupils feel that learning standard English dialect doesn't mean that they must discard their own" [79:382].

The teaching of poor children does not require unique skills, as does teaching the blind, for the handicap comes not from the children themselves but is placed upon them by the situations in which they live and the schools to which they go. But it does require broad life experiences which few middle-class teachers have had. Unless we stress this view of teacher education, we can unintentionally aggravate a potentially explosive division between the social classes and ethnic groups in our society.

## False Ideas about the Disadvantaged

So much has been written and said about the extreme want and educational starvation of these children that a false image has been created. It is easy to imagine that they are somehow emotionally and intellectually inferior. These children are basically the same as all other children. Though their experience may be different, they too are interested in their world, attached to their families, and have important hopes and aspirations. If these characteristics are not visible to their teachers, it is because the teachers see only with the narrow vision of the middle class.

Another false image of deprived children is that they are all alike. In truth they are as different from one another as the children of other elements of the population. The poor are different in life styles: the Appalachian white child, the Mexican child, the [black] child and the Indian child have distinct outlooks and modes of behavior, although the differences within these groups are as large as the differences among them. The black youth of the ghetto is greatly influenced, often controlled, by the norms and power of his peer group. The Appalachian youth is influenced more by his family and the adult community. Like the youth of the ghetto, he also is inclined to be resourceful and independent. The Mexican-American so closely identifies with his family and its cultural milieu that he is often more at variance with the norms of the school than either the Appalachian white or the [black] of the ghetto. The Indian child lives in a culture almost entirely apart from the culture of the white man or Appalachian, Mexican, or [black] variations.

If one considers affluent children, he will find differences among them as striking as those among the poor. There will be physical as well as cultural differences attributable to social origins, occupations of their parents, and family income. Many children of the very affluent have had a great deal of experience at sophisticated levels. To them school is apt to be dull and lack the sensational experiences to which they are accustomed. The children of the families from skilled occupations and proprietary groups are apt to be ambitious, although they do not always pursue the knowledge that could fulfill their ambitions. These are rather gross distinctions and in some cases they will not hold. But they will suggest the differences that often seem unexpectedly great to teachers moving from a "comfortable" school to a different one.

If we look again at disadvantaged children, we see that some of them come from families which are chronically poor. These people live on the barest necessities of life and are for the most part demoralized and hopeless. Many live in filth and degradation and would perish without some form of public aid. At this level of cultural existence children see little in the future except the kind of life their parents have had. The schools appear to offer them neither hope nor learning. For this hard core, poverty is a way of life.

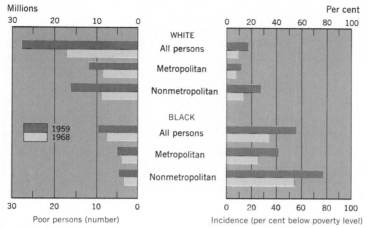

FIGURE 18-1   Number and percentage of persons in the United States in 1959 and 1968 classified as impoverished.

Economically, socially, and educationally disadvantaged children are not new to American society. Throughout American history since colonial days, disadvantaged youths and their families have made heroic efforts to avail themselves of schools.The existence of the free public school system itself can be attributed largely to the struggle of the laboring man to provide an education for his children. Even though the public school system is now well fixed in the American institutional structure, the struggle for an adequate program of education for the children of low-income groups continues.

## Disadvantages and Deprivations

It is futile to look at the disadvantaged as a homogeneous group. What is emerging from the mass of literature on the deprived is that it is more profitable, certainly for pedagogical purposes, to look at the social and economic factors which cause problems for children in relation to the school.

One of the central conditions which affects many disadvantaged school children is simply lack of money. Many studies indicate that the cost of schooling (dues, trips, out-of-pocket expense, collections for various causes, loss of family income, etc.) places an undue hardship on the child whose family is poor. If school is expensive, the child who cannot afford the cost of schooling must either avoid the cost and not participate in the school's program or accept the charity of the school. Either route is unacceptable. If the child does not participate, his experience is limited and his self-esteem may be damaged. If he accepts the charity of the school, the injury to his self-concept is apt to be even greater. For, as the Webbs pointed out long ago, charity degrades both the giver and the receiver.

The children of poverty suffer chronically from malnutrition. Depression, apathy, limited amounts of energy, and lethargy are but some of the effects of poor nutrition. The impact of malnutrition on the functioning of the child in school indicates the close interrelation between the school and community life of the child. The hunger which a child carries to school lessens his performance and affects his attitudes.

The disadvantaged child is often affected adversely by the instability of his family and the unemployment of his parents. There is considerable evidence showing the close connection between the degree of family stability and the child's ability to profit from schooling. It is very difficult in school for a child who comes from a home that is broken but has economic security, but it is almost devastating for one who comes from a home where there is neither family nor economic stability.

One of the conditions which induces a sense of futility among the disadvantaged is the failure of the helping professions to perform their tasks adequately among the poor whites, the black, the Indian, and the migrant. Legal services for these people are almost nonexistent. The record of police discrimination is one of the salient features of the Kerner Report. Medical services are often unavailable to the poor, causing some groups to forfeit, on the average, as much as a quarter of a century of their lives. The failure of the medical profession to respond to the needs of the poor stems partly from a desire to be compensated for services rendered, but it is also a commentary on the nature of our social priorities: profit is placed above service where people are concerned. The lack of response of psychiatrists and psychologists to the needs of the poor is notorious. Similar examples document the failure of human services to meet social responsibilities and show the classic bias that is built into our social system.

The massive evidence which has been assembled to document the plight of the [black] shows only too well the prejudices of the white man and the effects of racial discrimination upon black children. The recent Racial Isolation Report, the Coleman Report, and the Kerner Report add weight to years of scholarly findings and indicate the immense impact of segregation on the black children of society. Segregation has created in many [black] children a sense of inferiority, a negative self-image, and a feeling that blackness is a stigma.

When one takes all of these facts into account, the failure of deprived children to respond to traditional programs of schooling is understandable. Yet some conclude that the children's serious environmental deficits make adjusting to the work of the school impossible. Others believe that the curriculum, teachers, and school organization simply cannot be adapted to the uniquenesses of disadvantaged children. The blame can be placed on the child or on the school. But the fact of the school's

How may the attitudes, beliefs, and behavior of these children be affected as a result of their home environment? How can the school effectively meet their educational needs? *(Photograph by Carl Purcell, National Education Association.)*

ineffectiveness remains. The disadvantaged child seems to get progressively further behind in his achievement, in his adjustment to the demands of schooling, and in his relationships to teachers.

The school system itself is one of the conditions that accentuates the problems of the deprived child. Recent evidence from the disadvantaged themselves, in the Kerner Report, indicates that the school is not as high on the list of complaints as other social agencies. Still, the teaching profession would be foolish to ignore evidence in dropout rates, comparative scores on tests, turnover of teachers in poor and ghetto areas, and other measurements indicating a pattern of discrimination to which the schools wittingly or unwittingly contribute.

If the education of the teacher is looked at in the context of the great variation among the children of the American people, the enormous dimensions of the teacher's task become only too clear. The educational system, no less than the American people, is devoted to the idea of a common school. It is the only institution through which all the children of all the people share in the wide range of experience that is both the richness and the poverty of American life. The teacher who can work with the children of only one social stratum or minority group is inadequately prepared to teach in the common school. The idea that the backgrounds and interests of the child must be understood if he is to be properly taught must now be put into practice. Furthermore, skills and techniques of effective interaction with children and adults at all points on the social spectrum must be built into the competency of every teacher.

## The Disadvantaged and Racism

The problem of educating disadvantaged children can too easily become confused with the problems caused by the white man's prejudice and discriminations against the black man. The disadvantaged child is a product of his social class, and his deficiencies are attributable to the race of his parents only to the extent that white prejudice creates their poverty and other environmental limitations. The problem of educating the deprived child would exist if the total population of the country were either entirely white or entirely black. To be disadvantaged is to be a member of the lower social class, regardless of race or minority group.

Educational and economic deprivation is drastically increased by the existence of racism. Racism would deny any individual, because of color, the privilege of living in any part of the community he prefers, of being buried in any spot of earth he can afford, of holding a job for which he is fully competent, of getting an adequate education, and of associating freely with his friends regardless of their race.

Human beings have always set themselves apart from others on the dogma that some are by nature superior. This dogma was used as the justification of all forms of slavery, and, while a great proportion of the peoples of the earth have discarded it legally, there are still many who hold to it tenaciously. This dogma is the ultimate rationalization of the militant white when he is forced to justify his discriminations and crimes against the [black man]. He may not say it in so many words, but what he means is that, by nature, the blood of the white is superior to that of the black.

In racism, not only is the total group discriminated against, but the individual must carry the injustices which the white man's prejudices place upon the group. No matter how well the [black] may be educated or how wealthy he may be, the racist considers him to be inferior and enforces this belief in a thousand ways frequently too subtle to be perceived. In a democracy it is by the principle of achievement that the social position of an individual should be determined, not by his blood or his wealth. In actual practice, however, achievement has been combined with wealth. Racism has denied even the nation's most famous [blacks] the respect to which they were entitled by achievement.

The condemnation of the total group because of blood is the dogma of racial superiority that underlay Nazism. The basic idea of Nazism was not that the state is superior to the individual, but that the state is the instrument of the superior race in its efforts to reconstruct the world in its own image. In this sense, white prejudice in this country is much like the doctrine of racial superiority of the Nazi movement.

The [black] is not in the ghettos by his own choice. He is not in the work camps and the rural slums of the South because he wants to be there. He is in these places because that is where racist discriminations have placed him. The Irish once populated the ghettos [blacks] occupy today. The Italians and Jews also lived there. These people had their own schools, policemen, commercial enterprises, and small shops. In time they accumulated enough wealth and education to move out of the inner city to places more comfortable to live and rear children.

In these earlier ghettos there were jobs, industries, strong traditions, and morale to nourish and sustain the individual. But there are no jobs, no enterprises, and few traditions in the black ghettos, only hopelessness and loss of identity. The [black] has not been able to better himself while in the ghetto and to enjoy social mobility because American society is closed to him in countless ways. A great deal is said about our "open" society, but what we overlook is that it is open differentially to people according to their economic status and color. No one wishes to condemn the ideology of an open society just because American society at this point in its history is not completely open. It is the ideal by which men live and struggle to improve their social institutions and practices. The ideology must not be used to gloss over the hard fact that the ideal has yet to be realized.

As long as the political bureaucracies of the cities discriminate against the [black] in the appointment of police and teachers and in providing social services, and just as long as the financial system discriminates against the [black] by not giving him loans for business and housing, as long as real estate interests are able to build boundaries around the [black] by zoning and other means of exclusion, just that long will the ghettos continue to exist. The white man's hostility is deplorable enough, but even worse than hostility is his insidious patronage and discrimination in education, employment, and business, and countless other ways.

## Social Integration and the Schools

In recent years a great deal has been written about apartheid in South Africa. Actually it is only the word that is new in American culture. Segregation and political and economic discrimination against the black people have existed here for over 350 years, and until recently they were reinforced by legal enactments and court decisions. The legal and judicial barriers to racial integration are being reduced. Eventually white prejudice may begin to erode, and the time may not be too distant when many of the worst features of racial discrimination will be wiped out.

But at the very time when the nation is moving toward the elimination of its legal and judicial impediments to an open society, some black militants are moving to close ranks and to insist upon separation. Social change always lags far behind the promises and hopes of men. The suffering in the ghettos and in rural slums of the South is intolerable to a self-respecting people who constantly find their hopes and efforts to improve their lot thwarted by the prejudices and discriminations of the whites. But democracy cannot continue to survive in a society that follows a policy of segregation and isolation of its races. The very essence of democracy is that men are equal one to another and that this equality can be honored only in unfettered human association. Were the white militants who favor a doctrine of apartheid and the black militant who follow a separatist doctrine to succeed, the ideal of democracy in this country would perish. There would then be no guides left for those who criticize society and work for its improvement.

Social integration is a means and a goal. As a means, it is a partial solution to problems created by white prejudice. As a goal, effectively achieved, it is a true sign that massive prejudice has been eliminated. So it is with school integration. But a token integration of the schools is hardly more than a gesture.

School integration is more fundamental than the mere mingling of different races in a school building. Integration is the incorporation of individuals of different races as equals into a social group. Furthermore, school integration involves the hierarchical system by which the schools are administered and education carried on.

Malcolm X pointed out several years ago that school segregation meant not only the separation of the races into different buildings but also the control of the black schools by the white power group [147]. He went on to point out that integration simply brought the black and white children together and left the white power structure in control. At that time, he was arguing for black schools under black control. There is nothing undemocratic about a community predominantly [black] which exercises control over its schools in the same sense that a community predominantly white or upper middle class exercises control over its schools. As long as social and economic integration is denied the [black] there is no reason to deny him the privilege of managing the affairs which affect his life. No group can run the affairs of another without debilitating it. Human development depends upon the involvement of the individual in the affairs that concern him. The right of the [black] to participate in his own affairs cannot on any moral principle be denied. If integration of the schools is to occur, it must involve the participation of the [black] in the control and management of the schools as well as the classrooms.

Because of discrimination in business and housing, and lack of other human consideration, it may be many years before the black ghettos are dissolved or integrated. In the meantime, school integration must be pursued as vigorously as possible. When black and white children are bussed into mixed classes of high quality, both groups gain from the experience. The moving of [black] children into schools that are predominantly white and a corresponding transporting of white pupils into schools that are predominantly black must be increased so that larger, meaningful numbers are involved. But two-way movement is in and of itself insufficient. It is a step toward integration, not integration in its social and psychological sense.

## Teacher Preparation and School Integration

The problem of training teachers for schools in disadvantaged areas is not the same as the problem of preparing teachers to deal with racism in school and society. The teacher may be well prepared to work with children and parents who are victims of economic and social deprivation. He may know how to relate to them, to empathize with them, and he may understand quite fully the social and economic forces that cause their plight. He may correctly assess the experiential background of the children and tailor his instruction to their interests and needs. He may know what sort of content is most conducive to their development and he may know how to handle that content intellectually and with technological devices. He may know all these things and still be baffled by the problems in an integrated school which originate in racism.

He may not know how to handle discipline problems in a racially mixed group, especially if part of the group is from a culturally deprived area. If a [black] teacher is confronted by discipline problems with a white child in his classroom, the problem may be much more serious to him than the same conduct would be with a [black] child. He may be concerned with the reaction of the white parents, as well as the child, to the steps he takes. The same can be said of the white teacher who has an integrated class. In some integrated schools communication between the white and the black pupils is either nonexistent or has largely broken down. The problem of restoring communication in such a situation is one with which the whole school faculty must struggle.

The teacher must also face the question of racial prejudice in himself. The white teacher harbors many prejudices of which he is unaware. The [black] teacher may carry feelings of resentment and aggression that come with a feeling of imposed inferiority. It is necessary for the teacher to face his personal problems squarely and to include in his program of preparation experiences to shock him into realization of his prejudices and show him how to deal with them. Just as there are prejudices in the teacher's feelings and modes of thought, so too are these to be found in pupils and in the adults of the community.

Proper education of the teacher will lead him to examine his own human prejudices generally and, specifically, his racial prejudices and it will discipline him in the techniques of handling problems of interpersonal relations that arise from racial prejudices in his students and their parents.

## SUMMARY

This chapter has been concerned with some of the current educational issues and problems that are related to the rapidly changing social environment in which the school now functions. Teachers face the challenge of understanding these problems and of aiding in their solutions as schools strive to fulfill their function in a democratic society.

Today's student desires less conformity and more participation in his development. He wants to be heard and to be treated as a human being. Failure to recognize these facts frequently has resulted in organized protests upon the part of students. One very positive response to students has been the attempts by school administrators and teachers to provide opportunities for students to participate increasingly and more meaningfully in school government. Such participation can help to make the schools more responsive to the needs of students and at the same time prepare them to become participating members of a democratic society.

The current public desire for accountability in education is, in part, a demand that teachers be able to determine exactly the degree to which instructional objectives are achieved. The demand for objective measurement has produced experimentation with performance contracting in which private firms have been delegated instructional responsibility with payment contingent on guaranteed pupil performance.

Great differences exist throughout the United States in the educational opportunities afforded students. Various attempts are being made to remedy these inequalities through federally supported programs. An increasing awareness of these inequalities has focused attention upon the need for a better method of financing public education as well as a program of national assessment.

Teachers are confronted with the task of working more effectively with disadvantaged students and with the problem of racism in schools and in society. Disadvantaged youth often are viewed as being emotionally and intellectually inferior, when in reality they basically are the same as all youth. The problem of educating disadvantaged students often becomes confused with problems related to racism. Hence, the teacher is faced with the responsibility of critically examining his feelings and modes of thought so that he may be able to eradicate any subtle aspects of racism in his interpersonal relationships.

## QUESTIONS TO CONSIDER

1. What are some of the criticisms that elementary and secondary school students have of teachers and schools? How valid do these criticisms seem to be? What changes would you suggest?
2. To what extent are schools providing dehumanizing experiences for students? What are some examples of this dehumanization, and how would you correct each of them?
3. How do you propose to deal with some of the current educational problems such as student protests, relevance, student governance, drugs, and sex education?
4. In your opinion, what are the advantages and disadvantages of holding schools accountable for the achievement of pupils?
5. What are the arguments for and against performance contracting? What implications does it have for teachers and for the organization and administration of schools?
6. How will you attempt to foster a belief in the great American ideal of educational equality for all youth? Specifically, what changes in our educational system will you attempt to promote in order to make this ideal become more of a reality?
7. Upon what bases should public school authorities in large cities attempt to ensure that the public schools are racially balanced, even though this might result in students attending schools some distance from their homes?
8. What desirable and undesirable outcomes may result from the national assessment program? What possible effects may it have upon you as a teacher?
9. In addition to the many common characteristics to be found among children of minority groups, what differences may be found in the life-styles of Appalachian white, Mexican, blacks, and Indian children? How should the school attempt to respect these differences?
10. What are the arguments for and against bussing students to achieve racial balance in the schools? Which arguments do you think are sound? Unsound? Why?
11. Do you feel that teachers of culturally deprived children should be given some special type of training? Justify your position.
12. What are the most critical problems in the ghetto community? Which ones can the schools help solve? In what ways can the schools help solve them?
13. Define the term "racism." Have you seen racism in your high school? If yes, how did it manifest itself?
14. What competencies and qualities are needed by the white teacher to teach in a ghetto school? To which ones can teacher-education programs contribute most and how?
15. If you could do so today, what changes would you make in ghetto schools?

## PROBLEM SITUATION FOR INQUIRY*

As Mrs. Jones goes into different rooms in her role as resource teacher in a predominantly black school, the children usually greet her with smiles and applause. She first encountered hostility when she met Nanette.

From their first encounter, Nanette was stonily, silently, aggressively uncooperative, like a demonstrator in a sit-in. Mrs. Jones used every technique she could think of for drawing her out, but Nanette refused to be moved.

One day Mrs. Jones was trying to tell the children an inspiring story about a great black American and his contributions to our country. Nanette slumped in her chair. Mrs. Jones looked at her and she thumbed her nose at Mrs. Jones. At this point, Mrs. Jones interrupted the story at its peak and gave Nanette a piece of her mind. "If you're not interested in what

*Adapted from "Classroom Incident," *Today's Education,* vol. 58, no. 7, National Education Association, Washington, October, 1969, p. 67.

your own people have done to help make our country great, you ought to be ashamed."

Mrs. Jones has been bothered ever since. Why couldn't she have treated Nanette the way she would have treated any other child who was misbehaving? Or had she done just that? Would she or wouldn't she have been just as angry if a white child had thumbed her nose at her?

Mrs. Jones worries about the fact that she is worried. Does the whole matter bother her because there is in her some latent, unrecognized racism? She rather doubts that. She feels comfortable with the rest of her pupils, and she loves them all. Can it be that she regards black students in the context of *they* and *theirs* rather than of *we* and *ours*? It seems to her that human beings are successful in bridging a gap only when they forget there is one. She wonders if anyone can tell her how to do that. Can you?

## ACTIVITIES TO PURSUE

1. Interview some school dropouts, and attempt to determine the extent to which they feel that their school experiences were irrelevant.

2. Talk with school administrators and teachers regarding such problems as student protests, student governance, drugs, and sex education. Try to determine how they are attempting to deal with these problems.

3. If possible, visit a school that is using performance contracting. Talk with teachers, school administrators, pupils, and parents to determine how they feel about the use of performance contracting and its future role in education.

4. Organize a panel discussion on ways of equalizing educational opportunities throughout the United States.

5. Have a group of students collect data on the extent to which boys and girls in your state have equal educational opportunities. Discuss how any differences that exist may be corrected.

6. Make a careful study of the findings resulting from the national assessment program. What recommendations would you make to resolve some of the educational inequalities revealed in the data?

7. Visit some schools in which there are significant numbers of students from minority groups. In what ways are the teachers recognizing the needs of these students and providing appropriate educational experiences for them?

8. Visit in some ghetto schools and talk with students and teachers about evidences of racism. How will you attempt to avoid any racial tendencies in your interpersonal relationships when you become a teacher?

9. Select an American history, or English textbook, and study the table of contents, index, and pictures. What does the textbook contain on racial and ethnic groups in America? What do you think they should contain about racial and ethnic groups? Why?

10. Interview a black, Chicano, Indian, or Puerto Rican community leader to discover what he thinks are the critical educational needs of students and how well teachers are prepared to meet them.

11. Secure a listing of courses from a black studies or ethnic studies program. What courses do you think you should take in order to prepare for teaching in a school for students of the culturally different group chosen?

12. Secure a copy of *La Raza, The Liberator,* or the *Journal of American Indian Education* and read an article about one of the culturally different groups discussed in this chapter. Write a brief review of the article telling what you agree or disagree with and why.

13. Organize a panel of your classmates to discuss and deal with such topics as: the importance of quality education for urban students, ethnic studies in teacher education, needed improvements in the education of teachers for ghetto schools, community control of schools, and new conceptions of teachers and teaching for ghetto schools.

# RESOURCE SECTION FOR PART 6

Sample Application Form for a Teaching Position

Key Sources of Information on Available Positions

Suggested Readings

Suggested 16 mm Films

Figure Credits

## SAMPLE APPLICATION FORM FOR A TEACHING POSITION

APPLICATION BLANK

I. Name in full_____

    Present Address_____Telephone _____

    Permanent Address_____ Telephone _____

    Date of Birth_____Place of Birth_____

    Height_____ Weight_____ General Health _____

    Estimate of occupational time lost due to illness during the last 5 years_____

    List any physical defects_____ Do you wear glasses? _____

    Is your hearing normal?_____ Marital Status: Single_____ Married _____

    Widow (er)_____ Separated_____ Divorced_____ Number and ages of children_____

    _____

    Are you a citizen of the United States of America? _____

    If a war veteran or defense worker, give length of service_____ (months)

    Branch of service or activity _____

    Theatre of operation _____

    Rank_____ Type of work you did _____

    What foreign languages do you speak? _____

II. Present position _____

<table>
<tr><td>Grade</td><td>Subject</td></tr>
<tr><td>School</td><td>Place</td></tr>
</table>

    Present Salary_____ When can you accept a position? _____

    List position for which you are applying _____

    List in order of preference the subjects you like to teach:

      (a)_____ (b)_____ (c)_____ (d) _____

    Are you certified to teach in the state of New Jersey?_____

    Kind of certificate held_____ Major_____ Minor _____

    Are you willing to come to this school for an interview at your own expense? _____

## III. EDUCATIONAL PREPARATION PRIOR TO BEGINNING TEACHING

| School | Name | Location | Dates Attended | Course Major and Minor | Degree or Diploma | Date Graduated |
|---|---|---|---|---|---|---|
| Elementary | | | | | | |
| High School | | | | | | |
| College | | | | | | |

    Scholastic Honors _____

    High School and College _____

## IV. EDUCATIONAL TRAINING RECEIVED AFTER BEGINNING TEACHING

| Institution | Dates Attended | Course Major and Minor | Degree or Diploma | Date Graduated |
|---|---|---|---|---|
| | | | | |
| | | | | |
| | | | | |
| | | | | |
| | | | | |

*Source:* From Hanover Park Regional High School District, Hanover, N.J.

Scholastic Honors _____

At present matriculated for_____ degree, to be conferred about _____
by_____ University or College

   List and give extent of any special training you have had that is not mentioned above: e.g., music, art, industrial training, military courses while in military service, etc.

_____
_____
_____

### V. TEACHING EXPERIENCE (Do not include practice teaching)
                    List in order beginning with present position

| Period (years and dates) | School and Location | Grade or Subject Taught |
|---|---|---|
| | | |
| | | |
| | | |
| | | |
| | | |
| | | |
| | | |

   A. Student or Practice Teaching: _____
_____

   B. College, Part-Time, Substitute, Night or Summer, Etc._____
_____
_____

List the experiences you have had with children (other than the above)
    Camp _____
    Scouting _____
    Home _____
    Community_____
    Church _____
    Recreation _____
    Other _____
What type of work experience as an adult have you had other than teaching?(Business, trades, summer occupations, church work, social services, etc.)

| Dates From—— To—— | Employer and Location | Type of Work and/or Position | Years |
|---|---|---|---|
| | | | |
| | | | |
| | | | |

Were you trained for another profession or occupation before teaching? _____
If so, what?_____
Indicate the approximate number of credits taken in each of the following areas in your undergraduate courses:

   ——a. The humanities (other than literature: i.e., music, art, foreign literature, philosophy, etc.)

   ——b. The physical sciences (chemistry, physics, astronomy, etc.)

   ——c. Mathematics

   ——d. Social sciences (history, sociology, economics, anthropology)

List participation within the last two years in any professional activity for the improvement of the school or schools where you have been employed. (e.g., Curriculum Revision, Pupil Progress Report, etc.):

_____

(If not employed in a school system within the last two years, write "not so employed.")
List any professional organizations of which you are a member (mention any offices or positions of responsibility you have held in these organizations):

_____
_____
_____
_____

List the noneducational societies, organizations or clubs to which you belong (mention any offices or positions of responsibility you have held in these organizations):

_____
_____
_____
_____
_____
_____
_____

**VII.** List student activities, clubs, or athletic programs you would be competent to teach or sponsor.

_____
_____
_____
_____
_____
_____

## VI. INTERESTS AND HOBBIES

Indicate below any interests or hobbies you may have outside the professional field. Indicate briefly what professional and general magazine and book reading you have done in the past six months.

_____
_____
_____
_____
_____
_____

## VIII. TRAVEL

List below your most outstanding or interesting travels. (Include foreign countries)

| Year | To | Reason for Trip | Why Outstanding to You |
|------|------|------|------|
|  |  |  |  |
|  |  |  |  |
|  |  |  |  |
|  |  |  |  |
|  |  |  |  |

## IX. REFERENCES

These should be persons qualified and willing to give an honest appraisal of your fitness for the position you seek. Please include superintendents and principals with whom you have worked.

| Name | Address | Position or Occupation |
|------|---------|------------------------|
| A. Professional References: | | |
| 1. | | |
| 2. | | |
| 3. | | |
| 4. | | |

| | | |
|------|---------|------------------------|
| B. Personal References: | | |
| 1. | | |
| 2. | | |
| 3. | | |

# KEY SOURCES OF INFORMATION ON AVAILABLE POSITIONS

Listed below are some key sources of information on teaching positions that are available.

—College or university placement bureaus
—State departments of education, especially those having teacher-placement offices
—State education association headquarters, especially those having teacher-placement offices
—Personnel directors in specific school districts. The names and addresses of these officials may be secured from the *Education Directory, Part 2, Public School Systems,* published by the U.S. Office of Education, Superintendent of Documents, Government Printing Office, Washington, D.C., 20401
—*Association for School, College, and University Staffing,* located at the National Communication and Service Center, Inc., Box 166, Hershey, Pennsylvania, 17033
—*International Placement,* International School Services, 392 Fifth Avenue, New York, New York, 10018
—*U.S. Employment Service* offices located throughout the nation
—Commercial teacher agencies for which a complete listing may be secured by writing to the National Association of Teacher Agencies, 64 East Jackson Blvd., Chicago, Illinois, 60604

# SUGGESTED READINGS

*The number in parentheses following each suggestion denotes the chapter for which it is best suited.*

Bickel, Alexander M.: "Desegregation: Where Do We Go from Here?" *Phi Delta Kappan,* vol. 51, no. 10, pp. 518–522, Phi Delta Kappa, Bloomington, Ind., June, 1970. Suggests a variety of nationwide school desegregation efforts. (17)

"Black Leaders Speak Out on Black Education," *Today's Education,* vol. 58, no. 7, pp. 25–32, National Education Association, Washington, October, 1969. A special feature in which distinguished individuals discuss education of the blacks. (18)

Bottom, Raymond: *The Education of Disadvantaged Children,* Parker Publishing Company, West Nyack, N.Y., 1970. Presents an excellent discussion of the problems involved in educating disadvantaged children and offers many helpful suggestions. (18)

Brain, George B.: "National Assessment Moves Ahead," *Today's Education,* vol. 60, no. 2, p. 45, National Education Association, Washington, February, 1971. Reports on the first series of tests administered under the national assessment plan. (18)

Coles, Robert: *Teachers and the Children of Poverty,* Potomac Books, Inc., Publishers, Washington, 1970. Contains many helpful suggestions for teaching children from the lower-economic level. (18)

Donovan, Bernard E.: "Voucher Demonstration Project: Problems and Promise," *Phi Delta Kappan,* vol. 52, no. 4, p. 244, Phi Delta Kappa, Bloomington, Ind., December, 1970. Indicates problems involved in the use of the voucher system. (18)

"Drug Crisis Challenges Schools," *The Shape of Education for 1970-71,* vol. 12, pp. 9–14, National School Public Relations Association, Washington, 1970. Indicates that dissatisfaction and boredom propels many students to use drugs and that new understandings are needed by teachers. (18)

Fantini, Mario D.: *Designing Education for Tomorrow's Cities,* Holt, Rinehart and Winston, Inc., New York, 1970. Contains many suggestions for meeting the educational needs of urban children. (18)

Farias, Hector, Jr.: "Mexican-American Values and Attitudes Toward Education," *Phi Delta Kappan,* vol. 52, no. 10, pp. 602–604, Phi Delta Kappa, Bloomington, Ind., June, 1971. Cites specific cases to illustrate the need for teachers to understand the ethnic backgrounds of their students. (18)

Fuchs, Estelle: "Time to Redeem an Old Promise," *Saturday Review,* Saturday Review, Inc., N.Y., vol. 53, no. 4, pp. 54–57, 74–75, Jan. 24, 1970. Brief historical account of educational provisions for the American Indian in the United States. (18)

Gallup, George: "The Third Annual Survey of the Public's Attitudes Toward the Public Schools, 1971," *Phi Delta Kappan,* vol. 53, no. 1, pp. 30–44, Phi Delta Kappa, Bloomington, Ind., September, 1971. Presents the results of an opinion poll on such issues as performance contracts, accountability, voucher systems, integration, and school costs. (17 and 18)

Greenberg, Herbert M.: *Teaching with Feeling,* The Macmillan Company, Toronto, Ontario, 1969. Provides many insights into self-understanding and the understanding of others. (17 and 18)

Havighurst, Robert J.: "Curriculum for the Disadvantaged," *Phi Delta Kappan,* vol. 51, no. 7, pp. 371–373, Phi Delta Kappa, Bloomington, Ind., March, 1970. Predicts changes that could eliminate the need for a special curriculum for the disadvantaged child. (18)

*Historical Highlights in the Education of Black Americans,* National Education Association, Washington, n.d. An excellent booklet showing the continuity, from 1619 to the present, of movements in the education of black people in the United States. (18)

Hunt, Rolfe Lainer: "Teaching About Religion in the Public School," *Today's Education,* vol. 58, no. 9, pp. 24–26, National Education Association, Washington, December, 1969. Contains helpful suggestions on teaching about religion. (17)

Karmel, Louis J.: "Sex Education No! Sex Information Yes!" *Phi Delta Kappan,* vol. 52, no. 2, pp. 95–96, Phi Delta Kappa, Bloomington, Ind., October, 1970. Offers suggestions that may help both students and their elders to restore sex to a more wholesome perspective. (18)

Kliebard, Herbert M. (ed): *Religion and Education in America,* International Textbook Company, Scranton, Pa., 1969. A documentary treatment of the issue of church-state relations. (17)

*Man, Education and Manpower,* American Association of School Administrators, Washington, 1970. Analyzes the surfacing developments in vocational education. (17)

Morine, Harold: *A Primer for the Inner-City School,* McGraw-Hill Book Company, New York, 1970. Presents excellent suggestions for teaching in the inner city. (18)

Schrag, Peter: "End of the Impossible Dream," *Saturday Review,* Saturday Review, Inc., N.Y., Sept. 19, 1970, pp. 68–70, 92–96. Indicates that it was impossible to expect the school to remain somehow immune from the economic inequalities and social afflictions that plague the rest of mankind. (18)

Smith, B. Othanel: *Teachers for the Real World,* American Association of Colleges for Teacher Education, Washington, 1969. Presents an excellent discussion on the education of the culturally different. (18)

Stake, Robert E.: "Testing Hazards in Performance Contracting," *Phi Delta Kappan,* vol. 52, no. 10, pp. 583–589, Phi Delta Kappa, Bloomington, Ind., June, 1971. Offers a careful examination of statistical weaknesses and test limitations in performance contracting. (18)

Steinberg, Stephen: "The Language of Prejudice," *Today's Education,* vol. 60, no. 2, pp. 14–17, National Education Association, Washington, February, 1971. Discusses the deep-seated problem of prejudice and suggests means for overcoming it in school experiences. (18)

Stocker, Joseph, and Donald F. Wilson: "Accountability and the Classroom Teacher," *Today's Education,* vol. 60, no. 3, pp. 41–56, National Education Association, Washington, March, 1971. A special feature in which different educators discuss accountability from the standpoint of the classroom teacher. (18)

"The Teacher and the First Amendment," *NEA Research Bulletin,* vol. 48, no. 3, pp. 86–89, National Education Association, Research Division, Washington, October, 1970. Cites court cases relative to the First Amendment and the rights of teachers. (17)

Wagschal, Peter H.: "On the Irrelevance of Relevance," *Phi Delta Kappan,* vol. 51, no. 2, p. 61, Phi Delta Kappa, Bloomington, Ind., October, 1969. Provides an interpretation of the term "relevance" as it applies to the education of youth. (18)

"What's Right with American Education," *The Bulletin of the National Association of Secondary School Principals,* vol. 54, no. 346, National Association of Secondary School Principals, Washington, May, 1970. Contains a number of articles on such problems as drugs, performance criteria, student unrest, and instruction. (18)

Womer, Frank B., and Marjorie M. Mastie: "How Will National Assessment Change American Education?" *Phi Delta Kappan,* vol. 53, no. 2, pp. 118–120, Phi Delta Kappa, Bloomington, Ind., October, 1971. Illustrates the innumerable areas in which national assessment results may prove to have considerable utility. (18)

Wynne, Edward: "Student Unrest Reexamined," *Phi Delta Kappan,* vol. 53, no. 2, pp. 102–104, Phi Delta Kappa, Bloomington, Ind., October, 1971. Maintains that school should provide more meaningful experiences for youth. (18)

Young, Whitney M., Jr.: "Order or Chaos in Our Schools," *The National Elementary Principal,* vol. 49, no. 3, pp. 25–33, National Education Association, Department of Elementary School Principals, Washington, January, 1970. An analysis of the problem of unrest in schools as seen by the Executive Director of the National Urban League. (18)

## SUGGESTED 16 MM FILMS

*The number in parentheses following each suggestion denotes the chapter for which it is best suited.*

*America's Crises: The Hard Way* (National Educational Television, 59 min). Looks at the problem of poverty in the richest country in the world and emphasizes how today's poor are different from those of past generations. Focuses on slums, housing projects, public schools, and settlement houses in the St. Louis area. (18)

*America's Crises: Marked for Failure* (National Educational Television, 59 min). Discusses American education and examines the profound handicaps to learning that affect children from depressed areas. Describes a number of proposed solutions. Focuses on a prenursery pilot program in New York City schools. (18)

*America's Crises: The Young Americans* (National Educational Television, 59 min). Discusses the problems of American youth and examines who they are, what they want, where they fit in, how they affect society, and what they believe in and why. Features individual and group interviews with students in colleges, high schools, beach areas, and resort towns. Presents a frank questioning of traditional views on sex and youth's confused struggle to find a new morality. (18)

*Appalachia: Rich Land, Poor People* (National Educational Television, 59 min). Contrasts a land rich with coal, with the poverty of the residents who are denied adequate food, housing, and medical care. (18)

*Black & White Uptight* (Bailey Film Associates, 35 min, color). Points out the fallacious and misinformed thinking which spawns racial prejudice and hate. Documents the ways racial prejudice may be ingrained in society, how it is masked, and the ways it manifests itself. Notes the socioeconomic inequality which follows many black Americans from infancy onward, leading to discouragement, loss of ambition, and lifelong personality deficits. (18)

*The Difference Between Us* (National Educational Television, 60 min). Compares the secondary school education system in England and the United States. Discusses the differences in both approaches to advanced education. (17)

*Freedom to Learn* (National Education Association, 27 min). Shows how a teacher, charged by well-meaning parents with teaching communism in her classroom, explains that the purpose of teaching is to help children learn to think rather than to tell them *what* to think. Pictures Mrs. Orin's classroom activities and shows her students seeking facts and exchanging ideas. Points out that freedom to learn facts as they are is essential to a democratic way of life and that this freedom must be extended to children in the schools. (17)

*The Future and the Negro* (National Educational Television, 75 min). Presents a panel discussion on the subject of the Negro's future. Discusses the economic plight of the Negro in the United States and in the Negro nations. Emphasizes racism, which is felt to be deeply ingrained in people the world over. (18)

*Generation Without a Cause* (Star Film of Two Star Films, 50 min). Discusses the kind of young people who have grown up in the past twenty years of war, nuclear energy, and prosperity. Depicts the pressures and frustrations, the self-centeredness, conformity, and complacency in today's youth. Features one student who opposes the conformity and challenges the young people who accept the status quo and the comfort and security handed them by society. (18)

*Lonnie's Day* (Coronet Films, 14 min, color). Depicts one day in the life of an eight-year-old Negro boy who lives in a highrise ghetto apartment building. Shows the child at school, at home, and in his social group. (18)

*The Neglected* (International Film Bureau, 31 min). Suggests what poverty can do to the mental health of families and describes how the child protective agencies may help to change the family patterns which have threatened the physical and mental health of the children. (18)

*The Negro and the American Promise* (National Education Television, 59 min). Brings together four prominent Negro leaders who discuss the American Negro's movement for racial and social equality, and their own motivations, doctrines, methods, and goals. (18)

*No Reason to Stay* (Encyclopaedia Britannica Educational Corporation, 25 min). Dramatizes some of the classroom procedures and administrative indifferences which contribute to the lack of interest on the part of students and which can lead to their dropping out of school. (18)

*Philosophies of Education: Education for Moral Character* (National Education Television, 29 min). Suggests that the key to strong character is to define for young people the right things to do and to challenge them to build moral and spiritual strength with a positive approach. (17)

*Portrait of a Disadvantaged Child: Tommy Knight* (McGraw-Hill, 17 min). Documents the highlights of a day in the life of a slum child, Tommy Knight. Shows the contrasting home life in which two disadvantaged children live. Discusses the disadvantages Tommy must endure as the results of academic testing and the lack of background experience in subjects being taught. Introduces the viewer to the special problems, special needs, and strengths of the inner-city child. (18)

*Portrait of the Inner-city School: A Place to Learn* (McGraw-Hill, 18 min). Deals with problems of learning in an inner-city school. Points up the sharp areas of conflict between school practices and the cultural patterns of the pupils. Indicates positive attitudes which will help to facilitate adjustments in such schools. (18)

*The Search for America: Part 2, Our Problems in Education* (National Educational Television, 29 min). Discusses problems of American education and compares American schools with those in other countries. (17)

*The Troubled Cities* (National Educational Television, 60 min). Probes, in documentary style, the attempts which are being made to solve the problems which have been brought about by the urban population explosion. Cites slum areas, racial unbalance in the schools, and the needs of untrained or illiterate rural immigrants as some of the elements involved. (18)

*The Way It Is* (National Educational Television, 60 min). Documents the chaos of a ghetto school and what is being done in one particular school to remedy this situation. Focuses on Junior High School No. 5 in the Bedford-Stuyvesant section of Brooklyn. (18)

*Where Is Prejudice?* (National Educational Television, 60 min). Shows twelve college students of different races and faiths participating in a week-long workshop to test their common denial of prejudice. Reveals latent prejudices by candid discussion and questioning. (18)

## FIGURE CREDITS

FIGURE 17–1. (*Source:* "Teachers View Public Relations," *NEA Research Bulletin,* vol. 37, no. 2, National Education Association, Research Division, Washington, April, 1959, p. 39.)

FIGURE 18–1. (*Source: Statistical Abstract of the United States,* U.S. Department of Commerce, Bureau of the Census, Washington, 1970, p. 308.)

# 19 | RETROSPECT, INTROSPECT, AND PROSPECT

In ancient times the Romans had a famous god by the name of Janus, after whom the month of January was named. He was the god of gates and doorways. He was pictured with two faces, one looking forward and the other backward. People declared that he could look both ways at the same time. Perhaps everyone wishes that he had the ability to look both forward and backward so that he could clearly see the future and the past as he faces many of life's problems.

## YOUR STATUS IN PLANNING FOR TEACHING

In reading this book you have spent considerable time examining various aspects of teaching as a career. It was the intent of the author to present a realistic, relevant, and broad picture of the various components of the education profession. An honest attempt has been made to "tell it like it is." Attention has been focused primarily upon how to plan a career in education, how to gain the competencies required for teaching, and how to help perform the function of education in our democratic society. Often the process of stocktaking enables one to gain perspective and direction in one's thinking and planning. What then, in brief, have you gained as a result of your efforts?

### Progress in Your Planning

It should be evident that planning is an inescapable aspect of life which extends to all phases of living and continues throughout one's life. Furthermore, plans for the future are always tentative and are changed whenever developing situations seem to warrant it. Career planning is only one aspect of life planning. It necessitates the identification of the things that really seem important in an individual's life—that he clarify the values around which he wishes to rotate his life. A career in education should be tested to make certain that it is in harmony with the values he holds. As in all other professions, a career in education dictates certain requirements an individual must meet in order to be really successful and happy. After critical self-assessment in terms of these requirements, an individual then develops long-range as well as immediate plans in as much detail as possible for moving from where he is to where he wants to go—with the idea constantly in mind that modifications in the details of any master plan, or blueprint, are to be made as unforeseen situations develop.

## Clarification of Values and Nature of the Task

Why do you want to become a teacher? Because you have a desire to make a contribution to society? Because you feel that teaching provides an easy way of making a living? Because a position of authority inflates your ego? Because a friend once expressed the belief that you would make a successful teacher? Because you think the educational system in the United States needs to be revamped and you want to help change it? Because helping students learn and explore new horizons "turns you on"? Because teaching is a respected profession in our society? Why? Why do you want to be a teacher?

This text has attempted to help you by examining the work of a teacher in a broad context. In Chapter 1, the increasing importance of education in our society and the challenging role it will play in the future was noted. In chapters 5, 6, 9, and 12, the nature of a teacher's work, some professional obligations of teachers, and the type of administrative organization in which teachers perform their services were examined. Chapters 14, 15, and 16 stressed the sociological and philosophical foundations of education. Chapters 8, 10, 11, and 13 provided information regarding the economic, financial, and legal aspects of teaching.

Chapters 12 and 14 traced the evolution of educational practices and school organizational structures. Chapters 4, 5, and 6 discussed the wide variety of opportunities which a teacher has to assist the schools in meeting the tremendous challenges with which they are faced.

One might logically raise the question: Is all this essential for the preparation of a teacher? The answer depends upon the kind of teacher you want to be. Do you want to be a teaching technician, or do you want to be a professional educator with an effective voice in the policy and decision-making process of education?

## Analysis of Requirements for Teaching

Much attention has been devoted to a consideration of the personal and professional requirements for successful teaching. Chapter 2 specifically indicated those competencies generally associated with successful teachers and suggested plans for meeting those requirements. Chapter 3 outlined the requirements for teaching as they are affected by such matters as certification requirements specified by the various state departments of education, the requirements for graduation from teacher education institutions, and in-service education requirements essential for continued personal and professional growth.

## Appraising Your Prospects for Teaching

Throughout the book you have been encouraged to appraise yourself critically in light of the requirements for and demands made upon teachers. From your efforts you should have a relatively clear picture of your strengths and weaknesses for the profession and of how you can build up your good points and overcome your weaknesses.

If you have come to the conclusion that you are not suited to become a teacher, do not feel that your efforts have been wasted. In the first place you have saved yourself considerable time and money by not fully preparing for an occupation which probably would prove unsuitable for you. Also, you have spared yourself the unhappiness and frustration that would result from choosing the wrong occupation and having to readjust to another kind of work. Furthermore, the understandings you have gained regarding a career in education planning should help you to locate a more suitable occupation and to plan effectively in terms of the new field. In addition, you have gained further appreciation of the teacher's work and the function of education in our society. In the years that lie ahead, this should prove valuable to you for a number of reasons. You will be a taxpayer, and public schools are supported by taxation. You will be a member of some community in which school problems will be of general concern. You probably will be a member of some service group which holds more than casual interest in the education of boys and girls. It is highly probable that you will become a parent, in which case the education of your child will become of vital concern to you. In the final analysis, you should feel that you have gained much from your efforts.

## PLANS FOR THE FUTURE

In planning to teach, there are many things to which you will want to direct your attention as you move ahead. You may wish to plan in terms of the three major periods of life which were discussed in Chapter 2: (1) years in college, (2) years immediately following college, and (3) years in later life. Many suggestions have been made throughout this book, either directly or indirectly, that should help you in this planning. However, plans necessarily are highly personal in nature and must be worked out only by you. You may wish to keep in mind the few practical hints that follow, along with the many suggestions that have been indicated previously.

## Developing toward Student Teaching

Your attitude toward course work is of major importance in determining the value you will gain from it. For example, if you seek to gain from a history course a deep understanding of the social, economic, and political forces that have shaped society into the form in which we find it today, you certainly should be a better student of current problems, more capable in interpreting them to pupils, and better able to predict and shape future societal happenings. In the final analysis what you gain from your course work is a matter that rests largely with you.

Throughout the remainder of your college years, perhaps you will want to plan a variety of leadership experiences with boys and girls, in addition to those required in your program of teacher education, that will give you additional professional understandings, insights, and skills.

Your student teaching will probably prove to be the most important single course you take during your preparation for the profession. You should plan to make it of maximum benefit. Within limits you should be able to exercise some control over the semester, the grade level, and the subject area. Since most colleges and universities now have off-campus student teaching programs, you may have considerable latitude in the location of your student teaching assignment. If this be the case, ask to be assigned to a situation comparable to that in which you hope to begin teaching. In most cases, the evaluation of your student teaching experience prepared by your critic teacher and university supervisor becomes a part of your placement bureau record. Although prospective employers will review all your credentials, they generally treat your student teaching evaluation as the single most important part of your credentials. Since school districts may not seriously discuss a position with you until your student teaching experience has been completed, it may be undesirable to delay your student teaching until the final semester or quarter of your senior year.

Numerous opportunities for personal growth exist on every college campus and in its surrounding community. The library, the museum, the art gallery, the musical recitals, the various kinds of clinics, the entertainment and lecture series, the outstanding visitors, the conferences—these and many other resources normally are at your disposal. The extent to

Student teaching provides a "capstone" for the coursework, professional laboratory experiences, and other activities in which a prospective teacher has engaged during his undergraduate years. *(Photograph by Joe Di Dio, National Education Association.)*

which you avail yourself of them will depend upon the amount of individual initiative you wish to exercise.

College life also provides abundant opportunities for social growth, for understanding other students and working with them on common problems that require thought and planning, for using time and energy most effectively, and for establishing a healthy balance between work and recreational activities. Growth in these important areas is an individual matter and responsibility, for which thoughtful planning is essential.

## Locating a Position

In preparing to teach, certain actions may have a decided effect upon the position you secure. It would be wise for you to become well acquainted with several of your college instructors so that they will be able to write letters of recommendation regarding your promise as a teacher. College instructors hesitate to recommend highly those students with whom they are vaguely acquainted.

During the later stages of your preparation for teaching, you probably will register with your college placement office. The purpose of this office is to help graduates secure positions and to assist school administrators in arranging interviews. An attempt is made to locate teachers in positions for which they are well qualified and in which they can best succeed. This type of service usually is extended to the institution's graduates as long as they are interested in securing or changing positions. Usually no registration fee is charged for this service.

In registering with a placement office, you will be asked to provide references for recommendations as well as various personal and academic data on your training and background. The placement office uses these materials in referring you to the employing officials who have vacancies along the lines for which you are qualified. Obviously you should plan your college career so as to have as strong a set of placement credentials as possible. In addition to the letters of recommendation, your academic achievement, participation in cocurricular activities, and success in professional experiences (especially student teaching) enter as significant factors in your placement. Throughout your preparation for teaching, you are, in a sense, building the credentials upon which you will be recommended for various teaching positions. The need for careful planning in this regard is self-evident.

Your placement office will be concerned with the type and the general location of the teaching position you desire. Some important questions arise in regard to these matters. Do you prefer to teach in your home school system or in one located some distance away, possibly in another state or overseas? Do you prefer to teach in a strictly rural district, a town, a small city, or a large city school system? Are you interested in teaching disadvantaged pupils, or do you prefer to teach pupils that tend to be from average or above-average socioeconomic levels? The answers to these questions may have a significant bearing upon the nature of your plans for teaching and therefore warrant your early attention. The answers may necessitate considerable thought and effort on your part.

The responsibility for preparing the materials which go into your placement bureau folder rests with you. In many cases, these materials represent your initial contact with a prospective employer. Generally, school district personnel will review placement bureau credentials to decide who they want to invite to the district for an interview. What kind of first impression do you wish to make with a prospective employer? The care with which you prepare your credentials may make the difference in your moving beyond the initial screening stage to the interview stage.

A number of state departments of education and state education associations provide teacher-placement services or answer inquiries about openings. In some cases this service is free, and in other cases a nominal fee or a percentage of the first year's salary is charged. Many of the local and state offices of the United States Employment Service help place teachers at no charge. These offices serve as clearinghouses, enabling them to list vacancies in almost every state. The Resource Section for Part VI contains a list of key sources of information on available positions.

There are a number of reputable commercial placement bureaus that offer services to teachers on a national or a regional scale. A list of the accredited agencies may be obtained from the National Association of Teachers' Agencies, 64 E. Jackson Boulevard, Chicago, Illinois, 60604. Usually a fee is charged for registration. If you secure a position through the efforts of a commercial agency, you normally will be expected to pay a commission of approximately 5 per cent of your first year's salary.

If you should be interested in opportunities in overseas schools, military and territorial schools, or exchange positions abroad, you may be able to secure appropriate information from your placement office. *The Manual on Certification Requirements for School Personnel in the United States,* published by the National Commission on Teacher Education and Professional Standards of the National Education Association, also contains information on such opportunities, including a listing of the requirements, the kind of preparation needed, and the place to apply.

Many of the larger school systems have employing officials who visit placement offices throughout the nation in search of well-qualified teachers. The placement officials assist them in locating and in interviewing prospective candidates for the positions. On the other hand, a school official may write to the placement office requesting credentials of prospective teachers who meet the requirements for filling a vacancy existing in his school system. After examining the credentials of those recommended, the school official may invite one or more of the most promising candidates for an interview.

If you have a definite idea of a school system in which you may wish to secure a position, you may write requesting that your name be placed on file as a potential candidate in case a vacancy should develop along the lines of your qualifications. So long as you do not apply for a specific position known to be filled by another teacher, you would not be violating the code of ethics presented in Chapter 9. If you do not know the name of the school official to whom you should write, you may be able to get this information from the educational directory of your state or the *Education Directory, Part 2, Public School Systems,* U.S. Office of Education, Superintendent of Documents, Government Printing Office, Washington, D.C. If you make such a request of a superintendent, also indicate where he may secure your placement credentials and any other information that might be helpful to him in determining your qualifications and capabilities.

Regardless of any influential friends or relatives that you may have on the school board or in the community, you should scrupulously respect the official professional head of the school. You should conduct all your employment negotiations through him. Although it may appear to be absurd, many written applications for positions are not favorably considered because of poorly written letters, misspelled words, incorrect grammar, and tactless statements.

## The Interview

In most school districts, you may expect to be interviewed by more than one person. In small districts, you will probably meet with both the superintendent and the building principal. In larger districts, you may be interviewed by an assistant superintendent, the building principal, and a department head. Some districts also make it a practice of having teachers in the candidate's subject area participate in the interview.

In most cases, the person(s) conducting the interview will have reviewed previously your placement bureau credentials and/or a school district application blank which you have prepared and submitted. The interview is used by the school district to examine those things which often are not revealed in your credentials, such as: skill in communication, personal appearance, mannerisms, professional outlook, aspirations, technical competence, prejudices, and your plans for the future.

The interview gives you the opportunity to ask questions and to determine if you want to be a part of the school district teaching staff. It also gives you the opportunity to demonstrate to the employing officials that you are a well-qualified teacher. Thus, an interview is a two-way process. School district officials expect you to ask questions in addition to supplying answers to their questions.

What kinds of questions should you be prepared to answer in an interview? Although they vary greatly, it is safe to assume that you will be asked some of the following:

1. Why did you decide to become a teacher?
2. Why do you want to teach in our school?
3. What professional journals have you found to be especially helpful to you?
4. What books have you recently read?
5. Tell me about your philosophy of education.
6. Tell me about recent innovative instructional approaches in your subject area.
7. How do you plan to evaluate both the progress of your students and your progress as a teacher?
8. How do you view the role of the teacher? Do you see the teacher as a conveyor of information, as a resource person, or as a catalyst?
9. How do you plan to handle discipline problems when they arise?
10. What instructional strategies, techniques, or methods do you plan to use in your classes?
11. What new or different instructional approaches did you use in your student teaching?
12. What educational objectives would you seek to have your students achieve?
13. What do you intend to do in an effort to establish an effective working relationship with the students in your classes?
14. How do you feel about teacher strikes?

What kinds of questions should you ask the school district officials? The list is virtually endless. You can seek answers to many of your questions by doing your "homework" prior to the interview. Just as the school district officials have examined you prior to the interview by reviewing your credentials, you can examine the school district prior to the interview by looking at such things as the district school board policy handbook, the administrative handbook, the building policy and procedures manual, curriculum guides or course outlines, a student handbook, and possibly the school district budget. Prior to the interview, you may also find it helpful to: (1) tour the community, (2) informally talk with both adults and students about their schools, (3) examine the schools' physical facilities, (4) check on the availability and cost of housing, and (5) examine the recreational and cultural opportunities available in the community.

During the interview, you may want to ask the school officials some of the following questions:

1. What provisions does the district make for in-service education of teachers?
2. What is the teacher's role in curriculum development and in the selection of instructional materials?
3. What is the basis upon which teachers are evaluated in the district? Will I be given a copy of the evaluation?
4. To what extent are teachers in the district free to instigate and participate in responsible, well-planned experimental instructional approaches?
5. What instructional support services are available in the school, such as an instructional materials center containing facilities and personnel for preparing instructional materials of all kinds, audio-visual materials and equipment, clerical and typing assistance, teacher aides, guidance services, and learning resource center (library)?
6. What duties, other than regular teaching duties, are teachers expected to perform, such as sponsoring student activity groups, selling tickets at athletic contests, chaperoning dances, etc.?
7. In addition to salary, what fringe benefits, such as paid health, accident, and life insurance, does the district provide teachers?
8. What are the district policies concerning such things as tenure, sick leave, sabbatical leaves of absence, and transfer from one school to another within the district?
9. Is a teacher consulted about his assignment, or is he assigned to any school regardless of his preferences?
10. What is the history of public support of schools in the community?

## Entering into Teaching

Success and happiness in teaching require continuous planning, even though you have received your certificate and have secured an excellent position. In fact, the effort you put forth and the wisdom reflected in your planning will determine largely the extent to which you will realize the values inherent in a teaching career. Many teachers have found the following suggestions to be helpful to them in gaining happiness and satisfaction from their teaching:

1. *Become an integral part of the working situation.* In order to be most successful in his work and in improving conditions within the school, a teacher must first be accepted and respected by other members in the school and community. Unfortunately some beginning teachers feel an obligation to bring up to date all the other teachers and adminis-

Guiding the educational development of youth provides a constant challenge and source of enthusiasm for teachers. *(Photograph by Esther Bubley, National Education Association.)*

trators in their schools. They may try immediately to change things.
Obviously, such techniques do not contribute greatly to a program of
genuine progress in which a group moves forward together.

2. *Avoid the feeling that theory is one thing and that practice is
another.* Actually, theory provides direction in terms of which improvements in practice may take place. Practice, then, may be evaluated in
terms of the degree to which it is consistent with theory; therefore, a
teacher should not be discouraged if he finds theory to be relatively far in
advance of practice in his school. Such a condition should challenge
anyone to become effective in improving practice. In your attempts to
improve practice in your school, however, keep in mind that progress
within a school takes place rather slowly. During your first years of
teaching, therefore, you should feel very successful if you are able to
improve only a few of the general practices.

3. *Concentrate upon the positive aspects of a situation rather than
upon the weaknesses only.* It is difficult for anyone to maintain good
mental health if he is able to see only the difficulties, problems, and
shortcomings in a situation. There are always some good things to be
found.

4. *Approach your work with enthusiasm.* Enthusiasm is a contagious sort of thing which tends to facilitate learning and to improve
working conditions. It generally reflects a healthy attitude toward life, a
happy disposition, and a feeling of pride in one's work. It tends to release
energies through which greater accomplishments are made possible.

5. *Assume an experimental attitude toward your work.* Each day every teacher should seek to develop his competence as a teacher. Whenever anyone feels he has no more room for improvement, he has died professionally. Each year of teaching should be a new experience rather than a mere repetition of the preceding year.

6. *Expect changes to take place within the field of education.* Professional education of teachers will continue to advance. Educational research will continue to bring forth new understandings of human growth, new techniques, and new materials to be used. The nature of our society will also change as scientific, economic, political, and social advancements are made. These changes will bring forth new values, functions, and purposes in education. You may therefore assume that the future will be different, which calls for a positive, intelligent attitude toward change as it affects one's personal life and responsibilities as a teacher.

7. *Learn to differentiate the important from the unimportant tasks.* Some teachers lose perspective with respect to their primary function. As a result they tend to become lost in details which may or may not have real educational significance. For example, grading papers or various clerical duties may become more important than planning learning experiences of the pupils.

8. *Establish habits of orderliness, accuracy, and promptness.* If your daily routine become systematic and well arranged, you will be spared much confusion and irritation. Establish the habit of routinizing as many daily activities as possible, of anticipating problems, and of developing well-organized, yet flexible, plans for solving them promptly and accurately. By so doing, one gains an added sense of accomplishment and frees himself for other kinds of activities.

9. *Seek assistance on professional problems whenever needed.* There is little if any merit in not seeking help on problem situations. The sources of help are many—school administrators, supervisors, colleagues, books, and periodical literature. As anyone shares problems with others, he may gain insight into them, clarify his thinking, receive helpful suggestions, build self-confidence, and develop common interests and wholesome working relationships with others.

10. *Maintain a good sense of humor.* Look for the humorous side of life as well as the serious aspects. A sense of humor keeps anyone from taking himself too seriously. The ability to laugh often provides an excellent counterbalance for the many fears, anxieties, and disappointments normally encountered in life.

11. *Cultivate adequate, realistic self-concepts.* With all the stresses and strains involved in teaching, everyone has the problem of coping with the inner self. Every teacher experiences feelings of anger, hostility, and anxiety. It is important to identify the causes of these feelings and gain further skill in controlling and in resolving them so that a healthy positive outlook upon life and effective working relationships with others

may be maintained. Feelings of real success may be gained through identifying purposes which seem genuinely worthwhile and through attempting to make a realistic amount of progress in achieving them.

12.   *Continue to improve your perception of others.* Good teaching depends upon a teacher's sensitivity to and understanding of the pupils with whom he works as well as the interpretations he makes of their behavior. Every teacher should strive to gain increasing skill in making accurate judgments regarding the behavior of his pupils and his colleagues.

13.   *Continue to strengthen your academic background.* New knowledge is being created so fast that a teacher's academic background quickly becomes obsolete unless he continues to be a scholar, especially in his area of specialization. Continued growth in academic background gives a teacher added feelings of security and adequacy for meeting the growing interests and concerns of youth.

14.   *Know when to quit work for the day.* Conscientiousness and attention to duty are indeed admirable traits. However, some teachers work far into the night grading papers and performing similar school duties, thus exhausting their energies for the next day and warping their perspectives. Fatigue reflects itself in the mental attitude of the teacher and the emotional tone of the classroom, and this affects the education of pupils. It is important to establish a desirable balance between work and the activities that will restore physical and mental health.

15.   *Cultivate adult friends outside of the teaching profession.* Through day-to-day contacts with his colleagues, a teacher normally develops a number of friends within the profession. Since he shares with them so many common interests, and since it is so easy to talk shop, he may have a tendency to limit his contacts to teachers. Through the cultivation of friendships outside the profession, a teacher has the opportunity to widen his background of information, improve his human relationships, gain a broad and wholesome outlook upon life, and extend his influence in the community.

16.   *Build a satisfactory functional philosophy of life.* Everyone's life is governed according to certain fundamental ideas and beliefs which he holds in regard to the nature of the universe, his place within it, and his relationships with others. In view of this rapidly changing world, it is difficult indeed to develop a consistent and harmonious way of looking at life. It calls for searching thought and effort on the part of an individual if he is to maintain direction and peace of mind.

17.   *Never lose sight of the great challenge that a teacher has.* There may be times when you will feel discouraged. It may help you to remember that other good teachers have sometimes felt discouraged too—Jim Baker, for example. There were many times when Jim's smoothly functioning group of pupils seemed almost adult—and then again everything would seem to go wrong. He was not a philosopher, but every once in a while he remembered what a professor had said to him when he was trying to make up his mind about becoming a teacher:

Jim, teaching's not an ordinary job. It's a real adventure, filled with all the danger and excitement a spirited person could ask for. The teacher stands entrusted with the welfare and security of our country's greatest treasures—its youth. The people say to the teacher, "Here are our boys and girls; teach them what they must know to live in a world of varied races and cultures, in a world of uncertainty and change." From all the heritage of the race the teacher must select that which is to be passed on. From all the influences that surround his young charges he must choose those to encourage, those to ignore, those to fight. From all the possible and distant goals for which people may strive, he must choose the most worthy and magnify them for children's eyes. In the midst of conflicts and confusions, he must hold aloft democracy's lamp; he must keep it bright and help his pupils to walk in its light. Teaching is not for the immature or the timid. It is for those who care about what happens to the world and its children and who are prepared to do something about it. There's your job, Jim.

## SUMMARY

Throughout this book an earnest attempt has been made to help you in your orientation to the field of education and in planning your life work. The book has been written to encourage you to appraise critically and honestly both the profession and yourself. It is hoped that you feel rewarded for your efforts in reading it and that you like what you see in yourself and in the field of education.

## QUESTIONS TO CONSIDER

1.  What changes have you made, as a result of this course, in your plans for teaching?
2.  During this course, how have your views toward the function of the school changed?
3.  What are some illustrations of the concept that effective planning extends to all phases of living and continues throughout one's life?
4.  How can you gain from your college environment the greatest amount of growth toward teaching? To what extent are you using the resources available to you?
5.  Why do a number of teachers fail to assume an experimental attitude toward their work? How can you avoid such pitfalls?
6.  Why do some teachers feel that theory is one thing and that practice is another? What is the relationship between the two?
7.  What would be some advantages and disadvantages of teaching in your home community?
8.  Why should you file your application for a position with the superintendent of schools rather than with the president of the board of education?

## ACTIVITIES TO PURSUE

1.  Talk with some of your teachers who you feel have a wholesome outlook upon life and who have gained much enjoyment and satisfaction from teaching as a career. Try to determine the factors, conditions, and practices that have contributed to their success and happiness.
2.  Talk with some teachers who seem to regard teaching as a burdensome job from which they gain little or no satisfaction. In what ways do they differ from teachers who seem to derive much happiness from teaching? List any pitfalls which you will want to avoid.

3.  Consult with school administrators, college instructors, and placement officials regarding problems common to beginning teachers. You may be able to find research studies that have been made along this line. Plan ways in which you may be able to avoid many of these problems.
4.  Suggest to your instructor that some student teachers be invited to your class to discuss the kinds of pre-student teaching experiences that proved to be of most help to them. Incorporate into your plans any good ideas which you gain from the discussion.
5.  Suggest to your instructor that arrangements be made, if possible, for your class to view and discuss some good films concerned with student teaching.
6.  List or describe in detail the conditions which you hope will characterize your later life. What plans must you follow in order to achieve these conditions?
7.  Examine a number of blanks used in applying for a teaching position, including the one in the Resource Section for Part VI. What kinds of information are requested?
8.  Make a list of points you would want to keep in mind during an interview if you were applying for a position.
9.  Make a list of the things you would want to do ahead of time in preparation for an interview for a position in a school.
10. Now that you have completed this book, review critically any written plans you had made previously regarding your future. What changes must you make in order that they may be inclusive, adequate, realistic, and suitable for you?

## SUGGESTED READINGS

"The Beginning Teacher," *Today's Education,* vol. 60, no. 6, pp. 54–59, National Education Association, Washington, September, 1971. Contains questions and excerpts from four interviews with beginning teachers.

Foster, Walter S., and Norman C. Jacobs: *The Beginning Teacher: Problems and Issues,* Burgess Publishing Company, Minneapolis, Minn., 1970. Contains topics and questions that face many beginning elementary school teachers.

Greenberg, Herbert M.: *Teaching with Feeling,* The Macmillan Company, Toronto, Ontario, 1969. Although the entire book should be read, Chapter 6 should prove especially helpful in "Surviving the First Year."

James, Deborah: *The Taming: A Teacher Speaks,* McGraw-Hill Book Company, New York, 1969. Designed to help prospective teachers prepare for the conditions they may meet when they enter the school as a teacher.

Perry, William G., Jr.: *Forms of Intellectual and Ethical Development in the College Years,* Holt, Rinehart and Winston, Inc., New York, 1970. Contains many suggestions for college students as they seek intellectual and ethical maturity.

Shumsky, Abraham: *In Search of Teaching Styles,* Appleton-Century-Crofts, New York, 1968. Indicates how teachers can create better climates for learning.

Stinnett, T. M.: *Professional Problems of Teachers,* The Macmillan Company, Toronto, Ontario, 1969. Chapter 5 presents helpful suggestions in securing a position.

Wronski, Kendrick: "The Teacher I Want to Be," *Today's Education,* vol. 59, no. 6, p. 47, National Education Association, Washington, September, 1970. A description of a teacher by an FTA that won an award.

# REFERENCES

1. "AASA Blasts Parochiaid Vouchers," *Education U.S.A.,* National School Public Relations Association, Washington, Mar. 1, 1971.
2. *Adult Basic Education Program Statistics,* U.S. Office of Education, Washington, 1969.
3. *Adult Education: A New Imperative for Our Times,* National Education Association, Adult Education Association, Washington, 1961.
4. *Agreement between the Board of Education of the School District of the City of Detroit and the Detroit Federation of Teachers, Local 231, American Federation of Teachers, AFL-CIO, July 1, 1969-July 1, 1971,* Detroit Public School Center, 5057 Woodward Avenue, Detroit, Michigan, 1969.
5. Aiken, Wilford M.: *The Story of the Eight-year Study,* Harper and Row, Publishers, Inc., New York, 1942.
6. Alexander, William M.: *Are You a Good Teacher?* Holt, Rinehart and Winston, Inc., New York, 1959.
7. Alexander, William M.: *The Emergent Middle School,* Holt, Rinehart and Winston, Inc., New York, 1968.
8. Alexander, William M.: "The New School in the Middle," *Phi Delta Kappan,* vol. 50, no. 6, pp. 355–357, Phi Delta Kappa, Bloomington, Ind., February, 1969.
9. Allen, Paul M., William D. Barnes, Jerald L. Reece, and E. Wayne Roberson: *Teacher Self-appraisal: A Way of Looking Over Your Own Shoulder,* Charles A. Jones Publishing Company, Worthington, Ohio, 1970.
10. Amidon, Edmund, and Elizabeth Hunter: *Improving Teaching,* Holt, Rinehart and Winston, Inc., New York, 1966.
11. *Analysis of Teacher Tenure Provisions: State and Local,* National Education Association, Committee on Tenure and Academic Freedom, Washington, June, 1954, pp. 6–7.
12. Anderson, Robert H.: *Teaching in a World of Change,* Harcourt, Brace and World, Inc., New York, 1966.
13. *Annual List, 1970–1971,* National Council for Accreditation of Teacher Education, Washington, 1970.
14. "The Arguments on Merit Rating," *Research Memo 1950–30,* National Education Association, Research Division, Washington, December, 1959.
15. Armstrong, W. Earl, and T. M. Stinnett: *A Manual on Certification Requirements for School Personnel in the United States,* National Education Association, National Commission on Teacher Education and Professional Standards, Washington, 1964.
16. Bagley, William C.: "The Case for Essentialism in Education," *NEA Journal,* vol. 30, no. 7, pp. 201–202, National Education Association, Washington, October, 1941.
17. Bain, Helen: "Self-governance Must Come First, Then Accountability," *Phi Delta Kappan,* vol. 51, no. 8, p. 413, Phi Delta Kappa, Bloomington, Ind., April, 1970.
18. Barr, W. Montfort: *American Public School Finance,* American Book Company, New York, 1960.
19. Baxter, Bernice: *Teacher-Pupil Relationships,* The Macmillan Company, Toronto, Ontario, 1941.
20. Bayles, E. E., and B. L. Hood: *Growth of American Educational Thought and Practice,* Harper and Row, Publishers, Inc., New York, 1966.
21. Beggs, David, III: *Team Teaching: Bold New Venture,* Indiana University Press, Bloomington, Ind., 1964.
22. "Beginning Salaries for Teachers in Big Districts 1950–51 to 1970–71," *NEA*

*Research Bulletin,* vol. 48, no. 3, pp. 83–86, National Education Association, Research Division, Washington, October, 1970.

23. Benet, James, Christopher Arnold, Jonathan King, and James Robertson: *SCSD: The Project and the Schools,* Educational Facilities Laboratories, Inc., New York, 1967.

24. Bergevin, Paul: *A Philosophy for Adult Education,* The Seabury Press, New York, 1967.

25. Beyer, Evelyn: "Montessori in the Space Age," *NEA Journal,* vol. 52, no. 9, pp. 35–36, National Education Association, Washington, December, 1963.

26. Blaustein, Albert P., and Robert L. Zangrando (eds.): *Civil Rights and the American Negro,* Trident Press, New York, 1968.

27. Blocker, Clyde E., Robert H. Plummer, and Richard C. Richardson, Jr.: *The Two-year College: A Social Synthesis,* Prentice-Hall, Inc., Englewood Cliffs, N.J., 1965.

28. Bloom, Benjamin Samuel: *Stability and Change in Human Characteristics,* John Wiley and Sons, Inc., New York, 1964.

29. "Boardmen Reason: Share the Power with Students," *American School Board Journal,* vol. 157, no. 11, pp. 27–28, 30–31, National School Boards Association, Evanston, Ill., May, 1970.

30. Bossing, Nelson L., and Roscoe V. Cramer: *The Junior High School,* Houghton Mifflin Company, Boston, 1965.

31. Bowers, Harold J.: "Reciprocity in Teacher Certification," *NEA Journal,* vol. 39, no. 1, p. 14, National Education Association, Washington, January, 1950.

32. Bruner, Jerome S.: *The Process of Education,* Harvard University Press, Cambridge, Mass., 1965.

33. Bruner, Jerome S.: *Toward a Theory of Instruction,* The Belknap Press, Harvard University Press, Cambridge, Mass., 1966.

34. Burrup, Percy E.: *The Teacher and the Public School System,* Harper and Row, Publishers, Inc., New York, 1960.

35. Bushnell, Don D.: "Computers in Education," in Ronald Gross and Judith Murphy (eds.), *The Revolution in the Schools,* pp. 56–72, Harcourt, Brace and World, Inc., New York, 1964.

36. Butts, R. Freeman: "Search for Freedom: The Story of American Education," *NEA Journal,* vol. 49, no. 3, pp. 33–48, National Education Association, Washington, March, 1960.

37. Callahan, Raymond C.: *An Introduction to Education in American Society,* Alfred A. Knopf, Inc., New York, 1960.

38. "Catholic Schools Face Crises," *The Shape of Education for 1970–71,* vol. 12, pp. 24–29, National School Public Relations Association, Washington, 1970.

39. *The Central Purpose of American Education,* National Education Association, Educational Policies Commission, Washington, 1961.

40. Chambers, M. M.: "No Teacher Surplus," *Phi Delta Kappan,* vol. 52, no. 2, pp. 118–119, Phi Delta Kappa, Bloomington, Ind., October, 1970.

41. Chandler, B. J.: *Education and the Teacher,* Dodd, Mead and Company, Inc., New York, 1961.

42. "Citizenship Weaknesses Spotted by Assessment," *Education U.S.A.,* National School Public Relations Association, Washington, November 20, 1970.

43. "Class Size," *NEA Research Bulletin,* vol. 46, no. 2, pp. 35–36, National Education Association, Research Division, Washington, May, 1968.

44. "Classroom Teachers Speak on Differentiated Teaching Assignments," *Report of the Classroom Teachers National Study Conference,* National Education Association, Association of Classroom Teachers, Washington, 1969.

**45.** Combs, A. W.: *The Professional Education of Teachers,* Allyn and Bacon, Inc., Boston, Mass., 1965.

**46.** Committee on Education and Labor: *Federal Interest in Education,* House of Representatives, 87th Cong., 1st Sess., September, 1961.

**47.** "Community Control: A Sticky Wicket," *The Shape of Education for 1969–70,* vol. 11, pp. 10–15, National School Public Relations Association, Washington, 1969.

**48.** *Compact for Education,* Education Commission of the States, Duke University, Durham, N.C., 1966.

**49.** *Computers: New Era for Education,* National School Public Relations Association, Washington, 1968.

**50.** Conant, James Bryant: *The American High School Today,* McGraw-Hill Book Company, New York, 1959.

**51.** Conant, James Bryant: *The Education of American Teachers,* McGraw-Hill Book Company, New York, 1963.

**52.** Conant, James Bryant: *Shaping Educational Policy,* McGraw-Hill Book Company, New York, 1964.

**53.** *The Contemporary Challenge to American Education,* National Education Association, Educational Policies Commission, Washington, 1958.

**54.** "The Cost of Building in 1969–70: Out of Sight," *School Management,* vol. 14, no. 7, pp. 15–35, CCM Professional Magazines, Inc., Greenwich, Conn., July, 1970.

**55.** "Cost of Education Index, 1970–71," *School Management,* vol. 15, no. 1, pp. 10–15, CCM Professional Magazines, Inc., Greenwich, Conn., January, 1971.

**56.** Darling, Charles M.: *Perspectives for the 70's and 80's: Tomorrow's Problems Confronting Today's Management,* National Industrial Conference Board, Inc., New York, 1970.

**57.** Davis, E. Dale: *Focus on Secondary Education: An Introduction to Principles and Practices,* Scott, Foresman and Company, Chicago, 1966.

**58.** Davis, Thelma F.: "NEA Mutual Fund," *NEA Journal,* vol. 53, no. 8, pp. 29–30, National Education Association, Washington, November, 1964.

**59.** Dewey, John: *Democracy and Education,* The Macmillan Company, Toronto, Ontario, 1916.

**60.** Dewey, John: *Education Today,* G. P. Putnam's Sons, New York, 1940.

**61.** Di Nello, Marie C., and Harold L. Hawkins: *A Survey of the Revocation of Teacher Certificates,* Unpublished paper, College of Education, Texas A and M University, College Station, Texas, 1968.

**62.** "Differentiated Staffing in Schools," *Education U.S.A. Special Report,* National School Public Relations Association, Washington, 1970.

**63.** Dorros, Sidney: *Teaching As a Profession,* Charles E. Merrill Publishing Company, Columbus, Ohio, 1968.

**64.** Dreyer, Albert S., and David Rigler: "Cognitive Performance in Montessori and Nursery School Children," *The Journal of Educational Research,* vol. 62, no. 9, pp. 411–416, Dembar Educational Research Services, Inc., Madison, Wis., May–June, 1969.

**65.** "Drug Crisis Challenges Schools," *The Shape of Education for 1970–71,* vol. 12, pp. 9–14, National School Public Relations Association, Washington, 1970.

**66.** *Education Is Good Business,* American Association of School Administrators, Washington, 1966.

**67.** "Educational Technology," *New Directions for School Administrators,* California Association of School Administrators, Burlingame, California, January, 1969, pp. 25–31.

**68.** "Elementary Principals Set Policy Goals," *Education U.S.A.,* National School Public Relations Association, Washington, May 4, 1970.

**69.** Emans, Robert: "Teacher Attitudes As a Function of Values," *The Journal of Educational Research,* vol. 62, no. 10, pp. 459–463, Dembar Educational Research Services, Inc., Madison, Wis., July–August, 1969.

**70.** *Enforcement of the Code of Ethics of the Education Profession,* National Education Association, Committee on Professional Ethics, Washington, 1969.

**71.** Epstein, Benjamin: *The Principal's Role in Collective Negotiations Between Teachers and School Boards,* National Education Association, National Association of Secondary School Principals, Washington, 1965.

**72.** Eurich, Alvin C.: *America Is Opportunity: Effective Education for the Sixties,* an address at the 49th Annual Meeting, Chamber of Commerce of the United States, Washington, May, 1961.

**73.** "Extended-year Contracts for Teachers," *ERS Reporter,* National Education Association, American Association of School Administrators and the Research Division, Washington, September, 1964.

**74.** "Extra Pay and Dependency," *NEA Journal,* vol. 49, no. 8, pp. 52–54, National Education Association, Washington, November, 1960.

**75.** *Facts and Figures on Adult Education,* vol. 1, no. 1, National Education Association, Division of Adult Education Service, Washington, April, 1963.

**76.** "Facts on American Education," *NEA Research Bulletin,* vol. 48, no. 2, pp. 35–41, National Education Association, Research Division, Washington, May, 1970.

**77.** "Facts on American Education," *NEA Research Bulletin,* vol. 49, no. 2, pp. 47–55, 57, National Education Association, Research Division, Washington, May, 1971.

**78.** *Fall 1968 Statistics of Public Elementary and Secondary Day Schools,* U.S. Office of Education, Washington, 1969.

**79.** Fantini, Mario D., and Gerald Weinstein: *The Disadvantaged: Challenge to Education,* Harper and Row, Publishers, Inc., New York, 1968.

**80.** "Few States Certify Teachers for Growing Middle School," *Phi Delta Kappan,* vol. 51, no. 2, p. 102, Phi Delta Kappa, Bloomington, Ind., October, 1969.

**81.** "The Financial Rewards of Teaching," *NEA Research Bulletin,* vol. 38, no. 2, pp. 49–55, National Education Association, Research Division, Washington, May, 1960.

**82.** Finn, James D.: "The Good Guys and the Bad Guys," *Phi Delta Kappan,* vol. 40, no. 1, pp. 2–5, Phi Delta Kappa, Bloomington, Ind., October, 1958.

**83.** "First Assessment Results Analyzed," *Education U.S.A.,* National School Public Relations Association, Washington, August 3, 1970.

**84.** Flanders, Ned A.: *Interaction Analysis in the Classroom: A Manual for Observers, School of Education,* University of Michigan, Ann Arbor, Michigan, 1966.

**85.** Flanders, Ned A.: *Teacher Influence, Pupil Attitudes and Achievement: Studies in Interaction Analysis,* U.S. Office of Education, Cooperative Research Project, no. 397, Washington, 1960.

**86.** Floyd, William: *An Analysis of the Oral Questioning Activity in Selected Colorado Primary Classrooms,* Unpublished doctor's dissertation, Colorado State College, Greeley, Colorado, 1960.

**87.** Ford, Paul Leicester: *The Writings of Thomas Jefferson, II,* G. P. Putnam's Sons, New York, 1893.

**88.** *Fostering Mental Health in Our Schools,* 1950 Yearbook of the Association for Supervision and Curriculum Development, National Education Association, Washington, 1950.

**89.** Frasier, James E.: *An Introduction to the Study of Education,* 3d ed., Harper and Row, Publishers, Inc., New York, 1965.

90. Fuchs, Estelle: "Time to Redeem an Old Promise," *Saturday Review,* Saturday Review, Inc., N.Y., vol. 53, no. 4, January 24, 1970, pp. 54–57, 74–75.

91. Gallup, George: *How the Nation Views the Public Schools,* A CFK Ltd. Report, Gallup, International, Princeton, N.J., 1969.

92. Gallup, George: "Second Annual Survey of the Public's Attitude Toward the Public Schools," *Phi Delta Kappan,* vol. 52, no. 2, pp. 99–112, Phi Delta Kappa, Bloomington, Ind., October, 1970.

93. Gallup, George: "The Third Annual Survey of the Public's Attitudes Toward the Public Schools, 1971," *Phi Delta Kappan,* vol. 53, no. 1, pp. 30–44, Phi Delta Kappa, Bloomington, Ind., September, 1971.

94. "The Gallup Poll," *Washington Post,* Nov. 20, 1968, p. B 18.

95. Gardner, John W.: *Excellence: Can We Be Equal and Excellent Too?* Harper and Row, Publishers, Inc., New York, 1961.

96. Glass, Bentley: *The Time and the Timeless,* Basic Books, New York, 1970.

97. *Goals of the American Federation of Teachers AFL-CIO,* American Federation of Teachers, AFL-CIO, Washington, n.d.

98. Good, Carter V., (ed.): *Dictionary of Education,* 2d ed., McGraw-Hill Book Company, New York, 1959.

99. Good, Harry G.: *A History of Western Education,* The Macmillan Company, Toronto, Ontario, 1960.

100. Good, Thomas L., and Jere E. Brophy: "The Self-Fulfilling Prophecy," *Today's Education,* vol. 60, no. 4, pp. 52–53, National Education Association, Washington, April, 1971.

101. *A Good Start in School,* Department of Public Instruction, Bulletin 226, Indianapolis, Ind., 1958.

102. Goodlad, John I.: "The Future of Learning: Into the 21st Century," *AACTE Bulletin,* vol. 24, no. 1, pp. 1, 4–5, American Association of Colleges for Teacher Education, Washington, March, 1971.

103. Goodlad, John I., and Robert H. Anderson: *The Nongraded School,* Harcourt, Brace and World, Inc., New York, 1963.

104. Goodlad, John I., and Frances M. Klein: *Behind the Classroom Door,* Charles A. Jones Publishing Company, Worthington, Ohio, 1970.

105. "Governance for the Teaching Profession," *NEA National Commission on Teacher Education and Professional Standards,* no. 1, A working paper, National Education Association, Washington, November, 1970.

106. "Grade Organization Patterns," *ERS Reporter,* Educational Research Service, American Association of School Administrators and NEA Research Division, November, 1968.

107. Graybeal, William S.: "Teacher Surplus and Teacher Shortage," *Phi Delta Kappan,* vol. 53, no. 2, pp. 82–85, Phi Delta Kappa, Bloomington, Ind., October, 1971.

108. Gross, Edward, and Paul V. Grambsch: *University Goals and Academic Power,* American Council on Education, Washington, 1968.

109. "Group Insurance Is Growing," *NEA Journal,* vol. 55, no. 5, pp. 48–49, National Education Association, Washington, May, 1966.

110. *Guidelines for the Kindergarten,* Division of Planning and Research, Publication no. SC-343, Los Angeles City Schools, Los Angeles, 1970.

111. *Guidelines to Fringe Benefits for Members of the Teaching Profession,* National Education Association, Washington, 1969.

112. Haberman, Martin: "Behavioral Objectives: Bandwagon or Breakthrough," *The Journal of Teacher Education,* vol. 19, no. 1, pp. 91–94, National Education Association, Washington, Spring, 1968.

113. Hamachek, Don: "Characteristics of Good Teachers and Implications for Teacher Education," *Phi Delta Kappan,* vol. 50, no. 6, pp. 341–345, Phi Delta Kappa, Bloomington, Ind., February, 1969.

114. Harap, Henry: "Teacher Preparation: 5-year Programs," *School Life,* vol. 44, no. 2, pp. 18–21, U.S. Office of Education, Washington, October, 1961.

115. Harris, Norman C.: "Redoubled Efforts and Dimly Seen Goals," *Phi Delta Kappan,* vol. 46, no. 8, pp. 360–365, Phi Delta Kappa, Bloomington, Ind., April, 1965.

116. Havighurst, Robert J.: *Human Development and Education,* Longmans, Green and Company, Inc., New York, 1953.

117. Heald, James E., and Samuel A. Moore, II.: *The Teacher and Administrative Relationships in School Systems,* The Macmillan Company, Toronto, Ontario, 1968.

118. Heil, Louis, Marion Powell, and Irwin Feifer: *Characteristics of Teacher Behavior Related to the Achievement of Children in Several Elementary Grades,* Brooklyn College, Brooklyn, New York, 1960.

119. Heller, Celia S.: *Mexican American Youth,* Random House, New York, 1968.

120. Hemphill, John K., James M. Richards, and Richard E. Peterson: *Report of the Senior High School Principalship,* National Education Association, National Association of Secondary School Principals, Washington, 1965.

121. Hodgson, J. D.: "Manpower Patterns of the 70's," *Manpower,* vol. 3, no. 2, pp. 3–6, Superintendent of Documents, U.S. Government Printing Office, Washington, February, 1971.

122. *Hogs, Ax Handles and Woodpeckers,* American Association of School Administrators, Washington, 1958.

123. "How Early Should Education Start?" *The Shape of Education for 1969–70,* vol. 11, National School Public Relations Association, Washington, 1969.

124. *How Much Are Students Learning?* A Report from the Committee on Assessing the Progress of Education, University of Michigan, Ann Arbor, Michigan, November, 1968.

125. Hughes, James Monroe: *Education in America,* 2d ed., Harper and Row, Publishers, Inc., New York, 1965.

126. Hutchins, Robert M.: *The Conflict in Education,* Harper and Row, Publishers, Inc., New York, 1953.

127. *Imperatives in Education,* American Association of School Administrators, Washington, 1966.

128. *In Search of Excellence,* American Federation of Teachers, AFL-CIO, Washington, n.d.

129. Incollingo, Larry: "Sexplosion Erupts in U.S. Secondary Education," *Daily-Herald Telephone,* Section 2, p. 2, Bloomington, Ind., June 16, 1969.

130. "Innovations Fail to Reach Classroom, Study Says," *Education U.S.A.,* National School Public Relations Association, Washington, February 8, 1971.

131. "Instructional Technology," *Today's Education,* vol. 59, no. 8, pp. 33–40, National Education Association, Washington, November, 1970.

132. *An Introduction to Phi Delta Kappa,* Phi Delta Kappa, Bloomington, Ind. (brochure).

133. "It's 12-Month School for Atlanta," *The Shape of Education for 1969–70,* vol. 11, pp. 61–64, National School Public Relations Association, Washington, 1969.

134. Jersild, Arthur T., and Associates: *Education for Self-understanding: The Role of Psychology in the High School Program,* Teachers College Press, Columbia University, New York, 1953.

135. Johnstone, John W. C., and Ramon J. Rivera, *Volunteers for Learning,* Aldine Publishing Company, Chicago, 1965.

**136.** Kearney, Nolan C.: *Elementary School Objectives,* Russell Sage Foundation, New York, 1953.

**137.** Kirp, David L.: "The Poor, the Schools and Equal Protection," *Harvard Educational Review,* vol. 38, no. 4, pp. 635–688, Graduate School of Education, Harvard University, Cambridge, Mass., Fall, 1968.

**138.** Krathwohl, David R., Benjamin S. Bloom, and Bertram B. Masia: *Taxonomy of Educational Objectives, the Classification of Educational Goals, Handbook II: Affective Domain,* David McKay Company, Inc., New York, 1966. Reprinted by permission of David McKay Company, Inc.

**139.** Krech, David: "The Chemistry of Learning," *Saturday Review,* Saturday Review, Inc., N.Y., January 20, 1968.

**140.** Kreitlow, B. W.: *Long-term Study of Educational Effectiveness of Newly Formed Centralized Districts in Rural Areas,* Cooperative Research Project no. 375, Department of Agricultural and Extension Education, University of Wisconsin, Madison, Wis., September, 1962.

**141.** Lambert, Sam M.: *Inaugural Address,* Presidential Room, Statler-Hilton Hotel, Washington, Oct. 20, 1967.

**142.** "Leaves of Absence," *School Law Summaries,* National Education Association, Research Division, Washington, December, 1968.

**143.** "Leaves of Absence Provisions for Teachers," *NEA Research Memo 1969–22,* National Education Association, Research Division, Washington, October, 1969.

**144.** "Legality of Public Summer Schools," *NEA Research Bulletin,* vol. 43, no. 1, pp. 30–31, National Education Association, Research Division, Washington, February, 1965.

**145.** Lieberman, Myron: "Implications of the Coming NEA-AFT Merger," *Phi Delta Kappan,* vol. 50, no. 3, pp. 139–144, Phi Delta Kappa, Bloomington, Ind., November, 1968.

**146.** Lindsey, Margaret (ed.): *New Horizons for the Teaching Profession,* National Education Association, National Commission on Teacher Education and Professional Standards, Washington, 1961.

**147.** Little, Malcolm: *Malcolm X Speaks: Selected Speeches and Statements,* Merit Publishers, New York, 1965.

**148.** Locke, Robert W.: "Has the Education Industry Lost Its Nerve?" *Saturday Review,* Saturday Review, Inc., N.Y., January 16, 1971, pp. 42–44, 57, Copyright 1971.

**149.** McGee, Leo: "Early Efforts Toward Educating the Black Adult 1619–1850," *Adult Leadership,* vol. 19, no. 10, pp. 341–342, Adult Education Association, Washington, April, 1971.

**150.** McLure, William P.: *The Intermediate Administrative School District of the United States,* Bureau of Educational Research, College of Education, University of Illinois, Urbana, Ill., February, 1958.

**151.** "The Magnitude of the American Educational Establishment 1960–1970," *Saturday Review,* Saturday Review, Inc., N.Y., September 19, 1970, p. 67.

**152.** "Marlin Forsees Big Boost in Federal Aid," *Washington Monitor, Education U.S.A.,* National School Public Relations Association, March 1, 1971, p. 143.

**153.** Marshall, Robert A.: *The Story of Our Schools: A Short History of Public Education in the United States,* National Education Association, National Council for the Social Studies, Washington, 1962.

**154.** Massanari, Karl: "AACTE Explores Performance-based Teacher Education," *AACTE Bulletin,* vol. 24, no. 1, pp. 3, 6, and 8, American Association of Colleges for Teacher Education, Washington, March, 1971.

**155.** Mee, John F.: "The New Knowledge Industry," *The Review*, vol. 10, no. 2, pp. 10–22, Alumni Association of the College of Arts and Sciences—Graduate School, Indiana University, Bloomington, Ind., Winter, 1968.

**156.** "Merit Provisions in Teachers' Salary Schedules, 1969–70," *NEA Research Memo 1970–7*, National Education Association, Research Division, Washington, April, 1970.

**157.** "Methods of Evaluating Teachers," *NEA Research Bulletin*, vol. 43, no. 1, pp. 12–18, National Education Association, Research Division, Washington, February, 1965.

**158.** Michael, Donald N.: *The Next Generation: The Prospects Ahead for the Youth of Today and Tomorrow*, Random House, Inc., New York, 1965.

**159.** Michael, Donald N.: "Your Child and the World of Tomorrow," *NEA Journal*, vol. 55, no. 1, National Education Association, Washington, January, 1966 (supplement).

**160.** "Middle School Takes Shape As Research Poses Questions," *Education U.S.A.*, National School Public Relations Association, Washington, February 22, 1971, p. 133.

**161.** *Milestones in Teacher Education and Professional Standards*, National Education Association, National Commission on Teacher Education and Professional Standards, Washington, 1970.

**162.** Miller, Harriett: "Santa Barbara Has a Student School Board," *American School Board Journal*, vol. 157, no. 11, p. 29, National School Boards Association, Evanston, Ill., May, 1970.

**163.** "Minimum Annual Salaries for Teachers," *NEA Research Memo 1970–22*, National Education Association, Research Division, Washington, November, 1970.

**164.** Morphet, Edgar L., Roe L. Johns, and Theodore L. Reller: *Educational Organization and Administration*, Prentice-Hall, Inc., Englewood Cliffs, N.J., 1967.

**165.** Moustakas, Clark E., and Minnie P. Berson: *The Nursery School and Child Care Center*, Whiteside, Inc., New York, 1955.

**166.** "National Assessment Spreading to States," *Education U.S.A.*, National School Relations Association, Washington, August 3, 1970.

**167.** National Association of Public School Adult Education: *Public School Adult Education: A Guide for Administrators*, National Education Association, Washington, 1963.

**168.** *NEA Handbook for Local, State and National Associations 1970–71*, National Education Association, Washington, September, 1970.

**169.** *NEA Handbook for Local, State, and National Associations 1971–72*, National Education Association, Washington, October, 1971.

**170.** "Negotiations Moving to State Level?" *Convention Reporter*, American Association of School Administrators, Washington, February, 19, 1970.

**171.** *New England's First Fruits in Collections of the Massachusetts Historical Society for the Year 1792*, vol. 1, p. 242, T. R. Mavin, Printer, Boston, 1859.

**172.** "New Horizons in Teacher Education and Professional Standards," *NEA Journal*, vol. 50, no. 1, pp. 55–68, National Education Association, Washington, January, 1961.

**173.** "New Legislation to Spur Drug Education," *Washington Monitor, Education U.S.A.*, National School Public Relations Association, Washington, November 30, 1970, p. 77.

**174.** "News and Trends," *NEA Journal*, vol. 55, no. 1, p. 4, National Education Association, Washington, January, 1966.

**175.** "News and Trends," *NEA Journal*, vol. 56, no. 2, pp. 3–4, National Education Association, Washington, February, 1967.

**176.** "News and Trends," *Today's Education*, vol. 58, no. 1, pp. 3–4, National Education Association, Washington, January, 1969.

177. "News Front," *Education U.S.A.,* National School Public Relations Association, Washington, September 29, 1969, p. 26.

178. "News Front," *Education U.S.A.,* National School Public Relations Association, Washington, May 11, 1970, p. 206.

179. "News Front," *Education U.S.A.,* National School Public Relations Association, Washington, September 7, 1970.

180. "News Front," *Education U.S.A.,* National School Public Relations Association, Washington, December 14, 1970, p. 86.

181. "News Front," *Education U.S.A.,* National School Public Relations Association, Washington, February 22, 1971.

182. "News Front," *Education U.S.A.,* National School Public Relations Association, Washington, March 22, 1971.

183. Noar, Gertrude: *The Junior High School: Today, Tomorrow,* Prentice-Hall, Inc., Englewood Cliffs, N.J., 1961.

184. "Objectives of the National Congress of Parents and Teachers," *PTA Manual,* National Congress of Parents and Teachers, Chicago, 1965–66.

185. Olivero, James L., and Edward G. Buffie (eds.), *Educational Manpower: From Aides to Differentiated Staff Patterns,* Indiana University Press, Bloomington, Ind., 1970.

186. "Opinion Surveys Pinpoint Student Views," *Education U.S.A.,* National School Public Relations Association, December 14, 1970, p. 85.

187. Orlich, Donald C., and S. Samuel Shermis: *The Pursuit of Excellence: Introductory Readings in Education,* American Book Company, New York, 1965.

188. "Our Schools Aren't Good Enough," *The News Letter,* vol. 20, Bureau of Educational Research, Ohio State University, Columbus, Ohio, November, 1954.

189. *Pace Projects to Advance Creativity in Education: A Manual for Project Applicants,* Title III, Elementary and Secondary Education Act, Supplementary Centers and Services Program, U.S. Office of Education, Washington, 1965.

190. "Panel Blasts Vocational Education Effort," *Washington Monitor, Education U.S.A.,* National School Public Relations Association, Washington, September 8, 1969.

191. Perkins, Hugh V.: "Nongraded Programs: What Progress?" *Educational Leadership,* vol. 19, no. 3, pp. 166–169, 194, National Education Association, Association of Supervision and Curriculum Development, Washington, December, 1961.

192. Phoenix, Philip H.: *Philosophies of Education,* John Wiley and Sons, Inc., New York, 1961.

193. Piaget, Jean, and Bärbel Inhelder: *The Psychology of the Child,* Basic Books, New York, 1969.

194. *Policies and Criteria for the Approval of Secondary Schools,* North Central Association of Colleges and Secondary Schools, Chicago, 1966.

195. "Policy Statements on Salaries for School Personnel," *NEA Research Memo 1969–23,* National Education Association, Research Division, October, 1969.

196. Polley, Ira: "What's Right with American Education?" *Phi Delta Kappan,* vol. 51, no. 1, pp. 13–15, Phi Delta Kappa, Bloomington, Ind;, September, 1969.

197. "Population Trends and School Enrollments," *NEA Research Bulletin,* vol. 47, no. 1, pp. 25–28, National Education Association, Research Division, Washington, March, 1969.

198. "Population Trends Signal School Needs," *NEA Research Bulletin,* vol. 46, no. 1, pp. 24–28, National Education Association, Research Division, Washington, March, 1968.

199. *Preprimary Enrollment of Children under Six,* U.S. Office of Education, Washington, 1969.

**200.** The President's Commission on National Goals: *Goals for Americans,* Copyright 1960 by the American Assembly, Columbia University, New York. Reprinted by permission of Prentice-Hall, Inc., Englewood Cliffs, N.J.

**201.** "Professional Growth Requirements Specified in 1968–69 Salary Schedules (Reporting School Systems with Enrollments of 6,000 or More)," *NEA Research Memo 1969–10,* National Education Association, Research Division, Washington, April, 1969.

**202.** *Professional Organizations in American Education,* National Education Association, Educational Policies Commission, Washington, 1957.

**203.** "Profit and Loss in Education," *Saturday Review,* Saturday Review, Inc., N.Y., Aug. 15, 1970, p. 39.

**204.** *Projections of Educational Attainment in the United States: 1965 to 1985,* Current Population Reports, ser. P–25, no. 305, U.S. Bureau of the Census, Washington, April 14, 1965, pp. 1–16.

**205.** "Promising Innovations Hit Snags," *Education U.S.A.,* National School Public Relations Association, Washington, September 23, 1968.

**206.** "Purposes," *Educational Horizons,* vol. 43, no. 4, p. i, Pi Lambda Theta, Washington, Summer, 1965.

**207.** *The Purposes of Education in American Democracy,* National Education Association, Educational Policies Commission, Washington, 1938.

**208.** *The Pursuit of Excellence: Education and the Future of America.* Copyright 1958 by Rockefeller Brothers Fund, Inc. Reprinted with permission of Doubleday and Company, Inc.

**209.** Rajpol, Puran L.: "Relationship Between Expenditures and Quality Characteristics of Education in Public Schools," *The Journal of Educational Research,* vol. 63, no. 2, pp. 57–59, Dembar Educational Research Services, Inc., Madison, Wis., October, 1969.

**210.** "Rankings of the States, 1969," *Research Report 1969–R1,* National Education Association, Research Division, Washington, 1969.

**211.** "Rankings of the States, 1970," *Research Report 1970–R1,* National Education Association, Research Division, Washington, 1970.

**212.** "Rankings of the States, 1971," *Research Report 1971–R1,* National Education Association, Research Division, Washington, 1971.

**213.** Rathbone, M. J.: *Human Talent: The Great Investment,* Standard Oil Company (New Jersey), New Jersey, February 25, 1964.

**214.** *Recommended Standards for Teacher Education,* American Association of Colleges for Teacher Education, Washington, November, 1969.

**215.** Reeder, Ward G.: *A First Course in Education,* The Macmillan Company, Toronto, Ontario, 1946. (Quoted from Samuel Hall.)

**216.** Reisert, John E.: "Easy Answers to Tough Problems: The Conant Approach to Teacher Education," *The Hoosier Schoolmaster,* vol. 7, no. 3, pp. 1 and 5, Indiana Association of Junior and Senior High School Principals, Bloomington, Ind., April, 1964.

**217.** Reisert, John E.: "Migrating Educator? What about Your Teaching Credentials?" *Phi Delta Kappan,* vol. 47, no. 7, pp. 372–374, Phi Delta Kappa, Bloomington, Ind., March, 1968.

**218.** "Reporting Pupil Progress," *NEA Research Bulletin,* vol. 47, no. 3, pp. 75–76, National Education Association, Research Division, Washington, October, 1969.

**219.** "Reporting Pupil Progress to Parents," *NEA Research Bulletin,* vol. 49, no. 3, pp. 81–82, National Education Association, Research Division, Washington, October, 1971.

220. "Retirement Statistics, 1964," *NEA Research Bulletin,* vol. 42, no. 4, pp. 99–107, National Education Association, Research Division, Washington, December, 1964.

221. *Review of the American Educational System,* Hearing before the Subcommittee of the Committee on Appropriations, House of Representatives, 86th Cong. Sess., Washington, 1960.

222. Rickover, Hyman G.: "The World of the Uneducated," *The Saturday Evening Post,* November 28, 1959, p. 8.

223. Rippa, S. Alexander: *Education in a Free Society: An American History,* David McKay Company, Inc., New York, 1967.

224. Rosenthal, Robert, and Lenore Jacobson: *Pygmalion in the Classroom: Teacher Expectation and Pupils Intellectual Development,* Holt, Rinehart and Winston, New York, 1968.

225. Ryans, David G.: *Characteristics of Teachers,* American Council on Education, Washington, 1960. Used by permission.

226. Ryans, David G.: "Prediction of Teacher Effectiveness," *Encyclopedia of Educational Research,* 3d ed., The Macmillan Company, Toronto, Ontario, 1960, pp. 1,486–1,490.

227. "Salaries in Higher Education, 1969–70," *Research Report 1970–R6,* National Education Association, Research Division, Washington, 1970.

228. "Salaries of Beginning Teachers and Beginners in Other Professions," *NEA Research Bulletin,* vol. 49, no. 3, pp. 75–77, National Education Association, Research Division, Washington, October, 1971.

229. "Salary Schedule Supplements for Extra Duties 1969–70," *Research Report 1970–R4,* National Education Association, Research Division, Washington, 1970.

230. Salz, Arthur E.: "Local Control vs. Professionalism," *Phi Delta Kappan,* vol. 50, no. 6, pp. 332–334, Phi Delta Kappa, Bloomington, Ind., February, 1969.

231. "School Enrollment," *Financial Facts,* National Consumer Finance Association, Educational Services Division, Washington, April, 1971.

232. *Schools for the Sixties,* Project on Instruction of the National Education Association, McGraw-Hill Book Company, New York, 1963.

233. "Sensitivity Training: What's That?" *The Shape of Education for 1970–71,* vol. 12, pp. 45–49, National School Public Relations Association, Washington, 1970.

234. "Serious Protest Found in 18% of High Schools," *Education U.S.A.,* National School Public Relations Association, Washington, March 2, 1970, p. 145.

235. *Sesame Street Newsletter, No. 11,* 1865 Broadway, New York, November 8, 1970.

236. "Severance Pay for Professional School Employees," *NEA Research Bulletin,* vol. 47, no. 4, pp. 102–104, National Education Association, Research Division, Washington, December, 1969.

237. "Sex Education in the Schools," *Education U.S.A. Special Report,* National School Public Relations Association, Washington, 1969.

238. Shaffer, Helen B.: "Discipline in Public Schools," *Editorial Research Report 2,* pp. 635–652, ERIC Clearing House on Educational Management, University of Oregon, Eugene, Oregon, Aug. 27, 1969.

239. Shane, Harold G.: "Future-planning As a Means of Shaping Educational Change," in Robert M. McClure, and Herman Richey (eds.), *The Curriculum: Retrospect and Prospect,* The Seventieth Yearbook of the National Society for the Study of Education, Part I, The University of Chicago Press, Chicago, Ill., 1971, pp. 185–218.

240. Shane, Harold G.: "Future Shock and the Curriculum," *Phi Delta Kappan,* vol. 49, no. 2, pp. 67–70, Phi Delta Kappa, Bloomington, Ind., October, 1967.

241. Shane, Harold G.: *Résumé of Grouping in the Elementary School,* Indiana Association for Supervision and Curriculum Development, 1960. (Mimeographed.)

242. Shane, Harold G., and E. T. McSwain: *Evaluation and the Elementary Curriculum,* Holt, Rinehart and Winston, Inc., New York, 1958.

243. Shane, Harold G., and Owen N. Nelson: "What Will the Schools Become?" *Phi Delta Kappan,* vol. 52, no. 10, pp. 596–598, Phi Delta Kappa, Bloomington, Ind., June, 1971.

244. Shane, Harold G., and June Grant Shane: "Forecast for the 70's," *Today's Education,* vol. 58, no. 1, pp. 29–32, National Education Association, Washington, January, 1969.

245. Sheviakov, George V., and Fritz Redl: *Discipline for Today's Children and Youth,* National Education Association, Association for Supervision and Curriculum Development, Washington, 1956.

246. Simon, Kenneth A., and Marie G. Fullam: *Projections of Educational Statistics to 1978–79,* U.S. Office of Education, Washington, 1970.

247. Simon, Kenneth A., and Marie G. Fullam: *Projections of Educational Statistics to 1979–80,* U.S. Office of Education, Washington, 1971.

248. Simon, Kenneth, and W. Vance Grant: *Digest of Educational Statistics,* U.S. Office of Education, Washington, September, 1969.

249. Smith, B. Othanel: *Teachers for the Real World,* The American Association of Colleges for Teacher Education, Washington, 1969.

250. Smith, Louis M.: "Group Processes in Elementary and Secondary Schools," *What Research Says to the Teacher,* no. 19, National Education Association, Department of Classroom Teachers, American Educational Research Association, Washington, 1959.

251. Smith, Philip G.: *Philosophy of Education,* Harper and Row, Publishers, Inc., New York, 1965.

252. "State Sick Leave Provisions for Teachers," *NEA Research Bulletin,* vol. 47, no. 2, pp. 43–44, National Education Association, Research Division, Washington, May, 1969.

253. *Statistical Abstract of the United States, 1971,* U.S. Bureau of the Census, Washington, 1971.

254. Stinnett, T. M.: *A Manual on Certification Requirements for School Personnel in the United States,* National Education Association, National Commission on Teacher Education and Professional Standards, Washington, 1970.

255. Stinnett, T.M.: *Professional Problems of Teachers,* 3d ed., The Macmillan Company, Toronto, Ontario, 1969.

256. Stinnett, T. M.: "Reordering Goals and Roles: An Introduction," in *Unfinished Business of the Teaching Profession in the 1970's,* pp. 1–7, Phi Delta Kappa, Bloomington, Ind., 1971.

257. Stinnett, T. M.: "Teaching Professionalization: Challenge and Promise, Power of Professionalism in Teaching," *Bulletin of the School of Education,* vol. 40, no. 5, pp. 9–20, Indiana University, Bloomington, Ind., September, 1964.

258. Stinnett, T.M.: "What Is Relevant?" *The Inauguration of Sam M. Lambert,* National Education Association, Washington, October 20, 1967.

259. Stinnett, T. M., and Albert J. Huggett: *Professional Problems of Teachers,* The Macmillan Company, Toronto, Ontario, 1963.

260. Stoddard, George D.: *The Dual Progress Plan,* Harper and Row, Publishers, Inc., New York, 1961.

261. "Study Praises Differentiated Staffing," *Education U.S.A.,* National School Public Relations Association, Washington, March 15, 1971.

262. "Swings of the Educational Pendulum," *NASSP Convention Reporter, Education*

*U.S.A.*, National School Public Relations Association, Washington, January 23–27, 1971.

263. *T. M. Stinnett Speaks,* National Education Association, Department of Classroom Teachers, Washington, 1966.

264. "Tax-sheltered Annuities: Current Status," *NEA Research Bulletin,* vol. 42, no. 3, pp. 94–95, National Education Association, Research Division, Washington, October, 1964.

265. "Teacher Aides in Public Schools," *NEA Research Bulletin,* vol. 45, no. 2, pp. 37–39, National Education Association, Research Division, Washington, May, 1970.

266. "Teacher Job Shortage Ahead," *NEA Research Bulletin,* vol. 49, no. 3, pp. 69–74, National Education Association, Research Division, Washington, October, 1971.

267. *Teacher Leaves of Absence,* National Education Association, Research Division and Department of Classroom Teachers, Division Pamphlet 7, Washington, May, 1961.

268. "Teacher Mobility and Loss," *NEA Research Bulletin,* vol. 46, no. 6, pp. 118–126, National Education Association, Research Division, Washington, December, 1968.

269. "Teacher Opinion," *NEA Research Bulletin,* vol. 47, no. 3, pp. 70–72, National Education Association, Research Bulletin, Washington, October, 1969.

270. "Teacher Opinion Poll," *Today's Education,* vol. 60, no. 2, p. 27, National Education Association, Washington, February, 1971.

271. *Teacher Retirement,* National Education Association, Department of Classroom Teachers and Research Division, Discussion Pamphlet 2, Washington, November, 1957.

272. "Teacher Strikes, 1960–61 to 1969–70," *NEA Research Bulletin,* vol. 48, no. 3, pp. 69–72, National Education Association, Research Division, Washington, October, 1970.

273. "Teacher Supply and Demand in Public Schools, 1970," *Research Report 1970–R14,* National Education Association, Research Division, Washington, 1970.

274. "Teacher Supply and Demand in Universities, Colleges, and Junior Colleges, 1963–64 and 1964–65," *Research Report 1965–R4,* National Education Association, Research Division, Washington, April, 1965.

275. *Teacher Tenure,* National Education Association, Department of Classroom Teachers and the Research Division, Discussion Pamphlet 1, Washington, July, 1954.

276. "Teacher Tenure and Contracts," *Research Report 1971–R3,* National Education Association, Research Division, Washington, 1971.

277. "Technology in Education," *Education U.S.A. Special Report,* National School Public Relations Association, Washington, 1967.

278. "Technology in Education," *NEA Research Memo 1969–4,* National Education Association, Research Division, Washington, February, 1969.

279. Thayer, V. T.: *The Role of the School in American Society,* Dodd, Mead and Company, Inc., New York, 1960.

280. Thomas, Steven C.: "Valley View's 45–15 Year-round School," *Today's Education,* vol. 60, no. 8, pp. 42–43, National Education Association, Washington, November, 1971.

281. Thompson, Ronald B.: *Projections of Enrollments: Public and Private Colleges and Universities, 1970–1987,* American Association of Collegiate Registrars and Admissions Officers Office, One Dupont Circle, N.W., Washington, December, 1970.

282. Toffler, Alvin: *Future Shock,* Random House, New York, 1970.

283. Trump, J. Lloyd: *Guide to Better Schools: Focus on Change,* Rand McNally and Company, Chicago, 1961.

284. Turner, Richard L., and Nicholas A. Fattu: "Skills in Teaching, Assessed on the Criterion of Problem Solving," Bulletin of the School of Education, vol. 37, no. 3, Indiana University, Bloomington, Ind., May, 1961.

285. *200 Million Americans,* U.S. Department of Commerce, Superintendent of Documents, U.S. Government Printing Office, Washington, November, 1967.

286. Tyack, David B.: "Growing Up, Black: The Education of the Negro," pp. 186–196, in Stan Dropkin, Harold Full, and Ernest Schwarcz (eds.), *Contemporary American Education,* The Macmillan Company, Toronto, Ontario, 1965.

287. "Use of Drugs in Schools Poses Dread U.S. Problem," *Los Angeles Times,* Part 2, Los Angeles, Calif., February 19, 1970, p. 7.

288. Van Til, William: "The Key Word Is Relevance," *Today's Education,* vol. 58, no. 1, pp. 14–17, National Education Association, Washington, January, 1969.

289. *Washington Fastreport,* vol. 1, no. 2, p. 2, National School Boards Association, Washington, July 23, 1971.

290. Weigand, James (ed.): *Developing Teacher Competencies,* Prentice-Hall, Inc., Englewood Cliffs, N.J., 1971.

291. "What Teachers Think: A Summary of Teacher Opinion Poll Findings, 1960–1965," *Research Report 1965–R13,* National Education Association, Research Division, Washington, September, 1965.

292. "What the Kids Want," *Phi Delta Kappan,* vol. 51, no. 7, p. 407, Phi Delta Kappa, Bloomington, Ind., March, 1970.

293. "Which Schools Are Better," *NEA Research Bulletin,* vol. 41, no. 3, pp. 83–89, National Education Association, Research Division, Washington, October, 1963.

294. White, Leslie A.: "Man's Control over Civilization," *The Scientific Monthly,* vol. 66, March, 1948, p. 241.

295. Whitehead, Donald R.: "This Is Your Earth," *Indiana Alumni Magazine,* vol. 33, no. 6, pp. 10–13, Indiana University, Bloomington, Ind., March, 1970.

296. "Why Have Merit Plans for Teachers' Salaries Been Abandoned?" *Research Report 1961–R3,* National Education Association, Research Division, Washington, March, 1961.

297. Williamson, John A.: "Seniors Comment on Their Best and Poorest Teachers," *Colorado Journal of Educational Research,* vol. 7, no. 2, pp. 3–7, Bureau of Research, Colorado State College, Greeley, Colorado, Spring, 1968.

298. Witty, Paul A.: "Mental Hygiene in Modern Education," *Fifty-fourth Yearbook of the National Society for the Study of Education, Part II,* The University of Chicago Press, Chicago, 1955.

299. Witty, Paul A.: "The Teacher Who Has Helped Me Most," *NEA Journal,* vol. 36, no. 5, p. 386, National Education Association, Washington, May, 1947.

300. Woodson, Carter Godwin, and Charles H. Wesley: *The Negro in Our History,* 10th ed., Associated Publishers, Washington, 1962.

# INDEX

# INDEX